EVERYMAN'S LIBRARY

604

POETRY & DRAMA

Everyman, I will go with thee, and be thy guide,
In thy most need to go by thy side

JOHN DRYDEN, born in 1631; educated at Westminster and Trinity College, Cambridge; wrote equally admiring obituary on Cromwell and panegyric on return of Charles II. His first play was *The Wild Gallant*, 1663; his last, *Love Triumphant*, 1694. Became a member of the Royal Society, 1662, and poet laureate, 1670. Wrote Anglican propaganda under Charles II, Catholic propaganda under James II. He died in 1700.

WILLIAM WYCHERLEY, born in 1640 (?), was at various times an actor, a producer, a subaltern in the Duke of Buckingham's Foot, and a friend of the royal mistress, the Duchess of Cleveland. His first play, *Love in a Wood*, was acted in 1671; his last, *The Plain Dealer*, in 1674. He died in 1716.

WILLIAM CONGREVE, though educated in Ireland, was of English birth. Born in 1670, as a young man he collaborated with Dryden in his translations of the classics. His first play, *The Old Bachelor*, was produced in 1693; his last and best, *The Way of the World*, in 1700. He became rich and famous, the holder of many sinecures, and was the friend of Pope and of Voltaire. He died in 1729.

THOMAS OTWAY, born in 1652, went up to Oxford but did not proceed to a degree. As an actor he was a failure. His first play, *Alcibiades*, was acted in 1675; his last, *The Athiest*, in 1684. He was poor nearly all his life, and at one period enlisted and served in Holland, where he was commissioned. He died in 1685.

GEORGE FARQUHAR was born in 1678, son of a Londonderry clergyman; he was another unsuccessful actor and less successful army officer, whose first play, *Love and a Bottle*, was acted in 1698, and his last, *The Beaux-Stratagem*, in 1707; he died just after its first performance.

SIR JOHN VANBRUGH was born in 1664, to a solid City of London family of Flemish extraction. Studied architecture in France, was commissioned in the army in 1696; was a prisoner of war, 1690–2, and left the service, as a captain, in 1696, in which year his first play, *The Relapse*, was produced. In his capacity as an architect he designed Castle Howard, Blenheim, and Dalkeith Palace; he was knighted in 1714 and became Clarenceux King-of-arms. He died in 1726.

SIR GEORGE ETHEREDGE, born in 1634 or 1635, had his first play, *Love in a Tub*, produced in 1664. He entered the diplomatic service and became ambassador at Regensburg. He wrote only three plays. Little is known about his life, but 'gentle George' appears to have been an amiable, amorous, bibulous character who married money and bought his title.

RESTORATION PLAYS

INTRODUCTION BY
SIR EDMUND GOSSE

LONDON J. M. DENT & SONS LTD
NEW YORK E. P. DUTTON & CO INC

All rights reserved
Made in Great Britain
at the
Aldine Press · Letchworth · Herts
for
J. M. DENT & SONS LTD
Aldine House · Bedford Street · London
First published in Everyman's Library 1912
New edition first including *The Man of Mode* 1932
Last reprinted 1962

INTRODUCTION

THE tragedies and comedies of the Restoration constitutes a body of writing which is apt to suffer from comparison with an earlier school of English drama. But there was no continuity between the plays written under Charles I. and those written under Charles II., and the first thing to be done, in appreciating the latter, is to dismiss all consideration of the former. If the founder of the Restoration stage, William Davenant, was a relic of pre-Commonwealth times; if the earliest comic playwright of the new age, John Wilson, was a close disciple of Ben Jonson; if much of the richness of Jacobean language clung about the tragedies of Dryden; if Fletcher was still acted and Shakespeare sedulously adapted; these were accidental and not essential facts. What was essential was that for nearly twenty years stage-plays had not been represented in England, and that the tradition of acting—which is a very fragile thing, and needs to be handed down week by week and almost night by night—was broken and completely lost. In consequence, when there arose an irresistible public demand for the performance of drama in England, the revival could not come from memories of a stage, which had been already in decay a quarter of a century earlier, which none but elderly people had seen, and the character of which no one any longer recollected or cared to recollect.

There was, however, a stage with which all the politest Englishmen of the day were exactly familiar, on which indeed they had, until the moment of the restoration of their monarchy, seen acted the most moving and civilising spectacles. In considering the drama of England from 1665 to 1700, we waste time and lose our way if we try to connect what we see with the productions of the Elizabethan age. The first necessity of critical appreciation is to perceive that this drama is an offshoot of " classical " drama as developed in France, and as witnessed in Paris up to the moment of the king's return. The theatre in France had begun to dominate society in the second quarter of the seventeenth century, and it had moved in sympathy with the general craving for increased social refinement. The Hôtel de Bourgogne, with its long tradition from so far back as 1548, had "marked time," as we say now, until the personal taste of Louis XIV. had given a new and strong social prominence to the stage. The success of Corneille's *Mélite* in 1629 began the fashion for stately and ceremonious tragedy. The poet and the actor, Corneille and Mondory, the one inactive without the other, now played into one another's hands, and a crisis in the art of the world was marked by the great polite success of *Le Cid* in 1636.

It was soon after this that the exodus of English Royalists began, and in the main it was to Paris that they ultimately gravitated. Those of them who loved the theatre—and it must be recollected that every one whose tastes were in any measure theatrical was an adherent to the monarchy—all infatuated English playgoers arrived in Paris to find flourishing there a drama of a class entirely different from what they had left behind them languishing in London. They had left a stage that was rapidly fading into incoherence and folly; they found one which bore all the signs of youth and strength and logic. They watched such finished actors as Bellerose and Montfleury performing at the Bourgogne. In the very year in which the English Parliament published the sternly insolent ordinance forbidding all acting of stage-plays, the aristocratic English exiles had the exquisite pleasure of seeing Richelieu's theatre in the Palais Royal opened for spectacles of the highest refinement, where for the first time the impudence of audiences was kept in check and an air of good breeding made obligatory on the pit itself.

No wonder, then, that the civilising influence of the stage, as a beautiful instrument in the work of social refinement, should attract and interest the English emigrants in Paris. Small blame to them if this, indeed, became their chief solicitude in the thought of introducing at home—should they ever return to their Roundhead-ridden island—a drama built on the same lines as the French and possessing the same educational character. The poet had hitherto been a negligible citizen, the actor a mountebank and a vagabond, in English esteem. Here in Paris they found actors permitted to appear at court, and poets associating on equal terms with "the best people." They noticed, no doubt with ecstatic approval, the tragic dignity of Bellerose, and if they stayed long enough in France, they saw a genuine nobleman, the Sieur de Prine Fosse, become the darling of playgoers under the delicate pseudonym of Floridor.

In examining any period of literary art, it is imperative that we should ask ourselves, not, what do we ourselves like best, but what did the purveyors of all this elaborate entertainment design? We have formed a modern notion of " refinement " very different from that which was current in Europe in 1660. The simplicity of demeanour, the reduced emphasis, the moral severity, which we now regard as necessary for good behaviour, were not valued at our rate in the courts of the seventeenth century. To be " polite " was largely a matter of parade, of demeanour, even of clothes and ornaments. The fault of English society at the Restoration was its grossness, by which we must not be too ready to understand its immorality, nor even its indelicacy. It was slovenly in deportment, in thought, blunt in language. The rude manners of an earlier genera-tion had been reflected in the plays of Charles I.'s reign, and the revival of these pieces was resisted. Evelyn plainly puts it, that, in 1661, " the old plays began to disgust this refined age." The wit and polish of the French were set forward by the playwrights as the new objects of English imitation. Some one has said of the ideal theatre that it should be " the Corinthian capital of polished society," and that is what the founders of Restoration drama designed the stage of Davenant and Killigrew to be. There was little appeal made in it to the higher elements of spiritual life; " the springs of nature, passion, or imagination are but feebly touched," as Hazlitt notes. What was mainly attempted was to put the public in close contact with all that was attractive in the pomp of life, in its relation with birth and fashion. Tragedy was to represent, in super-human dignity, the solemn pageant of society; comedy was to paint, in more or less ridiculous colours, its elegancies and affectations. The object of the playwright, odd as it may sound to us, was, as Dryden says in his preface to *The Maiden Queen* (1668), " to show one great and absolute pattern of honour," and to avoid anything in language or manners which should approach to indecorum.

The literature which was produced in these conditions is not lightly to be dismissed as in its nature absurd because we are now wholly out of sympathy with the moral causes which inspired it. The London audiences, like the English dramatists, of the Restoration, looked upon the theatre as something quite distinct from nature. We can best appreciate their feeling if we regard tragedy, as they conceived it, as being an art halfway towards opera. We may be quite sure that sensible persons in the reign of Charles II. were as conscious as we are of the fact that even emperors and princes, under the influence of violent passion, do not spout and shout, nor stride across their palaces with measured gestures and emphatic declamation. But the noble convention of verse itself is already far upon the road of the non-natural, and if we admit the blank iambics of *Hamlet* we go very little further in admitting the rhymed couplets of *The Indian Emperor*. If the latter had been in their own class as good, or even half so good, as the former, there is little doubt that rhyme would have attached itself to tragedy in England as it did in France. No one complains because *Phèdre* is written in rhymed couplets.

But the misfortune was that the English playwrights of the Restoration, active and enthusiastic as they were, did not rise in technical merit to the level of classic tragedy. They missed altogether the harmonious beauty of the ideal Greek play; but they comprehended scarcely better what the finest French tragedians had revealed in the movement of the passions. To say the worst at once, what all the Restoration dramatists suffer from is a tendency to produce common and inadequate poetry. Their inefficiency lies upon them like a blight—dulness in Dryden, flatness in Otway, bombast in Lee. They aimed at subduing emotion to a level of pompous grandeur, but they lacked the splendour of the Greeks, the purity and elasticity of the French. Flat, bombastic, dull—so they are lamentably apt to appear to us when we read them, and in order to endure them we have to remind ourselves of a number of circumstances which justice demands that we should recognise. In particular, the effect of the rhymed verse, which modern critics almost always ridicule, should be judged on the stage itself. The rarity with which Restoration tragedies are given nowadays makes this difficult to do. But some years ago, a careful performance of Dryden's *Maiden Queen* on a London stage revealed to the surprise of the present writer the fact that the repercussion of the rhymes aided rather than impeded his intelligence of the evolution of the plot.

It must be remembered that, whether in rhymed or blank verse, tragedy under Charles II. was delivered in a kind of undulating sing-song. Some idea of its effect may perhaps be gained from Mr. Yeats' experiments in the delivery of verse in his Irish theatre. This was pleasing to the noble amateurs who patronised the stage, and it gave the audience, eager for self-improvement, an impression of being present in the best of company. The tradition of Elizabethan acting, as we have seen, was entirely lost, and when the theatres were opened again, it was necessary for Betterton (1635-1710), who was already without a rival the most capable actor in England, to go over to Paris to study, not merely his Dryden, but his Shakespeare parts. He is supposed to have visited the theatre of Molière, and perhaps in *Don Garcie de Navarre* he received impressions of the best way to represent tragi-comedy. But probably what pleased him best were not such French tragedies as we admire to-day, but those of Quinault and Thomas Corneille, with their languishing ardours of love and romantic travesties of history. These seem, at all events, to have inspired the founder of English "heroic" tragedy, Roger Boyle, first Earl of Orrery (1621-79), who had spent his youth in France, and whose *Henry V.*, in 1664, offered Betterton that part of Owen Tudor in which he is said to have laid the basis of his boundless reputation.

These plays are hardly comprehensible by us to-day, unless we understand them to represent, as we have said, a semi-operatic convention which had its civilising influence on manners. When Diderot asked his terrible questions: "Has any one ever spoken as we declaim? Do kings walk otherwise than does every man who walks well? Do princesses always hiss between their teeth when they talk?" he laid the axe to the root of the whole practice of classical histrionics. There was a radical absence of simplicity about the convention of tragedy, and a determined abuse of all the tricks of rhetoric, and these faults were more obvious in England than in France. But we must take the Restoration plays for what they had to give to a double English audience, composed of men of taste, nurtured in the principles of the French stage, and of coarse citizens, ready to be improved in mind and manners

by representations which sacrificed everything to pomp,
decorum, and refinement. The slow deaths of magnificent
tyrants, queens nobly canorous on the rack, the sacrifice of
royal infants upon pagan altars, no longer seem to us
moving or interesting subjects, but under Charles II., as
under Louis XIV., they took the large aspect of scenes
inspiring, to the sound of verbal music, the most exquisite
sentiments of loyalty and pity. The tragedy of the
Restoration was really a species of historical oratorio, and
to this rule the tender domestic plays of Otway, in which
there is no melody and no pomp, but a striving after the
humility of nature, offer almost the solitary exception.

Comedy after the Restoration was a slower growth than
tragedy. The Royalists came home with their pockets full
of tragedies, but Paris had not supplied them with many
pieces of diversion before 1660. It may be the habit to
insist, too peremptorily, that comedy did not exist in
France before Molière, but it is perfectly correct to say
that it held no position of importance or respect. Comedy
was not what polite people went to the theatre to see, nor
was it what English noblemen and their pleasant monarch
dreamed of introducing for the improvement of manners
on to the new London stage. It was by a very curious
accident, which may have definitely affected the history of
the English stage, that the return of the Royalists occurred
at the moment of the settlement of Molière in Paris, and the
development of a classic comedy among the French. The
opening of the splendid list of Molière's comedies with *Les
Précieuses Ridicules* (1659) coincided with the retirement of
Richard Cromwell and the formation of Lambert's Com-
mittee of Safety, events which drew all hearts and thoughts
of Englishmen in Paris towards their home; while Molière's
next triumph, in *Sganarelle*, was lost to the exiles in the
blaze and excitement of restoration. Paris, therefore,
became to them once more a foreign city exactly at the
moment when it was becoming the scene of the creation of
comedy.

Doubtless for that reason, although the influence and
imitation of Molière are felt in the early English comedies
to an extent to which critical justice has never been done,
yet that imitation and influence are blunter and less
intelligent than would have been the case had English-
speaking playgoers seen them in the original. When Molière

was ejected from the Petit Bourbon and went to the Palais
Royal, a thing new to Europe was revealed on the comic
stage, and it is a great pity that the English poets and
actors were not any longer on the spot to observe it.   Perhaps Orrery and Betterton were, but their thoughts were
habituated to tragedy and the tragic formulas.   Hence,
while Molière positively lifted France into moral light, the
English comic writers who followed him failed to civilise
the roughness of their audiences.   On the contrary, they
sank towards the level of their coarse auditors; they
flattered and cajoled the impudent *petits-maîtres*, the gross
citizens, whom they professed to satirise.   The French
comic stage fought for the respect of the audience, and we
see in *Les Fâcheux* the courage with which Molière took up
the battle against impudence.

However, although there is much to regret in the low
level of comedy between 1665 and 1700, there is much to
applaud.   To Molière was due the increasing naturalness of
the action in the plays of Shadwell and Dryden, to say
nothing of those of Wycherley and Congreve.   If we
eliminate Shakespeare and the purely poetic parts of the
Elizabethans, there is nothing in earlier English comedy to
compare with the best pieces of the Restoration stage,
whether in structure, language, or humour.   What is to be
regretted is the absence of grace.   If we compare what is
perhaps the most uniformly diverting of Dryden's comedies,
Sir Martin Mar-all (in which both Molière and Quinault
are heavily laid under contribution)—if we compare this
boisterous composition with *Les Plaideurs*, which was produced at Paris almost exactly at the same time, we may see
what English comedy lacked in comparison with French.
There are liveliness, a romping, dare-devil exhibition of
character, much dramatic high spirits, but a total absence
of that extraordinary elegance of mind and intellectual
high breeding which mark the no less gay and entertaining
comedy of Racine.

No English writer dared to rise in company with Molière
to the high flights of character-painting in comic verse.
Sir George Etheredge (1634-93) came first, and tried with
insufficient energy to raise his audiences to the Parisian
level.   His *Comical Revenge, or Love in a Tub* (1664), is the
earliest specimen we possess in English of classic comedy.
It is curious to read the contemporary comment on

Etheredge's plays; they " were esteemed by men of sense for the trueness of some of their characters, and the purity, freeness, and easy grace of their dialogue, but on their first appearance they were barbarously treated by the audience." It is a strange notion to us that Dorimant and Sir Fopling Flutter should be distasteful, on account of their refinement and the delicacy of the poet's treatment of them, to spectators at the Duke's Theatre in the reign of Charles and James. But we may conceive this first attempt at a Molièresque analysis of character to be as shocking to admirers of the old rough comedy as Ibsen and Madame Duse were fifteen years ago to lovers of the conventional play and of the stereotyped actor. Towards anything new in the theatrical world audiences are habitually "barbarous." Increased naturalness in writing or performing is always bitterly resisted at first.

There followed Wycherley (1640?-1716), a dramatic artist of more skill and weight than Etheredge, and more intelligently awake to the paramount merits of Molière. He set himself to create scenes of current social life as he cynically saw it, in a state of decomposition. His diagnosis of vice was scandalously farcical, and his picture of society under Charles II. was too heartless and too violent to be anything but a caricature. Nevertheless, Wycherley has vitality, and while we cross his vociferous stage, the curious and unholy men and women who hurtle against us seem living beings. His plays were closely adapted to the temper of the times, and their coarseness, which is offensive to our taste, was not apparent to his immediate contemporaries. Dryden praises " the satire, wit, and strength of manly Wycherley," and describes *The Plain Dealer* as " one of the most bold, most general, and most useful satires which has ever been presented in the English theatre." Thirty years later, one of the most austere of our moralists spoke of *The Country Wife* as " that very pleasant and instructive satire." This appreciation of the comedies of Wycherley continued to exist, without much abatement, until Macaulay made his celebrated attack on them, denying every species of value to the stage of this playwright. Macaulay went much too far in his diatribe. It is true that Wycherley sacrifices nature to artifice, and that he misses the variety, the depth, and the logic of Molière. Nevertheless, he deserves commendation for escaping from the kind of farcical comedy which consisted in dragging mere absurdities, "humours," across the footlights, and in an incessant rattle of extravagant language. He had studied the French with care, and he knew how to build up a comedy. His chief faults arose from his violence, his want of decorum.

His immediate contemporary, Thomas Shadwell (1640?-92), had less art than Wycherley, and he was strikingly less modern. Like all the rest of the comic playwrights of the Restoration, Shadwell studied Molière according to his lights, and he had travelled in France when the earliest of the new comedies were being produced in Paris. But his attitude towards French drama differs from that of Wycherley, who completely accepted the new classic form of comedy, while Shadwell was always reflecting how to plant buds of Molière on to the old worn stock of Ben Jonson. In his first play, *The Sullen Lovers* (1668), Shadwell says that he had already written most of his piece when he received " the report of a play of Molière's of three acts, called *Les Fascheux*," and that he stole two short scenes out of it. The date of *Les Fâcheux* is 1661, but these poets of the Restoration had a curious wish to have it supposed that they wrote their works in extreme youth. Wycherley o'ervaulted his own ambition in this respect so far as to pretend to have written *The Plain Dealer*, which is founded on *Le Misanthrope*, several years before 1666, when that play was produced in Paris. The attitude of all the English playwrights to Molière was so ungenerous that it is difficult to be patient with them. Shadwell has the impudence to say, in the preface to *The Miser* (1672), while admitting his debt to *L'Avare* (1668), " I think I may say without vanity, that Molière's part of it has not suffer'd in my hands, nor did I ever know a French Comedy made use of by the worst of our Poets, that was not better'd by 'em. 'Tis not barrenness of wit or invention that makes us borrow from the French, but laziness." In the face of such fatuity it is almost annoying to have to admit that Shadwell's bustling comedies have excellent qualities of humour.

But Congreve (1670-1729) was the one man who brought intellect to bear on the comic stage of the Restoration. His first merit resides in his style, in the extreme beauty of the language that he uses. This quality was first insisted upon by Hazlitt, who says, very happily, that *The Double Dealer* and *The Way of the World* " are a singular treat to those who have cultivated a taste for the niceties of English style; there is a peculiar flavour in the very words, which is hardly to be found in any other writer." In Congreve's first play, *The Old Bachelor* (1693), this beauty of language is already ripe, and illuminates the exuberant wit which sparkles from one artificial scene to another. In this play the working of a powerful mind is far more apparent than that of an observant eye or a sympathetic heart. The last Congreve never possessed, but his eye became exquisitely trained. In *The Double Dealer* (1694), where there is a still more scintillating, cruel, and prodigal display of wit, the observation of life is more apparent, but this reaches its highest point in *Love for Love* (1695), the most interesting comedy, and therefore the most interesting play, produced in England between the Commonwealth and the reign of George III. Congreve wrote but one other comedy, *The Way of the World* (1700), which had the unaccountable bad fortune to be damned, although it was a work of consummate wit and stage - craft. The fashion of the public, however, was changing, and Congreve, disgusted at what he called "that general taste which seems now to be predominant in the palates of our audience," withdrew in great dudgeon from the theatre, and would write no more plays, though he was still under the age of thirty.

This retirement, in the last year of the century, really marks the close of our period, but there were several dramatists who endeavoured, during the first decade of the eighteenth century, to carry on the tradition of the Restoration stage, while reconciling it to the altered taste which had driven Congreve from the boards. By examining the successes of these latest playwrights we may discover what it was which the shifting fashion of the age desired. Purely intellectual amusement, a direct appeal to the mind of the spectator, was no longer desired. Perhaps it never had been genuinely desired, and it is difficult to believe that Congreve's pyrotechnics were not always high over the heads of his audience. But with the opening of a new century playgoers began more and more to crave the humbler kind of amusement which was ultimately to be found in the novel of domestic manners. The great successes of the period were those of Sir John Vanbrugh(1672-1726), where the language is negligent, but where passages of everyday life are presented with marvellous fidelity; the rattling story is here the great matter, and not the delicate poise of wit or vanity of stage effect. In Congreve's plays we are always thinking of Congreve; in Vanbrugh's we do not ask who it is who presents the exciting adventures of Dick and Brass. Colley Cibber (1671-1757) was a lighter, more innocent, more insipid Vanbrugh, but in George Farquhar (1678-1707) the line of seventeenth - century dramatists closes in a figure of a very pleasing originality. Farquhar was what was then called "a pretty fellow"—a new type, a sentimental soldier, garrulous and tender, contrasting in a good-natured way with the hard and cynical types of satirist who had preceded him. He lies even further from literature than Vanbrugh, but he has great knowledge of life, and a brisk delivery. In him the step between the play and the novel was finally taken, and he himself perceived this. "Comedy," he says in 1702, "is no more at present than a well-framed tale handsomely told as an agreeable vehicle for counsel and reproof."

EDMUND GOSSE.

SELECT BIBLIOGRAPHY

(Titles are spelt as in the first editions)

JOHN DRYDEN. *All for Love: or, The World well Lost*, first acted 1677; published 1678; other editions, 1692, 1696, 1703, 1709, 1710, 1728, 1776, 1778, 1792, 1808, 1811, 1818, 1824, 1826, 1883. Translated into French by A. F. Prévost d'Exiles as *Tout pour l'Amour, ou le Monde bien perdu* (Paris), 1735.

THOMAS OTWAY. *Venice Preserv'd, or, A Plot Discover'd*, first acted February 1681–2; published 1682; other editions, 1696, 1704, 1711, 1735, 1750, 1776, 1778, 1791; revised by J. P. Kemble, 1795, 1811; other editions, 1797, 1808, 1811, 1815, 1818, 1824, 1829, 1834, 1850, 1864, 1883; edited from original quarto by R. Strong, 1885; another edition, 1899. Translated into French by P. A. de la Place as *Venise Sauvée* (Paris), 1747, 1782; by Baron A. G. P. Brugière de Barante (Paris), 1822; into Dutch by G. Muyser as *Het Gered Venetie* (Utrecht), 1755, 1760; into Italian by M. Leoni as *Venezia Salvata* (Firenze), 1817; into German by P. Hagen as *Die Verschworung gegen Venedig* (Leipzig), 1898; by H. von Hofmannsthal as *Das gerettete Venedig* (Berlin), 1905.

WILLIAM WYCHERLEY. *The Country-Wife*, first acted 1675; published 1675; other editions, 1683, 1688, 1695, 1736; altered by John Lee, 1765, 1786; by David Garrick, as *The Country Girl*, 1766, second edition 1767; other editions, 1777, 1791, 1808, 1816, 1819, 1824, 1834, 1835 (?), 1883.

SIR JOHN VANBRUGH. *The Provok'd Wife*, first acted May 1697; published 1697; other editions, 1699, 1709, 1710, 1711, 1727, 1734, 1735, 1743, 1770, 1776, 1777, 1778, 1797, 1808, 1811, 1824, 1864, 1883. Translated into French by C. Marguetel de Saint-Denis as *La femme poussée à bout* (Amsterdam), 1726, 1739.

WILLIAM CONGREVE. *The Way of the World*, first acted 1700; published 1700; second edition, 1706; other editions, 1711, 1735, 1776, 1797; revised by J. P. Kemble, 1800, 1815; other editions, 1811, 1815, 1824, 1864, 1883. Translated into German by J. J. C. Bode as *Der Lauf der Welt* (Leipzig), 1787.

GEORGE FARQUHAR. *The Beaux Stratagem*, first acted 1707; published 1707; other editions, 1711, 1748 (with life of author), 1768, 1776, 1778, 1797, 1808, 1815, 1818, 1824, 1829, 1883, 1898, 1906. Translated into German by J. Leonhardi as *Die Stuzerlist* (Berlin), 1782.

SIR GEORGE ETHEREGE. *The Man of Mode, or, Sr Fopling Flutter*, first acted June 1676; published 1676. Collected editions of Etherege's plays, 1704, 1715, 1735, 1888, 1927.

CONTENTS

ALL FOR LOVE

OR THE WORLD WELL LOST

A TRAGEDY

TO THE RIGHT HONOURABLE

THOMAS, EARL OF DANBY

Viscount Latimer, and Baron Osborne of Kiveton, in Yorkshire; Lord High Treasurer of England, one of His Majesty's Most Honourable Privy Council, and Knight of the Most Noble Order of the Garter.

MY LORD,—The gratitude of poets is so troublesome a virtue to great men, that you are often in danger of your own benefits: for you are threatened with some epistle, and not suffered to do good in quiet, or to compound for their silence whom you have obliged. Yet, I confess, I neither am nor ought to be surprised at this indulgence; for your lordship has the same right to favour poetry, which the great and noble have ever had—

Carmen amat, quisquis carmine digna gerit.

There is somewhat of a tie in nature betwixt those who are born for worthy actions, and those who can transmit them to posterity; and though ours be much the inferior part, it comes at least within the verge of alliance; nor are we unprofitable members of the commonwealth, when we animate others to those virtues, which we copy and describe from you.

It is indeed their interest, who endeavour the subversion of governments, to discourage poets and historians; for the best which can happen to them, is to be forgotten. But such who, under kings, are the fathers of their country, and by a just and prudent ordering of affairs preserve it, have the same reason to cherish the chroniclers of their actions, as they have to lay up in safety the deeds and evidences of their estates; for such records are their undoubted titles to the love and reverence of after ages. Your lordship's administration has already taken up a considerable part of the English annals; and many of its

I

most happy years are owing to it. His Majesty, the most knowing judge of men, and the best master, has acknowledged the ease and benefit he receives in the incomes of his treasury, which you found not only disordered, but exhausted. All things were in the confusion of a chaos, without form or method, if not reduced beyond it, even to annihilation; so that you had not only to separate the jarring elements, but (if that boldness of expression might be allowed me) to create them. Your enemies had so embroiled the management of your office, that they looked on your advancement as the instrument of your ruin. And as if the clogging of the revenue, and the confusion of accounts, which you found in your entrance, were not sufficient, they added their own weight of malice to the public calamity, by forestalling the credit which should cure it. Your friends on the other side were only capable of pitying, but not of aiding you; no further help or counsel was remaining to you, but what was founded on yourself; and that indeed was your security; for your diligence, your constancy, and your prudence, wrought most surely within, when they were not disturbed by any outward motion. The highest virtue is best to be trusted with itself; for assistance only can be given by a genius superior to that which it assists; and it is the noblest kind of debt, when we are only obliged to God and nature. This then, my lord, is your just commendation, that you have wrought out yourself a way to glory, by those very means that were designed for your destruction. You have not only restored but advanced the revenues of your master, without grievance to the subject; and, as if that were little yet, the debts of the exchequer, which lay heaviest both on the crown, and on private persons, have by your conduct been established in a certainty of satisfaction. An action so much the more great and honourable, because the case was without the ordinary relief of laws; above the hopes of the afflicted and beyond the narrowness of the treasury to redress, had it been managed by a less able hand. It is certainly the happiest, and most unenvied part of all your fortune, to do good to many, while you do injury to none; to receive at once the prayers of the subject, and the praises of the prince; and, by the care of your conduct, to give him means of exerting the chiefest (if any be the chiefest) of his royal virtues, his distributive justice to the deserving, and his bounty and compassion to the wanting. The disposition of princes towards their people cannot be better discovered than in the choice of their ministers; who, like the animal spirits betwixt the soul and body, participate somewhat of both natures, and make the communication which is betwixt them. A king, who is just and moderate in his nature, who rules according to the laws, whom God has made happy by forming the temper of his soul to the constitution of his government, and who makes us happy, by assuming over us no other sovereignty than that wherein our welfare and liberty consists; a prince, I say, of so excellent a character, and so suitable to the wishes of all good men, could not better have conveyed himself into his people's apprehensions, than in your lordship's person; who so lively express the same virtues, that you seem not so much a copy, as an emanation of him. Moderation is doubtless an establishment of greatness; but there is a steadiness of temper which is likewise requisite in a minister of state; so equal a mixture of both virtues, that he may stand like an isthmus betwixt the two encroaching seas of arbitrary power, and lawless anarchy. The undertaking would be difficult to any but an extraordinary genius, to stand at the line, and to divide the limits; to pay what is due to the great representative of the nation, and neither to enhance, nor to yield up, the undoubted prerogatives of the crown. These, my lord, are the proper virtues of a noble Englishman, as indeed they are properly English virtues; no people in the world being capable of using them, but we who have the happiness to be born under so equal, and so well-poised a government;—a government which has all the advantages of liberty beyond a commonwealth, and all the marks of kingly sovereignty, without the danger of a tyranny. Both my nature, as I am an Englishman, and my reason, as I am a man, have bred in me a loathing to that specious name of a republic; that mock appearance of a liberty, where all who have not part in the government, are slaves; and slaves they are of a viler note, than such as are subjects to an absolute dominion. For no Christian monarchy is so absolute, but it is circumscribed with laws; but when the executive power is in the law-makers, there is no further check upon them; and the people must suffer without a remedy, because they are oppressed by their representatives. If I must serve, the number of my masters, who were born my equals, would but add to the ignominy of my bondage. The nature of our government, above all others, is exactly suited both to the situation of our country, and the temper of the natives; an island being more proper for commerce and for defence, than for extending its dominions on the Continent; for what the valour of its inhabitants might gain, by reason of its remoteness, and the casualties of the seas, it could not so easily preserve. And, therefore, neither the arbitrary power of One, in a monarchy, nor of Many, in a commonwealth, could make us greater than we are. It is true, that vaster and more frequent taxes might be gathered, when the consent of the people was not asked or needed; but this were only by conquering abroad, to be poor at home; and the examples of our neighbours teach us, that they are not always the happiest subjects, whose kings extend their dominions farthest. Since therefore we cannot win by an offensive war, at least a land war, the model of our government seems naturally contrived for the defensive part; and the consent of a people is easily obtained to contribute to that power which must protect it. *Felices nimium, bona si sua nôrint, Angligenæ !* And yet there are not wanting malcontents among us, who, surfeiting themselves on too much happiness, would persuade the people that they might be happier by a change. It was indeed the policy of their old forefather, when himself was fallen from the station of glory, to seduce mankind into the same rebellion with him, by telling him he might yet be freer than he was; that is more free than his nature would allow, or, if I may so say, than God could make him. We have already all the liberty which freeborn subjects can enjoy, and all beyond it is but licence. But if it be liberty of conscience which they pretend, the moderation of our church is such, that its practice extends not to the severity of persecution; and its discipline is withal so easy, that it allows more freedom to dissenters than any of the sects would allow to it. In the meantime, what right can be pretended by these men to attempt innovation in church or state? Who made them the trustees, or to speak a little nearer their own language, the keepers of the liberty of England? If their call be extraordinary, let them convince us by working miracles; for ordinary vocation they can have none, to disturb the government under which they were born, and which protects them. He who has often changed his party, and always has made his interest the rule of it, gives little evidence of his sincerity for the public good; it is manifest he changes but for himself, and takes the people for tools to work his fortune. Yet the experience of all ages might let him know, that they who trouble the waters first, have seldom the benefit of the fishing; as they who began the late rebellion enjoyed not the fruit of their undertaking, but were crushed themselves by the usurpation of their own instrument. Neither is it enough for them to answer, that they only intend a reformation of the government, but not the subversion of it: on such pretence all insurrections have been founded; it is striking at the root of power, which is obedience. Every remonstrance of private men has the seed of treason in it; and discourses, which are couched in ambiguous terms, are therefore the more dangerous, because they do all the mischief of open sedition, yet are safe from the punishment of the laws. These, my lord, are considerations, which I should not pass so lightly over, had I room to manage them as they deserve; for no man can be so inconsiderable in a nation, as not to have a share in the welfare of it; and if he be a true Englishman, he must at the same time be fired with indignation, and revenge himself as he can on the disturbers of his country. And to whom could I more fitly apply myself than to your lordship, who have not only an inborn, but an hereditary loyalty? The memorable constancy and sufferings of your father, almost to the ruin of his estate, for the royal cause, were an earnest of that which such a parent and such an institution would produce in the person of a son. But so unhappy an occasion of manifesting your own zeal, in suffering for his present majesty, the providence of God, and the prudence of your administration, will, I hope, prevent; that, as your father's fortune waited on the unhappiness of his sovereign, so your own may participate of the better fate which attends his son. The relation which you have by alliance to the noble family of your lady, serves to confirm to you both this happy augury. For what can deserve a greater place in the English chronicle, than the loyalty and courage, the actions and death, of the general of an army, fighting for his prince and country? The honour and gallantry of the Earl of Lindsey is so illustrious a subject, that it is fit to adorn an heroic poem; for he was the proto-martyr of the cause, and the type of his unfortunate royal master.

Yet after all, my lord, if I may speak my thoughts, you are happy rather to us than to yourself; for the multiplicity, the cares, and the vexations of your employment, have betrayed you from yourself, and given you up into the possession of the public. You are robbed of your privacy and friends, and scarce any hour of your life you can call your own. Those, who envy your fortune, if they wanted not good-nature, might more justly pity it; and when they see you watched by a crowd of suitors, whose importunity it is impossible to avoid, would conclude, with reason, that you have lost much more in true content, than you have gained by dignity; and that a private gentleman is better attended by a single servant, than your lordship with so clamorous a train. Pardon me, my lord, if I speak like a philosopher on this subject; the fortune which makes a man uneasy, cannot make him happy; and a wise man must think himself uneasy, when few of his actions are in his choice.

This last consideration has brought me to another, and a very seasonable one for your relief; which is, that while I pity your want of leisure, I have impertinently detained you so long a time. I have put off my own business, which was my dedication, till it is so late, that I am now ashamed to begin it; and therefore I will say nothing of the poem, which I present to you, because I know not if you are like to have an hour, which, with a good conscience, you may throw away in perusing it; and for the author, I have only to beg the continuance of your protection to him, who is, my lord, your lordship's most obliged, most humble, and most obedient servant,

JOHN DRYDEN.

PREFACE

The death of Antony and Cleopatra is a subject which has been treated by the greatest wits of our nation, after Shakespeare; and by all so variously, that their example has given me the confidence to try myself in this bow of Ulysses amongst the crowd of suitors; and, withal, to take my own measures, in aiming at the mark. I doubt not but the same motive has prevailed with all of us in this attempt; I mean the excellency of the moral. For the chief persons represented were famous patterns of unlawful love; and their end accordingly was unfortunate. All reasonable men have long since concluded, that the hero of the poem ought not to be a character of perfect virtue, for then he could not, without injustice, be made unhappy; nor yet altogether wicked, because he could not then be pitied. I have therefore steered the middle course; and have drawn the character of Antony as favourably as Plutarch, Appian, and Dion Cassius would give me leave; the like I have observed in Cleopatra. That which is wanting to work up the pity to a greater height, was not afforded me by the story; for the crimes of love, which they both committed, were not occasioned by any necessity, or fatal ignorance, but were wholly voluntary; since our passions are, or ought to be, within our power. The fabric of the play is regular enough, as to the inferior parts of it; and the unities of time, place, and action, more exactly observed, than perhaps the English theatre requires. Particularly, the action is so much one, that it is the only of the kind without episode, or underplot; every scene in the tragedy conducing to the main design, and every act concluding with a turn of it. The greatest error in the contrivance seems to be in the person of Octavia; for, though I might use the privilege of a poet, to introduce her into Alexandria, yet I had not enough considered, that the compassion she moved to herself and children was destructive to that which I reserved for Antony and Cleopatra; whose mutual love being founded upon vice, must lessen the favour of the audience to them, when virtue and innocence were oppressed by it. And, though I justified Antony in some measure, by making Octavia's departure to proceed wholly from herself; yet the force of the first machine still remained; and the dividing of pity, like the cutting of a river into many channels, abated the strength of the natural stream. But this is an objection which none of my critics have urged against me; and therefore I might have let it pass, if I could have resolved to

7

have been partial to myself. The faults my enemies have found are rather cavils concerning little and not essential decencies; which a master of the ceremonies may decide betwixt us. The French poets, I confess, are strict observers of these punctilios. They would not, for example, have suffered Cleopatra and Octavia to have met; or, if they had met, there must have only passed betwixt them some cold civilities, but no eagerness of repartee, for fear of offending against the greatness of their characters, and the modesty of their sex. This objection I foresaw, and at the same time contemned; for I judged it both natural and probable, that Octavia, proud of her new-gained conquest, would search out Cleopatra to triumph over her; and that Cleopatra, thus attacked, was not of a spirit to shun the encounter. And it is not unlikely, that two exasperated rivals should use such satire as I have put into their mouths; for, after all, though the one were a Roman, and the other a queen, they were both women. It is true, some actions, though natural, are not fit to be represented; and broad obscenities in words ought in good manners to be avoided: expressions therefore are a modest clothing of our thoughts, as breeches and petticoats are of our bodies. If I have kept myself within the bounds of modesty, all beyond, it is but nicety and affectation; which is no more but modesty depraved into a vice. They betray themselves who are too quick of apprehension in such cases, and leave all reasonable men to imagine worse of them, than of the poet.

Honest Montaigne goes yet further: *Nous ne sommes que cérémonie ; la cérémonie nous emporte, et laissons la substance des choses. Nous nous tenons aux branches, et abandonnons le tronc et le corps. Nous avons appris aux dames de rougir, oyans seulement nommer ce qu'elles ne craignent aucunement à faire : Nous n'osons appeler à droit nos membres, et ne craignons pas de les employer à toute sorte de débauche. La cérémonie nous défend d'exprimer par paroles les choses licites et naturelles, et nous l'en croyons ; la raison nous défend de n'en faire point d'illicites et mauvaises, et personne ne l'en croit.* My comfort is, that by this opinion my enemies are but sucking critics, who would fain be nibbling ere their teeth are come.

Yet, in this nicety of manners does the excellency of French poetry consist. Their heroes are the most civil people breathing; but their good breeding seldom extends to a word of sense; all their wit is in their ceremony; they want the genius which animates our stage; and therefore it is but necessary, when they cannot please, that they should take care not to offend. But as the civilest man in the company is commonly the dullest, so these authors, while they are afraid to make you laugh or cry, out of pure good manners make you sleep. They are so careful not to exasperate a critic, that they never leave him any work; so busy with the broom, and make so clean a riddance that there

is little left either for censure or for praise. For no part of a
poem is worth our discommending, where the whole is insipid;
as when we have once tasted of palled wine, we stay not to
examine it glass by glass. But while they affect to shine in
trifles, they are often careless in essentials. Thus, their Hippolytus is so scrupulous in point of decency, that he will rather
expose himself to death, than accuse his stepmother to his father;
and my critics I am sure will commend him for it. But we of
grosser apprehensions are apt to think that this excess of
generosity is not practicable, but with fools and madmen. This
was good manners with a vengeance; and the audience is like to
be much concerned at the misfortunes of this admirable hero.
But take Hippolytus out of his poetic fit, and I suppose he would
think it a wiser part to set the saddle on the right horse, and
choose rather to live with the reputation of a plain-spoken,
honest man, than to die with the infamy of an incestuous villain.
In the meantime we may take notice, that where the poet ought
to have preserved the character as it was delivered to us by
antiquity, when he should have given us the picture of a rough
young man, of the Amazonian strain, a jolly huntsman, and
both by his profession and his early rising a mortal enemy to
love, he has chosen to give him the turn of gallantry, sent him
to travel from Athens to Paris, taught him to make love, and
transformed the Hippolytus of Euripides into Monsieur Hippo-
lyte. I should not have troubled myself thus far with French
poets, but that I find our *Chedreux* critics wholly form their
judgments by them. But for my part, I desire to be tried by
the laws of my own country; for it seems unjust to me, that the
French should prescribe here, till they have conquered. Our
little sonneteers, who follow them, have too narrow souls to
judge of poetry. Poets themselves are the most proper, though
I conclude not the only critics. But till some genius, as universal
as Aristotle, shall arise, one who can penetrate into all arts and
sciences, without the practice of them, I shall think it reasonable,
that the judgment of an artificer in his own art should be
preferable to the opinion of another man; at least where he is
not bribed by interest, or prejudiced by malice. And this, I
suppose, is manifest by plain inductions. For, first, the crowd
cannot be presumed to have more than a gross instinct, of what
pleases or displeases them. Every man will grant me this; but
then, by a particular kindness to himself, he draws his own
stake first, and will be distinguished from the multitude, of
which other men may think him one. But, if I come closer
to those who are allowed for witty men, either by the advantage
of their quality, or by common fame, and affirm that neither
are they qualified to decide sovereignly concerning poetry, I
shall yet have a strong party of my opinion; for most of them
severally will exclude the rest, either from the number of witty
men, or at least of able judges. But here again they are all

indulgent to themselves; and every one who believes himself a
wit, that is, every man, will pretend at the same time to a right
of judging.   But to press it yet further, there are many witty
men, but few poets; neither have all poets a taste of tragedy.
And this is the rock on which they are daily splitting.   Poetry,
which is a picture of nature, must generally please; but it is not
to be understood that all parts of it must please every man;
therefore is not tragedy to be judged by a witty man, whose
taste is only confined to comedy.   Nor is every man, who loves
tragedy, a sufficient judge of it; he must understand the
excellences of it too, or he will only prove a blind admirer, not
a critic.   From hence it comes that so many satires on poets,
and censures of their writings, fly abroad.   Men of pleasant
conversation (at least esteemed so), and endued with a trifling
kind of fancy, perhaps helped out with some smattering of Latin,
are ambitious to distinguish themselves from the herd of gentlemen, by their poetry—

Rarus enim fermè sensus communis in illâ
Fortunâ.

And is not this a wretched affectation, not to be contented
with what fortune has done for them, and sit down quietly with
their estates, but they must call their wits in question, and
needlessly expose their nakedness to public view?   Not considering that they are not to expect the same approbation from
sober men, which they have found from their flatterers after the
third bottle.   If a little glittering in discourse has passed them
on us for witty men, where was the necessity of undeceiving the
world?   Would a man who has an ill title to an estate, but yet
is in possession of it; would he bring it of his own accord, to be
tried at Westminster?   We who write, if we want the talent,
yet have the excuse that we do it for a poor subsistence; but
what can be urged in their defence, who, not having the vocation
of poverty to scribble, out of mere wantonness take pains to
make themselves ridiculous?   Horace was certainly in the right
where he said, " That no man is satisfied with his own condition."
A poet is not pleased, because he is not rich; and the rich are
discontented, because the poets will not admit them of their
number.   Thus the case is hard with writers.   If they succeed
not, they must starve; and if they do, some malicious satire is
prepared to level them, for daring to please without their leave.
But while they are so eager to destroy the fame of others, their
ambition is manifest in their concernment; some poem of their
own is to be produced, and the slaves are to be laid flat with
their faces on the ground, that the monarch may appear in the
greater majesty.

Dionysius and Nero had the same longings, but with all their
power they could never bring their business well about.   'Tis
true, they proclaimed themselves poets by sound of trumpet;

and poets they were, upon pain of death to any man who durst
call them otherwise. The audience had a fine time on't, you
may imagine; they sat in a bodily fear, and looked as demurely
as they could: for it was a hanging matter to laugh unseasonably;
and the tyrants were suspicious, as they had reason, that their
subjects had them in the wind; so, every man, in his own defence,
set as good a face upon the business as he could. It was known
beforehand that the monarchs were to be crowned laureates;
but when the show was over, and an honest man was suffered
to depart quietly, he took out his laughter which he had stifled,
with a firm resolution never more to see an emperor's play,
though he had been ten years a-making it. In the meantime
the true poets were they who made the best markets: for they had
wit enough to yield the prize with a good grace, and not contend
with him who had thirty legions. They were sure to be rewarded,
if they confessed themselves bad writers, and that was somewhat
better than to be martyrs for their reputation. Lucan's example
was enough to teach them manners; and after he was put to
death, for overcoming Nero, the emperor carried it without
dispute for the best poet in his dominions. No man was
ambitious of that grinning honour; for if he heard the malicious
trumpeter proclaiming his name before his betters, he knew there
was but one way with him. Mæcenas took another course, and
we know he was more than a great man, for he was witty too:
but finding himself far gone in poetry, which Seneca assures us
was not his talent, he thought it his best way to be well with
Virgil and with Horace; that at least he might be a poet at the
second hand; and we see how happily it has succeeded with
him; for his own bad poetry is forgotten, and their panegyrics
of him still remain. But they who should be our patrons are
for no such expensive ways to fame; they have much of the
poetry of Mæcenas, but little of his liberality. They are for
persecuting Horace and Virgil, in the persons of their successors;
for such is every man who has any part of their soul and fire,
though in a less degree. Some of their little zanies yet go
further; for they are persecutors even of Horace himself, as far
as they are able, by their ignorant and vile imitations of him;
by making an unjust use of his authority, and turning his
artillery against his friends. But how would he disdain to be
copied by such hands! I dare answer for him, he would be more
uneasy in their company, than he was with Crispinus, their
forefather, in the Holy Way; and would no more have allowed
them a place amongst the critics, than he would Demetrius the
mimic, and Tigellius the buffoon;

———— *Demetri, teque, Tigelli,*
Discipulorum inter jubeo plorare cathedras.

With what scorn would he look down on such miserable trans-
lators, who make doggerel of his Latin, mistake his meaning,

misapply his censures, and often contradict their own? He is fixed as a landmark to set out the bounds of poetry—

> ———— *Saxum antiquum, ingens,—*
> *Limes agro positus, litem ut discerneret arvis.*

But other arms than theirs, and other sinews are required, to raise the weight of such an author; and when they would toss him against enemies—

> *Genua labant, gelidus concrevit frigore sanguis.*
> *Tum lapis ipse viri, vacuum per inane volatus,*
> *Nec spatium evasit totum, nec pertulit ictum.*

For my part, I would wish no other revenge, either for myself, or the rest of the poets, from this rhyming judge of the twelve-penny gallery, this legitimate son of Sternhold, than that he would subscribe his name to his censure, or (not to tax him beyond his learning) set his mark. For, should he own himself publicly, and come from behind the lion's skin, they whom he condemns would be thankful to him, they whom he praises would choose to be condemned; and the magistrates, whom he has elected, would modestly withdraw from their employment, to avoid the scandal of his nomination. The sharpness of his satire, next to himself, falls most heavily on his friends, and they ought never to forgive him for commending them perpetually the wrong way, and sometimes by contraries. If he have a friend, whose hastiness in writing is his greatest fault, Horace would have taught him to have minced the matter, and to have called it readiness of thought, and a flowing fancy; for friendship will allow a man to christen an imperfection by the name of some neighbour virtue—

> *Vellem in amicitiâ sic erraremus ; et isti*
> *Errori nomen virtus posuisset honestum.*

But he would never have allowed him to have called a slow man hasty, or a hasty writer a slow drudge, as Juvenal explains it—

> ———— *Canibus pigris, scabieque vetustâ*
> *Lævibus, et siccæ lambentibus ora lucernæ,*
> *Nomen erit, Pardus, Tigris, Leo ; si quid adhuc est*
> *Quod fremit in terris violentius.*

Yet Lucretius laughs at a foolish lover, even for excusing the imperfections of his mistress—

> *Nigra* μελίχροος *est, immunda et fœtida* ἄκοσμος.
> *Balba loqui non quit,* τραυλίζει ; *muta pudens est,* etc.

But to drive it *ad Æthiopem cygnum* is not to be endured. I leave him to interpret this by the benefit of his French version on the other side, and without further considering him, than I have the rest of my illiterate censors, whom I have disdained to answer, because they are not qualified for judges. It remains that I acquaint the reader, that I have endeavoured in this play to follow the practice of the ancients, who, as Mr. Rymer has judiciously observed, are and ought to be our masters. Horace likewise gives it for a rule in his art of poetry—

——— *Vos exemplaria Græca*
Nocturnâ versate manu, versate diurnâ.

Yet, though their models are regular, they are too little for English tragedy; which requires to be built in a larger compass. I could give an instance in the *Œdipus Tyrannus*, which was the masterpiece of Sophocles; but I reserve it for a more fit occasion, which I hope to have hereafter. In my style, I have professed to imitate the divine Shakespeare; which that I might perform more freely, I have disencumbered myself from rhyme. Not that I condemn my former way, but that this is more proper to my present purpose. I hope I need not to explain myself, that I have not copied my author servilely. Words and phrases must of necessity receive a change in succeeding ages; but it is almost a miracle that much of his language remains so pure; and that he who began dramatic poetry amongst us, untaught by any, and as Ben Jonson tells us, without learning, should by the force of his own genius perform so much, that in a manner he has left no praise for any who come after him. The occasion is fair, and the subject would be pleasant to handle the difference of styles betwixt him and Fletcher, and wherein, and how far they are both to be imitated. But since I must not be over-confident of my own performance after him, it will be prudence in me to be silent. Yet, I hope, I may affirm, and without vanity, that, by imitating him, I have excelled myself throughout the play; and particularly, that I prefer the scene betwixt Antony and Ventidius in the first act, to anything which I have written in this kind.

PROLOGUE

WHAT flocks of critics hover here to-day,
As vultures wait on armies for their prey,
All gaping for the carcase of a play!
With croaking notes they bode some dire event,
And follow dying poets by the scent.
Ours gives himself for gone; y' have watched your time:
He fights this day unarmed,—without his rhyme;—
And brings a tale which often has been told;
As sad as Dido's; and almost as old.
His hero, whom you wits his bully call,
Bates of his mettle, and scarce rants at all:
He's somewhat lewd; but a well-meaning mind;
Weeps much; fights little; but is wond'rous kind.
In short, a pattern, and companion fit,
For all the keeping Tonies of the pit.
I could name more: a wife, and mistress too;
Both (to be plain) too good for most of you:
The wife well-natured, and the mistress true.

   Now, poets, if your fame has been his care,
Allow him all the candour you can spare.
A brave man scorns to quarrel once a-day;
Like Hectors in at every petty fray.
Let those find fault whose wit's so very small,
They've need to show that they can think at all;
Errors, like straws, upon the surface flow;
He who would search for pearls, must dive below.
Fops may have leave to level all they can;
As pigmies would be glad to lop a man.
Half-wits are fleas; so little and so light,
We scarce could know they live, but that they bite.
But, as the rich, when tired with daily feasts,
For change, become their next poor tenant's guests;
Drink hearty draughts of ale from plain brown bowls,
And snatch the homely rasher from the coals:
So you, retiring from much better cheer,
For once, may venture to do penance here.
And since that plenteous autumn now is past,
Whose grapes and peaches have indulged your taste,
Take in good part, from our poor poet's board,
Such rivelled fruits as winter can afford.

DRAMATIS PERSONÆ

Mark Antony.
Ventidius, his General.
Dolabella, his Friend.
Alexas, the Queen's Eunuch.
Serapion, Priest of Isis.
Myris, another Priest.
Servants to Antony.

Cleopatra, Queen of Egypt.
Octavia, Antony's Wife.
Charmion, } Cleopatra's Maids.
Iras,
Antony's two little Daughters.

SCENE—Alexandria.

ACT I

SCENE I.—*The Temple of Isis*

Enter SERAPION, MYRIS, Priests of Isis.

Serap. Portents and prodigies have grown so frequent,
That they have lost their name. Our fruitful Nile
Flowed ere the wonted season, with a torrent
So unexpected, and so wondrous fierce,
That the wild deluge overtook the haste
Even of the hinds that watched it: Men and beasts
Were borne above the tops of trees, that grew
On the utmost margin of the water-mark.
Then, with so swift an ebb the flood drove backward,
It slipt from underneath the scaly herd:
Here monstrous phocæ panted on the shore;
Forsaken dolphins there with their broad tails,
Lay lashing the departing waves: hard by them,
Sea horses floundering in the slimy mud,
Tossed up their heads, and dashed the ooze about them

Enter ALEXAS *behind them.*

Myr. Avert these omens, Heaven!
Serap. Last night, between the hours of twelve and one,
In a lone aisle of the temple while I walked,
A whirlwind rose, that, with a violent blast,
Shook all the dome: the doors around me clapt;
The iron wicket, that defends the vault,
Where the long race of Ptolemies is laid,
Burst open, and disclosed the mighty dead.
From out each monument, in order placed,
An armed ghost starts up: the boy-king last
Reared his inglorious head. A peal of groans
Then followed, and a lamentable voice
Cried, Egypt is no more! My blood ran back,
My shaking knees against each other knocked;
On the cold pavement down I fell entranced,
And so unfinished left the horrid scene.
Alex. And dreamed you this? or did invent the story,
                                        [*Showing himself.*
To frighten our Egyptian boys withal,
And train them up, betimes, in fear of priesthood?
Serap. My lord, I saw you not,

Nor meant my words should reach your ears; but what
I uttered was most true.

    Alex. A foolish dream,
Bred from the fumes of indigested feasts,
And holy luxury.

    Serap. I know my duty:
This goes no further.

    Alex. 'Tis not fit it should;
Nor would the times now bear it, were it true.
All southern, from yon hills, the Roman camp
Hangs o'er us black and threatening, like a storm
Just breaking on our heads.

    Serap. Our faint Egyptians pray for Antony:
But in their servile hearts they own Octavius.

    Myr. Why then does Antony dream out his hours,
And tempts not fortune for a noble day,
Which might redeem what Actium lost?

    Alex. He thinks 'tis past recovery.

    Serap. Yet the foe
Seems not to press the siege.

    Alex. Oh, there's the wonder.
Mæcenas and Agrippa, who can most
With Cæsar, are his foes. His wife Octavia,
Driven from his house, solicits her revenge;
And Dolabella, who was once his friend,
Upon some private grudge, now seeks his ruin:
Yet still war seems on either side to sleep.

    Serap. 'Tis strange that Antony, for some days past,
Has not beheld the face of Cleopatra;
But here, in Isis' temple, lives retired,
And makes his heart a prey to black despair.

    Alex. 'Tis true; and we much fear he hopes by absence
To cure his mind of love.

    Serap. If he be vanquished,
Or make his peace, Egypt is doomed to be
A Roman province; and our plenteous harvests
Must then redeem the scarceness of their soil.
While Antony stood firm, our Alexandria
Rivalled proud Rome (dominion's other seat),
And Fortune striding, like a vast Colossus,
Could fix an equal foot of empire here.

    Alex. Had I my wish, these tyrants of all nature,
Who lord it o'er mankind, should perish,—perish,
Each by the other's sword; but, since our will
Is lamely followed by our power, we must
Depend on one; with him to rise or fall.

    Serap. How stands the queen affected?

    Alex. Oh, she dotes,
She dotes, Serapion, on this vanquished man,

And winds herself about his mighty ruins;
Whom would she yet forsake, yet yield him up,
This hunted prey, to his pursuer's hands,
She might preserve us all: but 'tis in vain—
This changes my designs, this blasts my counsels,
And makes me use all means to keep him here,
Whom I could wish divided from her arms,
Far as the earth's deep centre. Well, you know
The state of things; no more of your ill omens
And black prognostics; labour to confirm
The people's hearts.

Enter VENTIDIUS, *talking aside with a* Gentleman *of* ANTONY'S.

   Serap. These Romans will o'erhear us.
But, who's that stranger? By his warlike port,
His fierce demeanour, and erected look,
He's of no vulgar note.
   Alex. Oh 'tis Ventidius,
Our emperor's great lieutenant in the East,
Who first showed Rome that Parthia could be conquered.
When Antony returned from Syria last,
He left this man to guard the Roman frontiers.
   Serap. You seem to know him well.
   Alex. Too well. I saw him at Cilicia first,
When Cleopatra there met Antony:
A mortal foe he was to us, and Egypt.
But,—let me witness to the worth I hate,—
A braver Roman never drew a sword;
Firm to his prince, but as a friend, not slave.
He ne'er was of his pleasures; but presides
O'er all his cooler hours, and morning counsels:
In short the plainness, fierceness, rugged virtue,
Of an old true-stampt Roman lives in him.
His coming bodes I know not what of ill
To our affairs. Withdraw to mark him better;
And I'll acquaint you why I sought you here,
And what's our present work.
[*They withdraw to a corner of the stage ; and* VENTIDIUS,
     with the other, comes forward to the front.
   Vent. Not see him, say you?
I say, I must, and will.
   Gent. He has commanded,
On pain of death, none should approach his presence.
   Vent. I bring him news will raise his drooping spirits,
Give him new life.
   Gent. He sees not Cleopatra.
   Vent. Would he had never seen her!
   Gent. He eats not, drinks not, sleeps not, has no use

Of anything, but thought; or if he talks,
'Tis to himself, and then 'tis perfect raving:
Then he defies the world, and bids it pass;
Sometimes he gnaws his lip, and curses loud
The boy Octavius; then he draws his mouth
Into a scornful smile, and cries, " Take all,
The world's not worth my care."

Vent. Just, just his nature.
Virtue's his path; but sometimes 'tis too narrow
For his vast soul; and then he starts out wide,
And bounds into a vice, that bears him far
From his first course, and plunges him in ills:
But, when his danger makes him find his fault,
Quick to observe, and full of sharp remorse,
He censures eagerly his own misdeeds,
Judging himself with malice to himself,
And not forgiving what as man he did,
Because his other parts are more than man.—
He must not thus be lost.

[ALEXAS *and the* Priests *come forward.*

Alex. You have your full instructions, now advance;
Proclaim your orders loudly.

Serap. Romans, Egyptians, hear the queen's command.
Thus Cleopatra bids: Let labour cease;
To pomp and triumphs give this happy day,
That gave the world a lord: 'tis Antony's.
Live, Antony; and Cleopatra live!
Be this the general voice sent up to heaven,
And every public place repeat this echo.

Vent. Fine pageantry!   [*Aside.*

Serap. Set out before your doors
The images of all your sleeping fathers,
With laurels crowned; with laurels wreathe your posts,
And strew with flowers the pavement; let the priests
Do present sacrifice; pour out the wine,
And call the gods to join with you in gladness.

Vent. Curse on the tongue that bids this general joy!
Can they be friends of Antony, who revel
When Antony's in danger? Hide, for shame,
You Romans, your great grandsires' images,
For fear their souls should animate their marbles,
To blush at their degenerate progeny.

Alex. A love, which knows no bounds, to Antony,
Would mark the day with honours, when all heaven
Laboured for him, when each propitious star
Stood wakeful in his orb, to watch that hour,
And shed his better influence. Her own birthday
Our queen neglected like a vulgar fate,
That passed obscurely by.

Vent. Would it had slept,
Divided far from this; till some remote
And future age had called it out, to ruin
Some other prince, not him!
    Alex. Your emperor,
Though grown unkind, would be more gentle, than
To upbraid my queen for loving him too well.
    Vent. Does the mute sacrifice upbraid the priest?
He knows him not his executioner.
Oh, she has decked his ruin with her love,
Led him in golden bands to gaudy slaughter,
And made perdition pleasing: She has left him
The blank of what he was.
I tell thee, eunuch, she has quite unmanned him.
Can any Roman see, and know him now,
Thus altered from the lord of half mankind,
Unbent, unsinewed, made a woman's toy,
Shrunk from the vast extent of all his honours,
And crampt within a corner of the world?
O Antony!
Thou bravest soldier, and thou best of friends!
Bounteous as nature; next to nature's God!
Couldst thou but make new worlds, so wouldst thou give them,
As bounty were thy being! rough in battle,
As the first Romans when they went to war;
Yet after victory more pitiful
Than all their praying virgins left at home!
    Alex. Would you could add, to those more shining virtues,
His truth to her who loves him.
    Vent. Would I could not!
But wherefore waste I precious hours with thee!
Thou art her darling mischief, her chief engine,
Antony's other fate. Go, tell thy queen,
Ventidius is arrived, to end her charms.
Let your Egyptian timbrels play alone,
Nor mix effeminate sounds with Roman trumpets.
You dare not fight for Antony; go pray
And keep your cowards' holiday in temples.
                     [*Exeunt* ALEXAS, SERAPION.

Re-enter the Gentleman *of* M. ANTONY.

    2 Gent. The emperor approaches, and commands,
On pain of death, that none presume to stay.
    1 Gent. I dare not disobey him.   [*Going out with the other.*
    Vent. Well, I dare.
But I'll observe him first unseen, and find
Which way his humour drives: The rest I'll venture.
                              [*Withdraws.*

Enter ANTONY, *walking with a disturbed motion before
he speaks.*

Ant. They tell me, 'tis my birthday, and I'll keep it
With double pomp of sadness.
'Tis what the day deserves, which gave me breath.
Why was I raised the meteor of the world,
Hung in the skies, and blazing as I travelled,
Till all my fires were spent; and then cast downward,
To be trod out by Cæsar?
     Vent. [*aside*]. On my soul,
'Tis mournful, wondrous mournful!
     Ant. Count thy gains.
Now, Antony, wouldst thou be born for this?
Glutton of fortune, thy devouring youth
Has starved thy wanting age.
     Vent. How sorrow shakes him!   [*Aside.*
So, now the tempest tears him up by the roots,
And on the ground extends the noble ruin.
               [ANTONY *having thrown himself down.*
Lie there, thou shadow of an emperor;
The place thou pressest on thy mother earth
Is all thy empire now: now it contains thee;
Some few days hence, and then 'twill be too large,
When thou'rt contracted in thy narrow urn,
Shrunk to a few cold ashes; then Octavia
(For Cleopatra will not live to see it),
Octavia then will have thee all her own,
And bear thee in her widowed hand to Cæsar;
Cæsar will weep, the crocodile will weep,
To see his rival of the universe
Lie still and peaceful there. I'll think no more on't.
     Ant. Give me some music: look that it be sad:
I'll soothe my melancholy, till I swell,
And burst myself with sighing.—   [*Soft music.*
'Tis somewhat to my humour: stay, I fancy
I'm now turned wild, a commoner of nature;
Of all forsaken, and forsaking all;
Live in a shady forest's sylvan scene,
Stretched at my length beneath some blasted oak,
I lean my head upon the mossy bark,
And look just of a piece as I grew from it;
My uncombed locks, matted like mistletoe,
Hang o'er my hoary face; a murmuring brook
Runs at my foot.
     Vent. Methinks I fancy
Myself there too.
     Ant. The herd come jumping by me,
And, fearless, quench their thirst, while I look on,

And take me for their fellow-citizen.
More of this image, more; it lulls my thoughts.

[Soft music again.

    Vent. I must disturb him; I can hold no longer.

[Stands before him.

    Ant. [starting up]. Art thou Ventidius?
    Vent. Are you Antony?
I'm liker what I was, than you to him
I left you last.
    Ant. I'm angry.
    Vent. So am I.
    Ant. I would be private: leave me.
    Vent. Sir, I love you,
And therefore will not leave you.
    Ant. Will not leave me!
Where have you learnt that answer? Who am I?
    Vent. My emperor; the man I love next Heaven:
If I said more, I think 'twere scarce a sin:
You're all that's good, and god-like.
    Ant. All that's wretched.
You will not leave me then?
    Vent. 'Twas too presuming
To say I would not; but I dare not leave you:
And, 'tis unkind in you to chide me hence
So soon, when I so far have come to see you.
    Ant. Now thou hast seen me, art thou satisfied?
For, if a friend, thou hast beheld enough;
And, if a foe, too much.
    Vent. Look, emperor, this is no common dew.   *[Weeping.*
I have not wept this forty years; but now
My mother comes afresh into my eyes;
I cannot help her softness.
    Ant. By heaven, he weeps! poor good old man, he weeps!
The big round drops course one another down
The furrows of his cheeks.—Stop them, Ventidius,
Or I shall blush to death: they set my shame,
That caused them, full before me.
    Vent. I'll do my best.
    Ant. Sure there's contagion in the tears of friends ·
See, I have caught it too. Believe me, 'tis not
For my own griefs, but thine.—Nay, father!
    Vent. Emperor.
    Ant. Emperor! Why, that's the style of victory;
The conqu'ring soldier, red with unfelt wounds,
Salutes his general so: but never more
Shall that sound reach my ears.
    Vent. I warrant you.
    Ant. Actium, Actium! Oh!——
    Vent. It sits too near you.

*B 604

Ant. Here, here it lies; a lump of lead by day,
And, in my short, distracted, nightly slumbers,
The hag that rides my dreams.——

   Vent. Out with it; give it vent.

   Ant. Urge not my shame.
I lost a battle,——

   Vent. So has Julius done.

   Ant. Thou favour'st me, and speak'st not half thou think'st;
For Julius fought it out, and lost it fairly:
But Antony——

   Vent. Nay, stop not.

   Ant. Antony,—
Well, thou wilt have it—like a coward, fled,
Fled while his soldiers fought; fled first, Ventidius.
Thou long'st to curse me, and I give thee leave.
I know thou cam'st prepared to rail.

   Vent. I did.

   Ant. I'll help thee.—I have been a man, Ventidius.

   Vent. Yes, and a brave one; but——

   Ant. I know thy meaning.
But I have lost my reason, have disgraced
The name of soldier, with inglorious ease.
In the full vintage of my flowing honours,
Sat still, and saw it prest by other hands.
Fortune came smiling to my youth, and wooed it,
And purple greatness met my ripened years.
When first I came to empire, I was borne
On tides of people, crowding to my triumphs;
The wish of nations, and the willing world
Received me as its pledge of future peace;
I was so great, so happy, so beloved,
Fate could not ruin me; till I took pains,
And worked against my fortune, chid her from me,
And turned her loose; yet still she came again.
My careless days, and my luxurious nights,
At length have wearied her, and now she's gone,
Gone, gone, divorced for ever. Help me, soldier,
To curse this madman, this industrious fool,
Who laboured to be wretched: Pr'ythee, curse me.

   Vent. No.

   Ant. Why?

   Vent. You are too sensible already
Of what you've done, too conscious of your failings;
And, like a scorpion, whipt by others first
To fury, sting yourself in mad revenge.
I would bring balm, and pour it in your wounds,
Cure your distempered mind, and heal your fortunes.

   Ant. I know thou would'st.

   Vent. I will.

Ant. Ha, ha, ha, ha!

Vent. You laugh.

Ant. I do, to see officious love
Give cordials to the dead.

Vent. You would be lost, then?

Ant. I am.

Vent. I say you are not. Try your fortune.

Ant. I have, to the utmost. Dost thou think me desperate,
Without just cause? No, when I found all lost
Beyond repair, I hid me from the world,
And learnt to scorn it here; which now I do
So heartily, I think it is not worth
The cost of keeping.

Vent. Cæsar thinks not so;
He'll thank you for the gift he could not take.
You would be killed like Tully, would you? do,
Hold out your throat to Cæsar, and die tamely.

Ant. No, I can kill myself; and so resolve.

Vent. I can die with you too, when time shall serve;
But fortune calls upon us now to live,
To fight, to conquer.

Ant. Sure thou dream'st, Ventidius.

Vent. No; 'tis you dream; you sleep away your hours
In desperate sloth, miscalled philosophy.
Up, up, for honour's sake; twelve legions wait you,
And long to call you chief: By painful journeys
I led them, patient both of heat and hunger,
Down from the Parthian marches to the Nile.
'Twill do you good to see their sunburnt faces,
Their scarred cheeks, and chopt hands: there's virtue in
    them.
They'll sell those mangled limbs at dearer rates
Than yon trim bands can buy.

Ant. Where left you them?

Vent. I said in Lower Syria.

Ant. Bring them hither;
There may be life in these.

Vent. They will not come.

Ant. Why didst thou mock my hopes with promised
    aids,
To double my despair? They're mutinous.

Vent. Most firm and loyal.

Ant. Yet they will not march
To succour me. O trifler!

Vent. They petition
You would make haste to head them.

Ant. I'm besieged.

Vent. There's but one way shut up: How came I hither?

Ant. I will not stir.

Vent. They would perhaps desire
A better reason.

Ant. I have never used
My soldiers to demand a reason of
My actions.　Why did they refuse to march?

Vent. They said they would not fight for Cleopatra.

Ant. What was't they said?

Vent. They said they would not fight for Cleopatra.
Why should they fight indeed, to make her conquer,
And make you more a slave? to gain you kingdoms,
Which, for a kiss, at your next midnight feast,
You'll sell to her?　Then she new-names her jewels,
And calls this diamond such or such a tax;
Each pendant in her ear shall be a province.

Ant. Ventidius, I allow your tongue free licence
On all my other faults; but, on your life,
No word of Cleopatra: she deserves
More worlds than I can lose.

Vent. Behold, you Powers,
To whom you have intrusted humankind!
See Europe, Afric, Asia, put in balance,
And all weighed down by one light, worthless woman!
I think the gods are Antonies, and give,
Like prodigals, this nether world away
To none but wasteful hands.

Ant. You grow presumptuous.

Vent. I take the privilege of plain love to speak.

Ant. Plain love! plain arrogance, plain insolence!
Thy men are cowards; thou, an envious traitor;
Who, under seeming honesty, hast vented
The burden of thy rank, o'erflowing gall.
O that thou wert my equal; great in arms
As the first Cæsar was, that I might kill thee
Without a stain to honour!

Vent. You may kill me;
You have done more already,—called me traitor.

Ant. Art thou not one?

Vent. For showing you yourself,
Which none else durst have done? but had I been
That name, which I disdain to speak again,
I needed not have sought your abject fortunes,
Come to partake your fate, to die with you.
What hindered me to have led my conquering eagles
To fill Octavius' bands?　I could have been
A traitor then, a glorious, happy traitor,
And not have been so called.

Ant. Forgive me, soldier;
I've been too passionate.

Vent. You thought me false;

Thought my old age betrayed you: Kill me, sir,
Pray, kill me; yet you need not, your unkindness
Has left your sword no work.
    Ant. I did not think so;
I said it in my rage: Pr'ythee, forgive me.
Why didst thou tempt my anger, by discovery
Of what I would not hear?
    Vent. No prince but you
Could merit that sincerity I used,
Nor durst another man have ventured it;
But you, ere love misled your wandering eyes,
Were sure the chief and best of human race,
Framed in the very pride and boast of nature;
So perfect, that the gods, who formed you, wondered
At their own skill, and cried—A lucky hit
Has mended our design. Their envy hindered,
Else you had been immortal, and a pattern,
When Heaven would work for ostentation's sake
To copy out again.
    Ant. But Cleopatra—
Go on; for I can bear it now.
    Vent. No more.
    Ant. Thou dar'st not trust my passion, but thou may'st;
Thou only lov'st, the rest have flattered me.
    Vent. Heaven's blessing on your heart for that kind word!
May I believe you love me? Speak again.
    Ant. Indeed I do. Speak this, and this, and this.
                              [Hugging him.
Thy praises were unjust; but, I'll deserve them,
And yet mend all. Do with me what thou wilt;
Lead me to victory! thou know'st the way.
    Vent. And, will you leave this——
    Ant. Pr'ythee, do not curse her,
And I will leave her; though, Heaven knows, I love
Beyond life, conquest, empire, all, but honour;
But I will leave her.
    Vent. That's my royal master;
And, shall we fight?
    Ant. I warrant thee, old soldier.
Thou shalt behold me once again in iron;
And at the head of our old troops, that beat
The Parthians, cry aloud—Come, follow me!
    Vent. Oh, now I hear my emperor! in that word
Octavius fell. Gods, let me see that day,
And, if I have ten years behind, take all:
I'll thank you for the exchange.
    Ant. O Cleopatra!
    Vent. Again?
    Ant. I've done: In that last sigh she went.

Cæsar shall know what 'tis to force a lover
From all he holds most dear.
   Vent. Methinks, you breathe
Another soul: Your looks are more divine;
You speak a hero, and you move a god.
   Ant. Oh, thou hast fired me; my soul's up in arms,
And mans each part about me: Once again,
That noble eagerness of fight has seized me;
That eagerness with which I darted upward
To Cassius' camp: In vain the steepy hill
Opposed my way; in vain a war of spears
Sung round my head, and planted on my shield;
I won the trenches, while my foremost men
Lagged on the plain below.
   Vent. Ye gods, ye gods,
For such another honour!
   Ant. Come on, my soldier!
Our hearts and arms are still the same: I long
Once more to meet our foes; that thou and I,
Like Time and Death, marching before our troops,
May taste fate to them; mow them out a passage,
And, entering where the foremost squadrons yield,
Begin the noble harvest of the field.   *[Exeunt.*

ACT II

SCENE I

Enter CLEOPATRA, IRAS, *and* ALEXAS.

   Cleo. What shall I do, or whither shall I turn?
Ventidius has o'ercome, and he will go.
   Alex. He goes to fight for you.
   Cleo. Then he would see me, ere he went to fight:
Flatter me not: If once he goes, he's lost,
And all my hopes destroyed.
   Alex. Does this weak passion
Become a mighty queen?
   Cleo. I am no queen:
Is this to be a queen, to be besieged
By yon insulting Roman, and to wait
Each hour the victor's chain? These ills are small:
For Antony is lost, and I can mourn
For nothing else but him. Now come, Octavius,
I have no more to lose! prepare thy bands;
I'm fit to be a captive: Antony
Has taught my mind the fortune of a slave.

Iras. Call reason to assist you.

Cleo. I have none,
And none would have: My love's a noble madness,
Which shows the cause deserved it. Moderate sorrow
Fits vulgar love, and for a vulgar man:
But I have loved with such transcendent passion,
I soared, at first, quite out of reason's view,
And now am lost above it. No, I'm proud
'Tis thus: Would Antony could see me now
Think you he would not sigh, though he must leave me?
Sure he would sigh; for he is noble-natured,
And bears a tender heart: I know him well.
Ah, no, I know him not; I knew him once,
But now 'tis past.

Iras. Let it be past with you:
Forget him, madam.

Cleo. Never, never, Iras.
He once was mine; and once, though now 'tis gone,
Leaves a faint image of possession still.

Alex. Think him inconstant, cruel, and ungrateful.

Cleo. I cannot: If I could, those thoughts were vain.
Faithless, ungrateful, cruel, though he be,
I still must love him.

Enter CHARMION.

Now, what news, my Charmion?
Will he be kind? and will he not forsake me?
Am I to live, or die?—nay, do I live?
Or am I dead? for when he gave his answer,
Fate took the word, and then I lived or died.

Char. I found him, madam——

Cleo. A long speech preparing?
If thou bring'st comfort, haste, and give it me,
For never was more need.

Iras. I know he loves you.

Cleo. Had he been kind, her eyes had told me so,
Before her tongue could speak it: Now she studies,
To soften what he said; but give me death,
Just as he sent it, Charmion, undisguised,
And in the words he spoke.

Char. I found him, then,
Encompassed round, I think, with iron statues;
So mute, so motionless his soldiers stood,
While awfully he cast his eyes about,
And every leader's hopes or fears surveyed:
Methought he looked resolved, and yet not pleased.
When he beheld me struggling in the crowd,
He blushed, and bade make way.

Alex. There's comfort yet.

Char. Ventidius fixed his eyes upon my passage
Severely, as he meant to frown me back,
And sullenly gave place: I told my message,
Just as you gave it, broken and disordered;
I numbered in it all your sighs and tears,
And while I moved your pitiful request,
That you but only begged a last farewell,
He fetched an inward groan; and every time
I named you, sighed, as if his heart were breaking,
But, shunned my eyes, and guiltily looked down;
He seemed not now that awful Antony,
Who shook an armed assembly with his nod;
But, making show as he would rub his eyes,
Disguised and blotted out a falling tear.

Cleo. Did he then weep? And was I worth a tear?
If what thou hast to say be not as pleasing,
Tell me no more, but let me die contented.

Char. He bid me say,—He knew himself so well,
He could deny you nothing, if he saw you;
And therefore——

Cleo. Thou wouldst say, he would not see me?

Char. And therefore begged you not to use a power,
Which he could ill resist; yet he should ever
Respect you, as he ought.

Cleo. Is that a word
For Antony to use to Cleopatra?
O that faint word, *respect!* how I disdain it!
Disdain myself, for loving after it!
He should have kept that word for cold Octavia.
Respect is for a wife: Am I that thing,
That dull, insipid lump, without desires,
And without power to give them?

Alex. You misjudge;
You see through love, and that deludes your sight;
As, what is straight, seems crooked through the water:
But I, who bear my reason undisturbed,
Can see this Antony, this dreaded man,
A fearful slave, who fain would run away,
And shuns his master's eyes: If you pursue him,
My life on't, he still drags a chain along
That needs must clog his flight.

Cleo. Could I believe thee!—

Alex. By every circumstance I know he loves.
True, he's hard prest, by interest and by honour;
Yet he but doubts, and parleys, and casts out
Many a long look for succour.

Cleo. He sends word,
He fears to see my face.

Alex. And would you more?

He shows his weakness who declines the combat,
And you must urge your fortune.   Could he speak
More plainly?   To my ears, the message sounds—
Come to my rescue, Cleopatra, come;
Come, free me from Ventidius; from my tyrant:
See me, and give me a pretence to leave him!—
I hear his trumpets. This way he must pass.
Please you, retire a while; I'll work him first,
That he may bend more easy.

   Cleo. You shall rule me;
But all, I fear, in vain.   [*Exit with* CHARMION *and* IRAS.

   Alex. I fear so too;
Though I concealed my thoughts, to make her bold;
But 'tis our utmost means, and fate befriend it! [*Withdraws.*

Enter Lictors *with Fasces; one bearing the Eagle; then enter*
ANTONY *with* VENTIDIUS, *followed by other* Commanders.

   Ant. Octavius is the minion of blind chance,
But holds from virtue nothing.

   Vent. Has he courage?

   Ant. But just enough to season him from coward.
Oh, 'tis the coldest youth upon a charge,
The most deliberate fighter! if he ventures
(As in Illyria once, they say, he did,
To storm a town), 'tis when he cannot choose;
When all the world have fixt their eyes upon him;
And then he lives on that for seven years after;
But, at a close revenge he never fails.

   Vent. I heard you challenged him.

   Ant. I did, Ventidius.
What think'st thou was his answer? 'Twas so tame!—
He said, he had more ways than one to die;
I had not.

   Vent. Poor!

   Ant. He has more ways than one;
But he would choose them all before that one.

   Vent. He first would choose an ague, or a fever.

   Ant. No; it must be an ague, not a fever;
He has not warmth enough to die by that.

   Vent. Or old age and a bed.

   Ant. Ay, there's his choice,
He would live, like a lamp, to the last wink,
And crawl upon the utmost verge of life.
O Hercules! Why should a man like this,
Who dares not trust his fate for one great action,
Be all the care of Heaven? Why should he lord it
O'er fourscore thousand men, of whom each one
Is braver than himself?

   Vent. You conquered for him;

Philippi knows it; there you shared with him
That empire, which your sword made all your own.

   Ant. Fool that I was, upon my eagle's wings
I bore this wren, till I was tired with soaring,
And now he mounts above me.
Good heavens, is this—is this the man who braves me?
Who bids my age make way? Drives me before him,
To the world's ridge, and sweeps me off like rubbish?

   Vent. Sir, we lose time; the troops are mounted all.

   Ant. Then give the word to march:
I long to leave this prison of a town,
To join thy legions; and, in open field,
Once more to show my face. Lead, my deliverer.

Enter ALEXAS.

   Alex. Great emperor,
In mighty arms renowned above mankind,
But, in soft pity to the opprest, a god;
This message sends the mournful Cleopatra
To her departing lord.

   Vent. Smooth sycophant!

   Alex. A thousand wishes, and ten thousand prayers,
Millions of blessings wait you to the wars;
Millions of sighs and tears she sends you too,
And would have sent
As many dear embraces to your arms,
As many parting kisses to your lips;
But those, she fears, have wearied you already.

   Vent. [*aside*]. False crocodile!

   Alex. And yet she begs not now, you would not leave her;
That were a wish too mighty for her hopes,
Too presuming
For her low fortune, and your ebbing love;
That were a wish for her more prosperous days,
Her blooming beauty, and your growing kindness.

   Ant. [*aside*]. Well, I must man it out:—What would the
      queen?

   Alex. First, to these noble warriors, who attend
Your daring courage in the chase of fame,—
Too daring, and too dangerous for her quiet,—
She humbly recommends all she holds dear,
All her own cares and fears,—the care of you.

   Vent. Yes, witness Actium.

   Ant. Let him speak, Ventidius.

   Alex. You, when his matchless valour bears him forward,
With ardour too heroic, on his foes,
Fall down, as she would do, before his feet;
Lie in his way, and stop the paths of death:
Tell him, this god is not invulnerable;

That absent Cleopatra bleeds in him;
And, that you may remember her petition,
She begs you wear these trifles, as a pawn,
Which, at your wished return, she will redeem
                              [*Gives jewels to the* Commanders.
With all the wealth of Egypt:
This to the great Ventidius she presents,
Whom she can never count her enemy,
Because he loves her lord.

 Vent. Tell her, I'll none on't;
I'm not ashamed of honest poverty;
Not all the diamonds of the east can bribe
Ventidius from his faith.   I hope to see
These and the rest of all her sparkling store,
Where they shall more deservingly be placed.

 Ant. And who must wear them then?

 Vent. The wronged Octavia.

 Ant. You might have spared that word.

 Vent. And he that bribe.

 Ant. But have I no remembrance?

 Alex. Yes, a dear one;
Your slave the queen——

 Ant. My mistress.

 Alex. Then your mistress;
Your mistress would, she says, have sent her soul,
But that you had long since; she humbly begs
This ruby bracelet, set with bleeding hearts,
The emblems of her own, may bind your arm.
                              [*Presenting a bracelet.*

 Vent. Now, my best lord,—in honour's name, I ask you,
For manhood's sake, and for your own dear safety,—
Touch not these poisoned gifts,
Infected by the sender; touch them not;
Myriads of bluest plagues lie underneath them,
And more than aconite has dipt the silk.

 Ant. Nay, now you grow too cynical, Ventidius:
A lady's favours may be worn with honour.
What, to refuse her bracelet! On my soul,
When I lie pensive in my tent alone,
'Twill pass the wakeful hours of winter nights,
To tell these pretty beads upon my arm,
To count for every one a soft embrace,
A melting kiss at such and such a time:
And now and then the fury of her love,
When——And what harm's in this?

 Alex. None, none, my lord,
But what's to her, that now 'tis past for ever.

 Ant. [*going to tie it*]. We soldiers are so awkward—help
  me tie it.

Alex. In faith, my lord, we courtiers too are awkward
In these affairs: so are all men indeed:
Even I, who am not one.   But shall I speak?

   Ant. Yes, freely.

   Alex. Then, my lord, fair hands alone
Are fit to tie it; she, who sent it can.

   Vent. Hell, death! this eunuch pander ruins you.
You will not see her?

                 [ALEXAS *whispers an* Attendant, *who goes out.*

   Ant. But to take my leave.

   Vent. Then I have washed an Æthiop. You're undone;
Y' are in the toils; y' are taken; y' are destroyed:
Her eyes do Cæsar's work.

   Ant. You fear too soon.
I'm constant to myself: I know my strength;
And yet she shall not think me barbarous neither,
Born in the depths of Afric: I am a Roman,
Bred in the rules of soft humanity.
A guest, and kindly used, should bid farewell.

   Vent. You do not know
How weak you are to her, how much an infant:
You are not proof against a smile, or glance;
A sigh will quite disarm you.

   Ant. See, she comes!
Now you shall find your error.—Gods, I thank you:
I formed the danger greater than it was,
And now 'tis near, 'tis lessened.

   Vent. Mark the end yet.

          Enter CLEOPATRA, CHARMION, *and* IRAS.

   Ant. Well, madam, we are met.

   Cleo. Is this a meeting?
Then, we must part?

   Ant. We must.

   Cleo. Who says we must?

   Ant. Our own hard fates.

   Cleo. We make those fates ourselves.

   Ant. Yes, we have made them; we have loved each other,
Into our mutual ruin.

   Cleo. The gods have seen my joys with envious eyes;
I have no friends in heaven; and all the world,
As 'twere the business of mankind to part us,
Is armed against my love: even you yourself
Join with the rest; you, you are armed against me.

   Ant. I will be justified in all I do
To late posterity, and therefore hear me.
If I mix a lie
With any truth, reproach me freely with it;
Else, favour me with silence.

 Cleo. You command me,
And I am dumb.
 Vent. I like this well; he shows authority.
 Ant. That I derive my ruin
From you alone——
 Cleo. O heavens! I ruin you!
 Ant. You promised me your silence, and you break it
Ere I have scarce begun.
 Cleo. Well, I obey you.
 Ant. When I beheld you first, it was in Egypt.
Ere Cæsar saw your eyes, you gave me love,
And were too young to know it; that I settled
Your father in his throne, was for your sake;
I left the acknowledgment for time to ripen.
Cæsar stept in, and, with a greedy hand,
Plucked the green fruit, ere the first blush of red,
Yet cleaving to the bough. He was my lord,
And was, beside, too great for me to rival;
But, I deserved you first, though he enjoyed you.
When, after, I beheld you in Cilicia,
An enemy to Rome, I pardoned you.
 Cleo. I cleared myself——
 Ant. Again you break your promise.
I loved you still, and took your weak excuses,
Took you into my bosom, stained by Cæsar,
And not half mine: I went to Egypt with you,
And hid me from the business of the world,
Shut out inquiring nations from my sight,
To give whole years to you.
 Vent. Yes, to your shame be't spoken.   [*Aside.*
 Ant. How I loved.
Witness, ye days and nights, and all ye hours,
That danced away with down upon your feet,
As all your business were to count my passion!
One day passed by, and nothing saw but love;
Another came, and still 'twas only love:
The suns were wearied out with looking on,
And I untired with loving.
I saw you every day, and all the day;
And every day was still but as the first,
So eager was I still to see you more.
 Vent. 'Tis all too true.
 Ant. Fulvia, my wife, grew jealous
(As she indeed had reason), raised a war
In Italy, to call me back.
 Vent. But yet
You went not.
 Ant. While within your arms I lay,
The world fell mouldering from my hands each hour,

And left me scarce a grasp—I thank your love for't.

Vent. Well pushed: that last was home.

Cleo. Yet may I speak?

Ant. If I have urged a falsehood, yes; else, not.
Your silence says, I have not.   Fulvia died
(Pardon, you gods, with my unkindness died);
To set the world at peace, I took Octavia,
This Cæsar's sister; in her pride of youth,
And flower of beauty, did I wed that lady,
Whom blushing I must praise, because I left her.
You called; my love obeyed the fatal summons:
This raised the Roman arms; the cause was yours.
I would have fought by land, where I was stronger;
You hindered it: yet, when I fought at sea,
Forsook me fighting; and (O stain to honour!
O lasting shame!) I knew not that I fled;
But fled to follow you.

Vent. What haste she made to hoist her purple sails!
And, to appear magnificent in flight,
Drew half our strength away.

Ant. All this you caused.
And, would you multiply more ruins on me?
This honest man, my best, my only friend,
Has gathered up the shipwreck of my fortunes;
Twelve legions I have left, my last recruits.
And you have watched the news, and bring your eyes
To seize them too.   If you have aught to answer,
Now speak, you have free leave.

Alex. [*aside*]. She stands confounded:
Despair is in her eyes.

Vent. Now lay a sigh in the way to stop his passage:
Prepare a tear, and bid it for his legions;
'Tis like they shall be sold.

Cleo. How shall I plead my cause, when you, my judge,
Already have condemned me?   Shall I bring
The love you bore me for my advocate?
That now is turned against me, that destroys me;
For love, once past, is, at the best, forgotten;
But oftener sours to hate: 'twill please my lord
To ruin me, and therefore I'll be guilty.
But, could I once have thought it would have pleased you,
That you would pry, with narrow searching eyes,
Into my faults, severe to my destruction,
And watching all advantages with care,
That serve to make me wretched?   Speak, my lord,
For I end here.   Though I deserved this usage,
Was it like you to give it?

Ant. Oh, you wrong me,
To think I sought this parting, or desired

To accuse you more than what will clear myself,
And justify this breach.

　　Cleo. Thus low I thank you;
And, since my innocence will not offend,
I shall not blush to own it.

　　Vent. After this,
I think she'll blush at nothing.

　　Cleo. You seemed grieved
(And therein you are kind), that Cæsar first
Enjoyed my love, though you deserved it better:
I grieve for that, my lord, much more than you;
For, had I first been yours, it would have saved
My second choice: I never had been his,
And ne'er had been but yours. But Cæsar first,
You say, possessed my love. Not so, my lord:
He first possessed my person; you, my love:
Cæsar loved me; but I loved Antony.
If I endured him after, 'twas because
I judged it due to the first name of men;
And, half constrained, I gave, as to a tyrant,
What he would take by force.

　　Vent. O Syren! Syren!
Yet grant that all the love she boasts were true,
Has she not ruined you? I still urge that,
The fatal consequence.

　　Cleo. The consequence indeed,
For I dare challenge him, my greatest foe,
To say it was designed: 'tis true, I loved you,
And kept you far from an uneasy wife,—
Such Fulvia was.
Yes, but he'll say, you left Octavia for me;—
And, can you blame me to receive that love,
Which quitted such desert, for worthless me?
How often have I wished some other Cæsar,
Great as the first, and as the second young,
Would court my love, to be refused for you!

　　Vent. Words, words; but Actium, sir; remember Actium.

　　Cleo. Even there, I dare his malice. True, I counselled
To fight at sea; but I betrayed you not.
I fled, but not to the enemy. 'Twas fear;
Would I had been a man, not to have feared!
For none would then have envied me your friendship,
Who envy me your love.

　　Ant. We are both unhappy:
If nothing else, yet our ill fortune parts us.
Speak: would you have me perish by my stay?

　　Cleo. If, as a friend, you ask my judgment, go;
If, as a lover, stay. If you must perish——
'Tis a hard word—but stay.

Vent. See now the effects of her so boasted love!
She strives to drag you down to ruin with her;
But, could she 'scape without you, oh, how soon
Would she let go her hold, and haste to shore,
And never look behind!

Cleo. Then judge my love by this.   [*Giving* ANTONY *a writing.*
Could I have borne
A life or death, a happiness or woe,
From yours divided, this had given me means.

Ant. By Hercules, the writing of Octavius!
I know it well: 'tis that proscribing hand,
Young as it was, that led the way to mine,
And left me but the second place in murder.—
See, see, Ventidius! here he offers Egypt,
And joins all Syria to it, as a present;
So, in requital, she forsake my fortunes,
And join her arms with his.

Cleo. And yet you leave me!
You leave me, Antony; and yet I love you,
Indeed I do: I have refused a kingdom;
That is a trifle;
For I could part with life, with anything,
But only you. Oh, let me die but with you!
Is that a hard request?

Ant. Next living with you,
'Tis all that Heaven can give.

Alex. He melts; we conquer.   [*Aside.*

Cleo. No; you shall go: your interest calls you hence;
Yes; your dear interest pulls too strong, for these
Weak arms to hold you here.   [*Takes his hand.*
Go; leave me, soldier
(For you're no more a lover): leave me dying:
Push me, all pale and panting, from your bosom,
And, when your march begins, let one run after,
Breathless almost for joy, and cry—She's dead.
The soldiers shout; you then, perhaps, may sigh,
And muster all your Roman gravity:
Ventidius chides; and straight your brow clears up,
As I had never been.

Ant. Gods, 'tis too much; too much for man to bear.

Cleo. What is't for me then,
A weak, forsaken woman, and a lover?—
Here let me breathe my last: envy me not
This minute in your arms: I'll die apace,
As fast as e'er I can, and end your trouble.

Ant. Die! rather let me perish; loosened nature
Leap from its hinges, sink the props of heaven,
And fall the skies, to crush the nether world!
My eyes, my soul, my all!   [*Embraces her.*

Vent. And what's this toy,
In balance with your fortune, honour, fame?

Ant. What is't, Ventidius?—it outweighs them all;
Why, we have more than conquered Cæsar now:
My queen's not only innocent, but loves me.
This, this is she, who drags me down to ruin!
" But, could she 'scape without me, with what haste
Would she let slip her hold, and make to shore,
And never look behind!"
Down on thy knees, blasphemer as thou art,
And ask forgiveness of wronged innocence.

Vent. I'll rather die, than take it. Will you go?

Ant. Go! whither? Go from all that's excellent?
Faith, honour, virtue, all good things forbid,
That I should go from her, who sets my love
Above the price of kingdoms! Give, you gods,
Give to your boy, your Cæsar,
This rattle of a globe to play withal,
This gewgaw world, and put him cheaply off:
I'll not be pleased with less than Cleopatra.

Cleo. She's wholly yours. My heart's so full of joy,
That I shall do some wild extravagance
Of love, in public; and the foolish world,
Which knows not tenderness, will think me mad.

Vent. O women! women! women! all the gods
Have not such power of doing good to man,
As you of doing harm.   [*Exit.*

Ant. Our men are armed:—
Unbar the gate that looks to Cæsar's camp:
I would revenge the treachery he meant me;
And long security makes conquest easy.
I'm eager to return before I go;
For, all the pleasures I have known beat thick
On my remembrance.—How I long for night!
    That both the sweets of mutual love may try,
    And triumph once o'er Cæsar ere we die.   [*Exeunt.*

ACT III

SCENE I

At one door enter CLEOPATRA, CHARMION, IRAS, *and* ALEXAS, *a*
Train of Egyptians: *at the other* ANTONY *and* Romans.
The entrance on both sides is prepared by music; the trumpets
first sounding on ANTONY'S *part: then answered by timbrels,*
etc., on CLEOPATRA'S. CHARMION *and* IRAS *hold a laurel*
wreath betwixt them. A Dance of Egyptians. *After the*
ceremony, CLEOPATRA *crowns* ANTONY.

Ant. I thought how those white arms would fold me in,
And strain me close, and melt me into love;
So pleased with that sweet image, I sprung forwards,
And added all my strength to every blow.
   Cleo. Come to me, come, my soldier, to my arms!
You've been too long away from my embraces;
But, when I have you fast, and all my own,
With broken murmurs, and with amorous sighs,
I'll say, you were unkind, and punish you,
And mark you red with many an eager kiss.
   Ant. My brighter Venus!
   Cleo. O my greater Mars!
   Ant. Thou join'st us well, my love!
Suppose me come from the Phlegræan plains,
Where gasping giants lay, cleft by my sword,
And mountain-tops paired off each other blow,
To bury those I slew. Receive me, goddess!
Let Cæsar spread his subtle nets; like Vulcan,
In thy embraces I would be beheld
By heaven and earth at once;
And make their envy what they meant their sport.
Let those, who took us, blush; I would love on,
With awful state, regardless of their frowns,
As their superior gods.
There's no satiety of love in thee:
Enjoyed, thou still art new; perpetual spring
Is in thy arms; the ripened fruit but falls,
And blossoms rise to fill its empty place;
And I grow rich by giving.

Enter VENTIDIUS, *and stands apart.*

   Alex. Oh, now the danger's past, your general comes!
He joins not in your joys, nor minds your triumphs;
But, with contracted brows, looks frowning on,
As envying your success.

Ant. Now, on my soul, he loves me; truly loves me:
He never flattered me in any vice,
But awes me with his virtue: even this minute,
Methinks, he has a right of chiding me.
Lead to the temple: I'll avoid his presence;
It checks too strong upon me.   [*Exeunt the rest.*
       [*As* ANTONY *is going,* VENTIDIUS *pulls him by the robe.*
Vent. Emperor!
Ant. 'Tis the old argument; I pr'ythee, spare me.
                                        [*Looking back.*
Vent. But this one hearing, emperor.
Ant. Let go
My robe; or, by my father Hercules——
Vent. By Hercules' father, that's yet greater,
I bring you somewhat you would wish to know.
Ant. Thou see'st we are observed; attend me here,
And I'll return.   [*Exit.*
Vent. I am waning in his favour, yet I love him;
I love this man, who runs to meet his ruin;
And sure the gods, like me, are fond of him:
His virtues lie so mingled with his crimes,
As would confound their choice to punish one,
And not reward the other.

Enter ANTONY.

Ant. We can conquer,
You see, without your aid.
We have dislodged their troops;
They look on us at distance, and, like curs
'Scaped from the lion's paws, they bay far off,
And lick their wounds, and faintly threaten war.
Five thousand Romans, with their faces upward,
Lie breathless on the plain.
Vent. 'Tis well; and he,
Who lost them, could have spared ten thousand more.
Yet if, by this advantage, you could gain
An easier peace, while Cæsar doubts the chance
Of arms——
Ant. Oh, think not on't, Ventidius!
The boy pursues my ruin, he'll no peace;
His malice is considerate in advantage.
Oh, he's the coolest murderer! so staunch,
He kills, and keeps his temper.
Vent. Have you no friend
In all his army, who has power to move him?
Mæcenas, or Agrippa, might do much.
Ant. They're both too deep in Cæsar's interests.
We'll work it out by dint of sword, or perish.

Vent. Fain I would find some other.

Ant. Thank thy love.

Some four or five such victories as this
Will save thy further pains.

Vent. Expect no more; Cæsar is on his guard:
I know, sir, you have conquered against odds;
But still you draw supplies from one poor town,
And of Egyptians: he has all the world,
And, at his beck, nations come pouring in,
To fill the gaps you make.   Pray, think again.

Ant. Why dost thou drive me from myself, to search
For foreign aids?—to hunt my memory,
And range all o'er a waste and barren place,
To find a friend?   The wretched have no friends.
Yet I had one, the bravest youth of Rome,
Whom Cæsar loves beyond the love of women:
He could resolve his mind, as fire does wax,
From that hard rugged image melt him down,
And mould him in what softer form he pleased.

Vent. Him would I see; that man, of all the world;
Just such a one we want.

Ant. He loved me too;
I was his soul; he lived not but in me:
We were so closed within each other's breasts,
The rivets were not found, that joined us first.
That does not reach us yet: we were so mixt,
As meeting streams, both to ourselves were lost;
We were one mass; we could not give or take,
But from the same; for he was I, I he.

Vent. He moves as I would wish him.   [*Aside.*

Ant. After this,
I need not tell his name;—'twas Dolabella.

Vent. He's now in Cæsar's camp.

Ant. No matter where,
Since he's no longer mine.   He took unkindly,
That I forbade him Cleopatra's sight,
Because I feared he loved her: he confessed,
He had a warmth, which, for my sake, he stifled;
For 'twere impossible that two, so one,
Should not have loved the same.   When he departed,
He took no leave; and that confirmed my thoughts.

Vent. It argues, that he loved you more than her,
Else he had stayed; but he perceived you jealous,
And would not grieve his friend: I know he loves you.

Ant. I should have seen him, then, ere now.

Vent. Perhaps
He has thus long been labouring for your peace.

Ant. Would he were here!

Vent. Would you believe he loved you?

I read your answer in your eyes, you would.
Not to conceal it longer, he has sent
A messenger from Cæsar's camp, with letters.

Ant. Let him appear.

Vent. I'll bring him instantly.

[*Exit* VENTIDIUS, *and re-enters immediately with* DOLABELLA.

　　Ant. 'Tis he himself! himself, by holy friendship!

　　　　　　　　　　　　　　　[*Runs to embrace him.*

Art thou returned at last, my better half?
Come, give me all myself!
Let me not live,
If the young bridegroom, longing for his night,
Was ever half so fond.

　　Dola. I must be silent, for my soul is busy
About a nobler work: she's new come home,
Like a long-absent man, and wanders o'er
Each room, a stranger to her own, to look
If all be safe.

　　Ant. Thou hast what's left of me;
For I am now so sunk from what I was,
Thou find'st me at my lowest water-mark.
The rivers that ran in, and raised my fortunes,
Are all dried up, or take another course:
What I have left is from my native spring;
I've still a heart that swells, in scorn of fate,
And lifts me to my banks.

　　Dola. Still you are lord of all the world to me.

　　Ant. Why, then I yet am so; for thou art all.
If I had any joy when thou wert absent,
I grudged it to myself; methought I robbed
Thee of thy part. But, O my Dolabella!
Thou hast beheld me other than I am.
Hast thou not seen my morning chambers filled
With sceptred slaves, who waited to salute me?
With eastern monarchs, who forgot the sun,
To worship my uprising?—menial kings
Ran coursing up and down my palace-yard,
Stood silent in my presence, watched my eyes,
And, at my least command, all started out,
Like racers to the goal.

　　Dola. Slaves to your fortune.

　　Ant. Fortune is Cæsar's now; and what am I?

　　Vent. What you have made yourself; I will not flatter.

　　Ant. Is this friendly done?

　　Dola. Yes; when his end is so, I must join with him;
Indeed I must, and yet you must not chide;
Why am I else your friend?

　　Ant. Take heed, young man,
How thou upbraid'st my love: The queen has eyes,

And thou too hast a soul.   Canst thou remember,
When, swelled with hatred, thou beheld'st her first,
As accessary to thy brother's death?
 Dola. Spare my remembrance; 'twas a guilty day,
And still the blush hangs here.
 Ant. To clear herself,
For sending him no aid, she came from Egypt.
Her galley down the silver Cydnus rowed,
The tackling silk, the streamers waved with gold;
The gentle winds were lodged in purple sails:
Her nymphs, like Nereids, round her couch were placed;
Where she, another sea-born Venus, lay.
 Dola. No more; I would not hear it.
 Ant. Oh, you must!
She lay, and leant her cheek upon her hand,
And cast a look so languishingly sweet,
As if, secure of all beholders' hearts,
Neglecting, she could take them: boys, like Cupids,
Stood fanning, with their painted wings, the winds,
That played about her face.   But if she smiled,
A darting glory seemed to blaze abroad,
That men's desiring eyes were never wearied,
But hung upon the object: To soft flutes
The silver oars kept time; and while they played,
The hearing gave new pleasure to the sight,
And both to thought.   'Twas heaven, or somewhat more:
For she so charmed all hearts, that gazing crowds
Stood panting on the shore, and wanted breath
To give their welcome voice.
Then, Dolabella, where was then thy soul?
Was not thy fury quite disarmed with wonder?
Didst thou not shrink behind me from those eyes
And whisper in my ear—Oh, tell her not
That I accused her with my brother's death?
 Dola. And should my weakness be a plea for yours?
Mine was an age when love might be excused,
When kindly warmth, and when my springing youth
Made it a debt to nature.   Yours——
 Vent. Speak boldly.
Yours, he would say, in your declining age,
When no more heat was left but what you forced,
When all the sap was needful for the trunk,
When it went down, then you constrained the course,
And robbed from nature, to supply desire;
In you (I would not use so harsh a word)
'Tis but plain dotage.
 Ant. Ha!
 Dola. 'Twas urged too home.—
But yet the loss was private, that I made;

'Twas but myself I lost: I lost no legions;
I had no world to lose, no people's love.
   Ant. This from a friend?
   Dola. Yes, Antony, a true one;
A friend so tender, that each word I speak
Stabs my own heart, before it reach your ear.
Oh, judge me not less kind, because I chide!
To Cæsar I excuse you.
   Ant. O ye gods!
Have I then lived to be excused to Cæsar?
   Dola. As to your equal.
   Ant. Well, he's but my equal:
While I wear this he never shall be more.
   Dola. I bring conditions from him.
   Ant. Are they noble?
Methinks thou shouldst not bring them else; yet he
Is full of deep dissembling; knows no honour
Divided from his interest. Fate mistook him;
For nature meant him for an usurer:
He's fit indeed to buy, not conquer kingdoms.
   Vent. Then, granting this,
What power was theirs, who wrought so hard a temper
To honourable terms?
   Ant. It was my Dolabella, or some god.
   Dola. Nor I, nor yet Mæcenas, nor Agrippa:
They were your enemies; and I, a friend,
Too weak alone; yet 'twas a Roman's deed.
   Ant. 'Twas like a Roman done: show me that man,
Who has preserved my life, my love, my honour;
Let me but see his face.
   Vent. That task is mine,
And, Heaven, thou know'st how pleasing.   [*Exit* VENTIDIUS.
   Dola. You'll remember
To whom you stand obliged?
   Ant. When I forget it,
Be thou unkind, and that's my greatest curse.
My queen shall thank him too.
   Dola. I fear she will not.
   Ant. But she shall do it: The queen, my Dolabella!
Hast thou not still some grudgings of thy fever?
   Dola. I would not see her lost.
   Ant. When I forsake her,
Leave me my better stars! for she has truth
Beyond her beauty. Cæsar tempted her,
At no less price than kingdoms, to betray me;
But she resisted all: and yet thou chidest me
For loving her too well. Could I do so?
   Dola. Yes; there's my reason.

Re-enter VENTIDIUS, *with* OCTAVIA, *leading* ANTONY'S
two little Daughters.

Ant. Where?—Octavia there!   [*Starting back*
Vent. What, is she poison to you?—a disease?
Look on her, view her well, and those she brings:
Are they all strangers to your eyes? has nature
No secret call, no whisper they are yours?
Dola. For shame, my lord, if not for love, receive them
With kinder eyes. If you confess a man,
Meet them, embrace them, bid them welcome to you.
Your arms should open, even without your knowledge,
To clasp them in; your feet should turn to wings,
To bear you to them; and your eyes dart out
And aim a kiss, ere you could reach the lips.
Ant. I stood amazed, to think how they came hither.
Vent. I sent for them; I brought them in unknown
To Cleopatra's guards.
Dola. Yet, are you cold?
Octav. Thus long I have attended for my welcome;
Which, as a stranger, sure I might expect.
Who am I?
Ant. Cæsar's sister.
Octav. That's unkind.
Had I been nothing more than Cæsar's sister,
Know, I had still remained in Cæsar's camp:
But your Octavia, your much injured wife,
Though banished from your bed, driven from your house,
In spite of Cæsar's sister, still is yours.
'Tis true, I have a heart disdains your coldness,
And prompts me not to seek what you should offer;
But a wife's virtue still surmounts that pride.
I come to claim you as my own; to show
My duty first; to ask, nay beg, your kindness:
Your hand, my lord; 'tis mine, and I will have it.
        [*Taking his hand.*
Vent. Do, take it; thou deserv'st it.
Dola. On my soul,
And so she does: she's neither too submissive,
Nor yet too haughty; but so just a mean
Shows, as it ought, a wife and Roman too.
Ant. I fear, Octavia, you have begged my life.
Octav. Begged it, my lord?
Ant. Yes, begged it, my ambassadress!
Poorly and basely begged it of your brother.
Octav. Poorly and basely I could never beg:
Nor could my brother grant.
Ant. Shall I, who, to my kneeling slave, could say,
Rise up, and be a king; shall I fall down

And cry,—Forgive me, Cæsar! Shall I set
A man, my equal, in the place of Jove,
As he could give me being? No; that word,
Forgive, would choke me up,
And die upon my tongue.

Dola. You shall not need it.

Ant. I will not need it. Come, you've all betrayed me,—
My friend too!—to receive some vile conditions.
My wife has bought me, with her prayers and tears;
And now I must become her branded slave.
In every peevish mood, she will upbraid
The life she gave: if I but look awry,
She cries—I'll tell my brother.

Octav. My hard fortune
Subjects me still to your unkind mistakes.
But the conditions I have brought are such,
You need not blush to take: I love your honour,
Because 'tis mine; it never shall be said,
Octavia's husband was her brother's slave.
Sir, you are free; free, even from her you loathe;
For, though my brother bargains for your love,
Makes me the price and cement of your peace,
I have a soul like yours; I cannot take
Your love as alms, nor beg what I deserve.
I'll tell my brother we are reconciled;
He shall draw back his troops, and you shall march
To rule the East: I may be dropt at Athens;
No matter where. I never will complain,
But only keep the barren name of wife,
And rid you of the trouble.

Vent. Was ever such a strife of sullen honour!
Both scorn to be obliged.

Dola. Oh, she has touched him in the tenderest part;
See how he reddens with despite and shame,
To be outdone in generosity!   } *Apart.*

Vent. See how he winks! how he dries up a tear,
That fain would fall!

Ant. Octavia, I have heard you, and must praise
The greatness of your soul;
But cannot yield to what you have proposed:
For I can ne'er be conquered but by love;
And you do all for duty. You would free me,
And would be dropt at Athens; was't not so?

Octav. It was, my lord.

Ant. Then I must be obliged
To one who loves me not; who, to herself,
May call me thankless and ungrateful man:—
I'll not endure it; no.

Vent. I am glad it pinches there.   [*Aside.*

Octav. Would you triumph o'er poor Octavia's virtue?
That pride was all I had to bear me up;
That you might think you owed me for your life,
And owed it to my duty, not my love.
I have been injured, and my haughty soul
Could brook but ill the man who slights my bed.

    Ant. Therefore you love me not.

    Octav. Therefore, my lord,
I should not love you.

    Ant. Therefore you would leave me?

    Octav. And therefore I should leave you—if I could.

    Dola. Her soul's too great, after such injuries,
To say she loves; and yet she lets you see it.
Her modesty and silence plead her cause.

    Ant. O Dolabella, which way shall I turn?
I find a secret yielding in my soul;
But Cleopatra, who would die with me,
Must she be left? Pity pleads for Octavia;
But does it not plead more for Cleopatra?

    Vent. Justice and pity both plead for Octavia;
For Cleopatra, neither.
One would be ruined with you; but she first
Had ruined you: The other, you have ruined,
And yet she would preserve you.
In everything their merits are unequal.

    Ant. O my distracted soul!

    Octav. Sweet Heaven compose it!—
Come, come, my lord, if I can pardon you,
Methinks you should accept it. Look on these:
Are they not yours? or stand they thus neglected,
As they are mine? Go to him, children, go;
Kneel to him, take him by the hand, speak to him;
For you may speak, and he may own you too,
Without a blush; and so he cannot all
His children: go, I say, and pull him to me,
And pull him to yourselves, from that bad woman.
You, Agrippina, hang upon his arms;
And you, Antonia, clasp about his waist:
If he will shake you off, if he will dash you
Against the pavement, you must bear it, children;
For you are mine, and I was born to suffer.

                       [Here the Children *go to him, etc.*

    Vent. Was ever sight so moving?—Emperor!

    Dola. Friend!

    Octav. Husband!

    Both Child. Father!

    Ant. I am vanquished: take me,
Octavia; take me, children; share me all.   *[Embracing them.*
I've been a thriftless debtor to your loves,

And run out much, in riot, from your stock;
But all shall be amended.
   Octav. O blest hour!
   Dola. O happy change!
   Vent. My joy stops at my tongue;
But it has found two channels here for one,
And bubbles out above.
   Ant. [*to* OCTAV.]. This is thy triumph; lead me where thou
     wilt;
Even to thy brother's camp.
   Octav. All there are yours.

       Enter ALEXAS *hastily.*

   Alex. The queen, my mistress, sir, and yours——
   Ant. 'Tis past.—
Octavia, you shall stay this night: To-morrow,
Cæsar and we are one.
     [*Exit leading* OCTAVIA; DOLABELLA *and the* Children *follow.*
   Vent. There's news for you; run, my officious eunuch,
Be sure to be the first; haste forward:
Haste, my dear eunuch, haste.   [*Exit.*
   Alex. This downright fighting fool, this thick-skulled hero,
This blunt, unthinking instrument of death,
With plain dull virtue has outgone my wit.
Pleasure forsook my earliest infancy;
The luxury of others robbed my cradle,
And ravished thence the promise of a man.
Cast out from nature, disinherited
Of what her meanest children claim by kind,
Yet greatness kept me from contempt: that's gone.
Had Cleopatra followed my advice,
Then he had been betrayed who now forsakes.
She dies for love; but she has known its joys:
Gods, is this just, that I, who know no joys,
Must die, because she loves?

   Enter CLEOPATRA, CHARMION, IRAS, *and Train.*

O madam, I have seen what blasts my eyes!
Octavia's here.
   Cleo. Peace with that raven's note.
I know it too; and now am in
The pangs of death.
   Alex. You are no more a queen;
Egypt is lost.
   Cleo. What tell'st thou me of Egypt?
My life, my soul is lost! Octavia has him!—
O fatal name to Cleopatra's love!
My kisses, my embraces now are hers;
While I——But thou hast seen my rival; speak,

Does she deserve this blessing? Is she fair?
Bright as a goddess? and is all perfection
Confined to her? It is.   Poor I was made
Of that coarse matter, which, when she was finished,
The gods threw by for rubbish.

   Alex. She is indeed a very miracle.

   Cleo. Death to my hopes, a miracle!

   Alex. A miracle;   [*Bowing.*
I mean of goodness; for in beauty, madam,
You make all wonders cease.

   Cleo. I was too rash:
Take this in part of recompense.   But, oh!   [*Giving a ring.*
I fear thou flatterest me.

   Char. She comes! she's here!

   Iras. Fly, madam, Cæsar's sister!

   Cleo. Were she the sister of the thunderer Jove,
And bore her brother's lightning in her eyes,
Thus would I face my rival.

     [*Meets* OCTAVIA *with* VENTIDIUS.   OCTAVIA *bears up to her.*
       Their Trains come up on either side.

   Octav. I need not ask if you are Cleopatra;
Your haughty carriage——

   Cleo. Shows I am a queen:
Nor need I ask you, who you are.

   Octav. A Roman:
A name, that makes and can unmake a queen.

   Cleo. Your lord, the man who serves me, is a Roman.

   Octav. He was a Roman, till he lost that name,
To be a slave in Egypt; but I come
To free him thence.

   Cleo. Peace, peace, my lover's Juno.
When he grew weary of that household clog,
He chose my easier bonds.

   Octav. I wonder not
Your bonds are easy: you have long been practised
In that lascivious art: He's not the first
For whom you spread your snares: Let Cæsar witness.

   Cleo. I loved not Cæsar; 'twas but gratitude
I paid his love: The worst your malice can,
Is but to say the greatest of mankind
Has been my slave.   The next, but far above him
In my esteem, is he whom law calls yours,
But whom his love made mine.

   Octav. I would view nearer   [*Coming up close to her.*
That face, which has so long usurped my right,
To find the inevitable charms, that catch
Mankind so sure, that ruined my dear lord.

   Cleo. Oh, you do well to search; for had you known
But half these charms, you had not lost his heart.

Octav. Far be their knowledge from a Roman lady,
Far from a modest wife! Shame of our sex,
Dost thou not blush to own those black endearments,
That make sin pleasing?

Cleo. You may blush, who want them.
If bounteous nature, if indulgent Heaven
Have given me charms to please the bravest man,
Should I not thank them? Should I be ashamed,
And not be proud? I am, that he has loved me;
And, when I love not him, Heaven change this face
For one like that.

Octav. Thou lov'st him not so well.

Cleo. I love him better, and deserve him more.

Octav. You do not; cannot: You have been his ruin.
Who made him cheap at Rome, but Cleopatra?
Who made him scorned abroad, but Cleopatra?
At Actium, who betrayed him? Cleopatra.
Who made his children orphans, and poor me
A wretched widow? only Cleopatra.

Cleo. Yet she, who loves him best, is Cleopatra.
If you have suffered, I have suffered more.
You bear the specious title of a wife,
To gild your cause, and draw the pitying world
To favour it: the world condemns poor me.
For I have lost my honour, lost my fame,
And stained the glory of my royal house,
And all to bear the branded name of mistress.
There wants but life, and that too I would lose
For him I love.

Octav. Be't so, then; take thy wish. [*Exit with her Train.*

Cleo. And 'tis my wish,
Now he is lost for whom alone I lived.
My sight grows dim, and every object dances,
And swims before me, in the maze of death.
My spirits, while they were opposed, kept up;
They could not sink beneath a rival's scorn!
But now she's gone, they faint.

Alex. Mine have had leisure
To recollect their strength, and furnish counsel,
To ruin her, who else must ruin you.

Cleo. Vain promiser!
Lead me, my Charmion; nay, your hand too, Iras.
My grief has weight enough to sink you both.
Conduct me to some solitary chamber,
And draw the curtains round;
Then leave me to myself, to take alone
My fill of grief:
There I till death will his unkindness weep;
As harmless infants moan themselves asleep. [*Exeunt.*

ACT IV

SCENE I

Enter ANTONY *and* DOLABELLA.

Dola. Why would you shift it from yourself on me?
Can you not tell her, you must part?
    Ant. I cannot.
I could pull out an eye, and bid it go,
And t'other should not weep.   O Dolabella,
How many deaths are in this word, *Depart !*
I dare not trust my tongue to tell her so:
One look of hers would thaw me into tears,
And I should melt, till I were lost again.
    Dola. Then let Ventidius;
He's rough by nature.
    Ant. Oh, he'll speak too harshly;
He'll kill her with the news: Thou, only thou.
    Dola. Nature has cast me in so soft a mould,
That but to hear a story, feigned for pleasure,
Of some sad lover's death, moistens my eyes,
And robs me of my manhood.   I should speak
So faintly, with such fear to grieve her heart,
She'd not believe it earnest.
    Ant. Therefore,——therefore
Thou only, thou art fit: Think thyself me;
And when thou speak'st (but let it first be long),
Take off the edge from every sharper sound,
And let our parting be as gently made,
As other loves begin: Wilt thou do this?
    Dola. What you have said so sinks into my soul,
That, if I must speak, I shall speak just so.
    Ant. I leave you then to your sad task: Farewell.
I sent her word to meet you. [*Goes to the door, and comes back.*
I forgot;
Let her be told, I'll make her peace with mine:
Her crown and dignity shall be preserved,
If I have power with Cæsar.——Oh, be sure
To think on that.
    Dola. Fear not, I will remember.
               [ANTONY *goes again to the door, and comes back.*
    Ant. And tell her, too, how much I was constrained;
I did not this, but with extremest force:
Desire her not to hate my memory,
For I still cherish hers;——insist on that.
    Dola. Trust me, I'll not forget it.

Ant. Then that's all.   [*Goes out, and returns again.*
Wilt thou forgive my fondness this once more?
Tell her, though we shall never meet again,
If I should hear she took another love,
The news would break my heart.—Now I must go;
For every time I have returned, I feel
My soul more tender; and my next command
Would be, to bid her stay, and ruin both.   [*Exit.*
     Dola. Men are but children of a larger growth;
Our appetites as apt to change as theirs,
And full as craving too, and full as vain;
And yet the soul, shut up in her dark room,
Viewing so clear abroad, at home sees nothing;
But, like a mole in earth, busy and blind,
Works all her folly up, and casts it outward
To the world's open view: Thus I discovered,
And blamed the love of ruined Antony;
Yet wish that I were he, to be so ruined.

Enter VENTIDIUS *above.*

     Vent. Alone, and talking to himself? concerned too?
Perhaps my guess is right; he loved her once,
And may pursue it still.
     Dola. O friendship! friendship!
Ill canst thou answer this; and reason, worse:
Unfaithful in the attempt; hopeless to win;
And if I win, undone: mere madness all.
And yet the occasion's fair.   What injury
To him, to wear the robe which he throws by!
     Vent. None, none at all.   This happens as I wish,
To ruin her yet more with Antony.

Enter CLEOPATRA, *talking with* ALEXAS; CHARMION,
IRAS *on the other side.*

     Dola. She comes!   What charms have sorrow on that face!
Sorrow seems pleased to dwell with so much sweetness;
Yet, now and then, a melancholy smile
Breaks loose, like lightning in a winter's night,
And shows a moment's day.
     Vent. If she should love him too! her eunuch there?
That porc'pisce bodes ill weather.   Draw, draw nearer,
Sweet devil, that I may hear.
     Alex. Believe me; try
          [DOLABELLA *goes over to* CHARMION *and* IRAS; *seems to
          talk with them.*
To make him jealous; jealousy is like
A polished glass held to the lips when life's in doubt;
If there be breath, 'twill catch the damp, and show it.

Cleo. I grant you, jealousy's a proof of love,
But 'tis a weak and unavailing medicine;
It puts out the disease, and makes it show,
But has no power to cure.

Alex. 'Tis your last remedy, and strongest too:
And then this Dolabella, who so fit
To practise on? He's handsome, valiant, young,
And looks as he were laid for nature's bait,
To catch weak women's eyes.
He stands already more than half suspected
Of loving you: the least kind word or glance
You give this youth, will kindle him with love:
Then, like a burning vessel set adrift,
You'll send him down amain before the wind,
To fire the heart of jealous Antony.

Cleo. Can I do this? Ah, no; my love's so true,
That I can neither hide it where it is,
Nor show it where it is not. Nature meant me
A wife; a silly, harmless, household dove,
Fond without art, and kind without deceit;
But Fortune, that has made a mistress of me,
Has thrust me out to the wide world, unfurnished
Of falsehood to be happy.

Alex. Force yourself.
The event will be, your lover will return,
Doubly desirous to possess the good
Which once he feared to lose.

Cleo. I must attempt it;
But oh, with what regret!

          [*Exit* ALEXAS. *She comes up to* DOLABELLA

Vent. So, now the scene draws near; they're in my reach.

Cleo. [*to* DOL.]. Discoursing with my women! might not I
Share in your entertainment?

Char. You have been
The subject of it, madam.

Cleo. How! and how?

Iras. Such praises of your beauty!

Cleo. Mere poetry.
Your Roman wits, your Gallus and Tibullus,
Have taught you this from Cytheris and Delia.

Dola. Those Roman wits have never been in Egypt;
Cytheris and Delia else had been unsung:
I, who have seen——had I been born a poet,
Should choose a nobler name.

Cleo. You flatter me.
But, 'tis your nation's vice: All of your country
Are flatterers, and all false. Your friend's like you.
I'm sure, he sent you not to speak these words.

Dola. No, madam; yet he sent me——

Cleo. Well, he sent you——

Dola. Of a less pleasing errand.

Cleo. How less pleasing?

Less to yourself, or me?

Dola. Madam, to both;

For you must mourn, and I must grieve to cause it.

Cleo. You, Charmion, and your fellow, stand at distance.——

Hold up, my spirits. [*Aside*]——Well, now your mournful
matter!

For I'm prepared, perhaps can guess it too.

Dola. I wish you would; for 'tis a thankless office,

To tell ill news: And I, of all your sex,

Most fear displeasing you.

Cleo. Of all your sex,

I soonest could forgive you, if you should.

Vent. Most delicate advances! Women! women!

Dear, damned, inconstant sex!

Cleo. In the first place,

I am to be forsaken; is't not so?

Dola. I wish I could not answer to that question.

Cleo. Then pass it o'er, because it troubles you:

I should have been more grieved another time.

Next, I'm to lose my kingdom——Farewell, Egypt!

Yet, is there any more?

Dola. Madam, I fear

Your too deep sense of grief has turned your reason.

Cleo. No, no, I'm not run mad; I can bear fortune:

And love may be expelled by other love,

As poisons are by poisons.

Dola. You o'erjoy me, madam,

To find your griefs so moderately borne.

You've heard the worst; all are not false like him.

Cleo. No; Heaven forbid they should.

Dola. Some men are constant.

Cleo. And constancy deserves reward, that's certain.

Dola. Deserves it not; but give it leave to hope.

Vent. I'll swear, thou hast my leave. I have enough:

But how to manage this! Well, I'll consider. [*Exit.*

Dola. I came prepared

To tell you heavy news; news, which I thought

Would fright the blood from your pale cheeks to hear:

But you have met it with a cheerfulness,

That makes my task more easy; and my tongue,

Which on another's message was employed,

Would gladly speak its own.

Cleo. Hold, Dolabella.

First tell me, were you chosen by my lord?

Or sought you this employment?

Dola. He picked me out; and, as his bosom friend,

* C 604

He charged me with his words.
    Cleo. The message then
I know was tender, and each accent smooth,
To mollify that rugged word, *Depart.*
    Dola. Oh, you mistake: He chose the harshest words;
With fiery eyes, and with contracted brows,
He coined his face in the severest stamp;
And fury shook his fabric, like an earthquake;
He heaved for vent, and burst like bellowing Ætna,
In sounds scarce human—" Hence away for ever,
Let her begone, the blot of my renown,
And bane of all my hopes ! "
    [All the time of this speech, Cleopatra *seems more and*
        more concerned, till she sinks quite down.
" Let her be driven, as far as men can think,
From man's commerce! she'll poison to the centre."
    Cleo. Oh, I can bear no more!
    Dola. Help, help!—O wretch! O cursed, cursed wretch!
What have I done!
    Char. Help, chafe her temples, Iras.
    Iras. Bend, bend her forward quickly.
    Char. Heaven be praised,
She comes again.
    Cleo. Oh, let him not approach me.
Why have you brought me back to this loathed being,
The abode of falsehood, violated vows,
And injured love? For pity, let me go;
For, if there be a place of long repose,
I'm sure I want it. My disdainful lord
Can never break that quiet; nor awake
The sleeping soul, with hollowing in my tomb
Such words as fright her hence.—Unkind, unkind!
    Dola. Believe me, 'tis against myself I speak;   *[Kneeling.*
That sure desires belief; I injured him:
My friend ne'er spoke those words. Oh, had you seen
How often he came back, and every time
With something more obliging and more kind,
To add to what he said; what dear farewells;
How almost vanquished by his love he parted,
And leaned to what unwillingly he left!
I, traitor as I was, for love of you
(But what can you not do, who made me false?)
I forged that lie; for whose forgiveness kneels
This self-accused, self-punished criminal.
    Cleo. With how much ease believe we what we wish!
Rise, Dolabella; if you have been guilty,
I have contributed, and too much love
Has made me guilty too.
The advance of kindness, which I made, was feigned,

To call back fleeting love by jealousy;
But 'twould not last. Oh, rather let me lose,
Than so ignobly trifle with his heart.
   Dola. I find your breast fenced round from human reach,
Transparent as a rock of solid crystal;
Seen through, but never pierced. My friend, my friend,
What endless treasure hast thou thrown away;
And scattered, like an infant, in the ocean,
Vain sums of wealth, which none can gather thence!
   Cleo. Could you not beg
An hour's admittance to his private ear?
Like one, who wanders through long barren wilds
And yet foreknows no hospitable inn
Is near to succour hunger, eats his fill,
Before his painful march;
So would I feed a while my famished eyes
Before we part; for I have far to go,
If death be far, and never must return.

VENTIDIUS with OCTAVIA, behind.

   Vent. From hence you may discover—oh, sweet, sweet!
Would you indeed? The pretty hand in earnest?
   Dola. I will, for this reward.   [*Takes her hand.*
Draw it not back.
'Tis all I e'er will beg.
   Vent. They turn upon us.
   Octav. What quick eyes has guilt!
   Vent. Seem not to have observed them, and go on.

They enter.

   Dola. Saw you the emperor, Ventidius?
   Vent. No.
I sought him; but I heard that he was private,
None with him but Hipparchus, his freedman.
   Dola. Know you his business?
   Vent. Giving him instructions,
And letters to his brother Cæsar.
   Dola. Well,
He must be found.   [*Exeunt* DOLABELLA *and* CLEOPATRA.
   Octav. Most glorious impudence!
   Vent. She looked, methought,
As she would say—Take your old man, Octavia;
Thank you, I'm better here.—
Well, but what use
Make we of this discovery?
   Octav. Let it die.
   Vent. I pity Dolabella; but she's dangerous;

Her eyes have power beyond Thessalian charms,
To draw the moon from heaven; for eloquence,
The sea-green Syrens taught her voice their flattery;
And, while she speaks, night steals upon the day,
Unmarked of those that hear: Then she's so charming,
Age buds at sight of her, and swells to youth:
The holy priests gaze on her when she smiles;
And with heaved hands, forgetting gravity,
They bless her wanton eyes: Even I, who hate her,
With a malignant joy behold such beauty;
And, while I curse, desire it. Antony
Must needs have some remains of passion still,
Which may ferment into a worse relapse,
If now not fully cured. I know, this minute,
With Cæsar he's endeavouring her peace.

   Octav. You have prevailed:——But for a further purpose
                                           [*Walks off.*
I'll prove how he will relish this discovery.
What, make a strumpet's peace! it swells my heart:
It must not, shall not be.

   Vent. His guards appear.
Let me begin, and you shall second me.

                  Enter ANTONY.

   Ant. Octavia, I was looking you, my love:
What, are your letters ready? I have given
My last instructions.

   Octav. Mine, my lord, are written.

   Ant. Ventidius.   [*Drawing him aside.*

   Vent. My lord?

   Ant. A word in private.—
When saw you Dolabella?

   Vent. Now, my lord,
He parted hence; and Cleopatra with him.

   Ant. Speak softly.—'Twas by my command he went,
To bear my last farewell.

   Vent. It looked indeed   [*Aloud.*
Like your farewell.

   Ant. More softly.—My farewell?
What secret meaning have you in those words
Of—My farewell? He did it by my order.

   Vent. Then he obeyed your order. I suppose   [*Aloud.*
You bid him do it with all gentleness,
All kindness, and all——love.

   Ant. How she mourned,
The poor forsaken creature!

   Vent. She took it as she ought; she bore **your** parting
As she did Cæsar's, as she would another's,

Were a new love to come.

 Ant. Thou dost belie her;   [*Aloud.*
Most basely, and maliciously belie her.

 Vent. I thought not to displease you; I have done.

 Octav. You seemed disturbed, my lord.   [*Coming up.*

 Ant. A very trifle.
Retire, my love.

 Vent. It was indeed a trifle.
He sent——

 Ant. No more. Look how thou disobey'st me;   [*Angrily.*
Thy life shall answer it.

 Octav. Then 'tis no trifle.

 Vent. [*to* OCTAV.]. 'Tis less; a very nothing: You too saw it,
As well as I, and therefore 'tis no secret.

 Ant. She saw it!

 Vent. Yes: She saw young Dolabella——

 Ant. Young Dolabella!

 Vent. Young, I think him young,
And handsome too; and so do others think him.
But what of that? He went by your command,
Indeed 'tis probable, with some kind message;
For she received it graciously; she smiled;
And then he grew familiar with her hand,
Squeezed it, and worried it with ravenous kisses;
She blushed, and sighed, and smiled, and blushed again;
At last she took occasion to talk softly,
And brought her cheek up close, and leaned on his;
At which, he whispered kisses back on hers;
And then she cried aloud—That constancy
Should be rewarded.

 Octav. This I saw and heard.

 Ant. What woman was it, whom you heard and saw
So playful with my friend?
Not Cleopatra?

 Vent. Even she, my lord.

 Ant. My Cleopatra?

 Vent. Your Cleopatra;
Dolabella's Cleopatra; every man's Cleopatra.

 Ant. Thou liest.

 Vent. I do not lie, my lord.
Is this so strange? Should mistresses be left,
And not provide against a time of change?
You know she's not much used to lonely nights.

 Ant. I'll think no more on't.
I know 'tis false, and see the plot betwixt you.—
You needed not have gone this way, Octavia.
What harms it you that Cleopatra's just?
She's mine no more. I see, and I forgive:
Urge it no further, love.

Octav. Are you concerned,
That she's found false?

Ant. I should be, were it so;
For, though 'tis past, I would not that the world
Should tax my former choice, that I loved one
Of so light note; but I forgive you both.

Vent. What has my age deserved, that you should think
I would abuse your ears with perjury?
If Heaven be true, she's false.

Ant. Though heaven and earth
Should witness it, I'll not believe her tainted.

Vent. I'll bring you, then, a witness
From hell, to prove her so.—Nay, go not back;
          [*Seeing* ALEXAS *just entering, and starting back.*
For stay you must and shall.

Alex. What means my lord?

Vent. To make you do what most you hate,—speak truth.
You are of Cleopatra's private counsel,
Of her bed-counsel, her lascivious hours;
Are conscious of each nightly change she makes,
And watch her, as Chaldeans do the moon,
Can tell what signs she passes through, what day.

Alex. My noble lord!

Vent. My most illustrious pander,
No fine set speech, no cadence, no turned periods,
But a plain homespun truth, is what I ask:
I did, myself, o'erhear your queen make love
To Dolabella.   Speak; for I will know,
By your confession, what more passed betwixt them;
How near the business draws to your employment;
And when the happy hour.

Ant. Speak truth, Alexas; whether it offend
Or please Ventidius, care not: Justify
Thy injured queen from malice: Dare his worst.

Octav. [*aside*]. See how he gives him courage! how he fears
To find her false! and shuts his eyes to truth,
Willing to be misled!

Alex. As far as love may plead for woman's frailty,
Urged by desert and greatness of the lover,
So far, divine Octavia, may my queen
Stand even excused to you for loving him
Who is your lord: so far, from brave Ventidius,
May her past actions hope a fair report.

Ant. 'Tis well, and truly spoken: mark, Ventidius.

Alex. To you, most noble emperor, her strong passion
Stands not excused, but wholly justified.
Her beauty's charms alone, without her crown,
From Ind and Meroe drew the distant vows
Of sighing kings; and at her feet were laid

The sceptres of the earth, exposed on heaps,
To choose where she would reign:
She thought a Roman only could deserve her,
And, of all Romans, only Antony;
And, to be less than wife to you, disdained
Their lawful passion.

Ant. 'Tis but truth.

Alex. And yet, though love, and your unmatched desert,
Have drawn her from the due regard of honour,
At last Heaven opened her unwilling eyes
To see the wrongs she offered fair Octavia,
Whose holy bed she lawlessly usurped.
The sad effects of this improsperous war
Confirmed those pious thoughts.

Vent. [*aside*]. Oh, wheel you there?
Observe him now; the man begins to mend,
And talk substantial reason.—Fear not, eunuch;
The emperor has given thee leave to speak.

Alex. Else had I never dared to offend his ears
With what the last necessity has urged
On my forsaken mistress; yet I must not
Presume to say, her heart is wholly altered.

Ant. No, dare not for thy life, I charge thee dare not
Pronounce that fatal word!

Octav. Must I bear this?   Good Heaven, afford me patience.
                                            [*Aside.*

Vent. On, sweet eunuch; my dear half-man, proceed.

Alex. Yet Dolabella
Has loved her long; he, next my god-like lord,
Deserves her best; and should she meet his passion,
Rejected, as she is, by him she loved——

Ant. Hence from my sight! for I can bear no more:
Let furies drag thee quick to hell; let all
The longer damned have rest; each torturing hand
Do thou employ, till Cleopatra comes;
Then join thou too, and help to torture her!
                        [*Exit* ALEXAS, *thrust out by* ANTONY.

Octav. 'Tis not well,
Indeed, my lord, 'tis much unkind to me,
To show this passion, this extreme concernment,
For an abandoned, faithless prostitute.

Ant. Octavia, leave me; I am much disordered:
Leave me, I say.

Octav. My lord!

Ant. I bid you leave me.

Vent. Obey him, madam: best withdraw a while,
And see how this will work.

Octav. Wherein have I offended you, my lord,
That I am bid to leave you?   Am I false,

Or infamous? Am I a Cleopatra?
Were I she,
Base as she is, you would not bid me leave you;
But hang upon my neck, take slight excuses,
And fawn upon my falsehood.
    Ant. 'Tis too much.
Too much, Octavia; I am pressed with sorrows
Too heavy to be borne; and you add more:
I would retire, and recollect what's left
Of man within, to aid me.
    Octav. You would mourn,
In private, for your love, who has betrayed you.
You did but half return to me: your kindness
Lingered behind with her. I hear, my lord,
You make conditions for her,
And would include her treaty. Wondrous proofs
Of love to me!
    Ant. Are you my friend, Ventidius?
Or are you turned a Dolabella too,
And let this fury loose?
    Vent. Oh, be advised,
Sweet madam, and retire.
    Octav. Yes, I will go; but never to return.
You shall no more be haunted with this Fury.
My lord, my lord, love will not always last,
When urged with long unkindness and disdain:
Take her again, whom you prefer to me;
She stays but to be called. Poor cozened man!
Let a feigned parting give her back your heart,
Which a feigned love first got; for injured me,
Though my just sense of wrongs forbid my stay,
My duty shall be yours.
To the dear pledges of our former love
My tenderness and care shall be transferred,
And they shall cheer, by turns, my widowed nights:
So, take my last farewell; for I despair
To have you whole, and scorn to take you half.   *[Exit.*
    Vent. I combat Heaven, which blasts my best designs:
My last attempt must be to win her back;
But oh! I fear in vain.   *[Exit.*
    Ant. Why was I framed with this plain, honest heart,
Which knows not to disguise its griefs and weakness,
But bears its workings outward to the world?
I should have kept the mighty anguish in,
And forced a smile at Cleopatra's falsehood:
Octavia had believed it, and had stayed.
But I am made a shallow-forded stream,
Seen to the bottom: all my clearness scorned,
And all my faults exposed.—See where he comes,

Enter DOLABELLA.

Who has profaned the sacred name of friend,
And worn it into vileness!
With how secure a brow, and specious form
He gilds the secret villain!   Sure that face
Was meant for honesty; but Heaven mismatched it,
And furnished treason out with nature's pomp,
To make its work more easy.
 Dola. O my friend!
 Ant. Well, Dolabella, you performed my message?
 Dola. I did, unwillingly.
 Ant. Unwillingly?
Was it so hard for you to bear our parting?
You should have wished it.
 Dola. Why?
 Ant. Because you love me.
And she received my message with as true,
With as unfeigned a sorrow as you brought it?
 Dola. She loves you, even to madness.
 Ant. Oh, I know it.
You, Dolabella, do not better know
How much she loves me.   And should I
Forsake this beauty?   This all-perfect creature?
 Dola. I could not, were she mine.
 Ant. And yet you first
Persuaded me: How come you altered since?
 Dola. I said at first I was not fit to go:
I could not hear her sighs, and see her tears,
But pity must prevail: And so, perhaps,
It may again with you; for I have promised,
That she should take her last farewell: And, see,
She comes to claim my word.

Enter CLEOPATRA.

 Ant. False Dolabella!
 Dola. What's false, my lord?
 Ant. Why, Dolabella's false,
And Cleopatra's false; both false and faithless.
Draw near, you well-joined wickedness, you serpents,
Whom I have in my kindly bosom warmed,
Till I am stung to death.
 Dola. My lord, have I
Deserved to be thus used?
 Cleo. Can Heaven prepare
A newer torment?   Can it find a curse
Beyond our separation?
 Ant. Yes, if fate

Be just, much greater: Heaven should be ingenious
In punishing such crimes.   The rolling stone,
And gnawing vulture, were slight pains, invented
When Jove was young, and no examples known
Of mighty ills; but you have ripened sin,
To such a monstrous growth, 'twill pose the gods
To find an equal torture.   Two, two such!—
Oh, there's no further name,—two such! to me,
To me, who locked my soul within your breasts,
Had no desires, no joys, no life, but you;
When half the globe was mine, I gave it you
In dowry with my heart; I had no use,
No fruit of all, but you: A friend and mistress
Was what the world could give.   O Cleopatra!
O Dolabella! how could you betray
This tender heart, which with an infant fondness
Lay lulled betwixt your bosoms, and there slept,
Secure of injured faith?
 Dola. If she has wronged you,
Heaven, hell, and you revenge it.
 Ant. If she has wronged me!
Thou wouldst evade thy part of guilt; but swear
Thou lov'st not her.
 Dola. Not so as I love you.
 Ant. Not so? Swear, swear, I say, thou dost not love her.
 Dola. No more than friendship will allow.
 Ant. No more?
Friendship allows thee nothing: Thou art perjured—
And yet thou didst not swear thou lov'st her not;
But not so much, no more.   O trifling hypocrite,
Who dar'st not own to her, thou dost not love,
Nor own to me, thou dost! Ventidius heard it;
Octavia saw it.
 Cleo. They are enemies.
 Ant. Alexas is not so: He, he confessed it;
He, who, next hell, best knew it, he avowed it.
Why do I seek a proof beyond yourself? [*To* DOLABELLA.
You, whom I sent to bear my last farewell,
Returned, to plead her stay.
 Dola. What shall I answer?
If to have loved be guilt, then I have sinned;
But if to have repented of that love
Can wash away my crime, I have repented.
Yet, if I have offended past forgiveness,
Let not her suffer: She is innocent.
 Cleo. Ah, what will not a woman do, who loves?
What means will she refuse, to keep that heart,
Where all her joys are placed?   'Twas I encouraged,

'Twas I blew up the fire that scorched his soul,
To make you jealous, and by that regain you.
But all in vain; I could not counterfeit:
In spite of all the dams my love broke o'er,
And drowned my heart again: fate took the occasion;
And thus one minute's feigning has destroyed
My whole life's truth.

   Ant. Thin cobweb arts of falsehood;
Seen, and broke through at first.

   Dola. Forgive your mistress.

   Cleo. Forgive your friend.

   Ant. You have convinced yourselves.
You plead each other's cause: What witness have you,
That you but meant to raise my jealousy?

   Cleo. Ourselves, and Heaven.

   Ant. Guilt witnesses for guilt. Hence, love and friendship!
You have no longer place in human breasts,
These two have driven you out: Avoid my sight!
I would not kill the man whom I have loved,
And cannot hurt the woman; but avoid me:
I do not know how long I can be tame;
For, if I stay one minute more, to think
How I am wronged, my justice and revenge
Will cry so loud within me, that my pity
Will not be heard for either.

   Dola. Heaven has but
Our sorrow for our sins; and then delights
To pardon erring man: Sweet mercy seems
Its darling attribute, which limits justice;
As if there were degrees in infinite,
And infinite would rather want perfection
Than punish to extent.

   Ant. I can forgive
A foe; but not a mistress and a friend.
Treason is there in its most horrid shape,
Where trust is greatest; and the soul resigned,
Is stabbed by its own guards: I'll hear no more;
Hence from my sight for ever!

   Cleo. How? for ever!
I cannot go one moment from your sight,
And must I go for ever?
My joys, my only joys, are centred here:
What place have I to go to? My own kingdom?
That I have lost for you: Or to the Romans?
They hate me for your sake: Or must I wander
The wide world o'er, a helpless, banished woman,
Banished for love of you; banished from you?
Ay, there's the banishment! Oh, hear me; hear me,
With strictest justice: For I beg no favour;

And if I have offended you, then kill me,
But do not banish me.

    Ant. I must not hear you.
I have a fool within me takes your part;
But honour stops my ears.

    Cleo. For pity hear me!
Would you cast off a slave who followed you?
Who crouched beneath your spurn?—He has no pity!
See, if he gives one tear to my departure;
One look, one kind farewell: O iron heart!
Let all the gods look down, and judge betwixt us,
If he did ever love!

    Ant. No more: Alexas!

    Dola. A perjured villain!

    Ant. [*to* CLEO.]. Your Alexas; yours.

    Cleo. Oh, 'twas his plot; his ruinous design,
To engage you in my love by jealousy.
Hear him; confront him with me; let him speak.

    Ant. I have; I have.

    Cleo. And if he clear me not——

    Ant. Your creature! one, who hangs upon your smiles!
Watches your eye, to say or to unsay,
Whate'er you please! I am not to be moved.

    Cleo. Then must we part? Farewell, my cruel lord!
The appearance is against me; and I go,
Unjustified, for ever from your sight.
How I have loved, you know; how yet I love,
My only comfort is, I know myself:
I love you more, even now you are unkind,
Than when you loved me most; so well, so truly
I'll never strive against it; but die pleased,
To think you once were mine.

    Ant. Good heaven, they weep at parting!
Must I weep too? that calls them innocent.
I must not weep; and yet I must, to think
That I must not forgive.——
Live, but live wretched; 'tis but just you should,
Who made me so: Live from each other's sight:
Let me not hear you meet. Set all the earth,
And all the seas, betwixt your sundered loves:
View nothing common but the sun and skies.
Now, all take several ways;

    And each your own sad fate, with mine, deplore;
    That you were false, and I could trust no more.

                                 [Exeunt severally.

ACT V

SCENE I

Enter CLEOPATRA, CHARMION, *and* IRAS.

Char. Be juster, Heaven; such virtue punished thus,
Will make us think that chance rules all above,
And shuffles, with a random hand, the lots,
Which man is forced to draw.
    Cleo. I could tear out these eyes, that gained his heart,
And had not power to keep it.   O the curse
Of doting on, even when I find it dotage!
Bear witness, gods, you heard him bid me go;
You, whom he mocked with imprecating vows
Of promised faith!——I'll die; I will not bear it.
You may hold me——
                [She pulls out her dagger, and they hold her.
But I can keep my breath; I can die inward,
And choke this love.

Enter ALEXAS.

Iras. Help, O Alexas, help!
The queen grows desperate; her soul struggles in her
With all the agonies of love and rage,
And strives to force its passage.
    Cleo. Let me go.
Art thou there, traitor!—O,
O for a little breath, to vent my rage,
Give, give me way, and let me loose upon him.
    Alex. Yes, I deserve it, for my ill-timed truth.
Was it for me to prop
The ruins of a falling majesty?
To place myself beneath the mighty flaw,
Thus to be crushed, and pounded into atoms,
By its o'erwhelming weight?   'Tis too presuming
For subjects to preserve that wilful power,
Which courts its own destruction.
    Cleo. I would reason
More calmly with you.   Did not you o'errule,
And force my plain, direct, and open love,
Into these crooked paths of jealousy?
Now, what's the event? Octavia is removed;
But Cleopatra's banished.   Thou, thou villain,
Hast pushed my boat to open sea; to prove,
At my sad cost, if thou canst steer it back.

It cannot be; I'm lost too far; I'm ruined:
Hence, thou impostor, traitor, monster, devil!—
I can no more: Thou, and my griefs, have sunk
Me down so low, that I want voice to curse thee.

    Alex. Suppose some shipwrecked seaman near the shore,
Dropping and faint with climbing up the cliff,
If, from above, some charitable hand
Pull him to safety, hazarding himself,
To draw the other's weight; would he look back,
And curse him for his pains? The case is yours;
But one step more, and you have gained the height.

    Cleo. Sunk, never more to rise.

    Alex. Octavia's gone, and Dolabella banished.
Believe me, madam, Antony is yours.
His heart was never lost, but started off
To jealousy, love's last retreat and covert;
Where it lies hid in shades, watchful in silence,
And listening for the sound that calls it back.
Some other, any man ('tis so advanced),
May perfect this unfinished work, which I
(Unhappy only to myself) have left
So easy to his hand.

    Cleo. Look well thou do't; else——

    Alex. Else, what your silence threatens.—Antony
Is mounted up the Pharos; from whose turret,
He stands surveying our Egyptian galleys,
Engaged with Cæsar's fleet. Now death or conquest!
If the first happen, fate acquits my promise;
If we o'ercome, the conqueror is yours. [*A distant shout within.*

    Char. Have comfort, madam: Did you mark that shout?
                                [*Second shout nearer.*

    Iras. Hark! they redouble it.

    Alex. 'Tis from the port.
The loudness shows it near: Good news, kind heavens!

    Cleo. Osiris make it so!

Enter SERAPION.

    Serap. Where, where's the queen?

    Alex. How frightfully the holy coward stares
As if not yet recovered of the assault,
When all his gods, and, what's more dear to him,
His offerings, were at stake.

    Serap. O horror, horror!
Egypt has been; our latest hour has come:
The queen of nations, from her ancient seat,
Is sunk for ever in the dark abyss:
Time has unrolled her glories to the last,
And now closed up the volume.

Cleo. Be more plain:
Say, whence thou comest; though fate is in thy face,
Which from thy haggard eyes looks wildly out,
And threatens ere thou speakest.
    Serap. I came from Pharos;
From viewing (spare me, and imagine it)
Our land's last hope, your navy——
    Cleo. Vanquished?
    Serap. No:
They fought not.
    Cleo. Then they fled.
    Serap. Nor that. I saw,
With Antony, your well-appointed fleet
Row out; and thrice he waved his hand on high,
And thrice with cheerful cries they shouted back:
'Twas then false Fortune, like a fawning strumpet,
About to leave the bankrupt prodigal,
With a dissembled smile would kiss at parting,
And flatter to the last; the well-timed oars,
Now dipt from every bank, now smoothly run
To meet the foe; and soon indeed they met,
But not as foes. In few,[1] we saw their caps
On either side thrown up; the Egyptian galleys,
Received like friends, passed through, and fell behind
The Roman rear: And now, they all come forward,
And ride within the port.
    Cleo. Enough, Serapion:
I've heard my doom.—This needed not, you gods:
When I lost Antony, your work was done;
'Tis but superfluous malice.—Where's my lord?
How bears he this last blow?
    Serap. His fury cannot be expressed by words:
Thrice he attempted headlong to have fallen
Full on his foes, and aimed at Cæsar's galley:
Withheld, he raves on you; cries,—He's betrayed.
Should he now find you——
    Alex. Shun him; seek your safety,
Till you can clear your innocence.
    Cleo. I'll stay.
    Alex. You must not; haste you to your monument,
While I make speed to Cæsar.
    Cleo. Cæsar! No,
I have no business with him.
    Alex. I can work him
To spare your life, and let this madman perish.
    Cleo. Base fawning wretch! wouldst thou betray him too?
Hence from my sight! I will not hear a traitor;
'Twas thy design brought all this ruin on us.—

Serapion, thou art honest; counsel me:
But haste, each moment's precious.

   Serap. Retire; you must not yet see Antony.
He who began this mischief,
'Tis just he tempt the danger; let him clear you:
And, since he offered you his servile tongue,
To gain a poor precarious life from Cæsar,
Let him expose that fawning eloquence,
And speak to Antony.

   Alex. O heavens! I dare not;
I meet my certain death.

   Cleo. Slave, thou deservest it.—
Not that I fear my lord, will I avoid him;
I know him noble: when he banished me,
And thought me false, he scorned to take my life;
But I'll be justified, and then die with him.

   Alex. O pity me, and let me follow you.

   Cleo. To death, if thou stir hence. Speak, if thou canst,
Now for thy life, which basely thou wouldst save;
While mine I prize at—this! Come, good Serapion.

      [*Exeunt* CLEOPATRA, SERAPION, CHARMION, *and* IRAS.

   Alex. O that I less could fear to lose this being,
Which, like a snowball in my coward hand,
The more 'tis grasped, the faster melts away.
Poor reason! what a wretched aid art thou!
For still, in spite of thee,
These two long lovers, soul and body, dread
Their final separation. Let me think:
What can I say, to save myself from death?
No matter what becomes of Cleopatra.

   Ant. Which way? where?   [*Within.*

   Vent. This leads to the monument.   [*Within.*

   Alex. Ah me! I hear him; yet I'm unprepared:
My gift of lying's gone;
And this court-devil, which I so oft have raised,
Forsakes me at my need. I dare not stay;
Yet cannot far go hence.

                            [*Exit.*

Enter ANTONY *and* VENTIDIUS.

   Ant. O happy Cæsar! thou hast men to lead:
Think not 'tis thou hast conquered Antony;
But Rome has conquered Egypt. I'm betrayed.

   Vent. Curse on this treacherous train!
Their soil and heaven infect them all with baseness:
And their young souls come tainted to the world
With the first breath they draw.

   Ant. The original villain sure no god created;
He was a bastard of the sun, by Nile,

Aped into man; with all his mother's mud
Crusted about his soul.

   Vent. The nation is
One universal traitor; and their queen
The very spirit and extract of them all.

   Ant. Is there yet left
A possibility of aid from valour?
Is there one god unsworn to my destruction?
The least unmortgaged hope? for, if there be,
Methinks I cannot fall beneath the fate
Of such a boy as Cæsar.
The world's one half is yet in Antony;
And from each limb of it, that's hewed away,
The soul comes back to me.

   Vent. There yet remain
Three legions in the town. The last assault
Lopt off the rest; if death be your design,—
As I must wish it now,—these are sufficient
To make a heap about us of dead foes,
An honest pile for burial.

   Ant. They are enough.
We'll not divide our stars; but, side by side,
Fight emulous, and with malicious eyes
Survey each other's acts: So every death
Thou giv'st, I'll take on me, as a just debt,
And pay thee back a soul.

   Vent. Now you shall see I love you. Not a word
Of chiding more. By my few hours of life,
I am so pleased with this brave Roman fate,
That I would not be Cæsar, to outlive you.
When we put off this flesh, and mount together,
I shall be shown to all the ethereal crowd,—
Lo, this is he who died with Antony!

   Ant. Who knows, but we may pierce through all their troops,
And reach my veterans yet? 'tis worth the 'tempting,
To o'erleap this gulf of fate,
And leave our wandering destinies behind.

        Enter ALEXAS, *trembling.*

   Vent. See, see, that villain!
See Cleopatra stamped upon that face,
With all her cunning, all her arts of falsehood!
How she looks out through those dissembling eyes!
How he sets his countenance for deceit,
And promises a lie, before he speaks!
Let me despatch him first.   [*Drawing.*

   Alex. O spare me, spare me!

   Ant. Hold; he's not worth your killing.—On thy life,
Which thou may'st keep, because I scorn to take it,

No syllable to justify thy queen;
Save thy base tongue its office.
   Alex. Sir, she is gone,
Where she shall never be molested more
By love, or you.
   Ant. Fled to her Dolabella!
Die, traitor! I revoke my promise! die! [*Going to kill him.*
   Alex. O hold! she is not fled.
   Ant. She is: my eyes
Are open to her falsehood; my whole life
Has been a golden dream of love and friendship;
But, now I wake, I'm like a merchant, roused
From soft repose, to see his vessel sinking,
And all his wealth cast over. Ungrateful woman!
Who followed me, but as the swallow summer,
Hatching her young ones in my kindly beams,
Singing her flatteries to my morning wake:
But, now my winter comes, she spreads her wings,
And seeks the spring of Cæsar.
   Alex. Think not so:
Her fortunes have, in all things, mixed with yours.
Had she betrayed her naval force to Rome,
How easily might she have gone to Cæsar,
Secure by such a bribe!
   Vent. She sent it first,
To be more welcome after.
   Ant. 'Tis too plain;
Else would she have appeared, to clear herself.
   Alex. Too fatally she has: she could not bear
To be accused by you; but shut herself
Within her monument; looked down and sighed;
While, from her unchanged face, the silent tears
Dropt, as they had not leave, but stole their parting.
Some indistinguished words she inly murmured;
At last, she raised her eyes; and, with such looks
As dying Lucrece cast——
   Ant. My heart forebodes——
   Vent. All for the best:—Go on.
   Alex. She snatched her poniard,
And, ere we could prevent the fatal blow,
Plunged it within her breast; then turned to me:
Go, bear my lord, said she, my last farewell;
And ask him, if he yet suspect my faith.
More she was saying, but death rushed betwixt.
She half pronounced your name with her last breath,
And buried half within her.
   Vent. Heaven be praised!
   Ant. Then art thou innocent, my poor dear love,
And art thou dead?

O those two words! their sound should be divided:
Hadst thou been false, and died; or hadst thou lived,
And hadst been true—But innocence and death!
This shows not well above. Then what am I,
The murderer of this truth, this innocence!
Thoughts cannot form themselves in words so horrid
As can express my guilt!

    Vent. Is't come to this? The gods have been too gracious;
And thus you thank them for it!

    Ant. [*to* ALEX.]. Why stayest thou here?
Is it for thee to spy upon my soul,
And see its inward mourning? Get thee hence
Thou art not worthy to behold, what now
Becomes a Roman emperor to perform.

    Alex. He loves her still:
His grief betrays it. Good! the joy to find
She's yet alive, completes the reconcilement.
I've saved myself, and her. But, oh! the Romans!
Fate comes too fast upon my wit,
Hunts me too hard, and meets me at each double.
                             [*Aside. Exit*

    Vent. Would she had died a little sooner, though!
Before Octavia went, you might have treated:
Now 'twill look tame, and would not be received.
Come, rouse yourself, and let's die warm together.

    Ant. I will not fight: there's no more work for war.
The business of my angry hours is done.

    Vent. Cæsar is at your gates.

    Ant. Why, let him enter;
He's welcome now.

    Vent. What lethargy has crept into your soul?

    Ant. 'Tis but a scorn of life, and just desire
To free myself from bondage.

    Vent. Do it bravely.

    Ant. I will; but not by fighting. O Ventidius!
What should I fight for now?—my queen is dead.
I was but great for her; my power, my empire,
Were but my merchandise to buy her love;
And conquered kings, my factors. Now she's dead,
Let Cæsar take the world,—
An empty circle, since the jewel's gone
Which made it worth my strife: my being's nauseous;
For all the bribes of life are gone away.

    Vent. Would you be taken?

    Ant. Yes, I would be taken;
But, as a Roman ought,—dead, my Ventidius:
For I'll convey my soul from Cæsar's reach,
And lay down life myself. 'Tis time the world
Should have a lord, and know whom to obey.

We two have kept its homage in suspense,
And bent the globe, on whose each side we trod,
Till it was dented inwards. Let him walk
Alone upon't: I'm weary of my part.
My torch is out; and the world stands before me,
Like a black desert at the approach of night:
I'll lay me down, and stray no farther on.
 Vent. I could be grieved,
But that I'll not outlive you: choose your death;
For, I have seen him in such various shapes,
I care not which I take: I'm only troubled,
The life I bear is worn to such a rag,
'Tis scarce worth giving. I could wish, indeed,
We threw it from us with a better grace;
That, like two lions taken in the toils,
We might at last thrust out our paws, and wound
The hunters that inclose us.
 Ant. I have thought on it.
Ventidius, you must live.
 Vent. I must not, sir.
 Ant. Wilt thou not live, to speak some good of me?
To stand by my fair fame, and guard the approaches
From the ill tongues of men?
 Vent. Who shall guard mine,
For living after you?
 Ant. Say, I command it.
 Vent. If we die well, our deaths will speak themselves
And need no living witness.
 Ant. Thou hast loved me,
And fain I would reward thee. I must die;
Kill me, and take the merit of my death,
To make thee friends with Cæsar.
 Vent. Thank your kindness.
You said I loved you; and in recompense,
You bid me turn a traitor: Did I think
You would have used me thus?—that I should die
With a hard thought of you?
 Ant. Forgive me, Roman.
Since I have heard of Cleopatra's death,
My reason bears no rule upon my tongue,
But lets my thoughts break all at random out.
I've thought better; do not deny me twice.
 Vent. By Heaven I will not.
Let it not be to outlive you.
 Ant. Kill me first,
And then die thou; for 'tis but just thou serve
Thy friend before thyself.
 Vent. Give me your hand.
We soon shall meet again. Now, farewell, emperor!—[*Embrace.*

Methinks that word's too cold to be my last:
Since death sweeps all distinctions, farewell, friend!
That's all——
I will not make a business of a trifle;
And yet I cannot look on you, and kill you;
Pray turn your face.

    Ant. I do: strike home, be sure.

    Vent. Home as my sword will reach.   [*Kills himself.*

    Ant. Oh, thou mistak'st;
That wound was not of thine; give it me back;
Thou robb'st me of my death.

    Vent. I do indeed;
But think 'tis the first time I e'er deceived you,
If that may plead my pardon.—And you, gods,
Forgive me, if you will; for I die perjured,
Rather than kill my friend.   [*Dies.*

    Ant. Farewell! Ever my leader, even in death!
My queen and thou have got the start of me,
And I'm the lag of honour.—Gone so soon?
Is Death no more? he used him carelessly,
With a familiar kindness: ere he knocked,
Ran to the door, and took him in his arms,
As who should say—You're welcome at all hours,
A friend need give no warning. Books had spoiled him;
For all the learned are cowards by profession.
'Tis not worth
My further thought; for death, for aught I know,
Is but to think no more. Here's to be satisfied.

                  [*Falls on his sword.*
I've missed my heart. O unperforming hand!
Thou never couldst have erred in a worse time.
My fortune jades me to the last; and death,
Like a great man, takes state, and makes me wait
For my admittance.——   [*Trampling within.*
Some, perhaps, from Cæsar:
If he should find me living, and suspect
That I played booty with my life! I'l mend
My work, ere they can reach me.   [*Rises upon his knees.*

     Enter CLEOPATRA, CHARMION, *and* IRAS.

    Cleo. Where is my lord? where is he?

    Char. There he lies,
And dead Ventidius by him.

    Cleo. My fears were prophets; I am come too late.
O that accursed Alexas!   [*Runs to him.*

    Ant. Art thou living?
Or am I dead before I knew, and thou
The first kind ghost that meets me?

Cleo. Help me seat him.
Send quickly, send for help!   [*They place him in a chair.*
    Ant. I am answered.
We live both.   Sit thee down, my Cleopatra:
I'll make the most I can of life, to stay
A moment more with thee.
    Cleo. How is it with you?
    Ant. 'Tis as with a man
Removing in a hurry; all packed up,
But one dear jewel that his haste forgot;
And he, for that, returns upon the spur:
So I come back for thee.
    Cleo. Too long, ye heavens, you have been cruel to me:
Now show your mended faith, and give me back
His fleeting life!
    Ant. It will not be, my love;
I keep my soul by force.
Say but, thou art not false.
    Cleo. 'Tis now too late
To say I'm true: I'll prove it, and die with you.
Unknown to me, Alexas feigned my death:
Which, when I knew, I hasted to prevent
This fatal conseqence.   My fleet betrayed
Both you and me.
    Ant. And Dolabella——
    Cleo. Scarce
Esteemed before he loved; but hated now.
    Ant. Enough: my life's not long enough for more.
Thou say'st, thou wilt come after: I believe thee;
For I can now believe whate'er thou sayest,
That we may part more kindly.
    Cleo. I will come:
Doubt not, my life, I'll come, and quickly too:
Cæsar shall triumph o'er no part of thee.
    Ant. But grieve not, while thou stayest,
My last disastrous times:
Think we have had a clear and glorious day
And Heaven did kindly to delay the storm,
Just till our close of evening.   Ten years' love,
And not a moment lost, but all improved
To the utmost joys,—what ages have we lived?
And now to die each other's; and, so dying,
While hand in hand we walk in groves below,
Whole troops of lovers' ghosts shall flock about us,
And all the train be ours.
    Cleo. Your words are like the notes of dying swans,
Too sweet to last.   Were there so many hours
For your unkindness, and not one for love?
    Ant. No, not a minute.—This one kiss—more worth

Than all I leave to Cæsar.   [*Dies.*

   Cleo. O tell me so again,
And take ten thousand kisses for that word.
My lord, my lord! speak, if you yet have being;
Sign to me, if you cannot speak; or cast
One look! Do anything that shows you live.

   Iras. He's gone too far to hear you;
And this you see, a lump of senseless clay,
The leavings of a soul.

   Char. Remember, madam,
He charged you not to grieve.

   Cleo. And I'll obey him.
I have not loved a Roman, not to know
What should become his wife; his wife, my Charmion!
For 'tis to that high title I aspire;
And now I'll not die less. Let dull Octavia
Survive, to mourn him dead: My nobler fate
Shall knit our spousals with a tie, too strong
For Roman laws to break.

   Iras. Will you then die?

   Cleo. Why shouldst thou make that question?

   Iras. Cæsar is merciful.

   Cleo. Let him be so
To those that want his mercy: My poor lord
Made no such covenant with him, to spare me
When he was dead. Yield me to Cæsar's pride?
What! to be led in triumph through the streets,
A spectacle to base plebeian eyes;
While some dejected friend of Antony's,
Close in a corner, shakes his head, and mutters
A secret curse on her who ruined him!
I'll none of that.

   Char. Whatever you resolve,
I'll follow, even to death.

   Iras. I only feared
For you; but more should fear to live without you.

   Cleo. Why, now, 'tis as it should be. Quick, my friends,
Despatch; ere this, the town's in Cæsar's hands:
My lord looks down concerned, and fears my stay,
Lest I should be surprised;
Keep him not waiting for his love too long.
You, Charmion, bring my crown and richest jewels:
With them, the wreath of victory I made
(Vain augury!) for him, who now lies dead:
You, Iras, bring the cure of all our ills.

   Iras. The aspics, madam?

   Cleo. Must I bid you twice?   [*Exit* CHARMION *and* IRAS.
'Tis sweet to die, when they would force life on me,
To rush into the dark abode of death,

And seize him first; if he be like my love,
He is not frightful, sure.
We're now alone, in secrecy and silence;
And is not this like lovers? I may kiss
These pale, cold lips; Octavia does not see me:
And, oh! 'tis better far to have him thus,
Than see him in her arms.—Oh, welcome, welcome!

Enter CHARMION *and* IRAS.

Char. What must be done?
Cleo. Short ceremony, friends;
But yet it must be decent. First, this laurel
Shall crown my hero's head: he fell not basely,
Nor left his shield behind him.—Only thou
Couldst triumph o'er thyself; and thou alone
Wert worthy so to triumph.
Char. To what end
These ensigns of your pomp and royalty?
Cleo. Dull, that thou art! why 'tis to meet my love;
As when I saw him first, on Cydnus' bank,
All sparkling, like a goddess: so adorned,
I'll find him once again; my second spousals
Shall match my first in glory. Haste, haste, both,
And dress the bride of Antony.
Char. 'Tis done.
Cleo. Now seat me by my lord. I claim this place;
For I must conquer Cæsar too, like him,
And win my share of the world.—Hail, you dear relics
Of my immortal love!
O let no impious hand remove you hence:
But rest for ever here! Let Egypt give
His death that peace, which it denied his life.—
Reach me the casket.
Iras. Underneath the fruit
The aspic lies.
Cleo. Welcome, thou kind deceiver! [*Putting aside the leaves.*
Thou best of thieves; who, with an easy key,
Dost open life, and, unperceived by us,
Even steal us from ourselves; discharging so
Death's dreadful office, better than himself;
Touching our limbs so gently into slumber,
That Death stands by, deceived by his own image,
And thinks himself but sleep.
Serap. The queen, where is she?   [*Within.*
The town is yielded, Cæsar's at the gates.
Cleo. He comes too late to invade the rights of death.
Haste, bare my arm, and rouse the serpent's fury.
                    [*Holds out her arm, and draws it back.*

Coward flesh,
Wouldst thou conspire with Cæsar to betray me,
As thou wert none of mine? I'll force thee to it,
And not be sent by him,
But bring, myself, my soul to Antony.
            [Turns aside, and then shows her arm bloody.
Take hence; the work is done.
   Serap. Break ope the door,   *[Within.*
And guard the traitor well.
   Char. The next is ours.
   Iras. Now, Charmion, to be worthy
Of our great queen and mistress.   *[They apply the aspics.*
   Cleo. Already, death, I feel thee in my veins:
I go with such a will to find my lord,
That we shall quickly meet.
A heavy numbness creeps through every limb,
And now 'tis at my head: My eyelids fall
And my dear love is vanquished in a mist.
Where shall I find him, where? O turn me to him,
And lay me on his breast!—Cæsar, thy worst;
Now part us, if thou canst.   *[Dies.*
     [IRAS *sinks down at her feet, and dies;* CHARMION
       stands behind her chair, as dressing her head.

Enter SERAPION, *two* Priests, ALEXAS *bound,* Egyptians.

   Priest. Behold, Serapion,
What havoc death has made!
   Serap. 'Twas what I feared.—
Charmion, is this well done?
   Char. Yes, 'tis well done, and like a queen, the last
Of her great race: I follow her.   *[Sinks down : dies.*
   Alex. 'Tis true,
She has done well: Much better thus to die,
Than live to make a holiday in Rome.
   Serap. See how the lovers sit in state together,
As they were giving laws to half mankind!
The impression of a smile, left in her face,
Shows she died pleased with him for whom she lived,
And went to charm him in another world.
Cæsar's just entering: grief has now no leisure.
Secure that villain, as our pledge of safety,
To grace the imperial triumph.—Sleep, blest pair,
Secure from human chance, long ages out,
While all the storms of fate fly o'er your tomb;
   And fame to late posterity shall tell,
   No lovers lived so great, or died so well.   *[Exeunt.*

EPILOGUE

Poets, like disputants, when reasons fail,
Have one sure refuge left—and that's to rail.
Fop, coxcomb, fool, are thundered through the pit;
And this is all their equipage of wit.
We wonder how the devil this difference grows,
Betwixt our fools in verse, and yours in prose:
For, 'faith, the quarrel rightly understood,
'Tis civil war with their own flesh and blood.
The threadbare author hates the gaudy coat;
And swears at the gilt coach, but swears afoot:
For 'tis observed of every scribbling man,
He grows a fop as fast as e'er he can;
Prunes up, and asks his oracle, the glass,
If pink or purple best become his face.
For our poor wretch, he neither rails nor prays;
Nor likes your wit just as you like his plays;
He has not yet so much of Mr. Bayes.
He does his best; and if he cannot please,
Would quietly sue out his *writ of ease*.
Yet, if he might his own grand jury call,
By the fair sex he begs to stand or fall.
Let Cæsar's power the men's ambition move,
But grace you him who lost the world for love!
Yet if some antiquated lady say,
The last age is not copied in his play;
Heaven help the man who for that face must drudge,
Which only has the wrinkles of a judge.
Let not the young and beauteous join with those;
For should you raise such numerous hosts of foes,
Young wits and sparks he to his aid must call;
'Tis more than one man's work to please you all.

THE COUNTRY WIFE

DRAMATIS PERSONÆ

Mr. HORNER.
Mr. HARCOURT.
Mr. DORILANT.
Mr. PINCHWIFE.
Mr. SPARKISH.
Sir JASPER FIDGET.
A Boy.
A Quack.
Waiters, Servants, and Attendants.

Mrs. MARGERY PINCHWIFE.
ALITHEA, Sister of Pinchwife.
Lady FIDGET.
Mrs. DAINTY FIDGET, Sister of Sir Jasper.
Mrs. SQUEAMISH.
Old Lady SQUEAMISH.
LUCY, Alithea's Maid.

SCENE—LONDON.

PROLOGUE

SPOKEN BY MR. HART

POETS, like cudgelled bullies, never do
At first or second blow submit to you;
But will provoke you still, and ne'er have done,
Till you are weary first with laying on.
The late so baffled scribbler of this day,
Though he stands trembling, bids me boldly say,
What we before most plays are used to do,
For poets out of fear first draw on you;
In a fierce prologue the still pit defy,
And, ere you speak, like Castril give the lie.
But though our Bayes's battles oft I've fought,
And with bruised knuckles their dear conquests bought;
Nay, never yet feared odds upon the stage,
In prologue dare not hector with the age;
But would take quarter from your saving hands,
Though Bayes within all yielding countermands,
Says, you confederate wits no quarter give,
Therefore his play shan't ask your leave to live.
Well, let the vain rash fop, by huffing so,
Think to obtain the better terms of you;
But we, the actors, humbly will submit,
Now, and at any time, to a full pit;
Nay, often we anticipate your rage,
And murder poets for you on our stage:
We set no guards upon our tiring-room,
But when with flying colours there you come,
We patiently, you see, give up to you
Our poets, virgins, nay, our matrons too.

THE COUNTRY WIFE

ACT I

SCENE I.—HORNER'S *Lodging*

Enter HORNER, *and* Quack *following him at a distance.*

Horn. [*aside*]. A quack is as fit for a pimp, as a midwife for a bawd; they are still but in their way, both helpers of nature.— [*Aloud.*] Well, my dear doctor, hast thou done what I desired?

Quack. I have undone you for ever with the women, and reported you throughout the whole town as bad as an eunuch, with as much trouble as if I had made you one in earnest.

Horn. But have you told all the midwives you know, the orange wenches at the playhouses, the city husbands, and old fumbling keepers of this end of the town? for they'll be the readiest to report it.

Quack. I have told all the chambermaids, waiting-women, tire-women, and old women of my acquaintance; nay, and whispered it as a secret to 'em, and to the whisperers of Whitehall; so that you need not doubt 'twill spread, and you will be as odious to the handsome young women as——

Horn. As the small-pox. Well——

Quack. And to the married women of this end of the town, as——

Horn. As the great one; nay, as their own husbands.

Quack. And to the city dames, as aniseed Robin, of filthy and contemptible memory; and they will frighten their children with your name, especially their females.

Horn. And cry, Horner's coming to carry you away. I am only afraid 'twill not be believed. You told 'em it was by an English-French disaster, and an English-French chirurgeon, who has given me at once not only a cure, but an antidote for the future against that damned malady, and that worse distemper, love, and all other women's evils?

Quack. Your late journey into France has made it the more credible, and your being here a fortnight before you appeared in public, looks as if you apprehended the shame, which I wonder you do not. Well, I have been hired by young gallants to belie 'em t'other way; but you are the first would be thought a man unfit for women.

Horn. Dear Mr. Doctor, let vain rogues be contented only to

85

be thought abler men than they are, generally 'tis all the pleasure they have; but mine lies another way.

Quack. You take, methinks, a very preposterous way to it, and as ridiculous as if we operators in physic should put forth bills to disparage our medicaments, with hopes to gain customers.

Horn. Doctor, there are quacks in love as well as physic, who get but the fewer and worse patients for their boasting; a good name is seldom got by giving it one's self; and women, no more than honour, are compassed by bragging. Come, come, Doctor, the wisest lawyer never discovers the merits of his cause till the trial; the wealthiest man conceals his riches, and the cunning gamester his play. Shy husbands and keepers, like old rooks, are not to be cheated but by a new unpractised trick: false friendship will pass now no more than false dice upon 'em; no, not in the city.

Enter Boy.

Boy. There are two ladies and a gentleman coming up. [*Exit.*

Horn. A pox! some unbelieving sisters of my former acquaintance, who, I am afraid, expect their sense should be satisfied of the falsity of the report. No—this formal fool and women!

Enter Sir JASPER FIDGET, Lady FIDGET, *and* Mrs. DAINTY FIDGET.

Quack. His wife and sister.

Sir Jasp. My coach breaking just now before your door, sir, I look upon as an occasional reprimand to me, sir, for not kissing your hands, sir, since your coming out of France, sir; and so my disaster, sir, has been my good fortune, sir; and this is my wife and sister, sir.

Horn. What then, sir?

Sir Jasp. My lady, and sister, sir.—Wife, this is Master Horner.

Lady Fid. Master Horner, husband!

Sir Jasp. My lady, my Lady Fidget, sir.

Horn. So, sir.

Sir Jasp. Won't you be acquainted with her, sir?—[*Aside.*] So, the report is true, I find, by his coldness or aversion to the sex; but I'll play the wag with him.—[*Aloud.*] Pray salute my wife, my lady, sir.

Horn. I will kiss no man's wife, sir, for him, sir; I have taken my eternal leave, sir, of the sex already, sir.

Sir Jasp. [*aside*]. Ha! ha! ha! I'll plague him yet.—[*Aloud.*] Not know my wife, sir?

Horn. I do know your wife, sir; she's a woman, sir, and consequently a monster, sir, a greater monster than a husband, sir.

Sir Jasp. A husband! how, sir?

Horn. So, sir; but I make no more cuckolds, sir.

[*Makes horns.*

Sir Jasp. Ha! ha! ha! Mercury! Mercury!

Lady Fid. Pray, Sir Jasper, let us be gone from this rude fellow.

Mrs. Dain. Who, by his breeding, would think he had ever been in France?

Lady Fid. Foh! he's but too much a French fellow, such as hate women of quality and virtue for their love to their husbands. Sir Jasper, a woman is hated by 'em as much for loving her husband as for loving their money. But pray let's be gone.

Horn. You do well, madam; for I have nothing that you came for. I have brought over not so much as a bawdy picture, no new postures, nor the second part of the *Ecole des Filles;* nor——

Quack. Hold, for shame, sir! what d'ye mean? you'll ruin yourself for ever with the sex—— [*Apart to* HORNER.

Sir Jasp. Ha! ha! ha! he hates women perfectly, I find.

Mrs. Dain. What pity 'tis he should!

Lady Fid. Ay, he's a base fellow for't. But affectation makes not a woman more odious to them than virtue.

Horn. Because your virtue is your greatest affectation, madam.

Lady Fid. How, you saucy fellow! would you wrong my honour?

Horn. If I could.

Lady Fid. How d'ye mean, sir?

Sir Jasp. Ha! ha! ha! no, he can't wrong your ladyship's honour, upon my honour. He, poor man—hark you in your ear—a mere eunuch. [*Whispers.*

Lady Fid. O filthy French beast! foh! foh! why do we stay? let's be gone: I can't endure the sight of him.

Sir Jasp. Stay but till the chairs come; they'll be here presently.

Lady Fid. No.

Sir Jasp. Nor can I stay longer. 'Tis, let me see, a quarter and half quarter of a minute past eleven. The council will be sat; I must away. Business must be preferred always before love and ceremony with the wise, Mr. Horner.

Horn. And the impotent, Sir Jasper.

Sir Jasp. Ay, ay, the impotent, Master Horner; hah! hah! hah!

Lady Fid. What, leave us with a filthy man alone in his lodgings?

Sir Jasp. He's an innocent man now, you know. Pray stay, I'll hasten the chairs to you.—Mr. Horner, your servant; I should be glad to see you at my house. Pray come and dine with me, and play at cards with my wife after dinner; you are fit for women at that game yet, ha! ha!—[*Aside.*] 'Tis as much a husband's prudence to provide innocent diversion for a wife as to hinder her unlawful pleasures; and he had better employ her than let her employ herself.—[*Aloud.*] Farewell.

Horn. Your servant, Sir Jasper.   [*Exit* Sir JASPER.

Lady Fid. I will not stay with him, foh!——

Horn. Nay, madam, I beseech you stay, if it be but to see I can be as civil to ladies yet as they would desire.

Lady Fid. No, no, foh! you cannot be civil to ladies.

Mrs. Dain. You as civil as ladies would desire?

Lady Fid. No, no, no, foh! foh! foh!

     [*Exeunt* Lady FIDGET *and* Mrs. DAINTY FIDGET.

Quack. Now, I think, I, or you yourself, rather, have done your business with the women.

Horn. Thou art an ass. Don't you see already, upon the report, and my carriage, this grave man of business leaves his wife in my lodgings, invites me to his house and wife, who before would not be acquainted with me out of jealousy?

Quack. Nay, by this means you may be the more acquainted with the husbands, but the less with the wives.

Horn. Let me alone; if I can but abuse the husbands, I'll soon disabuse the wives. Stay—I'll reckon you up the advantages I am like to have by my stratagem. First, I shall be rid of all my old acquaintances, the most insatiable sort of duns, that invade our lodgings in a morning; and next to the pleasure of making a new mistress is that of being rid of an old one, and of all old debts. Love, when it comes to be so, is paid the most unwillingly.

Quack. Well, you may be so rid of your old acquaintances; but how will you get any new ones?

Horn. Doctor, thou wilt never make a good chemist, thou art so incredulous and impatient. Ask but all the young fellows of the town if they do not lose more time, like huntsmen, in starting the game, than in running it down. One knows not where to find 'em; who will or will not. Women of quality are so civil, you can hardly distinguish love from good breeding, and a man is often mistaken: but now I can be sure she that shows an aversion to me loves the sport, as those women that are gone, whom I warrant to be right. And then the next thing is, your women of honour, as you call 'em, are only chary of their reputations, not their persons; and 'tis scandal they would avoid, not men. Now may I have, by the reputation of an eunuch, the privileges of one, and be seen in a lady's chamber in a morning as early as her husband; kiss virgins before their parents or lovers; and may be, in short, the *passe-partout* of the town. Now, doctor.

Quack. Nay, now you shall be the doctor; and your process is so new that we do not know but it may succeed.

Horn. Not so new neither; *probatum est*, doctor.

Quack. Well, I wish you luck, and many patients, whilst I go to mine.   [*Exit.*

Enter HARCOURT *and* DORILANT.

Har. Come, your appearance at the play yesterday has, I hope, hardened you for the future against the women's contempt, and the men's raillery; and now you'll abroad as you were wont.

Horn. Did I not bear it bravely?

Dor. With a most theatrical impudence, nay, more than the orange-wenches show there, or a drunken vizard-mask, or a great-bellied actress; nay, or the most impudent of creatures, an ill poet; or what is yet more impudent, a second-hand critic.

Horn. But what say the ladies? have they no pity?

Har. What ladies? The vizard-masks, you know, never pity a man when all's gone, though in their service.

Dor. And for the women in the boxes, you'd never pity them when 'twas in your power.

Har. They say 'tis pity but all that deal with common women should be served so.

Dor. Nay, I dare swear they won't admit you to play at cards with them, go to plays with 'em, or do the little duties which other shadows of men are wont to do for 'em.

Horn. What do you call shadows of men?

Dor. Half-men.

Horn. What, boys?

Dor. Ay, your old boys, old *beaux garçons*, who, like super-annuated stallions, are suffered to run, feed, and whinny with the mares as long as they live, though they can do nothing else.

Horn. Well, a pox on love and wenching! Women serve but to keep a man from better company. Though I can't enjoy them, I shall you the more. Good fellowship and friendship are lasting, rational, and manly pleasures.

Har. For all that, give me some of those pleasures you call effeminate too; they help to relish one another.

Horn. They disturb one another.

Har. No, mistresses are like books. If you pore upon them too much, they doze you, and make you unfit for company; but if used discreetly, you are the fitter for conversation by 'em.

Dor. A mistress should be like a little country retreat near the town; not to dwell in constantly, but only for a night and away, to taste the town the better when a man returns.

Horn. I tell you, 'tis as hard to be a good fellow, a good friend, and a lover of women, as 'tis to be a good fellow, a good friend, and a lover of money. You cannot follow both, then choose your side. Wine gives you liberty, loves takes it away.

Dor. Gad, he's in the right on't.

Horn. Wine gives you joy; love, grief and tortures, besides surgeons. Wine makes us witty; love, only sots. Wine makes us sleep; love breaks it.

Dor. By the world he has reason, Harcourt.

Horn. Wine makes——

Dor. Ay, wine makes us—makes us princes; love makes us beggars, poor rogues, egad—and wine——

Horn. So, there's one converted.—No, no, love and wine, oil and vinegar.

Har. I grant it; love will still be uppermost.

Horn. Come, for my part, I will have only those glorious manly pleasures of being very drunk and very slovenly.

Enter Boy.

Boy. Mr. Sparkish is below, sir.   [*Exit.*

Har. What, my dear friend! a rogue that is fond of me only, I think, for abusing him.

Dor. No, he can no more think the men laugh at him than that women jilt him; his opinion of himself is so good.

Horn. Well, there's another pleasure by drinking I thought not of,—I shall lose his acquaintance, because he cannot drink: and you know 'tis a very hard thing to be rid of him; for he's one of those nauseous offerers at wit, who, like the worst fiddlers, run themselves into all companies.

Har. One that, by being in the company of men of sense, would pass for one.

Horn. And may so to the short-sighted world; as a false jewel amongst true ones is not discerned at a distance. His company is as troublesome to us as a cuckold's when you have a mind to his wife's.

Har. No, the rogue will not let us enjoy one another, but ravishes our conversation; though he signifies no more to't than Sir Martin Mar-all's gaping, and awkward thrumming upon the lute, does to his man's voice and music.

Dor. And to pass for a wit in town shows himself a fool every night to us, that are guilty of the plot.

Horn. Such wits as he are, to a company of reasonable men, like rooks to the gamesters; who only fill a room at the table, but are so far from contributing to the play, that they only serve to spoil the fancy of those that do.

Dor. Nay, they are used like rooks too, snubbed, checked, and abused; yet the rogues will hang on.

Horn. A pox on 'em, and all that force nature, and would be still what she forbids 'em! Affectation is her greatest monster.

Har. Most men are the contraries to that they would seem. Your bully, you see, is a coward with a long sword; the little humbly-fawning physician, with his ebony cane, is he that destroys men.

Dor. The usurer, a poor rogue, possessed of mouldy bonds and mortgages; and we they call spendthrifts, are only wealthy, who lay out his money upon daily new purchases of pleasure.

Horn. Ay, your arrantest cheat is your trustee or executor; your jealous man, the greatest cuckold; your churchman the greatest atheist; and your noisy pert rogue of a wit, the greatest fop, dullest ass, and worst company, as you shall see; for here he comes.

Enter SPARKISH.

Spark. How is't, sparks? how is't? Well, faith, Harry, I must rally thee a little, ha! ha! ha! upon the report in town of thee, ha! ha! ha! I can't hold i'faith; shall I speak?

Horn. Yes; but you'll be so bitter then.

Spark. Honest Dick and Frank here shall answer for me; I will not be extreme bitter, by the universe.

Har. We will be bound in a ten thousand pound bond, he shall not be bitter at all.

Dor. Nor sharp, nor sweet.

Horn. What, not downright insipid?

Spark. Nay then, since you are so brisk, and provoke me, take what follows. You must know, I was discoursing and rallying with some ladies yesterday, and they happened to talk of the fine new signs in town——

Horn. Very fine ladies, I believe.

Spark. Said I, I know where the best new sign is.—Where? says one of the ladies.—In Covent Garden, I replied.—Said another, In what street?—In Russel Street, answered I.—Lord, says another, I'm sure there was never a fine new sign there yesterday.—Yes, but there was, said I again; and it came out of France, and has been there a fortnight.

Dor. A pox! I can hear no more, prithee.

Horn. No, hear him out; let him tune his crowd a while.

Har. The worst music, the greatest preparation.

Spark. Nay, faith, I'll make you laugh.—It cannot be, says a third lady.—Yes, yes, quoth I again.—Says a fourth lady——

Horn. Look to't, we'll have no more ladies.

Spark. No—then mark, mark, now. Said I to the fourth, Did you never see Mr. Horner? he lodges in Russel Street, and he's a sign of a man, you know, since he came out of France; ha! ha! ha!

Horn. But the devil take me if thine be the sign of a jest.

Spark. With that they all fell a-laughing, till they bepissed themselves. What, but it does not move you, methinks? Well, I see one had as good go to law without a witness, as break a jest without a laugher on one's side.—Come, come, sparks, but where do we dine? I have left at Whitehall an earl, to dine with you.

Dor. Why, I thought thou hadst loved a man with a title, better than a suit with a French trimming to't.

Har. Go to him again.

Spark. No, sir, a wit to me is the greatest title in the world.

Horn. But go dine with your earl, sir; he may be exceptious. We are your friends, and will not take it ill to be left, I do assure you.

Har. Nay, faith, he shall go to him.

Spark. Nay, pray, gentlemen.

Dor. We'll thrust you out, if you won't; what, disappoint anybody for us?

Spark. Nay, dear gentlemen, hear me.

Horn. No, no, sir, by no means; pray go, sir.

Spark. Why, dear rogues——

Dor. No, no.   [*They all thrust him out of the room.*

All. Ha! ha! ha!

Re-enter SPARKISH.

Spark. But, sparks, pray hear me. What, d'ye think I'll eat then with gay shallow fops and silent coxcombs? I think wit as necessary at dinner as a glass of good wine; and that's the reason I never have any stomach when I eat alone.—Come, but where do we dine?

Horn. Even where you will.

Spark. At Chateline's?

Dor. Yes, if you will.

Spark. Or at the Cock?

Dor. Yes, if you please.

Spark. Or at the Dog and Partridge?

Horn. Ay, if you have a mind to't; for we shall dine at neither.

Spark. Pshaw! with your fooling we shall lose the new play; and I would no more miss seeing a new play the first day, than I would miss sitting in the wit's row. Therefore I'll go fetch my mistress, and away.   [*Exit.*

Enter PINCHWIFE.

Horn. Who have we here? Pinchwife?

Pinch. Gentlemen, your humble servant.

Horn. Well, Jack, by thy long absence from the town, the grumness of thy countenance, and the slovenliness of thy habit, I should give thee joy, should I not, of marriage?

Pinch. [*aside*]. Death! does he know I'm married too? I thought to have concealed it from him at least.—[*Aloud.*] My long stay in the country will excuse my dress; and I have a suit of law that brings me up to town, that puts me out of humour. Besides, I must give Sparkish to-morrow five thousand pounds to lie with my sister.

Horn. Nay, you country gentlemen, rather than not purchase, will buy anything; and he is a cracked title, if we may quibble. Well, but am I to give thee joy? I heard thou wert married.

Pinch. What then?

Horn. Why, the next thing that is to be heard, is, thou'rt a cuckold.

Pinch. Insupportable name!   [*Aside.*

Horn. But I did not expect marriage from such a whoremaster as you; one that knew the town so much, and women so well.

Pinch. Why, I have married no London wife.

Horn. Pshaw! that's all one. That grave circumspection in marrying a country wife, is like refusing a deceitful pampered Smithfield jade, to go and be cheated by a friend in the country.

Pinch. [*aside*]. A pox on him and his simile!—[*Aloud.*] At least we are a little surer of the breed there, know what her keeping has been, whether foiled or unsound.

Horn. Come, come, I have known a clap gotten in Wales; and there are cousins, justices' clerks, and chaplains in the country, I won't say coachmen. But she's handsome and young?

Pinch. [*aside*]. I'll answer as I should do.—[*Aloud.*] No, no; she has no beauty but her youth, no attraction but her modesty: wholesome, homely, and huswifely; that's all.

Dor. He talks as like a grazier as he looks.

Pinch. She's too awkward, ill-favoured, and silly to bring to town.

Har. Then methinks you should bring her to be taught breeding.

Pinch. To be taught! no, sir, I thank you. Good wives and private soldiers should be ignorant—I'll keep her from your instructions, I warrant you.

Har. The rogue is as jealous as if his wife were not ignorant.
[*Aside.*

Horn. Why, if she be ill-favoured, there will be less danger here for you than by leaving her in the country. We have such variety of dainties that we are seldom hungry.

Dor. But they have always coarse, constant, swingeing stomachs in the country.

Har. Foul feeders indeed!

Dor. And your hospitality is great there.

Har. Open house; every man's welcome.

Pinch. So, so, gentlemen.

Horn. But prithee, why shouldst thou marry her? If she be ugly, ill-bred, and silly, she must be rich then.

Pinch. As rich as if she brought me twenty thousand pound out of this town; for she'll be as sure not to spend her moderate portion, as a London baggage would be to spend hers, let it be what it would: so 'tis all one. Then, because she's ugly, she's the likelier to be my own; and being ill-bred, she'll hate conversation; and since silly and innocent, will not know the difference betwixt a man of one-and-twenty and one of forty.

Horn. Nine—to my knowledge. But if she be silly, she'll expect as much from a man of forty-nine, as from him of one-and-twenty. But methinks wit is more necessary than beauty; and I think no young woman ugly that has it, and no handsome woman agreeable without it.

Pinch. 'Tis my maxim, he's a fool that marries; but he's a greater that does not marry a fool. What is wit in a wife good for, but to make a man a cuckold?

Horn. Yes, to keep it from his knowledge.

Pinch. A fool cannot contrive to make her husband a cuckold.

Horn. No; but she'll club with a man that can: and what is worse, if she cannot make her husband a cuckold, she'll make him jealous, and pass for one: and then 'tis all one.

Pinch. Well, well, I'll take care for one. My wife shall make me no cuckold, though she had your help, Mr. Horner. I understand the town, sir.

Dor. His help!   [*Aside.*

Har. He's come newly to town, it seems, and has not heard how things are with him.   [*Aside.*

Horn. But tell me, has marriage cured thee of whoring, which it seldom does?

Har. 'Tis more than age can do.

Horn. No, the word is, I'll marry and live honest: but a marriage vow is like a penitent gamester's oath, and entering into bonds and penalties to stint himself to such a particular small sum at play for the future, which makes him but the more eager; and not being able to hold out, loses his money again, and his forfeit to boot.

Dor. Ay, ay, a gamester will be a gamester whilst his money lasts, and a whoremaster whilst his vigour.

Har. Nay, I have known 'em, when they are broke, and can lose no more, keep a fumbling with the box in their hands to fool with only, and hinder other gamesters.

Dor. That had wherewithal to make lusty stakes.

Pinch. Well, gentlemen, you may laugh at me; but you shall never lie with my wife: I know the town.

Horn. But prithee, was not the way you were in better? is not keeping better than marriage?

Pinch. A pox on't! the jades would jilt me, I could never keep a whore to myself.

Horn. So, then you only married to keep a whore to yourself. Well, but let me tell you, women, as you say, are like soldiers, made constant and loyal by good pay, rather than by oaths and covenants. Therefore I'd advise my friends to keep rather than marry, since too I find, by your example, it does not serve one's turn; for I saw you yesterday in the eighteenpenny place with a pretty country-wench.

Pinch. How the devil! did he see my wife then? I sat there that she might not be seen. But she shall never go to a play again.   [*Aside.*

Horn. What! dost thou blush, at nine-and-forty, for having been seen with a wench?

Dor. No, faith, I warrant 'twas his wife, which he seated there out of sight; for he's a cunning rogue, and understands the town.

Har. He blushes. Then 'twas his wife; for men are now more ashamed to be seen with them in public than with a wench.

Pinch. Hell and damnation! I'm undone, since Horner has seen her, and they know 'twas she. *[Aside.*

Horn. But prithee, was it thy wife? She was exceeding pretty: I was in love with her at that distance.

Pinch. You are like never to be nearer to her. Your servant, gentlemen. *[Offers to go.*

Horn. Nay, prithee stay.

Pinch. I cannot; I will not.

Horn. Come, you shall dine with us.

Pinch. I have dined already.

Horn. Come, I know thou hast not: I'll treat thee, dear rogue; thou sha't spend none of thy Hampshire money to-day.

Pinch. Treat me! So, he uses me already like his cuckold.
[Aside.

Horn. Nay, you shall not go.

Pinch. I must; I have business at home. *[Exit.*

Har. To beat his wife. He's as jealous of her as a Cheapside husband of a Covent Garden wife.

Horn. Why, 'tis as hard to find an old whoremaster without jealousy and the gout, as a young one without fear, or the pox:—

> As gout in age from pox in youth proceeds,
> So wenching past, then jealousy succeeds;
> The worst disease that love and wenching breeds.
> *[Exeunt.*

ACT II

SCENE I.—*A Room in* PINCHWIFE'S *House*

Mrs. MARGERY PINCHWIFE *and* ALITHEA. PINCHWIFE *peeping behind at the door.*

Mrs. Pinch. Pray, sister, where are the best fields and woods to walk in, in London?

Alith. [*aside*]. A pretty question!—[*Aloud.*] Why, sister, Mulberry Garden and St. James's Park; and, for close walks, the New Exchange.

Mrs. Pinch. Pray, sister, tell me why my husband looks so grum here in town, and keeps me up so close, and will not let me go a-walking, nor let me wear my best gown yesterday.

Alith. O, he's jealous, sister.

Mrs. Pinch. Jealous! what's that?

Alith. He's afraid you should love another man.

Mrs. Pinch. How should he be afraid of my loving another man, when he will not let me see any but himself?

Alith. Did he not carry you yesterday to a play?

Mrs. Pinch. Ay; but we sat amongst ugly people. He would not let me come near the gentry, who sat under us, so that I could not see 'em. He told me, none but naughty women sat there, whom they toused and moused. But I would have ventured, for all that.

Alith. But how did you like the play?

Mrs. Pinch. Indeed I was weary of the play; but I liked hugeously the actors. They are the goodliest, properest men, sister!

Alith. O, but you must not like the actors, sister.

Mrs. Pinch. Ay, how should I help it, sister? Pray, sister, when my husband comes in, will you ask leave for me to go a-walking?

Alith. A-walking! ha! ha! Lord, a country-gentlewoman's pleasure is the drudgery of a footpost; and she requires as much airing as her husband's horses.—[*Aside.*] But here comes your husband: I'll ask, though I'm sure he'll not grant it.

Mrs. Pinch. He says he won't let me go abroad for fear of catching the pox.

Alith. Fy! the small-pox you should say.

Enter PINCHWIFE.

Mrs. Pinch. O my dear, dear bud, welcome home! Why dost thou look so fropish? who has nangered thee?

Pinch. You're a fool. [Mrs. PINCHWIFE *goes aside, and cries.*

Alith. Faith, so she is, for crying for no fault, poor tender creature!

Pinch. What, you would have her as impudent as yourself, as arrant a jilflirt, a gadder, a magpie; and to say all, a mere notorious town-woman?

Alith. Brother, you are my only censurer; and the honour of your family will sooner suffer in your wife there than in me, though I take the innocent liberty of the town.

Pinch. Hark you, mistress, do not talk so before my wife.— The innocent liberty of the town!

Alith. Why, pray, who boasts of any intrigue with me? what lampoon has made my name notorious? what ill women frequent my lodgings? I keep no company with any women of scandalous reputations.

Pinch. No, you keep the men of scandalous reputations company.

Alith. Where? would you not have me civil? answer 'em in a box at the plays, in the drawing-room at Whitehall, in St. James's Park, Mulberry Garden, or——

Pinch. Hold, hold! Do not teach my wife where the men are to be found: I believe she's the worse for your town-documents already. I bid you keep her in ignorance, as I do.

Mrs. Pinch. Indeed, be not angry with her, bud, she will tell me nothing of the town, though I ask her a thousand times a day.

Pinch. Then you are very inquisitive to know, I find?

Mrs. Pinch. Not I indeed, dear; I hate London. Our place-house in the country is worth a thousand of't: would I were there again!

Pinch. So you shall, I warrant. But were you not talking of plays and players when I came in?—[*To* ALITHEA.] You are her encourager in such discourses.

Mrs. Pinch. No, indeed, dear; she chid me just now for liking the playermen.

Pinch. [*aside*]. Nay, if she be so innocent as to own to me her liking them, there is no hurt in't.—[*Aloud.*] Come, my poor rogue, but thou likest none better than me?

Mrs. Pinch. Yes, indeed, but I do. The playermen are finer folks.

Pinch. But you love none better than me?

Mrs. Pinch. You are my own dear bud, and I know you. I hate a stranger.

Pinch. Ay, my dear, you must love me only; and not be like the naughty town-women, who only hate their husbands, and love every man else; love plays, visits, fine coaches, fine clothes, fiddles, balls, treats, and so lead a wicked town-life.

Mrs. Pinch. Nay, if to enjoy all these things be a town-life, London is not so bad a place, dear.

Pinch. How! if you love me, you must hate London.

Alith. The fool has forbid me discovering to her the pleasures of the town, and he is now setting her agog upon them himself. [*Aside.*

Mrs. Pinch. But, husband, do the town-women love the playermen too?

Pinch. Yes, I warrant you.

Mrs. Pinch. Ay, I warrant you.

Pinch. Why, you do not, I hope?

Mrs. Pinch. No, no, bud. But why have we no playermen in the country?

Pinch. Ha!—Mrs. Minx, ask me no more to go to a play.

Mrs. Pinch. Nay, why, love? I did not care for going: but when you forbid me, you make me, as 'twere, desire it.

Alith. So 'twill be in other things, I warrant. [*Aside.*

Mrs. Pinch. Pray let me go to a play, dear.

Pinch. Hold your peace, I wo' not.

Mrs. Pinch. Why, love?

Pinch. Why, I'll tell you.

Alith. Nay, if he tell her, she'll give him more cause to forbid her that place. [*Aside.*

Mrs. Pinch. Pray why, dear?

Pinch. First, you like the actors; and the gallants may like you.

Mrs. Pinch. What, a homely country girl! No, bud, nobody will like me.

Pinch. I tell you yes, they may.

Mrs. Pinch. No, no, you jest—I won't believe you: I will go.

Pinch. I tell you then, that one of the lewdest fellows in town, who saw you there, told me he was in love with you.

Mrs. Pinch. Indeed! who, who, pray who was't?

Pinch. I've gone too far, and slipped before I was aware; how overjoyed she is! [*Aside.*

Mrs. Pinch. Was it any Hampshire gallant, any of our neighbours? I promise you, I am beholden to him.

Pinch. I promise you, you lie; for he would but ruin you, as he has done hundreds. He has no other love for women but that; such as he look upon women, like basilisks, but to destroy 'em.

Mrs. Pinch. Ay, but if he loves me, why should he ruin me? answer me to that. Methinks he should not, I would do him no harm.

Alith. Ha! ha! ha!

Pinch. 'Tis very well; but I'll keep him from doing you any harm, or me either. But here comes company; get you in, get you in.

Mrs. Pinch. But, pray, husband, is he a pretty gentleman that loves me?

Pinch. In, baggage, in. [*Thrusts her in, and shuts the door.*

Enter SPARKISH *and* HARCOURT.

What, all the lewd libertines of the town brought to my lodging by this easy coxcomb! 'sdeath, I'll not suffer it.

Spark. Here, Harcourt, do you approve my choice?—[*To* ALITHEA.] Dear little rogue, I told you I'd bring you acquainted with all my friends, the wits and—— [HARCOURT *salutes her.*

Pinch. Ay, they shall know her, as well as you yourself will, I warrant you.

Spark. This is one of those, my pretty rogue, that are to dance at your wedding to-morrow; and him you must bid welcome ever, to what you and I have.

Pinch. Monstrous! [*Aside.*

Spark. Harcourt, how dost thou like her, faith? Nay, dear, do not look down; I should hate to have a wife of mine out of countenance at anything.

Pinch. Wonderful! [*Aside.*

Spark. Tell me, I say, Harcourt, how dost thou like her? Thou hast stared upon her enough, to resolve me.

Har. So infinitely well, that I could wish I had a mistress too, that might differ from her in nothing but her love and engagement to you.

Alith. Sir, Master Sparkish has often told me that his acquaintance were all wits and raillieurs, and now I find it.

Spark. No, by the universe, madam, he does not rally now; you may believe him. I do assure you, he is the honestest, worthiest, true-hearted gentleman—a man of such perfect honour, he would say nothing to a lady he does not mean.

Pinch. Praising another man to his mistress!   [*Aside.*

Har. Sir, you are so beyond expectation obliging, that——

Spark. Nay, egad, I am sure you do admire her extremely; I see't in your eyes.—He does admire you, madam.—By the world, don't you?

Har. Yes, above the world, or the most glorious part of it, her whole sex: and till now I never thought I should have envied you, or any man about to marry, but you have the best excuse for marriage I ever knew.

Alith. Nay, now, sir, I'm satisfied you are of the society of the wits and raillieurs, since you cannot spare your friend, even when he is but too civil to you; but the surest sign is, since you are an enemy to marriage,—for that I hear you hate as much as business or bad wine.

Har. Truly, madam, I was never an enemy to marriage till now, because marriage was never an enemy to me before.

Alith. But why, sir, is marriage an enemy to you now? because it robs you of your friend here? for you look upon a friend married, as one gone into a monastery, that is, dead to the world.

Har. 'Tis indeed, because you marry him; I see, madam, you can guess my meaning. I do confess heartily and openly, I wish it were in my power to break the match; by Heavens I would.

Spark. Poor Frank!

Alith. Would you be so unkind to me?

Har. No, no, 'tis not because I would be unkind to you.

Spark. Poor Frank! no gad, 'tis only his kindness to me.

Pinch. Great kindness to you indeed! Insensible fop, let a man make love to his wife to his face!   [*Aside.*

Spark. Come, dear Frank, for all my wife there, that shall be, thou shalt enjoy me sometimes, dear rogue. By my honour, we men of wit condole for our deceased brother in marriage, as much as for one dead in earnest: I think that was prettily said of me, ha, Harcourt?—But come, Frank, be not melancholy for me.

Har. No, I assure you, I am not melancholy for you.

Spark. Prithee, Frank, dost think my wife that shall be there, a fine person?

Har. I could gaze upon her till I became as blind as you are.

Spark. How as I am? how?

Har. Because you are a lover, and true lovers are blind, stock blind.

Spark. True, true; but by the world she has wit too, as well as beauty: go, go with her into a corner, and try if she has wit; talk to her anything, she's bashful before me.

Har. Indeed if a woman wants wit in a corner, she has it nowhere.

Alith. Sir, you dispose of me a little before your time——
[*Aside to* SPARKISH.

Spark. Nay, nay, madam, let me have an earnest of your obedience, or—go, go, madam——
[HARCOURT *courts* ALITHEA *aside.*

Pinch. How, sir! if you are not concerned for the honour of a wife, I am for that of a sister; he shall not debauch her. Be a pander to your own wife! bring men to her! let 'em make love before your face! thrust 'em into a corner together, then leave 'em in private! is this your town wit and conduct?

Spark. Ha! ha! ha! a silly wise rogue would make one laugh more than a stark fool, ha! ha! I shall burst. Nay, you shall not disturb 'em; I'll vex thee, by the world.
[*Struggles with* PINCHWIFE *to keep him from* HARCOURT *and* ALITHEA.

Alith. The writings are drawn, sir, settlements made; 'tis too late, sir, and past all revocation.

Har. Then so is my death.

Alith. I would not be unjust to him.

Har. Then why to me so?

Alith. I have no obligation to you.

Har. My love.

Alith. I had his before.

Har. You never had it; he wants, you see, jealousy, the only infallible sign of it.

Alith. Love proceeds from esteem; he cannot distrust my virtue: besides, he loves me, or he would not marry me.

Har. Marrying you is no more sign of his love than bribing your woman, that he may marry you, is a sign of his generosity. Marriage is rather a sign of interest than love; and he that marries a fortune covets a mistress, not loves her. But if you take marriage for a sign of love, take it from me immediately.

Alith. No, now you have put a scruple in my head; but in short, sir, to end our dispute, I must marry him, my reputation would suffer in the world else.

Har. No; if you do marry him, with your pardon, madam, your reputation suffers in the world, and you would be thought in necessity for a cloak.

Alith. Nay, now you are rude, sir.—Mr. Sparkish, pray come hither, your friend here is very troublesome, and very loving.

Har. Hold! hold!—— [*Aside to* ALITHEA.

Pinch. D'ye hear that?

Spark. Why, d'ye think I'll seem to be jealous, like a country bumpkin?

Pinch. No, rather be a cuckold, like a credulous cit.

Har. Madam, you would not have been so little generous as to have told him.

Alith. Yes, since you could be so little generous as to wrong him.

Har. Wrong him! no man can do't, he's beneath an injury: a bubble, a coward, a senseless idiot, a wretch so contemptible to all the world but you, that——

Alith. Hold, do not rail at him, for since he is like to be my husband, I am resolved to like him: nay, I think I am obliged to tell him you are not his friend.—Master Sparkish, Master Sparkish!

Spark. What, what?—[*To* HARCOURT.]   Now, dear rogue, has not she wit?

Har. Not so much as I thought, and hoped she had.

[*Speaks surlily.*

Alith. Mr. Sparkish, do you bring people to rail at you?

Har. Madam——

Spark. How! no; but if he does rail at me, 'tis but in jest, I warrant: what we wits do for one another, and never take any notice of it.

Alith. He spoke so scurrilously of you, I had no patience to hear him; besides, he has been making love to me.

Har. True, damned tell-tale woman!   [*Aside.*

Spark. Pshaw! to show his parts—we wits rail and make love often, but to show our parts: as we have no affections, so we have no malice, we——

Alith. He said you were a wretch below an injury——

Spark. Pshaw!

Har. Damned, senseless, impudent, virtuous jade! Well, since she won't let me have her, she'll do as good, she'll make me hate her.   [*Aside.*

Alith. A common bubble——

Spark. Pshaw!

Alith. A coward——

Spark. Pshaw, pshaw!

Alith. A senseless, drivelling idiot——

Spark. How! did he disparage my parts? Nay, then, my honour's concerned, I can't put up that, sir, by the world—brother, help me to kill him—[*Aside*] I may draw now, since we have the odds of him:—'tis a good occasion, too, before my mistress——   [*Offers to draw.*

Alith. Hold, hold!

Spark. What, what?

Alith. [*aside*]. I must not let 'em kill the gentleman neither, for his kindness to me: I am so far from hating him, that I wish my gallant had his person and understanding. Nay, if my honour——

Spark. I'll be thy death.

Alith. Hold, hold! Indeed, to tell the truth, the gentleman said after all, that what he spoke was but out of friendship to you.

Spark. How! say, I am, I am a fool, that is, no wit, out of friendship to me?

Alith. Yes, to try whether I was concerned enough for you; and made love to me only to be satisfied of my virtue, for your sake.

Har. Kind, however.   [*Aside.*

Spark. Nay, if it were so, my dear rogue, I ask thee pardon; but why would not you tell me so, faith?

Har. Because I did not think on't, faith.

Spark. Come, Horner does not come; Harcourt, let's be gone to the new play.—Come, madam.

Alith. I will not go, if you intend to leave me alone in the box, and run into the pit, as you use to do.

Spark. Pshaw! I'll leave Harcourt with you in the box to entertain you, and that's as good; if I sat in the box, I should be thought no judge but of trimmings.—Come away, Harcourt, lead her down.   [*Exeunt* SPARKISH, HARCOURT, *and* ALITHEA.

Pinch. Well, go thy ways, for the flower of the true town fops, such as spend their estates before they come to 'em, and are cuckolds before they're married. But let me go look to my own freehold.—How!

Enter Lady FIDGET, Mrs. DAINTY FIDGET, *and* Mrs. SQUEAMISH.

Lady Fid. Your servant, sir: where is your lady? We are come to wait upon her to the new play.

Pinch. New play!

Lady Fid. And my husband will wait upon you presently.

Pinch. [*aside*]. Damn your civility.—[*Aloud.*] Madam, by no means; I will not see Sir Jasper here, till I have waited upon him at home; nor shall my wife see you till she has waited upon your ladyship at your lodgings.

Lady Fid. Now we are here, sir?

Pinch. No, Madam.

Mrs. Dain. Pray, let us see her.

Mrs. Squeam. We will not stir till we see her.

Pinch. [*aside*]. A pox on you all!—[*Goes to the door, and returns.*] She has locked the door, and is gone abroad.

Lady Fid. No, you have locked the door, and she's within.

Mrs. Dain. They told us below she was here.

Pinch. [*aside*]. Will nothing do?—[*Aloud.*] Well, it must out then. To tell you the truth, ladies, which I was afraid to let you know before, lest it might endanger your lives, my wife has just now the small-pox come out upon her; do not be frightened; but pray be gone, ladies; you shall not stay here in danger of your lives; pray get you gone, ladies.

Lady Fid. No, no, we have all had 'em.

Mrs. Squeam. Alack, alack!

Mrs. Dain. Come, come, we must see how it goes with her; I understand the disease.

Lady Fid. Come!

Pinch. [*aside*]. Well, there is no being too hard for women at their own weapon, lying, therefore I'll quit the field.   [*Exit.*

Mrs. Squeam. Here's an example of jealousy!

Lady Fid. Indeed, as the world goes, I wonder there are no more jealous, since wives are so neglected.

Mrs. Dain. Pshaw! as the world goes, to what end should they be jealous?

Lady Fid. Foh! 'tis a nasty world.

Mrs. Squeam. That men of parts, great acquaintance, and quality, should take up with and spend themselves and fortunes in keeping little playhouse creatures, foh!

Lady Fid. Nay, that women of understanding, great acquaintance, and good quality, should fall a-keeping too of little creatures, foh!

Mrs. Squeam. Why, 'tis the men of quality's fault; they never visit women of honour and reputation as they used to do; and have not so much as common civility for ladies of our rank, but use us with the same indifferency and ill-breeding as if we were all married to 'em.

Lady Fid. She says true; 'tis an arrant shame women of quality should be so slighted; methinks birth—birth should go for something; I have known men admired, courted, and followed for their titles only.

Mrs. Squeam. Ay, one would think men of honour should not love, no more than marry, out of their own rank.

Mrs. Dain. Fy, fy, upon 'em! they are come to think cross breeding for themselves best, as well as for their dogs and horses.

Lady Fid. They are dogs and horses for't.

Mrs. Squeam. One would think, if not for love, for vanity a little.

Mrs. Dain. Nay, they do satisfy their vanity upon us sometimes; and are kind to us in their report, tell all the world they lie with us.

Lady Fid. Damned rascals, that we should be only wronged by 'em! To report a man has had a person, when he has not had a person, is the greatest wrong in the whole world that can be done to a person.

Mrs. Squeam. Well, 'tis an arrant shame noble persons should be so wronged and neglected.

Lady Fid. But still 'tis an arranter shame for a noble person to neglect her own honour, and defame her own noble person with little inconsiderable fellows, foh!

Mrs. Dain. I suppose the crime against our honour is the same with a man of quality as with another.

Lady Fid. How! no sure, the man of quality is likest one's husband, and therefore the fault should be the less.

Mrs. Dain. But then the pleasure should be the less.

Lady Fid. Fy, fy, fy, for shame, sister! whither shall we ramble? Be continent in your discourse, or I shall hate you.

Mrs. Dain. Besides, an intrigue is so much the more notorious for the man's quality.

Mrs. Squeam. 'Tis true that nobody takes notice of a private man, and therefore with him 'tis more secret; and the crime's the less when 'tis not known.

Lady Fid. You say true; i'faith, I think you are in the right on't: 'tis not an injury to a husband, till it be an injury to our honours; so that a woman of honour loses no honour with a private person; and to say truth——

Mrs. Dain. So, the little fellow is grown a private person—— with her——   [*Apart to* Mrs. SQUEAMISH.

Lady Fid. But still my dear, dear honour——

Enter Sir JASPER FIDGET, HORNER, *and* DORILANT.

Sir Jasp. Ay, my dear, dear of honour, thou hast still so much honour in thy mouth——

Horn. That she has none elsewhere.   [*Aside.*

Lady Fid. Oh, what d'ye mean to bring in these upon us?

Mrs. Dain. Foh! these are as bad as wits.

Mrs. Squeam. Foh!

Lady Fid. Let us leave the room.

Sir Jasp. Stay, stay; faith, to tell you the naked truth——

Lady Fid. Fy, Sir Jasper! do not use that word naked.

Sir Jasp. Well, well, in short I have business at Whitehall, and cannot go to the play with you, therefore would have you go——

Lady Fid. With those two to a play?

Sir Jasp. No, not with t'other, but with Mr. Horner; there can be no more scandal to go with him than with Mr. Tattle, or Master Limberham.

Lady Fid. With that nasty fellow! no—no.

Sir Jasp. Nay, prithee, dear, hear me.

[*Whispers to* Lady FIDGET.

Horn. Ladies——

[HORNER *and* DORILANT *draw near* Mrs. SQUEAMISH *and* Mrs. DAINTY FIDGET.

Mrs. Dain. Stand off.

Mrs. Squeam. Do not approach us.

Mrs. Dain. You herd with the wits, you are obscenity all over.

Mrs. Squeam. And I would as soon look upon a picture of Adam and Eve, without fig-leaves, as any of you, if I could help it; therefore keep off, and do not make us sick.

Dor. What a devil are these?

Horn. Why, these are pretenders to honour, as critics to wit, only by censuring others; and as every raw, peevish, out-of-humoured, affected, dull, tea-drinking, arithmetical fop, sets up for a wit by railing at men of sense, so these for honour, by railing at the court, and ladies of as great honour as quality.

Sir Jasp. Come, Mr. Horner, I must desire you to go with these ladies to the play, sir.

Horn. I, sir?

Sir Jasp. Ay, ay, come, sir.

Horn. I must beg your pardon, sir, and theirs; I will not be seen in women's company in public again for the world.

Sir Jasp. Ha, ha, strange aversion!

Mrs. Squeam. No, he's for women's company in private.

Sir Jasp. He—poor man—he—ha! ha! ha!

Mrs. Dain. 'Tis a greater shame amongst lewd fellows to be seen in virtuous women's company, than for the women to be seen with them.

Horn. Indeed, madam, the time was I only hated virtuous women, but now I hate the other too; I beg your pardon, ladies.

Lady Fid. You are very obliging, sir, because we would not be troubled with you.

Sir Jasp. In sober sadness, he shall go.

Dor. Nay, if he wo' not, I am ready to wait upon the ladies, and I think I am the fitter man.

Sir Jasp. You, sir! no, I thank you for that. Master Horner is a privileged man amongst the virtuous ladies, 'twill be a great while before you are so; he! he! he! he's my wife's gallant; he! he! he! No, pray withdraw, sir, for as I take it, the virtuous ladies have no business with you.

Dor. And I am sure he can have none with them. 'Tis strange a man can't come amongst virtuous women now, but upon the same terms as men are admitted into the Great Turk's seraglio. But heavens keep me from being an ombre player with 'em!—But where is Pinchwife? [*Exit.*

Sir Jasp. Come, come, man; what, avoid the sweet society of womankind? that sweet, soft, gentle, tame, noble creature, woman, made for man's companion——

Horn. So is that soft, gentle, tame, and more noble creature a spaniel, and has all their tricks; can fawn, lie down, suffer beating, and fawn the more; barks at your friends when they come to see you, makes your bed hard, gives you fleas, and the mange sometimes. And all the difference is, the spaniel's the more faithful animal, and fawns but upon one master.

Sir Jasp. He! he! he!

Mrs. Squeam. O the rude beast!

Mrs. Dain. Insolent brute!

Lady Fid. Brute! stinking, mortified, rotten French wether, to dare——

Sir Jasp. Hold, an't please your ladyship.—For shame, Master Horner! your mother was a woman—[*Aside*]. Now shall I never reconcile 'em.—[*Aside to* Lady FIDGET.] Hark you, madam, take my advice in your anger. You know you often want one to make up your drolling pack of ombre players, and you may cheat him easily; for he's an ill gamester, and con-

sequently loves play. Besides, you know you have but two old
civil gentlemen (with stinking breaths too) to wait upon you
abroad; take in the third into your service. The other are but
crazy; and a lady should have a supernumerary gentleman-
usher as a supernumerary coach-horse, lest sometimes you should
be forced to stay at home.

Lady Fid. But are you sure he loves play, and has money?

Sir Jasp. He loves play as much as you, and has money as
much as I.

Lady Fid. Then I am contented to make him pay for his
scurrility. Money makes up in a measure all other wants in
men.—Those whom we cannot make hold for gallants, we make
fine.   [*Aside.*

Sir Jasp. [*aside*]. So, so; now to mollify, wheedle him.—
[*Aside to* HORNER.] Master Horner, will you never keep civil
company? methinks 'tis time now, since you are only fit for them.
Come, come, man, you must e'en fall to visiting our wives,
eating at our tables, drinking tea with our virtuous relations
after dinner, dealing cards to 'em, reading plays and gazettes to
'em, picking fleas out of their smocks for 'em, collecting receipts,
new songs, women, pages, and footmen for 'em.

Horn. I hope they'll afford me better employment, sir.

Sir Jasp. He! he! he! 'tis fit you know your work before
you come into your place. And since you are unprovided of a
lady to flatter, and a good house to eat at, pray frequent mine,
and call my wife mistress, and she shall call you gallant,
according to the custom.

Horn. Who, I?

Sir Jasp. Faith, thou sha't for my sake; come, for my sake only.

Horn. For your sake——

Sir Jasp. Come, come, here's a gamester for you; let him be a
little familiar sometimes; nay, what if a little rude? Gamesters
may be rude with ladies, you know.

Lady Fid. Yes; losing gamesters have a privilege with women.

Horn. I always thought the contrary, that the winning
gamester had most privilege with women; for when you have
lost your money to a man, you'll lose anything you have, all you
have, they say, and he may use you as he pleases.

Sir Jasp. He! he! he! well, win or lose, you shall have your
liberty with her.

Lady Fid. As he behaves himself; and for your sake I'll give
him admittance and freedom.

Horn. All sorts of freedom, madam?

Sir Jasp. Ay, ay, ay, all sorts of freedom thou canst take.
And so go to her, begin thy new employment; wheedle her, jest
with her, and be better acquainted one with another.

Horn. [*aside*]. I think I know her already; therefore may
venture with her my secret for hers.

[HORNER *and* Lady FIDGET *whisper.*

Sir Jasp. Sister cuz, I have provided an innocent playfellow for you there.

Mrs. Dain. Who, he?

Mrs. Squeam. There's a playfellow, indeed!

Sir Jasp. Yes sure.—What, he is good enough to play at cards, blindman's-buff, or the fool with, sometimes!

Mrs. Squeam. Foh! we'll have no such playfellows.

Mrs. Dain. No, sir; you shan't choose playfellows for us, we thank you.

Sir Jasp. Nay, pray hear me.   [*Whispering to them.*

Lady Fid. But, poor gentleman, could you be so generous, so truly a man of honour, as for the sakes of us women of honour, to cause yourself to be reported no man? No man! and to suffer yourself the greatest shame that could fall upon a man, that none might fall upon us women by your conversation? but, indeed, sir, as perfectly, perfectly the same man as before your going into France, sir? as perfectly, perfectly, sir?

Horn. As perfectly, perfectly, madam. Nay, I scorn you should take my word; I desire to be tried only, madam.

Lady Fid. Well, that's spoken again like a man of honour: all men of honour desire to come to the test. But, indeed, generally you men report such things of yourselves, one does not know how or whom to believe; and it is come to that pass, we dare not take your words no more than your tailor's, without some staid servant of yours be bound with you. But I have so strong a faith in your honour, dear, dear, noble sir, that I'd forfeit mine for yours, at any time, dear sir.

Horn. No, madam, you should not need to forfeit it for me; I have given you security already to save you harmless, my late reputation being so well known in the world, madam.

Lady Fid. But if upon any future falling-out, or upon a suspicion of my taking the trust out of your hands, to employ some other, you yourself should betray your trust, dear sir? I mean, if you'll give me leave to speak obscenely, you might tell, dear sir.

Horn. If I did, nobody would believe me. The reputation of impotency is as hardly recovered again in the world as that of cowardice, dear madam.

Lady Fid. Nay, then, as one may say, you may do your worst, dear, dear sir.

Sir Jasp. Come, is your ladyship reconciled to him yet? have you agreed on matters? for I must be gone to Whitehall.

Lady Fid. Why, indeed, Sir Jasper, Master Horner is a thousand, thousand times a better man than I thought him. Cousin Squeamish, sister Dainty, I can name him now. Truly, not long ago, you know, I thought his very name obscenity; and I would as soon have lain with him as have named him.

Sir Jasp. Very likely, poor madam.

Mrs. Dain. I believe it.

Mrs. Squeam. No doubt on't.

Sir Jasp. Well, well—that your ladyship is as virtuous as any she, I know, and him all the town knows—he! he! he! therefore now you like him, get you gone to your business together, go, go to your business, I say, pleasure, whilst I go to my pleasure, business.

Lady Fid. Come, then, dear gallant.

Horn. Come away, my dearest mistress.

Sir Jasp. So, so; why, 'tis as I'd have it.   [*Exit.*

Horn. And as I'd have it.

Lady Fid. Who for his business from his wife will run,

Takes the best care to have her business done.

[*Exeunt.*

ACT III

SCENE I.—*A Room in* PINCHWIFE's *House*

Enter ALITHEA *and* Mrs. PINCHWIFE.

Alith. Sister, what ails you? you are grown melancholy.

Mrs. Pinch. Would it not make any one melancholy to see you go every day fluttering about abroad, whilst I must stay at home like a poor lonely sullen bird in a cage?

Alith. Ay, sister; but you came young, and just from the nest to your cage: so that I thought you liked it, and could be as cheerful in't as others that took their flight themselves early, and are hopping abroad in the open air.

Mrs. Pinch. Nay, I confess I was quiet enough till my husband told me what pure lives the London ladies live abroad, with their dancing, meetings, and junketings, and dressed every day in their best gowns; and I warrant you, play at nine-pins every day of the week, so they do.

Enter PINCHWIFE.

Pinch. Come, what's here to do? you are putting the town-pleasures in her head, and setting her a-longing.

Alith. Yes, after nine-pins. You suffer none to give her those longings you mean but yourself.

Pinch. I tell her of the vanities of the town like a confessor.

Alith. A confessor! just such a confessor as he that, by forbidding a silly ostler to grease the horse's teeth, taught him to do't.

Pinch. Come, Mrs. Flippant, good precepts are lost when bad examples are still before us: the liberty you take abroad makes her hanker after it, and out of humour at home. Poor wretch! she desired not to come to London; I would bring her.

Alith. Very well.

Pinch. She has been this week in town, and never desired till this afternoon to go abroad.

Alith. Was she not at a play yesterday?

Pinch. Yes; but she ne'er asked me; I was myself the cause of her going.

Alith. Then if she ask you again, you are the cause of her asking, and not my example.

Pinch. Well, to-morrow night I shall be rid of you; and the next day, before 'tis light, she and I'll be rid of the town, and my dreadful apprehensions.—Come, be not melancholy; for thou sha't go into the country after to-morrow, dearest.

Alith. Great comfort!

Mrs. Pinch. Pish! what d'ye tell me of the country for?

Pinch. How's this! what, pish at the country?

Mrs. Pinch. Let me alone; I am not well.

Pinch. O, if that be all—what ails my dearest?

Mrs. Pinch. Truly, I don't know: but I have not been well since you told me there was a gallant at the play in love with me.

Pinch. Ha!——

Alith. That's by my example too!

Pinch. Nay, if you are not well, but are so concerned, because a lewd fellow chanced to lie, and say he liked you, you'll make me sick too.

Mrs. Pinch. Of what sickness?

Pinch. O, of that which is worse than the plague, jealousy.

Mrs. Pinch. Pish, you jeer! I'm sure there's no such disease in our receipt-book at home.

Pinch. No, thou never met'st with it, poor innocent.—Well, if thou cuckold me, 'twill be my own fault—for cuckolds and bastards are generally makers of their own fortune. [*Aside.*

Mrs. Pinch. Well, but pray, bud, let's go to a play to-night.

Pinch. 'Tis just done, she comes from it. But why are you so eager to see a play?

Mrs. Pinch. Faith, dear, not that I care one pin for their talk there; but I like to look upon the player-men, and would see, if I could, the gallant you say loves me: that's all, dear bud.

Pinch. Is that all, dear bud?

Alith. This proceeds from my example!

Mrs. Pinch. But if the play be done, let's go abroad, however, dear bud.

Pinch. Come, have a little patience and thou shalt go into the country on Friday.

Mrs. Pinch. Therefore I would see first some sights to tell my neighbours of. Nay, I will go abroad, that's once.

Alith. I'm the cause of this desire too!

Pinch. But now I think on't, who, who was the cause of Horner's coming to my lodgings to-day? That was you.

Alith. No, you, because you would not let him see your handsome wife out of your lodging.

Mrs. Pinch. Why, O Lord! did the gentleman come hither to see me indeed?

Pinch. No, no.—You are not the cause of that damned question too, Mistress Alithea?—[*Aside.*] Well, she's in the right of it. He is in love with my wife—and comes after her—'tis so—but I'll nip his love in the bud; lest he should follow us into the country, and break his chariot-wheel near our house, on purpose for an excuse to come to't. But I think I know the town.

Mrs. Pinch. Come, pray, bud, let's go abroad before 'tis late; for I will go, that's flat and plain.

Pinch. [*aside*]. So! the obstinacy already of the town-wife; and I must, whilst she's here, humour her like one.—[*Aloud.*] Sister, how shall we do, that she may not be seen or known?

Alith. Let her put on her mask.

Pinch. Pshaw! a mask makes people but the more inquisitive, and is as ridiculous a disguise as a stage-beard: her shape, stature, habit will be known. And if we should meet with Horner, he would be sure to take acquaintance with us, must wish her joy, kiss her, talk to her, leer upon her, and the devil and all. No, I'll not use her to a mask, 'tis dangerous; for masks have made more cuckolds than the best faces that ever were known.

Alith. How will you do then?

Mrs. Pinch. Nay, shall we go? The Exchange will be shut, and I have a mind to see that.

Pinch. So—I have it—I'll dress her up in the suit we are to carry down to her brother, little Sir James; nay, I understand the town-tricks. Come, let's go dress her. A mask! no—a woman masked, like a covered dish, gives a man curiosity and appetite; when, it may be, uncovered, 'twould turn his stomach: no, no.

Alith. Indeed your comparison is something a greasy one: but I had a gentle gallant used to say, A beauty masked, like the sun in eclipse, gathers together more gazers than if it shined out.

[*Exeunt.*

SCENE II.—*The New Exchange*

Enter HORNER, HARCOURT, *and* DORILANT.

Dor. Engaged to women, and not sup with us!

Horn. Ay, a pox on 'em all!

Har. You were much a more reasonable man in the morning, and had as noble resolutions against 'em as a widower of a week's liberty.

Dor. Did I ever think to see you keep company with women in vain?

Horn. In vain: no—'tis since I can't love 'em, to be revenged on 'em.

Har. Now your sting is gone, you looked in the box amongst all those women like a drone in the hive; all upon you, shoved and ill-used by 'em all, and thrust from one side to t'other.

Dor. Yet he must be buzzing amongst 'em still, like other beetle-headed liquorish drones. Avoid 'em, and hate 'em, as they hate you.

Horn. Because I do hate 'em, and would hate 'em yet more, I'll frequent 'em. You may see by marriage, nothing makes a man hate a woman more than her constant conversation. In short, I converse with 'em, as you do with rich fools, to laugh at 'em and use 'em ill.

Dor. But I would no more sup with women, unless I could lie with 'em, than sup with a rich coxcomb, unless I could cheat him.

Horn. Yes, I have known thee sup with a fool for his drinking; if he could set out your hand that way only, you were satisfied, and if he were a wine-swallowing mouth, 'twas enough.

Har. Yes, a man drinks often with a fool, as he tosses with a marker, only to keep his hand in use. But do the ladies drink?

Horn. Yes, sir; and I shall have the pleasure at least of laying 'em flat with a bottle, and bring as much scandal that way upon 'em as formerly t'other.

Har. Perhaps you may prove as weak a brother among 'em that way as t'other.

Dor. Foh! drinking with women is as unnatural as scolding with 'em. But 'tis a pleasure of decayed fornicators, and the basest way of quenching love.

Har. Nay, 'tis drowning love, instead of quenching it. But leave us for civil women too!

Dor. Ay, when he can't be the better for 'em. We hardly pardon a man that leaves his friend for a wench, and that's a pretty lawful call.

Horn. Faith, I would not leave you for 'em, if they would not drink.

Dor. Who would disappoint his company at Lewis's for a gossiping?

Har. Foh! Wine and women, good apart, together are as nauseous as sack and sugar. But hark you, sir, before you go, a little of your advice; an old maimed general, when unfit for action, is fittest for counsel. I have other designs upon women than eating and drinking with them; I am in love with Sparkish's mistress, whom he is to marry to-morrow: now how shall I get her?

Enter SPARKISH, *looking about.*

Horn. Why, here comes one will help you to her.

Har. He! he, I tell you, is my rival, and will hinder my love.

Horn. No; a foolish rival and a jealous husband assist their rival's designs; for they are sure to make their women hate them, which is the first step to their love for another man.

Har. But I cannot come near his mistress but in his company.

Horn. Still the better for you; for fools are most easily cheated when they themselves are accessaries: and he is to be bubbled of his mistress as of his money, the common mistress, by keeping him company.

Spark. Who is that that is to be bubbled? Faith, let me snack; I han't met with a bubble since Christmas. 'Gad, I think bubbles are like their brother woodcocks, go out with the cold weather.

Har. A pox! he did not hear all, I hope.   [*Apart to* HORNER.

Spark. Come, you bubbling rogues you, where do we sup?— Oh, Harcourt, my mistress tells me you have been making fierce love to her all the play long: ha! ha!—But I——

Har. I make love to her!

Spark. Nay, I forgive thee, for I think I know thee, and I know her; but I am sure I know myself.

Har. Did she tell you so? I see all women are like these of the Exchange; who, to enhance the prize of their commodities, report to their fond customers offers which were never made 'em.

Horn. Ay, women are apt to tell before the intrigue, as men after it, and so show themselves the vainer sex. But hast thou a mistress, Sparkish? 'Tis as hard for me to believe it, as that thou ever hadst a bubble, as you bragged just now.

Spark. O, your servant, sir: are you at your raillery, sir? But we are some of us beforehand with you to-day at the play. The wits were something bold with you, sir; did you not hear us laugh?

Horn. Yes; but I thought you had gone to plays, to laugh at the poet's wit, not at your own.

Spark. Your servant, sir: no, I thank you. 'Gad, I go to a play as to a country treat; I carry my own wine to one, and my own wit to t'other, or else I'm sure I should not be merry at either. And the reason why we are so often louder than the players, is, because we think we speak more wit, and so become the poet's rivals in his audience: for to tell you the truth, we hate the silly rogues; nay, so much, that we find fault even with their bawdy upon the stage, whilst we talk nothing else in the pit as loud.

Horn. But why shouldst thou hate the silly poets? Thou hast too much wit to be one; and they, like whores, are only hated by each other: and thou dost scorn writing, I'm sure.

Spark. Yes; I'd have you to know I scorn writing: but women, women, that make men do all foolish things, make 'em write songs too. Everybody does it. 'Tis even as common with lovers, as playing with fans; and you can no more help rhyming to your Phillis, than drinking to your Phillis.

Har. Nay, poetry in love is no more to be avoided than jealousy.

Dor. But the poets damned your songs, did they?

Spark. Damn the poets! they have turned 'em into burlesque, as they call it. That burlesque is a hocus-pocus trick they have got, which, by the virtue of *Hictius doctius topsy turvy,* they make a wise and witty man in the world, a fool upon the stage you know not how: and 'tis therefore I hate 'em too, for I know not but it may be my own case; for they'll put a man into a play for looking asquint. Their predecessors were contented to make serving-men only their stage-fools: but these rogues must have gentlemen, with a pox to 'em, nay, knights; and, indeed, you shall hardly see a fool upon the stage but he's a knight. And to tell you the truth, they have kept me these six years from being a knight in earnest, for fear of being knighted in a play, and dubbed a fool.

Dor. Blame 'em not, they must follow their copy, the age.

Har. But why shouldst thou be afraid of being in a play, who expose yourself every day in the play-houses, and at public places?

Hor. 'Tis but being on the stage, instead of standing on a bench in the pit.

Dor. Don't you give money to painters to draw you like? and are you afraid of your pictures at length in a playhouse, where all your mistresses may see you?

Spark. A pox! painters don't draw the small-pox or pimples in one's face. Come, damn all your silly authors whatever, all books and booksellers, by the world; and all readers, courteous or uncourteous!

Har. But who comes here, Sparkish?

Enter PINCHWIFE *and* Mrs. PINCHWIFE *in man's clothes,*
ALITHEA *and* LUCY.

Spark. Oh, hide me! There's my mistress too.

[SPARKISH *hides himself behind* HARCOURT.

Har. She sees you.

Spark. But I will not see her. 'Tis time to go to Whitehall, and I must not fail the drawing-room.

Har. Pray, first carry me, and reconcile me to her.

Spark. Another time. Faith, the king will have supped.

Har. Not with the worse stomach for thy absence. Thou art one of those fools that think their attendance at the king's meals as necessary as his physicians, when you are more troublesome to him than his doctors or his dogs.

Spark. Pshaw! I know my interest, sir. Prithee hide me.

Horn. Your servant, Pinchwife.—What, he knows us not!

Pinch. Come along.   [*To his* Wife *aside.*

Mrs. Pinch. Pray, have you any ballads? give me sixpenny worth.

Bookseller. We have no ballads.

Mrs. Pinch. Then give me " Covent Garden Drollery," and a play or two—Oh, here's " Tarugo's Wiles," and " The Slighted Maiden "; [1] I'll have them.

Pinch. No; plays are not for your reading. Come along; will you discover yourself?   [*Apart to her.*

Horn. Who is that pretty youth with him, Sparkish?

Spark. I believe his wife's brother, because he's something like her: but I never saw her but once.

Horn. Extremely handsome; I have seen a face like it too. Let us follow 'em.

[*Exeunt* PINCHWIFE, Mrs. PINCHWIFE, ALITHEA, *and* LUCY; HORNER *and* DORILANT *following them.*

Har. Come, Sparkish, your mistress saw you, and will be angry you go not to her. Besides, I would fain be reconciled to her, which none but you can do, dear friend.

Spark. Well, that's a better reason, dear friend. I would not go near her now for her's or my own sake; but I can deny you nothing: for though I have known thee a great while, never go, if I do not love thee as well as a new acquaintance.

Har. I am obliged to you indeed, dear friend. I would be well with her, only to be well with thee still; for these ties to wives usually dissolve all ties to friends. I would be contented she should enjoy you a-nights, but I would have you to myself a-days as I have had, dear friend.

Spark. And thou shalt enjoy me a-days, dear, dear friend, never stir: and I'll be divorced from her, sooner than from thee. Come along.

Har. [*aside*]. So, we are hard put to't, when we make our rival our procurer; but neither she nor her brother would let me come near her now. When all's done, a rival is the best cloak to steal to a mistress under, without suspicion; and when we have once got to her as we desire, we throw him off like other cloaks.   [*Exit* SPARKISH, HARCOURT *following him.*

Re-enter PINCHWIFE *and* Mrs. PINCHWIFE.

Pinch. [*to* ALITHEA]. Sister, if you will not go, we must leave you.—[*Aside.*] The fool her gallant and she will muster up all the young saunterers of this place, and they will leave their dear sempstresses to follow us. What a swarm of cuckolds and cuckold-makers are here !—Come, let's be gone, Mistress Margery.

[1] " Covent Garden Drolery, Or a Colection of all the Choice Songs, Poems, Prologues, and Epilogues (Sung and Spoken at Courts and Theaters) never in Print before. Written by the refined'st Witts of the Age. And Collected by R[ichard] B[rome] Servant to His Majestie. London, Printed for James Magnes neer the Piazza in Russel-Street, 1672."—*Tarugo's Wiles, or the Coffee House ;* a comedy by Sir Thomas St. Serle, produced in 1668.—*The Slighted Maid,* a comedy by Sir Robert Stapleton, produced in 1663.

Mrs. Pinch. Don't you believe that; I han't half my bellyfull of sights yet.

Pinch. Then walk this way.

Mrs. Pinch. Lord, what a power of brave signs are here! stay—the Bull's-Head, the Ram's-Head, and the Stag's-Head, dear——

Pinch. Nay, if every husband's proper sign here were visible, they would be all alike.

Mrs. Pinch. What d'ye mean by that, bud?

Pinch. 'Tis no matter—no matter, bud.

Mrs. Pinch. Pray tell me: nay, I will know.

Pinch. They would be all Bulls, Stags, and Rams-heads.

[*Exeunt* PINCHWIFE *and* MRS. PINCHWIFE.

Re-enter SPARKISH, HARCOURT, ALITHEA, *and* LUCY,
at the other side.

Spark. Come, dear madam, for my sake you shall be reconciled to him.

Alith. For your sake I hate him.

Har. That's something too cruel, madam, to hate me for his sake.

Spark. Ay indeed, madam, too, too cruel to me, to hate my friend for my sake.

Alith. I hate him because he is your enemy; and you ought to hate him too, for making love to me, if you love me.

Spark. That's a good one! I hate a man for loving you! If he did love you, 'tis but what he can't help; and 'tis your fault, not his, if he admires you. I hate a man for being of my opinion! I'll n'er do't, by the world.

Alith. Is it for your honour, or mine, to suffer a man to make love to me, who am to marry you to-morrow?

Spark. Is it for your honour, or mine, to have me jealous? That he makes love to you, is a sign you are handsome; and that I am not jealous, is a sign you are virtuous. That I think is for your honour.

Alith. But 'tis your honour too I am concerned for.

Har. But why, dearest madam, will you be more concerned for his honour than he is himself? Let his honour alone, for my sake and his. He! he has no honour——

Spark. How's that?

Har. But what my dear friend can guard himself.

Spark. O ho—that's right again.

Har. Your care of his honour argues his neglect of it, which is no honour to my dear friend here. Therefore once more, let his honour go which way it will, dear madam.

Spark. Ay, ay; were it for my honour to marry a woman whose virtue I suspected, and could not trust her in a friend's hands?

Alith. Are you not afraid to lose me?

Har. He afraid to lose you, madam! No, no—you may see how the most estimable and most glorious creature in the world is valued by him. Will you not see it?

Spark. Right, honest Frank, I have that noble value for her that I cannot be jealous of her.

Alith. You mistake him. He means, you care not for me, nor who has me.

Spark. Lord, madam, I see you are jealous! Will you wrest a poor man's meaning from his words?

Alith. You astonish me, sir, with your want of jealousy.

Spark. And you make me giddy, madam, with your jealousy and fears, and virtue and honour. 'Gad, I see virtue makes a woman as troublesome as a little reading or learning.

Alith. Monstrous!

Lucy. Well, to see what easy husbands these women of quality can meet with! a poor chambermaid can never have such lady-like luck. Besides, he's thrown away upon her. She'll make no use of her fortune, her blessing, none to a gentleman, for a pure cuckold; for it requires good breeding to be a cuckold. [*Aside.*

Alith. I tell you then plainly, he pursues me to marry me.

Spark. Pshaw!

Har. Come, madam, you see you strive in vain to make him jealous of me. My dear friend is the kindest creature in the world to me.

Spark. Poor fellow!

Har. But his kindness only is not enough for me, without your favour, your good opinion, dear madam: 'tis that must perfect my happiness. Good gentleman, he believes all I say: would you would do so! Jealous of me! I would not wrong him nor you for the world.

Spark. Look you there. Hear him, hear him, and do not walk away so. [ALITHEA *walks carelessly to and fro.*

Har. I love you, madam, so——

Spark. How's that? Nay, now you begin to go too far indeed.

Har. So much, I confess, I say, I love you, that I would not have you miserable, and cast yourself away upon so unworthy and inconsiderable a thing as what you see here.

[*Clapping his hand on his breast, points at* SPARKISH.

Spark. No, faith, I believe thou wouldst not: now his meaning is plain; but I knew before thou wouldst not wrong me, nor her.

Har. No, no, Heavens forbid the glory of her sex should fall so low, as into the embraces of such a contemptible wretch, the least of mankind—my friend here—I injure him!

[*Embracing* SPARKISH.

Alith. Very well.

Spark. No, no, dear friend, I knew it.—Madam, you see he will rather wrong himself than me, in giving himself such names.

Alith. Do not you understand him yet?

Spark. Yes: how modestly he speaks of himself, poor fellow!

Alith. Methinks he speaks impudently of yourself, since—before yourself too; insomuch that I can no longer suffer his scurrilous abusiveness to you, no more than his love to me.

[*Offers to go.*

Spark. Nay, nay, madam, pray stay—his love to you! Lord, madam, has he not spoke yet plain enough?

Alith. Yes, indeed, I should think so.

Spark. Well then, by the world, a man can't speak civilly to a woman now, but presently she says, he makes love to her. Nay, madam, you shall stay, with your pardon, since you have not yet understood him, till he has made an eclaircissement of his love to you, that is, what kind of love it is. Answer to thy catechism, friend; do you love my mistress here?

Har. Yes, I wish she would not doubt it.

Spark. But how do you love her?

Har. With all my soul.

Alith. I thank him, methinks he speaks plain enough now.

Spark. [*to* ALITHEA]. You are out still.—But with what kind of love, Harcourt?

Har. With the best and the truest love in the world.

Spark. Look you there then, that is with no matrimonial love, I'm sure.

Alith. How's that? do you say matrimonial love is not best?

Spark. 'Gad, I went too far ere I was aware. But speak for thyself, Harcourt, you said you would not wrong me nor her.

Har. No, no, madam, e'en take him for Heaven's sake.

Spark. Look you there, madam.

Har. Who should in all justice be yours, he that loves you most.   [*Claps his hand on his breast.*

Alith. Look you there, Mr. Sparkish, who's that?

Spark. Who should it be?—Go on, Harcourt.

Har. Who loves you more than women titles, or fortune fools.

[*Points at* SPARKISH.

Spark. Look you there, he means me still, for he points at me.

Alith. Ridiculous!

Har. Who can only match your faith and constancy in love.

Spark. Ay.

Har. Who knows, if it be possible, how to value so much beauty and virtue.

Spark. Ay.

Har. Whose love can no more be equalled in the world, than that heavenly form of yours.

Spark. No.

Har. Who could no more suffer a rival, than your absence, and yet could no more suspect your virtue, than his own constancy in his love to you.

Spark. No.

Har. Who, in fine, loves you better than his eyes, that first made him love you.

Spark. Ay—Nay, madam, faith, you shan't go till——

Alith. Have a care, lest you make me stay too long.

Spark. But till he has saluted you; that I may be assured you are friends, after his honest advice and declaration. Come, pray, madam, be friends with him.

Re-enter PINCHWIFE *and* Mrs. PINCHWIFE.

Alith. You must pardon me, sir, that I am not yet so obedient to you.

Pinch. What, invite your wife to kiss men? Monstrous! are you not ashamed? I will never forgive you.

Spark. Are you not ashamed, that I should have more confidence in the chastity of your family than you have? You must not teach me, I am a man of honour, sir, though I am frank and free; I am frank, sir——

Pinch. Very frank, sir, to share your wife with your friends.

Spark. He is an humble, menial friend, such as reconciles the differences of the marriage bed; you know man and wife do not always agree; I design him for that use, therefore would have him well with my wife.

Pinch. A menial friend!—you will get a great many menial friends, by showing your wife as you do.

Spark. What then? It may be I have a pleasure in't, as I have to show fine cloths at a play-house, the first day, and count money before poor rogues.

Pinch. He that shows his wife or money, will be in danger of having them borrowed sometimes.

Spark. I love to be envied, and would not marry a wife that I alone could love; loving alone is as dull as eating alone. Is it not a frank age? and I am a frank person; and to tell you the truth, it may be, I love to have rivals in a wife, they make her seem to a man still but as a kept mistress; and so good night, for I must to Whitehall.—Madam, I hope you are now reconciled to my friend; and so I wish you a good night, madam, and sleep if you can: for to-morrow you know I must visit you early with a canonical gentleman. Good night, dear Harcourt.   [*Exit.*

Har. Madam, I hope you will not refuse my visit to-morrow, if it should be earlier with a canonical gentleman than Mr. Sparkish's.

Pinch. This gentlewoman is yet under my care, therefore you must yet forbear your freedom with her, sir.

      [*Coming between* ALITHEA *and* HARCOURT.

Har. Must, sir?

Pinch. Yes, sir, she is my sister.

Har. 'Tis well she is, sir—for I must be her servant, sir.— Madam——

Pinch. Come away, sister, we had been gone, if it had not been for you, and so avoided these lewd rake-hells, who seem to haunt us.

Re-enter HORNER *and* DORILANT.

Horn. How now, Pinchwife!

Pinch. Your servant.

Horn. What! I see a little time in the country makes a man turn wild and unsociable, and only fit to converse with his horses, dogs, and his herds.

Pinch. I have business, sir, and must mind it; your business is pleasure, therefore you and I must go different ways.

Horn. Well, you may go on, but this pretty young gentle-man——   [*Takes hold of* Mrs. PINCHWIFE.

Har. The lady——

Dor. And the maid——

Horn. Shall stay with us; for I suppose their business is the same with ours, pleasure.

Pinch. 'Sdeath, he knows her, she carries it so sillily! yet if he does not, I should be more silly to discover it first.   [*Aside.*

Alith. Pray, let us go, sir.

Pinch. Come, come——

Horn. [*to* Mrs. PINCHWIFE]. Had you not rather stay with us? —Prithee, Pinchwife, who is this pretty young gentleman?

Pinch. One to whom I'm a guardian.—[*Aside.*] I wish I could keep her out of your hands.

Horn. Who is he? I never saw anything so pretty in all my life.

Pinch. Pshaw! do not look upon him so much, he's a poor bashful youth, you'll put him out of countenance.—Come away, brother.   [*Offers to take her away.*

Horn. O, your brother!

Pinch. Yes, my wife's brother.—Come, come, she'll stay supper for us.

Horn. I thought so, for he is very like her I saw you at the play with, whom I told you I was in love with.

Mrs. Pinch. [*aside*]. O jeminy! is that he that was in love with me? I am glad on't, I vow, for he's a curious fine gentleman, and I love him already, too.—[*To* PINCHWIFE.] Is this he, bud?

Pinch. Come away, come away.   [*To his* Wife.

Horn. Why, what haste are you in? why won't you let me talk with him?

Pinch. Because you'll debauch him; he's yet young and innocent, and I would not have him debauched for anything in the world.—[*Aside.*] How she gazes on him! the devil!

Horn. Harcourt, Dorilant, look you here, this is the likeness of that dowdy he told us of, his wife; did you ever see a lovelier creature? The rogue has reason to be jealous of his wife, since she is like him, for she would make all that see her in love with her.

Har. And, as I remember now, she is as like him here as can be.

Dor. She is indeed very pretty, if she be like him.

Horn. Very pretty? a very pretty commendation!—she is a glorious creature, beautiful beyond all things I ever beheld.

*E 604

Pinch. So, so.

Har. More beautiful than a poet's first mistress of imagination.

Horn. Or another man's last mistress of flesh and blood.

Mrs. Pinch. Nay, now you jeer, sir; pray don't jeer me.

Pinch. Come, come.—[*Aside.*] By Heavens, she'll discover herself!

Horn. I speak of your sister, sir.

Pinch. Ay, but saying she was handsome, if like him, made him blush.—[*Aside.*] I am upon a rack!

Horn. Methinks he is so handsome he should not be a man.

Pinch. [*aside*]. O, there 'tis out! he has discovered her! I am not able to suffer any longer.—[*To his* Wife.] Come, come away, I say.

Horn. Nay, by your leave, sir, he shall not go yet.—[*Aside to them.*] Harcourt, Dorilant, let us torment this jealous rogue a little.

Har. Dor. How?

Horn. I'll show you.

Pinch. Come, pray let him go, I cannot stay fooling any longer; I tell you his sister stays supper for us.

Horn. Does she? Come then, we'll all go to sup with he and thee.

Pinch. No, now I think on't, having stayed so long for us, I warrant she's gone to bed.—[*Aside.*] I wish she and I were well out of their hands.—[*To his* Wife.] Come, I must rise early to-morrow, come.

Horn. Well then, if she be gone to bed, I wish her and you a good night. But pray, young gentleman, present my humble service to her.

Mrs. Pinch. Thank you heartily, sir.

Pinch. [*aside*]. 'Sdeath, she will discover herself yet in spite of me.—[*Aloud.*] He is something more civil to you, for your kindness to his sister, than I am, it seems.

Horn. Tell her, dear sweet little gentleman, for all your brother there, that you have revived the love I had for her at first sight in the playhouse.

Mrs. Pinch. But did you love her indeed, and indeed?

Pinch. [*aside*]. So, so.—[*Aloud.*] Away, I say.

Horn. Nay, stay.—Yes, indeed, and indeed, pray do you tell her so, and give her this kiss from me.   [*Kisses her.*

Pinch. [*aside*]. O Heavens! what do I suffer? Now 'tis too plain he knows her, and yet——

Horn. And this, and this——   [*Kisses her again.*

Mrs. Pinch. What do you kiss me for? I am no woman.

Pinch. [*aside*]. So, there, 'tis out.—[*Aloud.*] Come, I cannot, nor will stay any longer.

Horn. Nay, they shall send your lady a kiss too. Here, Harcourt, Dorilant, will you not?   [*They kiss her.*

Pinch. [*aside*]. How! do I suffer this? Was I not accusing another just now for this rascally patience, in permitting his wife to be kissed before his face? Ten thousand ulcers gnaw away their lips.—[*Aloud.*] Come, come.

Horn. Good night, dear little gentleman; madam, good night; farewell, Pinchwife.—[*Apart to* HARCOURT *and* DORILANT.] Did not I tell you I would raise his jealous gall?

[*Exeunt* HORNER, HARCOURT, *and* DORILANT.

Pinch. So, they are gone at last; stay, let me see first if the coach be at this door. [*Exit.*

Re-enter HORNER, HARCOURT, *and* DORILANT.

Horn. What, not gone yet? Will you be sure to do as I desired you, sweet sir?

Mrs. Pinch. Sweet sir, but what will you give me then?

Horn. Anything. Come away into the next walk.

[*Exit, haling away* Mrs. PINCHWIFE.

Alith. Hold! hold! what d'ye do?

Lucy. Stay, stay, hold——

Har. Hold, madam, hold, let him present him—he'll come presently; nay, I will never let you go till you answer my question.

Lucy. For God's sake, sir, I must follow 'em.

[ALITHEA *and* LUCY, *struggling with* HARCOURT *and* DORILANT.

Dor. No, I have something to present you with too, you shan't follow them.

Re-enter PINCHWIFE.

Pinch. Where?—how—what's become of?—gone!—whither?

Lucy. He's only gone with the gentleman, who will give him something, an't please your worship.

Pinch. Something!—give him something, with a pox!—where are they?

Alith. In the next walk only, brother.

Pinch. Only, only! where, where?

[*Exit and returns presently, then goes out again.*

Har. What's the matter with him? why so much concerned? But, dearest madam——

Alith. Pray let me go, sir; I have said and suffered enough already.

Har. Then you will not look upon, nor pity, my sufferings?

Alith. To look upon 'em, when I cannot help 'em, were cruelty, not pity; therefore, I will never see you more.

Har. Let me then, madam, have my privilege of a banished lover, complaining or railing, and giving you but a farewell reason why, if you cannot condescend to marry me, you should not take that wretch, my rival.

Alith. He only, not you, since my honour is engaged so far to him, can give me a reason why I should not marry him; but if he be true, and what I think him to me, I must be so to him. Your servant, sir.

Har. Have women only constancy when 'tis a vice, and are, like Fortune, only true to fools?

Dor. Thou sha't not stir, thou robust creature; you see I can deal with you, therefore you should stay the rather, and be kind.

[*To* LUCY, *who struggles to get from him.*

Re-enter PINCHWIFE.

Pinch. Gone, gone, not to be found! quite gone! ten thousand plagues go with 'em! Which way went they?

Alith. But into t'other walk, brother.

Lucy. Their business will be done presently sure, an't please your worship; it can't be long in doing, I'm sure on't.

Alith. Are they not there?

Pinch. No, you know where they are, you infamous wretch, eternal shame of your family, which you do not dishonour enough yourself you think, but you must help her to do it too, thou legion of bawds!

Alith. Good brother——

Pinch. Damned, damned sister!

Alith. Look you here, she's coming.

Re-enter Mrs. PINCHWIFE *running, with her hat full of oranges and dried fruit under her arm,* HORNER *following.*

Mrs. Pinch. O dear bud, look you here what I have got, see!

Pinch. And what I have got here too, which you can't see.

[*Aside, rubbing his forehead.*

Mrs. Pinch. The fine gentleman has given me better things yet.

Pinch. Has he so?—[*Aside.*] Out of breath and coloured!— I must hold yet.

Horn. I have only given your little brother an orange, sir.

Pinch. [to HORNER]. Thank you, sir.—[*Aside.*] You have only squeezed my orange, I suppose, and given it me again; yet I must have a city patience.—[*To his* Wife.] Come, come away.

Mrs. Pinch. Stay, till I have put up my fine things, bud.

Enter Sir JASPER FIDGET.

Sir Jasp. O, Master Horner, come, come, the ladies stay for you; your mistress, my wife, wonders you make not more haste to her.

Horn. I have stayed this half hour for you here, and 'tis your fault I am not now with your wife.

Sir Jasp. But, pray, don't let her know so much; the truth on't is, I was advancing a certain project to his majesty about— I'll tell you.

Horn. No, let's go, and hear it at your house. Good night, sweet little gentleman; one kiss more, you'll remember me now, I hope. *[Kisses her.*

Dor. What, Sir Jasper, will you separate friends? He promised to sup with us, and if you take him to your house, you'll be in danger of our company too.

Sir Jasp. Alas! gentlemen, my house is not fit for you; there are none but civil women there, which are not for your turn. He, you know, can bear with the society of civil women now, ha! ha! ha! besides, he's one of my family—he's—he! he! he!

Dor. What is he?

Sir Jasp. Faith, my eunuch, since you'll have it; he! he! he! *[Exeunt* Sir Jasper Fidget *and* Horner.

Dor. I rather wish thou wert his or my cuckold. Harcourt, what a good cuckold is lost there for want of a man to make him one? Thee and I cannot have Horner's privilege, who can make use of it.

Har. Ay, to poor Horner 'tis like coming to an estate at threescore, when a man can't be the better for't.

Pinch. Come.

Mrs. Pinch. Presently, bud.

Dor. Come, let us go too.—*[To* Alithea.] Madam, your servant.—*[To* Lucy.] Good night, strapper.

Har. Madam, though you will not let me have a good day or night, I wish you one; but dare not name the other half of my wish.

Alith. Good night, sir, for ever.

Mrs. Pinch. I don't know where to put this here, dear bud, you shall eat it; nay, you shall have part of the fine gentleman's good things, or treat, as you call it, when we come home.

Pinch. Indeed, I deserve it, since I furnished the best part of it. *[Strikes away the orange.*

The gallant treats presents, and gives the ball;
But 'tis the absent cuckold pays for all. *[Exeunt.*

ACT IV

SCENE I.—Pinchwife's *House in the morning*

Enter Alithea *dressed in new clothes, and* Lucy.

Lucy. Well—madam, now have I dressed you, and set you out with so many ornaments, and spent upon you ounces of essence and pulvillio; and all this for no other purpose but as people adorn and perfume a corpse for a stinking second-hand grave: such, or as bad, I think Master Sparkish's bed.

Alith. Hold your peace.

Lucy. Nay, madam, I will ask you the reason why you would banish poor Master Harcourt for ever from your sight; how could you be so hard-hearted?

Alith. 'Twas because I was not hard-hearted.

Lucy. No, no; 'twas stark love and kindness, I warrant.

Alith. It was so; I would see him no more because I love him.

Lucy. Hey day, a very pretty reason!

Alith. You do not understand me.

Lucy. I wish you may yourself.

Alith. I was engaged to marry, you see, another man, whom my justice will not suffer me to deceive or injure.

Lucy. Can there be a greater cheat or wrong done to a man than to give him your person without your heart? I should make a conscience of it.

Alith. I'll retrieve it for him after I am married a while.

Lucy. The woman that marries to love better, will be as much mistaken as the wencher that marries to live better. No, madam, marrying to increase love is like gaming to become rich; alas! you only lose what little stock you had before.

Alith. I find by your rhetoric you have been bribed to betray me.

Lucy. Only by his merit, that has bribed your heart, you see, against your word and rigid honour. But what a devil is this honour! 'tis sure a disease in the head, like the megrim or falling-sickness, that always hurries people away to do themselves mischief. Men lose their lives by it; women, what's dearer to 'em, their love, the life of life.

Alith. Come, pray talk you no more of honour, nor Master Harcourt; I wish the other would come to secure my fidelity to him and his right in me.

Lucy. You will marry him then?

Alith. Certainly, I have given him already my word, and will my hand too, to make it good, when he comes.

Lucy. Well, I wish I may never stick pin more, if he be not an arrant natural, to t'other fine gentleman.

Alith. I own he wants the wit of Harcourt, which I will dispense withal for another want he has, which is want of jealousy, which men of wit seldom want.

Lucy. Lord, madam, what should you do with a fool to your husband? You intend to be honest, don't you? then that husbandly virtue, credulity, is thrown away upon you.

Alith. He only that could suspect my virtue should have cause to do it; 'tis Sparkish's confidence in my truth that obliges me to be so faithful to him.

Lucy. You are not sure his opinion may last.

Alith. I am satisfied, 'tis impossible for him to be jealous after the proofs I have had of him. Jealousy in a husband—Heaven defend me from it! it begets a thousand plagues to a poor woman, the loss of her honour, her quiet, and her——

Lucy. And her pleasure.

Alith. What d'ye mean, impertinent?

Lucy. Liberty is a great pleasure, madam.

Alith. I say, loss of her honour, her quiet, nay, her life some-times; and what's as bad almost, the loss of this town; that is, she is sent into the country, which is the last ill-usage of a husband to a wife, I think.

Lucy [*aside*]. O, does the wind lie there?—[*Aloud.*] Then of necessity, madam, you think a man must carry his wife into the country, if he be wise. The country is as terrible, I find, to our young English ladies, as a monastery to those abroad; and on my virginity, I think they would rather marry a London jailer, than a high sheriff of a county, since neither can stir from his employment. Formerly women of wit married fools for a great estate, a fine seat, or the like; but now 'tis for a pretty seat only in Lincoln's Inn Fields, St. James's Fields, or the Pall Mall.

Enter SPARKISH, *and* HARCOURT, *dressed like a* Parson.

Spark. Madam, your humble servant, a happy day to you, and to us all.

Har. Amen.

Alith. Who have we here?

Spark. My chaplain, faith—O madam, poor Harcourt remem-bers his humble service to you; and, in obedience to your last commands, refrains coming into your sight.

Alith. Is not that he?

Spark. No, fy, no; but to show that he ne'er intended to hinder our match, has sent his brother here to join our hands. When I get me a wife, I must get her a chaplain, according to the custom; that is his brother, and my chaplain.

Alith. His brother!

Lucy. And your chaplain, to preach in your pulpit then——

[*Aside.*

Alith. His brother!

Spark. Nay, I knew you would not believe it.—I told you, sir, she would take you for your brother Frank.

Alith. Believe it!

Lucy. His brother! ha! ha! he! he has a trick left still, it seems.   [*Aside.*

Spark. Come, my dearest, pray let us go to church before the canonical hour is past.

Alith. For shame, you are abused still.

Spark. By the world, 'tis strange now you are so incredulous.

Alith. 'Tis strange you are so credulous.

Spark. Dearest of my life, hear me. I tell you this is Ned Harcourt of Cambridge, by the world; you see he has a sneaking college look. 'Tis true he's something like his brother Frank; and they differ from each other no more than in their age, for they were twins.

Lucy. Ha! ha! ha!

Alith. Your servant, sir; I cannot be so deceived, though you are. But come, let's hear, how do you know what you affirm so confidently?

Spark. Why I'll tell you all. Frank Harcourt coming to me this morning to wish me joy, and present his service to you, I asked him if he could help me to a parson. Whereupon he told me, he had a brother in town who was in orders; and he went straight away, and sent him, you see there, to me.

Alith. Yes, Frank goes and puts on a black coat, then tells you he is Ned; that's all you have for't.

Spark. Pshaw! pshaw! I tell you, by the same token, the midwife put her garter about Frank's neck, to know 'em asunder, they were so like.

Alith. Frank tells you this too?

Spark. Ay, and Ned there too: nay, they are both in a story.

Alith. So, so; very foolish.

Spark. Lord, if you won't believe one, you had best try him by your chambermaid there; for chambermaids must needs know chaplains from other men, they are so used to 'em.

Lucy. Let's see: nay, I'll be sworn he has the canonical smirk, and the filthy clammy palm of a chaplain.

Alith. Well, most reverend doctor, pray let us make an end of this fooling.

Har. With all my soul, divine heavenly creature, when you please.

Alith. He speaks like a chaplain indeed.

Spark. Why, was there not soul, divine, heavenly, in what he said?

Alith. Once more, most impertinent black coat, cease your persecution, and let us have a conclusion of this ridiculous love.

Har. I had forgot, I must suit my style to my coat, or I wear it in vain.   [*Aside.*

Alith. I have no more patience left; let us make once an end of this troublesome love, I say.

Har. So be it, seraphic lady, when your honour shall think it meet and convenient so to do.

Spark. 'Gad, I'm sure none but a chaplain could speak so, I think.

Alith. Let me tell you, sir, this dull trick will not serve your turn; though you delay our marriage, you shall not hinder it.

Har. Far be it from me, munificent patroness, to delay your marriage; I desire nothing more than to marry you presently, which I might do, if you yourself would; for my noble, good-natured, and thrice generous patron here would not hinder it.

Spark. No, poor man, not I, faith.

Har. And now, madam, let me tell you plainly nobody else shall marry you; by Heavens! I'll die first, for I'm sure I should die after it.

Lucy. How his love has made him forget his function, as I have seen it in real parsons!

Alith. That was spoken like a chaplain too? now you understand him, I hope.

Spark. Poor man, he takes it heinously to be refused; I can't blame him, 'tis putting an indignity upon him, not to be suffered; but you'll pardon me, madam, it shan't be; he shall marry us; come away, pray, madam.

Lucy. Ha! ha! he! more ado! 'tis late.

Alith. Invincible stupidity! I tell you, he would marry me as your rival, not as your chaplain.

Spark. Come, come, madam. [*Pulling her away.*

Lucy. I pray, madam, do not refuse this reverend divine the honour and satisfaction of marrying you; for I dare say, he has set his heart upon't, good doctor.

Alith. What can you hope or design by this?

Har. I could answer her, a reprieve for a day only, often revokes a hasty doom. At worst, if she will not take mercy on me, and let me marry her, I have at least the lover's second pleasure, hindering my rival's enjoyment, though but for a time. [*Aside.*

Spark. Come, madam, 'tis e'en twelve o'clock, and my mother charged me never to be married out of the canonical hours. Come, come; Lord, here's such a deal of modesty, I warrant, the first day.

Lucy. Yes, an't please your worship, married women show all their modesty the first day, because married men show all their love the first day. [*Exeunt.*

SCENE II.—*A Bedchamber in* PINCHWIFE'S *House*

PINCHWIFE *and* MRS. PINCHWIFE *discovered.*

Pinch. Come, tell me, I say.

Mrs. Pinch. Lord! han't I told it a hundred times over?

Pinch. [*aside*]. I would try, if in the repetition of the ungrateful tale, I could find her altering it in the least circumstance; for if her story be false, she is so too.—[*Aloud.*] Come, how was't, baggage?

Mrs. Pinch. Lord, what pleasure you take to hear it sure!

Pinch. No, you take more in telling it I find; but speak, how was't?

Mrs. Pinch. He carried me up into the house next to the Exchange.

Pinch. So, and you two were only in the room!

Mrs. Pinch. Yes, for he sent away a youth that was there, for some dried fruit, and China oranges.

Pinch. Did he so? Damn him for it—and for——

Mrs. Pinch. But presently came up the gentlewoman of the house.

Pinch. O, 'twas well she did; but what did he do whilst the fruit came?

Mrs. Pinch. He kissed me a hundred times, and told me he fancied he kissed my fine sister, meaning me, you know, whom he said he loved with all his soul, and bid me be sure to tell her so, and to desire her to be at her window, by eleven of the clock this morning, and he would walk under it at that time.

Pinch. And he was as good as his word, very punctual; a pox reward him for't.　　　　　　　　　　　　　　　　　　[*Aside.*

Mrs. Pinch. Well, and he said if you were not within, he would come up to her, meaning me, you know, bud, still.

Pinch. [*aside*]. So—he knew her certainly; but for this confession, I am obliged to her simplicity.—[*Aloud.*] But what, you stood very still when he kissed you?

Mrs. Pinch. Yes, I warrant you; would you have had me discovered myself?

Pinch. But you told me he did some beastliness to you, as you call it; what was't?

Mrs. Pinch. Why, he put——

Pinch. What?

Mrs. Pinch. Why, he put the tip of his tongue between my lips, and so mousled me—and I said, I'd bite it.

Pinch. An eternal canker seize it, for a dog!

Mrs. Pinch. Nay, you need not be so angry with him neither, for to say truth, he has the sweetest breath I ever knew.

Pinch. The devil! you were satisfied with it then, and would do it again?

Mrs. Pinch. Not unless he should force me.

Pinch. Force you, changeling! I tell you, no woman can be forced.

Mrs. Pinch. Yes, but she may sure, by such a one as he, for he's a proper, goodly, strong man; 'tis hard, let me tell you, to resist him.

Pinch. [*aside*]. So, 'tis plain she loves him, yet she has not love enough to make her conceal it from me; but the sight of him will increase her aversion for me and love for him; and that love instruct her how to deceive me and satisfy him, all idiot as she is. Love! 'twas he gave women first their craft, their art of deluding. Out of Nature's hands they came plain, open, silly, and fit for slaves, as she and Heaven intended 'em; but damned Love—well—I must strangle that little monster whilst I can deal with him.—[*Aloud.*] Go fetch pen, ink, and paper out of the next room.

Mrs. Pinch. Yes, bud.　　　　　　　　　　　　　　　　　[*Exit.*

Pinch. Why should women have more invention in love than men? It can only be, because they have more desires, more soliciting passions, more lust, and more of the devil.

Re-enter Mrs. PINCHWIFE.

Come, minx, sit down and write.

Mrs. Pinch. Ay, dear bud, but I can't do't very well.

Pinch. I wish you could not at all.

Mrs. Pinch. But what should I write for?

Pinch. I'll have you write a letter to your lover.

Mrs. Pinch. O Lord, to the fine gentleman a letter!

Pinch. Yes, to the fine gentleman.

Mrs. Pinch. Lord, you do but jeer: sure you jest.

Pinch. I am not so merry: come, write as I bid you.

Mrs. Pinch. What, do you think I am a fool?

Pinch. [*aside*]. She's afraid I would not dictate any love to him, therefore she's unwilling.—[*Aloud.*] But you had best begin.

Mrs. Pinch. Indeed, and indeed, but I won't, so I won't.

Pinch. Why?

Mrs. Pinch. Because he's in town; you may send for him if you will.

Pinch. Very well, you would have him brought to you; is it come to this? I say, take the pen and write, or you'll provoke me.

Mrs. Pinch. Lord, what d'ye make a fool of me for? Don't I know that letters are never writ but from the country to London, and from London into the country? Now he's in town, and I am in town too; therefore I can't write to him, you know.

Pinch. [*aside*]. So, I am glad it is no worse; she is innocent enough yet.—[*Aloud.*] Yes, you may, when your husband bids you, write letters to people that are in town.

Mrs. Pinch. O, may I so? then I'm satisfied.

Pinch. Come, begin:—" Sir "——   [*Dictates.*

Mrs. Pinch. Shan't I say, " Dear Sir? "—You know one says always something more than bare " Sir."

Pinch. Write as I bid you, or I will write whore with this penknife in your face.

Mrs. Pinch. Nay, good bud—" Sir "——   [*Writes.*

Pinch. " Though I suffered last night your nauseous, loathed kisses and embraces "—Write!

Mrs. Pinch. Nay, why should I say so? You know I told you he had a sweet breath.

Pinch. Write!

Mrs. Pinch. Let me but put out " loathed."

Pinch. Write, I say!

Mrs. Pinch. Well then.   [*Writes.*

Pinch. Let's see, what have you writ?—[*Takes the paper and reads.*] " Though I suffered last night your kisses and embraces "—Thou impudent creature! where is " nauseous " and " loathed ? "

Mrs. Pinch. I can't abide to write such filthy words.

Pinch. Once more write as I'd have you, and question it not, or I will spoil thy writing with this. I will stab out those eyes that cause my mischief.   [*Holds up the penknife.*

Mrs. Pinch. O Lord! I will.

Pinch. So—so—let's see now.—[*Reads.*] " Though I suffered last night your nauseous, loathed kisses and embraces "—go on—" yet I would not have you presume that you shall ever repeat them "—so——   [*She writes.*

Mrs. Pinch. I have writ it.

Pinch. On, then—" I then concealed myself from your knowledge, to avoid your insolencies."——   [*She writes.*

Mrs. Pinch. So——

Pinch. " The same reason, now I am out of your hands "——   [*She writes.*

Mrs. Pinch. So——

Pinch. " Makes me own to you my unfortunate, though innocent frolic, of being in man's clothes "——   [*She writes.*

Mrs. Pinch. So——

Pinch. " That you may for evermore cease to pursue her, who hates and detests you "——   [*She writes on.*

Mrs. Pinch. So—heigh!   [*Sighs.*

Pinch. What, do you sigh?—" detests you—as much as she loves her husband and her honour."

Mrs. Pinch. I vow, husband, he'll ne'er believe I should write such a letter.

Pinch. What, he'd expect a kinder from you? Come, now your name only.

Mrs. Pinch. What, shan't I say " Your most faithful humble servant till death? "

Pinch. No, tormenting fiend!—[*Aside.*] Her style, I find, would be very soft.—[*Aloud.*] Come, wrap it up now, whilst I go fetch wax and a candle; and write on the backside, " For Mr. Horner."   [*Exit.*

Mrs. Pinch. " For Mr. Horner."—So, I am glad he has told me his name. Dear Mr. Horner! but why should I send thee such a letter that will vex thee, and make thee angry with me?— Well, I will not send it.—Ay, but then my husband will kill me— for I see plainly he won't let me love Mr. Horner—but what care I for my husband?—I won't, so I won't, send poor Mr. Horner such a letter—But then my husband—but oh, what if I writ at bottom my husband made me write it?—Ay, but then my husband would see't—Can one have no shift? ah, a London woman would have had a hundred presently. Stay—what if I should write a letter, and wrap it up like this, and write upon't too? Ay, but then my husband would see't—I don't know what to do.—But yet evads I'll try, so I will—for I will not send this letter to poor Mr. Horner, come what will on't.

" Dear, sweet Mr. Horner "—[*Writes and repeats what she writes.*]—so—" my husband would have me send you a base,

rude, unmannerly letter; but I won't "—so—" and would have
me forbid you loving me; but I won't "—so—" and would have
me say to you, I hate you, poor Mr. Horner; but I won't tell a
lie for him "—there—" for I'm sure if you and I were in the
country at cards together "—so—" I could not help treading on
your toe under the table "—so—" or rubbing knees with you,
and staring in your face, till you saw me "—very well—" and
then looking down, and blushing for an hour together "—so—
" but I must make haste before my husband comes: and now
he has taught me to write letters, you shall have longer ones
from me, who am, dear, dear, poor, dear Mr. Horner, your most
humble friend, and servant to command till death,—Margery
Pinchwife."

Stay, I must give him a hint at bottom—so—now wrap it up
just like t'other—so—now write " For Mr. Horner "—But oh
now, what shall I do with it? for here comes my husband.

Re-enter PINCHWIFE.

Pinch. [*aside*]. I have been detained by a sparkish coxcomb,
who pretended a visit to me; but I fear 'twas to my wife—
[*Aloud.*] What, have you done?

Mrs. Pinch. Ay, ay, bud, just now.

Pinch. Let's see't: what d'ye tremble for? what, you would
not have it go?

Mrs. Pinch. Here—[*aside.*] No, I must not give him that:
so I had been served if I had given him this.

[*He opens and reads the first letter.*

Pinch. Come, where's the wax and seal?

Mrs. Pinch. [*aside*]. Lord, what shall I do now? Nay, then
I have it—[*aloud.*] Pray let me see't. Lord, you think me so
arrant a fool, I cannot seal a letter; I will do't, so I will.

[*Snatches the letter from him, changes it for the other, seals it,
and delivers it to him.*

Pinch. Nay, I believe you will learn that, and other things
too, which I would not have you.

Mrs. Pinch. So, han't I done it curiously?—[*Aside.*] I think
I have; there's my letter going to Mr. Horner, since he'll needs
have me send letters to folks.

Pinch. 'Tis very well; but I warrant, you would not have it
go now?

Mrs. Pinch. Yes, indeed, but I would, bud, now.

Pinch. Well, you are a good girl then. Come, let me lock you
up in your chamber, till I come back; and be sure you come not
within three strides of the window when I am gone, for I have a
spy in the street.—[*Exit* Mrs. PINCHWIFE, PINCHWIFE *locks the
door.*] At least, 'tis fit she think so. If we do not cheat women,
they'll cheat us, and fraud may be justly used with secret
enemies, of which a wife is the most dangerous; and he that has

a handsome one to keep, and a frontier town, must provide against treachery, rather than open force. Now I have secured all within, I'll deal with the foe without, with false intelligence.

[*Holds up the letter. Exit.*

SCENE III.—HORNER'S *Lodging*

Enter HORNER *and* Quack.

Quack. Well, sir, how fadges the new design? have you not the luck of all your brother projectors, to deceive only yourself at last?

Horn. No, good domine doctor, I deceive you, it seems, and others too; for the grave matrons, and old, rigid husbands think me as unfit for love, as they are; but their wives, sisters, and daughters know, some of 'em, better things already.

Quack. Already!

Horn. Already, I say. Last night I was drunk with half-a-dozen of your civil persons, as you call 'em, and people of honour, and so was made free of their society and dressing-rooms for ever hereafter; and am already come to the privileges of sleeping upon their pallets, warming smocks, tying shoes and garters, and the like, doctor, already, already, doctor.

Quack. You have made good use of your time, sir.

Horn. I tell thee, I am now no more interruption to 'em, when they sing, or talk bawdy, than a little squab French page who speaks no English.

Quack. But do civil persons and women of honour drink, and sing bawdy songs?

Horn. O, amongst friends, amongst friends. For your bigots in honour are just like those in religion; they fear the eye of the world more than the eye of Heaven; and think there is no virtue, but railing at vice, and no sin, but giving scandal. They rail at a poor, little, kept player, and keep themselves some young, modest pulpit comedian to be privy to their sins in their closets, not to tell 'em of them in their chapels.

Quack. Nay, the truth on't is, priests, amongst the women now, have quite got the better of us lay-confessors, physicians.

Horn. And they are rather their patients; but——

Enter Lady FIDGET, *looking about her.*

Now we talk of women of honour, here comes one. Step behind the screen there, and but observe, if I have not particular privileges with the women of reputation already, doctor, already.

[*Quack retires.*

Lady Fid. Well, Horner, am not I a woman of honour? you see, I'm as good as my word.

Horn. And you shall see, madam, I'll not be behind-hand with you in honour; and I'll be as good as my word too, if you please but to withdraw into the next room.

Lady Fid. But first, my dear sir, you must promise to have a care of my dear honour.

Horn. If you talk a word more of your honour, you'll make me incapable to wrong it. To talk of honour in the mysteries of love, is like talking of Heaven or the Deity, in an operation of witchcraft, just when you are employing the devil: it makes the charm impotent.

Lady Fid. Nay, fy! let us not be smutty. But you talk of mysteries and bewitching to me; I don't understand you.

Horn. I tell you, madam, the word money in a mistress's mouth, at such a nick of time, is not a more disheartening sound to a younger brother, than that of honour to an eager lover like myself.

Lady Fid. But you can't blame a lady of my reputation to be chary.

Horn. Chary! I have been chary of it already, by the report I have caused of myself.

Lady Fid. Ay, but if you should ever let other women know that dear secret, it would come out. Nay, you must have a great care of your conduct; for my acquaintance are so censorious (oh, 'tis a wicked, censorious world, Mr. Horner!), I say, are so censorious, and detracting, that perhaps they'll talk to the prejudice of my honour, though you should not let them know the dear secret.

Horn. Nay, madam, rather than they shall prejudice your honour, I'll prejudice theirs; and, to serve you, I'll lie with 'em all, make the secret their own, and then they'll keep it. I am a Machiavel in love, madam.

Lady Fid. O, no, sir, not that way.

Horn. Nay, the devil take me, if censorious women are to be silenced any other way.

Lady Fid. A secret is better kept, I hope, by a single person than a multitude; therefore pray do not trust anybody else with it, dear, dear Mr. Horner.   [*Embracing him.*

Enter Sir JASPER FIDGET.

Sir Jasp. How now!

Lady Fid. [*aside*]. O my husband!—prevented—and what's almost as bad, found with my arms about another man—that will appear too much—what shall I say?—[*Aloud.*] Sir Jasper, come hither: I am trying if Mr. Horner were ticklish, and he's as ticklish as can be. I love to torment the confounded toad; let you and I tickle him.

Sir Jasp. No, your ladyship will tickle him better without me, I suppose. But is this your buying china? I thought you had been at the china-house.

Horn. [*aside*]. China-house! that's my cue, I must take it.—
[*Aloud.*] A pox! can't you keep your impertinent wives at
home? Some men are troubled with the husbands, but I with
the wives; but I'd have you to know, since I cannot be your
journeyman by night, I will not be your drudge by day, to
squire your wife about, and be your man of straw, or scarecrow
only to pies and jays, that would be nibbling at your forbidden
fruit; I shall be shortly the hackney gentleman-usher of the
town.

Sir Jasp. [*aside*]. He! he! he! poor fellow, he's in the right
on't, faith. To squire women about for other folks is as ungrateful an employment, as to tell money for other folks.—
[*Aloud.*] He! he! he! be'n't angry, Horner.

Lady Fid. No, 'tis I have more reason to be angry, who am
left by you, to go abroad indecently alone; or, what is more
indecent, to pin myself upon such ill-bred people of your
acquaintance as this is.

Sir Jasp. Nay, prithee, what has he done?

Lady Fid. Nay, he has done nothing.

Sir Jasp. But what d'ye take ill, if he has done nothing?

Lady Fid. Ha! ha! ha! faith, I can't but laugh however;
why, d'ye think the unmannerly toad would come down to me
to the coach? I was fain to come up to fetch him, or go without
him, which I was resolved not to do; for he knows china very
well, and has himself very good, but will not let me see it, lest
I should beg some; but I will find it out, and have what I came
for yet.

Horn. [*apart to* Lady FIDGET, *as he follows her to the door*].
Lock the door, madam.—[*Exit* Lady FIDGET, *and locks the door.*]
—[*Aloud.*] So, she has got into my chamber and locked me out.
Oh the impertinency of woman-kind! Well, Sir Jasper, plain-
dealing is a jewel; if ever you suffer your wife to trouble me
again here, she shall carry you home a pair of horns; by my
lord mayor she shall; though I cannot furnish you myself, you
are sure, yet I'll find a way.

Sir Jasp. Ha! ha! he!—[*Aside.*] At my first coming in,
and finding her arms about him, tickling him it seems, I was
half jealous, but now I see my folly.—[*Aloud.*] He! he! he!
poor Horner.

Horn. Nay, though you laugh now, 'twill be my turn ere long.
Oh women, more impertinent, more cunning, and more mischievous than their monkeys, and to me almost as ugly!—Now
is she throwing my things about and rifling all I have; but I'll
get in to her the back way, and so rifle her for it.

Sir Jasp. Ha! ha! ha! poor angry Horner.

Horn. Stay here a little, I'll ferret her out to you presently,
I warrant.   [*Exit at the other door.*

    [Sir JASPER *talks through the door to his* Wife, *she answers
        from within.*

Sir Jasp. Wife! my Lady Fidget! wife! he is coming in to you the back way.

Lady Fid. Let him come, and welcome, which way he will.

Sir Jasp. He'll catch you, and use you roughly, and be too strong for you.

Lady Fid. Don't you trouble yourself, let him if he can.

Quack. [*aside*]. This indeed I could not have believed from him, nor any but my own eyes.

Enter Mrs. SQUEAMISH.

Mrs. Squeam. Where's this woman-hater, this toad, this ugly, greasy, dirty sloven?

Sir Jasp. [*aside*]. So, the women all will have him ugly: methinks he is a comely person, but his wants make his form contemptible to 'em; and 'tis e'en as my wife said yesterday, talking of him, that a proper handsome eunuch was as ridiculous a thing as a gigantic coward.

Mrs. Squeam. Sir Jasper, your servant: where is the odious beast?

Sir Jasp. He's within in his chamber, with my wife; she's playing the wag with him.

Mrs. Squeam. Is she so? and he's a clownish beast, he'll give her no quarter, he'll play the wag with her again, let me tell you: come, let's go help her.—What, the door's locked?

Sir Jasp. Ay, my wife locked it.

Mrs. Squeam. Did she so? let's break it open then.

Sir Jasp. No, no, he'll do her no hurt.

Mrs. Squeam. [*aside*]. But is there no other way to get in to 'em? whither goes this? I will disturb 'em.

[*Exit at another door.*

Enter Old Lady SQUEAMISH.

Lady Squeam. Where is this harlotry, this impudent baggage, this rambling tomrigg? O Sir Jasper, I'm glad to see you here; did you not see my vile grandchild come in hither just now?

Sir Jasp. Yes.

Lady Squeam. Ay, but where is she then? where is she? Lord, Sir Jasper, I have e'en rattled myself to pieces in pursuit of her: but can you tell what she makes here? they say below, no woman lodges here.

Sir Jasp. No.

Lady Squeam. No! what does she here then? say, if it be not a woman's lodging, what makes she here? But are you sure no woman lodges here?

Sir Jasp. No, nor no man neither, this is Mr. Horner's lodging.

Lady Squeam. Is it so, are you sure?

Sir Jasp. Yes, yes.

Lady Squeam. So; then there's no hurt in't, I hope. But where is he?

Sir Jasp. He's in the next room with my wife.

Lady Squeam. Nay, if you trust him with your wife, I may with my Biddy. They say, he's a merry harmless man now, e'en as harmless a man as ever came out of Italy with a good voice, and as pretty, harmless company for a lady, as a snake without his teeth.

Sir Jasp. Ay, ay, poor man.

Re-enter Mrs. SQUEAMISH.

Mrs. Squeam. I can't find 'em.—Oh, are you here, grandmother? I followed, you must know, my Lady Fidget hither; 'tis the prettiest lodging, and I have been staring on the prettiest pictures——

Re-enter Lady FIDGET *with a piece of china in her hand, and* HORNER *following.*

Lady Fid. And I have been toiling and moiling for the prettiest piece of china, my dear.

Horn. Nay, she has been too hard for me, do what I could.

Mrs. Squeam. Oh, lord, I'll have some china too. Good Mr. Horner, don't think to give other people china, and me none; come in with me too.

Horn. Upon my honour, I have none left now.

Mrs. Squeam. Nay, nay, I have known you deny your china before now, but you shan't put me off so. Come.

Horn. This lady had the last there.

Lady Fid. Yes indeed, madam, to my certain knowledge, he has no more left.

Mrs. Squeam. O, but it may be he may have some you could not find.

Lady Fid. What, d'ye think if he had had any left, I would not have had it too? for we women of quality never think we have china enough.

Horn. Do not take it ill, I cannot make china for you all, but I will have a roll-waggon for you too, another time.

Mrs. Squeam. Thank you, dear toad.

Lady Fid. What do you mean by that promise?

[*Aside to* HORNER.

Horn. Alas, she has an innocent, literal understanding.

[*Aside to* Lady FIDGET.

Lady Squeam. Poor Mr. Horner! he has enough to do to please you all, I see.

Horn. Ay, madam, you see how they use me.

Lady Squeam. Poor gentleman, I pity you.

Horn. I thank you, madam: I could never find pity, but from such reverend ladies as you are; the young ones will never spare a man.

Mrs. Squeam. Come, come, beast, and go dine with us; for we shall want a man at ombre after dinner.

Horn. That's all their use of me, madam, you see.

Mrs. Squeam. Come, sloven, I'll lead you, to be sure of you.
                                    [*Pulls him by the cravat.*

Lady Squeam. Alas, poor man, how she tugs him! Kiss, kiss her; that's the way to make such nice women quiet.

Horn. No, madam, that remedy is worse than the torment; they know I dare suffer anything rather than do it.

Lady Squeam. Prithee kiss her, and I'll give you her picture in little, that you admired so last night; prithee do.

Horn. Well, nothing but that could bribe me: I love a woman only in effigy, and good painting as much as I hate them.—I'll do't, for I could adore the devil well painted.
                                    [*Kisses* Mrs. SQUEAMISH.

Mrs. Squeam. Foh, you filthy toad! nay, now I've done jesting.

Lady Squeam. Ha! ha! ha! I told you so.

Mrs. Squeam. Foh! a kiss of his——

Sir Jasp. Has no more hurt in't than one of my spaniel's.

Mrs. Squeam. Nor no more good neither.

Quack. I will now believe anything he tells me.   [*Aside.*

Enter PINCHWIFE.

Lady Fid. O lord, here's a man! Sir Jasper, my mask, my mask! I would not be seen here for the world.

Sir Jasp. What, not when I am with you?

Lady Fid. No, no, my honour—let's be gone.

Mrs. Squeam. Oh grandmother, let's be gone; make haste, make haste, I know not how he may censure us.

Lady Fid. Be found in the lodging of anything like a man!—Away.
    [*Exeunt* Sir JASPER FIDGET, Lady FIDGET, Old Lady
        SQUEAMISH, *and* Mrs. SQUEAMISH.

Quack. What's here? another cuckold? he looks like one, and none else sure have any business with him.   [*Aside.*

Horn. Well, what brings my dear friend hither?

Pinch. Your impertinency.

Horn. My impertinency!—why, you gentlemen that have got handsome wives, think you have a privilege of saying anything to your friends, and are as brutish as if you were our creditors.

Pinch. No, sir, I'll ne'er trust you any way.

Horn. But why not, dear Jack? why diffide in me thou know'st so well?

Pinch. Because I do know you so well.

Horn. Han't I been always thy friend, honest Jack, always

ready to serve thee, in love or battle, before thou wert married, and am so still?

Pinch. I believe so, you would be my second now, indeed.

Horn. Well then, dear Jack, why so unkind, so grum, so strange to me? Come, prithee kiss me, dear rogue: gad, I was always, I say, and am still as much thy servant as——

Pinch. As I am yours, sir. What, you would send a kiss to my wife, is that it?

Horn. So, there 'tis—a man can't show his friendship to a married man, but presently he talks of his wife to you. Prithee, let thy wife alone, and let thee and I be all one, as we were wont. What, thou art as shy of my kindness as a Lombard Street alderman of a courtier's civility at Locket's!

Pinch. But you are over-kind to me, as kind as if I were your cuckold already; yet I must confess you ought to be kind and civil to me, since I am so kind, so civil to you, as to bring you this: look you there, sir. [*Delivers him a letter.*

Horn. What is't?

Pinch. Only a love-letter, sir.

Horn. From whom?—how! this is from your wife—hum—and hum—— [*Reads.*

Pinch. Even from my wife, sir: am I not wondrous kind and civil to you now too?—[*Aside.*] But you'll not think her so.

Horn. Ha! is this a trick of his or hers? [*Aside.*

Pinch. The gentleman's surprised I find.—What, you expected a kinder letter?

Horn. No faith, not I, how could I?

Pinch. Yes, yes, I'm sure you did. A man so well made as you are, must needs be disappointed, if the women declare not their passion at first sight or opportunity.

Horn. [*aside*]. But what should this mean? Stay, the post-script.—[*Reads aside.*] "Be sure you love me, whatsoever my husband says to the contrary, and let him not see this, lest he should come home and pinch me, or kill my squirrel."—It seems he knows not what the letter contains.

Pinch. Come, ne'er wonder at it so much.

Horn. Faith, I can't help it.

Pinch. Now, I think I have deserved your infinite friendship and kindness, and have showed myself sufficiently an obliging kind friend and husband; am I not so, to bring a letter from my wife to her gallant?

Horn. Ay, the devil take me, art thou, the most obliging, kind friend and husband in the world, ha! ha!

Pinch. Well, you may be merry, sir; but in short I must tell you, sir, my honour will suffer no jesting.

Horn. What dost thou mean?

Pinch. Does the letter want a comment? Then, know, sir, though I have been so civil a husband, as to bring you a letter from my wife, to let you kiss and court her to my face, I will not be a cuckold, sir, I will not.

Horn. Thou art mad with jealousy. I never saw thy wife in my life but at the play yesterday, and I know not if it were she or no. I court her, kiss her!

Pinch. I will not be a cuckold, I say; there will be danger in making me a cuckold.

Horn. Why, wert thou not well cured of thy last clap?

Pinch. I wear a sword.

Horn. It should be taken from thee, lest thou shouldst do thyself a mischief with it; thou art mad, man.

Pinch. As mad as I am, and as merry as you are, I must have more reason from you ere we part. I say again, though you kissed and courted last night my wife in man's clothes, as she confesses in her letter——

Horn. Ha! [*Aside.*

Pinch. Both she and I say, you must not design it again, for you have mistaken your woman, as you have done your man.

Horn. [*aside*]. O—I understand something now—[*Aloud.*] Was that thy wife! Why wouldst thou not tell me 'twas she? Faith, my freedom with her was your fault, not mine.

Pinch. Faith, so 'twas. [*Aside.*

Horn. Fy! I'd never do't to a woman before her husband's face, sure.

Pinch. But I had rather you should do't to my wife before my face, than behind my back; and that you shall never do.

Horn. No—you will hinder me.

Pinch. If I would not hinder you, you see by her letter she would.

Horn. Well, I must e'en acquiesce then, and be contented with what she writes.

Pinch. I'll assure you 'twas voluntarily writ; I had no hand in't you may believe me.

Horn. I do believe thee, faith.

Pinch. And believe her too, for she's an innocent creature, has no dissembling in her: and so fare you well, sir.

Horn. Pray, however, present my humble service to her, and tell her, I will obey her letter to a tittle, and fulfil her desires, be what they will, or with what difficulty soever I do't; and you shall be no more jealous of me, I warrant her, and you.

Pinch. Well then, fare you well; and play with any man's honour but mine, kiss any man's wife but mine, and welcome.

[*Exit.*

Horn. Ha! ha! ha! doctor.

Quack. It seems, he has not heard the report of you, or does not believe it.

Horn. Ha! ha!—now, doctor, what think you?

Quack. Pray let's see the letter—hum—" for—dear—love you——" [*Reads the letter.*

Horn. I wonder how she could contrive it! What say'st thou to't? 'tis an original.

Quack. So are your cuckolds too originals: for they are like no other common cuckolds, and I will henceforth believe it not impossible for you to cuckold the Grand Signior amidst his guards of eunuchs, that I say.

Horn. And I say for the letter, 'tis the first love-letter that ever was without flames, darts, fates, destinies, lying and dissembling in't.

Enter SPARKISH *pulling in* PINCHWIFE.

Spark. Come back, you are a pretty brother-in-law, neither go to church nor to dinner with your sister bride!

Pinch. My sister denies her marriage, and you see is gone away from you dissatisfied.

Spark. Pshaw! upon a foolish scruple, that our parson was not in lawful orders, and did not say all the common-prayer; but 'tis her modesty only I believe. But let all women be never so modest the first day, they'll be sure to come to themselves by night, and I shall have enough of her then. In the meantime, Harry Horner, you must dine with me: I keep my wedding at my aunt's in the Piazza.

Horn. Thy wedding! what stale maid has lived to despair of a husband, or what young one of a gallant?

Spark. O, your servant, sir—this gentleman's sister then,—no stale maid.

Horn. I'm sorry for't.

Pinch. How comes he so concerned for her?   [*Aside.*

Spark. You sorry for't? why, do you know any ill by her?

Horn. No, I know none but by thee; 'tis for her sake, not yours, and another man's sake that might have hoped, I thought.

Spark. Another man! another man! what is his name?

Horn. Nay, since 'tis past, he shall be nameless.—[*Aside.*] Poor Harcourt! I am sorry thou hast missed her.

Pinch. He seems to be much troubled at the match.   [*Aside.*

Spark. Prithee, tell me—Nay, you shan't go, brother.

Pinch. I must of necessity, but I'll come to you to dinner.
           [*Exit.*

Spark. But, Harry, what, have I a rival in my wife already? But with all my heart, for he may be of use to me hereafter; for though my hunger is now my sauce, and I can fall on heartily without, the time will come when a rival will be as good sauce for a married man to a wife, as an orange to veal.

Horn. O thou damned rogue! thou hast set my teeth on edge with thy orange.

Spark. Then let's to dinner—there I was with you again. Come.

Horn. But who dines with thee?

Spark. My friends and relations, my brother Pinchwife, you see, of your acquaintance.

Horn. And his wife?

Spark. No, 'gad, he'll ne'er let her come amongst us good fellows; your stingy country coxcomb keeps his wife from his friends, as he does his little firkin of ale, for his own drinking, and a gentleman can't get a smack on't; but his servants, when his back is turned, broach it at their pleasures, and dust it away, ha! ha! ha!—'Gad, I am witty, I think, considering I was married to-day, by the world; but come——

Horn. No, I will not dine with you, unless you can fetch her too.

Spark. Pshaw! what pleasure canst thou have with women now, Harry?

Horn. My eyes are not gone; I love a good prospect yet, and will not dine with you unless she does too; go fetch her, therefore, but do not tell her husband 'tis for my sake.

Spark. Well, I'll go try what I can do; in the meantime, come away to my aunt's lodging, 'tis in the way to Pinchwife's.

Horn. The poor woman has called for aid, and stretched forth her hand, doctor; I cannot but help her over the pale out of the briars. [*Exeunt.*

SCENE IV.—*A Room in* PINCHWIFE'S *House*

MRS. PINCHWIFE *alone, leaning on her elbow.—A table, pen, ink, and paper.*

Mrs. Pinch. Well, 'tis e'en so, I have got the London disease they call love; I am sick of my husband, and for my gallant. I have heard this distemper called a fever, but methinks 'tis like an ague; for when I think of my husband, I tremble, and am in a cold sweat, and have inclinations to vomit; but when I think of my gallant, dear Mr. Horner, my hot fit comes, and I am all in a fever indeed; and, as in other fevers, my own chamber is tedious to me, and I would fain be removed to his, and then methinks I should be well. Ah, poor Mr. Horner! Well, I cannot, will not stay here; therefore I'll make an end of my letter to him, which shall be a finer letter than my last, because I have studied it like anything. Oh sick, sick!

[*Takes the pen and writes.*

Enter PINCHWIFE, *who seeing her writing, steals softly behind her and looking over her shoulder, snatches the paper from her.*

Pinch. What, writing more letters?

Mrs. Pinch. O Lord, bud, why d'ye fright me so?

[*She offers to run out; he stops her, and reads.*

Pinch. How's this? nay, you shall not stir, madam:—"Dear, dear, dear Mr. Horner"—very well—I have taught you to write letters to good purpose—but let us see't. "First, I am to beg your pardon for my boldness in writing to you, which I'd have you to know I would not have done, had not you said first you loved me so extremely, which if you do, you will never suffer me to lie in the arms of another man whom I loathe, nauseate, and detest."—Now you can write these filthy words. But what follows?—"Therefore, I hope you will speedily find some way to free me from this unfortunate match, which was never, I assure you, of my choice, but I'm afraid 'tis already too far gone; however, if you love me, as I do you, you will try what you can do; but you must help me away before to-morrow, or else, alas! I shall be for ever out of your reach, for I can defer no longer our— our——" what is to follow "our"?—speak, what—our journey into the country I suppose—Oh woman, damned woman! and Love, damned Love, their old tempter! for this is one of his miracles; in a moment he can make those blind that could see, and those see that were blind, those dumb that could speak, and those prattle who were dumb before; nay, what is more than all, make these dough-baked, senseless, indocile animals, women, too hard for us their politic lords and rulers, in a moment. But make an end of your letter, and then I'll make an end of you thus, and all my plagues together.　　　　　[*Draws his sword.*

Mrs. Pinch. O Lord, O Lord, you are such a passionate man, bud!

Enter SPARKISH.

Spark. How now, what's here to do?

Pinch. This fool here now!

Spark. What! drawn upon your wife? You should never do that, but at night in the dark, when you can't hurt her. This is my sister-in-law, is it not? ay, faith, e'en our country Margery [*pulls aside her handkerchief*]; one may know her. Come, she and you must go dine with me; dinner's ready, come. But where's my wife? is she not come home yet? where is she?

Pinch. Making you a cuckold; 'tis that they all do, as soon as they can.

Spark. What, the wedding-day? no, a wife that designs to make a cully of her husband will be sure to let him win the first stake of love, by the world. But come, they stay dinner for us: come, I'll lead down our Margery.

Pinch. No—sir, go, we'll follow you.

Spark. I will not wag without you.

Pinch. This coxcomb is a sensible torment to me amidst the greatest in the world.　　　　　　　　　　　　　[*Aside.*

Spark. Come, come, Madam Margery.

Pinch. No; I'll lead her my way: what, would you treat your friends with mine, for want of your own wife?—[*Leads her to the other door, and locks her in and returns.*] I am contented my rage should take breath——　　　　　　　　　　　　[*Aside.*

Spark. I told Horner this.

Pinch. Come now.

Spark. Lord, how shy you are of your wife! but let me tell you, brother, we men of wit have amongst us a saying, that cuckolding, like the small-pox, comes with a fear; and you may keep your wife as much as you will out of danger of infection, but if her constitution incline her to't, she'll have it sooner or later, by the world, say they.

Pinch. [*aside*]. What a thing is a cuckold, that every fool can make him ridiculous!—[*Aloud.*] Well, sir—but let me advise you, now you are come to be concerned, because you suspect the danger, not to neglect the means to prevent it, especially when the greatest share of the malady will light upon your own head, for

> Hows'e'er the kind wife's belly comes to swell,
> The husband breeds for her, and first is ill.

[*Exeunt.*

ACT V

SCENE I.—PINCHWIFE's *House*

Enter PINCHWIFE *and* Mrs. PINCHWIFE.   *A table and candle.*

Pinch. Come, take the pen and make an end of the letter, just as you intended; if you are false in a tittle, I shall soon perceive it, and punish you as you deserve.—[*Lays his hand on his sword.*] Write what was to follow—let's see—" You must make haste, and help me away before to-morrow, or else I shall be for ever out of your reach, for I can defer no longer our "—What follows " our " ?

Mrs. Pinch. Must all out, then, bud?—Look you there, then.
                    [Mrs. PINCHWIFE *takes the pen and writes.*

Pinch. Let's see—" For I can defer no longer our—wedding— Your slighted Alithea."—What's the meaning of this? my sister's name to't? speak, unriddle.

Mrs. Pinch. Yes, indeed, bud.

Pinch. But why her name to't? speak—speak, I say.

Mrs. Pinch. Ay, but you'll tell her then again.   If you would not tell her again——

Pinch. I will not:—I am stunned, my head turns round.— Speak.

Mrs. Pinch. Won't you tell her, indeed, and indeed?

Pinch. No; speak, I say.

Mrs. Pinch. She'll be angry with me; but I had rather she should be angry with me than you, bud; and, to tell you the truth, 'twas she made me write the letter; and taught me what I should write.

Pinch. [aside]. Ha! I thought the style was somewhat better than her own.—[*Aloud.*] Could she come to you to teach you, since I had locked you up alone?

Mrs. Pinch. O, through the key-hole, bud.

Pinch. But why should she make you write a letter for her to him, since she can write herself?

Mrs. Pinch. Why, she said because—for I was unwilling to do it——

Pinch. Because what—because?

Mrs. Pinch. Because, lest Mr. Horner should be cruel, and refuse her; or be vain afterwards, and show the letter, she might disown it, the hand not being hers.

Pinch. [aside]. How's this? Ha!—then I think I shall come to myself again.—This changeling could not invent this lie: but if she could, why should she? she might think I should soon discover it.—Stay—now I think on't too, Horner said he was sorry she had married Sparkish; and her disowning her marriage to me makes me think she has evaded it for Horner's sake: yet why should she take this course? But men in love are fools; women may well be so—[*aloud.*] But hark you, madam, your sister went out in the morning, and I have not seen her within since.

Mrs. Pinch. Alack-a-day, she has been crying all day above, it seems, in a corner.

Pinch. Where is she? let me speak with her.

Mrs. Pinch. [aside]. O Lord, then she'll discover all!—[*Aloud.*] Pray hold, bud; what, d'ye mean to discover me? she'll know I have told you then. Pray, bud, let me talk with her first.

Pinch. I must speak with her, to know whether Horner ever made her any promise, and whether she be married to Sparkish or no.

Mrs. Pinch. Pray, dear bud, don't, till I have spoken with her, and told her that I have told you all; for she'll kill me else.

Pinch. Go then, and bid her come out to me.

Mrs. Pinch. Yes, yes, bud.

Pinch. Let me see——   [*Pausing.*

Mrs. Pinch. [aside]. I'll go, but she is not within to come to him: I have just got time to know of Lucy her maid, who first set me on work, what lie I shall tell next; for I am e'en at my wit's end.   [*Exit.*

Pinch. Well, I resolve it, Horner shall have her: I'd rather give him my sister than lend him my wife; and such an alliance will prevent his pretensions to my wife, sure. I'll make him of kin to her, and then he won't care for her.

Re-enter Mrs. PINCHWIFE.

Mrs. Pinch. O Lord, bud! I told you what anger you would make me with my sister.

Pinch. Won't she come hither?

Mrs. Pinch. No, no. Lack-a-day, she's ashamed to look you in the face: and she says, if you go in to her, she'll run away downstairs, and shamefully go herself to Mr. Horner, who has promised her marriage, she says; and she will have no other, so she won't.

Pinch. Did he so?—promise her marriage!—then she shall have no other. Go tell her so; and if she will come and discourse with me a little concerning the means, I will about it immediately. Go.—[*Exit* Mrs. PINCHWIFE.] His estate is equal to Sparkish's, and his extraction as much better than his, as his parts are; but my chief reason is, I'd rather be akin to him by the name of brother-in-law than that of cuckold.

Re-enter Mrs. PINCHWIFE.

Well, what says she now?

Mrs. Pinch. Why, she says, she would only have you lead her to Horner's lodging; with whom she first will discourse the matter before she talks with you, which yet she cannot do; for alack, poor creature, she says she can't so much as look you in the face, therefore she'll come to you in a mask. And you must excuse her, if she make you no answer to any question of yours, till you have brought her to Mr. Horner; and if you will not chide her, nor question her, she'll come out to you immediately.

Pinch. Let her come: I will not speak a word to her, nor require a word from her.

Mrs. Pinch. Oh, I forgot: besides, she says she cannot look you in the face, though through a mask; therefore would desire you to put out the candle.

Pinch. I agree to all. Let her make haste.—There, 'tis out.— [*Puts out the candle. Exit* Mrs. PINCHWIFE.] My case is something better: I'd rather fight with Horner for not lying with my sister, than for lying with my wife; and of the two, I had rather find my sister too forward than my wife. I expected no other from her free education, as she calls it, and her passion for the town. Well, wife and sister are names which make us expect love and duty, pleasure and comfort; but we find 'em plagues and torments, and are equally, though differently, troublesome to their keeper; for we have as much ado to get people to lie with our sisters as to keep 'em from lying with our wives.

Re-enter Mrs. PINCHWIFE *masked, and in hoods and scarfs, and a night-gown and petticoat of* ALITHEA'S.

What, are you come, sister? let us go then.—But first, let me lock up my wife. Mrs. Margery, where are you?

Mrs. Pinch. Here, bud.

Pinch. Come hither, that I may lock you up: get you in.—
[*Locks the door.*]　Come, sister, where are you now?

　　　[Mrs. PINCHWIFE *gives him her hand; but when he lets her*
　　　　go, she steals softly on to the other side of him, and is led
　　　　away by him for his Sister, ALITHEA.

SCENE II.—HORNER's *Lodging*

HORNER *and* QUACK.

Quack. What, all alone? not so much as one of your cuckolds
here, nor one of their wives! They use to take their turns with
you, as if they were to watch you.

Horn. Yes, it often happens that a cuckold is but his wife's
spy, and is more upon family duty when he is with her gallant
abroad, hindering his pleasure, than when he is at home with
her playing the gallant. But the hardest duty a married woman
imposes upon a lover is keeping her husband company always.

Quack. And his fondness wearies you almost as soon as hers.

Horn. A pox! keeping a cuckold company, after you have
had his wife, is as tiresome as the company of a country squire to
a witty fellow of the town, when he has got all his money.

Quack. And as at first a man makes a friend of the husband to
get the wife, so at last you are fain to fall out with the wife to
be rid of the husband.

Horn. Ay, most cuckold-makers are true courtiers; when once
a poor man has cracked his credit for 'em, they can't abide to
come near him.

Quack. But at first, to draw him in, are so sweet, so kind, so
dear! just as you are to Pinchwife. But what becomes of that
intrigue with his wife?

Horn. A pox! he's as surly as an alderman that has been bit;
and since he's so coy, his wife's kindness is in vain, for she's a
silly innocent.

Quack. Did she not send you a letter by him?

Horn. Yes; but that's a riddle I have not yet solved. Allow
the poor creature to be willing, she is silly too, and he keeps her
up so close——

Quack. Yes, so close, that he makes her but the more willing,
and adds but revenge to her love; which two, when met, seldom
fail of satisfying each other one way or other.

Horn. What! here's the man we are talking of, I think.

　　　Enter PINCHWIFE, *leading in his* Wife *masked, muffled,*
　　　　and in her Sister's *gown.*

Pshaw!

Quack. Bringing his wife to you is the next thing to bringing
a love-letter from her.

Horn. What means this?

Pinch. The last time, you know, sir, I brought you a love-letter; now, you see, a mistress; I think you'll say I am a civil man to you.

Horn. Ay, the devil take me, will I say thou art the civilest man I ever met with; and I have known some. I fancy I understand thee now better than I did the letter. But, hark thee, in thy ear——

Pinch. What?

Horn. Nothing but the usual question, man: is she sound, on thy word?

Pinch. What, you take her for a wench, and me for a pimp?

Horn. Pshaw! wench and pimp, paw words; I know thou art an honest fellow, and hast a great acquaintance among the ladies, and perhaps hast made love for me, rather than let me make love to thy wife.

Pinch. Come, sir, in short, I am for no fooling.

Horn. Nor I neither: therefore prithee, let's see her face presently. Make her show, man: art thou sure I don't know her?

Pinch. I am sure you do know her.

Horn. A pox! why dost thou bring her to me then?

Pinch. Because she's a relation of mine——

Horn. Is she, faith, man? then thou art still more civil and obliging, dear rogue.

Pinch. Who desired me to bring her to you.

Horn. Then she is obliging, dear rogue.

Pinch. You'll make her welcome for my sake, I hope.

Horn. I hope she is handsome enough to make herself welcome. Prithee let her unmask.

Pinch. Do you speak to her; she would never be ruled by me.

Horn. Madam—— [Mrs. PINCHWIFE *whispers to* HORNER.] She says she must speak with me in private. Withdraw, prithee.

Pinch. [*aside*]. She's unwilling, it seems, I should know all her indecent conduct in this business.—[*Aloud.*] Well then, I'll leave you together, and hope when I am gone, you'll agree; if not, you and I shan't agree, sir.

Horn. What means the fool? if she and I agree 'tis no matter what you and I do.

[*Whispers to* Mrs. PINCHWIFE, *who makes signs with her hand for him to be gone.*

Pinch. In the meantime I'll fetch a parson, and find out Sparkish, and disabuse him. You would have me fetch a parson, would you not? Well then—now I think I am rid of her, and shall have no more trouble with her—our sisters and daughters, like usurers' money, are safest when put out; but our wives, like their writings, never safe, but in our closets under lock and key.

[*Exit.*

Enter Boy.

Boy. Sir Jasper Fidget, sir, is coming up.   [*Exit.*
Horn. Here's the trouble of a cuckold now we are talking of.
A pox on him! has he not enough to do to hinder his wife's sport,
but he must other women's too?—Step in here, madam.
                    [*Exit* Mrs. PINCHWIFE.

Enter Sir JASPER FIDGET.

Sir Jasp. My best and dearest friend.
Horn. [*aside to* Quack]. The old style, doctor.—[*Aloud.*] Well,
be short, for I am busy. What would your impertinent wife
have now?
Sir Jasp. Well guessed, i'faith; for I do come from her.
Horn. To invite me to supper! Tell her, I can't come: go.
Sir Jasp. Nay, now you are out, faith; for my lady, and the
whole knot of the virtuous gang, as they call themselves, are
resolved upon a frolic of coming to you to-night in masquerade,
and are all dressed already.
Horn. I shan't be at home.
Sir Jasp. [*aside*]. Lord, how churlish he is to women!—
[*Aloud.*] Nay, prithee don't disappoint 'em; they'll think 'tis
my fault: prithee don't. I'll send in the banquet and the
fiddles. But make no noise on't; for the poor virtuous rogues
would not have it known, for the world, that they go a-masquerad-
ing; and they would come to no man's ball but yours.
Horn. Well, well—get you gone; and tell 'em, if they come,
'will be at the peril of their honour and yours.
Sir Jasp. He! he! he!—we'll trust you for that: farewell.
                    [*Exit.*

Horn. Doctor, anon you too shall be my guest,
    But now I'm going to a private feast.   [*Exeunt.*

SCENE III.—*The Piazza of Covent Garden*

Enter SPARKISH *with a letter in his hand,* PINCHWIFE *following.*

Spark. But who would have thought a woman could have
been false to me? By the world, I could not have thought it.
Pinch. You were for giving and taking liberty: she has taken
it only, sir, now you find in that letter. You are a frank person,
and so is she, you see there.
Spark. Nay, if this be her hand—for I never saw it.
Pinch. 'Tis no matter whether that be her hand or no; I am
sure this hand, at her desire, led her to Mr. Horner, with whom
I left her just now, to go fetch a parson to 'em at their desire too,

to deprive you of her for ever; for it seems yours was but a mock marriage.

Spark. Indeed, she would needs have it that 'twas Harcourt himself, in a parson's habit, that married us; but I'm sure he told me 'twas his brother Ned.

Pinch. O, there 'tis out; and you were deceived, not she: for you are such a frank person. But I must be gone.—You'll find her at Mr. Horner's. Go, and believe your eyes. [*Exit.*

Spark. Nay, I'll to her, and call her as many crocodiles, sirens, harpies, and other heathenish names, as a poet would do a mistress who had refused to hear his suit, nay more, his verses on her.—But stay, is not that she following a torch at t'other end of the Piazza? and from Horner's certainly—'tis so.

Enter ALITHEA *following a torch, and* LUCY *behind.*

You are well met, madam, though you don't think so. What‧ you have made a short visit to Mr. Horner? but I suppose you'll return to him presently, by that time the parson can be with him.

Alith. Mr. Horner and the parson, sir!

Spark. Come, madam, no more dissembling, no more jilting; for I am no more a frank person.

Alith. How's this?

Lucy. So, 'twill work, I see. [*Aside.*

Spark. Could you find out no easy country fool to abuse? none but me, a gentleman of wit and pleasure about the town? But it was your pride to be too hard for a man of parts, unworthy false woman! false as a friend that lends a man money to lose; false as dice, who undo those that trust all they have to 'em.

Lucy. He has been a great bubble, by his similes, as they say. [*Aside.*

Alith. You have been too merry, sir, at your wedding-dinner, sure.

Spark. What, d'ye mock me too?

Alith. Or you have been deluded.

Spark. By you.

Alith. Let me understand you.

Spark. Have you the confidence (I should call it something else, since you know your guilt) to stand my just reproaches? you did not write an impudent letter to Mr. Horner? who I find now has clubbed with you in deluding me with his aversion for women, that I might not, forsooth, suspect him for my rival.

Lucy. D'ye think the gentleman can be jealous now, madam? [*Aside.*

Alith. I write a letter to Mr. Horner!

Spark. Nay, madam, do not deny it. Your brother showed it me just now; and told me likewise, he left you at Horner's lodging to fetch a parson to marry you to him: and I wish you joy, madam, joy, joy; and to him too, much joy; and to myself more joy, for not marrying you.

Alith. [*aside*]. So, I find my brother would break off the match; and I can consent to't, since I see this gentleman can be made jealous.—[*Aloud.*] O Lucy, by his rude usage and jealousy, he makes me almost afraid I am married to him. Art thou sure 'twas Harcourt himself, and no parson, that married us?

Spark. No, madam, I thank you. I suppose, that was a contrivance too of Mr. Horner's and yours, to make Harcourt play the parson; but I would as little as you have him one now, no, not for the world. For, shall I tell you another truth? I never had any passion for you till now, for now I hate you. 'Tis true, I might have married your portion, as other men of parts of the town do sometimes: and so, your servant. And to show my unconcernedness, I'll come to your wedding, and resign you with as much joy, as I would a stale wench to a new cully; nay, with as much joy as I would after the first night, if I had been married to you. There's for you; and so your servant, servant.   [*Exit.*

Alith. How was I deceived in a man!

Lucy. You'll believe then a fool may be made jealous now? for that easiness in him that suffers him to be led by a wife, will likewise permit him to be persuaded against her by others.

Alith. But marry Mr. Horner! my brother does not intend it, sure: if I thought he did, I would take thy advice, and Mr. Harcourt for my husband. And now I wish, that if there be any over-wise woman of the town, who, like me, would marry a fool for fortune, liberty, or title, first, that her husband may love play, and be a cully to all the town but her, and suffer none but Fortune to be mistress of his purse; then, if for liberty, that he may send her into the country, under the conduct of some huswifely mother-in-law; and if for title, may the world give 'em none but that of cuckold.

Lucy. And for her greater curse, madam, may he not deserve it.

Alith. Away, impertinent! Is not this my old Lady Lanterlu's?

Lucy. Yes, madam.—[*Aside.*] And here I hope we shall find Mr. Harcourt.   [*Exeunt.*

SCENE IV.—HORNER's *Lodging.   A table, banquet, and bottles*

Enter HORNER, Lady FIDGET, Mrs. DAINTY FIDGET, *and* Mrs SQUEAMISH.

Horn. A pox! they are come too soon—before I have sent back my new mistress. All that I have now to do is to lock her in, that they may not see her.   [*Aside.*

Lady Fid. That we may be sure of our welcome, we have brought our entertainment with us, and are resolved to treat thee, dear toad.

Mrs. Dain. And that we may be merry to purpose, have left

Sir Jasper and my old Lady Squeamish quarrelling at home at backgammon.

Mrs. Squeam. Therefore let us make use of our time, lest they should chance to interrupt us.

Lady Fid. Let us sit then.

Horn. First, that you may be private, let me lock this door and that, and I'll wait upon you presently.

Lady Fid. No, sir, shut 'em only, and your lips for ever; for we must trust you as much as our women.

Horn. You know all vanity's killed in me; I have no occasion for talking.

Lady Fid. Now, ladies, supposing we had drank each of us two bottles, let us speak the truth of our hearts.

Mrs. Dain. and Mrs. Squeam. Agreed.

Lady Fid. By this brimmer, for truth is nowhere else to be found—[*aside to Horner*] not in thy heart, false man!

Horn. You have found me a true man, I'm sure.

[*Aside to* Lady FIDGET.

Lady Fid. [*aside to* HORNER]. Not every way.—But let us sit and be merry. [*Sings.*

> Why should our damned tyrants oblige us to live
> On the pittance of pleasure which they only give?
>> We must not rejoice
>> With wine and with noise:
> In vain we must wake in a dull bed alone,
> Whilst to our warm rival the bottle they're gone.
>> Then lay aside charms,
>> And take up these arms.
> 'Tis wine only gives 'em their courage and wit;
> Because we live sober, to men we submit.
>> If for beauties you'd pass,
>> Take a lick of the glass,
> 'Twill mend your complexions, and when they are gone,
> The best red we have is the red of the grape:
> Then, sisters, lay't on,
>> And damn a good shape.

Mrs. Dain. Dear brimmer! Well, in token of our openness and plain-dealing, let us throw our masks over our heads.

Horn. So, 'twill come to the glasses anon. [*Aside.*

Mrs. Squeam. Lovely brimmer! let me enjoy him first.

Lady Fid. No, I never part with a gallant till I've tried him. Dear brimmer! that makest our husbands short-sighted.

Mrs. Dain. And our bashful gallants bold.

Mrs. Squeam. And, for want of a gallant, the butler lovely in our eyes.—Drink, eunuch.

Lady Fid. Drink, thou representative of a husband.—Damn a husband!

Mrs. Dain. And, as it were a husband, an old keeper.

Mrs. Squeam. And an old grandmother.

Horn. And an English bawd, and a French surgeon.

Lady Fid. Ay, we have all reason to curse 'em.

Horn. For my sake, ladies?

Lady Fid. No, for our own; for the first spoils all young gallants' industry.

Mrs. Dain. And the other's art makes 'em bold only with common women.

Mrs. Squeam. And rather run the hazard of the vile distemper amongst them, than of a denial amongst us.

Mrs. Dain. The filthy toads choose mistresses now as they do stuffs, for having been fancied and worn by others.

Mrs. Squeam. For being common and cheap.

Lady Fid. Whilst women of quality, like the richest stuffs, lie untumbled, and unasked for.

Horn. Ay, neat, and cheap, and new, often they think best.

Mrs. Dain. No, sir, the beasts will be known by a mistress longer than by a suit.

Mrs. Squeam. And 'tis not for cheapness neither.

Lady Fid. No; for the vain fops will take up druggets and embroider 'em. But I wonder at the depraved appetites of witty men; they use to be out of the common road, and hate imitation. Pray tell me, beast, when you were a man, why you rather chose to club with a multitude in a common house for an entertainment, than to be the only guest at a good table.

Horn. Why, faith, ceremony and expectation are unsufferable to those that are sharp bent. People always eat with the best stomach at an ordinary, where every man is snatching for the best bit.

Lady Fid. Though he get a cut over the fingers.—But I have heard, that people eat most heartily of another man's meat, that is, what they do not pay for.

Horn. When they are sure of their welcome and freedom; for ceremony in love and eating is as ridiculous as in fighting: falling on briskly is all should be done on those occasions.

Lady Fid. Well then, let me tell you, sir, there is nowhere more freedom than in our houses; and we take freedom from a young person as a sign of good breeding; and a person may be as free as he pleases with us, as frolic, as gamesome, as wild as he will.

Horn. Han't I heard you all declaim against wild men?

Lady Fid. Yes; but for all that, we think wildness in a man as desirable a quality as in a duck or rabbit: a tame man! foh!

Horn. I know not, but your reputations frightened me as much as your faces invited me.

Lady Fid. Our reputation! Lord, why should you not think that we women make use of our reputation, as you men of yours, only to deceive the world with less suspicion? Our virtue is like the statesman's religion, the quaker's word, the gamester's oath, and the great man's honour; but to cheat those that trust us.

Mrs. Squeam. And that demureness, coyness, and modesty, that you see in our faces in the boxes at plays, is as much a sign of a kind woman, as a vizard-mask in the pit.

Mrs. Dain. For, I assure you, women are least masked when they have the velvet vizard on.

Lady Fid. You would have found us modest women in our denials only.

Mrs. Squeam. Our bashfulness is only the reflection of the men's.

Mrs. Dain. We blush when they are shamefaced.

Horn. I beg your pardon, ladies, I was deceived in you devilishly.   But why that mighty pretence to honour?

Lady Fid. We have told you; but sometimes 'twas for the same reason you men pretend business often, to avoid ill company, to enjoy the better and more privately those you love.

Horn. But why would you ne'er give a friend a wink then?

Lady Fid. Faith, your reputation frightened us, as much as ours did you, you were so notoriously lewd.

Horn. And you so seemingly honest.

Lady Fid. Was that all that deterred you?

Horn. And so expensive—you allow freedom, you say.

Lady Fid. Ay, ay.

Horn. That I was afraid of losing my little money, as well as my little time, both which my other pleasures required.

Lady Fid. Money! foh! you talk like a little fellow now: do such as we expect money?

Horn. I beg your pardon, madam, I must confess, I have heard that great ladies, like great merchants, set but the higher prices upon what they have, because they are not in necessity of taking the first offer.

Mrs. Dain. Such as we make sale of our hearts?

Mrs. Squeam. We bribed for our love? foh!

Horn. With your pardon, ladies, I know, like great men in offices, you seem to exact flattery and attendance only from your followers; but you have receivers about you, and such fees to pay, a man is afraid to pass your grants. Besides, we must let you win at cards, or we lose your hearts; and if you make an assignation, 'tis at a goldsmith's, jeweller's, or china-house; where for your honour you deposit to him, he must pawn his to the punctual cit, and so paying for what you take up, pays for what he takes up.

Mrs. Dain. Would you not have us assured of our gallants' love?

Mrs. Squeam. For love is better known by liberality than by jealousy.

Lady Fid. For one may be dissembled, the other not.—[*Aside.*]

But my jealousy can be no longer dissembled, and they are telling ripe.—[*Aloud.*]—Come, here's to our gallants in waiting, whom we must name, and I'll begin.   This is my false rogue.

[*Claps him on the back.*

Mrs. Squeam. How!

Horn. So, all will out now.   [*Aside.*

Mrs. Squeam. Did you not tell me, 'twas for my sake only you reported yourself no man?   [*Aside to* HORNER.

Mrs. Dain. Oh, wretch! did you not swear to me, 'twas for my love and honour you passed for that thing you do?

[*Aside to* HORNER.

Horn. So, so.

Lady Fid. Come, speak, ladies: this is my false villain.

Mrs. Squeam. And mine too.

Mrs. Dain. And mine.

Horn. Well then, you are all three my false rogues too, and there's an end on't.

Lady Fid. Well then, there's no remedy; sister sharers, let us not fall out, but have a care of our honour.   Though we get no presents, no jewels of him, we are savers of our honour, the jewel of most value and use, which shines yet to the world unsuspected, though it be counterfeit.

Horn. Nay, and is e'en as good as if it were true, provided the world think so; for honour, like beauty now, only depends on the opinion of others.

Lady Fid. Well, Harry Common, I hope you can be true to three.   Swear; but 'tis to no purpose to require your oath, for you are as often forsworn as you swear to new women.

Horn. Come, faith, madam, let us e'en pardon one another; for all the difference I find betwixt we men and you women, we forswear ourselves at the beginning of an amour, you as long as it lasts.

Enter Sir JASPER FIDGET, *and* Old Lady SQUEAMISH.

Sir Jasp. Oh, my Lady Fidget, was this your cunning, to come to Mr. Horner without me? but you have been nowhere else, I hope.

Lady Fid. No, Sir Jasper.

Lady Squeam. And you came straight hither, Biddy?

Mrs. Squeam. Yes, indeed, lady grandmother.

Sir Jasp. 'Tis well, 'tis well; I knew when once they were thoroughly acquainted with poor Horner, they'd ne'er be from him: you may let her masquerade it with my wife and Horner, and I warrant her reputation safe.

Enter Boy.

Boy. O, sir, here's the gentleman come, whom you bid me not suffer to come up, without giving you notice, with a lady too, and other gentlemen.

Horn. Do you all go in there, whilst I send 'em away; and, boy, do you desire 'em to stay below till I come, which shall be immediately.

[*Exeunt* Sir JASPER FIDGET, Lady FIDGET, Lady SQUEAMISH, Mrs. SQUEAMISH, *and* Mrs. DAINTY FIDGET.

Boy. Yes, sir.   [*Exit.*

[*Exit* HORNER *at the other door, and returns with* Mrs. PINCHWIFE.

Horn. You would not take my advice, to be gone home before your husband came back, he'll now discover all; yet pray, my dearest, be persuaded to go home, and leave the rest to my management; I'll let you down the back way.

Mrs. Pinch. I don't know the way home, so I don't.

Horn. My man shall wait upon you.

Mrs. Pinch. No, don't you believe that I'll go at all; what, are you weary of me already?

Horn. No, my life, 'tis that I may love you long, 'tis to secure my love, and your reputation with your husband; he'll never receive you again else.

Mrs. Pinch. What care I? d'ye think to frighten me with that? I don't intend to go to him again; you shall be my husband now.

Horn. I cannot be your husband, dearest, since you are married to him.

Mrs. Pinch. O, would you make me believe that? Don't I see every day at London here, women leave their first husbands, and go and live with other men as their wives? pish, pshaw! you'd make me angry, but that I love you so mainly.

Horn. So, they are coming up—In again, in, I hear 'em.— [*Exit* Mrs. PINCHWIFE.] Well, a silly mistress is like a weak place, soon got, soon lost, a man has scarce time for plunder; she betrays her husband first to her gallant, and then her gallant to her husband.

Enter PINCHWIFE, ALITHEA, HARCOURT, SPARKISH, LUCY, *and a* Parson.

Pinch. Come, madam, 'tis not the sudden change of your dress, the confidence of your asseverations, and your false witness there, shall persuade me I did not bring you hither just now; here's my witness, who cannot deny it, since you must be confronted.—Mr. Horner, did not I bring this lady to you just now?

Horn. Now must I wrong one woman for another's sake,— but that's no new thing with me, for in these cases I am still on the criminal's side against the innocent.   [*Aside.*

Alith. Pray speak, sir.

Horn. It must be so. I must be impudent, and try my luck; impudence uses to be too hard for truth.   [*Aside.*

Pinch. What, you are studying an evasion or excuse for her! Speak, sir.

Horn. No, faith, I am something backward only to speak in women's affairs or disputes.

Pinch. She bids you speak.

Alith. Ah, pray, sir, do, pray satisfy him.

Horn. Then truly, you did bring that lady to me just now.

Pinch. O ho!

Alith. How, sir?

Har. How, Horner?

Alith. What mean you, sir? I always took you for a man of honour.

Horn. Ay, so much a man of honour, that I must save my mistress, I thank you, come what will on't.   [*Aside.*

Spark. So, if I had had her, she'd have made me believe the moon had been made of a Christmas pie.

Lucy. Now could I speak, if I durst, and solve the riddle, who am the author of it.   [*Aside.*

Alith. O unfortunate woman! A combination against my honour! which most concerns me now, because you share in my disgrace, sir, and it is your censure, which I must now suffer, that troubles me, not theirs.

Har. Madam, then have no trouble, you shall now see 'tis possible for me to love too, without being jealous; I will not only believe your innocence myself, but make all the world believe it.—[*Aside to* HORNER.] Horner, I must now be concerned for this lady's honour.

Horn. And I must be concerned for a lady's honour too.

Har. This lady has her honour, and I will protect it.

Horn. My lady has not her honour, but has given it me to keep, and I will preserve it.

Har. I understand you not.

Horn. I would not have you.

Mrs. Pinch. What's the matter with 'em all?

                     [*Peeping in behind.*

Pinch. Come, come, Mr. Horner, no more disputing; here's the parson, I brought him not in vain.

Har. No, sir, I'll employ him, if this lady please.

Pinch. How! what d'ye mean?

Spark. Ay, what does he mean?

Horn. Why, I have resigned your sister to him, he has my consent.

Pinch. But he has not mine, sir; a woman's injured honour, no more than a man's, can be repaired or satisfied by any but him that first wronged it; and you shall marry her presently, or——

                     [*Lays his hand on his sword.*

Re-enter Mrs. PINCHWIFE.

Mrs. Pinch. O Lord, they'll kill poor Mr. Horner! besides, he shan't marry her whilst I stand by, and look on; I'll not lose my second husband so.

Pinch. What do I see?

Alith. My sister in my clothes!

Spark. Ha!

Mrs. Pinch. Nay, pray now don't quarrel about finding work for the parson, he shall marry me to Mr. Horner; or now, I believe, you have enough of me.   [*To* PINCHWIFE.

Horn. Damned, damned loving changeling!   [*Aside.*

Mrs. Pinch. Pray, sister, pardon me for telling so many lies of you.

Horn. I suppose the riddle is plain now.

Lucy. No, that must be my work.—Good sir, hear me.

    [*Kneels to* PINCHWIFE, *who stands doggedly with his hat over his eyes.*

Pinch. I will never hear woman again, but make 'em all silent thus——   [*Offers to draw upon his* Wife.

Horn. No, that must not be.

Pinch. You then shall go first, 'tis all one to me.

    [*Offers to draw on* HORNER, *but is stopped by* HARCOURT.

Har. Hold!

Re-enter Sir JASPER FIDGET, Lady FIDGET, Lady SQUEAMISH, Mrs. DAINTY FIDGET, *and* Mrs. SQUEAMISH.

Sir Jasp. What's the matter? what's the matter? pray, what's the matter, sir? I beseech you communicate, sir.

Pinch. Why, my wife has communicated, sir, as your wife may have done too, sir, if she knows him, sir.

Sir Jasp. Pshaw, with him! ha! ha! he!

Pinch. D'ye mock me, sir? a cuckold is a kind of a wild beast; have a care, sir.

Sir Jasp. No, sure, you mock me, sir. He cuckold you! it can't be, ha! ha! he! why, I'll tell you, sir——

     [*Offers to whisper.*

Pinch. I tell you again, he has whored my wife, and yours too, if he knows her, and all the women he comes near; 'tis not his dissembling, his hypocrisy, can wheedle me.

Sir Jasp. How! does he dissemble? is he a hypocrite? Nay, then—how—wife—sister, is he a hypocrite?

Lady Squeam. A hypocrite! a dissembler! Speak, young harlotry, speak, how?

Sir Jasp. Nay, then—O my head too!—O thou libidinous lady!

Lady Squeam. O thou harloting harlotry! hast thou done't then?

Sir Jasp. Speak, good Horner, art thou a dissembler, a rogue? hast thou——

Horn. So!

Lucy. I'll fetch you off, and her too, if she will but hold her tongue.   [*Apart to* HORNER.

Horn. Canst thou? I'll give thee——   [*Apart to* LUCY.

Lucy [*to* PINCHWIFE]. Pray have but patience to hear me, sir, who am the unfortunate cause of all this confusion. Your wife is innocent, I only culpable; for I put her upon telling you all these lies concerning my mistress, in order to the breaking off the match between Mr. Sparkish and her, to make way for Mr. Harcourt.

Spark. Did you so, eternal rotten tooth? Then, it seems, my mistress was not false to me, I was only deceived by you. Brother, that should have been, now man of conduct, who is a frank person now, to bring your wife to her lover, ha?

Lucy. I assure you, sir, she came not to Mr. Horner out of love, for she loves him no more——

Mrs. Pinch. Hold, I told lies for you, but you shall tell none for me, for I do love Mr. Horner with all my soul, and nobody shall say me nay; pray, don't you go to make poor Mr. Horner believe to the contrary; 'tis spitefully done of you, I'm sure.

Horn. Peace, dear idiot.   [*Aside to* Mrs. PINCHWIFE.

Mrs. Pinch. Nay, I will not peace.

Pinch. Not till I make you.

Enter DORILANT *and* Quack.

Dor. Horner, your servant; I am the doctor's guest, he must excuse our intrusion.

Quack. But what's the matter, gentlemen? for Heaven's sake, what's the matter?

Horn. Oh, 'tis well you are come. 'Tis a censorious world we live in; you may have brought me a reprieve, or else I had died for a crime I never committed, and these innocent ladies had suffered with me; therefore, pray satisfy these worthy, honourable, jealous gentlemen—that——   [*Whispers.*

Quack. O, I understand you, is that all?—Sir Jasper, by Heavens, and upon the word of a physician, sir——

    [*Whispers to* Sir JASPER.

Sir Jasp. Nay, I do believe you truly.—Pardon me, my virtuous lady, and dear of honour.

Lady Squeam. What, then all's right again?

Sir Jasp. Ay, ay, and now let us satisfy him too.

    [*They whisper with* PINCHWIFE.

Pinch. An eunuch! Pray, no fooling with me.

Quack. I'll bring half the chirurgeons in town to swear it.

Pinch. They!—they'll swear a man that bled to death through his wounds, died of an apoplexy.

Quack. Pray, hear me, sir—why, all the town has heard the report of him.

Pinch. But does all the town believe it?

Quack. Pray, inquire a little, and first of all these.

Pinch. I'm sure when I left the town, he was the lewdest fellow in't.

Quack. I tell you, sir, he has been in France since; pray, ask but these ladies and gentlemen, your friend Mr. Dorilant. Gentlemen and ladies, han't you all heard the late sad report of poor Mr. Horner?

All the Ladies. Ay, ay, ay.

Dor. Why, thou jealous fool, dost thou doubt it? he's an arrant French capon.

Mrs. Pinch. 'Tis false, sir, you shall not disparage poor Mr. Horner, for to my certain knowledge——

Lucy. O, hold!

Mrs. Squeam. Stop her mouth! [*Aside to* LUCY.

Lady Fid. Upon my honour, sir, 'tis as true——[*To* PINCHWIFE.

Mrs. Dain. D'ye think we would have been seen in his company?

Mrs. Squeam. Trust our unspotted reputations with him?

Lady Fid. This you get, and we too, by trusting your secret to a fool. [*Aside to* HORNER.

Horn. Peace, madam.—[*Aside to* Quack.] Well, doctor, is not this a good design, that carries a man on unsuspected, and brings him off safe?

Pinch. Well, if this were true—but my wife—— [*Aside.*

[DORILANT *whispers with* Mrs. PINCHWIFE.

Alith. Come, brother, your wife is yet innocent, you see; but have a care of too strong an imagination, lest, like an over-concerned timorous gamester, by fancying an unlucky cast, it should come. Women and fortune are truest still to those that trust 'em.

Lucy. And any wild thing grows but the more fierce and hungry for being kept up, and more dangerous to the keeper.

Alith. There's doctrine for all husbands, Mr. Harcourt.

Har. I edify, madam, so much, that I am impatient till I am one.

Dor. And I edify so much by example, I will never be one.

Spark. And because I will not disparage my parts, I'll ne'er be one.

Horn. And I, alas! can't be one.

Pinch. But I must be one—against my will to a country wife, with a country murrain to me!

Mrs. Pinch. And I must be a country wife still too, I find; for I can't, like a city one, be rid of my musty husband, and do what I list. [*Aside.*

Horn. Now, sir, I must pronounce your wife innocent, though I blush whilst I do it; and I am the only man by her now exposed to shame, which I will straight drown in wine, as you shall your suspicion; and the ladies' troubles we'll divert with a ballad.—Doctor, where are your maskers?

Lucy. Indeed, she's innocent, sir, I am her witness; and her end of coming out was but to see her sister's wedding; and what she has said to your face of her love to Mr. Horner, was but the usual innocent revenge on a husband's jealousy;—was it not, madam, speak?

Mrs. Pinch. [*aside to* LUCY *and* HORNER].   Since you'll have me tell more lies—[*Aloud.*]   Yes, indeed, bud.

Pinch. For my own sake fain I would all believe;
    Cuckolds, like lovers, should themselves deceive.
    But——   *Sighs.*
    His honour is least safe (too late I find)
    Who trusts it with a foolish wife or friend.

A Dance of Cuckolds.

Horn. Vain fops but court and dress, and keep a pother,
    To pass for women's men with one another;
    But he who aims by women to be prized,
    First by the men, you see, must be despised.   [*Exeunt.*

EPILOGUE

SPOKEN BY MRS. KNEP

Now you the vigorous, who daily here
O'er vizard-mask in public domineer,
And what you'd do to her, if in place where;
Nay, have the confidence to cry, " Come out! "
Yet when she says, " Lead on! " you are not stout;
But to your well-dressed brother straight turn round,
And cry, " Pox on her, Ned, she can't be sound! "
Then slink away, a fresh one to engage,
With so much seeming heat and loving rage,
You'd frighten listening actress on the stage;
Till she at last has seen you huffing come,
And talk of keeping in the tiring-room,
Yet cannot be provoked to lead her home.
Next, you Falstaffs of fifty, who beset
Your buckram maidenheads, which your friends get;
And whilst to them you of achievements boast,
They share the booty, and laugh at your cost.
In fine, you essenced boys, both old and young,
Who would be thought so eager, brisk, and strong,
Yet do the ladies, not their husbands wrong;
Whose purses for your manhood make excuse,
And keep your Flanders mares for show not use;
Encouraged by our woman's man to-day,
A Horner's part may vainly think to play;
And may intrigues so bashfully disown,
That they may doubted be by few or none;
May kiss the cards at picquet, ombre, loo,
And so be taught to kiss the lady too;
But, gallants, have a care, faith, what you do.
The world, which to no man his due will give,
You by experience know you can deceive,
And men may still believe you vigorous,
But then we women—there's no cozening us.

THE WAY OF THE WORLD

DRAMATIS PERSONÆ

FAINALL, in love with Mrs. Marwood . . Mr. BETTERTON.

MIRABELL, in love with Mrs. Millamant . . Mr. VERBRUGGEN.

WITWOUD } Followers of Mrs. Millamant . { Mr. BOWEN.
PETULANT } { Mr. BOWMAN.

Sir WILFULL WITWOUD, Half-brother to Witwoud, and Nephew to Lady Wishfort . . Mr. UNDERHILL.

WAITWELL, Servant to Mirabell . . . Mr. BRIGHT.

Lady WISHFORT, Enemy to Mirabell, for having
falsely pretended love to her . . . Mrs. LEIGH.

Mrs. MILLAMANT, a fine lady, Niece to Lady
Wishfort, and loves Mirabell . . . Mrs. BRACEGIRDLE.

Mrs. MARWOOD, Friend to Mr. Fainall, and likes
Mirabell . . . . Mrs. BARRY.

Mrs. FAINALL, Daughter to Lady Wishfort, and
wife to Fainall, formerly friend to Mirabell . Mrs. BOWMAN.

FOIBLE, Woman to Lady Wishfort . . . Mrs. WILLIS.

MINCING, Woman to Mrs. Millamant . . Mrs. PRINCE.

Dancers, Footmen, and Attendants.

SCENE—LONDON.

The time equal to that of the presentation.

RALPH, EARL OF MOUNTAGUE, &c.

My Lord,—Whether the world will arraign me of vanity, or not, that I have presumed to dedicate this comedy to your lordship, I am yet in doubt: though it may be it is some degree of vanity even to doubt of it. One who has at any time had the honour of your lordship's conversation, cannot be supposed to think very meanly of that which he would prefer to your perusal: yet it were to incur the imputation of too much sufficiency, to pretend to such a merit as might abide the test of your lordship's censure.

Whatever value may be wanting to this play while yet it is mine, will be sufficiently made up to it, when it is once become your lordship's; and it is my security, that I cannot have over-rated it more by my dedication, than your lordship will dignifie it by your patronage.

That it succeeded on the stage, was almost beyond my expectation; for but little of it was prepared for that general taste which seems now to be predominant in the pallats of our audience.

Those characters which are meant to be ridiculed in most of our comedies, are of fools so gross, that in my humble opinion, they should rather disturb than divert the well-natured and reflecting part of an audience; they are rather objects of charity than contempt; and instead of moving our mirth, they ought very often to excite our compassion.

This reflection moved me to design some characters, which should appear ridiculous not so much through a natural folly (which is incorrigible, and therefore not proper for the stage) as through an affected wit; a wit, which at the same time that it is affected, is also false. As there is some difficulty in the formation of a character of this nature, so there is some hazard which attends the progress of its success, upon the stage: for many come to a play, so over-charged with criticism, that they very often let fly their censure, when through their rashness they have mistaken their aim. This I had occasion lately to observe: for this play had been acted two or three days, before some of these hasty judges could find the leisure to distinguish betwixt the character of a Witwoud and a Truewit.

I must beg your lordship's pardon for this digression from the true course of this epistle; but that it may not seem altogether impertinent, I beg, that I may plead the occasion of it, in part of that excuse of which I stand in need, for recommending this comedy to your protection. It is only by the countenance of your lordship, and the *few* so qualified, that such who write with care and pains can hope to be distinguished: for the prostituted name of *poet* promiscuously levels all that bear it.

Terence, the most correct writer in the world, had a Scipio and a Lelius, if not to assist him, at least to support him in his reputation: and notwithstanding his extraordinary merit, it may be, their countenance was not more than necessary.

The purity of his stile, the delicacy of his turns, and the justness of his characters, were all of them beauties, which the greater part of his audience were incapable of tasting: some of the coursest strokes of Plautus, so severely censured by Horace, were more likely to affect the multitude; such, who come with expectation to laugh at the last act of a play, and are better entertained with two or three unseasonable jests, than with the artful solution of the fable.

As Terence excelled in his performances, so had he great advantages to encourage his undertakings; for he built most on the foundations of Menander: his plots were generally modelled, and his characters ready drawn to his hand. He copied Menander; and Menander had no less light in the formation of his characters, from the observations of Theophrastus, of whom he was a disciple; and Theophrastus it is known was not only the disciple, but the immediate successor of Aristotle, the first and greatest judge of poetry. These were great models to design by; and the further advantage which Terence possessed, towards giving his plays the due ornaments of purity of style and justness of manners, was not less considerable, from the freedom of conversation, which was permitted him with Lelius and Scipio, two of tne greatest and most polite men of his age. And indeed, the privilege of such a conversation is the only certain means of attaining to the perfection of dialogue.

If it has happened in any part of this comedy, that I have gained a turn of style, or expression more correct, or at least more corrigible than in those which I have formerly written, I must, with equal pride and gratitude, ascribe it to the honour of your lordship's admitting me into your conversation, and that of a society where everybody else was so well worthy of you, in your retirement last summer from the town: for it was immediately after, that this comedy was written. If I have failed in my performance, it is only to be regretted, where there were so many, not inferior either to a Scipio or a Lelius, that there should be one wanting, equal in capacity to a Terence.

If I am not mistaken, poetry is almost the only art which has not yet laid claim to your lordship's patronage. Architecture and painting, to the great honour of our country, have flourished under your influence and protection. In the meantime, poetry, the eldest sister of all arts, and parent of most, seems to have resigned her birthright, by having neglected to pay her duty to your lordship; and by permitting others of a later extraction to prepossess that place in your esteem, to which none can pretend a better title. Poetry, in its nature, is sacred to the good and great; the relation between them is reciprocal, and they are ever propitious to it. It is the privilege of poetry to address to them, and it is their prerogative alone to give it protection.

This received maxim is a general apology for all writers who consecrate their labours to great men: but I could wish, at this time, that this address were exempted from the common pretence of all dedications; and that as I can distinguish your lordship even among the most deserving, so this offering might become remarkable by some particular instance of respect, which should assure your lordship that I am, with all due sense of your extream worthiness and humanity, my lord, your lordship's most obedient and most obliged humble servant,

WILL. CONGREVE.

PROLOGUE

SPOKEN BY MR. BETTERTON

Of those few fools, who with ill stars are curst,
Sure scribling fools, called poets, fare the worst:
For they're a sort of fools which Fortune makes,
And after she has made 'em fools, forsakes.
With Nature's oafs 'tis quite a diff'rent case,
For Fortune favours all her Idiot-race:
In her own nest the Cuckow-eggs we find,
O'er which she broods to hatch the Changling-kind.
No portion for her own she has to spare,
So much she doats on her adopted care.

 Poets are bubbles, by the town drawn in,
Suffered at first some trifling stakes to win:
But what unequal hazards do they run!
Each time they write they venture all they've won: }
The squire that's buttered still, is sure to be undone. }
This author, heretofore, has found your favour,
But pleads no merit from his past behaviour.
To build on that might prove a vain presumption,
Should grants to poets made, admit resumption:
And in Parnassus he must lose his seat,
If that be found a forfeited estate.

 He owns, with toil, he wrought the following scenes,
But if they're naught ne'er spare him for his pains:
Damn him the more; have no commiseration
For dulness on mature deliberation.
He swears he'll not resent one hissed-off scene, }
Nor, like those peevish wits, his play maintain, }
Who, to assert their sense, your taste arraign. }
Some plot we think he has, and some new thought;
Some humour too, no farce; but that's a fault.
Satire, he thinks, you ought not to expect;
For so reformed a town, who dares correct?
To please, this time, has been his sole pretence,
He'll not instruct, lest it should give offence.
Should he by chance a knave or fool expose,
That hurts none here, sure here are none of those.
In short, our play shall (with your leave to shew it)
Give you one instance of a passive poet.
Who to your judgments yields all resignation;
So save or damn, after your own discretion.

THE WAY OF THE WORLD

ACT I

SCENE I.—*A Chocolate-house*

MIRABELL *and* FAINALL [*rising from Cards*], BETTY *waiting*.

Mira. You are a fortunate man, Mr. Fainall.

Fain. Have we done?

Mira. What you please. I'll play on to entertain you.

Fain. No, I'll give you your revenge another time, when you
are not so indifferent; you are thinking of something else now,
and play too negligently; the coldness of a losing gamester
lessens the pleasure of the winner. I'd no more play with a
man that slighted his ill fortune, than I'd make love to a woman
who undervalued the loss of her reputation.

Mira. You have a taste extreamly delicate, and are for
refining on your pleasures.

Fain. Prithee, why so reserved? Something has put you out
of humour.

Mira. Not at all: I happen to be grave to-day; and you are
gay; that's all.

Fain. Confess, Millamant and you quarrelled last night, after
I left you; my fair cousin has some humours that would tempt
the patience of a Stoick. What, some coxcomb came in, and
was well received by her, while you were by.

Mira. Witwoud and Petulant; and what was worse, her
aunt, your wife's mother, my evil genius; or to sum up all in
her own name, my old Lady Wishfort came in——

Fain. O there it is then—she has a lasting passion for you,
and with reason.—What, then my wife was there?

Mira. Yes, and Mrs. Marwood and three or four more, whom
I never saw before; seeing me, they all put on their grave faces,
whispered one another, then complained aloud of the vapours,
and after fell into a profound silence.

Fain. They had a mind to be rid of you.

Mira. For which reason I resolved not to stir. At last the
good old lady broke through her painful taciturnity, with an
invective against long visits. I would not have understood her
but Millamant joining in the argument, I rose and with a constrained smile told her I thought nothing was so easie as to know

when a visit began to be troublesome; she redened and I withdrew, without expecting her reply.

Fain. You were to blame to resent what she spoke only in
compliance with her aunt.

Mira. She is more mistress of herself, than to be under the
necessity of such a resignation.

Fain. What? though half her fortune depends upon her
marrying with my lady's approbation?

Mira. I was then in such a humour, that I should have been
better pleased if she had been less discreet.

Fain. Now I remember, I wonder not they were weary of you;
last night was one of their cabal-nights; they have 'em three
times a week, and meet by turns, at one another's apartments,
where they come together like the coroner's inquest, to sit upon
the murdered reputations of the week. You and I are excluded;
and it was once proposed that all the male sex should be excepted;
but somebody moved that to avoid scandal there might be one
man of the community; upon which motion Witwoud and
Petulant were enrolled members.

Mira. And who may have been the foundress of this sect?
My Lady Wishfort, I warrant, who publishes her detestation of
mankind; and full of the vigour of fifty-five, declares for a
friend and ratafia; and let posterity shift for itself, she'll breed
no more.

Fain. The discovery of your sham addresses to her, to conceal
your love to her neice, has provoked this separation: had you
dissembled better, things might have continued in the state of
nature.

Mira. I did as much as man could, with any reasonable conscience; I proceeded to the very last act of flattery with her, and
was guilty of a song in her commendation. Nay, I got a friend to
put her into a lampoon, and complement her with the imputation of an affair with a young fellow, which I carried so far,
that I told her the malicious town took notice that she was
grown fat of a sudden; and when she lay in of a dropsie, persuaded her she was reported to be in labour. The devil's in't,
if an old woman is to be flattered further, unless a man should
endeavour downright personally to debauch her; and that my
vertue forbad me. But for the discovery of this amour, I am
indebted to your friend, or your wife's friend, Mrs. Marwood.

Fain. What should provoke her to be your enemy, unless she
has made you advances, which you have slighted? Women do
not easily forgive omissions of that nature.

Mira. She was always civil to me, 'till of late; I confess I am
not one of those coxcombs who are apt to interpret a woman's
good manners to her prejudice; and think that she who does not
refuse 'em everything, can refuse 'em nothing.

Fain. You are a gallant man, Mirabell; and though you may
have cruelty enough, not to satisfie a lady's longing; you have

too much generosity, not to be tender of her honour. Yet you speak with an indifference which seems to be affected; and confesses you are conscious of a negligence.

Mira. You pursue the argument with a distrust that seems to be unaffected, and confesses you are conscious of a concern for which the lady is more indebted to you, than is your wife.

Fain. Fie, fie, friend, if you grow censorious I must leave you;—I'll look upon the gamesters in the next room.

Mira. Who are they?

Fain. Petulant and Witwoud.—Bring me some chocolate.

Mira. Betty, what says your clock?

Bet. Turned of the last canonical hour, sir.

Mira. How pertinently the jade answers me! Ha! almost one a clock! [*Looking on his watch.*] O, y'are come——

SCENE II

MIRABELL *and* FOOTMAN.

Mira. Well, is the grand affair over? You have been something tedious.

Serv. Sir, there's such coupling at Pancras, that they stand behind one another, as 'twere in a country dance. Ours was the last couple to lead up; and no hopes appearing of dispatch, besides, the parson growing hoarse, we were afraid his lungs would have failed before it came to our turn; so we drove round to Duke's Place; and there they were riveted in a trice.

Mira. So, so, you are sure they are married.

Serv. Married and bedded, sir: I am witness.

Mira. Have you the certificate?

Serv. Here it is, sir.

Mira. Has the tailor brought Waitwell's cloaths home, and the new liveries?

Serv. Yes, sir.

Mira. That's well. Do you go home again, d'ye hear, and adjourn the consummation 'till farther order; bid Waitwell shake his ears, and Dame Partlet rustle up her feathers, and meet me at one a clock by Rosamond's Pond; that I may see her before she returns to her lady: and as you tender your ears be secret.

SCENE III

MIRABELL, FAINALL, BETTY.

Fain. Joy of your success, Mirabell; you look pleased.

Mira. Ay; I have been engaged in a matter of some sort of mirth, which is not yet ripe for discovery. I am glad this is not a cabal-night. I wonder, Fainall, that you who are married, and of consequence should be discreet, will suffer your wife to be of such a party.

Fain. Faith, I am not jealous. Besides, most who are engaged are women and relations; and for the men, they are of a kind too contemptible to give scandal.

Mira. I am of another opinion. The greater the coxcomb, always the more the scandal: for a woman who is not a fool, can have but one reason for associating with a man who is one.

Fain. Are you jealous as often as you see Witwoud entertained by Millamant?

Mira. Of her understanding I am, if not of her person.

Fain. You do her wrong; for to give her her due, she has wit.

Mira. She has beauty enough to make any man think so; and complaisance enough not to contradict him who shall tell her so.

Fain. For a passionate lover, methinks you are a man somewhat too discerning in the failings of your mistress.

Mira. And for a discerning man, somewhat too passionate a lover; for I like her with all her faults; nay, like her for her faults. Her follies are so natural, or so artful, that they become her; and those affectations which in another woman would be odious, serve but to make her more agreeable. I'll tell thee, Fainall, she once used me with that insolence, that in revenge I took her to pieces; sifted her, and separated her failings; I studied 'em, and got 'em by rote. The catalogue was so large, that I was not without hopes, one day or other, to hate her heartily: to which end I so used myself to think of 'em, that at length, contrary to my design and expectation, they gave me every hour less and less disturbance; 'till in a few days it became habitual to me, to remember 'em without being displeased. They are now grown as familiar to me as my own frailties; and in all probability in a little time longer I shall like 'em as well.

Fain. Marry her, marry her; be half as well acquainted with her charms, as you are with her defects, and my life on't, you are your own man again.

Mira. Say you so?

Fain. I, I, I have experience: I have a wife, and so forth.

SCENE IV

[*To them*] Messenger.

Mess. Is one Squire Witwoud here?

Bet. Yes; what's your business?

Mess. I have a letter for him, from his brother, Sir Wilfull, which I am charged to deliver into his own hands.

Bet. He's in the next room, friend—that way.

SCENE V

MIRABELL, FAINALL, BETTY.

Mira. What, is the chief of that noble family in town, Sir Wilfull Witwoud?

Fain. He is expected to-day.   Do you know him?

Mira. I have seen him, he promises to be an extraordinary person; I think you have the honour to be related to him.

Fain. Yes; he is half-brother to this Witwoud by a former wife, who was sister to my Lady Wishfort, my wife's mother. If you marry Millamant, you must call cousins too.

Mira. I had rather be his relation than his acquaintance.

Fain. He comes to town in order to equip himself for travel.

Mira. For travel!   Why the man that I mean is above forty.

Fain. No matter for that; 'tis for the honour of England, that all Europe should know we have blockheads of all ages.

Mira. I wonder there is not an act of parliament to save the credit of the nation, and prohibit the exportation of fools.

Fain. By no means, 'tis better as 'tis; 'tis better to trade with a little loss, than to be quite eaten up, with being over-stocked.

Mira. Pray, are the follies of this knight-errant, and those of the squire his brother, anything related?

Fain. Not at all; Witwoud grows by the knight, like a medlar grafted on a crab.   One will melt in your mouth, and t'other set your teeth on edge; one is all pulp, and the other all core.

Mira. So one will be rotten before he be ripe, and the other will be rotten without ever being ripe at all.

Fain. Sir Wilfull is an odd mixture of bashfulness and obstinacy.—But when he's drunk, he's as loving as the monster in the "Tempest;" and much after the same manner.   To give t'other his due, he has something of good nature, and does not always want wit.

Mira. Not always; but as often as his memory fails him, and his commonplace of comparisons.   He is a fool with a good memory, and some few scraps of other folks' wit.   He is one whose conversation can never be approved, yet it is now and then to be endured.   He has indeed one good quality, he is not exceptious; for he so passionately affects the reputation of understanding raillery, that he will construe an affront into a jest; and call downright rudeness and ill language, satire and fire.

Fain. If you have a mind to finish his picture, you have an opportunity to do it at full length.   Behold the original.

SCENE VI

[*To them*] WITWOUD.

Wit. Afford me your compassion, my dears; pity me, Fainall, Mirabell, pity me.

Mira. I do from my soul.

Fain. Why, what's the matter?

Wit. No letters for me, Betty?

Bet. Did not a messenger bring you one but now, sir?

Wit. Ay, but no other?

Bet. No, sir.

Wit. That's hard, that's very hard;—a messenger, a mule, a beast of burden, he has brought me a letter from the fool my brother, as heavy as a panegyrick in a funeral sermon, or a copy of commendatory verses from one poet to another. And what's worse, 'tis as sure a forerunner of the author, as an epistle dedicatory.

Mira. A fool, and your brother, Witwoud!

Wit. Ay, ay, my half-brother. My half-brother he is, no nearer upon honour.

Mira. Then 'tis possible he may be but half a fool.

Wit. Good, good, Mirabell, *le drole!* Good, good, hang him, don't let's talk of him;—Fainall, how does your lady? Gad! I say anything in the world to get this fellow out of my head. I beg pardon that I should ask a man of pleasure, and the town, a question at once so foreign and domestick. But I talk like an old maid at a marriage, I don't know what I say: but she's the best woman in the world.

Fain. 'Tis well you don't know what you say, or else your commendation would go near to make me either vain or jealous.

Wit. No man in town lives well with a wife but Fainall. Your judgment, Mirabell?

Mira. You had better step and ask his wife, if you would be credibly informed.

Wit. Mirabell.

Mira. Ay.

Wit. My dear, I ask ten thousand pardons;—Gad I have forgot what I was going to say to you.

Mira. I thank you heartily, heartily.

Wit. No, but prithee excuse me,—my memory is such a memory.

Mira. Have a care of such apologies, Witwoud;—for I never knew a fool but he affected to complain, either of the spleen or his memory.

Fain. What have you done with Petulant?

Wit. He's reckoning his mony,—my mony it was—I have no luck to-day.

Fain. You may allow him to win of you at play;—for you are sure to be too hard for him at repartee: since you monopolise the wit that is between you, the fortune must be his of course.

Mira. I don't find that Petulant confesses the superiority of wit to be your talent, Witwoud.

Wit. Come, come, you are malicious now, and would breed debates—Petulant's my friend, and a very honest fellow, and a very pretty fellow, and has a smattering—faith and troth a pretty deal of an odd sort of a small wit: Nay, I'll do him justice. I'm his friend, I won't wrong him.—And if he had any judgment in the world,—he would not be altogether contemptible. Come, come, don't detract from the merits of my friend.

Fain. You don't take your friend to be over-nicely bred.

Wit. No, no, hang him, the rogue has no manners at all, that I must own—no more breeding than a bum-baily, that I grant you.—'Tis pity; the fellow has fire and life.

Mira. What, courage?

Wit. Hum, faith I don't know as to that,—I can't say as to that.—Yes, faith, in a controversie he'll contradict anybody.

Mira. Though 'twere a man whom he feared, or a woman whom he loved.

Wit. Well, well, he does not always think before he speaks;— We have all our failings; you are too hard upon him, you are, faith. Let me excuse him,—I can defend most of his faults, except one or two; one he has, that's the truth on't, if he were my brother, I could not acquit him—that indeed I could wish were otherwise.

Mira. Ay marry, what's that, Witwoud?

Wit. O pardon me—expose the infirmities of my friend.— No, my dear, excuse me there.

Fain. What I warrant he's unsincere, or 'tis some such trifle.

Wit. No, no, what if he be? 'Tis no matter for that, his wit will excuse that: a wit should no more be sincere, than a woman constant; one argues a decay of parts, as t'other of beauty.

Mira. Maybe you think him too positive?

Wit. No, no, his being positive is an incentive to argument, and keeps up conversation.

Fain. Too illiterate.

Wit. That! that's his happiness—his want of learning gives him the more opportunities to shew his natural parts.

Mira. He wants words.

Wit. Ay; but I like him for that now; for his want of words gives me the pleasure very often to explain his meaning.

Fain. He's impudent.

Wit. No, that's not it.

Mira. Vain.

Wit. No.

Mira. What, he speaks unseasonable truths sometimes, because he has not wit enough to invent an evasion.

Wit. Truths! Ha, ha, ha! No, no, since you will have it,— I mean, he never speaks truth at all,—that's all. He will lie like a chambermaid, or a woman of quality's porter. Now that is a fault.

SCENE VII

[*To them*] Coachman.

Coach. Is Master Petulant here, mistress?

Bet. Yes.

Coach. Three gentlewomen in a coach would speak with him.

Fain. O brave Petulant, three!

Bet. I'll tell him.

Coach. You must bring two dishes of chocolate and a glass of cinnamon-water.

SCENE VIII

MIRABELL, FAINALL, WITWOUD.

Wit. That should be for two fasting strumpets, and a bawd troubled with wind. Now you may know what the three are.

Mira. You are very free with your friend's acquaintance.

Wit. Ay, ay, friendship without freedom is as dull as love without enjoyment, or wine without toasting; but to tell you a secret, these are trulls whom he allows coach-hire, and something more by the week, to call on him once a day at publick places.

Mira. How!

Wit. You shall see he won't go to 'em because there's no more company here to take notice of him—Why this is nothing to what he used to do;—before he found out this way, I have known him call for himself——

Fain. Call for himself? What dost thou mean?

Wit. Mean, why he would slip you out of this chocolate-house, just when you had been talking to him—as soon as your back was turned—whip he was gone;—then trip to his lodging, clap on a hood and scarf, and a mask, slap into a hackney-coach, and drive hither to the door again in a trice; where he would send in for himself, that I mean, call for himself, wait for himself, nay and what's more, not finding himself, sometimes leave a letter for himself.

Mira. I confess this is something extraordinary—I believe he waits for himself now, he is so long a coming; O I ask his pardon.

SCENE IX

PETULANT, MIRABELL, FAINALL, WITWOUD, BETTY.

Bet. Sir, the coach stays.

Pet. Well, well; I come.—'Sbud a man had as good be a professed midwife, as a professed whoremaster, at this rate; to be knocked up and raised at all hours, and in all places. Pox on 'em, I won't come—D'ye hear, tell 'em I won't come.— Let 'em snivel and cry their hearts out.

Fain. You are very cruel, Petulant.

Pet. All's one, let it pass—I have a humour to be cruel.

Mira. I hope they are not persons of condition that you use at this rate.

Pet. Condition, condition's a dried fig, if I am not in humour. —By this hand, if they were your—a—a—your what-dee-call- 'ems themselves, they must wait or rub off, if I want appetite.

Mira. What-dee-call-'ems! What are they, Witwoud?

Wit. Empresses, my dear—by your what-dee-call-'ems he means sultana queens.

Pet. Ay, Roxolana's.

Mira. Cry you mercy.

Fain. Witwoud says they are——

Pet. What does he say th'are?

Wit. I; fine ladies I say.

Pet. Pass on, Witwoud—Harkee, by this light his relations— two co-heiresses his cousins, and an old aunt, who loves catter- wauling better than a conventicle.

Wit. Ha, ha, ha; I had a mind to see how the rogue would come off.—Ha, ha, ha; Gad I can't be angry with him, if he had said they were my mother and my sisters.

Mira. No!

Wit. No; the rogue's wit and readiness of invention charm me, dear Petulant.

Bet. They are gone, sir, in great anger.

Pet. Enough, let 'em trundel. Anger helps complexion, saves paint.

Fain. This continence is all dissembled; this is in order to have something to brag of the next time he makes court to Millamant, and swear he has abandoned the whole sex for her sake.

Mira. Have you not left off your impudent pretensions there yet? I shall cut your throat, sometime or other, Petulant, about that business.

Pet. Ay, ay, let that pass—there are other throats to be cut.—

Mira. Meaning mine, sir?

Pet. Not I—I mean nobody—I know nothing.—But there are

uncles and nephews in the world—and they may be rivals—
What then? All's one for that——

Mira. How! Harkee, Petulant, come hither—Explain, or I
shall call your interpreter.

Pet. Explain; I know nothing.—Why you have an uncle,
have you not, lately come to town, and lodges by my Lady
Wishfort's?

Mira. True.

Pet. Why that's enough—you and he are not friends; and if
he should marry and have a child, you may be disinherited, ha?

Mira. Where hast thou stumbled upon all this truth?

Pet. All's one for that; why then say I know something.

Mira. Come, thou art an honest fellow, Petulant, and shalt
make love to my mistress, thou shalt, faith. What hast thou
heard of my uncle?

Pet. I, nothing I. If throats are to be cut, let swords clash;
snug's the word, I shrug and am silent.

Mira. O raillery, raillery. Come, I know thou art in the
women's secrets.—What you're a cabalist, I know you staid at
Millamant's last night, after I went. Was there any mention
made of my uncle or me? Tell me; if thou hadst but good
nature equal to thy wit, Petulant, Tony Witwoud, who is now
thy competitor in fame, would shew as dim by thee as a dead
whiting's eye by a pearl of Orient; he would no more be seen
by thee, than Mercury is by the sun: Come, I'm sure thou wo't
tell me.

Pet. If I do, will you grant me common sense then, for the
future?

Mira. Faith I'll do what I can for thee, and I'll pray that
Heaven may grant it thee in the meantime.

Pet. Well, harkee.

Fain. Petulant and you both will find Mirabell as warm a
rival as a lover.

Wit. Pshaw, pshaw, that she laughs at Petulant is plain.
And for my part—but that it is almost a fashion to admire her,
I should—harkee—to tell you a secret, but let it go no further—
between friends, I shall never break my heart for her.

Fain. How!

Wit. She's handsome; but she's a sort of an uncertain woman.

Fain. I thought you had died for her.

Wit. Umh—no——

Fain. She has wit.

Wit. 'Tis what she will hardly allow anybody else—Now,
demme, I should hate that, if she were as handsome as Cleopatra.
Mirabell is not so sure of her as he thinks for.

Fain. Why do you think so?

Wit. We staid pretty late there last night; and heard something of an uncle to Mirabell, who is lately come to town,—and
is between him and the best part of his estate; Mirabell and he

are at some distance, as my Lady Wishfort has been told; and you know she hates Mirabell, worse than a Quaker hates a parrot, or than a fishmonger hates a hard frost. Whether this uncle has seen Mrs. Millamant or not, I cannot say; but there were items of such a treaty being in embrio; and if it should come to life, poor Mirabell would be in some sort unfortunately fobbed i'faith.

Fain. 'Tis impossible Millamant should harken to it.

Wit. Faith, my dear, I can't tell; she's a woman and a kind of a humorist.

Mira. And this is the sum of what you could collect last night.

Pet. The quintessence. Maybe Witwoud knows more, he stayed longer.—Besides they never mind him; they say anything before him.

Mira. I thought you had been the greatest favourite.

Pet. Ay, *tête à tête;* but not in publick, because I make remarks.

Mira. You do?

Pet. Ay, ay, pox I'm malicious, man. Now he's soft, you know, they are not in awe of him—the fellow's well bred, he's what you call a—what-d'ye-call-'em. A fine gentleman, but he's silly withal.

Mira. I thank you, I know as much as my curiosity requires. Fainall, are you for the Mall?

Fain. Ay, I'll take a turn before dinner.

Wit. Ay, we'll all walk in the Park, the ladies talked of being there.

Mira. I thought you were obliged to watch for your brother Sir Wilfull's arrival.

Wit. No, no, he comes to his aunt's, my Lady Wishfort; pox on him, I shall be troubled with him too; what shall I do with the fool?

Pet. Beg him for his estate; that I may beg you afterwards; and so have but one trouble with you both.

Wit. O rare Petulant; thou art as quick as fire in a frosty morning; thou shalt to the Mall with us; and we'll be very severe.

Pet. Enough, I'm in a humour to be severe.

Mira. Are you? Pray then walk by yourselves,—let not us be accessary to your putting the ladies out of countenance, with your senseless ribaldry; which you roar out aloud as often as they pass by you; and when you have made a handsome woman blush, then you think you have been severe.

Pet. What, what? Then let 'em either shew their innocence by not understanding what they hear, or else shew their discretion by not hearing what they would not be thought to understand.

Mira. But hast not thou then sense enough to know that thou ought'st to be most ashamed of thyself, when thou hast put another out of countenance?

Pet. Not I, by this hand—I always take blushing either for a sign of guilt, or ill breeding.

Mira. I confess you ought to think so. You are in the right, that you may plead the error of your judgment in defence of your practice.

Where modesty's ill manners, 'tis but fit
That impudence and malice pass for wit.

ACT II

SCENE I.—*St. James's Park*

Mrs. FAINALL *and* Mrs. MARWOOD.

Mrs. Fain. Ay, ay, dear Marwood, if we will be happy, we must find the means in ourselves, and among ourselves. Men are ever in extreams; either doating, or averse. While they are lovers, if they have fire and sense, their jealousies are insupportable: and when they cease to love (we ought to think at least) they loath; they look upon us with horror and distaste; they meet us like the ghosts of what we were, and as from such, fly from us.

Mrs. Mar. True, 'tis an unhappy circumstance of life, that love should ever die before us; and that the man so often should outlive the lover. But say what you will, 'tis better to be left, than never to have been loved. To pass our youth in dull indifference, to refuse the sweets of life because they once must leave us, is as preposterous as to wish to have been born old, because we one day must be old. For my part, my youth may wear and waste, but it shall never rust in my possession.

Mrs. Fain. Then it seems you dissemble an aversion to mankind, only in compliance to my mother's humour.

Mrs. Mar. Certainly. To be free; I have no taste of those insipid dry discourses, with which our sex of force must entertain themselves, apart from men. We may affect endearments to each other, profess eternal friendships, and seem to dote like lovers; but 'tis not in our natures long to persevere. Love will resume his empire in our breasts, and every heart, or soon or late, receive and readmit him as its lawful tyrant.

Mrs. Fain. Bless me, how have I been deceived! Why you profess a libertine.

Mrs. Mar. You see my friendship by my freedom. Come, be as sincere, acknowledge that your sentiments agree with mine.

Mrs. Fain. Never.

Mrs. Mar. You hate mankind?

Mrs. Fain. Heartily, inveterately

Mrs. Mar. Your husband?

Mrs. Fain. Most transcendently; ay, though I say it, meritoriously.

Mrs. Mar. Give me your hand upon it.

Mrs. Fain. There.

Mrs. Mar. I join with you; what I have said has been to try you.

Mrs. Fain. Is it possible? Dost thou hate those vipers men?

Mrs. Mar. I have done hating 'em, and am now come to despise 'em; the next thing I have to do, is eternally to forget 'em.

Mrs. Fain. There spoke the spirit of an Amazon, a Penthesilea.

Mrs. Mar. And yet I am thinking sometimes to carry my aversion further.

Mrs. Fain. How?

Mrs. Mar. Faith by marrying; if I could but find one that loved me very well, and would be thoroughly sensible of ill usage, I think I should do myself the violence of undergoing the ceremony.

Mrs. Fain. You would not make him a cuckold?

Mrs. Mar. No; but I'd make him believe I did, and that's as bad.

Mrs. Fain. Why had not you as good do it?

Mrs. Mar. O if he should ever discover it, he would then know the worst, and be out of his pain; but I would have him ever to continue upon the rack of fear and jealousie.

Mrs. Fain. Ingenious mischief! Would thou wert married to Mirabell.

Mrs. Mar. Would I were.

Mrs. Fain. You change colour.

Mrs. Mar. Because I hate him.

Mrs. Fain. So do I; but I can hear him named. But what reason have you to hate him in particular?

Mrs. Mar. I never loved him; he is, and always was, insufferably proud.

Mrs. Fain. By the reason you give for your aversion, one would think it dissembled; for you have laid a fault to his charge of which his enemies must acquit him.

Mrs. Mar. O then it seems you are one of his favourable enemies. Methinks you look a little pale, and now you flush again.

Mrs. Fain. Do I? I think I am a little sick o' the sudden.

Mrs. Mar. What ails you?

Mrs. Fain. My husband. Don't you see him? He turned short upon me unawares, and has almost overcome me.

SCENE II

[*To them*] FAINALL *and* MIRABELL.

Mrs. Mar. Ha, ha, ha; he comes opportunely for you.

Mrs. Fain. For you, for he has brought Mirabell with him.

Fain. My dear.

Mrs. Fain. My soul.

Fain. You don't look well to-day, child.

Mrs. Fain. D'ye think so?

Mira. He is the only man that does, madam.

Mrs. Fain. The only man that would tell me so at least; and the only man from whom I could hear it without mortification.

Fain. O my dear, I am satisfied of your tenderness; I know you cannot resent anything from me; especially what is an effect of my concern.

Mrs. Fain. Mr. Mirabell, my mother interrupted you in a pleasant relation last night: I would fain hear it out.

Mira. The persons concerned in that affair have yet a tolerable reputation.—I am afraid Mr. Fainall will be censorious.

Mrs. Fain. He has a humour more prevailing than his curiosity, and will willingly dispence with the hearing of one scandalous story, to avoid giving an occasion to make another by being seen to walk with his wife. This way, Mr. Mirabell, and I dare promise you will oblige us both.

SCENE III

FAINALL, MRS. MARWOOD.

Fain. Excellent creature! Well, sure if I should live to be rid of my wife, I should be a miserable man.

Mrs. Mar. Ay!

Fain. For having only that one hope, the accomplishment of it, of consequence must put an end to all my hopes; and what a wretch is he who must survive his hopes! Nothing remains when that day comes, but to sit down and weep like Alexander, when he wanted other worlds to conquer.

Mrs. Mar. Will you not follow 'em?

Fain. Faith, I think not.

Mrs. Mar. Pray let us; I have a reason.

Fain. You are not jealous?

Mrs. Mar. Of whom?

Fain. Of Mirabell.

Mrs. Mar. If I am, is it inconsistent with my love to you that I am tender of your honour?

Fain. You would intimate then, as if there were a fellow-feeling between my wife and him.

Mrs. Mar. I think she does not hate him to that degree she would be thought.

Fain. But he, I fear, is too insensible.

Mrs. Mar. It may be you are deceived.

Fain. It may be so. I do not now begin to apprehend it.

Mrs. Mar. What?

Fain. That I have been deceived, madam, and you are false.

Mrs. Mar. That I am false! What mean you?

Fain. To let you know I see through all your little arts—Come, you both love him; and both have equally dissembled your aversion. Your mutual jealousies of one another, have made you clash 'till you have both struck fire. I have seen the warm confession redening on your cheeks, and sparkling from your eyes.

Mrs. Mar. You do me wrong.

Fain. I do not—'twas for my ease to oversee and wilfully neglect the gross advances made him by my wife; that by permitting her to be engaged, I might continue unsuspected in my pleasures; and take you oftener to my arms in full security. But could you think, because the nodding husband would not wake, that e'er the watchful lover slept?

Mrs. Mar. And wherewithal can you reproach me?

Fain. With infidelity, with loving another, with love of Mirabell.

Mrs. Mar. 'Tis false. I challenge you to shew an instance that can confirm your groundless accusation. I hate him.

Fain. And wherefore do you hate him? He is insensible, and your resentment follows his neglect. An instance! The injuries you have done him are a proof: your interposing in his love. What cause had you to make discoveries of his pretended passion? To undeceive the credulous aunt, and be the officious obstacle of his match with Millamant?

Mrs. Mar. My obligations to my lady urged me: I had professed a friendship to her; and could not see her easie nature so abused by that dissembler.

Fain. What, was it conscience then? Professed a friendship! O the pious friendships of the female sex!

Mrs. Mar. More tender, more sincere, and more enduring, than all the vain and empty vows of men, whether professing love to us, or mutual faith to one another.

Fain. Ha, ha, ha; you are my wife's friend too.

Mrs. Mar. Shame and ingratitude! Do you reproach me? You, you upbraid me! Have I been false to her, through strict fidelity to you, and sacrificed my friendship to keep my love

*G 604

inviolate? And have you the baseness to charge me with the guilt, unmindful of the merit! To you it should be meritorious, that I have been vicious: And do you reflect that guilt upon me, which should lie buried in your bosom?

Fain. You misinterpret my reproof. I meant but to remind you of the slight account you once could make of strictest ties, when set in competition with your love to me.

Mrs. Mar. 'Tis false, you urged it with deliberate malice— 'twas spoke in scorn, and I never will forgive it.

Fain. Your guilt, not your resentment, begets your rage. If yet you loved, you could forgive a jealousie: but you are stung to find you are discovered.

Mrs. Mar. It shall be all discovered. You too shall be discovered; be sure you shall. I can but be exposed—if I do it myself I shall prevent your baseness.

Fain. Why, what will you do?

Mrs. Mar. Disclose it to your wife; own what has past between us.

Fain. Frenzy!

Mrs. Mar. By all my wrongs I'll do't—I'll publish to the world the injuries you have done me, both in my fame and fortune: With both I trusted you, you bankrupt in honour, as indigent of wealth.

Fain. Your fame I have preserved. Your fortune has been bestowed as the prodigality of your love would have it, in pleasures which we both have shared. Yet, had not you been false, I had e'er this repaid it—'Tis true—had you permitted Mirabell with Millamant to have stollen their marriage, my lady had been incensed beyond all means of reconcilement: Millamant had forfeited the moiety of her fortune; which then would have descended to my wife;—And wherefore did I marry, but to make lawful prize of a rich widow's wealth, and squander it on love and you?

Mrs. Mar. Deceit and frivolous pretence.

Fain. Death, am I not married? What's pretence? Am I not imprisoned, fettered? Have I not a wife? Nay, a wife that was a widow, a young widow, a handsome widow; and would be again a widow, but that I have a heart of proof, and something of a constitution to bustle through the ways of wedlock and this world. Will you yet be reconciled to truth and me?

Mrs. Mar. Impossible. Truth and you are inconsistent—I hate you, and shall for ever.

Fain. For loving you?

Mrs. Mar. I loath the name of love after such usage; and next to the guilt with which you would asperse me, I scorn you most. Farewell.

Fain. Nay, we must not part thus.

Mrs. Mar. Let me go.

Fain. Come, I'm sorry.

Mrs. Mar. I care not—let me go—break my hands, do—I'd leave 'em to get loose.

Fain. I would not hurt you for the world. Have I no other hold to keep you here?

Mrs. Mar. Well, I have deserved it all.

Fain. You know I love you.

Mrs. Mar. Poor dissembling!—O that—Well, it is not yet——

Fain. What? What is it not? What is it not yet? It is not yet too late——

Mrs. Mar. No, it is not yet too late—I have that comfort.

Fain. It is, to love another.

Mrs. Mar. But not to loath, detest, abhor mankind, myself and the whole treacherous world.

Fain. Nay, this is extravagance.—Come, I ask your pardon—no tears—I was to blame, I could not love you and be easie in my doubts—pray forbear—I believe you; I'm convinced I've done you wrong; and any way, every way will make amends;—I'll hate my wife yet more, damn her, I'll part with her, rob her of all she's worth, and we'll retire somewhere, anywhere, to another world, I'll marry thee—be pacified.—'Sdeath they come, hide your face, your tears—you have a mask, wear it a moment. This way, this way, be persuaded.

SCENE IV

MIRABELL *and* Mrs. FAINALL.

Mrs. Fain. They are here yet.

Mira. They are turning into the other walk.

Mrs. Fain. While I only hated my husband, I could bear to see him; but since I have despised him, he's too offensive.

Mira. O you should hate with prudence.

Mrs. Fain. Yes, for I have loved with indiscretion.

Mira. You should have just so much disgust for your husband as may be sufficient to make you relish your lover.

Mrs. Fain. You have been the cause that I have loved without bounds, and would you set limits to that aversion, of which you have been the occasion? Why did you make me marry this man?

Mira. Why do we daily commit disagreeable and dangerous actions? To save that idol reputation. If the familiarities of our loves had produced that consequence, of which you were apprehensive, where could you have fixed a father's name with credit, but on a husband? I knew Fainall to be a man lavish of his morals, an interested and professing friend, a false and a designing lover; yet one whose wit and outward fair behaviour have gained a reputation with the town, enough to make that woman stand excused, who has suffered herself to be won by his addresses. A better man ought not to have been sacrificed to the occasion; a worse had not answered to the purpose. When you are weary of him, you know your remedy.

Mrs. Fain. I ought to stand in some degree of credit with you, Mirabell.

Mira. In justice to you, I have made you privy to my whole design, and put it in your power to ruin or advance my fortune.

Mrs. Fain. Whom have you instructed to represent your pretended uncle?

Mira. Waitwell, my servant.

Mrs. Fain. He is an humble servant to foible my mother's woman, and may win her to your interest.

Mira. Care is taken for that—she is won and worn by this time. They were married this morning.

Mrs. Fain. Who?

Mira. Waitwell and Foible. I would not tempt my servant to betray me by trusting him too far. If your mother, in hopes to ruin me, should consent to marry my pretended uncle, he might, like Mosca in the "Fox," stand upon terms; so I made him sure before-hand.

Mrs. Fain. So, if my poor mother is caught in a contract, you will discover the imposture betimes; and release her by producing a certificate of her gallant's former marriage.

Mira. Yes, upon condition that she consent to my marriage with her niece, and surrender the moiety of her fortune in her possession.

Mrs. Fain. She talked last night of endeavouring at a match between Millamant and your uncle.

Mira. That was by Foible's direction, and my instruction, that she might seem to carry it more privately.

Mrs. Fain. Well, I have an opinion of your success; for I believe my lady will do anything to get an husband; and when she has this, which you have provided for her, I suppose she will submit to anything to get rid of him.

Mira. Yes, I think the good lady would marry anything that resembled a man, though 'twere no more than what a butler could pinch out of a napkin.

Mrs. Fain. Female frailty! We must all come to it, if we live to be old, and feel the craving of a false appetite when the true is decayed.

Mira. An old woman's appetite is depraved like that of a girl—'tis the green-sickness of a second childhood; and like the faint offer of a latter spring, serves but to usher in the fall; and withers in an affected bloom.

Mrs. Fain. Here's your mistress.

SCENE V

[To them] Mrs. MILLAMANT, WITWOUD, MINCING.

Mira. Here she comes i'faith full sail, with her fan spread and streamers out, and a shoal of fools for tenders—Ha, no, I cry her mercy.

Mrs. Fain. I see but one poor empty sculler; and he tows her woman after him.

Mira. You seem to be unattended, madam,—you used to have the *beau-mond* throng after you; and a flock of gay fine perukes hovering round you.

Wit. Like moths about a candle—I had like to have lost my comparison for want of breath.

Milla. O I have denied myself airs to-day. I have walked as fast through the croud——

Wit. As a favourite just disgraced; and with as few followers.

Milla. Dear Mr. Witwoud, truce with your similitudes: for I am as sick of 'em——

Wit. As a physician of a good air—I cannot help it, madam, though 'tis against myself.

Milla. Yet again! Mincing, stand between me and his wit.

Wit. Do, Mrs. Mincing, like a skreen before a great fire. I confess I do blaze to-day, I am too bright.

Mrs. Fain. But, dear Millamant, why were you so long?

Milla. Long! Lord, have I not made violent haste? I have asked every living thing I met for you; I have enquired after you, as after a new fashion.

Wit. Madam, truce with your similitudes—No, you met her husband, and did not ask him for her.

Mira. By your leave, Witwoud, that were like enquiring after an old fashion, to ask a husband for his wife.

Wit. Hum, a hit, a hit, a palpable hit, I confess it.

Mrs. Fain. You were dressed before I came abroad.

Milla. Ay, that's true—O but then I had—Mincing, what had I? Why was I so long?

Minc. O mem, your laship staid to peruse a pacquet of letters.

Milla. O ay, letters—I had letters—I am persecuted with letters—I hate letters—nobody knows how to write letters; and yet one has 'em, one does not know why—they serve one to pin up one's hair.

Wit. Is that the way? Pray, madam, do you pin up your hair with all your letters? I find I must keep copies.

Milla. Only with those in verse, Mr. Witwoud. I never pin up my hair with prose. I think I tried once, Mincing.

Minc. O mem, I shall never forget it.

Milla. Ay, poor Mincing tift and tift all the morning.

Minc. 'Till I had the cramp in my fingers, I'll vow, mem. And all to no purpose. But when your laship pins it up with poetry, it sits so pleasant the next day as anything, and is so pure and so crips.

Wit. Indeed, so crips?

Minc. You're such a critick, Mr. Witwoud.

Milla. Mirabell, did you take exceptions last night? O ay, and went away—Now I think on't I'm angry—no, now I think on't I'm pleased—for I believe I gave you some pain.

Mira. Does that please you?

Milla. Infinitely; I love to give pain.

Mira. You would affect a cruelty which is not in your nature; your true vanity is in the power of pleasing.

Milla. O I ask your pardon for that—one's cruelty is one's power, and when one parts with one's cruelty, one parts with one's power; and when one has parted with that, I fancy one's old and ugly.

Mira. Ay, ay, suffer your cruelty to ruin the object of your power, to destroy your lover—and then how vain, how lost a thing you'll be? Nay, 'tis true: you are no longer handsome when you've lost your lover; your beauty dies upon the instant: For beauty is the lover's gift; 'tis he bestows your charms—your glass is all a cheat. The ugly and the old, whom the looking-glass mortifies, yet after commendation can be flattered by it, and discover beauties in it: for that reflects our praises, rather than your face.

Milla. O the vanity of these men! Fainall, d'ye hear him? If they did not commend us, we were not handsome! Now you must know they could not commend one, if one was not handsome. Beauty the lover's gift—Lord, what is a lover, that it can give? Why one makes lovers as fast as one pleases, and they live as long as one pleases, and they die as soon as one pleases: and then if one pleases one makes more.

Wit. Very pretty. Why you make no more of making of lovers, madam, than of making so many card-matches.

Milla. One no more owes one's beauty to a lover, than one's wit to an eccho: they can but reflect what we look and say; vain empty things if we are silent or unseen, and want a being.

Mira. Yet, to those two vain empty things, you owe two the greatest pleasures of your life.

Milla. How so?

Mira. To your lover you owe the pleasure of hearing yourselves praised; and to an eccho the pleasure of hearing yourselves talk.

Wit. But I know a lady that loves talking so incessantly, she won't give an eccho fair play; she has that everlasting rotation of tongue, that an eccho must wait 'till she dies, before it can catch her last words.

Milla. O fiction; Fainall, let us leave these men.

Mira. Draw off Witwoud.   [*Aside to* Mrs. Fainall.
Mrs. Fain. Immediately; I have a word or two for Mr. Witwoud.

SCENE VI

Millamant, Mirabell, Mincing.

Mira. I would beg a little private audience too—you had the tyranny to deny me last night; though you knew I came to impart a secret to you that concerned my love.

Milla. You saw I was engaged.

Mira. Unkind. You had the leisure to entertain a herd of fools; things who visit you from their excessive idleness; bestowing on your easiness that time, which is the incumbrance of their lives. How can you find delight in such society? It is impossible they should admire you, they are not capable: or if they were, it should be to you as a mortification; for sure to please a fool is some degree of folly.

Milla. I please myself—besides, sometimes to converse with fools is for my health.

Mira. Your health! Is there a worse disease than the conversation of fools?

Milla. Yes, the vapours; fools are physick for it, next to *assa-fœtida.*

Mira. You are not in a course of fools?

Milla. Mirabell, if you persist in this offensive freedom, you'll displease me—I think I must resolve after all, not to have you—we shan't agree.

Mira. Not in our physick it may be.

Milla. And yet our distemper in all likelihood will be the same; for we shall be sick of one another. I shan't endure to be reprimanded, nor instructed; 'tis so dull to act always by advice, and so tedious to be told of one's faults—I can't bear it. Well, I won't have you, Mirabell—I'm resolved—I think—You may go—ha, ha, ha. What would you give, that you could help loving me?

Mira. I would give something that you did not know, I could not help it.

Milla. Come, don't look grave then. Well, what do you say to me?

Mira. I say that a man may as soon make a friend by his wit, or a fortune by his honesty, as win a woman with plain-dealing and sincerity.

Milla. Sententious Mirabell! Prithee don't look with that violent and inflexible wise face, like Solomon at the dividing of the child in an old tapestry hanging.

Mira. You are merry, madam, but I would persuade you for a moment to be serious.

Milla. What, with that face? No, if you keep your countenance, 'tis impossible I should hold mine. Well, after all, there is something very moving in a lovesick face. Ha, ha, ha—Well I won't laugh, don't be peevish—Heigho! Now I'll be melancholy, as melancholy as a watch-light. Well, Mirabell, if ever you will win me woo me now—Nay, if you are so tedious, fare you well;—I see they are walking away.

Mira. Can you not find in the variety of your disposition one moment——

Milla. To hear you tell me Foible's married, and your plot like to speed.—No.

Mira. But how you came to know it——

Milla. Without the help of the devil, you can't imagine; unless she should tell me herself. Which of the two it may have been, I will leave you to consider; and when you have done thinking of that, think of me.

SCENE VII

Mirabell *alone.*

Mira. I have something more—Gone—think of you! To think of a whirlwind, though 'twere in a whirlwind, were a case of more steady contemplation; a very tranquility of mind and mansion. A fellow that lives in a windmill, has not a more whimsical dwelling than the heart of a man that is lodged in a woman. There is no point of the compass to which they cannot turn, and by which they are not turned; and by one as well as another; for motion not method is their occupation. To know this, and yet continue to be in love, is to be made wise from the dictates of reason, and yet persevere to play the fool by the force of instinct.—O here come my pair of turtles.—what, billing so sweetly! Is not Valentine's Day over with you yet?

SCENE VIII

[*To him*] Waitwell, Foible.

Mira. Sirrah, Waitwell, why sure you think you were married for your own recreation, and not for my conveniency.

Wait. Your pardon, sir. With submission, we have indeed been solacing in lawful delights; but still with an eye to business, sir. I have instructed her as well as I could. If she can take your directions as readily as my instructions, sir, your affairs are in a prosperous way.

Mira. Give you joy, Mrs. Foible.

Foib. O-las, sir, I'm so ashamed—I'm afraid my lady has been in a thousand inquietudes for me. But I protest, sir, I made as much haste as I could.

Wait. That she did indeed, sir. It was my fault that she did not make more.

Mira. That I believe.

Foib. But I told my lady as you instructed me, sir. That I had a prospect of seeing Sir Rowland your uncle; and that I would put her ladiship's picture in my pocket to shew him; which I'll be sure to say has made him so enamoured of her beauty, that he burns with impatience to lye at her ladiship's feet and worship the original.

Mira. Excellent Foible! Matrimony has made you eloquent in love.

Wait. I think she has profited, sir. I think so.

Foib. You have seen Madam Millamant, sir?

Mira. Yes.

Foib. I told her, sir, because I did not know that you might find an opportunity; she had so much company last night.

Mira. Your diligence will merit more—In the meantime——

[*Gives mony.*

Foib. O dear sir, your humble servant.

Wait. Spouse.

Mira. Stand off, sir, not a penny.—Go on and prosper, Foible—the lease shall be made good and the farm stocked, if we succeed.

Foib. I don't question your generosity, sir: and you need not doubt of success. If you have no more commands, sir, I'll be gone; I'm sure my lady is at her toilet, and can't dress 'till I come.—O dear, I'm sure that [*looking out*] was Mrs. Marwood that went by in a mask; if she has seen me with you I'm sure she'll tell my lady. I'll make haste home and prevent her. Your servant, sir. B'w'y, Waitwell.

SCENE IX

MIRABELL, WAITWELL.

Wait. Sir Rowland if you please. The jade's so pert upon her preferment she forgets herself.

Mira. Come, sir, will you endeavour to forget yourself—and transform into Sir Rowland.

Wait. Why, sir; it will be impossible I should remember myself—married, knighted and attended all in one day! 'Tis enough to make any man forget himself. The difficulty will be how to recover my acquaintance and familiarity with my former self; and fall from my transformation to a reformation into

Waitwell. Nay, I shan't be quite the same Waitwell neither—for now I remember me, I'm married, and can't be my own man again.

> Ay there's my grief; that's the sad change of life;
> To lose my title, and yet keep my wife.

ACT III

SCENE I.—*A Room in* Lady WISHFORT's *House.*

Lady WISHFORT *at her toilet,* PEG *waiting.*

Lady. Merciful, no news of Foible yet?

Peg. No, madam.

Lady. I have no more patience—if I have not fretted myself 'till I am pale again, there's no veracity in me. Fetch me the red—the red, do you hear, sweetheart? An errant ash colour, as I'm a person. Look you how this wench stirs! Why dost thou not fetch me a little red? Didst thou not hear me, mopus?

Peg. The red ratafia does your ladiship mean, or the cherry-brandy?

Lady. Ratafia, fool. No, fool. Not the ratafia, fool—grant me patience! I mean the Spanish paper, idiot, complexion darling. Paint, paint, paint, dost thou understand that, changeling, dangling thy hands like bobbins before thee? Why dost thou not stir, puppet? thou wooden thing upon wires.

Peg. Lord, madam, your ladiship is so impatient—I cannot come at the paint, madam, Mrs. Foible has locked it up, and carried the key with her.

Lady. A pox take you both—fetch me the cherry-brandy then.

SCENE II

Lady WISHFORT.

I'm as pale and as faint, I look like Mrs. Qualmsick the curate's wife, that's always breeding—Wench, come, come, wench, what art thou doing, sipping? tasting? Save thee, dost thou not know the bottle?

SCENE III

Lady WISHFORT, PEG *with a bottle and china cup.*

Peg. Madam, I was looking for a cup.

Lady. A cup, save thee, and what a cup hast thou brought!

Dost thou take me for a fairy, to drink out of an acorn? Why didst thou not bring thy thimble? Hast thou ne'er a brass thimble clinking in thy pocket with a bit of nutmeg? I warrant thee. Come, fill, fill.—So—again. See who that is.—[*One knocks.*] Set down the bottle first. Here, here, under the table—What, wouldst thou go with the bottle in thy hand like a tapster. As I'm a person, this wench has lived in an inn upon the road, before she came to me, like Maritornes the Asturian in *Don Quixote.* No Foible yet?

Peg. No, madam, Mrs. Marwood.

Lady. O Marwood, let her come in. Come in, good Marwood.

SCENE IV

[*To them*] Mrs. MARWOOD.

Mrs. Mar. I'm surprized to find your ladiship in *dishabillé* at this time of day.

Lady. Foible's a lost thing; has been abroad since morning, and never heard of since.

Mrs. Mar. I saw her but now, as I came masked through the Park, in conference with Mirabell.

Lady. With Mirabell! You call my blood into my face, with mentioning that traitor. She durst not have the confidence. I sent her to negotiate an affair, in which if I'm detected I'm undone. If that wheadling villain has wrought upon Foible to detect me, I'm ruined. Oh my dear friend, I'm a wretch of wretches if I'm detected.

Mrs. Mar. O madam, you cannot suspect Mrs. Foible's integrity.

Lady. O, he carries poison in his tongue that would corrupt integrity itself. If she has given him an opportunity, she has as good as put her integrity into his hands. Ah, dear Marwood, what's integrity to an opportunity?—Hark! I hear her.—Dear friend, retire into my closet, that I may examine her with more freedom—You'll pardon me, dear friend, I can make bold with you—There are books over the chimney—Quarles and Pryn, and the *Short View of the Stage,* with Bunyan's works to entertain you.—Go, you thing, and send her in.　　　　　　[*To* PEG.

SCENE V

Lady WISHFORT, FOIBLE.

Lady. O Foible, where hast thou been? what hast thou been doing?

Foib. Madam, I have seen the party.

Lady. But what hast thou done?

Foib. Nay, 'tis your ladiship has done, and are to do; I have only promised. But a man so enamoured—so transported! Well, if worshipping of pictures be a sin—poor Sir Rowland, I say.

Lady. The miniature has been counted like—But hast thou not betrayed me, Foible? Hast thou not detected me to that faithless Mirabell?—What hadst thou to do with him in the Park? Answer me, has he got nothing out of thee?

Foib. So, the devil has been beforehand with me, what shall I say?—Alas, madam, could I help it, if I met that confident thing? Was I in fault? If you had heard how he used me, and all upon your ladiship's account, I'm sure you would not suspect my fidelity. Nay, if that had been the worst I could have born: but he had a fling at your ladiship too; and then I could not hold: but i'faith I gave him his own.

Lady. Me? What did the filthy fellow say?

Foib. O madam; 'tis a shame to say what he said—with his taunts and his fleers, tossing up his nose. Humh (says he), what you are a hatching some plot (says he), you are so early abroad, or catering (says he), ferreting for some disbanded officer, I warrant—half pay is but thin subsistance (says he)—Well, what pension does your lady propose? Let me see (says he), what she must come down pretty deep now, she's superannuated (says he) and——

Lady. Ods my life, I'll have him, I'll have him murdered. I'll have him poisoned. Where does he eat? I'll marry a drawer to have him poisoned in his wine. I'll send for Robin from Lockets—immediately.

Foib. Poison him? Poisoning's too good for him. Starve him, madam, starve him; marry Sir Rowland, and get him disinherited. O you would bless yourself, to hear what he said.

Lady. A villain, superannuated!

Foib. Humh (says he), I hear you are laying designs against me too (says he), and Mrs. Millamant is to marry my uncle (he does not suspect a word of your ladiship); but (says he) I'll fit you for that, I warrant you (says he), I'll hamper you for that (says he), you and your old frippery too (says he), I'll handle you——

Lady. Audacious villain! handle me, would he durst—Frippery? old frippery! Was there ever such a foul-mouthed fellow? I'll be married to-morrow, I'll be contracted to-night.

Foib. The sooner the better, madam.

Lady. Will Sir Rowland be here, say'st thou? when, Foible?

Foib. Incontinently, madam. No new sheriff's wife expects the return of her husband after knighthood, with that impatience in which Sir Rowland burns for the dear hour of kissing your ladiship's hand after dinner.

Lady. Frippery! superannuated frippery! I'll frippery the villain; I'll reduce him to frippery and rags: a tatterdemallion —I hope to see him hung with tatters, like a Long-Lane penthouse, or a gibbet-thief. A slander-mouthed railer: I warrant the spendthrift prodigal's in debt as much as the million lottery, or the whole court upon a birthday. I'll spoil his credit with his tailor. Yes, he shall have my niece with her fortune, he shall.

Foib. He! I hope to see him lodge in Ludgate first, and angle into Black-Fryars for brass farthings, with an old mitten.

Lady. Ay, dear Foible; thank thee for that, dear Foible. He has put me out of all patience. I shall never recompose my features to receive Sir Rowland with any oeconomy of face. This wretch has fretted me that I am absolutely decayed. Look, Foible.

Foib. Your ladiship has frowned a little too rashly, indeed, madam. There are some cracks discernible in the white vernish.

Lady. Let me see the glass—Cracks, say'st thou? Why, I am arrantly fleaed—I look like an old peeled wall. Thou must repair me, Foible, before Sir Rowland comes; or I shall never keep up to my picture.

Foib. I warrant you, madam; a little art once made your picture like you; and now a little of the same art must make you like your picture. Your picture must sit for you, madam.

Lady. But art thou sure Sir Rowland will not fail to come? Or will a not fail when he does come? Will he be importunate, Foible, and push? For if he should not be importunate—I shall never break decorums—I shall die with confusion, if I am forced to advance—Oh no, I can never advance—I shall swoon if he should expect advances. No, I hope Sir Rowland is better bred, than to put a lady to the necessity of breaking her forms. I won't be too coy neither.—I won't give him despair—but a little disdain is not amiss; a little scorn is alluring.

Foib. A little scorn becomes your ladiship.

Lady. Yes, but tenderness becomes me best—a sort of a dyingness—You see that picture has a sort of a—Ha, Foible? A swimmingness in the eyes—Yes, I'll look so—my niece affects it; but she wants features. Is Sir Rowland handsome? Let my toilet be removed—I'll dress above. I'll receive Sir Rowland here. Is he handsome? Don't answer me. I won't know: I'll be surprized. I'll be taken by surprize.

Foib. By storm, madam. Sir Rowland's a brisk man.

Lady. Is he! O then he'll importune, if he's a brisk man. I shall save decorums if Sir Rowland importunes. I have a mortal terror at the apprehension of offending against decorums. O I'm glad he's a brisk man. Let my things be removed, good Foible.

SCENE VI

Mrs. FAINALL, FOIBLE.

Mrs. Fain. O Foible, I have been in a fright, lest I should come too late. That devil, Marwood, saw you in the Park with Mirabell, and I'm afraid will discover it to my lady.

Foib. Discover what, madam?

Mrs. Fain. Nay, nay, put not on that strange face. I am privy to the whole design, and know that Waitwell, to whom thou wert this morning married, is to personate Mirabell's uncle, and as such, winning my lady, to involve her in those difficulties from which Mirabell only must release her, by his making his conditions to have my cousin and her fortune left to her own disposal.

Foib. O dear madam, I beg your pardon. It was not my confidence in your ladiship that was deficient; but I thought the former good correspondence between your ladiship and Mr. Mirabell, might have hindered his communicating this secret.

Mrs. Fain. Dear Foible, forget that.

Foib. O dear madam, Mr. Mirabell is such a sweet winning gentleman—But your ladiship is the pattern of generosity.— Sweet lady, to be so good! Mr. Mirabell cannot chuse but be grateful. I find your ladiship has his heart still. Now, madam, I can safely tell your ladiship our success, Mrs. Marwood had told my lady; but I warrant I managed myself. I turned it all for the better. I told my lady that Mr. Mirabell railed at her. I laid horrid things to his charge, I'll vow; and my lady is so incensed, that she'll be contracted to Sir Rowland to-night, she says;—I warrant I worked her up, that he may have her for asking for, as they say of a Welsh maiden-head.

Mrs. Fain. O rare Foible!

Foib. Madam, I beg your ladiship to acquaint Mr. Mirabell of his success. I would be seen as little as possible to speak to him—besides, I believe Madam Marwood watches me.—She has a month's mind; but I know Mr. Mirabell can't abide her.— [*Calls.*] John—remove my lady's toilet. Madam, your servant. My lady is so impatient, I fear she'll come for me, if I stay.

Mrs. Fain. I'll go with you up the back stairs, lest I should meet her.

SCENE VII

Mrs. MARWOOD *alone.*

Mrs. Mar. Indeed, Mrs. Engine, is it thus with you? Are you become a go-between of this importance? Yes, I shall watch you. Why this wench is the *pass-par-toute*, a very master-key to everybody's strong box. My friend Fainall, have you carried it so swimmingly? I thought there was something in it; but it seems it's over with you. Your loathing is not from a want of appetite then, but from a surfeit. Else you could never be so cool to fall from a principal to be an assistant; to procure for him! A pattern of generosity, that I confess. Well, Mr. Fainall, you have met with your match.— O man, man! Woman, woman! The devil's an ass: if I were a painter, I would draw him like an idiot, a driveler with a bib and bells. Man should have his head and horns, and woman the rest of him. Poor simple fiend! Madam Marwood has a month's mind, but he can't abide her—'Twere better for him you had not been his confessor in that affair; without you could have kept his counsel closer. I shall not prove another pattern of generosity—he has not obliged me to that with those excesses of himself; and now I'll have none of him. Here comes the good lady, panting ripe; with a heart full of hope, and a head full of care, like any chymist upon the day of projection.

SCENE VIII

[*To her*] Lady WISHFORT.

Lady. O dear Marwood, what shall I say for this rude forgetfulness—but my dear friend is all goodness.

Mrs. Mar. No apologies, dear madam. I have been very well entertained.

Lady. As I'm a person I am in a very chaos to think I should so forget myself—but I have such an olio of affairs really I know not what to do.—[*Calls*]—Foible—I expect my nephew Sir Wilfull every moment too:—Why, Foible—He means to travel for improvement.

Mrs. Mar. Methinks Sir Wilfull should rather think of marrying than travelling at his years. I hear he is turned of forty.

Lady. O he's in less danger of being spoiled by his travels—I am against my nephew's marrying too young. It will be time enough when he comes back, and has acquired discretion to chuse for himself.

Mrs. Mar. Methinks Mrs. Millamant and he would make a very fit match. He may travel afterwards. 'Tis a thing very usual with young gentlemen.

Lady. I promise you I have thought on't—and since 'tis your judgment, I'll think on't again. I assure you I will; I value your judgment extreamly. On my word I'll propose it.

SCENE IX

[*To them*] FOIBLE.

Lady. Come, come, Foible—I had forgot my nephew will be here before dinner—I must make haste.

Foib. Mr. Witwoud and Mr. Petulant are come to dine with your ladiship.

Lady. O dear, I can't appear 'till I am dressed. Dear Marwood, shall I be free with you again, and beg you to entertain 'em. I'll make all imaginable haste. Dear friend, excuse me.

SCENE X

Mrs. Marwood, Mrs. Millamant, Mincing.

Milla. Sure never anything was so unbred as that odious man.—Marwood, your servant.

Mrs. Mar. You have a colour, what's the matter?

Milla. That horrid fellow Petulant has provoked me into a flame—I have broke my fan—Mincing, lend me yours;—Is not all the powder out of my hair?

Mrs. Mar. No. What has he done?

Milla. Nay, he has done nothing; he has only talked—Nay, he has said nothing neither; but he has contradicted everything that has been said. For my part, I thought Witwoud and he would have quarrelled.

Minc. I vow, mem, I thought once they would have fitt.

Milla. Well, 'tis a lamentable thing I swear, that one has not the liberty of chusing one's acquaintance as one does one's cloaths.

Mrs. Mar. If we had that liberty, we should be as weary of one set of acquaintance, though never so good, as we are of one suit, though never so fine. A fool and a doily stuff would now and then find days of grace, and be worn for variety.

Milla. I could consent to wear 'em, if they would wear alike; but fools never wear out—they are such *drap-de-berry* things! Without one could give 'em to one's chambermaid after a day or two.

Mrs. Mar. 'Twere better so indeed. Or what think you of the play-house? A fine gay glosly fool should be given there, like a new masking habit, after the masquerade is over, and we have done with the disguise. For a fool's visit is always a disguise; and never admitted by a woman of wit, but to blind her affair with a lover of sense. If you would but appear barefaced now, and own Mirabell; you might as easily put off Petulant and Witwoud, as your hood and scarf. And indeed 'tis time, for the town has found it: the secret is grown too big for the pretence: 'tis like Mrs. Primly's great belly; she may lace it down before, but it burnishes on her hips. Indeed, Millamant, you can no more conceal it, than my Lady Strammel can her face, that goodly face, which in defiance of her Rhenish-wine tea, will not be comprehended in a mask.

Milla. I'll take my death, Marwood, you are more censorious than a decayed beauty, or a discarded toast; Mincing, tell the men they may come up. My aunt is not dressing here; their folly is less provoking than your malice.

SCENE XI

MILLAMANT, MARWOOD.

Milla. The town has found it. What has it found? That Mirabell loves me is no more a secret, than it is a secret that you discovered it to my aunt, or than the reason why you discovered it is a secret.

Mrs. Mar. You are nettled.

Milla. You're mistaken. Ridiculous!

Mrs. Mar. Indeed, my dear, you'll tear another fan, if you don't mitigate those violent airs.

Milla. O silly! Ha, ha, ha. I could laugh immoderately. Poor Mirabell! His constancy to me has quite destroyed his complaisance for all the world beside. I swear, I never enjoined it him, to be so coy—If I had the vanity to think he would obey me, I would command him to shew more gallantry—'tis hardly well bred to be so particular on one hand, and so insensible on the other. But I despair to prevail, and so let him follow his own way. Ha, ha, ha. Pardon me, dear creature, I must laugh, ha, ha, ha; though I grant you 'tis a little barbarous, ha, ha, ha.

Mrs. Mar. What pity 'tis, so much fine railery, and delivered with so significant gesture, should be so unhappily directed to miscarry.

Milla. Hæ! Dear creature, I ask your pardon—I swear I did not mind you.

Mrs. Mar. Mr. Mirabell and you both may think it a thing impossible, when I shall tell him by telling you——

Milla. O dear, what? for it is the same thing, if I hear it— ha, ha, ha.

Mrs. Mar. That I detest him, hate him, madam.

Milla. O madam, why so do I—and yet the creature loves me, ha, ha, ha. How can one forbear laughing to think of it— I am a Sybil if I am not amazed to think what he can see in me. I'll take my death, I think you are handsomer—and within a year or two as young.—If you could but stay for me, I should overtake you—but that cannot be—Well, that thought makes me melancholick—now I'll be sad.

Mrs. Mar. Your merry note may be changed sooner than you think.

Milla. D'ye say so? Then I'm resolved I'll have a song to keep up my spirits.

SCENE XII

[*To them*] MINCING.

Minc. The gentlemen stay but to comb, madam; and will wait on you.

Milla. Desire Mrs. —— that is in the next room to sing the song I would have learnt yesterday.   You shall hear it, madam —Not that there's any great matter in it—but 'tis agreeable to my humour.

SONG

Set by Mr. John Eccles.

I

Love's but the frailty of the mind,
When 'tis not with ambition joined;
A sickly flame, which if not fed expires;
And feeding, wastes in self-consuming fires.

II

'Tis not to wound a wanton boy
Or am'rous youth, that gives the joy;
But 'tis the glory to have pierced a swain,
For whom inferior beauties sighed in vain.

III

Then I alone the conquest prize,
When I insult a rival's eyes:
If there's delight in love, 'tis when I see
That heart which others bleed for, bleed for me.

SCENE XIII

[*To them*] PETULANT, WITWOUD.

Milla. Is your animosity composed, gentlemen?

Wit. Raillery, raillery, madam, we have no animosity—we hit off a little wit now and then, but no animosity—The falling out of wits is like the falling out of lovers—We agree in the main, like treble and base.   Ha, Petulant!

Pet. Ay, in the main—but when I have a humour to contradict——

Wit. Ay, when he has a humour to contradict, then I contradict too. What, I know my cue. Then we contradict one another like two battledores; for contradictions beget one another like Jews.

Pet. If he says black's black—if I have a humour to say 'tis blue—let that pass—all's one for that. If I have a humour to prove it, it must be granted.

Wit. Not positively must—but it may—it may.

Pet. Yes, it positively must, upon proof positive.

Wit. Ay, upon proof positive it must; but upon proof presumptive it only may. That's a logical distinction now, madam.

Mrs. Mar. I perceive your debates are of importance, and very learnedly handled.

Pet. Importance is one thing, and learning's another; but a debate's a debate, that I assert.

Wit. Petulant's an enemy to learning; he relies altogether on his parts.

Pet. No, I'm no enemy to learning; it hurts not me.

Mrs. Mar. That's a sign indeed it's no enemy to you.

Pet. No, no, it's no enemy to anybody, but them that have it.

Milla. Well, an illiterate man's my aversion, I wonder at the impudence of any illiterate man, to offer to make love.

Wit. That I confess I wonder at too.

Milla. Ah! to marry an ignorant! that can hardly read or write.

Pet. Why should a man be any further from being married though he can't read, than he is from being hanged? The ordinary's paid for setting the psalm, and the parish-priest for reading the ceremony. And for the rest which is to follow in both cases, a man may do it without book—so all's one for that.

Milla. D'ye hear the creature? Lord, here's company, I'll be gone.

SCENE XIV

Sir WILFULL WITWOUD *in a riding dress*, Mrs. MARWOOD, PETULANT, WITWOUD, Footman.

Wit. In the name of Bartlemew and his fair, what have we here?

Mrs. Mar. 'Tis your brother, I fancy. Don't you know him?

Wit. Not I—Yes, I think it is he—I've almost forgot him; I have not seen him since the Revolution.

Foot. Sir, my lady's dressing. Here's company; if you please to walk in, in the meantime.

Sir Wil. Dressing! What, it's but morning here I warrant with you in London; we should count it towards afternoon in our parts, down in Shropshire.—Why then belike my aunt han't dined yet—ha, friend?

Foot. Your aunt, sir?

Sir Wil. My aunt, sir, yes, my aunt, sir, and your lady, sir; your lady is my aunt, sir—Why, what do'st thou not know me, friend? Why then send somebody hither that does. How long hast thou lived with thy lady, fellow, ha?

Foot. A week, sir; longer than anybody in the house, except my lady's woman.

Sir Wil. Why then belike thou dost not know thy lady, if thou see'st her, ha, friend?

Foot. Why truly, sir, I cannot safely swear to her face in a morning, before she is dressed. 'Tis like I may give a shrewd guess at her by this time.

Sir Wil. Well, prithee try what thou canst do; if thou canst not guess, enquire her out, do'st hear, fellow? And tell her, her nephew, Sir Wilfull Witwoud, is in the house.

Foot. I shall, sir.

Sir Wil. Hold ye, hear me, friend; a word with you in your ear, prithee who are these gallants?

Foot. Really, sir, I can't tell; here come so many here, 'tis hard to know 'em all.

SCENE XV

Sir WILFULL WITWOUD, PETULANT, WITWOUD, Mrs. MARWOOD.

Sir Wil. Oons this fellow knows less than a starling; I don't think a' knows his own name.

Mrs. Mar. Mr. Witwoud, your brother is not behind-hand in forgetfulness—I fancy he has forgot you too.

Wit. I hope so—the devil take him that remembers first, I say.

Sir Wil. Save you, gentlemen and lady.

Mrs. Mar. For shame, Mr. Witwoud; why won't you speak to him?—And you, sir.

Wit. Petulant, speak.

Pet. And you, sir.

Sir Wil. No offence, I hope.   [*Salutes* MARWOOD.

Mrs. Mar. No, sure, sir.

Wit. This is a vile dog, I see that already. No offence! Ha, ha, ha, to him; to him, Petulant, smoke him.

Pet. It seems as if you had come a journey, sir; hem, hem.

[*Surveying him round.*

Sir Wil. Very likely, sir, that it may seem so.

Pet. No offence, I hope, sir.

Wit. Smoke the boots, the boots; Petulant, the boots; ha, ha, ha.

Sir Wil. Maybe not, sir; thereafter as 'tis meant, sir.

Pet. Sir, I presume upon the information of your boots.

Sir Wil. Why, 'tis like you may, sir: if you are not satisfied with the information of my boots, sir, if you will step to the stable, you may enquire further of my horse, sir.

Pet. Your horse, sir! Your horse is an ass, sir!

Sir Wil. Do you speak by way of offence, sir?

Mrs. Mar. The gentleman's merry, that's all, sir.—S'life, we shall have a quarrel betwixt an horse and an ass, before they find one another out. You must not take anything amiss from your friends, sir. You are among your friends here, though it may be you don't know it.—If I am not mistaken, you are Sir Wilfull Witwoud.

Sir Wil. Right, lady; I am Sir Wilfull Witwoud, so I write myself; no offence to anybody, I hope; and nephew to the Lady Wishfort of this mansion.

Mrs. Mar. Don't you know this gentleman, sir?

Sir Wil. Hum! What, sure 'tis not—Yea, by'r lady, but 'tis —'Sheart, I know not whether 'tis or no—Yea, but 'tis, by the Rekin. Brother Antony! What, Tony, i'faith! What do'st thou not know me? By'r Lady, nor I thee, thou art so be-cravated, and so beperriwiged—'Sheart, why do'st not speak? Art thou o'erjoyed?

Wit. Odso, brother, is it you? Your servant, brother.

Sir Wil. Your servant! Why yours, sir. Your servant again—'Sheart, and your friend and servant to that—And a—(*puff*) and a flap dragon for your service, sir: and a hare's foot, and a hare's scut for your service, sir; an you be so cold and so courtly!

Wit. No offence, I hope, brother.

Sir Wil. 'Sheart, sir, but there is, and much offence.—A pox, is this your Inns o' Court breeding, not to know your friends and your relations, your elders, and your betters?

Wit. Why, brother Wilfull of Salop, you may be as short as a Shrewsbury cake, if you please. But I tell you 'tis not modish to know relations in town. You think you're in the country, where great lubberly brothers slabber and kiss one another when they meet, like a call of serjeants—'Tis not the fashion here; 'tis not indeed, dear brother.

Sir Wil. The fashion's a fool; and you're a fop, dear brother. 'Sheart, I've suspected this—By'r Lady I conjectured you were a fop, since you began to change the stile of your letters, and write in a scrap of paper gilt round the edges, no bigger than a subpæna. I might expect this when you left off Honoured Brother; and hoping you are in good health, and so forth—to begin with a Rat me, knight, I'm so sick of a last night's debauch —O'ds heart, and then tell a familiar tale of a cock and a bull, and a whore and a bottle, and so conclude—You could write news before you were out of your time, when you lived with

honest Pumple-Nose, the attorney of Furnival's Inn—You could
intreat to be remembered then to your friends round the Rekin.
We could have Gazettes then, and Dawks's Letter, and the
Weekly Bill, 'till of late days.

Pet. 'Slife, Witwoud, were you ever an attorney's clerk? Of
the family of the Furnivals. Ha, ha, ha!

Wit. Ay, ay, but that was but for a while. Not long, not
long; pshaw, I was not in my own power then. An orphan,
and this fellow was my guardian; ay, ay, I was glad to consent
to that man to come to London. He had the disposal of me
then. If I had not agreed to that, I might have been bound
prentice to a felt-maker in Shrewsbury; this fellow would have
bound me to a maker of felts.

Sir Wil. 'Sheart, and better than to be bound to a maker of
fops; where, I suppose, you have served your time; and now
you may set up for yourself.

Mrs. Mar. You intend to travel, sir, as I'm informed.

Sir Wil. Belike I may, madam. I may chance to sail upon
the salt seas, if my mind hold.

Pet. And the wind serve.

Sir Wil. Serve or not serve, I shan't ask license of you, sir;
nor the weather-cock your companion. I direct my discourse
to the lady, sir. 'Tis like my aunt may have told you, madam—
Yes, I have settled my concerns, I may say now, and am minded
to see foreign parts. If an how that the peace holds, whereby
that is taxes abate.

Mrs. Mar. I thought you had designed for France at all
adventures.

Sir Wil. I can't tell that; 'tis like I may, and 'tis like I may
not. I am somewhat dainty in making a resolution,—because
when I make it I keep it. I don't stand shill I, shall I, then;
if I say't, I'll do't: But I have thoughts to tarry a small matter
in town, to learn somewhat of your lingo first, before I cross the
seas. I'd gladly have a spice of your French as they say,
whereby to hold discourse in foreign countries.

Mrs. Mar. Here's an academy in town for that use.

Sir Wil. There is? 'Tis like there may.

Mrs. Mar. No doubt you will return very much improved.

Wit. Yes, refined like a Dutch skipper from a whale-fishing.

SCENE XVI

[*To them*] Lady WISHFORT *and* FAINALL.

Lady. Nephew, you are welcome.

Sir Wil. Aunt, your servant.

Fain. Sir Wilfull, your most faithful servant.

Sir Wil. Cousin Fainall, give me your hand.

Lady. Cousin Witwoud, your servant; Mr. Petulant, your servant—nephew, you are welcome again. Will you drink anything after your journey, nephew, before you eat? Dinner's almost ready.

Sir Wil. I'm very well I thank you, aunt—however, I thank you for your courteous offer. 'Sheart, I was afraid you would have been in the fashion too, and have remembered to have forgot your relations. Here's your Cousin Tony, belike, I mayn't call him brother for fear of offence.

Lady. O he's a rallier, nephew—my cousin's a wit; and your great wits always rally their best friends to chuse. When you have been abroad, nephew, you'll understand raillery better.

[Fain, *and* Mrs. Marwood *talk apart.*

Sir Wil. Why then let him hold his tongue in the meantime; and rail when that day comes.

SCENE XVII

[*To them*] Mincing.

Minc. Mem, I come to acquaint your laship that dinner is impatient.

Sir Wil. Impatient? Why then belike it won't stay 'till I pull off my boots. Sweetheart, can you help me to a pair of slippers?—My man's with his horses, I warrant.

Lady. Fie, fie, nephew, you would not pull off your boots here—go down into the hall—dinner shall stay for you.—My nephew's a little unbred, you'll pardon him, madam—Gentlemen, will you walk? Marwood?

Mrs. Mar. I'll follow you, madam,—before Sir Wilfull is ready.

SCENE XVIII

Marwood, Fainall.

Fain. Why then Foible's a bawd, an errant, rank, matchmaking bawd. And I, it seems, am a husband, a rank-husband; and my wife a very errant, rank-wife,—all in the way of the world. 'Sdeath, to be a cuckold by anticipation, a cuckold in embrio? Sure I was born with budding antlers like a young satyr, or a citizen's child. 'Sdeath, to be outwitted, to be outjilted—out-matrimonied—If I had kept my speed like a stag, 'twere somewhat—but to crawl after, with my horns like a snail, and be outstripped by my wife—'tis scurvy wedlock.

Mrs. Mar. Then shake it off, you have often wished for an opportunity to part;—and now you have it. But first prevent their plot,—the half of Millamant's fortune is too considerable to be parted with, to a foe, to Mirabell.

Fain. Dam him, that had been mine, had you not made that fond discovery—that had been forfeited, had they been married. My wife had added lustre to my horns, by that encrease of fortune, I could have worn 'em tipt with gold, though my forehead had been furnished like a deputy-lieutenant's hall.

Mrs. Mar. They may prove a cap of maintenance to you still, if you can away with your wife. And she's no worse than when you had her—I dare swear she had given up her game, before she was married.

Fain. Hum! That may be——

Mrs. Mar. You married her to keep you; and if you can contrive to have her keep you better than you expected, why should you not keep her longer than you intended?

Fain. The means, the means.

Mrs. Mar. Discover to my lady your wife's conduct; threaten to part with her—my lady loves her, and will come to any composition to save her reputation. Take the opportunity of breaking it, just upon the discovery of this imposture. My lady will be enraged beyond bounds, and sacrifice niece, and fortune, and all at that conjuncture. And let me alone to keep her warm; if she should flag in her part, I will not fail to prompt her.

Fain. Faith, this has an appearance.

Mrs. Mar. I'm sorry I hinted to my lady to endeavour a match between Millamant and Sir Wilfull, that may be an obstacle.

Fain. O for that matter leave me to manage him; I'll disable him for that, he will drink like a Dane: after dinner, I'll set his hand in.

Mrs. Mar. Well, how do you stand affected towards your lady?

Fain. Why faith I'm thinking of it.—Let me see—I am married already; so that's over—My wife has plaid the jade with me—well, that's over too—I never loved her, or if I had, why that would have been over too by this time—Jealous of her I cannot be, for I am certain; so there's an end of jealousie. Weary of her, I am and shall be—No, there's no end of that; no, no, that were too much to hope. Thus far concerning my repose. Now for my reputation—As to my own, I married not for it; so that's out of the question.—And as to my part in my wife's—why she had parted with hers before; so bringing none to me, she can take none from me; 'tis against all rule of play, that I should lose to one who has not wherewithal to stake.

Mrs. Mar. Besides, you forget, marriage is honourable.

Fain. Hum! Faith and that's well thought on; marriage is honourable, as you say; and if so, wherefore should cuckoldom be a discredit, being derived from so honourable a root?

Mrs. Mar. Nay, I know not; if the root be honourable, why not the branches?

Fain. So, so, why this point's clear.—Well, how do we proceed?

Mrs. Mar. I will contrive a letter which shall be delivered to my lady at the time when that rascal who is to act Sir Rowland is with her. It shall come as from an unknown hand—for the less I appear to know of the truth, the better I can play the incendiary. Besides, I would not have Foible provoked if I could help it,—because you know she knows some passages—nay, I expect all will come out—but let the mine be sprung first, and then I care not if I am discovered.

Fain. If the worst come to the worst, I'll turn my wife out to grass—I have already a deed of settlement of the best part of her estate; which I wheadled out of her; and that you shall partake at least.

Mrs. Mar. I hope you are convinced that I hate Mirabell now: you'll be no more jealous?

Fain. Jealous, no,—by this kiss—let husbands be jealous; but let the lover still believe: or if he doubt, let it be only to endear his pleasure, and prepare the joy that follows, when he proves his mistress true. But let husbands' doubts convert to endless jealousie; or if they have belief, let it corrupt to superstition, and blind credulity. I am single, and will herd no more with 'em. True, I wear the badge, but I'll disown the order. And since I take my leave of 'em, I care not if I leave 'em a common motto to their common crest.

All husbands must, or pain, or shame, endure;
The wife too jealous are, fools too secure.

ACT IV

SCENE I.—[*Scene continues*]

Lady WISHFORT *and* FOIBLE.

Lady. Is Sir Rowland coming, say'st thou, Foible? and are things in order?

Foib. Yes, madam. I have put wax-lights in the sconces; and placed the footmen in a row in the hall, in their best liveries, with the coachman and postilion to fill up the equipage.

Lady. Have you pullvilled the coachman and postilion, that they may not stink of the stable, when Sir Rowland comes by?

Foib. Yes, madam.

Lady. And are the dancers and the music ready, that he may be entertained in all points with correspondence to his passion?

Foib. All is ready, madam.

Lady. And—well—and how do I look, Foible?

Foib. Most killing well, madam.

Lady. Well, and how shall I receive him? In what figure shall I give his heart the first impression? There is a great deal in the first impression. Shall I sit?—No, I won't sit—I'll walk —ay, I'll walk from the door upon his entrance; and then turn full upon him—No, that will be too sudden. I'll lye—ay, I'll lye down—I'll receive him in my little dressing-room, there's a couch—yes, yes, I'll give the first impression on a couch—I won't lye neither, but loll and lean upon one elbow; with one foot a little dangling off, jogging in a thoughtful way—yes— and then as soon as he appears, start, ay, start and be surpriz..d, and rise to meet him in a pretty disorder—yes—O, nothing is more alluring than a levee from a couch in some confusion— it shews the foot to advantage, and furnishes with blushes, and re-composing airs beyond comparison. Hark! There's a coach.

Foib. 'Tis he, madam.

Lady. O dear, has my nephew made his addresses to Millamant? I ordered him.

Foib. Sir Wilfull is set in to drinking, madam, in the parlour.

Lady. Ods my life, I'll send him to her. Call her down, Foible; bring her hither. I'll send him as I go—When they are together, then come to me, Foible, that I may not be too long alone with Sir Rowland.

SCENE II

Mrs. MILLAMANT, Mrs. FAINALL, FOIBLE.

Foib. Madam, I stayed here, to tell your ladiship that Mr. Mirabell has waited this half-hour for an opportunity to talk with you. Though my lady's orders were to leave you and Sir Wilfull together. Shall I tell Mr. Mirabell that you are at leisure?

Milla. No—What would the dear man have? I am thoughtful, and would amuse myself,—bid him come another time.

> There never yet was woman made,
> Nor shall, but to be cursed.

[Repeating and walking about.

That's hard!

Mrs. Fain. You are very fond of Sir John Suckling to-day, Millamant, and the poets.

Milla. He? Ay, and filthy verses—so I am.

Foib. Sir Wilfull is coming, madam. Shall I send Mr. Mirabell away?

Milla. Ay, if you please, Foible, send him away,—or send him hither,—just as you will, dear Foible.—I think I'll see him— Shall I? Ay, let the wretch come.

Thyrsis, a youth of the inspired train. [*Repeating.*
Dear Fainall, entertain Sir Wilfull—thou hast philosophy to undergo a fool, thou art married and hast patience—I would confer with my own thoughts.

Mrs. Fain. I am obliged to you, that you would make me your proxy in this affair; but I have business of my own.

SCENE III

[*To them*] Sir WILFULL.

Mrs. Fain. O Sir Wilfull; you are come at the critical instant. There's your mistress up to the ears in love and contemplation, pursue your point, now or never.

Sir Wil. Yes; my aunt will have it so,—I would gladly have been encouraged with a bottle or two, because I'm somewhat wary at first, before I am acquainted—[*This while* MILLA. *walks about repeating to herself.*] But I hope, after a time, I shall break my mind—that is upon further acquaintance.—So for the present, cousin, I'll take my leave—if so be you'll be so kind to make my excuse, I'll return to my company——

Mrs. Fain. O fie, Sir Wilfull! What, you must not be daunted.

Sir Wil. Daunted, no, that's not it, it is not so much for that —for if so be that I set on't, I'll do't. But only for the present, 'tis sufficient 'till further acquaintance, that's all—your servant.

Mrs. Fain. Nay, I'll swear you shall never lose so favourable an opportunity, if I can help it. I'll leave you together, and lock the door.

SCENE IV

Sir WILFULL, MILLAMANT.

Sir Wil. Nay, nay, cousin,—I have forgot my gloves.—What d'ye do? 'Sheart, a' has locked the door indeed, I think—Nay, Cousin Fainall, open the door—Pshaw, what a vixon trick is this?—Nay, now a' has seen me too—cousin, I made bold to pass through as it were—I think this door's inchanted——

Milla. [*repeating*].

I prithee spare me, gentle boy,
Press me no more for that slight toy.

Sir Wil. Anan? Cousin, your servant.
Milla.   That foolish trifle of a heart——
Sir Wilfull!

Sir Wil. Yes—your servant. No offence, I hope, cousin.
Milla. [*repeating.*]

> I swear it will not do its part,
> Though thou dost thine, employ'st thy power and art.

Natural, easie Suckling!
Sir Wil. Anan? Suckling? No such suckling neither, cousin,
nor stripling: I thank Heaven, I'm no minor.
Milla. Ah, rustick, ruder than Gothick.
Sir Wil. Well, well, I shall understand your lingo one of these
days, cousin, in the meanwhile I must answer in plain English.
Milla. Have you any business with me, Sir Wilfull?
Sir Wil. Not at present, cousin.—Yes, I made bold to see, to
come and know if that how you were disposed to fetch a walk
this evening, if so be that I might not be troublesome, I would
have sought a walk with you.
Milla. A walk? What then?
Sir Wil. Nay, nothing—only for the walk's sake, that's all——
Milla. I nauseate walking; 'tis a country diversion, I loath
the country and everything that relates to it.
Sir Wil. Indeed! Hah! Look ye, look ye, you do? Nay,
'tis like you may—Here are choice of pastimes here in town, as
plays and the like, that must be confessed indeed——
Milla. Ah l'etourdie ! I hate the town too.
Sir Wil. Dear heart, that's much—Hah! that you should
hate 'em both! Hah! 'tis like you may; there are some can't
relish the town, and others can't away with the country,—'tis
like you may be one of those, cousin.
Milla. Ha, ha, ha. Yes, 'tis like I may.—You have nothing
further to say to me?
Sir Wil. Not at present, cousin.—'Tis like when I have an
opportunity to be more private, I may break my mind in some
measure—I conjecture you partly guess—However, that's as
time shall try,—but spare to speak and spare to speed, as they
say.
Milla. If it is of no great importance, Sir Wilfull, you will
oblige me to leave me: I have just now a little business——
Sir Wil. Enough, enough, cousin: yes, yes, all a case—when
you're disposed, when you're disposed. Now's as well as another
time; and another time as well as now. All's one for that.—
Yes, yes, if your concerns call you, there's no haste; it will keep
cold as they say—Cousin, your servant.—I think this door's
locked.
Milla. You may go this way, sir.
Sir Wil. Your servant, then with your leave I'll return to my
company.
Milla. Ay, ay; ha, ha, ha.

> Like Phœbus sung the no less am'rous boy.

SCENE V

MILLAMANT, MIRABELL.

Mira.   Like Daphne she, as lovely and as coy.
Do you lock yourself up from me, to make my search more
curious? Or is this pretty artifice contrived, to signifie that
here the chace must end, and my pursuit be crowned, for you
can fly no further?

Milla. Vanity! No—I'll fly and be followed to the last
moment, though I am upon the very verge of matrimony, I
expect you should sollicit me as much as if I were wavering at
the grate of a monastery, with one foot over the threshold. I'll
be sollicited to the very last, nay and afterwards.

Mira. What, after the last?

Milla. O, I should think I was poor and had nothing to
bestow, if I were reduced to an inglorious ease, and freed from
the agreeable fatigues of sollicitation.

Mira. But do not you know, that when favours are conferred
upon instant and tedious sollicitation, that they diminish in
their value, and that both the giver loses the grace, and the
receiver lessens his pleasure?

Milla. It may be in things of common application; but never
sure in love. O, I hate a lover that can dare to think he draws
a moment's air, independent on the bounty of his mistress.
There is not so impudent a thing in nature, as the sawcy look of
an assured man, confident of success. The pedantick arrogance
of a very husband has not so pragmatical an air. Ah! I'll
never marry, unless I am first made sure of my will and pleasure.

Mira. Would you have 'em both before marriage? Or will
you be contented with the first now, and stay for the other 'till
after grace?

Milla. Ah, don't be impertinent—My dear liberty, shall I
leave thee? My faithful solitude, my darling contemplation,
must I bid you then adieu? Ay-h, adieu—my morning thoughts,
agreeable wakings, indolent slumbers, all ye *douceurs*, ye *someils
du matin*, adieu—I can't do't, 'tis more than impossible—
Positively, Mirabell, I'll lye abed in a morning as long as I please.

Mira. Then I'll get up in a morning as early as I please.

Milla. Ah! Idle creature, get up when you will—And d'ye
hear, I won't be called names after I'm married; positively I
won't be called names.

Mira. Names!

Milla. Ay, as wife, spouse, my dear, joy, jewel, love, sweetheart, and the rest of that nauseous cant, in which men and their
wives are so fulsomly familiar—I shall never bear that—Good
Mirabell, don't let us be familiar or fond, nor kiss before folks,
like my Lady Fadler and Sir Francis: nor go to Hide Park

together the first Sunday in a new chariot, to provoke eyes and whispers; and then never be seen there together again; as if we were proud of one another the first week, and ashamed of one another ever after. Let us never visit together, nor go to a play together, but let us be very strange and well bred: let us be as strange as if we had been married a great while; and as well bred as if we were not married at all.

Mira. Have you any more conditions to offer? Hitherto your demands are pretty reasonable.

Milla. Trifles,—as liberty to pay and receive visits to and from whom I please; to write and receive letters, without interrogatories or wry faces on your part; to wear what I please; and chuse conversation with regard only to my own taste; to have no obligation upon me to converse with wits that I don't like, because they are your acquaintance; or to be intimate with fools because they may be your relations. Come to dinner when I please, dine in my dressing-room when I'm out of humour, without giving a reason. To have my closet inviolate; to be sole empress of my tea-table, which you must never presume to approach without first asking leave. And lastly, wherever I am, you shall always knock at the door before you come in. These articles subscribed, if I continue to endure you a little longer, I may by degrees dwindle into a wife.

Mira. Your bill of fare is something advanced in this latter account. Well, have I liberty to offer conditions—that when you are dwindled into a wife, I may not be beyond measure enlarged into a husband?

Milla. You have free leave, propose your utmost, speak and spare not.

Mira. I thank you. *Inprimis* then, I covenant that your acquaintance be general; that you admit no sworn confident, or intimate of your own sex; no she friend to skreen her affairs under your countenance, and tempt you to make trial of a mutual secresie. No decoy-duck to wheadle you a *fop—scrambling* to the play in a mask—then bring you home in a pretended fright, when you think you shall be found out—and rail at me for missing the play, and disappointing the frolick which you had to pick me up and prove my constancy.

Milla. Detestable *inprimis!* I go to the play in a mask!

Mira. *Item*, I article, that you continue to like your own face as long as I shall: and while it passes currant with me, that you endeavour not to new coin it. To which end, together with all vizards for the day, I prohibit all masks for the night, made of oiled-skins and I know not what—hog's bones, hare's gall, pig water, and the marrow of a roasted cat. In short, I forbid all commerce with the gentlewoman in *what-d'ye-call-it* Court. *Item*, I shut my doors against all bauds with baskets, and pennyworths of *muslin, china, fans, atlasses*, etc.—*Item*, when you shall be breeding——

Milla. Ah! name it not.

Mira. Which may be presumed, with a blessing on our endeavours——

Milla. Odious endeavours!

Mira. I denounce against all strait lacing, squeezing for a shape, 'till you mould my boy's head like a sugar-loaf; and instead of a man-child, make me father to a crooked-billet. Lastly, to the dominion of the *tea-table* I submit.—But with *proviso*, that you exceed not in your province; but restrain yourself to native and simple *tea-table* drinks, as *tea, chocolate,* and *coffee.* As likewise to genuine and authorised *tea-table* talk—such as mending of fashions, spoiling reputations, railing at absent friends, and so forth—but that on no account you encroach upon the men's prerogative, and presume to drink healths, or toast fellows; for prevention of which, I banish all *foreign forces,* all auxiliaries to the *tea-table,* as *orange-brandy,* all *anniseed, cinamon, citron* and *Barbado's-waters,* together with *ratafia* and the most noble spirit of *clary.*—But for *couslip-wine, poppy-water,* and all *dormitives,* those I allow.—These *provisos* admitted, in other things I may prove a tractable and complying husband.

Milla. O horrid *provisos!* filthy strong waters! I toast fellows, odious men! I hate your odious *provisos.*

Mira. Then we're agreed. Shall I kiss your hand upon the contract? and here comes one to be a witness to the sealing of the deed.

SCENE VI

[To them] Mrs. FAINALL.

Milla. Fainall, what shall I do? Shall I have him? I think I must have him.

Mrs. Fain. Ay, ay, take him, take him, what should you do?

Milla. Well then—I'll take my death I'm in a horrid fright—Fainall, I shall never say it—Well—I think—I'll endure you.

Mrs. Fain. Fy, fy, have him, have him, and tell him so in plain terms: for I am sure you have a mind to him.

Milla. Are you? I think I have—and the horrid man looks as if he thought so too—Well, you ridiculous thing you, I'll have you—I won't be kissed, nor I won't be thanked—Here, kiss my hand though—so, hold your tongue now, don't say a word.

Mrs. Fain. Mirabell, there's a necessity for your obedience; —you have neither time to talk nor stay. My mother is coming; and in my conscience, if she should see you, would fall into fits, and maybe not recover time enough to return to Sir Rowland; who, as Foible tells me, is in a fair way to succeed. Therefore spare your extacies for another occasion, and slip down the back stairs, where Foible waits to consult you.

Milla. Ay, go, go. In the meantime I suppose you have said something to please me.

Mira. I am all obedience.

SCENE VII

MILLAMANT, MRS. FAINALL.

Mrs. Fain. Yonder Sir Wilfull's drunk; and so noisie that my mother has been forced to leave Sir Rowland to appease him; but he answers her only with singing and drinking—What they may have done by this time I know not; but Petulant and he were upon quarrelling as I came by.

Milla. Well, if Mirabell should not make a good husband, I am a lost thing; for I find I love him violently.

Mrs. Fain. So it seems; for you mind not what's said to you. —If you doubt him, you had best take up with Sir Wilfull.

Milla. How can you name that superannuated lubber? foh!

SCENE VIII

[*To them*] WITWOUD *from drinking*.

Mrs. Fain. So, is the fray made up, that you have left 'em?

Wit. Left 'em? I could stay no longer—I have laughed like ten christnings—I am tipsie with laughing—if I had staid any longer I should have burst,—I must have been let out and pieced in the sides like an unsized camlet—Yes, yes, the fray is composed; my lady came in like a *noli prosequi*, and stopt the proceedings.

Milla. What was the dispute?

Wit. That's the jest; there was no dispute. They could neither of 'em speak for rage; and so fell a sputtering at one another like two roasting apples.

SCENE IX

[*To them*] PETULANT *drunk*.

Wit. Now, Petulant? all's over, all's well? Gad, my head begins to whim it about—Why dost thou not speak? thou art both as drunk and as mute as a fish.

Pet. Look you, Mrs. Millamant—if you can love me, dear nymph—say it—and that's the conclusion—pass on, or pass off,—that's all.

Wit. Thou hast uttered volumes, folios, in less than *decimo sexto*, my dear Lacedemonian. Sirrah, Petulant, thou art an epitomiser of words.

Pet. Witwoud—you are an annihilator of sense.

Wit. Thou art a retailer of phrases; and dost deal in remnants of remnants, like a maker of pincushions—thou art in truth (metaphorically speaking) a speaker of shorthand.

Pet. Thou art (without a figure) just one half of an ass, and Baldwin yonder, thy half-brother, is the rest—a gemini of asses split, would make just four of you.

Wit. Thou dost bite, my dear mustard-seed; kiss me for that.

Pet. Stand off—I'll kiss no more males,—I have kissed your *twin* yonder in a humour of reconciliation, 'till he (*hiccup*) rises upon my stomach like a radish.

Milla. Eh! filthy creature—what was the quarrel?

Pet. There was no quarrel—there might have been a quarrel.

Wit. If there had been words enow between 'em to have expressed provocation, they had gone together by the ears like a pair of castanets.

Pet. You were the quarrel.

Milla. Me!

Pet. If I have a humour to quarrel, I can make less matters conclude premises.—If you are not handsom, what then; if I have a humour to prove it?—If I shall have my reward, say so; if not, fight for your face the next time yourself—I'll go sleep.

Wit. Do, wrap thyself up like a woodlouse, and dream revenge—and hear me, if thou canst learn to write by to-morrow morning, pen me a challenge—I'll carry it for thee.

Pet. Carry your mistress's monkey a spider,—go flea dogs, and read romances—I'll go to bed to my maid.

Mrs. Fain. He's horridly drunk—how came you all in this pickle?

Wit. A plot, a plot, to get rid of the knight,—your husband's advice; but he sneaked off.

SCENE X

Sir WILFULL *drunk*, Lady WISHFORT, WITWOUD, MILLAMANT, Mrs. FAINALL.

Lady. Out upon't, out upon't, at years of discretion, and comport yourself at this rantipole rate.

Sir Wil. No offence, aunt.

Lady. Offence? As I'm a person, I'm ashamed of you—Fogh! how you stink of wine! D'ye think my niece will ever endure such a *borachio!* you're an absolute *borachio.*

Sir Wil. Borachio!

Lady. At a time when you should commence an amour, and put your best foot foremost——

Sir Wil. 'Sheart, an you grutch me your liquor, make a bill—give me more drink, and take my purse. [*Sings.*

> Prithee fill me the glass
> 'Till it laugh in my face,
> With ale that is potent and mellow;
> He that whines for a lass
> Is an ignorant ass,
> For a *bumper* has not its fellow.

But if you would have me marry my cousin, say the word, and I'll do't—Wilfull will do't, that's the word—Wilfull will do't, that's my crest—my motto I have forgot.

Lady. My nephew's a little overtaken, cousin—but 'tis with drinking your health—O' my word you are obliged to him——

Sir Wil. In vino veritas, aunt:—If I drunk your health to-day, cousin, I am a *borachio.* But if you have a mind to be married say the word, and send for the piper, Wilfull will do't. If not, dust it away, and let's have t'other round—Tony, 'odsheart, where's Tony—Tony's an honest fellow, but he spits after a bumper, and that's a fault. [*Sings.*

> We'll drink and we'll never ha' done, boys,
> Put the glass then around with the sun, boys,
> Let Apollo's example invite us;
> For he's drunk every night,
> And that makes him so bright,
> That he's able next morning to light us.

The sun's a good pimple, an honest soaker, he has a cellar at your Antipodes. If I travel, aunt, I touch at your Antipodes—your Antipodes are a good rascally sort of topsie-turvy fellows—if I had a bumper I'd stand upon my head and drink a health to 'em—A match or no match, cousin, with the hard name—aunt, Wilfull will do't. If she has her maidenhead let her look to't; if she has not, let her keep her own counsel in the meantime, and cry out at the nine months' end.

Milla. Your pardon, madam, I can stay no longer—Sir Wilfull grows very powerful. Egh! how he smells! I shall be overcome if I stay. Come, cousin.

SCENE XI

Lady WISHFORT, Sir WILFULL WITWOUD,
Mr. WITWOUD, FOIBLE.

Lady. Smells! he would poison a tallow-chandler and his family. Beastly creature, I know not what to do with him.—Travel, quoth a; ay travel, travel, get thee gone, get thee but

far enough, to the Saracens, or the Tartars, or the Turks—for
thou art not fit to live in a Christian commonwealth, thou
beastly pagan.

Sir Wil. Turks, no; no Turks, aunt: your Turks are infidels,
and believe not in the grape. Your Mahometan, your Mussul-
man is a dry stinkard—no offence, aunt. My map says that
your Turk is not so honest a man as your Christian—I cannot
find by the map that your mufti is orthodox—whereby it is a
plain case, that orthodox is a hard word, aunt, and (*hiccup*)
Greek for claret. [*Sings.*

> To drink is a Christian diversion
> Unknown to the Turk or the Persian:
> Let Mahometan fools
> Live by heathenish rules,
> And be damned over tea-cups and coffee.
> But let British lads sing,
> Crown a health to the king,
> And a fig for your sultan and Sophy.

Ah, Tony! [FOIBLE *whispers* Lady WISHFORT.

Lady. Sir Rowland impatient? Good lack! what shall I do
with this beastly tumbril?—Go lie down and sleep, you sot—or
as I'm a person, I'll have you bastinadoed with broom-sticks.
Call up the wenches with broom-sticks.

Sir Wil. Ahey? Wenches, where are the wenches?

Lady. Dear Cousin Witwoud, get him away, and you will bind
me to you inviolably. I have an affair of moment that invades
me with some precipitation.—You will oblige me to all futurity.

Wit. Come, knight—pox on him, I don't know what to say to
him—will you go to a cock-match?

Sir Wil. With a wench, Tony? Is she a shake-bag, sirrah?
Let me bite your cheek for that.

Wit. Horrible! He has a breath like a bagpipe—Ay, ay,
come, will you march, my Salopian?

Sir Wil. Lead on, little Tony—I'll follow thee, my Anthony,
my Tantony. Sirrah, thou shalt be my Tantony, and I'll be
thy pig.

—And a fig for your sultan and Sophy.

Lady. This will never do. It will never make a match—at
least before he has been abroad.

SCENE XII

Lady WISHFORT, WAITWELL *disguised as for* Sir ROWLAND.

Lady. Dear Sir Rowland, I am confounded with confusion at
the retrospection of my own rudeness,—I have more pardons to

ask than the pope distributes in the year of jubile. But I hope where there is likely to be so near an alliance, we may unbend the severity of decorum, and dispense with a little ceremony.

Wait. My impatience, madam, is the effect of my transport; —and 'till I have the possession of your adorable person, I am tantalised on the rack; and do but hang, madam, on the tenter of expectation.

Lady. You have excess of gallantry, Sir Rowland; and press things to a conclusion, with a most prevailing vehemence.— But a day or two for decency of marriage——

Wait. For decency of funeral, madam. The delay will break my heart—or if that should fail, I shall be poisoned. My nephew will get an inkling of my designs, and poison me,—and I would willingly starve him before I die—I would gladly go out of the world with that satisfaction.—That would be some comfort to me, if I could but live so long as to be revenged on that unnatural viper.

Lady. Is he so unnatural, say you? Truly I would contribute much both to the saving of your life, and the accomplishment of your revenge—not that I respect myself; though he has been a perfidious wretch to me.

Wait. Perfidious to you!

Lady. O Sir Rowland, the hours that he has died away at my feet, the tears that he has shed, the oaths that he has sworn, the palpitations that he has felt, the trances and the tremblings, the ardors and the ecstacies, the kneelings, and the risings, the heart-heavings and the hand-gripings, the pangs and the pathetick regards of his protesting eyes! Oh, no memory can register.

Wait. What, my rival! Is the rebel my rival? a' dies.

Lady. No, don't kill him at once, Sir Rowland, starve him gradually inch by inch.

Wait. I'll do't. In three weeks he shall be bare-foot; in a month out at knees with begging an alms,—he shall starve upward and upward, 'till he has nothing living but his head, and then go out in a stink like a candle's end upon a save-all.

Lady. Well, Sir Rowland, you have the way,—you are no novice in the labyrinth of love—you have the clue—But as I am a person, Sir Rowland, you must not attribute my yielding to any sinister appetite, or indigestion of widow-hood; nor impute my complacency to any lethargy of continence—I hope you do not think me prone to any iteration of nuptials——

Wait. Far be it from me——

Lady. If you do, I protest I must recede—or think that I have made a prostitution of decorums, but in the vehemence of compassion, and to save the life of a person of so much importance——

Wait. I esteem it so——

Lady. Or else you wrong my condescension——

Wait. I do not, I do not——
Lady. Indeed you do.
Wait. I do not, fair shrine of virtue.
Lady. If you think the least scruple of caruality was an ingredient——
Wait. Dear madam, no. You are all camphire and frankincense, all chastity and odour.
Lady. Or that——

SCENE XIII

[*To them*] FOIBLE.

Foib. Madam, the dancers are ready, and there's one with a letter, who must deliver it into your own hands.
Lady. Sir Rowland, will you give me leave? Think favourably, judge candidly, and conclude you have found a person who would suffer racks in honour's cause, dear Sir Rowland, and will wait on you incessantly.

SCENE XIV

WAITWELL, FOIBLE.

Wait. Fie, fie!—What a slavery have I undergone; spouse, hast thou any cordial, I want spirits.
Foib. What a washy rogue art thou, to pant thus for a quarter of an hour's lying and swearing to a fine lady?
Wait. O, she is the antidote to desire. Spouse, thou wilt fare the worse for't—I shall have no appetite to iteration of nuptials this eight and forty hours—By this hand I'd rather be a chairman in the dog-days, than act Sir Rowland 'till this time to-morrow.

SCENE XV

[*To them*] Lady *with a letter.*

Lady. Call in the dancers;—Sir Rowland, we'll sit, if you please, and see the entertainment   [*Dance.*
Now with your permission, Sir Rowland, I will peruse my letter—I would open it in your presence, because I would not make you uneasie. If it should make you uneasie I would burn it—speak if it does—but you may see, the superscription is like a woman's hand.
Foib. By heaven! Mrs. Marwood's, I know it,—my heart akes—get it from her——   [*To him.*

Wait. A woman's hand? No, madam, that's no woman's hand, I see that already. That's somebody whose throat must be cut.

Lady. Nay, Sir Rowland, since you give me a proof of your passion by your jealousie, I promise you I'll make a return, by a frank communication—You shall see it—we'll open it together —look you here.

[*Reads.*] " Madam, though unknown to you,"—Look you there, 'tis from nobody that I know—" I have that honour for your character, that I think myself obliged to let you know you are abused. He who pretends to be Sir Rowland is a cheat and a rascal——" Oh heavens! what's this?

Foib. Unfortunate, all's ruined.

Wait. How, how, let me see, let me see [*reading*], " A rascal and disguised, and suborned for that imposture,"—O villany! O villany!—" by the contrivance of——"

Lady. I shall faint, I shall die, oh!

Foib. Say 'tis your nephew's hand.—Quickly, his plot, swear, swear it.   [*To him.*

Wait. Here's a villain! Madam, don't you perceive it, don't you see it?

Lady. Too well, too well. I have seen too much.

Wait. I told you at first I knew the hand—A woman's hand? The rascal writes a sort of a large hand; your Roman hand—I saw there was a throat to be cut presently. If he were my son, as he is my nephew, I'd pistol him——

Foib. O treachery! But are you sure, Sir Rowland, it is his writing?

Wait. Sure? Am I here? do I live? do I love this pearl of India? I have twenty letters in my pocket from him, in the same character.

Lady. How!

Foib. O what luck it is, Sir Rowland, that you were present at this juncture! This was the business that brought Mr. Mirabell disguised to Madam Millamant this afternoon. I thought something was contriving, when he stole by me and would have hid his face.

Lady. How, how!—I heard the villain was in the house indeed; and now I remember, my niece went away abruptly, when Sir Wilfull was to have made his addresses.

Foib. Then, then, madam, Mr. Mirabell waited for her in her chamber; but I would not tell your ladiship to discompose you when you were to receive Sir Rowland.

Wait. Enough, his date is short.

Foib. No, good Sir Rowland, don't incur the law.

Wait. Law! I care not for law. I can but die, and 'tis in a good cause—my lady shall be satisfied of my truth and innocence, though it cost me my life.

Lady. No, dear Sir Rowland, don't fight, if you should be

killed I must never shew my face; or hanged—O consider my reputation, Sir Rowland—No, you shan't fight.—I'll go in and examine my niece; I'll make her confess. I conjure you, Sir Rowland, by all your love, not to fight.

Wait. I am charmed, madam, I obey. But some proof you must let me give you;—I'll go for a black box, which contains the writings of my whole estate, and deliver that into your hands.

Lady. Ay, dear Sir Rowland, that will be some comfort, bring the black box.

Wait. And may I presume to bring a contract to be signed this night? May I hope so far?

Lady. Bring what you will; but come alive, pray come alive. O this is a happy discovery.

Wait. Dead or alive I'll come—and married we will be in spight of treachery; ay, and get an heir that shall defeat the last remaining glimpse of hope in my abandoned nephew. Come, my buxom widow:

> E'er long you shall substantial proof receive
> That I'm an arrant knight——

Foib. Or arrant knave.

ACT V

SCENE I.—[*Scene continues*]

Lady WISHFORT *and* FOIBLE.

Lady. Out of my house, out of my house, thou viper. thou serpent, that I have fostered; thou bosom traitress, that I raised from nothing—begone, begone, begone, go, go,—that I took from washing of old gause and weaving of dead hair, with a bleak blue nose, over a chafing-dish of starved embers, and dining behind a traver's rag, in a shop no bigger than a bird-cage,—go, go, starve again, do, do.

Foib. Dear madam, I'll beg pardon on my knees.

Lady. Away, out, out, go set up for yourself again—do, drive a trade, do, with your threepenny-worth of small ware, flaunting upon a packthread, under a brandy-feller's bulk, or against a dead wall by a ballad-monger. Go, hang out an old frisoneer-gorget with a yard of yellow colberteen again; do; an old gnawed mask, two rows of pins and a child's fiddle; a glass necklace with the beads broken, and a quilted nightcap with one ear. Go, go, drive a trade.—These were your commodities, you treacherous trull, this was the merchandize you dealt in, when

I took you into my house, placed you next myself, and made you governante of my whole family. You have forgot this, have you, now you have feathered your nest?

Foib. No, no, dear madam. Do but hear me, have but a moment's patience—I'll confess all. Mr. Mirabell seduced me; I am not the first that he has wheadled with his dissembling tongue; your ladiship's own wisdom has been deluded by him, then how should I, a poor ignorant, defend myself? O madam, if you knew but what he promised me, and how he assured me your ladiship should come to no damage—or else the wealth of the Indies should not have bribed me to conspire against so good, so sweet, so kind a lady as you have been to me.

Lady. No damage? What, to betray me, to marry me to a cast-serving-man; to make me a receptacle, an hospital for a decayed pimp? No damage? O thou frontless impudence, more than a big-bellied actress.

Foib. Pray do but hear me, madam, he could not marry your ladiship, madam—no indeed, his marriage was to have been void in law; for he was married to me first, to secure your ladiship. He could not have bedded your ladiship; for if he had consummated with your ladiship, he must have run the risque of the law, and been put upon his clergy—Yes indeed, I enquired of the law in that case before I would meddle or make.

Lady. What, then I have been your property, have I? I have been convenient to you, it seems,—while you were catering for Mirabell; I have been broaker for you? What, have you made a passive bawd of me?—This exceeds all precedent; I am brought to fine uses, to become a botcher of second-hand marriages between Abigails and Andrews! I'll couple you. Yes, I'll baste you together, you and your Philander. I'll Duke's Place you, as I'm a person. Your turtle is in custody already: you shall coo in the same cage, if there be constable or warrant in the parish.

Foib. O that ever I was born, O that I was ever married,— a bride, ay, I shall be a Bridewell-bride. Oh!

SCENE II

Mrs FAINALL, FOIBLE.

Mrs. Fain. Poor Foible, what's the matter?

Foib. O madam, my lady's gone for a constable; I shall be had to a justice, and put to Bridewell to beat hemp; poor Waitwell's gone to prison already.

Mrs. Fain. Have a good heart, Foible, Mirabell's gone to give security for him. This is all Marwood's and my husband's doing.

Foib. Yes, yes; I know it, madam; she was in my lady's

closet, and overheard all that you said to me before dinner. She sent the letter to my lady; and that missing effect, Mr. Fainall laid this plot to arrest Waitwell, when he pretended to go for the papers; and in the meantime Mrs. Marwood declared all to my lady.

Mrs. Fain. Was there no mention made of me in the letter? —My mother does not suspect my being in the confederacy? I fancy Marwood has not told her, though she has told my husband.

Foib. Yes, madam; but my lady did not see that part: we stifled the letter before she read so far. Has that mischievous devil told Mr. Fainall of your ladiship then?

Mrs. Fain. Ay, all's out, my affair with Mirabell, everything discovered. This is the last day of our living together, that's my comfort.

Foib. Indeed, madam, and so 'tis a comfort if you knew all,— he has been even with your ladiship; which I could have told you long enough since, but I love to keep peace and quietness by my good will: I had rather bring friends together than set 'em at distance. But Mrs. Marwood and he are nearer related than ever their parents thought for.

Mrs. Fain. Say'st thou so, Foible? Canst thou prove this?

Foib. I can take my oath of it, madam, so can Mrs. Mincing; we have had many a fair word from Madam Marwood, to conceal something that passed in our chamber one evening when you were at Hide Park;—and we were thought to have gone a walking: but we went up unawares,—though we were sworn to secresie too; Madam Marwood took a book and swore us upon it: but it was but a book of poems,—so long as it was not a Bible-oath, we may break it with a safe conscience.

Mrs. Fain. This discovery is the most opportune thing I could wish. Now Mincing?

SCENE III

[To them] MINCING.

Minc. My lady would speak with Mrs. Foible, mem. Mr. Mirabell is with her; he has set your spouse at liberty, Mrs. Foible, and would have you hide yourself in my lady's closet, 'till my old lady's anger is abated. O, my old lady is in a perilous passion at something Mr. Fainall has said; he swears, and my old lady cries. There's a fearful hurricane I vow. He says, mem, how that he'll have my lady's fortune made over to him, or he'll be divorced.

Mrs. Fain. Does your lady or Mirabell know that?

Minc. Yes, mem, they have sent me to see if Sir Wilfull be sober, and to bring him to them. My lady is resolved to have him I think, rather than lose such a vast sum as six thousand pound. O, come, Mrs. Foible, I hear my old lady.

Mrs. Fain. Foible, you must tell Mincing that she must prepare to vouch when I call her.

Foib. Yes, yes, madam.

Minc. O yes, mem, I'll vouch anything for your ladiship's service, be what it will.

SCENE IV

Mrs. FAINALL, Lady WISHFORT, MARWOOD.

Lady. O my dear friend, how can I enumerate the benefits that I have received from your goodness? To you I owe the timely discovery of the false vows of Mirabell; to you I owe the detection of the impostor Sir Rowland. And now you are become an intercessor with my son-in-law, to save the honour of my house, and compound for the frailties of my daughter. Well, friend, you are enough to reconcile me to the bad world, or else I would retire to desarts and solitudes; and feed harmless sheep by groves and purling streams. Dear Marwood, let us leave the world, and retire by ourselves and be shepherdesses.

Mrs. Mar. Let us first dispatch the affair in hand, madam. We shall have leisure to think of retirement afterwards. Here is one who is concerned in the treaty.

Lady. O daughter, daughter, is it possible thou should'st be my child, bone of my bone, and flesh of my flesh, and as I may say, another me, and yet transgress the most minute particle of severe virtue? Is it possible you should lean aside to iniquity, who have been cast in the direct mold of virtue? I have not only been a mold but a pattern for you, and a model for you, after you were brought into the world.

Mrs. Fain. I don't understand your ladiship.

Lady. Not understand? Why, have you not been naught? Have you not been sophisticated? Not understand? Here I am ruined to compound for your caprices and your cuckoldoms. I must pawn my plate and my jewels, and ruin my niece, and all little enough——

Mrs. Fain. I am wronged and abused, and so are you. 'Tis a false accusation, as false as hell, as false as your friend there, ay, or your friend's friend, my false husband.

Mrs. Mar. My friend, Mrs. Fainall? Your husband my friend, what do you mean?

Mrs. Fain. I know what I mean, madam, and so do you; and so shall the world at a time convenient.

Mrs. Mar. I am sorry to see you so passionate, madam. More temper would look more like innocence. But I have done. I am sorry my zeal to serve your ladiship and family should admit of misconstruction, or make me liable to affronts. You will pardon me, madam, if I meddle no more with an affair in which I am not personally concerned.

Lady. O dear friend, I am so ashamed that you should meet with such returns—You ought to ask pardon on your knees, ungrateful creature; she deserves more from you, than all your life can accomplish—O don't leave me destitute in this perplexity;—no, stick to me, my good genius.

Mrs. Fain. I tell you, madam, you're abused—Stick to you? ay, like a leach, to suck your best blood—she'll drop off when she's full. Madam, you shan't pawn a bodkin, nor part with a brass counter, in composition for me. I defie 'em all. Let 'em prove their aspersions: I know my own innocence, and dare stand a trial.

SCENE V

Lady WISHFORT, MARWOOD.

Lady. Why, if she should be innocent, if she should be wronged after all, ha? I don't know what to think,—and I promise you, her education has been unexceptionable—I may say it; for I chiefly made it my own care to initiate her very infancy in the rudiments of virtue, and to impress upon her tender years a young odium and aversion to the very sight of men,—ay, friend, she would ha' shrieked if she had but seen a man, 'till she was in her teens. As I'm a person 'tis true.—She was never suffered to play with a male-child, though but in coats; nay, her very babies were of the feminine gender,—O, she never looked a man in the face but her own father, or the chaplain, and him we made a shift to put upon her for a woman, by the help of his long garments, and his sleek face; 'till she was going in her fifteen.

Mrs. Mar. 'Twas much she should be deceived so long.

Lady. I warrant you, or she would never have born to have been catechised by him; and have heard his long lectures against singing and dancing, and such debaucheries; and going to filthy plays; and prophane musick-meetings, where the lewd trebles squeek nothing but bawdy, and the bases roar blasphemy. O, she would have swooned at the sight or name of an obscene play-book—and can I think after all this, that my daughter can be naught? What, a whore? And thought it excommunication to set her foot within the door of a play-house. O dear friend, I can't believe it, no, no; as she says, let him prove it, let him prove it.

Mrs. Mar. Prove it, madam? What, and have your name prostituted in a publick court; yours and your daughter's reputation worried at the bar by a pack of bawling lawyers?

To be ushered in with an *O yes* of scandal; and have your case opened by an old fumbling leacher in a quoif like a man midwife, to bring your daughter's infamy to light; to be a theme for legal punsters, and quiblers by the statute; and become a jest, against a rule of court, where there is no precedent for a jest in any record; not even in Doomsday Book: to discompose the gravity of the bench, and provoke naughty interrogatories in more naughty law Latin; while the good judge, tickled with the proceeding, simpers under a grey beard, and figes off and on his cushion as if he had swallowed cantharides, or sate upon cowitch.

Lady. O, 'tis very hard!

Mrs. Mar. And then to have my young revellers of the Temple take notes, like prentices at a conventicle; and after talk it over again in Commons, or before drawers in an eating-house.

Lady. Worse and worse.

Mrs. Mar. Nay, this is nothing; if it would end here 'twere well. But it must after this be consigned by the shorthand writers to the publick press; and from thence be transferred to the hands, nay, into the throats and lungs of hawkers, with voices more licentious than the loud flounder-man's: and this you must hear 'till you are stunned; nay, you must hear nothing else for some days.

Lady. O, 'tis insupportable. No, no, dear friend, make it up, make it up; ay, ay, I'll compound. I'll give up all, myself and my all, my niece and her all—anything, everything for composition.

Mrs. Mar. Nay, madam, I advise nothing, I only lay before you, as a friend, the inconveniencies which perhaps you have overseen. Here comes Mr. Fainall, if he will be satisfied to huddle up all in silence, I shall be glad. You must think I would rather congratulate than condole with you.

SCENE VI

Fainall, Lady Wishfort, Mrs. Marwood.

Lady. Ay, ay, I do not doubt it, dear Marwood: no, no, I do not doubt it.

Fain. Well, madam; I have suffered myself to be overcome by the importunity of this lady your friend; and am content you shall enjoy your own proper estate during life; on condition you oblige yourself never to marry, under such penalty as I think convenient.

Lady. Never to marry?

Fain. No more Sir Rowlands,—the next imposture may not be so timely detected.

Mrs. Mar. That condition, I dare answer, my lady will con sent to, without difficulty; she has already but too much experienced the perfidiousness of men. Besides, madam, when we retire to our pastoral solitude we shall bid adieu to all other thoughts.

Lady. Ay, that's true; but in case of necessity; as of health, or some such emergency——

Fain. O, if you are prescribed marriage, you shall be considered; I will only reserve to myself the power to chuse for you. If your physick be wholsome, it matters not who is your apothecary. Next, my wife shall settle on me the remainder of her fortune, not made over already; and for her maintenance depend entirely on my discretion.

Lady. This is most inhumanly savage; exceeding the barbarity of a Muscovite husband.

Fain. I learned it from his czarish majesty's retinue, in a winter evening's conference over brandy and pepper, amongst other secrets of matrimony and policy, as they are at present practised in the northern hemisphere. But this must be agreed unto, and that positively. Lastly, I will be endowed, in right of my wife, with that six thousand pound, which is the moiety of Mrs. Millamant's fortune in your possession; and which she has forfeited (as will appear by the last will and testament of your deceased husband, Sir Jonathan Wishfort) by her disobedience in contracting herself against your consent or knowledge; and by refusing the offered match with Sir Wilfull Witwoud, which you, like a careful aunt, had provided for her.

Lady. My nephew was *non compos;* and could not make his addresses.

Fain. I come to make demands—I'll hear no objections.

Lady. You will grant me time to consider?

Fain. Yes, while the instrument is drawing, to which you must set your hand 'till more sufficient deeds can be perfected: which I will take care shall be done with all possible speed. In the meanwhile I will go for the said instrument, and 'till my return you may ballance this matter in your own discretion.

SCENE VII

Lady WISHFORT, Mrs. MARWOOD.

Lady. This insolence is beyond all precedent, all parallel; must I be subject to this merciless villain?

Mrs. Mar. 'Tis severe indeed, madam, that you should smart for your daughter's wantonness.

Lady. 'Twas against my consent that she married this barbarian, but she would have him, though her year was not out.—Ah! her first husband, my son Languish, would not have carried it thus. Well, that was my choice, this is hers; she is matched now with a witness—I shall be mad, dear friend, is there no comfort for me? Must I live to be confiscated at this rebel-rate?—Here come two more of my Egyptian plagues too.

SCENE VIII

To them] MILLAMANT, Sir WILFULL.

Sir Wil. Aunt, your servant.

Lady. Out, caterpillar, call not me aunt; I know thee not.

Sir Wil. I confess I have been a little in disguise, as they say —'Sheart! and I'm sorry for't. What would you have? I hope I committed no offence, aunt—and if I did I am willing to make satisfaction; and what can a man say fairer? If I have broke anything I'll pay for't, an it cost a pound. And so let that content for what's past, and make no more words. For what's to come, to pleasure you I'm willing to marry my cousin. So pray let's all be friends, she and I are agreed upon the matter before a witness.

Lady. How's this, dear niece? Have I any comfort? Can this be true?

Milla. I am content to be a sacrifice to your repose, madam; and to convince you that I had no hand in the plot, as you were misinformed, I have laid my commands on Mirabell to come in person, and be a witness that I give my hand to this flower of knighthood; and for the contract that passed between Mirabell and me, I have obliged him to make a resignation of it in your ladiship's presence;—he is without, and waits your leave for admittance.

Lady. Well, I'll swear I am something revived at this testimony of your obedience; but I cannot admit that traitor,—I fear I cannot fortify myself to support his appearance. He is as terrible to me as a Gorgon; if I see him I fear I shall turn to stone, petrifie incessantly.

Milla. If you disoblige him he may resent your refusal, and insist upon the contract still. Then 'tis the last time he will be offensive to you.

Lady. Are you sure it will be the last time?—If I were sure of that—shall I never see him again?

Milla. Sir Wilfull, you and he are to travel together, are you not?

Sir Wil. 'Sheart, the gentleman's a civil gentleman, aunt, let him come in; why, we are sworn brothers and fellow-travellers. —We are to be Pylades and Orestes, he and I—he is to be my interpreter in foreign parts. He has been over-seas once already;

and with proviso that I marry my cousin, will cross 'em once again, only to bear me company.—'Sheart, I'll call him in,—an I set on't once, he shall come in; and see who'll hinder him.

[*Goes to the door and hems.*

Mrs. Mar. This is precious fooling, if it would pass; but I'll know the bottom of it.

Lady. O dear Marwood, you are not going?

Mar. Not far, madam; I'll return immediately.

SCENE IX

Lady WISHFORT, MILLAMANT, Sir WILFULL, MIRABELL.

Sir Wil. Look up, man, I'll stand by you, 'sbud, an she do frown, she can't kill you;—besides—harkee, she dare not frown desperately, because her face is none of her own; 'sheart, and she should her forehead would wrinkle like the coat of a cream-cheese; but mum for that, fellow-traveller.

Mira. If a deep sense of the many injuries I have offered to so good a lady, with a sincere remorse, and a hearty contrition, can but obtain the least glance of compassion, I am too happy —Ah, madam, there was a time—but let it be forgotten—I confess I have deservedly forfeited the high place I once held, of sighing at your feet; nay, kill me not, by turning from me in disdain—I come not to plead for favour;—nay, not for pardon; I am a suppliant only for pity—I am going where I never shall behold you more——

Sir Wil. How, fellow-traveller!—You shall go by yourself then.

Mira. Let me be pitied first; and afterwards forgotten—I ask no more.

Sir Wil. By'r Lady, a very reasonable request, and will cost you nothing, aunt.—Come, come, forgive and forget, aunt, why you must an you are a Christian.

Mira. Consider, madam, in reality, you could not receive much prejudice; it was an innocent device; though I confess it had a face of guiltiness, it was at most an artifice which love contrived—and errors which love produces have ever been accounted venial. At least think it is punishment enough, that I have lost what in my heart I hold most dear, that to your cruel indignation I have offered up this beauty, and with her my peace and quiet; nay, all my hopes of future comfort.

Sir Wil. An he does not move me, would I may never be o' the quorum,—an it were not as good a deed as to drink, to give her to him again, I would I might never take shipping—Aunt, if you don't forgive quickly, I shall melt, I can tell you that. My contract went no farther than a little mouth-glew, and that's hardly dry;—one doleful sigh more from my fellow-traveller and 'tis dissolved.

Lady. Well, nephew, upon your account—Ah, he has a false insinuating tongue—Well, sir, I will stifle my just resentment at my nephew's request.—I will endeavour what I can to forget,—but on proviso that you resign the contract with my niece immediately.

Mira. It is in writing and with papers of concern; but I have sent my servant for it, and will deliver it to you, with all acknowledgments for your transcendent goodness.

Lady. Oh, he has witchcraft in his eyes and tongue;—when I did not see him I could have bribed a villain to his assassination; but his appearance rakes the embers which have so long lain smothered in my breast.——   [*Aside.*

SCENE X

[*To them*] FAINALL, Mrs. MARWOOD.

Fain. Your date of deliberation, madam, is expired. Here is the instrument, are you prepared to sign?

Lady. If I were prepared, I am not impowered. My niece exerts a lawful claim, having matched herself by my direction to Sir Wilfull.

Fain. That sham is too gross to pass on me—though 'tis imposed on you, madam.

Milla. Sir, I have given my consent.

Mira. And, sir, I have resigned my pretensions.

Sir Wil. And, sir, I assert my right; and will maintain it in defiance of you, sir, and of your instrument. 'Sheart, an you talk of an instrument, sir, I have an old fox by my thigh shall hack your instrument of ram vellam to shreds, sir. It shall not be sufficient for a mittimus or a tailor's measure; therefore withdraw your instrument, sir, or by'r Lady I shall draw mine.

Lady. Hold, nephew, hold.

Milla. Good Sir Wilfull, respite your valour.

Fain. Indeed? Are you provided of your guard, with your single beef-eater there? But I'm prepared for you; and insist upon my first proposal. You shall submit your own estate to my management, and absolutely make over my wife's to my sole use; as pursuant to the purport and tenor of this other covenant.—I suppose, madam, your consent is not requisite in this case; nor, Mr. Mirabell, your resignation; nor, Sir Wilfull, your right—you may draw your fox if you please sir, and make a bear-garden flourish somewhere else: for here it will not avail. This, my Lady Wishfort, must be subscribed, or your darling daughter's turned adrift, like a leaky hulk to sink or swim, as she and the current of this lewd town can agree.

Lady. Is there no means, no remedy, to stop my ruin? Ungrateful wretch! dost thou not owe thy being, thy subsistance, to my daughter's fortune?

Fain. I'll answer you when I have the rest of it in my possession.

Mira. But that you would not accept of a remedy from my hands—I own I have not deserved you should owe any obligation to me; or else perhaps I could davise——

Lady. O what? what? to save me and my child from ruin, from want, I'll forgive all that's past; nay, I'll consent to anything to come, to be delivered from this tyranny.

Mira. Ay, madam; but that is too late, my reward is intercepted. You have disposed of her, who only could have made me a compensation for all my services;—but be it as it may, I am resolved I'll serve you, you shall not be wronged in this savage manner.

Lady. How! Dear Mr. Mirabell, can you be so generous at last! But it is not possible. Harkee, I'll break my nephew's match, you shall have my niece yet, and all her fortune, if you can but save me from this imminent danger.

Mira. Will you? I take you at your word. I ask no more. I must have leave for two criminals to appear.

Lady. Ay, ay, anybody, anybody.

Mira. Foible is one, and a penitent.

SCENE XI

[*To them*] Mrs. FAINALL, FOIBLE, MINCING.

MIRA. *and* Lady *go to* Mrs. FAIN. *and* FOIBLE.

Mrs. Mar. O my shame! these corrupt things are brought hither to expose me.   [*To* FAIN.

Fain. If it must all come out, why let 'em know it, 'tis but *the way of the world.* That shall not urge me to relinquish or abate one title of my terms, no, I will insist the more.

Foib. Yes indeed, madam, I'll take my Bible-oath of it.

Minc. And so will I, mem.

Lady. O Marwood, Marwood, art thou false? my friend deceive me? Hast thou been a wicked accomplice with that profligate man?

Mrs. Mar. Have you so much ingratitude and injustice, to give credit against your friend, to the aspersions of two such mercenary truls?

Minc. Mercenary, mem? I scorn your words. 'Tis true we found you and Mr. Fainall in the blue garret; by the same token, you swore us to secresie upon Messalinas's poems. Mercenary? No, if we would have been mercenary, we should have held our tongues; you would have bribed us sufficiently.

Fain. Go, you are an insignificant thing.—Well, what are you the better for this! Is this Mr. Mirabell's expedient? I'll be put off no longer—You, thing, that was a wife, shall smart for this. I will not leave thee wherewithal to hide thy shame: your body shall be naked as your reputation.

Mrs. Fain. I despise you, and defie your malice—you have aspersed me wrongfully—I have proved your falsehood—go you and your treacherous—I will not name it, but starve together—perish.

Fain. Not while you are worth a groat, indeed, my dear. Madam, I'll be fooled no longer.

Lady. Ah, Mr. Mirabell, this is small comfort, the detection of this affair.

Mira. O in good time—Your leave for the other offender and penitent to appear, madam.

SCENE XII

[To them] WAITWELL *with a box of writings.*

Lady. O Sir Rowland—Well, rascal.

Wait. What your ladiship pleases.—I have brought the black box at last, madam.

Mira. Give it me.   Madam, you remember your promise.

Lady. Ay, dear sir.

Mira. Where are the gentlemen?

Wait. At hand, sir, rubbing their eyes,—just risen from sleep.

Fain. S'death, what's this to me? I'll not wait your private concerns.

SCENE XIII

[To them] PETULANT, WITWOUD.

Pet. How now? what's the matter? who's hand's out?

Wit. Hey day! what, are you all got together, like players at the end of the last act?

Mira. You may remember, gentlemen, I once requested your hands as witnesses to a certain parchment.

Wit. Ay, I do, my hand I remember—Petulant set his mark.

Mira. You wrong him, his name is fairly written, as shall appear—You do not remember, gentlemen, anything of what that parchment contained?   *[Undoing the box.*

Wit. No.

Pet. Not I. I writ, I read nothing.

Mira. Very well, now you shall know—Madam, your promise

Lady. Ay, ay, sir, upon my honour

Mira. Mr. Fainall, it is now time that you should know that your lady, while she was at her own disposal, and before you had by your insinuations wheadled her out of a pretended settlement of the greatest part of her fortune——

Fain. Sir! pretended!

Mira. Yes, sir. I say that this lady while a widow, having it seems received some cautions respecting your inconstancy and tyranny of temper, which from her own partial opinion and fondness of you she could never have suspected—she did, I say, by the wholesome advice of friends and of sages learned in the laws of this land, deliver this same as her act and deed to me in trust, and to the uses within mentioned. You may read if you please—[*holding out the parchment*] though perhaps what is written on the back may serve your occasions.

Fain. Very likely, sir. What's here? Damnation!

[*Reads.*] "A deed of conveyance of the whole estate real of Arabella Languish, widow, in trust to Edward Mirabell."—Confusion!

Mira. Even so, sir, 'tis *the way of the world*, sir; of the widows of the world. I suppose this deed may bear an elder date than what you have obtained from your lady.

Fain. Perfidious fiend! then thus I'll be revenged.——

[*Offers to run at* Mrs. FAIN.

Sir Wil. Hold, sir, now you may make your bear-garden flourish somewhere else, sir.

Fain. Mirabell, you shall hear of this, sir, be sure you shall.—Let me pass, oaf.

Mrs. Fain. Madam, you seem to stifle your resentment: you had better give it vent.

Mrs. Mar. Yes, it shall have vent—and to your confusion, or I'll perish in the attempt.

SCENE XIV (THE LAST)

Lady WISHFORT, MILLAMANT, MIRABELL, Mrs. FAINALL, Sir WILFULL, PETULANT, WITWOUD, FOIBLE, MINCING, WAITWELL.

Lady. O daughter, daughter, 'tis plain thou hast inherited thy mother's prudence.

Mrs. Fain. Thank Mr. Mirabell, a cautious friend, to whose advice all is owing.

Lady. Well, Mr. Mirabell, you have kept your promise—and I must perform mine.—First I pardon for your sake Sir Rowland there and Foible—the next thing is to break the matter to my nephew—and how to do that——

Mira. For that, madam, give yourself no trouble,—let me have your consent—Sir Wilfull is my friend; he has had compassion upon lovers, and generously engaged a volunteer in this action, for our service; and now designs to prosecute his travels.

Sir Wil. 'Sheart, aunt, I have no mind to marry. My cousin's a fine lady, and the gentleman loves her, and she loves him, and they deserve one another; my resolution is to see foreign parts—I have set on't—and when I'm set on't, I must do't. And if these two gentlemen would travel too, I think they may be spared.

Pet. For my part, I say little—I think things are best off or on.

Wit. I gad, I understand nothing of the matter,—I'm in a maze yet, like a dog in a dancing-school.

Lady. Well, sir, take her, and with her all the joy I can give you.

Milla. Why does not the man take me? Would you have me give myself to you over again?

Mira. Ay, and over and over again.—[*Kisses her hand.*] I would have you as often as possibly I can. Well, Heaven grant I love you not too well, that's all my fear.

Sir Wil. 'Sheart, you'll have time enough to toy after you're married; or if you will toy now, let us have a dance in the meantime; that we who are not lovers may have some other employment, besides looking on.

Mira. With all my heart, dear Sir Wilfull. What shall we do for musick?

Foib. O sir, some that were provided for Sir Rowland's entertainment are yet within call.   [*A dance.*

Lady. As I am a person I can hold out no longer;—I have wasted my spirits so to-day already, that I am ready to sink under the fatigue; and I cannot but have some fears upon me yet, that my son Fainall will pursue some desperate course.

Mira. Madam, disquiet not yourself on that account; to my knowledge his circumstances are such, he must of force comply. For my part, I will contribute all that in me lyes to a reunion; in the meantime, madam [*to* Mrs. FAIN.], let me before these witnesses restore to you this deed of trust; it may be a means, well managed, to make you live easily together.

> From hence let those be warned, who mean to wed;
> Lest mutual falshood stain the bridal-bed:
> For each deceiver to his cost may find,
> That marriage frauds too oft are paid in kind.
>
>   [*Exeunt omnes.*

EPILOGUE

AFTER our epilogue this crowd dismisses,
I'm thinking how this play'll be pulled to pieces.
But pray consider, e'er you doom its fall,
How hard a thing 'twould be, to please you all.
There are some criticks so with spleen diseased,
They scarcely come inclining to be pleased:
And sure he must have more than mortal skill,
Who pleases any one against his will.
Then, all bad poets we are sure are foes,
And how their number's swelled the town well knows:
In shoals, I've marked 'em judging in the pit;
Though they're on no pretence for judgment fit,
But that they have been damned for want of wit.
Since when, they by their own offences taught,
Set up for spies on plays, and finding fault.
Others there are whose malice we'd prevent;
Such, who watch plays, with scurrilous intent
To mark out who by Characters are meant.
And though no perfect likeness they can trace;
Yet each pretends to know the Copied Face.
These, with false glosses feed their own ill-nature,
And turn to Libel, what was meant a Satire.
May such malicious Fops this fortune find,
To think themselves alone the Fools designed:
If any are so arrogantly vain,
To think they singly can support a Scene,
And furnish Fool enough to entertain.
For well the learned and the judicious know,
That Satire scorns to stoop so meanly low,
As any one abstracted Fop to show.
For, as when painters form a matchless face,
They from each Fair one catch some different grace;
And shining features in one portrait blend,
To which no single beauty must pretend:
So poets oft, do in one piece expose
Whole *belles assemblées* of *cocquets* and *beaux*.

VENICE   PRESERVED

DRAMATIS PERSONÆ

DUKE OF VENICE.
PRIULI, Father to Belvidera, a Senator.
ANTONIO, a Fine Speaker in the Senate.
JAFFEIR
PIERRE
RENAULT
BEDAMAR
SPINOSA
THEODORE
ELIOT
REVILLIDO   } Conspirators.
DURAND
MEZZANA
BRAMVEIL
TERNON
BRABE
RETROSI

BELVIDERA.
AQUILINA.

Two Women, Attendants on Belvidera.
Two Women, Servants to Aquilina.
The Council of Ten.
Officer.
Guards.
Friar.
Executioner and Rabble.

EPISTLE DEDICATORY

MADAM,—Were it possible for me to let the world know how entirely your Grace's goodness has devoted a poor man to your service; were there words enough in speech to express the mighty sense I have of your great bounty towards me; surely I should write and talk of it for ever: but your Grace has given me so large a theme, and laid so very vast a foundation, that imagination wants stock to build upon it. I am as one dumb when I would speak of it, and when I strive to write, I want a scale of thought sufficient to comprehend the height of it. Forgive me, then, madam, if (as a poor peasant once made a present of an apple to an emperor) I bring this small tribute, the humble growth of my little garden, and lay it at your feet. Believe it is paid you with the utmost gratitude, believe that so long as I have thought to remember how very much I owe your generous nature, I will ever have a heart that shall be grateful for it too: Your grace, next Heaven, deserves it amply from me; that gave me life, but on a hard condition, till your extended favour taught me to prize the gift, and took the heavy burthen it was clogged with from me: I mean hard fortune: when I had enemies, that with malicious power kept back and shaded me from those royal beams, whose warmth is all I have, or hope to live by; your noble pity and compassion found me, where I was far cast backward from my blessing; down in the rear of Fortune, called me up, placed me in the shine, and I have felt its comfort. You have in that restored me to my native right, for a steady faith, and loyalty to my prince, was all the inheritance my father left me, and however hardly my ill-fortune deal with me, 'tis what I prize so well that I ne'er pawned it yet, and hope I ne'er shall part with it. Nature and Fortune were certainly in league when you were born, and as the first took care to give you beauty enough to enslave the hearts of all the world, so the other resolved to do its merit justice, that none but a monarch, fit to rule that world, should e'er possess it, and in it he had an empire. The young prince you have given him, by his blooming virtues, early declares the mighty stock he came from; and as you have taken all the pious care of a dear mother and a prudent guardian to give him a noble and generous education; may it succeed according to his merits and your wishes: may he grow up to be a bulwark to his illustrious father, and a patron to his loyal subjects, with wisdom and learning to assist him, whenever called to his councils, to defend his right against the encroachments of republicans in his senates, to cherish such men as shall be able to vindicate the royal cause, that good and fit servants to the crown may never be lost for want of a protector. May he have courage and conduct, fit to fight his battles abroad, and terrify his rebels at home; and that all these may be yet more sure, may he never, during the spring-time of his years, when these growing virtues ought with care to be cherished, in order to their ripening; may he never meet with vicious natures, or the tongues of faithless, sordid, insipid flatterers, to blast 'em: To conclude; may he be as great as the hand of Fortune (with his honour) shall be able to make him: and may your grace, who are so good a mistress, and so noble a patroness, never meet with a less grateful servant than, madam, your grace's entirely devoted creature,

THOMAS OTWAY.

PROLOGUE

In these distracted times, when each man dreads
The bloody stratagems of busy heads;
When we have feared three years we know not what,
Till witnesses began to die o' th' rot,
What made our poet meddle with a plot?
Was't that he fancied, for the very sake
And name of plot, his trifling play might take?
For there's not in't one inch-board evidence,
But 'tis, he says, to reason plain and sense,
And that he thinks a plausible defence.
Were Truth by Sense and Reason to be tried,
Sure all our swearers might be laid aside:
No, of such tools our author has no need,
To make his plot, or make his play succeed;
He, of black Bills, has no prodigious tales,
Or Spanish pilgrims cast ashore in Wales;
Here's not one murther'd magistrate at least,
Kept rank like ven'son for a city feast,
Grown four days stiff, the better to prepare
And fit his pliant limbs to ride in chair:
Yet here's an army raised, though under ground,
But no man seen, nor one commission found;
Here is a traitor too, that's very old,
Turbulent, subtle, mischievous, and bold,
Bloody, revengeful, and to crown his part,
Loves fumbling with a wench, with all his heart;
Till after having many changes passed,
In spite of age (thanks heaven) is hanged at last:
Next is a senator that keeps a whore,
In Venice none a higher office bore;
To lewdness every night the letcher ran,
Show me, all London, such another man,
Match him at Mother Creswold's if you can.
O Poland, Poland! had it been thy lot,
T' have heard in time of this Venetian plot,
Thou surely chosen hadst one king from thence,
And honoured them as thou hast England since.

VENICE PRESERVED

OR, A PLOT DISCOVERED

ACT I

SCENE I

Enter Priuli *and* Jaffeir.

Priu. No more! I'll hear no more; begone and leave.
Jaff. Not hear me! by my sufferings but you shall!
My lord, my lord! I'm not that abject wretch
You think me: Patience! where's the distance throws
Me back so far, but I may boldly speak
In right, though proud oppression will not hear me!
Priu. Have you not wrong'd me?
Jaff.   Could my nature e'er
Have brook'd injustice or the doing wrongs,
I need not now thus low have bent myself
To gain a hearing from a cruel father!
Wronged you?
Priu.   Yes! wronged me, in the nicest point:
The honour of my house; you have done me wrong;
You may remember (for I now will speak,
And urge its baseness): when you first came home
From travel, with such hopes, as made you looked on
By all men's eyes, a youth of expectation;
Pleased with your growing virtue, I received you:
Courted, and sought to raise you to your merits:
My house, my table, nay my fortune too,
My very self, was yours; you might have used me
To your best service; like an open friend,
I treated, trusted you, and thought you mine;
When in requital of my best endeavours,
You treacherously practised to undo me,
Seduced the weakness of my age's darling,
My only child, and stole her from my bosom:
O Belvidera!
Jaff.   'Tis to me you owe her,
Childless you had been else, and in the grave,
Your name extinct, nor no more Priuli heard of.

You may remember, scarce five years are past,
Since in your brigandine you sailed to see
The Adriatic wedded by our Duke,
And I was with you: your unskilful pilot
Dashed us upon a rock; when to your boat
You made for safety; entered first yourself;
The affrighted Belvidera following next,
As she stood trembling on the vessel side,
Was by a wave washed off into the deep,
When instantly I plunged into the sea,
And buffeting the billows to her rescue,
Redeemed her life with half the loss of mine:
Like a rich conquest in one hand I bore her,
And with the other dashed the saucy waves,
That thronged and pressed to rob me of my prize:
I brought her, gave her to your despairing arms:
Indeed you thanked me; but a nobler gratitude
Rose in her soul: for from that hour she loved me,
Till for her life she paid me with herself.

   Priu. You stole her from me, like a thief you stole her,
At dead of night; that curséd hour you chose
To rifle me of all my heart held dear.
May all your joys in her prove false like mine;
A sterile fortune, and a barren bed,
Attend you both; continual discord make
Your days and nights bitter and grievous: still
May the hard hand of a vexatious need
Oppress, and grind you; till at last you find
The curse of disobedience all your portion.

   Jaff. Half of your curse you have bestowed in vain,
Heaven has already crowned our faithful loves
With a young boy, sweet as his mother's beauty.
May he live to prove more gentle than his grandsire,
And happier than his father!

   Priu.   Rather live
To bait thee for his bread, and din your ears
With hungry cries: whilst his unhappy mother
Sits down and weeps in bitterness of want.

   Jaff. You talk as if 'twould please you.

   Priu.   'Twould by Heaven.
Once she was dear indeed; the drops that fell
From my sad heart, when she forgot her duty,
The fountain of my life was not so precious:
But she is gone, and if I am a man
I will forget her.

   Jaff. Would I were in my grave!

   Priu   And she too with thee;
For, living here, you're but my cursed remembrancers
I once was happy.

Jaff. You use me thus, because you know my soul
Is fond of Belvidera: you perceive
My life feeds on her, therefore thus you treat me;
Oh! could my soul ever have known satiety:
Were I that thief, the doer of such wrongs
As you upbraid me with, what hinders me,
But I might send her back to you with contumely,
And court my fortune where she would be kinder!
   Priu. You dare not do't——
   Jaff.   Indeed, my lord, I dare not.
My heart that awes me is too much my master:
Three years are past since first our vows were plighted,
During which time, the world must bear me witness,
I have treated Belvidera like your daughter,
The daughter of a senator of Venice;
Distinction, place, attendance, and observance,
Due to her birth, she always has commanded;
Out of my little fortune I have done this;
Because (though hopeless e'er to win your nature)
The world might see, I loved her for herself,
Not as the heiress of the great Priuli——
   Priu. No more!
   Jaff.   Yes! all, and then adieu for ever
There's not a wretch that lives on common charity
But's happier than me: for I have known
The luscious sweets of plenty; every night
Have slept with soft content about my head,
And never waked but to a joyful morning;
Yet now must fall like a full ear of corn,
Whose blossom scaped, yet's withered in the ripening.
   Priu. Home and be humble, study to retrench;
Discharge the lazy vermin of thy hall,
Those pageants of thy folly,
Reduce the glittering trappings of thy wife
To humble weeds, fit for thy little state;
Then to some suburb cottage both retire;
Drudge, to feed loathsome life: get brats, and starve——
Home, home, I say.——   [*Exit* PRIULI.
   Jaff.   Yes, if my heart would let me—
This proud, this swelling heart: home I would go,
But that my doors are hateful to my eyes,
Filled and dammed up with gaping creditors,
Watchful as fowlers when their game will spring;
I have now not fifty ducats in the world,
Yet still I am in love, and pleased with ruin.
O Belvidera! oh, she is my wife—
And we will bear our wayward fate together,
But ne'er know comfort more.

Enter PIERRE.

Pierr.   My friend, good morrow!
How fares the honest partner of my heart?
What, melancholy! not a word to spare me?
    Jaff. I'm thinking, Pierre, how that damned starving quality
Called Honesty got footing in the world.
    Pierr. Why, powerful Villainy first set it up,
For its own ease and safety: honest men
Are the soft easy cushions on which knaves
Repose and fatten: were all mankind villains,
They'd starve each other; lawyers would want practice,
Cut-throats rewards: each man would kill his brother
Himself, none would be paid or hanged for murder:
Honesty was a cheat invented first
To bind the hands of bold deserving rogues,
That fools and cowards might sit safe in power,
And lord it uncontrolled above their betters.
    Jaff. Then Honesty is but a notion.
    Pierr.   Nothing else,
Like wit, much talked of, not to be defined:
He that pretends to most, too, has least share in't;
'Tis a ragged virtue: Honesty! no more on't.
    Jaff. Sure thou art honest?
    Pierr.   So indeed men think me?
But they're mistaken, Jaffeir; I am a rogue
As well as they;
A fine gay bold-faced villain, as thou seest me;
'Tis true, I pay my debts when they're contracted;
I steal from no man; would not cut a throat
To gain admission to a great man's purse,
Or a whore's bed; I'd not betray my friend,
To get his place or fortune: I scorn to flatter
A blown-up fool above me, or crush the wretch beneath me,
Yet, Jaffeir, for all this, I am a villain!
    Jaff. A villain——
    Pierr.   Yes, a most notorious villain:
To see the suff'rings of my fellow-creatures,
And own myself a man: to see our senators
Cheat the deluded people with a show
Of Liberty, which yet they ne'er must taste of;
They say, by them our hands are free from fetters,
Yet whom they please they lay in basest bonds;
Bring whom they please to Infamy and Sorrow;
Drive us like wracks down the rough tide of power,
Whilst no hold's left to save us from destruction;
All that bear this are villains; and I one,
Not to rouse up at the great call of nature,
And check the growth of these domestic spoilers,

That makes us slaves and tells us 'tis our charter.
    Jaff. O Aquilina! Friend, to lose such beauty,
The dearest purchase of thy noble labours;
She was thy right by conquest, as by love.
    Pierr. O Jaffeir! I'd so fixed my heart upon her,
That wheresoe'er I framed a scheme of life
For time to come, she was my only joy
With which I wished to sweeten future cares;
I fancied pleasures, none but one that loves
And dotes as I did can imagine like 'em:
When in the extremity of all these hopes,
In the most charming hour of expectation,
Then when our eager wishes soar the highest,
Ready to stoop and grasp the lovely game,
A haggard owl, a worthless kite of prey,
With his foul wings sailed in and spoiled my quarry.
    Jaff. I know the wretch, and scorn him as thou hat'st him.
    Pierr. Curse on the common good that's so protected!
Where every slave that heaps up wealth enough
To do much wrong, becomes a lord of right:
I, who believed no ill could e'er come near me,
Found in the embraces of my Aquilina
A wretched old but itching senator;
A wealthy fool, that had bought out my title,
A rogue, that uses beauty like a lambskin,
Barely to keep him warm: that filthy cuckoo too
Was in my absence crept into my nest,
And spoiling all my brood of noble pleasure.
    Jaff. Didst thou not chase him thence?
    Pierr.   I did, and drove
The rank old bearded Hirco stinking home:
The matter was complained of in the Senate,
I summoned to appear, and censured basely,
For violating something they call *privilege*—
This was the recompense of my service:
Would I'd been rather beaten by a coward!
A soldier's mistress Jaffeir's his religion,
When that's profaned, all other ties are broken;
That even dissolves all former bonds of service,
And from that hour I think myself as free
To be the foe as e'er the friend of Venice.—
Nay, dear Revenge, whene'er thou call'st I'm ready.
    Jaff. I think no safety can be here for virtue,
And grieve, my friend, as much as thou to live
In such a wretched state as this of Venice;
Where all agree to spoil the public good,
And villains fatten with the brave man's labours.
    Pierr. We have neither safety, unity, nor peace,
For the foundation's lost of common good;

Justice is lame as well as blind amongst us;
The laws (corrupted to their ends that make 'em)
Serve but for instruments of some new tyranny,
That every day starts up to enslave us deeper:
Now could this glorious cause but find out friends
To do it right! O Jaffeir! then might'st thou
Not wear these seals of woe upon thy face.
The proud Priuli should be taught humanity,
And learn to value such a son as thou art.
I dare not speak! But my heart bleeds this moment!

    Jaff. Cursed be the cause, though I thy friend be part on't:
Let me partake the troubles of thy bosom,
For I am used to misery, and perhaps
May find a way to sweeten 't to thy spirit.

    Pierr. Too soon it will reach thy knowledge——

    Jaff.   Then from thee
Let it proceed. There's virtue in thy friendship
Would make the saddest tale of sorrow pleasing,
Strengthen my constancy, and welcome ruin.

    Pierr. Then thou art ruined!

    Jaff.   That I long since knew,
I and ill-fortune have been long acquaintance.

    Pierr. I passed this very moment by thy doors,
And found them guarded by a troop of villains;
The sons of public rapine were destroying:
They told me, by the sentence of the law
They had commission to seize all thy fortune,
Nay more, Priuli's cruel hand hath signed it.
Here stood a ruffian with a horrid face
Lording it o'er a pile of massy plate,
Tumbled into a heap for public sale:
There was another making villainous jests
At thy undoing; he had ta'en possession
Of all thy ancient most domestic ornaments,
Rich hangings, intermixed and wrought with gold;
The very bed, which on thy wedding-night
Received thee to the arms of Belvidera,
The scene of all thy joys, was violated
By the coarse hands of filthy dungeon villains,
And thrown amongst the common lumber.

    Jaff. Now, thanks Heaven——

    Pierr. Thank Heaven! for what?

    Jaff.   That I am not worth a ducat.

    Pierr. Curse thy dull stars, and the worse fate of Venice,
Where brothers, friends, and fathers, all are false;
Where there's no trust, no truth; where Innocence
Stoops under vile Oppression, and Vice lords it:
Hadst thou but seen, as I did, how at last
Thy beauteous Belvidera, like a wretch

That's doomed to banishment, came weeping forth,
Shining through tears, like April suns in showers
That labour to o'ercome the cloud that loads 'em,
Whilst two young virgins, on whose arms she leaned,
Kindly looked up, and at her grief grew sad,
As if they catched the sorrows that fell from her:
Even the lewd rabble that were gathered round
To see the sight, stood mute when they beheld her;
Governed their roaring throats and grumbled pity:
I could have hugged the greasy rogues: they pleased me.

    Jaff. I thank thee for this story, from my soul,
Since now I know the worst that can befall me:
Ah, Pierre! I have a heart, that could have borne
The roughest wrong my fortune could have done me:
But when I think what Belvidera feels,
The bitterness her tender spirit tastes of,
I own myself a coward: bear my weakness,
If throwing thus my arms about thy neck,
I play the boy, and blubber in thy bosom.
Oh! I shall drown thee with my sorrows!

    Pierr.   Burn!
First burn, and level Venice to thy ruin.
What! starve like beggars' brats in frosty weather,
Under a hedge, and whine ourselves to death!
Thou, or thy cause, shall never want assistance,
Whilst I have blood or fortune fit to serve thee;
Command my heart: thou art every way its master.

    Jaff. No: there's a secret pride in bravely dying.

    Pierr. Rats die in holes and corners, dogs run mad;
Man knows a braver remedy for sorrow:
Revenge! the attribute of gods, they stamped it
With their great image on our natures; die!
Consider well the cause that calls upon thee:
And if thou'rt base enough, die then: remember
Thy Belvidera suffers: Belvidera!
Die!—damn first!—what! be decently interred
In a churchyard, and mingle thy brave dust
With stinking rogues that rot in dirty winding-sheets,
Surfeit-slain fools, the common dung o' th' soil.

    Jaff. Oh!

    Pierr.   Well said, out with't, swear a little——

    Jaff.   Swear!
By sea and air! by earth, by heaven and hell,
I will revenge my Belvidera's tears!
Hark thee, my friend—Priuli—is—a Senator!

    Pierr. A dog!

    Jaff.   Agreed.

    Pierr.   Shoot him.

    Jaff.   With all my heart.

No more: where shall we meet at night?
    Pierr.   I'll tell thee;
On the *Rialto* every night at twelve
I take my evening's walk of meditation,
There we two will meet, and talk of precious
Mischief——
    Jaff.   Farewell.
    Pierr.   At twelve.
    Jaff.   At any hour, my plagues
Will keep me waking.   [*Exit* PIERRE.
Tell me why, good Heaven,
Thou mad'st me what I am, with all the spirit,
Aspiring thoughts and elegant desires
That fill the happiest man? Ah! rather why
Didst thou not form me sordid as my fate,
Base-minded, dull, and fit to carry burdens?
Why have I sense to know the curse that's on me?
Is this just dealing, Nature? Belvidera!

                Enter BELVIDERA.

Poor Belvidera!
    Belv. Lead me, lead me, my virgins!
To that kind voice. My lord, my love, my refuge!
Happy my eyes, when they behold thy face:
My heavy heart will leave its doleful beating
At sight of thee, and bound with sprightful joys.
O smile, as when our loves were in their spring,
And cheer my fainting soul.
    Jaff.   As when our loves
Were in their spring? has then my fortune changed?
Art thou not Belvidera, still the same,
Kind, good, and tender, as my arms first found thee?
If thou art altered, where shall I have harbour?
Where ease my loaded heart? Oh! where complain?
    Belv. Does this appear like change, or love decaying?
When thus I throw myself into thy bosom,
With all the resolution of a strong truth:
Beats not my heart, as 'twould alarum thine
To a new charge of bliss; I joy more in thee,
Than did thy mother when she hugged thee first,
And blessed the gods for all her travail past.
    Jaff. Can there in women be such glorious faith?
Sure all ill-stories of thy sex are false:
O woman! lovely woman! Nature made thee
To temper man: we had been brutes without you:
Angels are painted fair, to look like you;
There's in you all that we believe of heaven,
Amazing brightness, purity and truth,

Eternal joy, and everlasting love.

 Belv. If love be treasure, we'll be wondrous rich;
I have so much, my heart will surely break with 't;
Vows cannot express it; when I would declare
How great's my joy, I am dumb with the big thought;
I swell, and sigh, and labour with my longing.
O lead me to some desert wide and wild,
Barren as our misfortunes, where my soul
May have its vent: where I may tell aloud
To the high heavens, and ever list'ning planet,
With what a boundless stock my bosom's fraught!
Where I may throw my eager arms about thee,
Give loose to love with kisses, kindling joy,
And let off all the fire that's in my heart.

 Jaff. O Belvidera! double I'm a beggar,
Undone by fortune, and in debt to thee;
Want! worldly Want! that hungry meagre fiend
Is at my heels, and chases me in view;
Canst thou bear cold and hunger? can these limbs,
Framed for the tender offices of love,
Endure the bitter gripes of smarting poverty?
When banished by our miseries abroad
(As suddenly we shall be), to seek out
(In some far climate where our names are strangers)
For charitable succour; wilt thou then,
When in a bed of straw we shrink together,
And the bleak winds shall whistle round our heads,
Wilt thou then talk thus to me? Wilt thou then
Hush my cares thus, and shelter me with love?

 Belv. Oh, I will love thee, even in madness love thee.
Though my distracted senses should forsake me,
I'd find some intervals, when my poor heart
Should 'suage itself and be let loose to thine.
Though the bare earth be all our resting-place,
Its roots our food, some clift our habitation,
I'll make this arm a pillow for thy head;
As thou sighing liest, and swelled with sorrow,
Creep to thy bosom, pour the balm of love
Into thy soul, and kiss thee to thy rest;
Then praise our God, and watch thee till the morning.

 Jaff. Hear this, you heavens, and wonder how you made her!
Reign, reign, ye monarchs that divide the world,
Busy rebellion ne'er will let you know
Tranquillity and happiness like mine;
Like gaudy ships, th' obsequious billows fall
And rise again, to lift you in your pride;
They wait but for a storm and then devour you:
I, in my private bark, already wrecked,
Like a poor merchant driven on unknown land,

That had by chance packed up his choicest treasure
In one dear casket, and saved only that:

> Since I must wander further on the shore,
> Thus hug my little, but my precious store;
> Resolved to scorn, and trust my fate no more.

              [Exeunt.

ACT II

[SCENE I]

Enter PIERRE *and* AQUILINA.

Aquil. By all thy wrongs, thou'rt dearer to my arms
Than all the wealth of Venice: prithee stay,
And let us love to-night.
    Pierr.   No: there's fool,
There's fool about thee: when a woman sells
Her flesh to fools, her beauty's lost to me;
They leave a taint, a sully where they've past,
There's such a baneful quality about 'em,
E'en spoils complexions with their own nauseousness.
They infect all they touch; I cannot think
Of tasting anything a fool has palled.
    Aquil. I loathe and scorn that fool thou mean'st, as much
Or more than thou canst; but the beast has gold
That makes him necessary: power too,
To qualify my character, and poise me
Equal with peevish virtue, that beholds
My liberty with envy: in their hearts
Are loose as I am; but an ugly power
Sits in their faces, and frights pleasures from 'em.
    Pierr. Much good may't do you, madam, with your Senator.
    Aquil. My Senator! why, canst thou think that wretch
E'er filled thy Aquilina's arms with pleasure?
Think'st thou, because I sometimes give him leave
To foil himself at what he is unfit for;
Because I force myself to endure and suffer him,
Think'st thou I love him? No, by all the joys
Thou ever gav'st me, his presence is my penance;
The worst thing an old man can be's a lover,
A mere *memento mori* to poor woman.
I never lay by his decrepit side,
But all that night I pondered on my grave.
    Pierr. Would he were well sent thither!

Aquil.   That's my wish too:
For then, my Pierre, I might have cause with pleasure
To play the hypocrite: oh! how I could weep
Over the dying dotard, and kiss him too,
In hopes to smother him quite; then, when the time
Was come to pay my sorrows at his funeral,
For he's already made me heir to treasures,
Would make me out-act a real widow's whining:
How could I frame my face to fit my mourning,
With wringing hands attend him to his grave,
Fall swooning on his hearse: take mad possession
Even of the dismal vault where he lay buried,
There like the Ephesian matron dwell, till thou,
My lovely soldier, com'st to my deliverance;
Then throwing up my veil, with open arms
And laughing eyes, run to new-dawning joy.

   Pierr. No more! I have friends to meet me here to-night,
And must be private. As you prize my friendship
Keep up your coxcomb: let him not pry nor listen
Nor fisk about the house as I have seen him,
Like a tame mumping squirrel with a bell on;
Curs will be abroad to bite him if you do.

   Aquil. What friends to meet? may I not be of your council?
   Pierr. How! a woman ask questions out of bed?
Go to your Senator, ask him what passes
Amongst his brethren, he'll hide nothing from you;
But pump not me for politics. No more!
Give order that whoever in my name
Comes here, receive admittance: so good-night.

   Aquil. Must we ne'er meet again! Embrace no more!
Is love so soon and utterly forgotten?
   Pierr. As you henceforward treat your fool, I'll think on't.
   Aquil. Curst be all fools, and doubly curst myself,
The worst of fools—I die if he forsakes me;
And now to keep him, heaven or hell instruct me.   [*Exeunt.*

[SCENE II.]—*The Rialto*

Enter JAFFEIR.

   Jaff. I am here, and thus, the shades of night around me,
I look as if all hell were in my heart,
And I in hell. Nay, surely 'tis so with me;—
For every step I tread, methinks some fiend
Knocks at my breast, and bids it not be quiet:
I've heard, how desperate wretches, like myself,
Have wandered out at this dead time of night
To meet the foe of mankind in his walk:

Sure I'm so curst, that, tho' of Heaven forsaken,
No minister of darkness cares to tempt me.
Hell! hell! why sleepest thou?

Enter PIERRE.

Pierr.   Sure I have stayed too long:
The clock has struck, and I may lose my proselyte.
Speak, who goes there?
    Jaff.   A dog, that comes to howl
At yonder moon: what's he that asks the question?
    Pierr. A friend to dogs, for they are honest creatures
And ne'er betray their masters; never fawn
On any that they love not: well met, friend:
Jaffeir!
    Jaff. The same.   O Pierre! thou art come in season,
I was just going to pray.
    Pierr.   Ah, that's mechanic,
Priests make a trade on't, and yet starve by it too:
No praying, it spoils business, and time's precious;
Where's Belvidera?
    Jaff.   For a day or two
I've lodged her privately, till I see further
What fortune will do with me?   Prithee, friend,
If thou wouldst have me fit to hear good counsel,
Speak not of Belvidera——
    Pierr.   Speak not of her.
    Jaff. Oh no!
    Pierr. Nor name her.   May be I wish her well.
    Jaff. Who well?
    Pierr.   Thy wife, thy lovely Belvidera;
I hope a man may wish his friend's wife well,
And no harm done!
    Jaff.   Y' are merry, Pierre!
    Pierr.   I am so:
Thou shalt smile too, and Belvidera smile;
We'll all rejoice; here's something to buy pins,
Marriage is chargeable.
    Jaff.   I but half wished
To see the Devil, and he's here already.
Well!
What must this buy, rebellion, murder, treason?
Tell me which way I must be damned for this.
    Pierr. When last we parted, we had no qualms like these,
But entertained each other's thoughts like men,
Whose souls were well acquainted.   Is the world
Reformed since our last meeting?   what new miracles
Have happened?   has Priuli's heart relented?
Can he be honest?
    Jaff.   Kind Heaven! let heavy curses

Gall his old age; cramps, aches, rack his bones,
And bitterest disquiet wring his heart;
Oh, let him live till life become his burden!
Let him groan under't long, linger an age
In the worst agonies and pangs of death,
And find its ease, but late.

    Pierr.   Nay, couldst thou not
As well, my friend, have stretched the curse to all
The Senate round, as to one single villain?

    Jaff. But curses stick not: could I kill with cursing,
By Heaven! I know not thirty heads in Venice
Should not be blasted; Senators should rot
Like dogs on dunghills; but their wives and daughters
Die of their own diseases. Oh, for a curse
To kill with!

    Pierr.   Daggers, daggers are much better!

    Jaff. Ha!

    Pierr.   Daggers.

    Jaff.   But where are they?

    Pierr.   Oh, a thousand
May be disposed in honest hands in Venice.

    Jaff. Thou talk'st in clouds.

    Pierr.   But yet a heart half wronged
As thine has been, would find the meaning, Jaffeir.

    Jaff. A thousand daggers, all in honest hands;
And have not I a friend will stick one here?

    Pierr. Yes, if I thought thou wert not to be cherished
To a nobler purpose, I'd be that friend.
But thou hast better friends, friends whom thy wrongs
Have made thy friends; friends worthy to be called so;
I'll trust thee with a secret: there are spirits
This hour at work. But as thou art a man,
Whom I have picked and chosen from the world,
Swear, that thou wilt be true to what I utter,
And when I have told thee, that which only gods
And men like gods are privy to, then swear,
No chance or change shall wrest it from my bosom.

    Jaff. When thou wouldst bind me, is there need of oaths?
(Greensickness girls lose maidenheads with such counters)
For thou'rt so near my heart, that thou mayst see
Its bottom, sound its strength, and firmness to thee:
Is coward, fool, or villain, in my face?
If I seem none of these, I dare believe
Thou wouldst not use me in a little cause,
For I am fit for honour's toughest task;
Nor ever yet found fooling was my province;
And for a villainous inglorious enterprise,
I know thy heart so well, I dare lay mine
Before thee, set it to what point thou wilt.

Pierr. Nay, it's cause thou wilt be fond of, Jaffeir.
For it is founded on the noblest basis,
Our liberties, our natural inheritance;
There's no religion, no hypocrisy in't;
We'll do the business, and ne'er fast and pray for't:
Openly act a deed, the world shall gaze
With wonder at, and envy when it's done.

Jaff. For liberty!

Pierr.   For liberty, my friend!
Thou shalt be freed from base Priuli's tyranny,
And thy sequestered fortunes healed again.
I shall be freed from opprobrious wrongs,
That press me now, and bend my spirit downward:
All Venice free, and every growing merit
Succeed to its just right: fools shall be pulled
From Wisdom's seat; those baleful unclean birds,
Those lazy owls, who (perched near Fortune's top)
Sit only watchful with their heavy wings
To cuff down new-fledged virtues, that would rise
To nobler heights, and make the grove harmonious.

Jaff. What can I do?

Pierr.   Canst thou not kill a Senator?

Jaff. Were there one wise or honest, I could kill him
For herding with that nest of fools and knaves;
By all my wrongs, thou talk'st as if revenge
Were to be had, and the brave story warms me.

Pierr. Swear, then!

Jaff.   I do, by all those glittering stars
And yond great ruling planet of the night!
By all good powers above, and ill below!
By love and friendship, dearer than my life!
No power or death shall make me false to thee.

Pierr. Here we embrace, and I'll unlock my heart.
A council's held hard by, where the destruction
Of this great Empire's hatching: there I'll lead thee!
But be a man, for thou'rt to mix with men
Fit to disturb the peace of all the world,
And rule it when it's wildest——

Jaff.   I give thee thanks
For this kind warning: yes, I will be a man,
And charge thee, Pierre, whene'er thou seest my fears
Betray me less, to rip this heart of mine
Out of my breast, and show it for a coward's.
Come, let's begone, for from this hour I chase
All little thoughts, all tender human follies
Out of my bosom: vengeance shall have room:
Revenge!

Pierr. And liberty!

Jaff.   Revenge! revenge!   [*Exeunt.*

[SCENE III.]—*The Scene changes to* AQUILINA'S *house,*
the Greek Courtesan

Enter RENAULT.

Renault. Why was my choice ambition, the first ground
A wretch can build on? it's indeed at distance
A good prospect, tempting to the view,
The height delights us, and the mountain top
Looks beautiful, because it's nigh to heaven,
But we ne'er think how sandy's the foundation,
What storm will batter, and what tempest shake us!
Who's there?

Enter SPINOSA.

Spin.   Renault, good morrow! for by this time
I think the scale of night has turned the balance,
And weighs up morning: has the clock struck twelve?
Ren. Yes, clocks will go as they are set.   But Man,
Irregular Man's ne'er constant, never certain:
I've spent at least three precious hours of darkness
In waiting dull attendance; 'tis the curse
Of diligent virtue to be mixed like mine,
With giddy tempers, souls but half resolved.
Spin. Hell seize that soul amongst us, it can frighten!
Ren. What's then the cause that I am here alone?
Why are we not together?

Enter ELIOT.

                    O sir, welcome!
You are an Englishman: when treason's hatching
One might have thought you'd not have been behindhand.
In what whore's lap have you been lolling?
Give but an Englishman his whore and ease,
Beef and sea-coal fire, he's yours for ever.
Eliot. Frenchman, you are saucy.
Ren.   How!

Enter BEDAMAR *the* Ambassador, THEODORE, BRAMVEIL, DURAND,
BRABE, REVILLIDO, MEZZANA, TERNON, RETROSI, Conspirators.

Beda.   At difference, fie!
Is this a time for quarrels?   Thieves and rogues
Fall out and brawl: should men of your high calling,
Men separated by the choice of Providence,
From the gross heap of mankind, and set here
In this great assembly as in one great jewel,
To adorn the bravest purpose it e'er smiled on,
Should you like boys wrangle for trifles?

Ren.   Boys!

Beda. Renault, thy hand!

Ren.   I thought I'd given my heart
Long since to every man that mingles here;
But grieve to find it trusted with such tempers,
That can't forgive my froward age its weakness.

Beda. Eliot, thou once hadst virtue; I have seen
Thy stubborn temper bend with godlike goodness,
Not half thus courted: 'tis thy nation's glory,
To hug the foe that offers brave alliance.
Once more embrace, my friends—we'll all embrace—
United thus, we are the mighty engine
Must twist this rooted Empire from its basis!
Totters it not already?

Eliot.   Would it were tumbling!

Beda. Nay, it shall down: this night we seal its ruin.

Enter PIERRE.

O Pierre! thou art welcome!
Come to my breast, for by its hopes thou look'st
Lovelily dreadful, and the fate of Venice
Seems on thy sword already.   O my Mars!
The poets that first feigned a god of war
Sure prophesied of thee.

Pierr.   Friends! was not Brutus
(I mean that Brutus who in open senate
Stabbed the first Cæsar that usurped the world)
A gallant man?

Ren.   Yes, and Catiline too;
Though story wrong his fame: for he conspired
To prop the reeling glory of his country:
His cause was good.

Beda.   And ours as much above it,
As Renault thou art superior to Cethegus,
Or Pierre to Cassius.

Pierr.   Then to what we aim at
When do we start? or must we talk for ever?

Beda. No, Pierre, the deed's near birth: Fate seems to have
    set
The business up, and given it to our care;
I hope there's not a heart nor hand amongst us
But is firm and ready.

All.   All!
We'll die with Bedamar.

Beda.   O men,
Matchless, as will your glory be hereafter.
The game is for a matchless prize, if won;
If lost, disgraceful ruin.

Ren.   What can lose it?

The public stock's a beggar; one Venetian
Trusts not another: look into their stores
Of general safety; empty magazines,
A tattered fleet, a murmuring unpaid army,
Bankrupt nobility, a harassed commonalty,
A factious, giddy, and divided Senate,
Is all the strength of Venice: let's destroy it;
Let's fill their magazines with arms to awe them,
Man out their fleet, and make their trade maintain it;
Let loose the murmuring army on their masters,
To pay themselves with plunder; lop their nobles
To the base roots, whence most of 'em first sprung;
Enslave the rout, whom smarting will make humble;
Turn out their droning Senate, and possess
That seat of empire which our souls were framed for.

   Pierr. Ten thousand men are armed at your nod,
Commanded all by leaders fit to guide
A battle for the freedom of the world;
This wretched state has starved them in its service,
And by your bounty quickened, they're resolved
To serve your glory, and revenge their own!
They've all their different quarters in this city,
Watch for th' alarm, and grumble 'tis so tardy.

   Beda. I doubt not, friend, but thy unwearied diligence
Has still kept waking, and it shall have ease;
After this night it is resolved we meet
No more, till Venice own us for her lords.

   Pierr. How lovely the Adriatic whore,
Dressed in her flames, will shine! devouring flames!
Such as shall burn her to the watery bottom
And hiss in her foundation.

   Beda.   Now if any
Amongst us that owns this glorious cause,
Have friends or interest, he'd wish to save,
Let it be told, the general doom is sealed;
But I'd forego the hopes of a world's empire,
Rather than wound the bowels of my friend.

   Pierr. I must confess you there have touched my weakness,
I have a friend; hear it, such a friend!
My heart was ne'er shut to him: nay, I'll tell you,
He knows the very business of this hour;
But he rejoices in the cause, and loves it,
We've changed a vow to live and die together,
And he's at hand to ratify it here.

   Ren.   How! all betrayed?
   Pierr. No—I've dealt nobly with you;
I've brought my all into the public stock;
I had but one friend, and him I'll share amongst you!
Receive and cherish him: or if, when seen

And searched, you find him worthless, as my tongue
Has lodged this secret in his faithful breast,
To ease your fears I wear a dagger here
Shall rip it out again, and give you rest.
Come forth, thou only good I e'er could boast of.

Enter JAFFEIR *with a Dagger.*

Beda. His presence bears the show of manly virtue.
Jaff. I know you'll wonder all, that thus uncalled,
I dare approach this place of fatal counsels;
But I'm amongst you, and by Heaven it glads me,
To see so many virtues thus united,
To restore justice and dethrone oppression.
Command this sword, if you would have it quiet,
Into this breast; but if you think it worthy
To cut the throats of reverend rogues in robes,
Send me into the cursed assembled Senate;
It shrinks not, though I meet a father there;
Would you behold this city flaming? Here's
A hand shall bear a lighted torch at noon
To the Arsenal, and set its gates on fire.
Ren. You talk this well, sir.
Jaff.   Nay—by Heaven I'll do this.
Come, come, I read distrust in all your faces;
You fear me a villain, and indeed it's odd
To hear a stranger talk thus at first meeting,
Of matters, that have been so well debated;
But I come ripe with wrongs as you with counsels,
I hate this Senate, am a foe to Venice;
A friend to none, but men resolved like me,
To push on mischief; oh, did you but know me,
I need not talk thus!
Beda.   Pierre! I must embrace him,
My heart beats to this man as if it knew him.
Ren. I never lov'd these huggers.
Jaff.   Still I see
The cause delights me not. Your friends survey me,
As I were dangerous—but I come armed
Against all doubt, and to your trust will give
A pledge, worth more than all the world can pay for.
My Belvidera! Ho! My Belvidera!
Beda. What wonder next?
Jaff.   Let me entreat you,
As I have henceforth hopes to call ye friends,
That all but the ambassador, [and] this
Grave guide of councils, with my friend that owns me,
Withdraw a while to spare a woman's blushes.
                [*Exeunt all but* BEDAMAR, RENAULT, JAFFEIR, PIERRE.

Beda. Pierre, whither will this ceremony lead us?
Jaff. My Belvidera! ho! my Belvidera!

Enter BELVIDERA.

Belv. Who calls so loud at this late peaceful hour?
That voice was wont to come in gentler whispers,
And fill my ears with the soft breath of love:
Thou hourly image of my thoughts, where art thou?
Jaff. Indeed 'tis late.
Belv.   Oh! I have slept and dreamt,
And dreamt again: where hast thou been, thou loiterer?
Tho' my eyes closed, my arms have still been opened;
Stretched every way betwixt my broken slumbers,
To search if thou wert come to crown my rest;
There's no repose without thee: Oh, the day
Too soon will break, and wake us to our sorrow;
Come, come to bed, and bid thy cares good-night.
Jaff. O Belvidera! we must change the scene
In which the past delights of life were tasted:
The poor sleep little, we must learn to watch
Our labours late, and early every morning,
Midst winter frosts; then clad and fed with sparing,
Rise to our toils, and drudge away the day.
Belv. Alas! where am I! whither is't you lead me!
Methinks I read distraction in your face!
Something less gentle than the fate you tell me:
You shake and tremble too! your blood runs cold!
Heavens guard my love, and bless his heart with patience.
Jaff. That I have patience, let our fate bear witness,
Who has ordained it so, that thou and I,
(Thou the divinest Good man e'er possessed,
And I the wretched'st of the race of man)
This very hour, without one tear, must part.
Belv. Part! must we part? Oh! am I then forsaken?
Will my love cast me off? have my misfortunes
Offended him so highly, that he'll leave me?
Why drag you from me; whither are you going?
My dear! my life! my love!
Jaff.   O friends!
Belv. Speak to me.
Jaff.   Take her from my heart;
She'll gain such hold else, I shall ne'er get loose.
I charge thee take her, but with tender'st care
Relieve her troubles and assuage her sorrows.
Ren. Rise, madam! and command amongst your servants!
Jaff. To you, sirs, and your honours, I bequeath her,
And with her this, when I prove unworthy—   [*Gives a dagger.*
You know the rest:—then strike it to her heart;

And tell her, he, who three whole happy years
Lay in her arms, and each kind night repeated
The passionate vows of still-increasing love,
Sent that reward for all her truth and sufferings.

   Belv. Nay, take my life, since he has sold it cheaply;
Or send me to some distant clime your slave,
But let it be far off, lest my complainings
Should reach his guilty ears, and shake his peace.

   Jaff. No, Belvidera, I've contrived thy honour.
Trust to my faith, and be but fortune kind
To me, as I'll preserve that faith unbroken,
When next we meet, I'll lift thee to a height,
Shall gather all the gazing world about thee,
To wonder what strange virtue placed thee there.
But if we ne'er meet more——

      Belv.   O thou unkind one,
Never meet more? have I deserved this from you?
Look on me, tell me, speak, thou dear deceiver,
Why am I separated from thy love?
If I am false, accuse me; but if true,
Don't, prithee, don't in poverty forsake me,
But pity the sad heart, that's torn with parting.
Yet hear me! yet recall me——

            [*Exeunt* RENAULT, BEDAMAR, *and* BELVIDERA.

   Jaff.   O my eyes!
Look not that way, but turn yourselves awhile
Into my heart, and be wean'd all together.
My friend, where art thou?

   Pierr.   Here, my honour's brother.

   Jaff. Is Belvidera gone?

   Pierr.   Renault has led her
Back to her own apartment: but, by Heaven!
Thou must not see her more till our work's over.

   Jaff. No.

   Pierr.   Not for your life.

   Jaff.   O Pierre, wert thou but she,
How I could pull thee down into my heart,
Gaze on thee till my eye-strings cracked with love,
Till all my sinews with its fire extended,
Fixed me upon the rack of ardent longing;
Then swelling, sighing, raging to be blest,
Come like a panting turtle to thy breast,
On thy soft bosom, hovering, bill and play,
Confess the cause why last I fled away;
     Own 'twas a fault, but swear to give it o'er
     And never follow false ambition more.   [*Exeunt ambo.*

ACT III

[SCENE II]

Enter AQUILINA *and her* Maid.

Aquil. Tell him I am gone to bed: tell him I am not at home; tell him I've better company with me, or anything; tell him, in short, I will not see him, the eternal, troublesome, vexatious fool: he's worse company than an ignorant physician—I'll not be disturbed at these unseasonable hours.

Maid. But madam! He's here already, just entered the doors.

Aquil. Turn him out again, you unnecessary, useless, giddy-brained ass! If he will not begone, set the house a-fire and burn us both: I had rather meet a toad in my dish than that old hideous animal in my chamber to-night.

Enter ANTONIO.

Anto. Nacky, Nacky, Nacky—how dost do, Nacky? Hurry durry. I am come, little Nacky; past eleven o'clock, a late hour; time in all conscience to go to bed, Nacky—Nacky, did I say? Ay Nacky; Aquilina, lina, lina, quilina, quilina, quilina, Aquilina, Naquilina, Naquilina, Acky, Acky, Nacky, Nacky, Queen Nacky—come let's to bed—you Fubbs, you Pugg you— you little Puss—Purree Tuzzey—I am a Senator.

Aquil. You are a fool, I am sure.

Anto. May be so too, sweetheart. Never the worse Senator for all that. Come Nacky, Nacky, let's have a game at rump, Nacky.

Aquil. You would do well, signor, to be troublesome here no longer, but leave me to myself: be sober and go home, sir.

Anto. Home, Madonna!

Aquil. Ay, home, sir. Who am I?

Anto. Madonna, as I take it you are my—you are—thou art my little Nicky Nacky . . . that's all!

Aquil. I find you are resolved to be troublesome, and so to make short of the matter in few words, I hate you, detest you, loathe you, I am weary of you, sick of you—hang you, you are an old, silly, impertinent, impotent, solicitous coxcomb, crazy in your head, and lazy in your body, love to be meddling with everything, and if you had not money, you are good for nothing.

Anto. Good for nothing! Hurry durry, I'll try that presently. Sixty-one years old, and good for nothing: that's brave.—[*To the maid.*] Come, come, come, Mistress fiddle-faddle, turn you out for a season; go turn out, I say, it is our will and pleasure

to be private some moments—out, out when you are bid to.—
[*Puts her out and locks the door.*]   Good for nothing, you say.

Aquil. Why, what are you good for?

Anto. In the first place, madam, I am old, and consequently
very wise, very wise, Madonna, d'ye mark that? in the second
place, take notice, if you please, that I am a Senator, and when
I think fit can make speeches, Madonna.   Hurry durry, I can
make a speech in the Senate-house now and then—would make
your hair stand on end, Madonna.

Aquil. What care I for your speeches in the Senate-house: if
you would be silent here, I should thank you.

Anto. Why, I can make speeches to thee too, my lovely
Madonna; for example—my cruel fair one.

[*Takes out a purse of gold and at every pause shakes it.*
Since it is my fate, that you should with your servant angry
prove; tho' late at night—I hope 'tis not too late with this to
gain reception for my love—there's for thee, my little Nicky
Nacky—take it, here take it—I say take it, or I'll fling it at your
head—how now, rebel!

Aquil. Truly, my illustrious Senator, I must confess your
honour is at present most profoundly eloquent indeed.

Anto. Very well; come, now let's sit down and think upon't
a little—come sit I say—sit down by me a little, my Nicky
Nacky, ha !—[*Sits down.*]   Hurry durry—good for nothing——

Aquil. No, sir, if you please I can know my distance and
stand.

Anto. Stand: how?   Nacky up and I down!   Nay, then, let
me exclaim with the poet,

> Show me a case more pitiful who can,
> A standing woman, and a falling man.

Hurry durry—not sit down—see this, ye gods—You won't sit
down?

Aquil. No, sir.

Anto. Then look you now, suppose me a bull, a *basan*-bull,
the bull of bulls, or any bull.   Thus up I get and with my brows
thus bent—I broo, I say I broo, I broo, I broo.   You won't sit
down, will you ?—I broo—[*Bellows like a bull, and drives her about.*

Aquil. Well, sir, I must endure this.   Now your [*she sits down*]
honour has been a bull, pray what beast will your worship please
to be next?

Anto. Now I'll be a Senator again, and thy lover, little Nicky
Nacky! [*He sits by her.*]   Ah toad, toad, toad, toad! spit in
my face a little, Nacky—spit in my face prithee, spit in my face,
never so little: spit but a little bit—spit, spit, spit, spit, when
you are bid, I say; do prithee spit—now, now, now, spit: what,
you won't spit, will you ?   Then I'll be a dog.

Aquil. A dog, my lord ?

Anto. Ay, a dog—and I'll give thee this t'other purse to let

me be a dog—and to use me like a dog a little. Hurry durry—
I will—here 'tis.   [*Gives the purse.*

Aquil. Well, with all my heart. But let me beseech your
dogship to play your tricks over as fast as you can, that you may
come to stinking the sooner, and be turned out of doors as you
deserve.

Anto. Ay, ay—no matter for that—that—[*He gets under the
table*]—shan't move me——Now, bow wow wow, bow wow . . .
                                              [*Barks like a dog.*

Aquil. Hold, hold, hold, sir, I beseech you: what is't you do?
If curs bite, they must be kicked, sir. Do you see, kicked thus.

Anto. Ay, with all my heart: do kick, kick on, now I am
under the table, kick again—kick harder—harder yet, bow wow
wow, wow, bow—'od I'll have a snap at thy shins—bow wow
wow, wow, bow—'od she kicks bravely.——

Aquil. Nay, then I'll go another way to work with you: and
I think here's an instrument fit for the purpose.

                                    [*Fetches a whip and bell.*
What, bite your mistress, sirrah! out, out of doors, you dog, to
kennel and be hanged—bite your mistress by the legs, you
rogue——   [*She whips him.*

Anto. Nay, prithee Nacky, now thou art too loving: Hurry
durry, 'od I'll be a dog no longer.

Aquil. Nay, none of your fawning and grinning: but be gone,
or here's the discipline: what, bite your mistress by the legs,
you mongrel? out of doors—hout hout, to kennel, sirrah! go.

Anto. This is very barbarous usage, Nacky, very barbarous:
look you, I will not go—I will not stir from the door, that I
resolve—hurry durry, what, shut me out? [*She whips him out.*

Aquil. Ay, and if you come here any more to-night I'll have
my footmen lug you, you cur: what, bite your poor mistress
Nacky, sirrah!

Enter Maid.

Maid. Heavens, madam! What's the matter?
                            [*He howls at the door like a dog.*
Aquil. Call my footmen hither presently.

Enter two Footmen.

Maid. They are here already, madam, the house is all alarmed
with a strange noise, that nobody knows what to make of.

Aquil. Go all of you and turn that troublesome beast in the
next room out of my house—If I ever see him within these walls
again, without my leave for his admittance, you sneaking rogues,
I'll have you poisoned all, poisoned, like rats; every corner of
the house shall stink of one of you; go, and learn hereafter to
know my pleasure. So now for my Pierre:

              Thus when godlike lover was displeased,
              We sacrifice our fool and he's appeased.   [*Exeunt.*

SCENE II

Enter BELVIDERA.

Belv. I'm sacrificed! I am sold! betray'd to shame!
Inevitable ruin has enclosed me!
No sooner was I to my bed repaired
To weigh, and (weeping) ponder my condition,
But the old hoary wretch, to whose false care
My peace and honour was entrusted, came
(Like Tarquin) ghastly with infernal lust.
O thou, Roman Lucrece! thou couldst find friends
To vindicate thy wrong,
I never had but one, and he's proved false;
He that should guard my virtue, has betrayed it;
Left me! undone me!   O that I could hate him!
Where shall I go!   O whither whither wander?

Enter JAFFEIR.

Jaff. Can Belvidera want a resting place
When these poor arms are open to receive her?
Oh, 'tis in vain to struggle with desires
Strong as my love to thee; for every moment
I'm from thy sight, the heart within my bosom
Moans like a tender infant in its cradle
Whose nurse has left it;   come, and with the songs
Of gentle love persuade it to its peace.
Belv. I fear the stubborn wanderer will not own me,
'Tis grown a rebel to be ruled no longer,
Scorns the indulgent bosom that first lulled it,
And like a disobedient child disdains
The soft authority of Belvidera.
Jaff. There was a time——
Belv.   Yes, yes, there was a time
When Belvidera's tears, her cries, and sorrows,
Were not despised;   when if she chanced to sigh,
Or look but sad—there was indeed a time
When Jaffeir would have ta'en her in his arms,
Eased her declining head upon his breast,
And never left her till he found the cause.
But let her now weep seas,
Cry, till she rend the earth;   sigh till she burst
Her heart asunder;   still he bears it all;
Deaf as the wind, and as the rocks unshaken.
Jaff. Have I been deaf?   am I that rock unmoved,
Against whose root tears beat and sighs are sent?
In vain have I beheld thy sorrows calmly!

Witness against me, heavens, have I done this?
Then bear me in a whirlwind back again,
And let that angry dear one ne'er forgive me!
O thou too rashly censur'st of my love!
Couldst thou but think how I have spent this night,
Dark and alone, no pillow to my head,
Rest in my eyes, nor quiet in my heart,
Thou wouldst not, Belvidera, sure thou wouldst not
Talk to me thus, but like a pitying angel
Spreading thy wings come settle on my breast,
And hatch warm comfort there ere sorrows freeze it.

Belv. Why, then, poor mourner, in what baleful corner
Hast thou been talking with that witch the night?
On what cold stone hast thou been stretched along,
Gathering the grumbling winds about thy head,
To mix with theirs the accents of thy woes!
Oh, now I find the cause my love forsakes me!
I am no longer fit to bear a share
In his concernments: my weak female virtue
Must not be trusted; 'tis too frail and tender.

Jaff. O Portia! Portia! what a soul was thine!

Belv. That Portia was a woman, and when Brutus,
Big with the fate of Rome (Heaven guard thy safety!)
Concealed from her the labours of his mind,
She let him see her blood was great as his,
Flowed from a spring as noble, and a heart
Fit to partake his troubles, as his love:
Fetch, fetch that dagger back, the dreadful dower
Thou gav'st last night in parting with me; strike it
Here to my heart; and as the blood flows from it
Judge if it run not pure as Cato's daughter's.

Jaff. Thou art too good, and I indeed unworthy,
Unworthy so much virtue: teach me how
I may deserve such matchless love as thine,
And see with what attention I'll obey thee.

Belv. Do not despise me: that's the all I ask.

Jaff. Despise thee! Hear me——

Belv.   Oh, thy charming tongue
Is but too well acquainted with my weakness,
Knows, let it name but love, my melting heart
Dissolves within my breast; till with closed eyes
I reel into thy arms, and all's forgotten.

Jaff. What shall I do?

Belv.   Tell me! be just, and tell me
Why dwells that busy cloud upon thy face?
Why am I made a stranger? why that sigh,
And I not know the cause? Why, when the world
Is wrapt in rest, why chooses then my love
To wander up and down in horrid darkness

Loathing his bed, and these desiring arms?
Why are these eyes bloodshot with tedious watching?
Why starts he now? and looks as if he wished
His fate were finished? Tell me, ease my fears;
Lest when we next time meet, I want the power
To search into the sickness of thy mind,
But talk as wildly then as thou look'st now.

    Jaff. O Belvidera!

    Belv. Why was I last night delivered to a villain?

    Jaff. Ha, a villain!

    Belv. Yes! to a villain! Why at such an hour
Meets that assembly all made up of wretches
That look as hell had drawn 'em into league?
Why, I in this hand, and in that a dagger,
Was I delivered with such dreadful ceremonies?
" *To you, sirs, and to your honour I bequeath her,*
And with her this : whene'er I prove unworthy,
You know the rest, then strike it to her heart " ?
Oh! why's that *rest* concealed from me? must I
Be made the hostage of a hellish trust?
For such I know I am; that's all my value?
But by the love and loyalty I owe thee,
I'll free thee from the bondage of these slaves,
Straight to the Senate, tell 'em all I know,
All that I think, all that my fears inform me!

    Jaff. Is this the Roman virtue! this the blood
That boasts its purity with Cato's daughter's!
Would she have e'er betrayed her Brutus?

    Belv.   No:
For Brutus trusted her: wert thou so kind,
What would not Belvidera suffer for thee?

    Jaff. I shall undo myself, and tell thee all.

    Belv. Look not upon me, as I am a woman,
But as a bone, thy wife, thy friend, who long
Has had admission to thy heart, and there
Studied the virtues of thy gallant nature;
Thy constancy, thy courage and thy truth,
Have been my daily lesson: I have learnt them,
Am bold as thou, can suffer or despise
The worst of fates for thee, and with thee share them.

    Jaff. O you divinest Powers! look down and hear
My prayers! instruct me to reward this virtue!
Yet think a little ere thou tempt me further:
Think I have a tale to tell, will shake thy nature,
Melt all this boasted constancy thou talk'st of
Into vile tears and despicable sorrows:
Then if thou shouldst betray me!

    Belv.   Shall I swear?

    Jaff. No: do not swear: I would not violate

Thy tender nature with so rude a bond:
But as thou hopest to see me live my days,
And love thee long, lock this within thy breast;
I've bound myself by all the strictest sacraments
Divine and human——
   Belv.   Speak!
   Jaff.   To kill thy father——
   Belv. My father!
   Jaff.   Nay, the throats of the whole Senate
Shall bleed, my Belvidera: he amongst us
That spares his father, brother, or his friend,
Is damned: how rich and beauteous will the face
Of Ruin look, when these wide streets run blood;
I and the glorious partners of my fortune
Shouting, and striding o'er the prostrate dead,
Still to new waste; whilst thou, far off in safety,
Smiling, shalt see the wonders of our daring,
And when night comes, with praise and love receive me.
   Belv. Oh!
   Jaff.   Have a care, and shrink not even in thought!
For if thou dost——
   Belv.   I know it, thou wilt kill me.
Do, strike thy sword into this bosom: lay me
Dead on the earth, and then thou wilt be safe:
Murder my father! tho' his cruel nature
Has persecuted me to my undoing,
Driven me to basest wants, can I behold him,
With smiles of vengeance, butchered in his age?
The sacred fountain of my life destroyed?
And canst thou shed the blood that gave me being,
Nay, be a traitor too, and sell thy country?
Can thy great heart descend so vilely low,
Mix with hired slaves, bravos, and common stabbers,
Nose-slitters, alley-lurking villains! join
With such a crew and take a ruffian's wages
To cut the throats of wretches as they sleep?
   Jaff. Thou wrong'st me, Belvidera! I've engaged
With men of souls: fit to reform the ills
Of all mankind: there's not a heart amongst them,
But's as stout as death, yet honest as the nature
Of man first made, ere fraud and vice were fashions.
   Belv. What's he, to whose curst hands last night thou gav'st me?
Was that well done? Oh! I could tell a story
Would rouse thy lion-heart out of its den
And make it rage with terrifying fury.
   Jaff. Speak on, I charge thee!
   Belv.   O my love! if e'er
Thy Belvidera's peace deserved thy care,
Remove me from this place: last night, last night——

Jaff. Distract me not, but give me all the truth.

Belv. No sooner wert thou gone, and I alone,
Left in the power of that old son of mischief;
No sooner was I lain on my sad bed,
But that vile wretch approached me; loose, unbuttoned,
Ready for violation: then my heart
Throbb'd with its fears: oh, how I wept and sighed
And shrunk and trembled; wished in vain for him
That should protect me. Thou, alas! wert gone!

Jaff. Patience, sweet Heaven, till I make vengeance sure!

Belv. He drew the hideous dagger forth thou gav'st him,
And with upbraiding smiles, he said, "*Behold it ;
This is the pledge of a false husband's love :*"
And in my arms then pressed, and would have clasped me;
But with my cries I scared his coward heart,
Till he withdrew, and muttered vows to hell.
These are thy friends! with these thy life, thy honour,
Thy love, all's staked, and all will go to ruin.

Jaff. No more: I charge thee keep this secret close;
Clear up thy sorrows, look as if thy wrongs
Were all forgot, and treat him like a friend,
As no complaint were made. No more, retire;
Retire, my life, and doubt not of my honour;
I'll heal its failings and deserve thy love.

Belv. Oh, should I part with thee, I fear thou wilt
In anger leave me, and return no more.

Jaff. Return no more! I would not live without thee
Another night to purchase the creation.

Belv. When shall we meet again?

Jaff.   Anon at twelve!
I'll steal myself to thy expecting arms,
Come like a travelled dove and bring thee peace.

Belv. Indeed!

Jaff.   By all our loves!

Belv.   'Tis hard to part:
But sure no falsehood ever looked so fairly.
Farewell—remember twelve.   [*Exit* BELVIDERA

Jaff.   Let Heaven forget me
When I remember not thy truth, thy love.
How curst is my condition, tossed and justled,
From every corner; Fortune's common fool,
The jest of rogues, an instrumental ass
For villains to lay loads of shame upon,
And drive about just for their ease and scorn.

Enter PIERRE.

Pierr. Jaffeir!

Jaff.   Who calls!

Pierr.   A friend, that could have wished

T' have found thee otherwise employed: what, hunt
A wife on the dull soil! sure a staunch husband
Of all hounds is the dullest? wilt thou never,
Never be weaned from caudles and confections?
What feminine tale hast thou been listening to,
Of unaired shirts; catarrhs and toothache got
By thin-soled shoes? Damnation! that a fellow
Chosen to be a sharer in the destruction
Of a whole people, should sneak thus in corners
To ease his fulsome lusts, and fool his mind.

   Jaff. May not a man then trifle out an hour
With a kind woman and not wrong his calling?

   Pierr. Not in a cause like ours.

   Jaff.   Then, friend, our cause
Is in a damned condition: for I'll tell thee,
That canker-worm called Lechery has touched it,
'Tis tainted vilely: wouldst thou think it, Renault
(That mortified old withered winter rogue)
Loves simple fornication like a priest;
I found him out for watering at my wife:
He visited her last night like a kind guardian:
Faith, she has some temptations, that's the truth on't.

   Pierr. He durst not wrong his trust!

   Jaff.   'Twas something late, though,
To take the freedom of a lady's chamber.

   Pierr. Was she in bed?

   Jaff.   Yes, faith, in virgin sheets
White as her bosom, Pierre, dished neatly up,
Might tempt a weaker appetite to taste.
Oh, how the old fox stunk, I warrant thee,
When the rank fit was on him!

   Pierr.   Patience guide me!
He used no violence?

   Jaff.   No, no! out on't, violence!
Played with her neck; brushed her with his grey-beard,
Struggled and towzed, tickled her till she squeaked a little
May be, or so—but not a jot of violence——

   Pierr. Damn him!

   Jaff.   Ay, so say I: but hush, no more on't—
All hitherto is well, and I believe
Myself no monster yet: though no man knows
What fate he's born to: sure 'tis near the hour
We all should meet for our concluding orders:
Will the ambassador be here in person?

   Pierr. No: he has sent commission to that villain, Renault,
To give the executing charge.
I'd have thee be a man, if possible,
And keep thy temper; for a brave revenge
Ne'er comes too late.

Jaff.   Fear not, I'm cool as patience:
Had he completed my dishonour, rather
Than hazard the success our hopes are ripe for,
I'd bear it all with mortifying virtue.

Pierr. He's yonder coming this way through the hall;
His thoughts seem full.

Jaff.   Prithee retire, and leave me
With him alone: I'll put him to some trial,
See how his rotten part will bear the touching.

Pierr. Be careful, then.   [*Exit* PIERRE.

Jaff.   Nay, never doubt, but trust me.
What, be a devil! take a damning oath
For shedding native blood! can there be a sin
In merciful repentance? O this villain!

Enter RENAULT.

Ren. Perverse! and peevish! what a slave is Man!
To let his itching flesh thus get the better of him!
Despatch the tool her husband—that were well.
Who's there?

Jaff.   A man.

Ren.   My friend, my near ally!
The hostage of your faith, my beauteous charge, is very well.

Jaff. Sir, are you sure of that?
Stands she in perfect health? beats her pulse even?
Neither too hot nor cold?

Ren.   What means that question?

Jaff. Oh, women have fantastic constitutions,
Inconstant as their wishes, always wavering,
And ne'er fixed; was it not boldly done
Even at first sight to trust the thing I loved
(A tempting treasure too!) with youth so fierce
And vigorous as thine? but thou art honest.

Ren. Who dares accuse me?

Jaff.   Cursed be him that doubts
Thy virtue: I have tried it, and declare,
Were I to choose a guardian of my honour
I'd put it into thy keeping; for I know thee.

Ren. Know me!

Jaff.   Ay, know thee: there's no falsehood in thee.
Thou lookst just as thou art: let us embrace.
Now wouldst thou cut my throat or I cut thine?

Ren. You dare not do't.

Jaff.   You lie, sir.

Ren.   How!

Jaff.   No more.
'Tis a base world, and must reform, that's all.

Enter Spinosa, Theodore, Eliot, Revillido, Durand,
　　Bramveil, *and the rest of the* Conspirators.

Ren. Spinosa, Theodore!
Spin.　　　　　　The same.
Ren. You are welcome!
Spin.　　　　　　You are trembling, sir.
Ren. 'Tis a cold night indeed, I am aged,
Full of decay and natural infirmities;　　　[Pierre *re-enters.*
We shall be warm, my friend, I hope, to-morrow.
Pierr. 'Twas not well done, thou shouldst have stroked him
And not have galled him.
Jaff.　　　　　Damn him, let him chew on't.
Heaven! where am I? beset with cursed fiends,
That wait to damn me: what a devil's man,
When he forgets his nature—hush, my heart.
Ben. My friends, 'tis late: are we assembled all?
Where's Theodore?
Theo.　　　　At hand.
Ren.　　　　　　Spinosa.
Spin.　　　　　　　　Here.
Ren. Bramveil.
Bram.　　　I'm ready.
Ren.　　　　　　Durand and Brabe.
Dur.　　　　　　　　　　Command us,
We are both prepared!
Ren.　　　　　Mezzana, Revillido,
Ternon, Retrosi; oh, you are men, I find,
Fit to behold your fate, and meet her summons.
To-morrow's rising sun must see you all
Decked in your honours! are the soldiers ready?
Omn. All, all.
Ren. You, Durand, with your thousand must possess
St. Mark's: you, captain, know your charge already:
'Tis to secure the ducal palace: you,
Brabe, with a hundred more must gain the Secque.
With the like number Bramveil to the Procuralle.
Be all this done with the least tumult possible,
Till in each place you post sufficient guards:
Then sheathe your swords in every breast you meet.
Jaff. O reverend cruelty! damn'd bloody villain!
Ren. During this execution, Durand, you
Must in the midst keep your battalia fast,
And, Theodore, be sure to plant the cannon
That may command the streets; whilst Revillido,
Mezzana, Ternon, and Retrosi, guard you.
This done, we'll give the general alarm,
Apply petards, and force the ars'nal gates;
Then fire the city round in several places,

Or with our cannon, if it dare resist,
Batter't to ruin. But 'bove all I charge you
Shed blood enough, spare neither sex nor age,
Name nor condition; if there live a Senator
After to-morrow, tho' the dullest rogue
That e'er said nothing, we have lost our ends;
If possible, let's kill the very name
Of Senator, and bury it in blood.

    Jaff. Merciless, horrid slave!—Ay, blood enough!
Shed blood enough, old Renault: how thou charm'st me!

    Ren. But one thing more, and then farewell till Fate
Join us again, or separate us ever:
First, let's embrace, Heav'n knows who next shall thus
Wing ye together: but let's all remember
We wear no common cause upon our swords;
Let each man think that on his single virtue
Depends the good and fame of all the rest,
Eternal honour or perpetual infamy.
Let's remember through what dreadful hazards
Propitious Fortune hitherto has led us,
How often on the brink of some discovery
Have we stood tottering, and yet kept our ground
So well, the busiest searchers ne'er could follow
Those subtle tracks which puzzled all suspicion:
You droop, sir.

    Jaff. No: with a most profound attention
I've heard it all, and wonder at thy virtue.

    Ren. Tho' there be yet few hours 'twixt them and Ruin,
Are not the Senate lulled in full security,
Quiet and satisfied, as fools are always!
Never did so profound repose forerun
Calamity so great: nay, our good fortune
Has blinded the most piercing of mankind;
Strengthened the fearful'st, charm'd the most suspectful,
Confounded the most subtle; for we live,
We live, my friends, and quickly shall our life
Prove fatal to these tyrants: let's consider
That we destroy oppression, avarice,
A people nursed up equally with vices
And loathsome lusts, which Nature most abhors,
And such as without shame she cannot suffer.

    Jaff. O Belvidera, take me to thy arms
And show me where's my peace, for I have lost it.
                                  [*Exit* JAFFEIR.

    Ren. Without the least remorse then let's resolve
With fire and sword t' exterminate these tyrants,
And when we shall behold those curst tribunals,
Stained by the tears and sufferings of the innocent,
Burning with flames rather from Heav'n than ours,

The raging furious and unpitying soldier
Pulling his reeking dagger from the bosoms
Of gasping wretches; death in every quarter,
With all that sad disorder can produce,
To make a spectacle of horror: then,
Then let us call to mind, my dearest friends,
That there is nothing pure upon the earth,
That the most valued things have most alloys,
And that in change of all those vile enormities,
Under whose weight this wretched country labours,
The means are only in our hands to crown them.

   Pierr. And may those Powers above that are propitious
To gallant minds record this cause, and bless it.

   Ren. Thus happy, thus secure of all we wish for,
Should there, my friends, be found amongst us one
False to this glorious enterprise, what fate,
What vengeance were enough for such a villain?

   Eliot. Death here without repentance, hell hereafter.

   Ren. Let that be my lot, if as here I stand
Lifted by Fate amongst her darling sons,
Tho' I'd one only brother, dear by all
The strictest ties of nature; tho' one hour
Had given us birth, one fortune fed our wants,
One only love, and that but of each other,
Still filled our minds: could I have such a friend
Joined in this cause, and had but ground to fear
Meant foul play; may this right hand drop from me,
If I'd not hazard all my future peace,
And stab him to the heart before you: who
Would not do less? Wouldst not thou, Pierre, the same?

   Pierr. You've singled me, sir, out for this hard question,
As if 'twere started only for my sake!
Am I the thing you fear? Here, here's my bosom,
Search it with all your swords! am I a traitor?

   Ren. No: but I fear your late commended friend
Is little less: come, sirs, 'tis now no time
To trifle with our safety. Where's this Jaffeir?

   Spin. He left the room just now in strange disorder.

   Ren. Nay, there's danger in him: I observ'd him,
During the time I took for explanation,
He was transported from most deep attention
To a confusion which he could not smother.
His looks grew full of sadness and surprise,
All which betrayed a wavering spirit in him,
That laboured with reluctancy and sorrow;
What's requisite for safety must be done
With speedy execution: he remains
Yet in our power: I for my own part wear
A dagger.

Pierr. Well.

Ren.   And I could wish it!

Pierr.   Where?

Ren. Buried in his heart.

Pierr.   Away! we're yet all friends;
No more of this, 'twill breed ill blood amongst us.

Spin. Let us all draw our swords, and search the house,
Pull him from the dark hole where he sits brooding
O'er his cold fears, and each man kill his share of him.

Pierr. Who talks of killing? who's he'll shed the blood
That's dear to me! is't you? or you? or you, sir?
What, not one speak? how you stand gaping all
On your grave oracle, your wooden god there;
Yet not a word: then, sir, I'll tell you a secret,
Suspicion's but at best a coward's virtue!   [*To* RENAULT.

Ren. A coward——   [*Handles his sword.*

Pierr.   Put, put up the sword, old man,
Thy hand shakes at it; come, let's heal this breach,
I am too hot; we yet may live as friends.

Spin. Till we are safe, our friendship cannot be so.

Pierr. Again: who's that?

Spin.   'Twas I.

Theo.   And I.

Revill.   And I.

Eliot.   And all.

Ren. Who are on my side?

Spin.   Every honest sword;
Let's die like men and not be sold like slaves.

Pierr. One such word more, by Heav'n I'll to the Senate
And hang ye all, like dogs in clusters.
Why peep your coward swords half out their shells?
Why do you not all brandish them like mine?
You fear to die, and yet dare talk of killing?

Ren. Go to thy Senate and betray us, hasten,
Secure thy wretched life, we fear to die
Less than thou dar'st be honest.

Pierr.   That's rank falsehood.
Fear'st not thou death? fie, there's a knavish itch
in that salt blood, an utter foe to smarting.
Had Jaffeir's wife proved kind, he'd still been true.
Foh—how that stinks?
Thou die! thou kill my friend, or thou, or thou,
Or thou, with that lean wither'd wretched face!
Away! disperse all to your several charges,
And meet to-morrow where your honour calls you;
I'll bring that man, whose blood you so much thirst for,
And you shall see him venture for you fairly—
Hence, hence, I say.   [*Exit* RENAULT *angrily.*

Spin.   I fear we've been to blame;

And done too much.

   Theo. 'Twas too far urged against the man you loved.

   Revill. Here, take our swords and crush 'em with your feet.

   Spin. Forgive us, gallant friend.

   Pierr.   Nay, now ye've found
The way to melt and cast me as you will:
I'll fetch this friend and give him to your mercy:
Nay, he shall die if you will take him from me;
For your repose I'll quit my heart's jewel,
But would not have him torn away by villains
And spiteful villainy.

   Spin.   No; may you both
For ever live and fill the world with fame!

   Pierr. Now you are too kind. Whence rose all this discord?
Oh, what a dangerous precipice have we scaped!
How near a fall was all we had long been building!
What an eternal blot had stained our glories,
If one, the bravest and the best of men,
Had fallen a sacrifice to rash suspicion,
Butchered by those whose cause he came to cherish:
Oh, could you know him all as I have known him,
How good he is, how just, how true, how brave,
You would not leave this place till you had seen him;
Humbled yourselves before him, kissed his feet,
And gained remission for the worst of follies;
   Come but to-morrow all your doubts shall end,
   And to your loves me better recommend,
   That I've preserved your fame, and saved my friend.
                                   [Exeunt omnes.

ACT IV

[SCENE I]

Enter JAFFEIR *and* BELVIDERA.

   Jaff. Where dost thou lead me? Every step I move,
Methinks I tread upon some mangled limb
Of a rack'd friend: O my dear charming ruin!
Where are we wandering?

   Belv.   To eternal honour;
To do a deed shall chronicle thy name,
Among the glorious legends of those few
That have sav'd sinking nations: thy renown
Shall be the future song of all the virgins,
Who by thy piety have been preserved

From horrid violation: every street
Shall be adorn'd with statues to thy honour,
And at thy feet this great inscription written,
Remember him that propp'd the fall of Venice.

Jaff. Rather, remember him, who after all
The sacred bonds of oaths and holier friendship,
In fond compassion to a woman's tears
Forgot his manhood, virtue, truth and honour,
To sacrifice the bosom that relieved him.
Why wilt thou damn me?

Belv.   O inconstant man!
How will you promise? how will you deceive?
Do return back, replace me in my bondage,
Tell all thy friends how dangerously thou lov'st me,
And let thy dagger do its bloody office;
O that kind dagger, Jaffeir, how 'twill look
Stuck through my heart, drench'd in my blood to th' hilts!
Whilst these poor dying eyes shall with their tears
No more torment thee, then thou wilt be free:
Or if thou think'st it nobler, let me live
Till I'm a victim to the hateful lust
Of that infernal devil, that old fiend
That's damned himself and would undo mankind:
Last night, my love——

Jaff.   Name, name it not again,
It shows a beastly image to my fancy,
Will wake me into madness. Oh, the villain!
That durst approach such purity as thine
On terms so vile: destruction, swift destruction
Fall on my coward-head, and make my name
The common scorn of fools if I forgive him;
If I forgive him, if I not revenge
With utmost rage and most unstaying fury,
Thy suffering, thou dear darling of my life.

Belv. Delay no longer, then, but to the Senate;
And tell the dismal'st story ever utter'd,
Tell 'em what bloodshed, rapines, desolations,
Have been prepared, how near's the fatal hour!
Save thy poor country, save the reverend blood
Of all its nobles, which to-morrow's dawn
Must else see shed: save the poor tender lives
Of all those little infants which the swords
Of murtherers are whetting for this moment:
Think thou already hearst their dying screams,
Think that thou seest their sad distracted mothers
Kneeling before thy feet, and begging pity
With torn dishevell'd hair and streaming eyes,
Their naked mangled breasts besmear'd with blood,
And even the milk with which their fondled babes,

Softly they hush'd, dropping in anguish from 'em.
Think thou seest this, and then consult thy heart.
   Jaff. Oh!
   Belv. Think too, if [that] thou lose this present minute,
What miseries the next day bring upon thee.
Imagine all the horrors of that night,
Murder and rapine, waste and desolation,
Confusedly ranging.   Think what then may prove
My lot! the ravisher may then come safe,
And midst the terror of the public ruin
Do a damn'd deed; perhaps to lay a train
May catch thy life; then where will be revenge,
The dear revenge that's due to such a wrong?
   Jaff. By all Heaven's powers, prophetic truth dwells in thee,
For every word thou speak'st strikes through my heart
Like a new light, and shows it how't has wandered;
Just what thou'st made me, take me, Belvidera,
And lead me to the place where I'm to say
This bitter lesson, where I must betray
My truth, my virtue, constancy and friends:
Must I betray my friends!   Ah, take me quickly,
Secure me well before that thought's renewed;
If I relapse once more, all's lost for ever.
   Belv. Hast thou a friend more dear than Belvidera?
   Jaff. No, thou'rt my soul itself; wealth, friendship, honour,
All present joys, and earnest of all future,
Are summ'd in thee: methinks when in thy arms
Thus leaning on thy breast, one minute's more
Than a long thousand years of vulgar hours.
Why was such happiness not given me pure?
Why dash'd with cruel wrongs, and bitter wantings?
Come, lead me forward now like a tame lamb
To sacrifice, thus in his fatal garlands,
Deck'd fine and pleas'd, the wanton skips and plays,
   Trots by the enticing flattering priestess' side,
   And much transported with his little pride,
   Forgets his dear companions of the plain
   Till, by her bound, he's on the altar lain,
   Yet then too hardly bleats, such pleasure's in the pain.

Enter Officer and six Guards.

   Offic. Stand, who goes there?
   Belv. Friends.
   Jaff. Friends, Belvidera! hide me from my friends:
By heaven, I'd rather see the face of hell,
Than meet the man I love.
   Offic.   But what friends are you?
   Belv. Friends to the Senate and the State of Venice.
   Offic. My orders are to seize on all I find

*K 604

At this late hour, and bring 'em to the Council,
Who now are sitting.
    Jaff.   Sir, you shall be obeyed.
Hold, brutes, stand off, none of your paws upon me.
Now the lot's cast, and Fate do what thou wilt!
                              [Exeunt guarded.

SCENE [II.]—*The Senate-house*

Where appear sitting, the Duke of VENICE, PRIULI,
    ANTONIO, *and eight other* Senators.

    Duke. Antony, Priuli, Senators of Venice,
Speak; why are we assembled here this night?
What have you to inform us of, concerns
The State of Venice, honour, or its safety?
    Priu. Could words express the story I have to tell you,
Fathers, these tears were useless, these sad tears
That fall from my old eyes; but there is cause
We all should weep; tear off these purple robes,
And wrap ourselves in sackcloth, sitting down
On the sad earth, and cry aloud to Heaven.
Heaven knows if yet there be an hour to come
Ere Venice be no more.
    All Senators.   How!
    Priu.   Nay, we stand
Upon the very brink of gaping ruin.
Within this city's formed a dark conspiracy,
To massacre us all, our wives and children,
Kindred and friends, our palaces and temples
To lay in ashes: nay, the hour too, fix'd;
The swords, for aught I know, drawn e'en this moment,
And the wild waste begun: from unknown hands
I had this warning: but if we are men
Let's not be tamely butchered, but do something
That may inform the world in after ages,
Our virtue was not ruin'd though we were.   *[A noise without.*
Room, room, make room for some prisoners——
    Second Senator. Let's raise the city.

             Enter Officer *and* Guard.

    Priu.   Speak there, what disturbance?
    Offic. Two prisoners have the guard seiz'd in the streets,
Who say they come to inform this reverend Senate
About the present danger.

      Enter JAFFEIR *and* BELVIDERA *guarded.*

    All.   Give 'em entrance——
Well, who are you?

Jaff.   A villain.
Anto.   Short and pithy.
The man speaks well.
    Jaff.   Would every man that hears me
Would deal so honestly, and own his title.
    Duke. 'Tis rumour'd that a plot has been contriv'd
Against this State; that you have a share in't too.
If you're a villain, to redeem your honour,
Unfold the truth and be restored with mercy.
    Jaff. Think not that I to save my life come hither,
I know its value better; but in pity
To all those wretches whose unhappy dooms
Are fix'd and seal'd. You see me here before you,
The sworn and covenanted foe of Venice;
But use me as my dealings may deserve
And I may prove a friend.
    Duke.   The slave capitulates;
Give him the tortures.
    Jaff.   That you dare not do,
Your fears won't let you, nor the longing itch
To hear a story which you dread the truth of,
Truth which the fear of smart shall ne'er get from me.
Cowards are scared with threat'nings; boys are whipp'd
Into confessions: but a steady mind
Acts of itself, ne'er asks the body counsel.
Give him the tortures! Name but such a thing
Again, by Heaven I'll shut these lips for ever,
Not all your racks, your engines, or your wheels
Shall force a groan away—that you may guess at.
    Anto. A bloody-minded fellow, I'll warrant;
A damn'd bloody-minded fellow.
    Duke. Name your conditions.
    Jaff.   For myself full pardon,
Besides the lives of two and twenty friends,   [*Delivers a list.*
Whose names are here enrolled: nay, let their crimes
Be ne'er so monstrous, I must have the oaths
And sacred promise of this reverend Council,
That in a full assembly of the Senate
The thing I ask be ratified. Swear this,
And I'll unfold the secrets of your danger.
    All. We'll swear.
    Duke.   Propose the oath.
    Jaff.   By all the hopes
Ye have of peace and happiness hereafter,
Swear.
    All. We all swear.
    Jaff.   To grant me what I've asked,
Ye swear.
    All. We swear.

Jaff.   And as ye keep the oath,
May you and your posterity be blest
Or curst for ever.

All.   Else be curst for ever.

Jaff. Then here's the list, and with't the full disclose
Of all that threatens you.   [*Delivers another paper.*
                    Now Fate, thou hast caught me.

Anto. Why, what a disgraceful catalogue of cut-throats is
    here!
I'll warrant you not one of these fellows but has a face like a lion.
I dare not so much as read their names over.

Duke. Give orders that all diligent search be made
To seize these men, their characters are public;
The paper intimates their rendezvous
To be at the house of a famed Grecian courtesan
Called Aquilina; see that place secured.

Anto. What, my Nicky Nacky, Hurry Durry, Nicky Nacky
    in the plot—I'll make a speech.   Most noble Senators,
What headlong apprehension drives you on,
Right noble, wise and truly solid senators,
To violate the laws and rights of nations?
The lady is a lady of renown.
'Tis true, she holds a house of fair reception,
And though I say't myself, as many more
Can say as well as I.

Second Senator.   My lord, long speeches
Are frivolous here when dangers are so near us;
We all well know your interest in that lady,
The world talks loud on't.

Anto.   Verily, I have done,
I say no more.

Duke.   But since he has declared
Himself concerned, pray, captain, take great caution
To treat the fair one as becomes her character,
And let her bed-chamber be searched with decency.
You, Jaffeir, must with patience bear till morning
To be our prisoner.

Jaff.   Would the chains of death
Had bound me fast ere I had known this minute.
I've done a deed will make my story hereafter
Quoted in competition with all ill ones:
The history of my wickedness shall run
Down through the low traditions of the vulgar,
And boys be taught to tell the tale of Jaffeir.

Duke. Captain, withdraw your prisoner.

Jaff.   Sir, if possible,
Lead me where my own thoughts themselves may lose me,
Where I may doze out what I've left of life,

Forget myself and this day's guilt and falsehood.
Cruel remembrance, how shall I appease thee!   [*Exit guarded.*

Noise without :
More traitors ; room, room, make room there.

Duke. How's this? guards!
Where are our guards? shut up the gates, the treason's
Already at our doors.

Enter Officer.

Offic.   My lords, more traitors:
Seized in the very act of consultation;
Furnished with arms and instruments of mischief.
Bring in the prisoners.

Enter PIERRE, RENAULT, THEODORE, ELIOT, REVILLIDO,
and other Conspirators, *in fetters, guarded.*

Pierr.   You, my lords and fathers
(As you are pleased to call yourselves) of Venice;
If you sit here to guide the course of Justice,
Why these disgraceful chains upon the limbs
That have so often laboured in your service?
Are these the wreaths of triumph ye bestow
On those that bring you conquests home and honours?
Duke. Go on: you shall be heard, sir.
Anto. And be hanged too, I hope.
Pierr. Are these the trophies I've deserv'd for fighting
Your battles with confederated powers?
When winds and seas conspir'd to overthrow you,
And brought the fleets of Spain to your own harbours;
When you, great Duke, shrunk trembling in your palace,
And saw your wife, th' Adriatic, plough'd
Like a lewd whore by bolder prows than yours,
Stepp'd not I forth, and taught your loose Venetians,
The task of honour and the way to greatness,
Rais'd you from your capitulating fears
To stipulate the terms of sued-for peace?
And this my recompense? If I'm a traitor
Produce my charge; or show the wretch that's base enough
And brave enough to tell me I'm a traitor.
Duke. Know you one Jaffeir?   [*All the* Conspirators *murmur.*
Pierr.   Yes, and know his virtue,
His justice, truth; his general worth and sufferings
From a hard father taught me first to love him.

Enter JAFFEIR *guarded.*

Duke. See him brought forth.
Pierr.   My friend too bound! nay then
Our fate has conquered us, and we must fall.

Why droops the man whose welfare's so much mine
They're but one thing? these reverend tyrants, Jaffeir,
Call us all traitors: art thou one, my brother?

Jaff. To thee I am the falsest, veriest slave
That e'er betrayed a generous trusting friend,
And gave up honour to be sure of ruin.
All our fair hopes which morning was to have crown'd
Has this curs'd tongue o'erthrown.

Pierr.   So, then, all's over;
Venice has lost her freedom; I my life;
No more, farewell.

Duke.   Say, will you make confession
Of your vile deeds and trust the Senate's mercy?

Pierr. Cursed be your Senate: cursed your constitution:
The curse of growing factions and division
Still vex your councils, shake your public safety,
And make the robes of government you wear,
Hateful to you, as these base chains to me.

Duke. Pardon or death?

Pierr.   Death, honourable death!

Ren. Death's the best thing we ask or you can give.

All Conspir. No shameful bonds, but honourable death.

Duke. Break up the council: captain, guard your prisoners.
Jaffeir, you are free, but these must wait for judgment.

                              [*Exeunt all the* Senators.

Pierr. Come, where's my dungeon? lead me to my straw:
It will not be the first time I've lodged hard
To do your Senate service.

Jaff.   Hold one moment.

Pierr. Who's he disputes the judgment of the Senate?
Presumptuous rebel—on——   [*Strikes* JAFFEIR.

Jaff.   By Heaven, you stir not.
I must be heard, I must have leave to speak;
Thou hast disgrac'd me, Pierre, by a vile blow:
Had not a dagger done thee nobler justice?
But use me as thou wilt, thou canst not wrong me,
For I am fallen beneath the basest injuries;
Yet look upon me with an eye of mercy,
With pity and with charity behold me;
Shut not thy heart against a friend's repentance,
But as there dwells a god-like nature in thee
Listen with mildness to my supplications.

Pierr. What whining monk art thou? what holy cheat,
That wouldst encroach upon my credulous ears
And cant'st thus vilely? hence. I know thee not.
Dissemble and be nasty: leave me, hypocrite.

Jaff. Not know me, Pierre?

Pierr.   No, I know thee not: what art thou?

Jaff. Jaffeir, thy friend, thy once loved, valued friend!

Though now deservedly scorned, and used most hardly.

Pierr. Thou Jaffeir! Thou my once loved valued friend?
By heavens, thou liest; the man, so call'd, my friend,
Was generous, honest, faithful, just and valiant,
Noble in mind, and in his person lovely,
Dear to my eyes and tender to my heart:
But thou a wretched, base, false, worthless coward,
Poor even in soul, and loathsome in thy aspect,
All eyes must shun thee, and all hearts detest thee.
Prithee avoid, nor longer cling thus round me,
Like something baneful, that my nature's chill'd at.

Jaff. I have not wrong'd thee, by these tears I have not.
But still am honest, true, and hope too, valiant:
My mind still full of thee, therefore still noble;
Let not thy eyes then shun me, nor thy heart
Detest me utterly; oh, look upon me,
Look back and see my sad sincere submission!
How my heart swells, as even 'twould burst my bosom;
Fond of its gaol, and labouring to be at thee!
What shall I do? what say to make thee hear me?

Pierr. Hast thou not wronged me? dar'st thou call thyself
Jaffeir, that once loved, valued friend of mine,
And swear thou hast not wronged me? whence these chains?
Whence the vile death which I may meet this moment?
Whence this dishonour, but from thee, thou false one?

Jaff. All's true, yet grant one thing, and I've done asking.

Pierr. What's that?

Jaff.   To take thy life on such conditions
The Council have propos'd: thou and thy friends
May yet live long, and to be better treated.

Pierr. Life! ask my life! confess! record myself
A villain for the privilege to breathe,
And carry up and down this cursed city
A discontented and repining spirit,
Burthensome to itself a few years longer,
To lose it, may be, at last in a lewd quarrel
For some new friend, treacherous and false as thou art!
No, this vile world and I have long been jangling,
And cannot part on better terms than now,
When only men like thee are fit to live in't.

Jaff. By all that's just——

Pierr.   Swear by some other powers,
For thou hast broke that sacred oath too lately.

Jaff. Then by that hell I merit, I'll not leave thee,
Till to thyself at least thou'rt reconciled,
However thy resentment deal with me.

Pierr. Not leave me!

Jaff.   No, thou shalt not force me from thee.
Use me reproachfully, and like a slave,

Tread on me, buffet me, heap wrongs on wrongs
On my poor head: I'll bear it all with patience,
Shall weary out thy most unfriendly cruelty,
Lie at thy feet and kiss 'em though they spurn me,
Till, wounded by my sufferings, thou relent,
And raise me to thy arms with dear forgiveness.

 Pierr. Art thou not——
 Jaff.   What?
 Pierr.   A traitor?
 Jaff.   Yes.
 Pierr.   A villain?
 Jaff. Granted.
 Pierr.   A coward, a most scandalous coward,
Spiritless, void of honour, one who has sold
Thy everlasting fame for shameless life?
 Jaff. All, all, and more, much more: my faults are numberless
 Pierr. And wouldst thou have me live on terms like thine?
Base as thou art false——
 Jaff.   No, 'tis to me that's granted.
The safety of thy life was all I aim'd at,
In recompense for faith and trust so broken.
 Pierr. I scorn it more because preserv'd by thee.
And as when first my foolish heart took pity
On thy misfortunes, sought thee in thy miseries,
Relieved thy wants, and raised thee from thy state
Of wretchedness in which thy fate had plung'd thee,
To rank thee in my list of noble friends;
All I received in surety for thy truth,
Were unregarded oaths; and this, this dagger,
Given with a worthless pledge, thou since hast stol'n,
So I restore it back to thee again,
Swearing by all those powers which thou hast violated,
Never from this curs'd hour to hold communion,
Friendship or interest with thee, though our years
Were to exceed those limited the world.
Take it—farewell—for now I owe thee nothing.
 Jaff. Say thou wilt live, then.
 Pierr.   For my life, dispose it
Just as thou wilt, because 'tis what I'm tired with.
 Jaff. O Pierre!
 Pierr.   No more.
 Jaff.   My eyes won't lose the sight of thee,
But languish after thine, and ache with gazing.
 Pierr. Leave me—nay, then, thus, thus, I throw thee from me
And curses, great as is thy falsehood, catch thee.
 Jaff. Amen.
He's gone, my father, friend, preserver,
And here's the portion he has left me. *[Holds the dagger up.*
This dagger, well remembered, with this dagger

I gave a solemn vow of dire importance,
Parted with this and Belvidera together;
Have a care, mem'ry, drive that thought no farther;
No, I'll esteem it as a friend's last legacy,
Treasure it up within this wretched bosom,
Where it may grow acquainted with my heart,
That when they meet, they start not from each other.
So; now for thinking: a blow, call'd traitor, villain,
Coward, dishonourable coward, fough!
O for a long sound sleep, and so forget it!
Down, busy devil.—

Enter BELVIDERA.

Belv.   Whither shall I fly?
Where hide me and my miseries together?
Where's now the Roman constancy I boasted?
Sunk into trembling fears and desperation!
Not daring now to look up to that dear face
Which used to smile even on my faults, but down
Bending these miserable eyes to earth,
Must move in penance, and implore much mercy.
Jaff. Mercy, kind Heaven, has surely endless stores
Hoarded for thee of blessings yet untasted;
Let wretches loaded hard with guilt as I am,
Bow [with] the weight and groan beneath the burthen,
Creep with a remnant of that strength they've left,
Before the footstool of that Heaven they've injured.
O Belvidera! I'm the wretched'st creature
E'er crawled on earth: now if thou hast virtue, help me,
Take me into thy arms, and speak the words of peace
To my divided soul, that wars within me,
And raises every sense to my confusion;
By Heav'n, I'm tottering on the very brink
Of peace; and thou art all the hold I've left.
Belv. Alas! I know thy sorrows are most mighty;
I know thou'st cause to mourn; to mourn, my Jaffeir,
With endless cries, and never-ceasing wailings,
Thou'st lost——
Jaff.   Oh, I have lost what can't be counted;
My friend too, Belvidera, that dear friend,
Who, next to thee, was all my health rejoiced in,
Has used me like a slave; shamefully used me;
'Twould break thy pitying heart to hear the story.
What shall I do? resentment, indignation,
Love, pity, fear and mem'ry, how I've wronged him,
Distract my quiet with the very thought on't,
And tear my heart to pieces in my bosom.
Belv. What has he done?
Jaff.   Thou'dst hate me, should I tell thee.

Belv. Why?

Jaff. Oh, he has us'd me! yet, by Heaven, I bear it:
He has us'd me, Belvidera, but first swear
That when I've told thee, thou'lt not loathe me utterly,
Though vilest blots and stains appear upon me;
But still at least with charitable goodness,
Be near me in the pangs of my affliction,
Not scorn me, Belvidera, as he has done.

Belv. Have I then e'er been false that now I'm doubted?
Speak, what's the cause I'm grown into distrust,
Why thought unfit to hear my love's complaining?

Jaff. Oh!

Belv. Tell me.

Jaff.   Bear my failings, for they are many.
O my dear angel! in that friend I've lost
All my soul's peace; for every thought of him
Strikes my sense hard, and deads it in my brains;
Wouldst thou believe it?

Belv.   Speak!

Jaff.   Before we parted,
Ere yet his guards had led him to his prison,
Full of severest sorrows for his suff'rings,
With eyes o'erflowing and a bleeding heart,
Humbling myself almost beneath my nature,
As at his feet I kneel'd, and sued for mercy,
Forgetting all our friendship, all the dearness,
In which we've lived so many years together,
With a reproachful hand, he dashed a blow,
He struck me, Belvidera, by Heaven, he struck me,
Buffeted, called me traitor, villain, coward.
Am I a coward? am I a villain? tell me:
Thou'rt the best judge, and mad'st me, if I am so.
Damnation: coward!

Belv.   Oh! forgive him, Jaffeir.
And if his sufferings wound thy heart already,
What will they do to-morrow?

Jaff.   Hah!

Belv.   To-morrow,
When thou shalt see him stretch'd in all the agonies
Of a tormenting and a shamful death,
His bleeding bowels, and his broken limbs,
Insulted o'er by a vile butchering villain;
What will thy heart do then? oh, sure 'twill stream
Like my eyes now.

Jaff.   What means thy dreadful story?
Death, and to-morrow? broken limbs and bowels!
Insulted o'er by a vile butchering villain!
By all my fears I shall start out to madness,
With barely guessing if the truth's hid longer.

Belv. The faithless Senators, 'tis they've decreed it:
They say according to our friend's request,
They shall have death, and not ignoble bondage:
Declare their promised mercy all as forfeited,
False to their oaths, and deaf to intercession;
Warrants are passed for public death to-morrow.

Jaff. Death! doomed to die! condemned unheard! unpleaded!

Belv. Nay, cruell'st racks and torments are preparing,
To force confessions from their dying pangs.
Oh, do not look so terribly upon me,
How your lips shake, and all your face disordered!
What means my love?

Jaff. Leave me, I charge thee, leave me—strong temptations
Wake in my heart.

Belv.   For what?

Jaff.   No more, but leave me.

Belv. Why?

Jaff. Oh! by Heaven I love you with that fondness
I would not have thee stay a moment longer,
Near these curs'd hands; are they not cold upon thee?

    [*Pulls the dagger half out of his bosom and puts it back again.*

Belv. No, everlasting comfort's in thy arms.
To lean thus on thy breast is softer ease
Than downy pillows deck'd with leaves of roses.

Jaff. Alas! thou think'st not of the thorns 'tis filled with:
Fly ere they [gall] thee: there's a lurking serpent,
Ready to leap and sting thee to thy heart;
Art thou not terrified?

Belv.   No.

Jaff.   Call to mind,
What thou hast done, and whither thou hast brought me.

Belv. Hah!

Jaff. Where's my friend? my friend, thou smiling mischief?
Nay, shrink not, now 'tis too late, thou shouldst have fled
When thy guilt first had cause, for dire revenge
Is up and raging for my friend. He groans,
Hark how he groans, his screams are in my ears
Already; see, they've fix'd him on the wheel,
And now they tear him—Murther! perjur'd Senate!
Murther—Oh!—hark thee, traitress, thou hast done this:

    [*Fumbling for his dagger.*

Thanks to thy tears and false persuading love.
How her eyes speak! O thou bewitching creature!
Madness cannot hurt thee: come, thou little trembler,
Creep, even into my heart, and there lie safe:
'Tis thy own citadel—ha!—yet stand off,
Heaven must have justice, and my broken vows
Will sink me else beneath its reaching mercy;
I'll wink and then 'tis done——

Belv.   What means the lord
Of me, my life and love? what's in thy bosom,
                [*Draws the dagger, offers to stab her.*
Thou grasp'st at so?   Nay, why am I thus treated?
What wilt thou do?   Ah! do not kill me, Jaffeir,
Pity these panting breasts, and trembling limbs,
That used to clasp thee when thy looks were milder,
That yet hang heavy on my unpurg'd soul,
And plunge it not into eternal darkness.
    Jaff.   No, Belvidera, when we parted last
I gave this dagger with thee as in trust
To be thy portion, if I e'er proved false.
On such condition was my truth believ'd:
But now 'tis forfeited and must be paid for.
                [*Offers to stab her again.*

    Belv. Oh, mercy!   [*Kneeling.*
    Jaff.   Nay, no struggling.
    Belv.   Now, then, kill me.
                [*Leaps upon his neck and kisses him.*
While thus I cling about thy cruel neck,
Kiss thy revengeful lips and die in joys
Greater than any I can guess hereafter.
    Jaff.   I am, I am a coward; witness 't, heaven,
Witness it, earth, and every being witness;
'Tis but one blow; yet, by immortal love,
I cannot bear a thought to harm thee;
              [*He throws away the dagger and embraces her.*
The seal of Providence is sure upon thee,
And thou wert born for yet unheard-of wonders:
Oh, thou wert either born to save or damn me!
By all the power that's given thee o'er my soul,
By thy resistless tears and conquering smiles,
By the victorious love that still waits on thee,
Fly to thy cruel father: save my friend,
Or all our future quiet's lost for ever:
Fall at his feet, cling round his reverend knees;
Speak to him with thy eyes, and with thy tears
Melt his hard heart, and wake dead nature in him;
Crush him in thy arms, and torture him with thy softness:
    Nor, till thy prayers are granted, set him free,
    But conquer him, as thou hast vanquish'd me.
                [*Exeunt ambo.*

ACT V

[SCENE I]

Enter PRIULI, *solus.*

Priu. Why, cruel Heaven, have my unhappy days
Been lengthen'd to this sad one?   Oh, dishonour
And deathless infamy is fall'n upon me!
Was it my fault?   Am I a traitor?   No.
But then, my only child, my daughter, wedded;
There my best blood runs foul, and a disease
Incurable has seized upon my memory,
To make it rot and stink to after ages.
Cursed be the fatal minute when I got her;
Or would that I'd been anything but man,
And raised an issue which would ne'er have wrong'd me.
The miserablest creatures, man excepted,
Are not the less esteemed, though their posterity
Degenerate from the virtues of their fathers;
The vilest beasts are happy in their offsprings,
While only man gets traitors, whores and villains.
Cursed be the names, and some swift blow from Fate
Lay his head deep, where mine may be forgotten.

Enter BELVIDERA *in a long mourning veil.*

Belv. He's there, my father, my inhuman father,
That, for three years, has left an only child
Exposed to all the outrages of Fate,
And cruel ruin—oh!——

Priu.   What child of sorrow
Art thou that com'st thus wrapt in weeds of sadness,
And mov'st as if thy steps were towards a grave?

Belv. A wretch, who from the very top of happiness
Am fallen into the lowest depths of misery,
And want your pitying hand to raise me up again.

Priu. Indeed thou talk'st as thou hadst tasted sorrows;
Would I could help thee!

Belv.   'Tis greatly in your power.
The world, too, speaks you charitable, and I,
Who ne'er asked alms before, in that dear hope
Am come a-begging to you, sir.

Priu.   For what?

Belv. O well regard me, is this voice a strange one?
Consider, too, when beggars once pretend
A case like mine, no little will content 'em.

Priu. What wouldst thou beg for?

Belv.   Pity and forgiveness;   [*Throws up her veil.*
By the kind tender names of child and father,
Hear my complaints and take me to your love.

Priu. My daughter?

Belv.   Yes, your daughter, by a mother
Virtuous and noble, faithful to your honour,
Obedient to your will, kind to your wishes,
Dear to your arms: by all the joys she gave you,
When in her blooming years she was your treasure,
Look kindly on me; in my face behold
The lineaments of hers you've kiss'd so often,
Pleading the cause of your poor cast-off child.

Priu. Thou art my daughter?

Belv.   Yes—and you've oft told me,
With smiles of love and chaste paternal kisses,
I'd much resemblance of my mother.

Priu.   Oh!
Hadst thou inherited her matchless virtues
I'd been too bless'd.

Belv.   Nay, do not call to memory
My disobedience, but let pity enter
Into your heart, and quite deface the impression;
For could you think how mine's perplexed, what sadness,
Fears and despairs distract the peace within me,
Oh, you would take me in your dear, dear arms,
Hover with strong compassion o'er your young one,
To shelter me with a protecting wing,
From the black gather'd storm, that's just, just breaking.

Priu. Don't talk thus.

Belv.   Yes, I must, and you must hear too.
I have a husband.

Priu.   Damn him.

Belv.   Oh, do not curse him!
He would not speak so hard a word towards you,
On any terms, [howe'er] he deal with me.

Priu. Ha! what means my child?

Belv. Oh, there's but this short moment
'Twixt me and Fate, yet send me not with curses
Down to my grave, afford me one kind blessing
Before we part: just take me in your arms,
And recommend me with a prayer to Heaven,
That I may die in peace, and when I'm dead——

Priu. How my soul's catched!

Belv.   Lay me, I beg you, lay me
By the dear ashes of my tender mother:
She would have pitied me, had Fate yet spared her.

Priu. By heaven, my aching heart forebodes much mischief;
Tell me thy story, for I'm still thy father.

Belv. No, I'm contented.

Priu.   Speak.

Belv.   No matter.

Priu.   Tell me.
By yon blest Heaven, my heart runs o'er with fondness.

Belv. Oh!

Priu.   Utter't.

Belv.   O my husband, my dear husband
Carries a dagger in his once kind bosom,
To pierce the heart of your poor Belvidera.

Priu. Kill thee?

Belv.   Yes, kill me.   When he pass'd his faith
And covenant, against your State and Senate,
He gave me up as hostage for his truth,
With me a dagger and a dire commission
Whene'er he failed, to plunge it through this bosom.
I learnt the danger, chose the hour of love
To attempt his heart, and bring it back to honour.
Great love prevail'd and bless'd me with success:
He came, confessed, betrayed his dearest friends
For promis'd mercy; now they're doomed to suffer,
Gall'd with remembrance of what then was sworn,
If they are lost, he vows to appease the gods
With this poor life, and make my blood the atonement.

Priu. Heavens!

Belv.   Think you saw what pass'd at our last parting;
Think you beheld him like a raging lion,
Pacing the earth and tearing up his steps,
Fate in his eyes, and roaring with the pain
Of burning fury; think you saw his one hand
Fix'd on my throat, while the extended other
Grasp'd a keen threat'ning dagger: oh, 'twas thus
We last embrac'd, when, trembling with revenge,
He dragg'd me to the ground, and at my bosom
Presented horrid death, cried out: "My friends,
Where are my friends?" swore, wept, rag'd, threaten'd, lov'd,
For he yet loved, and that dear love preserved me,
To this last trial of a father's pity.
I fear not death, but cannot bear a thought
That that dear hand should do the unfriendly office;
If I was ever then your care, now hear me;
Fly to the Senate, save the promised lives
Of his dear friends, ere mine be made the sacrifice.

Priu. O my heart's comfort!

Belv.   Will you not, my father?
Weep not, but answer me.

Priu.   By Heaven, I will.
Not one of 'em but what shall be immortal.
Canst thou forgive me all my follies past,

I'll henceforth be indeed a father; never,
Never more thus expose, but cherish thee,
Dear as the vital warmth that feeds my life,
Dear as these eyes that weep in fondness o'er thee.
Peace to thy heart.　　Farewell.

Belv.　　　　　　　　　　　　Go, and remember
'Tis Belvidera's life her father pleads for.　　[*Exeunt severally.*

Enter ANTONIO.

Hum, hum, ha,

Signor Priuli, my lord Priuli, my lord, my lord, my lord:
[how] we lords love to call one another by our titles!　My lord,
my lord, my lord—pox on him, I am a lord as well as he; and
so let him fiddle—I'll warrant him he's gone to the Senate-house,
and I'll be there too, soon enough for somebody.　'Od, here's a
tickling speech about the plot, I'll prove there's a plot with a
vengeance—would I had it without book; let me see—

Most reverend Senators,

That there is a plot, surely by this time, no man that hath
eyes or understanding in his head will presume to doubt, 'tis as
plain as the light in the cucumber—no—hold there—cucumber
does not come in yet—'tis as plain as the light in the sun, or as
the man in the moon, even at noonday; it is indeed a pumpkin-
plot, which, just as it was mellow, we have gathered, and now we
have gathered it, prepared and dressed it, shall we throw it like
a pickled cucumber out at the window?　no: that it is not only
a bloody, horrid, execrable, damnable and audacious plot, but it
is, as I may so say, a saucy plot: and we all know, most reverend
fathers, that what is sauce for a goose is sauce for a gander:
therefore, I say, as those bloodthirsty ganders of the conspiracy
would have destroyed us geese of the Senate, let us make haste
to destroy them, so I humbly move for hanging—ha!　hurry
durry—I think this will do, tho' I was something out, at first,
about the sun and the cucumber.

Enter AQUILINA.

Aquil. Good-morrow, Senator.

Anto. Nacky, my dear Nacky, morrow, Nacky, 'od I am very
brisk, very merry, very pert, very jovial—ha-a-a-a-a—kiss me,
Nacky; how dost thou do, my little Tory, rory strumpet, kiss
me, I say, hussy, kiss me.

Aquil. Kiss me, Nacky, hang you, sir, coxcomb, hang you, sir.

Anto. Hayty, tayty, is it so indeed, with all my heart, faith—
hey then up go we, faith—*hey then up go we,* dum dum derum
dump.　　　　　　　　　　　　　　　　　　　　　　　　[*Sings.*

Aquil. Signior.

Anto. Madonna.

Aquil. Do you intend to die in your bed——?

Anto. About threescore years hence, much may be done, my
dear.

Aquil. You'll be hanged, signior.

Anto. Hanged, sweetheart, prithee be quiet, hanged quotha,
that's a merry conceit, with all my heart, why thou jok'st, Nacky,
thou art given to joking, I'll swear; well, I protest, Nacky, nay,
I must protest, and will protest that I love joking dearly, man.
And I love thee for joking, and I'll kiss thee for joking, and
towse thee for joking, and 'od, I have a devilish mind to take thee
aside about that business for joking too, 'od I have, and *Hey
then up go we*, dum dum derum dump.   [*Sings.*

Aquil. See you this, sir?   [*Draws a dagger.*

Anto. O Lud, a dagger! O Lud! it is naturally my aversion,
I cannot endure the sight on't, hide it for Heaven's sake, I cannot
look that way till it be gone—hide it, hide it, oh, oh, hide it!

Aquil. Yes, in your heart I'll hide it.

Anto. My heart; what, hide a dagger in my heart's blood?

Aquil. Yes, in thy heart, thy throat, thou pampered devil;
Thou hast help'd to spoil my peace, and I'll have vengeance
On thy cursed life, for all the bloody Senate,
The perjur'd faithless Senate: where's my lord,
My happiness, my love, my god, my hero,
Doom'd by thy accursed tongue, amongst the rest,
T' a shameful wrack? By all the rage that's in me
I'll be whole years in murthering thee.

Anto.   Why, Nacky,
Wherefore so passionate? what have I done? what's the
matter, my dear Nacky? am not I thy love, thy happiness, thy
lord, thy hero, thy Senator, and everything in the world, Nacky?

Aquil. Thou! think'st thou, thou art fit to meet my joys;
To bear the eager clasps of my embraces?
Give me my Pierre, or——

Anto. Why, he's to be hang'd, little Nacky,
Trussed up for treason, and so forth, child.

Aquil. Thou liest: stop down thy throat that hellish sentence,
Or 'tis thy last: swear that my love shall live,
Or thou art dead.

Anto.   Ah-h-h-h.

Aquil.   Swear to recall his doom,
Swear at my feet, and tremble at my fury.

Anto. I do. Now if she would but kick a little bit, one kick
now.

Ah-h-h-h.

Aquil.   Swear, or——

Anto.   I do, by these dear fragrant foots
And little toes, sweet as, e-e-e-e my Nacky Nacky Nacky.

Aquil. How!

Anto. Nothing but untie thy shoe-string a little, faith and
troth,

That's all, that's all, as I hope to live, Nacky, that's all.

Aquil. Nay, then——

Anto.   Hold, hold, thy love, thy lord, thy hero
Shall be preserv'd and safe.

Aquil.   Or may this poniard
Rust in thy heart.

Anto.   With all my soul.

Aquil.   Farewell——
                    [*Exit* AQUILINA.

Anto. Adieu. Why, what a bloody-minded, inveterate,
termagant strumpet have I been plagued with! Oh-h-h yet
more! nay then I die, I die—I am dead already.
                    [*Stretches himself out.*

Enter JAFFEIR.

Jaff. Final destruction seize on all the world:
Bend down, ye heavens, and shutting round this earth,
Crush the vile globe into its first confusion;
Scorch it, with elemental flames, to one curst cinder,
And all us little creepers in't, called men,
Burn, burn to nothing: but let Venice burn
Hotter than all the rest: here kindle hell
Ne'er to extinguish, and let souls hereafter
Groan here, in all those pains which mine feels now.

Enter BELVIDERA.

Belv. My life——   [*Meeting him.*
Jaff.   My plague——   [*Turning from her.*
Belv.   Nay then I see my ruin
If I must die!

Jaff.   No, Death's this day too busy,
Thy father's ill-timed mercy came too late.
I thank thee for thy labours though and him too,
But all my poor betray'd unhappy friends
Have summons to prepare for Fate's black hour;
And yet I live.

Belv.   Then be the next my doom.
I see thou'st pass'd my sentence in thy heart,
And I'll no longer weep or plead against it,
But with the humblest, most obedient patience
Meet thy dear hands, and kiss 'em when they wound me;
Indeed I'm willing, but I beg thee do it
With some remorse, and where thou giv'st the blow,
View me with eyes of a relenting love,
And show me pity, for 'twill sweeten justice.

Jaff. Show pity to thee?

Belv.   Yes, and when thy hands,
Charg'd with my fate, come trembling to the deed,
As thou hast done a thousand thousand dear times,

To this poor breast, when kinder rage has brought thee,
When our stinged hearts have leaped to meet each other,
And melting kisses sealed our lips together,
When joys have left me gasping in thy arms,
So let my death come now, and I'll not shrink from't.

Jaff. Nay, Belvidera, do not fear my cruelty,
Nor let the thoughts of death perplex thy fancy,
But answer me to what I shall demand
With a firm temper and unshaken spirit.

Belv. I will when I've done weeping——

Jaff.				Fie, no more on't—
How long is't since the miserable day
We wedded first——

Belv.			Oh-h-h!

Jaff.				Nay, keep in thy tears,
Lest they unman me too.

Belv.			Heaven knows I cannot;
The words you utter sound so very sadly
These streams will follow——

Jaff.			Come, I'll kiss 'em dry, then.

Belv. But was't a miserable day?

Jaff.				A curs'd one.

Belv. I thought it otherwise, and you've oft sworn
In the transporting hours of warmest love
When sure you spoke the truth, you've sworn you blessed it.

Jaff. 'Twas a rash oath.

Belv.			Then why am I not curs'd too?

Jaff. No, Belvidera; by the eternal truth,
I dote with too much fondness.

Belv.			Still so kind?
Still then do you love me?

Jaff.			Nature, in her workings,
Inclines not with more ardour to creation,
Than I do now towards thee: man ne'er was bless'd,
Since the first pair first met, as I have been.

Belv. Then sure you will not curse me.

Jaff.				No, I'll bless thee.
I came on purpose, Belvidera, to bless thee.
'Tis now, I think, three years we've liv'd together.

Belv. And may no fatal minute ever part us,
Till, reverend grown, for age and love, we go
Down to one grave, as our last bed, together,
There sleep in peace till an eternal morning.

Jaff. When will that be?			[*Sighing.*

Belv.			I hope long ages hence.

Jaff. Have I not hitherto (I beg thee tell me
Thy very fears) used thee with tender'st love?
Did e'er my soul rise up in wrath against thee?
Did e'er I frown when Belvidera smiled,

Or, by the least unfriendly word, betray
A bating passion? have I ever wronged thee?
    Belv. No.
    Jaff.   Has my heart, or have my eyes e'er wandered
To any other woman?
    Belv.   Never, never—
I were the worst of false ones should I accuse thee;
I own I've been too happy, bless'd above
My sex's charter.
    Jaff. Did I not say I came to bless thee?
    Belv. Yes.
    Jaff.   Then hear me, bounteous Heaven!
Pour down your blessings on this beauteous head,
Where everlasting sweets are always springing,
With a continual giving hand: let peace,
Honour, and safety, always hover round her:
Feed her with plenty, let her eyes ne'er see
A sight of sorrow, nor her heart know mourning:
Crown all her days with joy, her nights with rest,
Harmless as her own thoughts; and prop her virtue,
To bear the loss of one that too much lov'd,
And comfort her with patience in our parting.
    Belv. How, parting! parting!
    Jaff.   Yes, for ever parting.
I have sworn, Belvidera, by yon heaven,
That best can tell how much I lose to leave thee,
We part this hour for ever.
    Belv.   Oh, call back
Your cruel blessings, stay with me and curse me!
    Jaff. No, 'tis resolv'd.
    Belv.   Then hear me too, just Heaven!
Pour down your curses on this wretched head
With never-ceasing vengeance: let despair,
Danger or infamy, nay, all surround me:
Starve me with wantings: let my eyes ne'er see
A sight of comfort, nor my heart know peace,
But dash my days with sorrow, night with horrors
Wild as my own thoughts now, and let loose fury
To make me mad enough for what I lose,
If I must lose him; if I must, I will not.
O turn and hear me!
    Jaff.   Now hold, heart, or never.
    Belv. By all the tender days we've liv'd together;
By all our charming nights, and joys that crown'd 'em:
Pity my sad condition, speak, but speak.
    Jaff. Oh-h-h!
    Belv.   By these arms that now cling round thy neck:
By this dear kiss and by ten thousand more,
By these poor streaming eyes——

Jaff.   Murther! unhold me:

                                       [Draws his dagger.

By the immortal destiny that doom'd me
To this curs'd minute, I'll not live one longer.
Resolve to let me go or see me fall——

    Belv. Hold, sir, be patient.

    Jaff.   Hark, the dismal bell

                                       [Passing bell tolls.

Tolls out for death; I must attend its call too,
For my poor friend, my dying Pierre expects me:
He sent a message to require I'd see him
Before he died, and take his last forgiveness.
Farewell for ever.   *[Going out looks back at her.*

    Belv.   Leave thy dagger with me.

Bequeath me something.—Not one kiss at parting?
O my poor heart, when wilt thou break?

    Jaff.   Yet stay,

We have a child, as yet a tender infant.
Be a kind mother to him when I am gone:
Breed him in virtue and the paths of honour,
But let him never know his father's story:
I charge thee guard him from the wrongs my fate
May do his future fortune or his name.
Now—nearer yet—   *[Approaching each other.*
O that my arms were riveted
Thus round thee ever! But my friends, my oath!
This and no more.   *[Kisses her.*

    Belv.   Another, sure another,
For that poor little one you've ta'en care of,
I'll give't him truly.

    Jaff.   So, now farewell.

    Belv.   For ever?

    Jaff. Heaven knows for ever; all good angels guard thee.

                                          [Exit.

    Belv. All ill ones sure had charge of me this moment.
Curs'd be my days, and doubly curs'd my nights,
Which I must now mourn out in widow'd tears;
Blasted be every herb and fruit and tree;
Curs'd be the rain that falls upon the earth,
And may the general curse reach man and beast;
Oh, give me daggers, fire or water!
How I could bleed, how burn, how drown, the waves
Huzzing and booming round my sinking head,
Till I descended to the peaceful bottom!
Oh, there's all quiet, here all rage and fury:
The air's too thin, and pierces my weak brain:
I long for thick substantial sleep: hell, hell,
Burst from the centre, rage and roar aloud,
If thou art half so hot, so mad as I am.

Enter PRIULI *and* Servants.

Who's there?   [*They seize her.*
    Priu. Run, seize and bring her safely home.
Guard her as you would life: alas, poor creature!
    Belv. What? to my husband then conduct me quickly.
Are all things ready? shall we die most gloriously?
Say not a word of this to my old father.
Murmuring streams, soft shades, and springing flowers,
Lutes, laurels, seas of milk, and ships of amber.   [*Exit.*

[SCENE II]

*Scene opening discovers a Scaffold and a Wheel prepared for the
    executing of* PIERRE, *then enter other* Officers, PIERRE *and*
    Guards, *a Friar,* Executioner, *and a great rabble.*

    Offic. Room, room there—stand all by, make room for the
prisoner.
    Pierr. My friend not come yet?
    Father. Why are you so obstinate?
    Pierr. Why you so troublesome, that a poor wretch
Can't die in peace,
But you, like ravens, will be croaking round him?
    Fath. Yet, Heaven——
    Pierr.   I tell thee Heaven and I are friends.
I ne'er broke peace with't yet, by cruel murthers,
Rapine or perjury, or vile deceiving,
But lived in moral justice towards all men,
Nor am a foe to the most strong believers,
Howe'er my own short-sighted faith confine me.
    Fath. But an all-seeing Judge——
    Pierr.   You say my conscience
Must be mine accuser: I've search'd that conscience,
And find no records there of crimes that scare me.
    Fath. 'Tis strange you should want faith.
    Pierr.   You want to lead
My reason blindfold, like a hamper'd lion,
Check'd of its nobler vigour; then, when baited
Down to obedient tameness, make it couch,
And show strange tricks, which you call signs of faith.
So silly souls are gull'd and you get money.
Away, no more: Captain, I would hereafter
This fellow write no lies of my conversion,
Because he has crept upon my troubled hours.

Enter JAFFEIR.

    Jaff. Hold: eyes, be dry!
Heart, strengthen me to bear

This hideous sight, and humble me, to take
The last forgiveness of a dying friend,
Betray'd by my vile falsehood, to his ruin.
O Pierre!

    Pierr.   Yet nearer.

    Jaff.   Crawling on my knees,
And prostrate on the earth, let me approach thee:
How shall I look up to thy injured face,
That always used to smile, with friendship on me?
It darts an air of so much manly virtue,
That I, methinks, look little in thy sight,
And stripes are fitter for me than embraces.

    Pierr. Dear to my arms, though thou'st undone my fame,
I cannot forget to love thee; prithee, Jaffeir,
Forgive that filthy blow my passion dealt thee;
I'm now preparing for the land of peace,
And fain would have the charitable wishes
Of all good men, like thee, to bless my journey.

    Jaff. Good! I am the vilest creature; worse than e'er
Suffer'd the shameful fate thou'rt going to taste of.
Why was I sent for to be used thus kindly?
Call, call me villain, as I am, describe
The foul complexion of my hateful deeds,
Lead me to the rack, and stretch me in thy stead,
I've crimes enough to give it its full load,
And do it credit. Thou wilt not spoil the use on't,
And honest men hereafter bear its figure
About 'em, as a charm from treacherous friendship.

    Offic. The time grows short, your friends are dead already.

    Jaff. Dead!

    Pierr.   Yes, dead, Jaffeir, they've all died like men too,
Worthy their character.

    Jaff.   And what must I do?

    Pierr. O Jaffeir!

    Jaff.   Speak aloud thy burthen'd soul,
And tell thy troubles to thy tortured friend.

    Pierr. Couldst thou yet be a friend, a generous friend,
I might hope comfort from thy noble sorrows.
Heav'n knows I want a friend.

    Jaff.   And I a kind one,
That would not thus scorn my repenting virtue,
Or think when he's to die, my thoughts are idle.

    Pierr. No! live, I charge thee, Jaffeir.

    Jaff.   Yes, I'll live,
But it shall be to see thy fall revenged
At such a rate, as Venice long shall groan for.

    Pierr. Wilt thou?

    Jaff.   I will, by Heav'n.

    Pierr.   Then still thou'rt noble,

And I forgive thee, oh—yet—shall I trust thee?

Jaff. No: I've been false already.

Pierr.   Dost thou love me?

Jaff. Rip up my heart, and satisfy thy doubtings.

Pierr. Curse on this weakness.   [*He weeps.*

Jaff.   Tears! Amazement! Tears!
I never saw thee melted thus before,
And know there's something labouring in thy bosom
That must have vent: though I'm a villain, tell me.

Pierr. Seest thou that engine?   [*Pointing to the Wheel.*

Jaff. Why?

Pierr. Is't fit a soldier, who has liv'd with honour,
Fought nations' quarrels, and been crown'd with conquest,
Be exposed a common carcase on a wheel?

Jaff. Ha!

Pierr.   Speak! is't fitting?

Jaff.   Fitting?

Pierr.   Yes, is't fitting?

Jaff. What's to be done?

Pierr.   I'd have thee undertake
Something that's noble, to preserve my memory
From the disgrace that's ready to attaint it.

Offic. The day grows late, sir.

Pierr.   I'll make haste! O Jaffeir,
Though thou'st betray'd me, do me some way justice.

Jaff. No more of that: thy wishes shall be satisfied.
I have a wife, and she shall bleed, my child too
Yield up his little throat, and all t' appease thee——
                    [*Going away,* PIERRE *holds him.*

Pierr. No—this—no more!   [*He whispers* JAFFEIR.

Jaff.   Ha! is't then so?

Pierr.   Most certainly.

Jaff. I'll do't.

Pierr.   Remember.

Offic.   Sir.

Pierr.   Come, now I'm ready.
                    [*He and* JAFFEIR *ascend the scaffold.*
Captain, you should be a gentleman of honour.
Keep off the rabble, that I may have room
To entertain my fate and die with decency.
Come! [*Takes off his gown,* Executioner *prepares to bind him.*

Fath. Son!

Pierr.   Hence, tempter.

Offic.   Stand off, priest.

Pierr. I thank you, sir.

                    You'll think on't.   [*To* JAFFEIR.

Jaff. 'Twon't grow stale before to-morrow.

Pierr. Now, Jaffeir! now I am going. Now;—
                    [*Executioner having bound him.*

Jaff.   Have at thee,
Thou honest heart, then—here—   [*Stabs him.*
And this is well too.   [*Then stabs himself.*
    Fath.   Damnable deed!
    Pierr. Now thou hast indeed been faithful.
This was done nobly—we've deceived the Senate.
    Jaff. Bravely.
    Pierr.   Ha! ha! ha!—oh! oh!——   [*Dies.*
    Jaff.   Now, you curs'd rulers,
Thus of the blood ye've shed I make libation,
And sprinkle it mingling: may it rest upon you,
And all your race: be henceforth peace a stranger
Within your walls; let plagues and famine waste
Your generations—O poor Belvidera!
Sir, I have a wife, bear this in safety to her.
A token that with my dying breath I blessed her,
And the dear little infant left behind me.
I'm sick—I'm quiet——   [JAFFEIR *dies.*
    Offic.   Bear this news to the Senate,
And guard their bodies till there's farther order:
Heaven grant I die so well!   [*Scene shuts upon them.*

Soft music. Enter BELVIDERA *distracted, led by two of*
her women, PRIULI *and Servants.*

    Priu. Strengthen her heart with patience, pitying Heaven.
    Belv. Come come come come come, nay, come to bed!
Prithee my love.   The winds! hark how they whistle!
And the rain beats: oh, how the weather shrinks me!
You are angry now, who cares? pish, no indeed.
Choose then, I say you shall not go, you shall not;
Whip your ill nature; get you gone then! oh,
                              [JAFFEIR'S *ghost rises.*
Are you return'd?   See, father, here he's come again!
Am I to blame to love him?   O thou dear one!   [*Ghost sinks.*
Why do you fly me? are you angry still, then?
Jaffeir! where art thou?   Father, why do you do thus?
Stand off, don't hide him from me.   He's here somewhere.

Enter Officer *and others.*

Stand off, I say! what, gone? remember't Tyrant!
I may revenge myself for this trick one day.
I'll do't—I'll do't! Renault's a nasty fellow.
Hang him, hang him, hang him.
    Priu. News, what news?   [Officer *whispers* PRIULI.
    Offic.   Most sad, sir.
Jaffeir, upon the scaffold, to prevent

A shameful death, stabb'd Pierre, and next himself:
Both fell together.

    [The ghosts of JAFFEIR *and* PIERRE *rise together, both bloody.*

Priu.   Daughter.

Belv.   Ha, look there!
My husband bloody, and his friend too! Murther!
Who has done this? speak to me, thou sad vision, *[Ghosts sink.*
On these poor trembling knees I beg it.   Vanish'd!
Here they went down; oh, I'll dig, dig the den up.
You shan't delude me thus.   Ho, Jaffeir, Jaffeir,
Peep up and give me but a look.   I have him!
I've got him, father: oh, how I'll s[n]uggle him!
My love! my dear! my blessing! help me, help me!
They've hold on me, and drag me to the bottom.
Nay—now they pull so hard—farewell——   *[She dies.*

    Maid.   She's dead.
Breathless and dead.

    Priu.   Then guard me from the sight on't;
Lead me into some place that's fit for mourning;
Where the free air, light, and the cheerful sun
May never enter: hang it round with black:
Set up one taper that may last a day
As long as I've to live: and there leave me.
    Sparing no tears when you this tale relate,
    But bid all cruel fathers dread my fate.

        [Curtain falls.   Exeunt omnes.

EPILOGUE

The text is done, and now for application,
And when that's ended pass your approbation.
Though the conspiracy's prevented here,
Methinks I see another hatching there;
And there's a certain faction fain would sway,
If they had strength enough, and damn this play,
But this the author bade me boldly say:
If any take his plainness in ill part,
He's glad on't from the bottom of his heart;
Poets in honour of the truth should write,
With the same spirit brave men for it fight;
And though against him causeless hatreds rise,
And daily where he goes of late, he spies
The scowls of sullen and revengeful eyes;
'Tis what he knows with much contempt to bear,
And serves a cause too good to let him fear:
He fears no poison from an incensed drab,
No ruffian's five-foot sword, nor rascal's stab;
Nor any other snares of mischief laid,
Not a Rose-alley cudgel-ambuscade,
From any private cause where malice reigns,
Or general pique all blockheads have to brains:
Nothing shall daunt his pen when Truth does call,
No, not the picture mangler at Guildhall.
The rebel tribe, of which that vermin's one,
Have now set forward and their course begun;
And while that Prince's figure they deface,
  As they before had massacred his name,
Durst their base fears but look him in the face,
  They'd use his Person as they've used his fame;
A face, in which such lineaments they read
Of that great Martyr's, whose rich blood they shed,
That their rebellious hate they still retain,
And in his Son would murther Him again:
With indignation then, let each brave heart,
Rouse and unite to take his injured part;
Till royal love and goodness call him home,
And songs of triumph meet him as he come;
Till Heaven his honour and our peace restore,
And villains never wrong his virtue more.

APPENDIX

PROLOGUE

To His Royal Highness
Upon his first appearance at the Duke's Theatre
since his Return from Scotland

Written by **Mr. Dryden.**   *Spoken by* **Mr. Smith.**

In those cold Regions which no Summers chear,
When brooding darkness covers half the year,
To hollow Caves the shivering Natives go;
Bears range abroad, and hunt in tracks of Snow:
But when the tedious Twilight wears away,
And stars grow paler at th' approach of Day,
The longing Crowds to frozen Mountains run,
Happy who first can see the glimmering Sun!
The surly Salvage Offspring disappear;
And curse the bright Successour of the year.
Yet, though rough Bears in Covert seek defence, ⎫
White Foxes stay, with seeming Innocence: ⎬
That crafty kind with daylight can dispense. ⎭
Still we are throng'd so full with Reynard's race,
That Loyal Subjects scarce can find a place:
Thus modest Truth is cast behind the Crowd:
Truth speaks too Low; Hypocrisie too Loud.
Let 'em be first, to flatter in success;
Duty can stay; but Guilt has need to press.
Once, when true Zeal the Sons of God did call,
To make their solemn show at Heaven's White-hall,
The fawning Devil appear'd among the rest,
And made as good a Courtier as the best.
The friends of Job, who rail'd at him before,
Came Cap in hand when he had three time more.
Yet late Repentance may, perhaps, be true;
Kings can forgive if Rebels can but sue:
A Tyrant's Pow'r in rigour is exprest:
The Father yearns in the true Prince's Breast.
We grant an Ore'grown Whig no grace can mend;
But most are Babes, that know not they offend.
The Crowd, to restless motion still enclin'd,
Are Clouds, that rack according to the Wind.

Driv'n by their Chiefs, they storms of Hailstones pour:
Then mourn, and soften to a silent showre.
O welcome to this much offending Land
The Prince that brings forgiveness in his hand!
Thus Angels on Glad Messages appear:
Their first salute commands us not to fear:
Thus Heav'n, that cou'd constrain us to obey,
(With rev'rence if we might presume to say,) }
Seems to relax the rights of Sov'reign sway;
Permits to Man the choice of Good and Ill;
And makes us Happy by our own Free-will.

THE EPILOGUE

Written by Mr. Otway to his Play call'd *Venice Preserv'd, or, A Plot Discover'd;* spoken upon his Royal Highness the Duke of York's coming to the Theatre, Friday, April 21, 1682

WHEN too much Plenty, Luxury, and Ease,
Had surfeited this Isle to a Disease;
When noisome Blaines did its best parts orespread,
And on the rest their dire Infection shed;
Our Great Physician, who the Nature knew
Of the Distemper, and from whence it grew,
Fix't for Three Kingdoms quiet (Sir) on You:
He cast his searching Eyes o'er all the Frame,
And finding whence before one sickness came,
How once before our Mischiefs foster'd were,
Knew well Your Vertue, and apply'd You there:
Where so Your Goodness, so Your Justice sway'd,
You but appear'd, and the wild Plague was stay'd.
When from the filthy Dunghil-faction bred,
New form'd Rebellion durst rear up its head,
Answer me all: who struck the Monster dead?
      See, see, the injur'd PRINCE, and bless his Name,
Think on the Martyr from whose Loynes he came:
Think on the Blood was shed for you before,
And curse the Paricides that thirst for more.
His foes are yours, then of their wiles beware:
Lay, lay him in your Hearts, and guard him there;
Where let his Wrongs your Zeal for him Improve;
He wears a Sword will justifie your Love.
With Blood still ready for your good t' expend,
And has a Heart that ne're forgot his friend.
His Duteous Loyalty before you lay,
And learn of him, unmurm'ring to obey.
Think what he'as born, your Quiet to restore;
Repent your madness and rebell no more.
No more let Bout'feu's hope to lead Petitions,
Scriv'ners to be Treas'rures; Pedlars Politicians;
Nor ev'ry fool, whose wife has tript at Court,
Pluck up a Spirit, and turn Rebell for't.
      In Lands where Cuckolds multiply like ours,
What Prince can be too Jealous of their powers,
Or can too often think himself alarm'd?
They're male contents that ev'rywhere go arm'd:

And when the horned Herd's together got,
Nothing portends a Commonwealth like that.

Cast, cast your Idols off, your Gods of wood,
Er'e yet Philistins fatten with your blood:
Renounce your Priests of Baal with Amen-faces,
Your Wapping Feasts and your Mile-End High-places.
Nail all your Medals on the Gallows Post,
In recompense th' Original was lost:
At these, illustrious Repentance pay,
In his kind hands your humble Offrings lay:
Let Royal Pardon be by him implor'd,
Th' Attoning Brother of your Anger'd Lord:
He only brings a medicine fit to aswage
A people's folly, and rowz'd Monarch's rage;
An Infant Prince yet lab'ring in the womb, }
Fated with wond'rous happiness to come, }
He goes to fetch the mighty blessing home: }
Send all your wishes with him, let the Ayre }
With gentle breezes waft it safely here, }
The Seas, like what they'l carry, calm and fair: }
Let the Illustrious Mother touch our Land
Mildly, as hereafter may her Son Command;
While our glad Monarch welcomes her to shoar,
With kind assurance; she shall part no more.

Be the Majestick Babe then smiling born,
And all good signs of Fate his Birth adorn,
So live and grow, a constant pledg to stand
Of Cæsar's Love to an obedient Land.

THE BEAUX-STRATAGEM

ADVERTISEMENT

THE reader may find some faults in this play, which my illness prevented the amending of; but there is great amends made in the representation, which cannot be matched, no more than the friendly and indefatigable care of Mr. Wilks, to whom I chiefly owe the success of the play.

GEORGE FARQUHAR.

DRAMATIS PERSONÆ

With names of the original actors and actresses.

THOMAS AIMWELL FRANCIS ARCHER	Two gentlemen of broken fortunes, the first as master, and the second as servant	Mr. MILLS. Mr. WILKS.
Count BELLAIR	A French Officer, prisoner at Lichfield	Mr. BOMAN.
Squire SULLEN	A Country Blockhead, brutal to his Wife	Mr. VERBRUGGEN.
Sir CHARLES FREE-MAN	A Gentleman from London, brother to Mrs. Sullen	Mr. KEEN.
FOIGARD	A Priest, Chaplain to the French Officers	Mr. BOWEN.
GIBBET	A Highwayman	Mr. CIBBER.
HOUNSLOW BAGSHOT	His Companions.	
BONIFACE	Landlord of the Inn	Mr. BULLOCK.
SCRUB	Servant to Squire Sullen	Mr. NORRIS.
Lady BOUNTIFUL	An old, civil, Country Gentlewoman, that cures all her neighbours of all distempers, and foolishly fond of her son, Squire Sullen	Mrs. POWELL.
Mrs. SULLEN	Her Daughter-in-law, wife to Squire Sullen	Mrs. OLDFIELD.
DORINDA	Lady Bountiful's Daughter	Mrs. BRADSHAW.
GIPSY	Maid to the Ladies	Mrs. MILLS.
CHERRY	The Landlord's Daughter in the Inn	Mrs. BICKNELL.

Tapster, Coach-passengers, Countryman, Country-woman, and Servants.

SCENE—LICHFIELD.

PROLOGUE

SPOKEN BY MR. WILKS

WHEN strife disturbs, or sloth corrupts an age,
Keen satire is the business of the stage.
When the *Plain-Dealer* writ, he lash'd those crimes,
Which then infested most—the modish times:
But now, when faction sleeps, and sloth is fled,
And all our youth in active fields are bred;
When through Great Britain's fair extensive round,
The trumps of fame, the notes of UNION sound;
When Anna's sceptre points the laws their course,
And her example gives her precepts force:
There scarce is room for satire; all our lays
Must be, or songs of triumph, or of praise.
But as in grounds best cultivated, tares
And poppies rise among the golden ears;
Our product so, fit for the field or school,
Must mix with nature's favourite plant—a fool:
A weed that has to twenty summers ran,
Shoots up in stalk, and vegetates to man.
Simpling our author goes from field to field,
And culls such fools as may diversion yield;
And, thanks to Nature, there's no want of those,
For rain or shine, the thriving coxcomb grows.
Follies to-night we show ne'er lash'd before,
Yet such as nature shows you every hour;
Nor can the pictures give a just offence,
For fools are made for jests to men of sense.

THE BEAUX-STRATAGEM

ACT I

SCENE I.—*A Room in* BONIFACE'S *Inn*

Enter BONIFACE *running.*

Bon. Chamberlain! maid! Cherry! daughter Cherry! all asleep! all dead?

Enter CHERRY *running.*

Cher. Here, here! why d'ye bawl so, father? d'ye think we have no ears?

Bon. You deserve to have none, you young minx! The company of the Warrington coach has stood in the hall this hour, and nobody to show them to their chambers.

Cher. And let 'em wait farther; there's neither red-coat in the coach, nor footman behind it.

Bon. But they threaten to go to another inn to-night.

Cher. That they dare not, for fear the coachman should overturn them to-morrow.—Coming! coming!—Here's the London coach arrived.

Enter several people with trunks, bandboxes, and other luggage, and cross the stage.

Bon. Welcome, ladies!

Cher. Very welcome, gentlemen!—Chamberlain, show the *Lion* and the *Rose.*   [*Exit with the company.*

Enter AIMWELL *in a riding-habit, and* ARCHER *as footman, carrying a portmantle.*

Bon. This way, this way, gentlemen!

Aim. [*to* ARCHER]. Set down the things; go to the stable, and see my horses well rubbed.

Arch. I shall, sir.   [*Exit.*

Aim. You're my landlord, I suppose?

Bon. Yes, sir, I'm old Will Boniface, pretty well known upon this road, as the saying is.

Aim. O Mr. Boniface, your servant!

Bon. O sir!—What will your honour please to drink, as the saying is?

Aim. I have heard your town of Lichfield much famed for ale; I think I'll taste that.

Bon. Sir, I have now in my cellar ten tun of the best ale in Staffordshire; 'tis smooth as oil, sweet as milk, clear as amber, and strong as brandy; and will be just fourteen year old the fifth day of next March, old style.

Aim. You're very exact, I find, in the age of your ale.

Bon. As punctual, sir, as I am in the age of my children. I'll show you such ale!—Here, tapster [*enter* Tapster], broach number 1706, as the saying is.—Sir, you shall taste my *Anno Domini.*—I have lived in Lichfield, man and boy, above eight-and-fifty years, and, I believe, have not consumed eight-and-fifty ounces of meat.

Aim. At a meal, you mean, if one may guess your sense by your bulk.

Bon. Not in my life, sir: I have fed purely upon ale; I have eat my ale, drank my ale, and I always sleep upon ale.

Enter Tapster *with a bottle and glass, and exit.*

Now, sir, you shall see!—[*Filling out a glass.*] Your worship's health.—[*Drinks.*] Ha! delicious, delicious! fancy it burgundy, only fancy it, and 'tis worth ten shillings a quart.

Aim. [*drinks*]. 'Tis confounded strong!

Bon. Strong! it must be so, or how should we be strong that drink it?

Aim. And have you lived so long upon this ale, landlord?

Bon. Eight-and-fifty years, upon my credit, sir—but it killed my wife, poor woman, as the saying is.

Aim. How came that to pass?

Bon. I don't know how, sir; she would not let the ale take its natural course, sir; she was for qualifying it every now and then with a dram, as the saying is; and an honest gentleman that came this way from Ireland, made her a present of a dozen bottles of usquebaugh—but the poor woman was never well after: but, howe'er, I was obliged to the gentleman, you know.

Aim. Why, was it the usquebaugh that killed her?

Bon. My Lady Bountiful said so. She, good lady, did what could be done; she cured her of three tympanies, but the fourth carried her off. But she's happy, and I'm contented, as the saying is.

Aim. Who's that Lady Bountiful you mentioned?

Bon. Ods my life, sir, we'll drink her health.—[*Drinks.*] My Lady Bountiful is one of the best of women. Her last husband, Sir Charles Bountiful, left her worth a thousand pound a year; and, I believe, she lays out one-half on't in charitable uses for the good of her neighbours. She cures rheumatisms, ruptures, and broken shins in men; green-sickness, obstructions, and fits of the mother, in women; the king's evil, chincough, and chilblains, in children: in short, she has cured more people in and about Lichfield within ten years than the doctors have killed in twenty; and that's a bold word.

Aim. Has the lady been any other way useful in her generation?

Bon. Yes, sir; she has a daughter by Sir Charles, the finest woman in all our country, and the greatest fortune. She has a son too, by her first husband, Squire Sullen, who married a fine lady from London t'other day; if you please, sir, we'll drink his health.

Aim. What sort of a man is he?

Bon. Why, sir, the man's well enough; says little, thinks less, and does—nothing at all, faith. But he's a man of a great estate, and values nobody.

Aim. A sportsman, I suppose?

Bon. Yes, sir, he's a man of pleasure; he plays at whisk and smokes his pipe eight-and-forty hours together sometimes.

Aim. And married, you say?

Bon. Ay, and to a curious woman, sir. But he's a—he wants it here, sir.   *[Pointing to his forehead.*

Aim. He has it there, you mean?

Bon. That's none of my business; he's my landlord, and so a man, you know, would not—But—ecod, he's no better than—Sir, my humble service to you.—[*Drinks.*] Though I value not a farthing what he can do to me; I pay him his rent at quarter-day; I have a good running-trade; I have but one daughter, and I can give her—but no matter for that.

Aim. You're very happy, Mr. Boniface. Pray, what other company have you in town?

Bon. A power of fine ladies; and then we have the French officers.

Aim. Oh, that's right, you have a good many of those gentlemen: pray, how do you like their company?

Bon. So well, as the saying is, that I could wish we had as many more of 'em; they're full of money, and pay double for everything they have. They know, sir, that we paid good round taxes for the taking of 'em, and so they are willing to reimburse us a little. One of 'em lodges in my house.

Re-enter ARCHER.

Arch. Landlord, there are some French gentlemen below that ask for you.

Bon. I'll wait on 'em.—[*Aside to* ARCHER.] Does your master stay long in town, as the saying is?

Arch. I can't tell, as the saying is.

Bon. Come from London?

Arch. No.

Bon. Going to London, mayhap?

Arch. No.

Bon. [*aside*]. An odd fellow this.—[*To* AIMWELL.] I beg your worship's pardon, I'll wait on you in half a minute. [*Exit.*

Aim. The coast's clear, I see.—Now, my dear Archer, welcome to Lichfield!

Arch. I thank thee, my dear brother in iniquity.

Aim. Iniquity! prithee, leave canting; you need not change your style with your dress.

Arch. Don't mistake me, Aimwell, for 'tis still my maxim, that there is no scandal like rags, nor any crime so shameful as poverty.

Aim. The world confesses it every day in its practice though men won't own it for their opinion. Who did that worthy lord, my brother, single out of the side-box to sup with him t'other night?

Arch. Jack Handicraft, a handsome, well-dressed, mannerly, sharping rogue, who keeps the best company in town.

Aim. Right! And, pray, who married my lady Manslaughter t'other day, the great fortune?

Arch. Why, Nick Marrabone, a professed pickpocket, and a good bowler; but he makes a handsome figure, and rides in his coach, that he formerly used to ride behind.

Aim. But did you observe poor Jack Generous in the Park last week?

Arch. Yes, with his autumnal periwig, shading his melancholy face, his coat older than anything but its fashion, with one hand idle in his pocket, and with the other picking his useless teeth; and, though the Mall was crowded with company, yet was poor Jack as single and solitary as a lion in a desert.

Aim. And as much avoided, for no crime upon earth but the want of money.

Arch. And that's enough. Men must not be poor; idleness is the root of all evil; the world's wide enough, let 'em bustle. Fortune has taken the weak under her protection, but men of sense are left to their industry.

Aim. Upon which topic we proceed, and, I think, luckily hitherto. Would not any man swear now, that I am a man of quality, and you my servant, when if our intrinsic value were known——

Arch. Come, come, we are the men of intrinsic value who can strike our fortunes out of ourselves, whose worth is independent of accidents in life, or revolutions in government: we have heads to get money and hearts to spend it.

Aim. As to our hearts, I grant ye, they are as willing tits as any within twenty degrees: but I can have no great opinion of our heads from the service they have done us hitherto, unless it be that they have brought us from London hither to Lichfield, made me a lord and you my servant.

Arch. That's more than you could expect already. But what money have we left?

Aim. But two hundred pound.

Arch. And our horses, clothes, rings, etc.—Why, we have very good fortunes now for moderate people; and, let me tell you, that this two hundred pound, with the experience that we are now masters of, is a better estate than the ten we have spent. —Our friends, indeed, began to suspect that our pockets were low, but we came off with flying colours, showed no signs of want either in word or deed.

Aim. Ay, and our going to Brussels was a good pretence enough for our sudden disappearing; and, I warrant you, our friends imagine that we are gone a-volunteering.

Arch. Why, faith, if this prospect fails, it must e'en come to that. I am for venturing one of the hundreds, if you will, upon this knight-errantry; but, in case it should fail, we'll reserve t'other to carry us to some counterscarp, where we may die, as we lived, in a blaze.

Aim. With all my heart; and we have lived justly, Archer; we can't say that we have spent our fortunes, but that we have enjoyed 'em.

Arch. Right! so much pleasure for so much money. We have had our pennyworths; and, had I millions, I would go to the same market again.—O London! London!—Well, we have had our share, and let us be thankful: past pleasures, for aught I know, are best, such as we are sure of; those to come may disappoint us.

Aim. It has often grieved the heart of me to see how some inhuman wretches murder their kind fortunes; those that, by sacrificing all to one appetite, shall starve all the rest. You shall have some that live only in their palates, and in their sense of tasting shall drown the other four: others are only epicures in appearances, such who shall starve their nights to make a figure a days, and famish their own to feed the eyes of others: a contrary sort confine their pleasures to the dark, and contract their specious acres to the circuit of a muff-string.

Arch. Right! But they find the Indies in that spot where they consume 'em, and I think your kind keepers have much the best on't: for they indulge the most senses by one expense, there's the seeing, hearing, and feeling, amply gratified; and, some philosophers will tell you, that from such a commerce there arises a sixth sense, that gives infinitely more pleasure than the other five put together.

Aim. And to pass to the other extremity, of all keepers I think those the worst that keep their money.

Arch. Those are the most miserable wights in being, they destroy the rights of nature, and disappoint the blessings of Providence. Give me a man that keeps his five senses keen and bright as his sword, that has 'em always drawn out in their just order and strength, with his reason as commander at the head of 'em, that detaches 'em by turns upon whatever party of pleasure agreeably offers, and commands 'em to retreat upon the least appearance of disadvantage or danger! For my part, I can stick to my bottle while my wine, my company, and my reason, hold good; I can be charmed with Sappho's singing without falling in love with her face: I love hunting, but would not, like Actæon, be eaten up by my own dogs; I love a fine house, but let another keep it; and just so I love a fine woman.

Aim. In that last particular you have the better of me.

Arch. Ay, you're such an amorous puppy, that I'm afraid you'll spoil our sport; you can't counterfeit the passion without feeling it.

Aim. Though the whining part be out of doors in town, 'tis still in force with the country ladies: and let me tell you, Frank, the fool in that passion shall outdo the knave at any time.

Arch. Well, I won't dispute it now; you command for the day, and so I submit: at Nottingham, you know, I am to be master.

Aim. And at Lincoln, I again.

Arch. Then, at Norwich I mount, which, I think, shall be our last stage; for, if we fail there, we'll embark for Holland, bid adieu to Venus, and welcome Mars.

Aim. A match!—Mum!

Re-enter BONIFACE.

Bon. What will your worship please to have for supper?

Aim. What have you got?

Bon. Sir, we have a delicate piece of beef in the pot, and a pig at the fire.

Aim. Good supper-meat, I must confess. I can't eat beef, landlord.

Arch. And I hate pig.

Aim. Hold your prating, sirrah! do you know who you are?

Bon. Please to bespeak something else; I have everything in the house.

Aim. Have you any veal?

Bon. Veal! sir, we had a delicate loin of veal on Wednesday last.

Aim. Have you got any fish or wildfowl?

Bon. As for fish, truly, sir, we are an inland town, and in-differently provided with fish, that's the truth on't; and then for wildfowl—we have a delicate couple of rabbits.

Aim. Get me the rabbits fricasseed.

Bon. Fricasseed! Lard, sir, they'll eat much better smothered with onions.

Arch. Psha! Damn your onions!

Aim. Again, sirrah!—Well, landlord, what you please. But hold, I have a small charge of money, and your house is so full of strangers, that I believe it may be safer in your custody than mine; for when this fellow of mine gets drunk he minds nothing. —Here, sirrah, reach me the strong-box.

Arch. Yes, sir.—[*Aside.*] This will give us a reputation.

[*Brings* AIMWELL *the box.*

Aim. Here, landlord; the locks are sealed down both for your security and mine; it holds somewhat above two hundred pound: if you doubt it, I'll count it to you after supper; but be sure you lay it where I may have it at a minute's warning; for my affairs are a little dubious at present; perhaps I may be gone in half an hour, perhaps I may be your guest till the best part of that be spent; and pray order your ostler to keep my horses always saddled. But one thing above the rest I must beg, that you would let this fellow have none of your *Anno Domini*, as you call it; for he's the most insufferable sot.—Here, sirrah, light me to my chamber. [*Exit, lighted by* ARCHER.

Bon. Cherry! daughter Cherry!

Re-enter CHERRY.

Cher. D'ye call, father?

Bon. Ay, child, you must lay by this box for the gentleman: 'tis full of money.

Cher. Money! all that money! why, sure, father, the gentleman comes to be chosen parliament-man. Who is he?

Bon. I don't know what to make of him; he talks of keeping his horses ready saddled, and of going perhaps at a minute's warning, or of staying perhaps till the best part of this be spent.

Cher. Ay, ten to one, father, he's a highwayman.

Bon. A highwayman! upon my life, girl, you have hit it, and this box is some new-purchased booty. Now, could we find him out, the money were ours.

Cher. He don't belong to our gang.

Bon. What horses have they?

Cher. The master rides upon a black.

Bon. A black! ten to one the man upon the black mare; and since he don't belong to our fraternity, we may betray him with a safe conscience: I don't think it lawful to harbour any rogues but my own. Look'ee, child, as the saying is, we must go cunningly to work, proofs we must have; the gentleman's servant loves drink, I'll ply him that way, and ten to one loves a wench: you must work him t'other way.

Cher. Father, would you have me give my secret for his?

Bon. Consider, child, there's two hundred pound to boot.— [*Ringing without.*] Coming! coming!—Child, mind your business.

[*Exit.*

Cher. What a rogue is my father! My father! I deny it. My mother was a good, generous, free-hearted woman, and I can't tell how far her good nature might have extended for the good of her children. This landlord of mine, for I think I can call him no more, would betray his guest, and debauch his daughter into the bargain—by a footman too!

Re-enter ARCHER.

Arch. What footman, pray, mistress, is so happy as to be the subject of your contemplation?

Cher. Whoever he is, friend, he'll be but little the better for't.

Arch. I hope so, for, I'm sure, you did not think of me.

Cher. Suppose I had?

Arch. Why, then, you're but even with me; for the minute I came in, I was a-considering in what manner I should make love to you.

Cher. Love to me, friend!

Arch. Yes, child.

Cher. Child! manners!—If you kept a little more distance, friend, it would become you much better.

Arch. Distance! good-night, sauce-box.   [*Going.*

Cher. [*aside*]. A pretty fellow! I like his pride.—[*Aloud.*] Sir, pray, sir, you see, sir [ARCHER *returns*], I have the credit to be entrusted with your master's fortune here, which sets me a degree above his footman; I hope, sir, you an't affronted?

Arch. Let me look you full in the face, and I'll tell you whether you can affront me or no. 'Sdeath, child, you have a pair of delicate eyes, and you don't know what to do with 'em!

Cher. Why, sir, don't I see everybody?

Arch. Ay, but if some women had 'em, they would kill everybody. Prithee, instruct me, I would fain make love to you, but I don't know what to say.

Cher. Why, did you never make love to anybody before?

Arch. Never to a person of your figure, I can assure you, madam: my addresses have been always confined to people within my own sphere, I never aspired so high before.   [*Sings.*

> But you look so bright,
> And are dress'd so tight,
> That a man would swear you're right,
> As arm was e'er laid over.
>   Such an air
>   You freely wear
>   To ensnare,
> As makes each guest a lover!
>
> Since then, my dear, I'm your guest,
>   Prithee give me of the best
>   Of what is ready drest:
> Since then, my dear, etc.

Cher. [*aside*]. What can I think of this man?—[*Aloud.*] Will you give me that song, sir?

Arch. Ay, my dear, take it while 'tis warm.—[*Kisses her.*] Death and fire! her lips are honeycombs.

Cher. And I wish there had been bees too, to have stung you for your impudence.

Arch. There's a swarm of Cupids, my little Venus, that has done the business much better.

Cher. [*aside*]. This fellow is misbegotten as well as I.— [*Aloud.*] What's your name, sir?

Arch. [*aside*]. Name! egad, I have forgot it.—[*Aloud.*] Oh! Martin.

Cher. Where were you born?

Arch. In St. Martin's parish.

Cher. What was your father?

Arch. St. Martin's parish.

Cher. Then, friend, good-night.

Arch. I hope not.

Cher. You may depend upon't.

Arch. Upon what?

Cher. That you're very impudent.

Arch. That you're very handsome.

Cher. That you're a footman.

Arch. That you're an angel.

Cher. I shall be rude.

Arch. So shall I.

Cher. Let go my hand.

Arch. Give me a kiss. [*Kisses her.*

[*Call without.*] Cherry! Cherry!

Cher. I'm—my father calls; you plaguy devil, how durst you stop my breath so? Offer to follow me one step, if you dare. [*Exit.*

Arch. A fair challenge, by this light! this is a pretty fair opening of an adventure; but we are knight-errants, and so Fortune be our guide. [*Exit.*

ACT II

SCENE I.—*A Gallery in* Lady BOUNTIFUL'S *House*

Enter Mrs. SULLEN *and* DORINDA, *meeting.*

Dor. Morrow, my dear sister; are you for church this morning?

Mrs. Sul. Anywhere to pray; for Heaven alone can help me. But I think, Dorinda, there's no form of prayer in the liturgy against bad husbands.

Dor. But there's a form of law in Doctors-Commons; and I swear, sister Sullen, rather than see you thus continually discontented, I would advise you to apply to that: for besides the part that I bear in your vexatious broils, as being sister to the husband, and friend to the wife, your example gives me such an impression of matrimony, that I shall be apt to condemn my person to a long vacation all its life. But supposing, madam, that you brought it to a case of separation, what can you urge against your husband? My brother is, first, the most constant man alive.

Mrs. Sul. The most constant husband, I grant ye.

Dor. He never sleeps from you.

Mrs. Sul. No, he always sleeps with me.

Dor. He allows you a maintenance suitable to your quality.

Mrs. Sul. A maintenance! do you take me, madam, for an hospital child, that I must sit down, and bless my benefactors for meat, drink, and clothes? As I take it, madam, I brought your brother ten thousand pounds, out of which I might expect some pretty things, called pleasures.

Dor. You share in all the pleasures that the country affords.

Mrs. Sul. Country pleasures! racks and torments! Dost think, child, that my limbs were made for leaping of ditches, and clambering over stiles? or that my parents, wisely foreseeing my future happiness in country pleasures, had early instructed me in rural accomplishments of drinking fat ale, playing at whisk, and smoking tobacco with my husband? or of spreading of plasters, brewing of diet-drinks, and stilling rosemary-water, with the good old gentlewoman my mother-in-law?

Dor. I'm sorry, madam, that it is not more in our power to divert you; I could wish, indeed, that our entertainments were a little more polite, or your taste a little less refined. But, pray, madam, how came the poets and philosophers, that laboured so much in hunting after pleasure, to place it at last in a country life?

Mrs. Sul. Because they wanted money, child, to find out the pleasures of the town. Did you ever see a poet or philosopher worth ten thousand pounds? if you can show me such a man, I'll lay you fifty pounds you'll find him somewhere within the weekly bills. Not that I disapprove rural pleasures, as the poets have painted them; in their landscape, every Phillis has her Corydon, every murmuring stream, and every flowery mead, gives fresh alarms to love. Besides, you'll find, that their couples were never married:—but yonder I see my Corydon, and a sweet swain it is, Heaven knows! Come, Dorinda, don't be angry, he's my husband, and your brother; and, between both, is he not a sad brute?

Dor. I have nothing to say to your part of him, you're the best judge.

Mrs. Sul. O sister, sister! if ever you marry, beware of a sullen, silent sot, one that's always musing, but never thinks. There's some diversion in a talking blockhead; and since a

woman must wear chains, I would have the pleasure of hearing
'em rattle a little. Now you shall see, but take this by the way.
He came home this morning at his usual hour of four, wakened
me out of a sweet dream of something else, by tumbling over the
tea-table, which he broke all to pieces; after his man and he had
rolled about the room, like sick passengers in a storm, he comes
flounce into bed, dead as a salmon into a fishmonger's basket;
his feet cold as ice, his breath hot as a furnace, and his hands and
his face as greasy as his flannel night-cap. O matrimony! He
tosses up the clothes with a barbarous swing over his shoulders,
disorders the whole economy of my bed, leaves me half naked,
and my whole night's comfort is the tuneable serenade of that
wakeful nightingale, his nose! Oh, the pleasure of counting the
melancholy clock by a snoring husband! But now, sister, you
shall see how handsomely, being a well-bred man, he will beg
my pardon.

Enter Squire SULLEN.

Squire Sul. My head aches consumedly.

Mrs. Sul. Will you be pleased, my dear, to drink tea with us
this morning? it may do your head good.

Squire Sul. No.

Dor. Coffee, brother?

Squire Sul. Psha!

Mrs. Sul. Will you please to dress, and go to church with me?
the air may help you.

Squire Sul. Scrub!   [*Calls.*

Enter SCRUB.

Scrub. Sir!

Squire Sul. What day o' th' week is this?

Scrub. Sunday, an't please your worship.

Squire Sul. Sunday! bring me a dram; and d'ye hear, set
out the venison-pasty and a tankard of strong beer upon the
hall-table, I'll go to breakfast.   [*Going.*

Dor. Stay, stay, brother, you shan't get off so; you were very
naught last night, and must make your wife reparation; come,
come, brother, won't you ask pardon?

Squire Sul. For what?

Dor. For being drunk last night.

Squire Sul. I can afford it, can't I?

Mrs. Sul. But I can't, sir.

Squire Sul. Then you may let it alone.

Mrs. Sul. But I must tell you, sir, that this is not to be borne.

Squire Sul. I'm glad on't.

Mrs. Sul. What is the reason, sir, that you use me thus
inhumanly?

Squire Sul. Scrub!

Scrub. Sir!

Squire Sul. Get things ready to shave my head.   [*Exit.*

Mrs. Sul. Have a care of coming near his temples, Scrub, for fear you meet something there that may turn the edge of your razor.—[*Exit* SCRUB.]   Inveterate stupidity! did you ever know so hard, so obstinate a spleen as his? O sister, sister! I shall never ha' good of the beast till I get him to town; London, dear London, is the place for managing and breaking a husband.

Dor. And has not a husband the same opportunities there for humbling a wife?

Mrs. Sul. No, no, child, 'tis a standing maxim in conjugal discipline, that when a man would enslave his wife, he hurries her into the country; and when a lady would be arbitrary with her husband, she wheedles her booby up to town. A man dare not play the tyrant in London, because there are so many examples to encourage the subject to rebel. O Dorinda! Dorinda! a fine woman may do anything in London: o' my conscience, she may raise an army of forty thousand men.

Dor. I fancy, sister, you have a mind to be trying your power that way here in Lichfield; you have drawn the French count to your colours already.

Mrs. Sul. The French are a people that can't live without their gallantries.

Dor. And some English that I know, sister, are not averse to such amusements.

Mrs. Sul. Well, sister, since the truth must out, it may do as well now as hereafter; I think, one way to rouse my lethargic, sottish husband, is to give him a rival: security begets negligence in all people, and men must be alarmed to make 'em alert in their duty. Women are like pictures, of no value in the hands of a fool, till he hears men of sense bid high for the purchase.

Dor. This might do, sister, if my brother's understanding were to be convinced into a passion for you; but, I fancy, there's a natural aversion on his side; and I fancy, sister, that you don't come much behind him, if you dealt fairly.

Mrs. Sul. I own it, we are united contradictions, fire and water: but I could be contented, with a great many other wives, to humour the censorious mob, and give the world an appearance of living well with my husband, could I bring him but to dissemble a little kindness to keep me in countenance.

Dor. But how do you know, sister, but that, instead of rousing your husband by this artifice to a counterfeit kindness, he should awake in a real fury?

Mrs. Sul. Let him: if I can't entice him to the one, I would provoke him to the other.

Dor. But how must I behave myself between ye?

Mrs. Sul. You must assist me.

Dor. What, against my own brother?

Mrs. Sul. He's but half a brother, and I'm your entire friend. If I go a step beyond the bounds of honour, leave me; till then,

I expect you should go along with me in everything; while I trust my honour in your hands, you may trust your brother's in mine. The count is to dine here to-day.

Dor. 'Tis a strange thing, sister, that I can't like that man.

Mrs. Sul. You like nothing; your time is not come; Love and Death have their fatalities, and strike home one time or other: you'll pay for all one day, I warrant ye. But come, my lady's tea is ready, and 'tis almost church time. [*Exeunt.*

SCENE II.—*A Room in* BONIFACE'S *Inn*

Enter AIMWELL *dressed, and* ARCHER.

Aim. And was she the daughter of the house?

Arch. The landlord is so blind as to think so; but I dare swear she has better blood in her veins.

Aim. Why dost think so?

Arch. Because the baggage has a pert *je ne sais quoi ;* she reads plays, keeps a monkey, and is troubled with vapours.

Aim. By which discoveries I guess that you know more of her.

Arch. Not yet, faith; the lady gives herself airs; forsooth, nothing under a gentleman!

Aim. Let me take her in hand.

Arch. Say one word more o' that, and I'll declare myself, spoil your sport there, and everywhere else; look ye, Aimwell, every man in his own sphere.

Aim. Right; and therefore you must pimp for your master.

Arch. In the usual forms, good sir, after I have served myself. —But to our business. You are so well dressed, Tom, and make so handsome a figure, that I fancy you may do execution in a country church; the exterior part strikes first, and you're in the right to make that impression favourable.

Aim. There's something in that which may turn to advantage. The appearance of a stranger in a country church draws as many gazers as a blazing-star; no sooner he comes into the cathedral, but a train of whispers runs buzzing round the congregation in a moment: *Who is he? Whence comes he? Do you know him?* Then I, sir, tips me the verger with half-a-crown; he pockets the simony, and inducts me into the best pew in the church; I pull out my snuff-box, turn myself round, bow to the bishop, or the dean, if he be the commanding-officer; single out a beauty, rivet both my eyes to hers, set my nose a-bleeding by the strength of imagination, and show the whole church my concern, by my endeavouring to hide it; after the sermon, the whole town gives me to her for a lover, and by persuading the lady that I am a-dying for her, the tables are turned, and she in good earnest falls in love with me.

Arch. There's nothing in this, Tom, without a precedent;

but instead of riveting your eyes to a beauty, try to fix 'em upon a fortune; that's our business at present.

Aim. Psha! no woman can be a beauty without a fortune. Let me alone, for I am a marksman.

Arch. Tom!

Aim. Ay.

Arch. When were you at church before, pray?

Aim. Um—I was there at the coronation.

Arch. And how can you expect a blessing by going to church now?

Aim. Blessing! nay, Frank, I ask but for a wife.   [*Exit.*

Arch. Truly, the man is not very unreasonable in his demands.
                                    [*Exit at the opposite door.*

Enter BONIFACE *and* CHERRY.

Bon. Well, daughter, as the saying is, have you brought Martin to confess?

Cher. Pray, father, don't put me upon getting anything out of a man; I'm but young, you know, father, and I don't understand wheedling.

Bon. Young! why, you jade, as the saying is, can any woman wheedle that is not young? your mother was useless at five-and-twenty. Not wheedle! would you make your mother a whore, and me a cuckold, as the saying is? I tell you, his silence confesses it, and his master spends his money so freely, and is so much a gentleman every manner of way, that he must be a highwayman.

Enter GIBBET, *in a cloak.*

Gib. Landlord, landlord, is the coast clear?

Bon. O Mr. Gibbet, what's the news?

Gib. No matter, ask no questions, all fair and honourable.— Here, my dear Cherry.—[*Gives her a bag.*] Two hundred sterling pounds, as good as any that ever hanged or saved a rogue; lay 'em by with the rest; and here—three wedding or mourning rings, 'tis much the same, you know—here, two silver-hilted swords; I took those from fellows that never show any part of their swords but the hilts—here is a diamond necklace which the lady hid in the privatest place in the coach, but I found it out— this gold watch I took from a pawnbroker's wife; it was left in her hands by a person of quality: there's the arms upon the case.

Cher. But who had you the money from?

Gib. Ah! poor woman! I pitied her;—from a poor lady just eloped from her husband. She had made up her cargo, and was bound for Ireland, as hard as she could drive; she told me of her husband's barbarous usage, and so I left her half-a-crown. But I had almost forgot, my dear Cherry, I have a present for you.

Cher. What is't?

Gib. A pot of ceruse, my child, that I took out of a lady's under-pocket.

Cher. What, Mr. Gibbet, do you think that I paint?

Gib. Why, you jade, your betters do; I'm sure the lady that I took it from had a coronet upon her handkerchief. Here, take my cloak, and go, secure the premises.

Cher. I will secure 'em.   [*Exit.*

Bon. But, hark'ee, where's Hounslow and Bagshot?

Gib. They'll be here to-night.

Bon. D'ye know of any other gentlemen o' the pad on this road?

Gib. No.

Bon. I fancy that I have two that lodge in the house just now.

Gib. The devil! how d'ye smoke 'em?

Bon. Why, the one is gone to church.

Gib. That's suspicious, I must confess.

Bon. And the other is now in his master's chamber; he pretends to be servant to the other; we'll call him out and pump him a little.

Gib. With all my heart.

Bon. Mr. Martin! Mr. Martin!   [*Calls*

Enter ARCHER, *combing a periwig and singing.*

Gib. The roads are consumed deep, I'm as dirty as Old Brentford at Christmas.—A good pretty fellow that; whose servant are you, friend?

Arch. My master's.

Gib. Really!

Arch. Really.

Gib. That's much.—The fellow has been at the bar by his evasions.—But pray, sir, what is your master's name?

Arch. Tall, all, dall!—[*Sings and combs the periwig.*] This is the most obstinate curl——

Gib. I ask you his name?

Arch. Name, sir—*tall, all, dall!*—I never asked him his name in my life.—*Tall, all, dall!*

Bon. What think you now?   [*Aside to* GIBBET.

Gib. [*aside to* BONIFACE]. Plain, plain, he talks now as if he were before a judge.—[*To* ARCHER.] But pray, friend, which way does your master travel?

Arch. A-horseback.

Gib. [*aside*]. Very well again, an old offender, right.—[*To* ARCHER.] But, I mean, does he go upwards or downwards?

Arch. Downwards, I fear, sir.—*Tall, all!*

Gib. I'm afraid my fate will be a contrary way.

Bon. Ha! ha! ha! Mr. Martin, you're very arch. This gentleman is only travelling towards Chester, and would be glad of your company, that's all.—Come, captain, you'll stay to-night, I suppose? I'll show you a chamber—come, captain.

Gib. Farewell, friend!

Arch. Captain, your servant.—[*Exeunt* BONIFACE *and* GIBBET.]
Captain! a pretty fellow! 'Sdeath, I wonder that the officers
of the army don't conspire to beat all scoundrels in red but
their own.

Re-enter CHERRY.

Cher. [*aside*]. Gone, and Martin here! I hope he did not
listen; I would have the merit of the discovery all my own,
because I would oblige him to love me.—[*Aloud.*]   Mr. Martin,
who was that man with my father?

Arch. Some recruiting serjeant, or whipped-out trooper, I
suppose.

Cher. All's safe, I find.   [*Aside.*

Arch. Come, my dear, have you conned over the catechise I
taught you last night?

Cher. Come, question me.

Arch. What is love?

Cher. Love is I know not what, it comes I know not how, and
goes I know not when.

Arch. Very well, an apt scholar.—[*Chucks her under the chin.*]
Where does love enter?

Cher. Into the eyes.

Arch. And where go out?

Cher. I won't tell ye.

Arch. What are the objects of that passion?

Cher. Youth, beauty, and clean linen.

Arch. The reason?

Cher. The two first are fashionable in nature, and the third
at court.

Arch. That's my dear.—What are the signs and tokens of
that passion?

Cher. A stealing look, a stammering tongue, words improbable,
designs impossible, and actions impracticable.

Arch. That's my good child, kiss me.—What must a lover do
to obtain his mistress?

Cher. He must adore the person that disdains him, he must
bribe the chambermaid that betrays him, and court the footman
that laughs at him.   He must—he must——

Arch. Nay, child, I must whip you if you don't mind your
lesson; he must treat his——

Cher. Oh ay!—he must treat his enemies with respect, his
friends with indifference, and all the world with contempt; he
must suffer much, and fear more; he must desire much, and
hope little; in short, he must embrace his ruin, and throw
himself away.

Arch. Had ever man so hopeful a pupil as mine!—Come, my
dear, why is love called a riddle?

Cher. Because, being blind, he leads those that see, and, though a child, he governs a man.

Arch. Mighty well!—And why is Love pictured blind?

Cher. Because the painters out of the weakness or privilege of their art chose to hide those eyes that they could not draw.

Arch. That's my dear little scholar, kiss me again.—And why should Love, that's a child, govern a man?

Cher. Because that a child is the end of love.

Arch. And so ends Love's catechism.—And now, my dear, we'll go in and make my master's bed.

Cher. Hold, hold, Mr. Martin! You have taken a great deal of pains to instruct me, and what d'ye think I have learned by it?

Arch. What?

Cher. That your discourse and your habit are contradictions, and it would be nonsense in me to believe you a footman any longer.

Arch. 'Oons, what a witch it is!

Cher. Depend upon this, sir, nothing in this garb shall ever tempt me; for, though I was born to servitude, I hate it. Own your condition, swear you love me, and then——

Arch. And then we shall go make my master's bed?

Cher. Yes.

Arch. You must know, then, that I am born a gentleman, my education was liberal; but I went to London a younger brother, fell into the hands of sharpers, who stripped me of my money, my friends disowned me, and now my necessity brings me to what you see.

Cher. Then take my hand—promise to marry me before you sleep, and I'll make you master of two thousand pounds.

Arch. How?

Cher. Two thousand pounds that I have this minute in my own custody; so, throw off your livery this instant, and I'll go find a parson.

Arch. What said you? a parson!

Cher. What! do you scruple?

Arch. Scruple! no, no, but—Two thousand pounds, you say?

Cher. And better.

Arch. [*aside*]. 'Sdeath, what shall I do?—[*Aloud.*] But hark'ee, child, what need you make me master of yourself and money, when you may have the same pleasure out of me, and still keep your fortune in your hands?

Cher. Then you won't marry me?

Arch. I would marry you, but——

Cher. O sweet sir, I'm your humble servant, you're fairly caught! Would you persuade me that any gentleman who could bear the scandal of wearing a livery would refuse two thousand pounds, let the condition be what it would? no, no, sir. But I hope you'll pardon the freedom I have taken, since it was only to inform myself of the respect that I ought to pay you. [*Going.*

Arch. [*aside*]. Fairly bit, by Jupiter!—[*Aloud.*] Hold! hold!
—And have you actually two thousand pounds?

Cher. Sir, I have my secrets as well as you; when you please
to be more open I shall be more free, and be assured that I have
discoveries that will match yours, be what they will. In the
meanwhile, be satisfied that no discovery I make shall ever hurt
you, but beware of my father!   [*Exit.*

Arch. So! we're like to have as many adventures in our inn
as Don Quixote had in his. Let me see—two thousand pounds
—if the wench would promise to die when the money were spent,
egad, one would marry her; but the fortune may go off in a year
or two, and the wife may live—Lord knows how long. Then
an innkeeper's daughter! ay, that's the devil—there my pride
brings me off.

> For whatsoe'er the sages charge on pride,
> The angels' fall, and twenty faults beside,
> On earth, I'm sure, 'mong us of mortal calling,
> Pride saves man oft, and woman too, from falling.

          [*Exit.*

ACT III

SCENE I.—*The Gallery in* Lady Bountiful's *House*

Enter Mrs. Sullen *and* Dorinda.

Mrs. Sul. Ha! ha! ha! my dear sister, let me embrace thee!
now we are friends indeed; for I shall have a secret of yours as
a pledge for mine—now you'll be good for something, I shall
have you conversable in the subjects of the sex.

Dor. But do you think that I am so weak as to fall in love
with a fellow at first sight?

Mrs. Sul. Psha! now you spoil all; why should not we be as
free in our friendships as the men? I warrant you, the gentleman has got to his confidant already, has avowed his passion,
toasted your health, called you ten thousand angels, has run
over your lips, eyes, neck, shape, air, and everything, in a
description that warms their mirth to a second enjoyment.

Dor. Your hand, sister, I an't well.

Mrs. Sul. So—she's breeding already—come, child, up with
it—hem a little—so—now tell me, don't you like the gentleman
that we saw at church just now?

Dor. The man's well enough.

Mrs. Sul. Well enough! is he not a demigod, a Narcissus, a
star, the man i' the moon?

Dor. O sister, I'm extremely ill!

Mrs. Sul. Shall I send to your mother, child, for a little of her cephalic plaster to put to the soles of your feet, or shall I send to the gentleman for something for you? Come, unlace your stays, unbosom yourself. The man is perfectly a pretty fellow; I saw him when he first came into church.

Dor. I saw him too, sister, and with an air that shone, me-thought, like rays about his person.

Mrs. Sul. Well said, up with it!

Dor. No forward coquette behaviour, no airs to set him off, no studied looks nor artful posture—but Nature did it all——

Mrs. Sul. Better and better!—one touch more—come!

Dor. But then his looks—did you observe his eyes?

Mrs. Sul. Yes, yes, I did.—His eyes, well, what of his eyes?

Dor. Sprightly, but not wandering; they seemed to view, but never gazed on anything but me.—And then his looks so humble were, and yet so noble, that they aimed to tell me that he could with pride die at my feet, though he scorned slavery anywhere else.

Mrs. Sul. The physic works purely!—How d'ye find yourself now, my dear?

Dor. Hem! much better, my dear.—Oh, here comes our Mercury!

Enter SCRUB.

Well, Scrub, what news of the gentleman?

Scrub. Madam, I have brought you a packet of news.

Dor. Open it quickly, come.

Scrub. In the first place I inquired who the gentleman was; they told me he was a stranger. Secondly, I asked what the gentleman was; they answered and said, that they never saw him before. Thirdly, I inquired what countryman he was; they replied, 'twas more than they knew. Fourthly, I de-manded whence he came; their answer was, they could not tell. And, fifthly, I asked whither he went; and they replied, they knew nothing of the matter,—and this is all I could learn.

Mrs. Sul. But what do the people say? can't they guess?

Scrub. Why, some think he's a spy, some guess he's a mounte-bank, some say one thing, some another: but, for my own part, I believe he's a Jesuit.

Dor. A Jesuit! why a Jesuit?

Scrub. Because he keeps his horses always ready saddled, and his footman talks French.

Mrs. Sul. His footman!

Scrub. Ay, he and the count's footman were jabbering French like two intriguing ducks in a mill-pond; and I believe they talked of me, for they laughed consumedly.

Dor. What sort of livery has the footman?

Scrub. Livery! Lord, madam, I took him for a captain, he's so bedizzened with lace! And then he has tops to his shoes, up to his mid leg, a silver-headed cane dangling at his knuckles; he carries his hands in his pockets just so—[*walks in the French air*]—and has a fine long periwig tied up in a bag.—Lord, madam, he's clear another sort of man than I!

Mrs. Sul. That may easily be.—But what shall we do now, sister?

Dor. I have it—this fellow has a world of simplicity, and some cunning, the first hides the latter by abundance.—Scrub!

Scrub. Madam!

Dor. We have a great mind to know who this gentleman is, only for our satisfaction.

Scrub. Yes, madam, it would be a satisfaction, no doubt.

Dor. You must go and get acquainted with his footman, and invite him hither to drink a bottle of your ale because you're butler to-day.

Scrub. Yes, madam, I am butler every Sunday.

Mrs. Sul. O brave! sister, o' my conscience, you understand the mathematics already. 'Tis the best plot in the world: your mother, you know, will be gone to church, my spouse will be got to the ale-house with his scoundrels, and the house will be our own—so we drop in by accident, and ask the fellow some questions ourselves. In the country, you know, any stranger is company, and we're glad to take up with the butler in a country-dance, and happy if he'll do us the favour.

Scrub. O madam, you wrong me! I never refused your ladyship the favour in my life.

Enter GIPSY.

Gip. Ladies, dinner's upon table.

Dor. Scrub, we'll excuse your waiting—go where we ordered you.

Scrub. I shall.   [*Exeunt.*

SCENE II.—*A Room in* BONIFACE'S *Inn*

Enter AIMWELL *and* ARCHER.

Arch. Well, Tom, I find you're a marksman.

Aim. A marksman! who so blind could be, as not discern a swan among the ravens?

Arch. Well, but hark'ee, Aimwell!

Aim. Aimwell! call me Oroondates, Cesario, Amadis, all that romance can in a lover paint, and then I'll answer. O Archer! I read her thousands in her looks, she looked like Ceres in her harvest: corn, wine and oil, milk and honey, gardens, groves, and purling streams played on her plenteous face.

Arch. Her face! her pocket, you mean; the corn, wine, and oil lies there. In short, she has ten thousand pounds, that's the English on't.

Aim. Her eyes——

Arch. Are demi-cannons, to be sure; so I won't stand their battery.   [*Going.*

Aim. Pray excuse me, my passion must have vent.

Arch. Passion! what a plague, d'ye think these romantic airs will do our business? Were my temper as extravagant as yours, my adventures have something more romantic by half.

Aim. Your adventures!

Arch. Yes,

The nymph that with her twice ten hundred pounds,
With brazen engine hot, and quoif clear-starched,
Can fire the guest in warming of the bed——

There's a touch of sublime Milton for you, and the subject but an innkeeper's daughter! I can play with a girl as an angler does with his fish; he keeps it at the end of his line, runs it up the stream, and down the stream, till at last he brings it to hand, tickles the trout, and so whips it into his basket.

Enter BONIFACE.

Bon. Mr. Martin, as the saying is—yonder's an honest fellow below, my Lady Bountiful's butler, who begs the honour that you would go home with him and see his cellar.

Arch. Do my *baise-mains* to the gentleman, and tell him I will do myself the honour to wait on him immediately.

        [*Exit* BONIFACE.

Aim. What do I hear?

Soft Orpheus play, and fair Toftida sing!

Arch. Psha! damn your raptures; I tell you, here's a pump going to be put into the vessel, and the ship will get into harbour, my life on't. You say, there's another lady very handsome there?

Aim. Yes, faith.

Arch. I'm in love with her already.

Aim. Can't you give me a bill upon Cherry in the meantime?

Arch. No, no, friend, all her corn, wine, and oil is ingrossed to my market. And once more I warn you, to keep your anchorage clear of mine; for if you fall foul of me, by this light you shall go to the bottom! What! make prize of my little frigate, while I am upon the cruise for you!——

Aim. Well, well, I won't.   [*Exit* ARCHER.

Re-enter BONIFACE.

Landlord, have you any tolerable company in the house, I don't care for dining alone?

Bon. Yes, sir, there's a captain below, as the saying is, that arrived about an hour ago.

Aim. Gentlemen of his coat are welcome everywhere; will you make him a compliment from me and tell him I should be glad of his company?

Bon. Who shall I tell him, sir, would——

Aim. [*aside*]. Ha! that stroke was well thrown in!—[*Aloud.*] I'm only a traveller, like himself, and would be glad of his company, that's all.

Bon. I obey your commands, as the saying is.   [*Exit.*

Re-enter ARCHER.

Arch. 'Sdeath! I had forgot; what title will you give yourself?

Aim. My brother's, to be sure; he would never give me anything else, so I'll make bold with his honour this bout:—you know the rest of your cue.

Arch. Ay, ay.   [*Exit.*

Enter GIBBET.

Gib. Sir, I'm yours.

Aim. 'Tis more than I deserve, sir, for I don't know you.

Gib. I don't wonder at that, sir, for you never saw me before— [*aside*] I hope.

Aim. And pray, sir, how came I by the honour of seeing you now?

Gib. Sir, I scorn to intrude upon any gentleman—but my landlord——

Aim. O sir, I ask your pardon, you're the captain he told me of?

Gib. At your service, sir.

Aim. What regiment, may I be so bold?

Gib. A marching regiment, sir, an old corps.

Aim. [*aside*]. Very old, if your coat be regimental.—[*Aloud.*] You have served abroad, sir?

Gib. Yes, sir—in the plantations, 'twas my lot to be sent into the worst service; I would have quitted it indeed, but a man of honour, you know—Besides, 'twas for the good of my country that I should be abroad:—anything for the good of one's country —I'm a Roman for that.

Aim. [*aside*]. One of the first; I'll lay my life.—[*Aloud.*] You found the West Indies very hot, sir?

Gib. Ay, sir, too hot for me.

Aim. Pray, sir, han't I seen your face at Will's coffee-house?

Gib. Yes, sir, and at White's too.

Aim. And where is your company now, captain?

Gib. They an't come yet.

Aim. Why, d'ye expect 'em here?

Gib. They'll be here to-night, sir.

Aim. Which way do they march?

Gib. Across the country.—[*Aside.*] The devil's in't, if I han't said enough to encourage him to declare! But I'm afraid he's not right; I must tack about.

Aim. Is your company to quarter in Lichfield?

Gib. In this house, sir.

Aim. What! all?

Gib. My company's but thin, ha! ha! ha! we are but three, ha! ha! ha!

Aim. You're merry, sir.

Gib. Ay, sir, you must excuse me, sir; I understand the world, especially the art of travelling: I don't care, sir, for answering questions directly upon the road—for I generally ride with a charge about me.

Aim. Three or four, I believe.   [*Aside.*

Gib. I am credibly informed that there are highwaymen upon this quarter; not, sir, that I could suspect a gentleman of your figure—but truly, sir, I have got such a way of evasion upon the road, that I don't care for speaking truth to any man.

Aim. [*aside*]. Your caution may be necessary.—[*Aloud.*] Then I presume you're no captain?

Gib. Not I, sir; captain is a good travelling name, and so I take it; it stops a great many foolish inquiries that are generally made about gentlemen that travel, it gives a man an air of something, and makes the drawers obedient:—and thus far I am a captain, and no farther.

Aim. And pray, sir, what is your true profession?

Gib. O sir, you must excuse me!—upon my word, sir, I don't think it safe to tell ye.

Aim. Ha! ha! ha! upon my word I commend you.

Re-enter BONIFACE.

Well, Mr. Boniface, what's the news?

Bon. There's another gentleman below, as the saying is, that hearing you were but two, would be glad to make the third man, if you would give him leave.

Aim. What is he?

Bon. A clergyman, as the saying is.

Aim. A clergyman! is he really a clergyman? or is it only his travelling name, as my friend the captain has it?

Bon. O sir, he's a priest, and chaplain to the French officers in town.

Aim. Is he a Frenchman?

Bon. Yes, sir, born at Brussels.

Gib. A Frenchman, and a priest! I won't be seen in his company, sir; I have a value for my reputation, sir.

Aim. Nay, but, captain, since we are by ourselves—can he speak English, landlord?

Bon. Very well, sir; you may know him, as the saying is, to be a foreigner by his accent, and that's all.

Aim. Then he has been in England before?

Bon. Never, sir; but he's a master of languages, as the saying is; he talks Latin—it does me good to hear him talk Latin.

Aim. Then you understand Latin, Mr. Boniface?

Bon. Not I, sir, as the saying is; but he talks it so very fast, that I'm sure it must be good.

Aim. Pray, desire him to walk up.

Bon. Here he is, as the saying is.

Enter FOIGARD.

Foi. Save you, gentlemens, bote.

Aim. [*aside*]. A Frenchman!—[*To Foigard.*] Sir, your most humble servant.

Foi. Och, dear joy, I am your most faithful shervant, and yours alsho.

Gib. Doctor, you talk very good English, but you have a mighty twang of the foreigner.

Foi. My English is very vell for the vords, but we foreigners, you know, cannot bring our tongues about the pronunciation so soon.

Aim. [*aside*]. A foreigner! a downright Teague, by this light! —[*Aloud.*] Were you born in France, doctor?

Foi. I was educated in France, but I was borned at Brussels; I am a subject of the King of Spain, joy.

Gib. What King of Spain, sir? speak;

Foi. Upon my shoul, joy, I cannot tell you as yet.

Aim. Nay, captain, that was too hard upon the doctor; he's a stranger.

Foi. Oh, let him alone, dear joy; I am of a nation that is not easily put out of countenance.

Aim. Come, gentlemen, I'll end the dispute.—Here, landlord, is dinner ready?

Bon. Upon the table, as the saying is.

Aim. Gentlemen—pray—that door——

Foi. No, no, fait, the captain must lead.

Aim. No, doctor, the church is our guide.

Gib. Ay, ay, so it is.

[*Exit* FOIGARD *foremost, the others following.*

SCENE III.—*The Gallery in* Lady BOUNTIFUL'S *House*

Enter ARCHER *and* SCRUB *singing, and hugging one another, the latter with a tankard in his hand.* GIPSY *listening at a distance.*

Scrub. Tall, all, dall!—Come, my dear boy, let's have that song once more.

Arch. No, no, we shall disturb the family.—But will you be sure to keep the secret?

Scrub. Pho! upon my honour, as I'm a gentleman.

Arch. 'Tis enough. You must know, then, that my master is the Lord Viscount Aimwell; he fought a duel t'other day in London, wounded his man so dangerously that he thinks fit to withdraw till he hears whether the gentleman's wounds be mortal or not. He never was in this part of England before, so he chose to retire to this place, that's all.

Gip. And that's enough for me.   [*Exit.*

Scrub. And where were you when your master fought?

Arch. We never know of our masters' quarrels.

Scrub. No! if our masters in the country here receive a challenge, the first thing they do is to tell their wives; the wife tells the servants, the servants alarm the tenants, and in half an hour you shall have the whole county in arms.

Arch. To hinder two men from doing what they have no mind for.—But if you should chance to talk now of my business?

Scrub. Talk! ay, sir, had I not learned the knack of holding my tongue, I had never lived so long in a great family.

Arch. Ay, ay, to be sure there are secrets in all families.

Scrub. Secrets! ay;—but I'll say no more. Come, sit down, we'll make an end of our tankard: here——

                                        [*Gives* ARCHER *the tankard.*

Arch. With all my heart; who knows but you and I may come to be better acquainted, eh? Here's your ladies' healths; you have three, I think, and to be sure there must be secrets among 'em.   [*Drinks.*

Scrub. Secrets! ay, friend.—I wish I had a friend!

Arch. Am not I your friend? come, you and I will be sworn brothers.

Scrub. Shall we?

Arch. From this minute. Give me a kiss:—and now, brother Scrub——

Scrub. And now, brother Martin, I will tell you a secret that will make your hair stand on end. You must know that I am consumedly in love.

Arch. That's a terrible secret, that's the truth on't.

Scrub. That jade, Gipsy, that was with us just now in the cellar, is the arrantest whore that ever wore a petticoat; and I'm dying for love of her.

Arch. Ha! ha! ha!—Are you in love with her person or her virtue, brother Scrub?

Scrub. I should like virtue best, because it is more durable than beauty: for virtue holds good with some women long, and many a day after they have lost it.

Arch. In the country, I grant ye, where no woman's virtue is lost, till a bastard be found.

Scrub. Ay, could I bring her to a bastard, I should have her all to myself; but I dare not put it upon that lay, for fear of being sent for a soldier. Pray, brother, how do you gentlemen in London like that same Pressing Act?

Arch. Very ill, brother Scrub; 'tis the worst that ever was made for us. Formerly I remember the good days, when we could dun our masters for our wages, and if they refused to pay us, we could have a warrant to carry 'em before a Justice: but now if we talk of eating, they have a warrant for us, and carry us before three Justices.

Scrub. And to be sure we go, if we talk of eating; for the Justices won't give their own servants a bad example. Now this is my misfortune—I dare not speak in the house, while that jade Gipsy dings about like a fury.—Once I had the better end of the staff.

Arch. And how comes the change now?

Scrub. Why, the mother of all this mischief is a priest.

Arch. A priest!

Scrub. Ay, a damned son of a whore of Babylon, that came over hither to say grace to the French officers, and eat up our provisions. There's not a day goes over his head without a dinner or supper in this house.

Arch. How came he so familiar in the family?

Scrub. Because he speaks English as if he had lived here all his life, and tells lies as if he had been a traveller from his cradle.

Arch. And this priest, I'm afraid, has converted the affections of your Gipsy?

Scrub. Converted! ay, and perverted, my dear friend: for, I'm afraid, he has made her a whore and a papist! But this is not all; there's the French count and Mrs. Sullen, they're in the confederacy, and for some private ends of their own, to be sure.

Arch. A very hopeful family yours, brother Scrub! I suppose the maiden lady has her lover too?

Scrub. Not that I know: she's the best on 'em, that's the truth on't: but they take care to prevent my curiosity, by giving me so much business, that I'm a perfect slave. What d'ye think is my place in this family?

Arch. Butler, I suppose.

Scrub. Ah, Lord help you! I'll tell you. Of a Monday I drive the coach, of a Tuesday I drive the plough, on Wednesday I follow the hounds, a Thursday I dun the tenants, on Friday I go to market, on Saturday I draw warrants, and a Sunday I draw beer.

Arch. Ha! ha! ha! if variety be a pleasure in life, you have enough on't, my dear brother. But what ladies are those?

Scrub. Ours, ours; that upon the right hand is Mrs. Sullen, and the other is Mrs. Dorinda. Don't mind 'em; sit still, man.

Enter Mrs. SULLEN *and* DORINDA.

Mrs. Sul. I have heard my brother talk of my Lord Aimwell; but they say that his brother is the finer gentleman.

Dor. That's impossible, sister.

Mrs. Sul. He's vastly rich, but very close, they say.

Dor. No matter for that; if I can creep into his heart, I'll open his breast, I warrant him: I have heard say, that people may be guessed at by the behaviour of their servants; I could wish we might talk to that fellow.

Mrs. Sul. So do I; for I think he's a very pretty fellow. Come this way, I'll throw out a lure for him presently.

> [DORINDA *and* Mrs. SULLEN *walk a turn towards the opposite side of the stage.*

Arch. [*aside*]. Corn, wine, and oil indeed!—But, I think, the wife has the greatest plenty of flesh and blood; she should be my choice.—Ay, ay, say you so!—[Mrs. SULLEN *drops her glove,* ARCHER *runs, takes it up and gives to her.*] Madam—your ladyship's glove.

Mrs. Sul. O sir, I thank you!—[*To* DORINDA.] What a handsome bow the fellow has!

Dor. Bow! why, I have known several footmen come down from London set up here for dancing-masters, and carry off the best fortunes in the country.

Arch. [*aside*]. That project, for aught I know, had been better than ours.—[*To* SCRUB.] Brother Scrub, why don't you introduce me?

Scrub. Ladies, this is the strange gentleman's servant that you saw at church to-day; I understood he came from London, and so I invited him to the cellar, that he might show me the newest flourish in whetting my knives.

Dor. And I hope you have made much of him?

Arch. Oh yes, madam, but the strength of your ladyship's liquor is a little too potent for the constitution of your humble servant.

Mrs. Sul. What, then you don't usually drink ale?

Arch. No, madam; my constant drink is tea, or a little wine and water. 'Tis prescribed me by the physician for a remedy against the spleen.

Scrub. Oh la! Oh la! a footman have the spleen!

Mrs. Sul. I thought that distemper had been only proper to people of quality?

Arch. Madam, like all other fashions it wears out, and so descends to their servants; though in a great many of us, I believe, it proceeds from some melancholy particles in the blood, occasioned by the stagnation of wages.

Dor. [*aside to* Mrs. SULLEN]. How affectedly the fellow talks! —[*To* ARCHER.] How long, pray, have you served your present master?

Arch. Not long; my life has been mostly spent in the service of the ladies.

Mrs. Sul. And pray, which service do you like best?

Arch. Madam, the ladies pay best; the honour of serving them is sufficient wages; there is a charm in their looks that delivers a pleasure with their commands, and gives our duty the wings of inclination.

Mrs. Sul. [*aside*]. That flight was above the pitch of a livery. —[*Aloud.*] And, sir, would not you be satisfied to serve a lady again?

Arch. As a groom of the chamber, madam, but not as a footman.

Mrs. Sul. I suppose you served as footman before?

Arch. For that reason I would not serve in that post again; for my memory is too weak for the load of messages that the ladies lay upon their servants in London. My Lady Howd'ye, the last mistress I served, called me up one morning, and told me, " Martin, go to my Lady Allnight with my humble service; tell her I was to wait on her ladyship yesterday, and left word with Mrs. Rebecca, that the preliminaries of the affair she knows of are stopped till we know the concurrence of the person that I know of, for which there are circumstances wanting which we shall accommodate at the old place; but that in the meantime there is a person about her ladyship, that from several hints and surmises, was accessory at a certain time to the disappointments that naturally attend things, that to her knowledge are of more importance——"

Mrs. Sul., Dor. Ha! ha! ha! where are you going, sir?

Arch. Why, I han't half done!—The whole howd'ye was about half an hour long; so I happened to misplace two syllables, and was turned off, and rendered incapable.

Dor. [*aside to* Mrs. SULLEN]. The pleasantest fellow, sister, I ever saw!—[*To* ARCHER.] But, friend, if your master be married, I presume you still serve a lady?

Arch. No, madam, I take care never to come into a married family! the commands of the master and mistress are always so contrary, that 'tis impossible to please both.

Dor. There's a main point gained: my lord is not married, I find.   [*Aside.*

Mrs. Sul. But I wonder, friend, that in so many good services, you had not a better provision made for you.

Arch. I don't know how, madam. I had a lieutenancy offered me three or four times; but that is not bread, madam— I live much better as I do.

Scrub. Madam, he sings rarely! I was thought to do pretty well here in the country till he came; but alack a day, I'm nothing to my brother Martin!

Dor. Does he?—Pray, sir, will you oblige us with a song?

Arch. Are you for passion or humour?

Scrub. Oh le! he has the purest ballad about a trifle——

Mrs. Sul. A trifle! pray, sir, let's have it.

Arch. I'm ashamed to offer you a trifle, madam; but since you command me—

[*Sings to the tune of* " *Sir Simon the King.*"

A trifling song you shall hear,
Begun with a trifle and ended:
All trifling people draw near,
And I shall be nobly attended.

Were it not for trifles, a few,
That lately have come into play;
The men would want something to do,
And the women want something to say.

What makes men trifle in dressing?
Because the ladies (they know)
Admire, by often possessing,
That eminent trifle, a beau.

When the lover his moments has trifled,
The trifle of trifles to gain:
No sooner the virgin is rifled,
But a trifle shall part 'em again.

What mortal man would be able
At White's half an hour to sit?
Or who could bear a tea-table,
Without talking of trifles for wit?

The court is from trifles secure,
Gold keys are no trifles, we see:
White rods are no trifles, I'm sure,
Whatever their bearers may be.

But if you will go to the place,
Where trifles abundantly breed,
The levee will show you His Grace
Makes promises trifles indeed.

A coach with six footmen behind,
I count neither trifle nor sin:
But, ye gods! how oft do we find
A scandalous trifle within.

A flask of champagne, people think it
A trifle, or something as bad:
But if you'll contrive how to drink it,
You'll find it no trifle, egad!

A parson's a trifle at sea,
A widow's a trifle in sorrow:
A peace is a trifle to-day,
Who knows what may happen to-morrow

A black coat a trifle may cloke,
Or to hide it, the red may endeavour:
But if once the army is broke,
We shall have more trifles than ever.

The stage is a trifle, they say,
The reason, pray carry along,
Because at every new play,
The house they with trifles so throng.

> But with people's malice to trifle,
> And to set us all on a foot:
> The author of this is a trifle,
> And his song is a trifle to boot.

Mrs. Sul. Very well, sir, we're obliged to you.—Something for a pair of gloves.   [*Offering him money.*

Arch. I humbly beg leave to be excused: my master, madam, pays me; nor dare I take money from any other hand, without injuring his honour, and disobeying his commands.

[*Exit* ARCHER *and* SCRUB.

Dor. This is surprising! Did you ever see so pretty a well-bred fellow?

Mrs. Sul. The devil take him for wearing that livery!

Dor. I fancy, sister, he may be some gentleman, a friend of my lord's, that his lordship has pitched upon for his courage, fidelity, and discretion, to bear him company in this dress, and who ten to one was his second too.

Mrs. Sul. It is so, it must be so, and it shall be so!—for I like him.

Dor. What! better than the Count?

Mrs. Sul. The Count happened to be the most agreeable man upon the place; and so I chose him to serve me in my design upon my husband. But I should like this fellow better in a design upon myself.

Dor. But now, sister, for an interview with this lord and this gentleman; how shall we bring that about?

Mrs. Sul. Patience! you country ladies give no quarter if once you be entered. Would you prevent their desires, and give the fellows no wishing-time? Look'ee, Dorinda, if my Lord Aimwell loves you or deserves you, he'll find a way to see you, and there we must leave it. My business comes now upon the tapis. Have you prepared your brother?

Dor. Yes, yes.

Mrs. Sul. And how did he relish it?

Dor. He said little, mumbled something to himself, promised to be guided by me—but here he comes.

Enter Squire SULLEN.

Squire Sul. What singing was that I heard just now?

Mrs. Sul. The singing in your head, my dear; you complained of it all day.

Squire Sul. You're impertinent.

Mrs. Sul. I was ever so, since I became one flesh with you.

Squire Sul. One flesh! rather two carcasses joined unnaturally together.

Mrs. Sul. Or rather a living soul coupled to a dead body.

Dor. So, this is fine encouragement for me!

Squire Sul. Yes, my wife shows you what you must do.

Mrs. Sul. And my husband shows you what you must suffer.

Squire Sul. 'Sdeath, why can't you be silent?

Mrs. Sul. 'Sdeath, why can't you talk?

Squire Sul. Do you talk to any purpose?

Mrs. Sul. Do you think to any purpose?

Squire Sul. Sister, hark'ee!—[*Whispers.*]   I shan't be home till it be late.   [*Exit.*

Mrs. Sul. What did he whisper to ye?

Dor. That he would go round the back way, come into the closet, and listen as I directed him.   But let me beg you once more, dear sister, to drop this project; for as I told you before, instead of awaking him to kindness, you may provoke him to a rage; and then who knows how far his brutality may carry him?

Mrs. Sul. I'm provided to receive him, I warrant you.   But here comes the Count: vanish!   [*Exit* DORINDA.

Enter Count BELLAIR.

Don't you wonder, Monsieur le Count, that I was not at church this afternoon?

Count Bel. I more wonder, madam, that you go dere at all, or how you dare to lift those eyes to heaven that are guilty of so much killing.

Mrs. Sul. If Heaven, sir, has given to my eyes with the power of killing the virtue of making a cure, I hope the one may atone for the other.

Count Bel. Oh, largely, madam, would your ladyship be as ready to apply the remedy as to give the wound.   Consider, madam, I am doubly a prisoner; first to the arms of your general, then to your more conquering eyes.   My first chains are easy—there a ransom may redeem me; but from your fetters I never shall get free.

Mrs. Sul. Alas, sir! why should you complain to me of your captivity, who am in chains myself?   You know, sir, that I am bound, nay, must be tied up in that particular that might give you ease: I am like you, a prisoner of war—of war, indeed—I have given my parole of honour!   would you break yours to gain your liberty?

Count Bel. Most certainly I would, were I a prisoner among the Turks; dis is your case, you're a slave, madam, slave to the worst of Turks, a husband.

Mrs. Sul. There lies my foible, I confess; no fortifications, no courage, conduct, nor vigilancy, can pretend to defend a place where the cruelty of the governor forces the garrison to mutiny.

Count Bel. And where de besieger is resolved to die before de place.—Here will I fix [*kneels*];—with tears, vows, and prayers assault your heart and never rise till you surrender; or if I must storm—Love and St. Michael!—And so I begin the attack.

Mrs. Sul. Stand off!—[*Aside.*]   Sure he hears me not!—And I could almost wish he did not!—The fellow makes love very

prettily.—[*Aloud.*] But, sir, why should you put such a value
upon my person, when you see it despised by one that knows it
so much better?

Count Bel. He knows it not, though he possesses it; if he but
knew the value of the jewel he is master of he would always
wear it next his heart, and sleep with it in his arms.

Mrs. Sul. But since he throws me unregarded from him——

Count Bel. And one that knows your value well comes by and
takes you up, is it not justice?   [*Goes to lay hold of her.*

Enter Squire SULLEN *with his sword drawn.*

Squire Sul. Hold, villain, hold!

Mrs. Sul. [*presenting a pistol*]. Do you hold!

Squire Sul. What! murder your husband, to defend your
bully!

Mrs. Sul. Bully! for shame, Mr. Sullen, bullies wear long
swords, the gentleman has none; he's a prisoner, you know. I
was aware of your outrage, and prepared this to receive your
violence; and, if occasion were, to preserve myself against the
force of this other gentleman.

Count Bel. O madam, your eyes be bettre firearms than your
pistol; they nevre miss.

Squire Sul. What! court my wife to my face!

Mrs. Sul. Pray, Mr. Sullen, put up; suspend your fury for a
minute.

Squire Sul. To give you time to invent an excuse!

Mrs. Sul. I need none.

Squire Sul. No, for I heard every syllable of your discourse.

Count Bel. Ah! and begar, I tink the dialogue was vera pretty.

Mrs. Sul. Then I suppose, sir, you heard something of your
own barbarity?

Squire Sul. Barbarity! 'oons, what does the woman call
barbarity? Do I ever meddle with you?

Mrs. Sul. No.

Squire Sul. As for you, sir, I shall take another time.

Count Bel. Ah, begar, and so must I.

Squire Sul. Look'ee, madam, don't think that my anger
proceeds from any concern I have for your honour, but for my
own, and if you can contrive any way of being a whore without
making me a cuckold, do it and welcome.

Mrs. Sul. Sir, I thank you kindly, you would allow me the
sin but rob me of the pleasure. No, no, I'm resolved never to
venture upon the crime without the satisfaction of seeing you
punished for't.

Squire Sul. Then will you grant me this, my dear? Let anybody else do you the favour but that Frenchman, for I mortally
hate his whole generation.   [*Exit.*

Count Bel. Ah, sir, that be ungrateful, for begar, I love some
of yours.—Madam——   [*Approaching her.*

Mrs. Sul. No, sir.

Count Bel. No, sir! garzoon, madam, I am not your husband.

Mrs. Sul. 'Tis time to undeceive you, sir. I believed your addresses to me were no more than an amusement, and I hope you will think the same of my complaisance; and to convince you that you ought, you must know that I brought you hither only to make you instrumental in setting me right with my husband, for he was planted to listen by my appointment.

Count Bel. By your appointment?

Mrs. Sul. Certainly.

Count Bel. And so, madam, while I was telling twenty stories to part you from your husband, begar, I was bringing you together all the while?

Mrs. Sul. I ask your pardon, sir, but I hope this will give you a taste of the virtue of the English ladies.

Count Bel. Begar, madam, your virtue be vera great, but garzoon, your honeste be vera little.

Re-enter DORINDA.

Mrs. Sul. Nay, now, you're angry, sir.

Count Bel. Angry!—*Fair Dorinda* [*Sings " Fair Dorinda,"*
the opera tune, and addresses DORINDA.] Madam, when your ladyship want a fool, send for me. *Fair Dorinda, Revenge, etc.*
[*Exit singing.*

Mrs. Sul. There goes the true humour of his nation—resentment with good manners, and the height of anger in a song! Well, sister, you must be judge, for you have heard the trial.

Dor. And I bring in my brother guilty.

Mrs. Sul. But I must bear the punishment. 'Tis hard, sister.

Dor. I own it; but you must have patience.

Mrs. Sul. Patience! the cant of custom—Providence sends no evil without a remedy. Should I lie groaning under a yoke I can shake off, I were accessory to my ruin, and my patience were no better than self-murder.

Dor. But how can you shake off the yoke? your divisions don't come within the reach of the law for a divorce.

Mrs. Sul. Law! what law can search into the remote abyss of nature? what evidence can prove the unaccountable disaffections of wedlock? Can a jury sum up the endless aversions that are rooted in our souls, or can a bench give judgment upon antipathies?

Dor. They never pretended, sister; they never meddle, but in case of uncleanness.

Mrs. Sul. Uncleanness! O sister! casual violation is a transient injury, and may possibly be repaired, but can radical hatreds be ever reconciled? No, no, sister, nature is the first lawgiver, and when she has set tempers opposite, not all the golden links of wedlock nor iron manacles of law can keep 'em fast.

Wedlock we own ordain'd by Heaven's decree,
But such as Heaven ordain'd it first to be;—
Concurring tempers in the man and wife
As mutual helps to draw the load of life.
View all the works of Providence above,
The stars with harmony and concord move;
View all the works of Providence below,
The fire, the water, earth, and air, we know,
All in one plant agree to make it grow.
Must man, the chiefest work of art divine,
Be doom'd in endless discord to repine?
No, we should injure Heaven by that surmise,
Omnipotence is just, were man but wise.   [*Exeunt.*

ACT IV

SCENE I.—*The Gallery in* Lady BOUNTIFUL'S *House*

MRS. SULLEN *discovered alone.*

Mrs. Sul. Were I born an humble Turk, where women have
no soul nor property, there I must sit contented. But in
England, a country whose women are its glory, must women be
abused? where women rule, must women be enslaved? Nay,
cheated into slavery, mocked by a promise of comfortable
society into a wilderness of solitude! I dare not keep the
thought about me. Oh, here comes something to divert me.

Enter a Countrywoman.

Wom. I come, an't please your ladyship—you're my Lady
Bountiful, an't ye?

Mrs. Sul. Well, good woman, go on.

Wom. I have come seventeen long mail to have a cure for my
husband's sore leg.

Mrs. Sul. Your husband! what, woman, cure your husband!

Wom. Ay, poor man, for his sore leg won't let him stir from
home.

Mrs. Sul. There, I confess, you have given me a reason.
Well, good woman, I'll tell you what you must do. You must
lay your husband's leg upon a table, and with a chopping-knife
you must lay it open as broad as you can, then you must take
out the bone, and beat the flesh soundly with a rolling-pin, then
take salt, pepper, cloves, mace, and ginger, some sweet-herbs,
and season it very well, then roll it up like brawn, and put it
into the oven for two hours.

Wom. Heavens reward your ladyship!—I have two little babies too that are piteous bad with the graips, an't please ye.

Mrs. Sul. Put a little pepper and salt in their bellies, good woman.

Enter Lady BOUNTIFUL.

I beg your ladyship's pardon for taking your business out of your hands; I have been a-tampering here a little with one of your patients.

Lady Boun. Come, good woman, don't mind this mad creature; I am the person that you want, I suppose. What would you have, woman?

Mrs. Sul. She wants something for her husband's sore leg.

Lady Boun. What's the matter with his leg, goody?

Wom. It come first, as one might say, with a sort of dizziness in his foot, then he had a kind of laziness in his joints, and then his leg broke out, and then it swelled, and then it closed again, and then it broke out again, and then it festered, and then it grew better, and then it grew worse again.

Mrs. Sul. Ha! ha! ha!

Lady Boun. How can you be merry with the misfortunes of other people?

Mrs. Sul. Because my own make me sad, madam.

Lady Boun. The worst reason in the world, daughter; your own misfortunes should teach you to pity others.

Mrs. Sul. But the woman's misfortunes and mine are nothing alike; her husband is sick, and mine, alas! is in health.

Lady Boun. What! would you wish your husband sick?

Mrs. Sul. Not of a sore leg, of all things.

Lady Boun. Well, good woman, go to the pantry, get your bellyful of victuals, then I'll give you a receipt of diet-drink for your husband. But d'ye hear, goody, you must not let your husband move too much?

Wom. No, no, madam, the poor man's inclinable enough to lie still. [*Exit.*

Lady Boun. Well, daughter Sullen, though you laugh, I have done miracles about the country here with my receipts.

Mrs. Sul. Miracles indeed, if they have cured anybody; but I believe, madam, the patient's faith goes farther toward the miracle than your prescription.

Lady Boun. Fancy helps in some cases; but there's your husband, who has as little fancy as anybody, I brought him from death's door.

Mrs. Sul. I suppose, madam, you made him drink plentifully of ass's milk.

Enter DORINDA, *who runs to* Mrs. SULLEN.

Dor. News, dear sister! news! news!

Enter ARCHER, *running.*

Arch. Where, where is my Lady Bountiful?—Pray, which is
the old lady of you three?

Lady Boun. I am.

Arch. O madam, the fame of your ladyship's charity, goodness, benevolence, skill and ability, have drawn me hither to
implore your ladyship's help in behalf of my unfortunate master,
who is this moment breathing his last.

Lady Boun. Your master! where is he?

Arch. At your gate, madam. Drawn by the appearance of
your handsome house to view it nearer, and walking up the
avenue within five paces of the court-yard, he was taken ill of a
sudden with a sort of I know not what, but down he fell, and
there he lies.

Lady Boun. Here, Scrub! Gipsy! all run, get my easy-chair
down stairs, put the gentleman in it, and bring him in quickly!
quickly!

Arch. Heaven will reward your ladyship for this charitable act.

Lady Boun. Is your master used to these fits?

Arch. O yes, madam, frequently: I have known him have
five or six of a night.

Lady Boun. What's his name?

Arch. Lord, madam, he's a-dying! a minute's care or neglect
may save or destroy his life.

Lady Boun. Ah, poor gentleman!—Come, friend, show me
the way; I'll see him brought in myself.   [*Exit with* ARCHER.

Dor. O sister, my heart flutters about strangely! I can
hardly forbear running to his assistance.

Mrs. Sul. And I'll lay my life he deserves your assistance
more than he wants it. Did not I tell you that my lord would
find a way to come at you? Love's his distemper, and you
must be the physician; put on all your charms, summon all
your fire into your eyes, plant the whole artillery of your looks
against his breast, and down with him.

Dor. O sister! I'm but a young gunner; I shall be afraid to
shoot, for fear the piece should recoil, and hurt myself.

Mrs. Sul. Never fear, you shall see me shoot before you, if
you will.

Dor. No, no, dear sister; you have missed your mark so
unfortunately, that I shan't care for being instructed by you.

Enter AIMWELL *in a chair carried by* ARCHER *and* SCRUB, *and
counterfeiting a swoon;* Lady BOUNTIFUL *and* GIPSY *following.*

Lady Boun. Here, here, let's see the hartshorn drops.—
Gipsy, a glass of fair water! His fit's very strong.—Bless me,
how his hands are clinched!

Arch. For shame, ladies, what d'ye do? why don't you help
us?—[*To* DORINDA.] Pray, madam, take his hand, and open

it, if you can, whilst I hold his head. [DORINDA *takes his hand.*

Dor. Poor gentleman!—Oh!—he has got my hand within his, and squeezes it unmercifully——

Lady Boun. 'Tis the violence of his convulsion, child.

Arch. Oh, madam, he's perfectly possessed in these cases—he'll bite if you don't have a care.

Dor. Oh, my hand! my hand!

Lady Boun. What's the matter with the foolish girl? I have got his hand open, you see, with a great deal of ease.

Arch. Ay, but, madam, your daughter's hand is somewhat warmer than your ladyship's, and the heat of it draws the force of the spirits that way.

Mrs. Sul. I find, friend, you're very learned in these sorts of fits.

Arch. 'Tis no wonder, madam, for I'm often troubled with them myself; I find myself extremely ill at this minute.

[*Looking hard at* Mrs. SULLEN.

Mrs. Sul. I fancy I could find a way to cure you. [*Aside.*

Lady Boun. His fit holds him very long.

Arch. Longer than usual, madam.—Pray, young lady, open his breast and give him air.

Lady Boun. Where did his illness take him first, pray?

Arch. To-day at church, madam.

Lady Boun. In what manner was he taken?

Arch. Very strangely, my lady. He was of a sudden touched with something in his eyes, which, at the first, he only felt, but could not tell whether 'twas pain or pleasure.

Lady Boun. Wind, nothing but wind!

Arch. By soft degrees it grew and mounted to his brain, there his fancy caught it; there formed it so beautiful, and dressed it up in such gay, pleasing colours, that his transported appetite seized the fair idea, and straight conveyed it to his heart. That hospitable seat of life sent all its sanguine spirits forth to meet, and opened all its sluicy gates to take the stranger in.

Lady Boun. Your master should never go without a bottle to smell to.—Oh—he recovers! The lavender-water—some feathers to burn under his nose—Hungary water to rub his temples.—Oh, he comes to himself!—Hem a little, sir, hem.—Gipsy! bring the cordial-water.

[AIMWELL *seems to awake in amaze.*

Dor. How d'ye, sir?

Aim. Where am I? [*Rising.*

Sure I have pass'd the gulf of silent death,
And now I land on the Elysian shore!—
Behold the goddess of those happy plains,
Fair Proserpine—let me adore thy bright divinity.

[*Kneels to* DORINDA, *and kisses her hand.*

Mrs. Sul. So, so, so! I knew where the fit would end!

Aim. Eurydice perhaps—

> How could thy Orpheus keep his word,
> And not look back upon thee?
> No treasure but thyself could sure have bribed him
> To look one minute off thee.

Lady Boun. Delirious, poor gentleman!

Arch. Very delirious, madam, very delirious.

Aim. Martin's voice, I think.

Arch. Yes, my lord.—How does your lordship?

Lady Boun. Lord! did you mind that, girls?

         [*Aside to* Mrs. SULLEN *and* DORINDA.

Aim. Where am I?

Arch. In very good hands, sir. You were taken just now with one of your old fits, under the trees, just by this good lady's house; her ladyship had you taken in, and has miraculously brought you to yourself, as you see.

Aim. I am so confounded with shame, madam, that I can now only beg pardon; and refer my acknowledgments for your ladyship's care till an opportunity offers of making some amends. I dare be no longer troublesome.—Martin! give two guineas to the servants.   [*Going.*

Dor. Sir, you may catch cold by going so soon into the air; you don't look, sir, as if you were perfectly recovered.

     [*Here* ARCHER *talks to* Lady BOUNTIFUL *in dumb show.*

Aim. That I shall never be, madam; my present illness is so rooted that I must expect to carry it to my grave.

Mrs. Sul. Don't despair, sir; I have known several in your distemper shake it off with a fortnight's physic.

Lady Boun. Come, sir, your servant has been telling me that you're apt to relapse if you go into the air: your good manners shan't get the better of ours—you shall sit down again, sir. Come, sir, we don't mind ceremonies in the country—here, sir, my service t'ye.—You shall taste my water; 'tis a cordial I can assure you, and of my own making—drink it off, sir.—[AIMWELL *drinks.*] And how d'ye find yourself now, sir?

Aim. Somewhat better—though very faint still.

Lady Boun. Ay, ay, people are always faint after these fits.—Come, girls, you shall show the gentleman the house.—'Tis but an old family building, sir; but you had better walk about, and cool by degrees, than venture immediately into the air. You'll find some tolerable pictures.—Dorinda, show the gentleman the way. I must go to the poor woman below.   [*Exit.*

Dor. This way, sir.

Aim. Ladies, shall I beg leave for my servant to wait on you, for he understands pictures very well?

Mrs. Sul. Sir, we understand originals as well as he does pictures, so he may come along.

     [*Exeunt all but* SCRUB, AIMWELL *leading* DORINDA.

Enter FOIGARD.

Foi. Save you, Master Scrub!

Scrub. Sir, I won't be saved your way—I hate a priest, I abhor the French, and I defy the devil. Sir, I'm a bold Briton, and will spill the last drop of my blood to keep out popery and slavery.

Foi. Master Scrub, you would put me down in politics, and so I would be speaking with Mrs. Shipsy.

Scrub. Good Mr. Priest, you can't speak with her; she's sick, sir, she's gone abroad, sir, she's—dead two months ago, sir.

Re-enter GIPSY.

Gip. How now, impudence! how dare you talk so saucily to the doctor?—Pray, sir, don't take it ill; for the common people of England are not so civil to strangers, as——

Scrub. You lie! you lie! 'tis the common people that are civilest to strangers.

Gip. Sirrah, I have a good mind to—get you out, I say!

Scrub. I won't.

Gip. You won't, sauce-box!—Pray, doctor, what is the captain's name that came to your inn last night?

Scrub. [*aside*]. The captain! ah, the devil, there she hampers me again; the captain has me on one side and the priest on t'other: so between the gown and the sword, I have a fine time on't.—But, *Cedunt arma togæ.*   [*Going.*

Gip. What, sirrah, won't you march?

Scrub. No, my dear, I won't march—but I'll walk.—[*Aside.*] And I'll make bold to listen a little too.

                          [*Goes behind the side-scene and listens.*

Gip. Indeed, doctor, the Count has been barbarously treated, that's the truth on't.

Foi. Ah, Mrs. Gipsy, upon my shoul, now, gra, his complainings would mollify the marrow in your bones, and move the bowels of your commiseration! He veeps, and he dances, and he fistles, and he swears, and he laughs, and he stamps, and he sings; in conclusion, joy, he's afflicted *à-la-Française*, and a stranger would not know whider to cry or to laugh with him.

Gip. What would you have me do, doctor?

Foi. Noting, joy, but only hide the Count in Mrs. Sullen's closet when it is dark.

Gip. Nothing! is that nothing? it would be both a sin and a shame, doctor.

Foi. Here is twenty louis-d'ors, joy, for your shame; and I will give you an absolution for the shin.

Gip. But won't that money look like a bribe?

Foi. Dat is according as you shall tauk it. If you receive the money beforehand, 'twill be *logicè*, a bribe; but if you stay till afterwards, 'twill be only a gratification.

Gip. Well, doctor, I'll take it *logicè*. But what must I do with my conscience, sir?

Foi. Leave dat wid me, joy; I am your priest, gra; and your conscience is under my hands.

Gip. But should I put the Count into the closet——

Foi. Vel, is dere any shin for a man's being in a closhet? one may go to prayers in a closhet.

Gip. But if the lady should come into her chamber, and go to bed?

Foi. Vel, and is dere any shin in going to bed, joy?

Gip. Ay, but if the parties should meet, doctor?

Foi. Vel den—the parties must be responsible. Do you be gone after putting the Count into the closhet; and leave the shins wid themselves. I will come with the Count to instruct you in your chamber.

Gip. Well, doctor, your religion is so pure! Methinks I'm so easy after an absolution, and can sin afresh with so much security, that I'm resolved to die a martyr to't. Here's the key of the garden door, come in the back way when 'tis late, I'll be ready to receive you; but don't so much as whisper, only take hold of my hand; I'll lead you, and do you lead the Count, and follow me. [*Exeunt.*

Scrub [*coming forward*]. What witchcraft now have these two imps of the devil been a-hatching here? "There's twenty louis-d'ors"; I heard that, and saw the purse.—But I must give room to my betters. [*Exit.*

Re-enter AIMWELL, *leading* DORINDA, *and making love in dumb show;* MRS. SULLEN *and* ARCHER *following.*

Mrs. Sul. [*to* ARCHER]. Pray, sir, how d'ye like that piece?

Arch. Oh, 'tis Leda! You find, madam, how Jupiter comes disguised to make love——

Mrs. Sul. But what think you there of Alexander's battles?

Arch. We only want a Le Brun, madam, to draw greater battles, and a greater general of our own. The Danube, madam, would make a greater figure in a picture than the Granicus; and we have our Ramillies to match their Arbela.

Mrs. Sul. Pray, sir, what head is that in the corner there?

Arch. O madam, 'tis poor Ovid in his exile.

Mrs. Sul. What was he banished for?

Arch. His ambitious love, madam.—[*Bowing.*] His misfortune touches me.

Mrs. Sul. Was he successful in his amours?

Arch. There he has left us in the dark. He was too much a gentleman to tell.

Mrs. Sul. If he were secret, I pity him.

Arch. And if he were successful, I envy him.

Mrs. Sul. How d'ye like that Venus over the chimney?

Arch. Venus! I protest, madam, I took it for your picture; but now I look again, 'tis not handsome enough.

Mrs. Sul. Oh, what a charm is flattery! If you would see my picture, there it is over that cabinet. How d'ye like it?

Arch. I must admire anything, madam, that has the least resemblance of you. But, methinks, madam—[*He looks at the picture and* Mrs. SULLEN *three or four times, by turns.*] Pray, madam, who drew it?

Mrs. Sul. A famous hand, sir.

[*Here* AIMWELL *and* DORINDA *go off.*

Arch. A famous hand, madam!—Your eyes, indeed, are featured there; but where's the sparking moisture, shining fluid, in which they swim? The picture, indeed, has your dimples; but where's the swarm of killing Cupids that should ambush there? The lips too are figured out; but where's the carnation dew, the pouting ripeness that tempts the taste in the original?

Mrs. Sul. Had it been my lot to have matched with such a man!   [*Aside.*

Arch. Your breasts too—presumptuous man! what, paint Heaven!—Apropos, madam, in the very next picture is Salmoneus, that was struck dead with lightning, for offering to imitate Jove's thunder; I hope you served the painter so, madam?

Mrs. Sul. Had my eyes the power of thunder, they should employ their lightning better.

Arch. There's the finest bed in that room, madam! I suppose 'tis your ladyship's bedchamber.

Mrs. Sul. And what then, sir?

Arch. I think the quilt is the richest that ever I saw. I can't at this distance, madam, distinguish the figures of the embroidery; will you give me leave, madam?

Mrs. Sul. [*aside*]. The devil take his impudence!—Sure, if I gave him an opportunity, he durst not offer it?—I have a great mind to try.—[*Going : returns.*] 'Sdeath, what am I doing?—And alone, too!—Sister! sister!   [*Runs out.*

Arch. I'll follow her close—

For where a Frenchman durst attempt to storm,
A Briton sure may well the work perform.   [*Going.*

Re-enter SCRUB.

Scrub. Martin! brother Martin!

Arch. O brother Scrub, I beg your pardon, I was not a-going: here's a guinea my master ordered you.

Scrub. A guinea! hi! hi! hi! a guinea! eh—by this light it is a guinea! But I suppose you expect one-and-twenty shillings in change?

Arch. Not at all; I have another for Gipsy.

Scrub. A guinea for her! faggot and fire for the witch! Sir, give me that guinea, and I'll discover a plot.

Arch. A plot!

Scrub. Ay, sir, a plot, and a horrid plot! First, it must be a plot, because there's a woman in't: secondly, it must be a plot, because there's a priest in't: thirdly, it must be a plot, because there's French gold in't: and fourthly, it must be a plot, because I don't know what to make on't.

Arch. Nor anybody else, I'm afraid, brother Scrub.

Scrub. Truly, I'm afraid so too; for where there's a priest and a woman, there's always a mystery and a riddle. This I know, that here has been the doctor with a temptation in one hand and an absolution in the other, and Gipsy has sold herself to the devil; I saw the price paid down, my eyes shall take their oath on't.

Arch. And is all this bustle about Gipsy?

Scrub. That's not all; I could hear but a word here and there; but I remember they mentioned a Count, a closet, a back-door, and a key.

Arch. The Count!—Did you hear nothing of Mrs. Sullen?

Scrub. I did hear some word that sounded that way; but whether it was Sullen or Dorinda, I could not distinguish.

Arch. You have told this matter to nobody, brother?

Scrub. Told! no, sir, I thank you for that; I'm resolved never to speak one word *pro* nor *con*, till we have a peace.

Arch. You're i' the right, brother Scrub. Here's a treaty afoot between the Count and the lady: the priest and the chambermaid are the plenipotentiaries. It shall go hard but I find a way to be included in the treaty.—Where's the doctor now?

Scrub. He and Gipsy are this moment devouring my lady's marmalade in the closet.

Aim. [*from without*]. Martin! Martin!

Arch. I come, sir, I come.

Scrub. But you forget the other guinea, brother Martin.

Arch. Here, I give it with all my heart.

Scrub. And I take it with all my soul.—[*Exit* ARCHER.] Ecod, I'll spoil your plotting, Mrs. Gipsy! and if you should set the captain upon me, these two guineas will buy me off. [*Exit.*

Re-enter Mrs. SULLEN *and* DORINDA, *meeting.*

Mrs. Sul. Well, sister!

Dor. And well, sister!

Mrs. Sul. What's become of my lord?

Dor. What's become of his servant?

Mrs. Sul. Servant! he's a prettier fellow, and a finer gentleman by fifty degrees, than his master.

Dor. O' my conscience, I fancy you could beg that fellow at the gallows-foot!

Mrs. Sul. O' my conscience I could, provided I could put a friend of yours in his room.

Dor. You desired me, sister, to leave you, when you transgressed the bounds of honour.

Mrs. Sul. Thou dear censorious country girl! what dost mean? You can't think of the man without the bedfellow, I find.

Dor. I don't find anything unnatural in that thought: while the mind is conversant with flesh and blood, it must conform to the humours of the company.

Mrs. Sul. How a little love and good company improves a woman! Why, child, you begin to live—you never spoke before.

Dor. Because I was never spoke to.—My lord has told me that I have more wit and beauty than any of my sex; and truly I begin to think the man is sincere.

Mrs. Sul. You're in the right, Dorinda; pride is the life of a woman, and flattery is our daily bread; and she's a fool that won't believe a man there, as much as she that believes him in anything else. But I'll lay you a guinea that I had finer things said to me than you had.

Dor. Done! What did your fellow say to ye?

Mrs. Sul. My fellow took the picture of Venus for mine.

Dor. But my lover took me for Venus herself.

Mrs. Sul. Common cant! Had my spark called me a Venus directly, I should have believed him a footman in good earnest.

Dor. But my lover was upon his knees to me.

Mrs. Sul. And mine was upon his tiptoes to me.

Dor. Mine vowed to die for me.

Mrs. Sul. Mine swore to die with me.

Dor. Mine spoke the softest moving things.

Mrs. Sul. Mine had his moving things too.

Dor. Mine kissed my hand ten thousand times.

Mrs. Sul. Mine has all that pleasure to come.

Dor. Mine offered marriage.

Mrs. Sul. O Lard! d'ye call that a moving thing?

Dor. The sharpest arrow in his quiver, my dear sister! Why, my ten thousand pounds may lie brooding here this seven years, and hatch nothing at last but some ill-natured clown like yours. Whereas, if I marry my Lord Aimwell, there will be title, place, and precedence, the Park, the play, and the drawing-room, splendour, equipage, noise, and flambeaux.—*Hey, my Lady Aimwell's servants there !—Lights, lights to the stairs !—My Lady Aimwell's coach put forward !—Stand by, make room for her ladyship !*—Are not these things moving?—What! melancholy of a sudden?

Mrs. Sul. Happy, happy sister! your angel has been watchful for your happiness, whilst mine has slept regardless of his charge. Long smiling years of circling joys for you, but not one hour for me! [*Weeps.*

Dor. Come, my dear, we'll talk of something else.

Mrs. Sul. O Dorinda! I own myself a woman, full of my sex, a gentle, generous soul, easy and yielding to soft desires; a spacious heart, where love and all his train might lodge. And must the fair apartment of my breast be made a stable for a brute to lie in?

Dor. Meaning your husband, I suppose?

Mrs. Sul. Husband! no; even husband is too soft a name for him.—But, come, I expect my brother here to-night or to-morrow; he was abroad when my father married me; perhaps he'll find a way to make me easy.

Dor. Will you promise not to make yourself easy in the meantime with my lord's friend?

Mrs. Sul. You mistake me, sister. It happens with us as among the men, the greatest talkers are the greatest cowards? and there's a reason for it; those spirits evaporate in prattle, which might do more mischief if they took another course.—Though, to confess the truth, I do love that fellow;—and if I met him dressed as he should be, and I undressed as I should be —look'ee, sister, I have no supernatural gifts—I can't swear I could resist the temptation; though I can safely promise to avoid it; and that's as much as the best of us can do. [*Exeunt.*

SCENE II.—*A Room in* BONIFACE'S *Inn*

Enter AIMWELL *and* ARCHER *laughing.*

Arch. And the awkward kindness of the good motherly old gentlewoman——

Aim. And the coming easiness of the young one—'Sdeath, 'tis pity to deceive her!

Arch. Nay, if you adhere to these principles, stop where you are.

Aim. I can't stop; for I love her to distraction.

Arch. 'Sdeath, if you love her a hair's-breadth beyond discretion, you must go no further.

Aim. Well, well, anything to deliver us from sauntering away our idle evenings at White's, Tom's, or Will's, and be stinted to bare looking at our old acquaintance, the cards; because our impotent pockets can't afford us a guinea for the mercenary drabs.

Arch. Or be obliged to some purse-proud coxcomb for a scandalous bottle, where we must not pretend to our share of the discourse, because we can't pay our club o' th' reckoning.—Damn it, I had rather sponge upon Morris, and sup upon a dish of bohea scored behind the door!

Aim. And there expose our want of sense by talking criticisms, as we should our want of money by railing at the government.

Arch. Or be obliged to sneak into the side-box, and between both houses steal two acts of a play, and because we han't money to see the other three, we come away discontented, and damn the whole five.

Aim. And ten thousand such rascally tricks—had we outlived our fortunes among our acquaintance.—But now——

Arch. Ay, now is the time to prevent all this:—strike while the iron is hot.—This priest is the luckiest part of our adventure; he shall marry you, and pimp for me.

Aim. But I should not like a woman that can be so fond of a Frenchman.

Arch. Alas, sir! Necessity has no law. The lady may be in distress; perhaps she has a confounded husband, and her revenge may carry her farther than her love. Egad, I have so good an opinion of her, and of myself, that I begin to fancy strange things: and we must say this for the honour of our women, and indeed of ourselves, that they do stick to their men as they do to their *Magna Charta*. If the plot lies as I suspect, I must put on the gentleman.—But here comes the doctor—I shall be ready. [*Exit.*

Enter FOIGARD.

Foi. Sauve you, noble friend.

Aim. O sir, your servant! Pray, doctor, may I crave your name?

Foi. Fat naam is upon me? My naam is Foigard, joy.

Aim. Foigard! a very good name for a clergyman. Pray, Doctor Foigard, were you ever in Ireland?

Foi. Ireland! no, joy. Fat sort of plaace is dat saam Ireland? Dey say de people are catched dere when dey are young.

Aim. And some of 'em when they are old:—as for example.— [*Takes* FOIGARD *by the shoulder.*] Sir, I arrest you as a traitor against the government; you're a subject of England, and this morning showed me a commission, by which you served as chaplain in the French army. This is death by our law, and your reverence must hang for it.

Foi. Upon my shoul, noble friend, dis is strange news you tell me! Fader Foigard a subject of England! de son of a burgo-master of Brussels, a subject of England! ubooboo—

Aim. The son of a bog-trotter in Ireland! Sir, your tongue will condemn you before any bench in the kingdom.

Foi. And is my tongue all your evidensh, joy?

Aim. That's enough.

Foi. No, no, joy, for I vill never spake English no more.

Aim. Sir, I have other evidence.—Here, Martin!

Re-enter ARCHER.

You know this fellow?

Arch. [*in a brogue*]. Saave you, my dear cussen, how does your health?

Foi. [*aside*]. Ah! upon my shoul dere is my countryman, and his brogue will hang mine.—[*To* ARCHER.] *Mynheer, Ick wet neat watt hey zacht, Ick universton ewe neat, sacramant!*

Aim. Altering your language won't do, sir; this fellow knows your person, and will swear to your face.

Foi. Faash! fey, is dere a brogue upon my faash too?

Arch. Upon my soulvation dere ish, joy!—But cussen Mackshane, vil you not put a remembrance upon me?

Foi. Mackshane! by St. Paatrick, dat ish my naam shure enough! [*Aside.*

Aim. I fancy, Archer, you have it. [*Aside to* ARCHER.

Foi. The devil hang you, joy! by fat acquaintance are you my cussen?

Arch. Oh, de devil hang yourshelf, joy! you know we were little boys togeder upon de school, and your foster-moder's son was married upon my nurse's chister, joy, and so we are Irish cussens.

Foi. De devil taake de relation! vel, joy, and fat school was it?

Arch. I tinks it vas—aay—'twas Tipperary.

Foi. No, no, joy; it vas Kilkenny.

Aim. That's enough for us—self-confession,—come, sir, must deliver you into the hands of the next magistrate.

Arch. He sends you to jail, you're tried next assizes, and away you go swing into purgatory.

Foi. And is it so wid you, cussen?

Arch. It vil be sho wid you, cussen, if you don't immediately confess the secret between you and Mrs. Gipsy. Look'ee, sir, the gallows or the secret, take your choice.

Foi. The gallows! upon my shoul I hate that saam gallow, for it is a diseash dat is fatal to our family. Vel, den, dere is nothing, shentlemens, but Mrs. Shullen would spaak wid the Count in her chamber at midnight, and dere is no haarm, joy, for I am to conduct the Count to the plash, myshelf.

Arch. As I guessed.—Have you communicated the matter to the Count?

Foi. I have not sheen him since.

Arch. Right again! Why then, doctor—you shall conduct me to the lady instead of the Count.

Foi. Fat, my cussen to the lady! upon my shoul, gra, dat is too much upon the brogue.

Arch. Come, come, doctor; consider we have got a rope about your neck, and if you offer to squeak, we'll stop your windpipe, most certainly: we shall have another job for you in a day or two, I hope.

Aim. Here's company coming this way; let's into my chamber and there concert our affairs farther.

Arch. Come, my dear cussen, come along. [*Exeunt.*

Enter BONIFACE, HOUNSLOW, *and* BAGSHOT *at one door,* GIBBET *at the opposite.*

Gib. Well, gentlemen, 'tis a fine night for our enterprise.

Houn. Dark as hell.

Bag. And blows like the devil; our landlord here has showed us the window where we must break in, and tells us the plate stands in the wainscot cupboard in the parlour.

Bon. Ay, ay, Mr. Bagshot, as the saying is, knives and forks, and cups and cans, and tumblers and tankards. There's one tankard, as the saying is, that's near upon as big as me; it was a present to the squire from his godmother, and smells of nutmeg and toast like an East-India ship.

Houn. Then you say we must divide at the stairhead?

Bon. Yes, Mr. Hounslow, as the saying is. At one end of that gallery lies my Lady Bountiful and her daughter, and at the other Mrs. Sullen. As for the squire——

Gib. He's safe enough, I have fairly entered him, and he's more than half seas over already. But such a parcel of scoundrels are got about him now, that, egad, I was ashamed to be seen in their company.

Bon. 'Tis now twelve, as the saying is—gentlemen, you must set out at one.

Gib. Hounslow, do you and Bagshot see our arms fixed, and I'll come to you presently.

Houn., Bag. We will.   [*Exeunt.*

Gib. Well, my dear Bonny, you assure me that Scrub is a coward?

Bon. A chicken, as the saying is. You'll have no creature to deal with but the ladies.

Gib. And I can assure you, friend, there's a great deal of address and good manners in robbing a lady; I am the most a gentleman that way that ever travelled the road.—But, my dear Bonny, this prize will be a galleon, a Vigo business.—I warrant you we shall bring off three or four thousand pounds.

Bon. In plate, jewels, and money, as the saying is, you may.

Gib. Why then, Tyburn, I defy thee! I'll get up to town, sell off my horse and arms, buy myself some pretty employment in the household, and be as snug and as honest as any courtier of 'em all.

Bon. And what think you then of my daughter Cherry for a wife?

Gib. Look'ee, my dear Bonny—Cherry *is the Goddess I adore,* as the song goes; but it is a maxim, that man and wife should never have it in their power to hang one another; for if they should, the Lord have mercy on 'em both!   [*Exeunt.*

ACT V

SCENE I.—*A Room in* BONIFACE'S *Inn*

Knocking without, enter BONIFACE.

Bon. Coming! Coming!—A coach and six foaming horses at this time o' night! some great man, as the saying is, for he scorns to travel with other people.

Enter Sir CHARLES FREEMAN.

Sir Chas. What, fellow! a public house, and abed when other people sleep?

Bon. Sir, I an't abed, as the saying is.

Sir Chas. Is Mr. Sullen's family abed, think'ee?

Bon. All but the squire himself, sir, as the saying is; he's in the house.

Sir Chas. What company has he?

Bon. Why, sir, there's the constable, Mr. Gage the exciseman, the hunch-backed barber, and two or three other gentlemen.

Sir Chas. I find my sister's letters gave me the true picture of her spouse.   [*Aside.*

Enter Squire SULLEN, *drunk.*

Bon. Sir, here's the squire.

Squire Sul. The puppies left me asleep—Sir!

Sir Chas. Well, sir.

Squire Sul. Sir, I am an unfortunate man—I have three thousand pounds a year, and I can't get a man to drink a cup of ale with me.

Sir Chas. That's very hard.

Squire Sul. Ay, sir; and unless you have pity upon me, and smoke one pipe with me, I must e'en go home to my wife, and I had rather go to the devil by half.

Sir Chas. But I presume, sir, you won't see your wife to-night; she'll be gone to bed. You don't use to lie with your wife in that pickle?

Squire Sul. What! not lie with my wife! why, sir, do you take me for an atheist or a rake?

Sir Chas. If you hate her, sir, I think you had better lie from her.

Squire Sul. I think so too, friend. But I'm a justice of peace, and must do nothing against the law.

Sir Chas. Law! as I take it, Mr. Justice, nobody observes law for law's sake, only for the good of those for whom it was made.

Squire Sul. But, if the law orders me to send you to jail, you must lie there, my friend.

Sir Chas. Not unless I commit a crime to deserve it.

Squire Sul. A crime? 'oons, an't I married?

Sir Chas. Nay, sir, if you call a marriage a crime, you must disown it for a law.

Squire Sul. Eh! I must be acquainted with you, sir.—But, sir, I should be very glad to know the truth of this matter.

Sir Chas. Truth, sir, is a profound sea, and few there be that dare wade deep enough to find out the bottom on't. Besides, sir, I'm afraid the line of your understanding mayn't be long enough.

Squire Sul. Look'ee, sir, I have nothing to say to your sea of truth, but, if a good parcel of land can entitle a man to a little truth, I have as much as any He in the country.

Bon. I never heard your worship, as the saying is, talk so much before.

Squire Sul. Because I never met with a man that I liked before.

Bon. Pray, sir, as the saying is, let me ask you one question: are not man and wife one flesh?

Sir Chas. You and your wife, Mr. Guts, may be one flesh, because ye are nothing else; but rational creatures have minds that must be united.

Squire Sul. Minds!

Sir Chas. Ay, minds, sir; don't you think that the mind takes place of the body?

Squire Sul. In some people.

Sir Chas. Then the interest of the master must be consulted before that of his servant.

Squire Sul. Sir, you shall dine with me to-morrow!—'Oons, I always thought that we were naturally one.

Sir Chas. Sir, I know that my two hands are naturally one, because they love one another, kiss one another, help one another in all the actions of life; but I could not say so much if they were always at cuffs.

Squire Sul. Then 'tis plain that we are two.

Sir Chas. Why don't you part with her, sir?

Squire Sul. Will you take her, sir?

Sir Chas. With all my heart.

Squire Sul. You shall have her to-morrow morning, and a venison-pasty into the bargain.

Sir Chas. You'll let me have her fortune too?

Squire Sul. Fortune! why, sir, I have no quarrel at her fortune: I only hate the woman, sir, and none but the woman shall go.

Sir Chas. But her fortune, sir——

Squire Sul. Can you play at whisk, sir?

Sir Chas. No, truly, sir.

Squire Sul. Nor at all-fours?

Sir Chas. Neither.

Squire Sul. [*aside*]. 'Oons! where was this man bred?—
[*Aloud.*] Burn me, sir! I can't go home, 'tis but two o'clock.

Sir Chas. For half an hour, sir, if you please; but you must consider 'tis late.

Squire Sul. Late! that's the reason I can't go to bed.—
Come, sir! [*Exeunt.*

Enter CHERRY, *runs across the stage, and knocks at* AIMWELL's *chamber door. Enter* AIMWELL *in his nightcap and gown.*

Aim. What's the matter? you tremble, child; you're frighted.

Cher. No wonder, sir—But, in short, sir, this very minute a gang of rogues are gone to rob my Lady Bountiful's house.

Aim. How!

Cher. I dogged 'em to the very door, and left 'em breaking in.

Aim. Have you alarmed anybody else with the news?

Cher. No, no, sir, I wanted to have discovered the whole plot, and twenty other things, to your man Martin; but I have searched the whole house, and can't find him: where is he?

Aim. No matter, child; will you guide me immediately to the house?

Cher. With all my heart, sir; my Lady Bountiful is my godmother, and I love Mrs. Dorinda so well——

Aim. Dorinda! the name inspires me, the glory and the danger shall be all my own.—Come, my life, let me but get my sword. [*Exeunt.*

SCENE II.—*A Bedchamber in* Lady BOUNTIFUL's *House*

Mrs. SULLEN *and* DORINDA *discovered undressed; a table and lights.*

Dor. 'Tis very late, sister, no news of your spouse yet?

Mrs. Sul. No, I'm condemned to be alone till towards four, and then perhaps I may be executed with his company.

Dor. Well, my dear, I'll leave you to your rest; you'll go directly to bed, I suppose?

Mrs. Sul. I don't know what to do.—Heigh-ho!

Dor. That's a desiring sigh, sister.

Mrs. Sul. This is a languishing hour, sister.

Dor. And might prove a critical minute if the pretty fellow were here.

Mrs. Sul. Here! what, in my bedchamber at two o'clock o' th' morning, I undressed, the family asleep, my hated husband abroad, and my lovely fellow at my feet!—O 'gad, sister!

Dor. Thoughts are free, sister, and them I allow you.—So, my dear, good night.

Mrs. Sul. A good rest to my dear Dorinda!—[*Exit* DORINDA.]
Thoughts free! are they so? Why, then suppose him here,
dressed like a youthful, gay, and burning bridegroom,

[*Here* ARCHER *steals out of a closet behind.*

with tongue enchanting, eyes bewitching, knees imploring.—
[*Turns a little on one side and sees* ARCHER *in the posture she
describes.*]—Ah!—[*Shrieks, and runs to the other side of the stage.*]
Have my thoughts raised a spirit?—What are you, sir, a man
or a devil?

Arch. A man, a man, madam.   [*Rising.*

Mrs. Sul. How shall I be sure of it?

Arch. Madam, I'll give you demonstration this minute.

[*Takes her hand.*

Mrs. Sul. What, sir! do you intend to be rude?

Arch. Yes, madam, if you please.

Mrs. Sul. In the name of wonder, whence came ye?

Arch. From the skies, madam—I'm a Jupiter in love, and you
shall be my Alcmena.

Mrs. Sul. How came you in?

Arch. I flew in at the window, madam; your cousin Cupid
lent me his wings, and your sister Venus opened the casement.

Mrs. Sul. I'm struck dumb with wonder!

Arch. And I—with admiration!   [*Looks passionately at her.*

Mrs. Sul. What will become of me?

Arch. How beautiful she looks!—The teeming jolly Spring
smiles in her blooming face, and, when she was conceived, her
mother smelt to roses, looked on lilies—

Lilies unfold their white, their fragrant charms,
When the warm sun thus darts into their arms.

[*Runs to her.*

Mrs. Sul. Ah!   [*Shrieks.*

Arch. 'Oons, madam, what d'ye mean? you'll raise the
house.

Mrs. Sul. Sir, I'll wake the dead before I bear this!—What!
approach me with the freedom of a keeper! I'm glad on't, your
impudence has cured me.

Arch. If this be impudence—[*Kneels.*] I leave to your partial
self; no panting pilgrim, after a tedious, painful voyage, e'er
bowed before his saint with more devotion.

Mrs. Sul. [*aside*]. Now, now, I'm ruined if he kneels!—
[*Aloud.*] Rise, thou prostrate engineer, not all thy undermining
skill shall reach my heart.—Rise, and know I am a woman
without my sex; I can love to all the tenderness of wishes, sighs,
and tears—but go no farther.—Still, to convince you that I'm
more than woman, I can speak my frailty, confess my weakness
even for you, but——

Arch. For me!   [*Going to lay hold on her.*

Mrs. Sul. Hold, sir! build not upon that; for my most mortal

hatred follows if you disobey what I command you now.—
Leave me this minute.—[*Aside.*] If he denies I'm lost.

Arch. Then you'll promise——

Mrs. Sul. Anything another time.

Arch. When shall I come?

Mrs. Sul. To-morrow—when you will.

Arch. Your lips must seal the promise.

Mrs. Sul. Psha!

Arch. They must! they must!—[*Kisses her.*] Raptures and
paradise!—And why not now, my angel? the time, the place,
silence, and secrecy, all conspire. And the now conscious stars
have preordained this moment for my happiness.

[*Takes her in his arms.*

Mrs. Sul. You will not! cannot, sure!

Arch. If the sun rides fast, and disappoints not mortals of
to-morrow's dawn, this night shall crown my joys.

Mrs. Sul. My sex's pride assist me!

Arch. My sex's strength help me!

Mrs. Sul. You shall kill me first!

Arch. I'll die with you.   [*Carrying her off.*

Mrs. Sul. Thieves! thieves! murder!

Enter Scrub *in his breeches, and one shoe.*

Scrub. Thieves! thieves! murder! popery!

Arch. Ha! the very timorous stag will kill in rutting time.

[*Draws, and offers to stab* Scrub.

Scrub [*kneeling*]. O pray, sir, spare all I have, and take my life!

Mrs. Sul. [*holding* Archer's *hand*]. What does the fellow
mean?

Scrub. O madam, down upon your knees, your marrow-bones!
—he's one of 'em.

Arch. Of whom?

Scrub. One of the rogues—I beg your pardon, one of the
honest gentlemen that just now are broke into the house.

Arch. How!

Mrs. Sul. I hope you did not come to rob me?

Arch. Indeed I did, madam, but I would have taken nothing
but what you might ha' spared; but your crying "Thieves"
has waked this dreaming fool, and so he takes 'em for granted.

Scrub. Granted! 'tis granted, sir; take all we have.

Mrs. Sul. The fellow looks as if he were broke out of Bedlam.

Scrub. 'Oons, madam, they're broke into the house with fire
and sword! I saw them, heard them; they'll be here this
minute.

Arch. What, thieves!

Scrub. Under favour, sir, I think so.

Mrs. Sul. What shall we do, sir?

Arch. Madam, I wish your ladyship a good night.

Mrs. Sul. Will you leave me?

Arch. Leave you! Lord, madam, did not you command me to be gone just now, upon pain of your immortal hatred?

Mrs. Sul. Nay, but pray, sir——   [*Takes hold of him.*

Arch. Ha! ha! ha! now comes my turn to be ravished.—You see now, madam, you must use men one way or other; but take this by the way, good madam, that none but a fool will give you the benefit of his courage, unless you'll take his love along with it.—How are they armed, friend?

Scrub. With sword and pistol, sir.

Arch. Hush!—I see a dark lantern coming through the gallery.—Madam, be assured I will protect you, or lose my life.

Mrs. Sul. Your life! no, sir, they can rob me of nothing that I value half so much; therefore now, sir, let me entreat you to be gone.

Arch. No, madam, I'll consult my own safety for the sake of yours; I'll work by stratagem. Have you courage enough to stand the appearance of 'em?

Mrs. Sul. Yes, yes, since I have 'scaped your hands, I can face anything.

Arch. Come hither, brother Scrub! don't you know me?

Scrub. Eh, my dear brother, let me kiss thee.

[*Kisses* ARCHER.

Arch. This way—here——

[ARCHER *and* SCRUB *hide behind the bed.*

Enter GIBBET, *with a dark lantern in one hand, and a pistol in the other.*

Gib. Ay, ay, this is the chamber, and the lady alone.

Mrs. Sul. Who are you, sir? what would you have? d'ye come to rob me?

Gib. Rob you! alack a day, madam, I'm only a younger brother, madam; and so, madam, if you make a noise, I'll shoot you through the head; but don't be afraid, madam.—[*Laying his lantern and pistol upon the table.*] These rings, madam; don't be concerned, madam, I have a profound respect for you, madam; your keys, madam; don't be frighted, madam, I'm the most of a gentleman.—[*Searching her pockets.*] This necklace, madam; I never was rude to any lady;—I have a veneration—for this necklace——

[*Here* ARCHER *having come round, and seized the pistol, takes* GIBBET *by the collar, trips up his heels, and claps the pistol to his breast.*

Arch. Hold, profane villain, and take the reward of thy sacrilege!

Gib. Oh! pray, sir, don't kill me; I an't prepared.

Arch. How many is there of 'em, Scrub?

Scrub. Five-and-forty, sir.

Arch. Then I must kill the villain, to have him out of the way.

Gib. Hold, hold, sir, we are but three, upon my honour.

Arch. Scrub, will you undertake to secure him?

Scrub. Not I, sir; kill him, kill him!

Arch. Run to Gipsy's chamber, there you'll find the doctor; bring him hither presently.—[*Exit* SCRUB, *running.*] Come, rogue, if you have a short prayer, say it.

Gib. Sir, I have no prayer at all; the government has provided a chaplain to say prayers for us on these occasions.

Mrs. Sul. Pray, sir, don't kill him: you fright me as much as him.

Arch. The dog shall die, madam, for being the occasion of my disappointment.—Sirrah, this moment is your last.

Gib. Sir, I'll give you two hundred pounds to spare my life.

Arch. Have you no more, rascal?

Gib. Yes, sir, I can command four hundred, but I must reserve two of 'em to save my life at the sessions.

Re-enter SCRUB *and* FOIGARD.

Arch. Here, doctor, I suppose Scrub and you between you may manage him. Lay hold of him, doctor.

　　　　　　　　　　　　　　　[FOIGARD *lays hold of* GIBBET.

Gib. What! turned over to the priest already!—Look'ee, doctor, you come before your time; I an't condemned yet, I thank ye.

Foi. Come, my dear joy, I vill secure your body and your shoul too; I vill make you a good Catholic, and give you an absolution.

Gib. Absolution! can you procure me a pardon, doctor?

Foi. No, joy.

Gib. Then you and your absolution may go to the devil.

Arch. Convey him into the cellar, there bind him:—take the pistol, and if he offers to resist, shoot him through the head— and come back to us with all the speed you can.

Scrub. Ay, ay, come, doctor, do you hold him fast, and I'll guard him.　　　　[*Exit* FOIGARD *with* GIBBET, SCRUB *following.*

Mrs. Sul. But how came the doctor——

Arch. In short, madam—[*Shrieking without.*] 'Sdeath! the rogues are at work with the other ladies—I'm vexed I parted with the pistol; but I must fly to their assistance.—Will you stay here, madam, or venture yourself with me?

Mrs. Sul. [*taking him by the arm*]. Oh, with you, dear sir, with you.　　　　　　　　　　　　　　　　　[*Exeunt.*

SCENE III.—*Another Bedchamber in the same*

Enter HOUNSLOW *and* BAGSHOT, *with swords drawn, haling in* Lady BOUNTIFUL *and* DORINDA.

Houn. Come, come, your jewels, mistress!

Bag. Your keys, your keys, old gentlewoman!

Enter AIMWELL *and* CHERRY.

Aim. Turn this way, villains! I durst engage an army in such a cause. [*He engages them both.*

Dor. O madam, had I but a sword to help the brave man!

Lady Boun. There's three or four hanging up in the hall; but they won't draw. I'll go fetch one, however. [*Exit.*

Enter ARCHER *and* Mrs. SULLEN.

Arch. Hold, hold, my lord! every man his bird, pray.

   [*They engage man to man ;* HOUNSLOW *and* BAGSHOT *are thrown and disarmed.*

Cher. [*aside*]. What! the rogues taken! then they'll impeach my father: I must give him timely notice. [*Runs out.*

Arch. Shall we kill the rogues ?

Aim. No, no, we'll bind them.

Arch. Ay, ay.—[*To* Mrs. SULLEN, *who stands by him.*] Here, madam, lend me your garter.

Mrs. Sul. [*aside*]. The devil's in this fellow! he fights, loves, and banters, all in a breath.—[*Aloud.*] Here's a cord that the rogues brought with 'em, I suppose.

Arch. Right, right, the rogue's destiny, a rope to hang himself.—Come, my lord—this is but a scandalous sort of an office [*Binding the* Highwaymen *together*], if our adventures should end in this sort of hangman-work; but I hope there is something in prospect, that——

Enter SCRUB.

Arch. Well, Scrub, have you secured your Tartar ?

Scrub. Yes, sir, I left the priest and him disputing about religion.

Aim. And pray carry these gentlmeen to reap the benefit of the controversy.

   [*Delivers the prisoners to* SCRUB, *who leads them out.*

Mrs. Sul. Pray, sister, how came my lord here ?

Dor. And pray, how came the gentleman here ?

Mrs. Sul. I'll tell you the greatest piece of villainy—

   [*They talk in dumb show.*

Aim. I fancy, Archer, you have been more successful in your adventures than the housebreakers.

Arch. No matter for my adventure, yours is the principal.— Press her this minute to marry you—now while she's hurried between the palpitation of her fear and the joy of her deliverance, now while the tide of her spirits is at high-flood—throw yourself at her feet, speak some romantic nonsense or other—address her, like Alexander in the height of his victory, confound her senses, bear down her reason, and away with her.—The priest is now in the cellar, and dare not refuse to do the work.

Re-enter Lady BOUNTIFUL.

Aim. But how shall I get off without being observed?

Arch. You a lover, and not find a way to get off!—Let me see——

Aim. You bleed, Archer.

Arch. 'Sdeath, I'm glad on't; this wound will do the business. I'll amuse the old lady and Mrs. Sullen about dressing my wound, while you carry off Dorinda.

Lady Boun. Gentlemen, could we understand how you would be gratified for the services——

Arch. Come, come, my lady, this is no time for compliments; I'm wounded, madam.

Lady Boun., Mrs. Sul. How! wounded!

Dor. I hope, sir, you have received no hurt?

Aim. None but what you may cure——

                 [*Makes love in dumb show.*

Lady Boun. Let me see your arm, sir—I must have some powder-sugar to stop the blood.—O me! an ugly gash; upon my word, sir, you must go into bed.

Arch. Ay, my lady, a bed would do very well.—[*To* Mrs. SULLEN.] Madam, will you do me the favour to conduct me to a chamber.

Lady Boun. Do, do, daughter—while I get the lint and the probe and the plaster ready.

       [*Runs out one way,* AIMWELL *carries off* DORINDA *another.*

Arch. Come, madam, why don't you obey your mother's commands?

Mrs. Sul. How can you, after what is passed, have the confidence to ask me?

Arch. And if you go to that, how can you, after what is passed, have the confidence to deny me? Was not this blood shed in your defence, and my life exposed for your protection? Look'ee, madam, I'm none of your romantic fools, that fight giants and monsters for nothing; my valour is downright Swiss; I'm a soldier of fortune, and must be paid.

Mrs. Sul. 'Tis ungenerous in you, sir, to upbraid me with your services!

Arch. 'Tis ungenerous in you, madam, not to reward 'em.

Mrs. Sul. How! at the expense of my honour?

Arch. Honour! can honour consist with ingratitude? If you would deal like a woman of honour, do like a man of honour. D'ye think I would deny you in such a case?

Enter a Servant.

Serv. Madam, my lady ordered me to tell you, that your brother is below at the gate.   [*Exit.*

Mrs. Sul. My brother! Heavens be praised!—Sir, he shall thank you for your services; he has it in his power.

Arch. Who is your brother, madam?

Mrs. Sul. Sir Charles Freeman.—You'll excuse me, sir; I must go and receive him. [*Exit.*

Arch. Sir Charles Freeman! 'sdeath and hell! my old acquaintance. Now unless Aimwell has made good use of his time, all our fair machine goes souse into the sea like the Eddystone.

[*Exit.*

SCENE IV.—*The Gallery in the same house*

Enter AIMWELL *and* DORINDA.

Dor. Well, well, my lord, you have conquered; your late generous action will, I hope, plead for my easy yielding; though I must own, your lordship had a friend in the fort before.

Aim. The sweets of Hybla dwell upon her tongue!—Here, doctor——

Enter FOIGARD, *with a book.*

Foi. Are you prepared boat?

Dor. I'm ready. But first, my lord, one word.—I have a frightful example of a hasty marriage in my own family; when I reflect upon't it shocks me. Pray, my lord, consider a little——

Aim. Consider! do you doubt my honour or my love?

Dor. Neither: I do believe you equally just as brave: and were your whole sex drawn out for me to choose, I should not cast a look upon the multitude if you were absent. But, my lord, I'm a woman; colours, concealments may hide a thousand faults in me, therefore know me better first; I hardly dare affirm I know myself in anything except my love.

Aim. [*aside*]. Such goodness who could injure! I find myself unequal to the task of villain; she has gained my soul, and made it honest like her own.—I cannot, cannot hurt her.— [*Aloud.*] Doctor, retire.—[*Exit* FOIGARD.] Madam, behold your lover and your proselyte, and judge of my passion by my conversion!—I'm all a lie, nor dare I give a fiction to your arms; I'm all counterfeit, except my passion.

Dor. Forbid it, Heaven! a counterfeit!

Aim. I am no lord, but a poor needy man, come with a mean, a scandalous design to prey upon your fortune; but the beauties of your mind and person have so won me from myself that, like a trusty servant, I prefer the interest of my mistress to my own.

Dor. Sure I have had the dream of some poor mariner, a sleepy image of a welcome port, and wake involved in storms!— Pray, sir, who are you?

Aim. Brother to the man whose title I usurped, but stranger to his honour or his fortune.

Dor. Matchless honesty!—Once I was proud, sir, of your

wealth and title, but now am prouder that you want it: now I can show my love was justly levelled, and had no aim but love. —Doctor, come in.

Enter FOIGARD *at one door,* GIPSY *at another,*
who whispers DORINDA.

[*To* FOIGARD.]   Your pardon, sir, we shan't want you now.—
[*To* AIMWELL.]   Sir, you must excuse me—I'll wait on you presently.   [*Exit with* GIPSY.

Foi. Upon my shoul, now, dis is foolish.   [*Exit.*

Aim. Gone! and bid the priest depart!—It has an ominous look.

Enter ARCHER.

Arch. Courage, Tom!—Shall I wish you joy?
Aim. No.
Arch. 'Oons, man, what ha' you been doing?
Aim. O Archer! my honesty, I fear, has ruined me.
Arch. How?
Aim. I have discovered myself.
Arch. Discovered! and without my consent? What! have I embarked my small remains in the same bottom with yours, and you dispose of all without my partnership?
Aim. O Archer! I own my fault.
Arch. After conviction—'tis then too late for pardon.—You may remember, Mr. Aimwell, that you proposed this folly: as you begun, so end it. Henceforth I'll hunt my fortune single— so farewell!
Aim. Stay, my dear Archer, but a minute.
Arch. Stay! what, to be despised, exposed, and laughed at! No, I would sooner change conditions with the worst of the rogues we just now bound, than bear one scornful smile from the proud knight that once I treated as my equal.
Aim. What knight?
Arch. Sir Charles Freeman, brother to the lady that I had almost—but no matter for that, 'tis a cursed night's work, and so I leave you to make the best on't.   [*Going.*
Aim. Freeman!—One word, Archer. Still I have hopes; methought she received my confession with pleasure.
Arch. 'Sdeath, who doubts it?
Aim. She consented after to the match; and still I dare believe she will be just.
Arch. To herself, I warrant her, as you should have been.
Aim. By all my hopes she comes, and smiling comes!

Re-enter DORINDA, *mighty gay.*

Dor. Come, my dear lord—I fly with impatience to your arms —the minutes of my absence were a tedious year. Where's this priest?

Re-enter FOIGARD.

Arch. 'Oons, a brave girl!

Dor. I suppose, my lord, this gentleman is privy to our affairs?

Arch. Yes, yes, madam, I'm to be your father.

Dor. Come, priest, do your office.

Arch. Make haste, make haste, couple 'em any way.—[*Takes* AIMWELL'S *hand.*] Come, madam, I'm to give you——

Dor. My mind's altered; I won't.

Arch. Eh!

Aim. I'm confounded!

Foi. Upon my shoul, and sho is myshelf.

Arch. What's the matter now, madam?

Dor. Look'ee, sir, one generous action deserves another.— This gentleman's honour obliged him to hide nothing from me; my justice engages me to conceal nothing from him. In short, sir, you are the person that you thought you counterfeited; you are the true Lord Viscount Aimwell, and I wish your Lordship joy.—Now, priest, you may be gone; if my Lord is pleased now with the match, let his Lordship marry me in the face of the world.

Aim., Arch. What does she mean?

Dor. Here's a witness for my truth.

Enter Sir CHARLES FREEMAN *and* Mrs. SULLEN.

Sir Chas. My dear Lord Aimwell, I wish you joy.

Aim. Of what?

Sir Chas. Of your honour and estate. Your brother died the day before I left London; and all your friends have writ after you to Brussels;—among the rest I did myself the honour.

Arch. Hark'ee, sir knight, don't you banter now?

Sir Chas. 'Tis truth, upon my honour.

Aim. Thanks to the pregnant stars that formed this accident.

Arch. Thanks to the womb of time that brought it forth!— away with it!

Aim. Thanks to my guardian angel that led me to the prize!
[*Taking* DORINDA'S *hand.*

Arch. And double thanks to the noble Sir Charles Freeman.— My Lord, I wish you joy.—My Lady, I wish you joy.—Egad, Sir Freeman, you're the honestest fellow living!—'Sdeath, I'm grown strange airy upon this matter!—My Lord, how d'ye?— A word, my Lord; don't you remember something of a previous agreement, that entitles me to the moiety of this lady's fortune, which I think will amount to five thousand pounds?

Aim. Not a penny, Archer; you would ha' cut my throat just now, because I would not deceive this lady.

Arch. Ay, and I'll cut your throat again, if you should deceive her now.

Aim. That's what I expected; and to end the dispute, the

lady's fortune is ten thousand pounds, we'll divide stakes: take the ten thousand pounds or the lady.

Dor. How! is your Lordship so indifferent?

Arch. No, no, no, madam! his Lordship knows very well that I'll take the money; I leave you to his Lordship, and so we're both provided for.

Enter Count BELLAIR.

Count Bel. *Mesdames et Messieurs*, I am your servant trice humble! I hear you be rob here.

Aim. The ladies have been in some danger, sir.

Count Bel. And, begar, our inn be rob too!

Aim. Our inn! by whom?

Count Bel. By the landlord, begar!—Garzoon, he has rob himself, and run away!

Arch. Robbed himself!

Count Bel. Ay, begar, and me too of a hundre pound.

Arch. A hundred pounds?

Count Bel. Yes, that I owed him.

Aim. Our money's gone, Frank.

Arch. Rot the money! my wench is gone.—[*To* Count BELLAIR.] *Savez-vous quelquechose de Mademoiselle Cherry?*

Enter a Countryman *with a strong-box and a letter.*

Coun. Is there one Martin here?

Arch. Ay, ay—who wants him?

Coun. I have a box here, and letter for him.

Arch. [*taking the box*]. Ha! ha! ha! what's here? Legerde-main!—By this light, my lord, our money again!—But this unfolds the riddle.—[*Opening the letter.*] Hum, hum, hum!—Oh, 'tis for the public good, and must be communicated to the company.   [*Reads.*

"MR. MARTIN.—My father being afraid of an impeachment by the rogues that are taken to-night, is gone off; but if you can procure him a pardon, he'll make great discoveries that may be useful to the country. Could I have met you instead of your master to-night, I would have delivered myself into your hands, with a sum that much exceeds that in your strong-box, which I have sent you, with an assurance to my dear Martin that I shall ever be his most faithful friend till death.—CHERRY BONIFACE."

There's a *billet-doux* for you! As for the father, I think he ought to be encouraged; and for the daughter—pray, my Lord, persuade your bride to take her into her service instead of Gipsy.

Aim. I can assure you, madam, your deliverance was owing to her discovery.

Dor. Your command, my Lord, will do without the obliga-tion. I'll take care of her.

Sir Chas. This good company meets opportunely in favour of a design I have in behalf of my unfortunate sister. I intend to part her from her husband—gentlemen, will you assist me?

Arch. Assist you! 'sdeath, who would not?

Count Bel. Assist! garzoon, we all assist!

Enter Squire SULLEN.

Squire Sul. What's all this? They tell me, spouse, that you had like to have been robbed.

Mrs. Sul. Truly, spouse, I was pretty near it, had not these two gentlemen interposed.

Squire Sul. How came these gentlemen here?

Mrs. Sul. That's his way of returning thanks, you must know.

Count Bel. Garzoon, the question be apropos for all dat.

Sir Chas. You promised last night, sir, that you would deliver your lady to me this morning.

Squire Sul. Humph!

Arch. Humph! what do you mean by humph? Sir, you shall deliver her—in short, sir, we have saved you and your family; and if you are not civil, we'll unbind the rogues, join with 'em, and set fire to your house. What does the man mean? not part with his wife!

Count Bel. Ay, garzoon, de man no understan common justice.

Mrs. Sul. Hold, gentlemen, all things here must move by consent, compulsion would spoil us; let my dear and I talk the matter over, and you shall judge it between us.

Squire Sul. Let me know first who are to be our judges. Pray, sir, who are you?

Sir Chas. I am Sir Charles Freeman, come to take away your wife.

Squire Sul. And you, good sir?

Aim. Thomas, Viscount Aimwell, come to take away your sister.

Squire Sul. And you, pray, sir?

Arch. Francis Archer, esquire, come——

Squire Sul. To take away my mother, I hope. Gentlemen, you're heartily welcome; I never met with three more obliging people since I was born!—And now, my dear, if you please, you shall have the first word.

Arch. And the last, for five pounds!

Mrs. Sul. Spouse!

Squire Sul. Rib!

Mrs. Sul. How long have we been married?

Squire Sul. By the almanac, fourteen months; but by my account, fourteen years.

Mrs. Sul. 'Tis thereabout by my reckoning.

Count Bel. Garzoon, their account will agree.

Mrs. Sul. Pray, spouse, what did you marry for?

Squire Sul. To get an heir to my estate.

*N 604

Sir Chas. And have you succeeded?

Squire Sul. No.

Arch. The condition fails of his side.—Pray, madam, what did you marry for?

Mrs. Sul. To support the weakness of my sex by the strength of his, and to enjoy the pleasures of an agreeable society.

Sir Chas. Are your expectations answered?

Mrs. Sul. No.

Count Bel. A clear case! a clear case!

Sir Chas. What are the bars to your mutual contentment?

Mrs. Sul. In the first place, I can't drink ale with him.

Squire Sul. Nor can I drink tea with her.

Mrs. Sul. I can't hunt with you.

Squire Sul. Nor can I dance with you.

Mrs. Sul. I hate cocking and racing.

Squire Sul. And I abhor ombre and piquet.

Mrs. Sul. Your silence is intolerable.

Squire Sul. Your prating is worse.

Mrs. Sul. Have we not been a perpetual offence to each other? a gnawing vulture at the heart?

Squire Sul. A frightful goblin to the sight?

Mrs. Sul. A porcupine to the feeling?

Squire Sul. Perpetual wormwood to the taste?

Mrs. Sul. Is there on earth a thing we could agree in?

Squire Sul. Yes—to part.

Mrs. Sul. With all my heart.

Squire Sul. Your hand.

Mrs. Sul. Here.

Squire Sul. These hands joined us, these shall part us.—Away!

Mrs. Sul. North.

Squire Sul. South.

Mrs. Sul. East.

Squire Sul. West—far as the poles asunder.

Count Bel. Begar, the ceremony be vera pretty!

Sir Chas. Now, Mr. Sullen, there wants only my sister's fortune to make us easy.

Squire Sul. Sir Charles, you love your sister, and I love her fortune; every one to his fancy.

Arch. Then you won't refund;

Squire Sul. Not a stiver.

Arch. Then I find, madam, you must e'en go to your prison again.

Count Bel. What is the portion?

Sir Chas. Ten thousand pounds, sir.

Count Bel. Garzoon, I'll pay it, and she shall go home wid me.

Arch. Ha! ha! ha! French all over.—Do you know, sir, what ten thousand pounds English is?

Count Bel. No, begar, not justement.

Arch. Why, sir, 'tis a hundred thousand livres.

Count Bel. A hundre tousand livres! Ah! garzoon, me canno' do't, your beauties and their fortunes are both too much for me.

Arch. Then I will.—This night's adventure has proved strangely lucky to us all—for Captain Gibbet in his walk had made bold, Mr. Sullen, with your study and escritoir, and had taken out all the writings of your estate, all the articles of marriage with this lady, bills, bonds, leases, receipts to an infinite value: I took 'em from him, and I deliver 'em to Sir Charles.

[*Gives* Sir CHARLES FREEMAN *a parcel of papers and parchments.*

Squire Sul. How, my writings!—my head aches consumedly. —Well, gentlemen, you shall have her fortune, but I can't talk. If you have a mind, Sir Charles, to be merry, and celebrate my sister's wedding and my divorce, you may command my house —but my head aches consumedly.—Scrub, bring me a dram.

Arch. [*to* Mrs. SULLEN]. Madam, there's a country dance to the trifle that I sung to-day; your hand, and we'll lead it up.

Here a Dance.

'Twould be hard to guess which of these parties is the better pleased, the couple joined, or the couple parted; the one rejoicing in hopes of an untasted happiness, and the other in their deliverance from an experienced misery.

> Both happy in their several states we find,
> Those parted by consent, and those conjoined.
> Consent, if mutual, saves the lawyer's fee.
> Consent is law enough to set you free. [*Exeunt omnes.*

EPILOGUE

Designed to be spoken in " The Beaux-Stratagem."

IF to our play your judgment can't be kind,
Let its expiring author pity find:
Survey his mournful case with melting eyes,
Nor let the bard be damn'd before he dies.
Forbear, you fair, on his last scene to frown,
But his true exit with a plaudit crown;
Then shall the dying poet cease to fear
The dreadful knell, while your applause he hear.
At Leuctra so the conquering Theban died,
Claim'd his friends' praises, but their tears denied:
Pleased in the pangs of death he greatly thought
Conquest with loss of life but cheaply bought.
The difference this, the Greek was one would fight,
As brave, though not so gay, as Serjeant Kite;
Ye sons of Will's, what's that to those who write?
To Thebes alone the Grecian owed his bays,
You may the bard above the hero raise,
Since yours is greater than Athenian praise.

THE PROVOKED WIFE

A COMEDY IN FIVE ACTS

DRAMATIS PERSONÆ

LORD RAKE	HEARTFREE	LADY BRUTE	MADEMOISELLE
SIR JOHN BRUTE	CONSTANT	LADY FANCIFUL	CORNET
COLONEL BULLY	RAZOR	BELINDA	Servants

THE PROVOKED WIFE

ACT I

SCENE I.—Sir JOHN BRUTE's *House*

Enter Sir JOHN BRUTE.

Sir J. What cloying meat is love, when matrimony's the sauce to it! Two years' marriage has debauched my five senses. Everything I see, everything I hear, everything I feel, everything I smell, and everything I taste, methinks, has wife in't. No boy was ever so weary of his tutor, no girl of her bib, no nun of doing penance, or old maid of being chaste, as I am of being married. Sure, there's a secret curse entailed upon the very name of wife. My lady is a young lady, a fine lady, a witty lady, a virtuous lady, and yet, I hate her. There is but one thing on earth I loath beyond her, that's fighting. Would my courage come up to a fourth part of my ill-nature, I'd stand buff to her relations, and thrust her out of doors. But marriage has sunk me down to such an ebb of resolution, I dare not draw my sword, though even to get rid of my wife. But here she comes.

Enter Lady BRUTE.

Lady B. Do you dine at home to-day, Sir John?

Sir J. Why? Do you expect I should tell you what I don't know myself?

Lady B. I thought there was no harm in asking you.

Sir J. If thinking wrong were an excuse for impertinence, women might be justified in most things they say or do.

Lady B. I am sorry I have said anything to displease you.

Sir J. Sorrow for things past, is of as little importance to me, as my dining at home or abroad ought to be to you.

Lady B. My inquiry was only that I might have provided what you liked.

Sir J. Six to four you had been in the wrong there again; for what I liked yesterday I don't like to-day, and what I like to-day, 'tis odds I mayn't like to-morrow.

Lady B. But if I had asked you what you liked?

Sir J. Why, then, there would be more asking about it than the thing is worth.

Lady B. I wish I did but know how I might please you.

381

Sir J. Ay, but that sort of knowledge is not a wife's talent.

Lady B. Whatever my talent is, I'm sure my will has ever been to make you easy.

Sir J. If women were to have their wills, the world would be finely governed.

Lady B. What reason have I given you to use me as you do of late? It once was otherwise: you married me for love.

Sir J. And you me for money: so you have your reward, and I have mine.

Lady B. What is it that disturbs you?

Sir J. A parson.

Lady B. Why, what has he done to you?

Sir J. He has married me, and be d——d to him!   [*Exit.*

Lady B. The devil's in the fellow, I think. I was told before I married him, that thus 'twould be. The surly puppy! Yet, he's a fool for it: for hitherto, he has been no monster: but who knows how far he may provoke me? Or, who can tell? perhaps, a good part of what I suffer from my husband may be a judgment upon me for my cruelty to my lover. But, hold! let me go no further: I think I have a right to alarm this surly brute of mine: but, if I know my heart, it will never let me go so far as to injure him.

Enter BELINDA.

Good-morrow, dear cousin.

Bel. Good-morrow, madam; you look pleased this morning.

Lady B. I am so.

Bel. With what, pray?

Lady B. With my husband.

Bel. Drown husbands! for your's is a provoking fellow: as he went out just now, I prayed him to tell me what time of day 'twas; and he asked me if I took him for the church clock, that was obliged to tell all the parish.

Lady B. He has been saying some good obliging things to me, too. In short, Belinda, he has used me so barbarously of late, that I could almost resolve to play the downright wife, and cuckold him.

Bel. That would be downright, indeed.

Lady B. Why, after all, there's more to be said for't than you'd imagine, child. He is the first aggressor, not I.

Bel. Ah! but, you know, we must return good for evil.

Lady. B. That may be a mistake in the translation. Pr'ythee, be of my opinion, Belinda; for I'm positive I'm in the right; and if you'll keep up the prerogative of a woman, you'll likewise be positive you are in the right, whenever you do anything you have a mind to. But I shall play the fool, and jest on, till I make you begin to think I am in earnest.

Bel. I sha'n't take the liberty, madam, to think of anything that you desire to keep a secret from me.

SCENE I.] The Provoked Wife 383

Lady B. Alas! my dear, I have no secrets. My heart could never yet confine my tongue.

Bel. Your eyes, you mean; for I am sure I have seen them gadding, when your tongue has been locked up safe enough.

Lady B. My eyes gadding! Pr'ythee, after who, child?

Bel. Why, after one that thinks you hate him, as much as I know you love him.

Lady B. Constant, you mean?

Bel. I do so.

Lady B. Lord! what should put such a thing into your head.

Bel. That which puts things into most people's heads,— observation.

Lady B. Why, what have you observed, in the name of wonder?

Bel. I have observed you blush when you met him; force yourself away from him; and then be out of humour with everything about you: in a word, never was a poor creature so spurred on by desire, or so reined in with fear.

Lady B. How strong is fancy!

Bel. How weak is woman!

Lady B. Pr'ythee, niece, have a better opinion of your aunt's inclination.

Bel. Dear aunt, have a better opinion of your niece's understanding.

Lady B. You'll make me angry.

Bel. You'll make me laugh.

Lady B. Then you are resolved to persist?

Bel. Positively.

Lady B. And all I can say——

Bel. Will signify nothing.

Lady B. Though I should swear 'twere false——

Bel. I should think it true.

Lady B. Then let us forgive; [*kissing her*] for we have both offended: I, in making a secret; you in discovering it.

Bel. Good-nature may do much: but you have more reason to forgive one, than I have to pardon t'other.

Lady B. 'Tis true, Belinda, you have given me so many proofs of your friendship, that my reserve has been, indeed, a crime; and, as a proof of my repentance, I own, Belinda, I am in danger. But whatever you may have observed, I have dissembled so well as to keep him ignorant. So, you see, I'm no coquet, Belinda. For 'tis an unreasonable thing to engage a man in a disease, which we beforehand resolve we will never apply a cure to.

Bel. 'Tis true; but, then, a woman must abandon one of the supreme blessings of her life. For I am fully convinced, no man has half that pleasure in gallanting a mistress, as a woman has in jilting a gallant.

Lady B. The happiest woman, then, on earth must be our neighbour.

Bel. Oh! the impertinent composition! She has vanity and affectation enough to make her a ridiculous original.

Lady B. She concludes all men her captives; and whatever course they take, it serves to confirm her in that opinion.

Bel. If they shun her, she thinks 'tis modesty, and takes it for a proof of their passion.

Lady B. And if they are rude to her, 'tis conduct, and done to prevent town-talk.

Bel. All their actions and their words, she takes for granted, aim at her.

Lady B. And pities all other women, because she thinks they envy her.

Bel. Pray, out of pity to ourselves, let us find a better subject, for I'm weary of this. Do you think your husband inclined to jealousy?

Lady B. Oh! no; he does not love me well enough for that. Lord! how wrong men's maxims are! They are seldom jealous of their wives, unless they are very fond of them: whereas, they ought to consider the women's inclinations, for there depends their fate. Well, men may talk; but they are not so wise as we: that's certain.

Bel. At least in our affairs.

Lady B. Nay, I believe we should outdo them in the business of the state, too: for, methinks, they do and undo, and make but bad work on't.

Bel. Why, then, don't we get into the intrigues of government, as well as they?

Lady B. Because we have intrigues of our own, that make us more sport, child. And so, let's in and consider of them.

[*Exeunt.*

SCENE II.—*A Dressing Room*

Lady FANCIFUL, MADEMOISELLE, *and* CORNET, *discovered.*

Lady F. How do I look this morning?

Cor. Your ladyship looks very ill, truly.

Lady F. Lard! how ill-natured thou art, Cornet, to tell me so, though the thing should be true. Don't you know, that I have humility enough to be but too easily out of conceit with myself? Hold the glass: I dare say that will have more manners than you have. Mademoiselle, let me have your opinion too.

Madem. My opinion pe, matam, dat your ladyship never look so well in your life.

Lady F. Well, the French are the prettiest, obliging people! they say the most acceptable, well-mannered things—and never flatter.

Madem. Your ladyship say great justice, inteed.

Lady F. Nay, everything is just in my house, but Cornet. The very looking-glass gives her the dementi.   But I'm almost afraid it flatters me, it makes me look so engaging.

[*Looking affectedly in the glass.*

Madem. Inteed, matam, your face pe handsomer den all de looking-glass in de world, croyez moi.

Lady F. But is it possible my eyes can be so languishing, and so very full of fire?

Madem. Matam, if de glass was burning-glass, I believe your eyes set de fire in de house.

Lady F. You may take that night-gown, mademoiselle.   Get out of the room, Cornet.   I can't endure you.   [*Exit* CORNET.] This wench, methinks, does look so insufferably ugly!

Madem. Everyting look ugly, matam, dat stand by your latyship.

Lady F. No, really, mademoiselle, methinks you look mighty pretty.

Madem. Ah! matam, de moon have no eclat, ven de sun appear.

Lady F. Oh! pretty expression!   Have you ever been in love, mademoiselle?

Madem. Oui, matam.   [*Sighing.*

Lady F. And were you beloved again?

Madem. No, matam.

Lady F. Oh! ye gods! what an unfortunate creature should I be in such a case!   But nature has made me nice, for my own defence; I am nice, strangely nice, mademoiselle: I believe, were the merit of whole mankind bestowed upon one single person, I should still think the fellow wanted something to make it worth my while to take notice of him; and yet, I could love, nay, fondly love, were it possible to have a thing made on purpose for me, for I am not cruel, mademoiselle; I am only nice.

Madem. Ah! matam, I wish I was fine gentleman, for your sake.   I do all de ting in de world to get a little way into your heart.   I make song, I make verse, I give you de serenade, I give great many present to mademoiselle; I no eat, I no sleep, I be lean, I be mad, I hang myself, I drown myself.   Ah! ma chère dame, que je vous aimerois!   [*Embracing her.*

Lady F. Well, the French have strange, obliging ways with them; you may take those two pair of gloves, mademoiselle.

Madem. Me humbly tank my sweet lady.

Enter a Servant *with a letter.*

Serv. Madam, here's a letter for your ladyship.   [*Exit.*

Lady F. 'Tis thus I am importuned every morning, mademoiselle.   Pray, how do the French ladies, when they are thus accablées?

Madem. Matam, dey never complain.   Au contraire, when one Frense laty have got a hundred lover, den she do all she can to get a hundred more.

Lady F. Well, let me die, I think they have le bon goat. For 'tis an unutterable pleasure to be adored by all the men, and envied by all the women. Yet, I'll swear, I'm concerned at the torture I give them. Lard! why was I formed to make the whole creation uneasy? But let me read my letter. [*Reads.*] " If you have a mind to hear of your faults, instead of being praised for your virtues, take the pains to walk in the Green Walk in St. James's Park, with your woman, an hour hence. You'll there meet one, who hates you for some things, as he could love you for others; and, therefore, is willing to endeavour your reformation. If you come to the place I mention, you'll know who I am; if you don't, you never shall: so take your choice." This is strangely familiar, mademoiselle! now have I a provoking fancy to know who this impudent fellow is.

Madem. Den take your scarf and your mask, and go to de rendezvous. De Frense laty do justement comme ça.

Lady F. Rendezvous! What, rendezvous with a man, mademoiselle?

Madem. Eh! pourquoi non?

Lady F. What, and a man, perhaps, I never saw in my life!

Madem. Tant mieux: c'est, donc, quelque chose de nouveau

Lady F. Why, how do I know what designs he may have? He may intend to ravish me, for aught I know.

Madem. Ravish! Bagatelle! I would fain see one impudent rogue ravish mademoiselle. Oui, je le voudrois.

Lady F. Oh! but my reputation, mademoiselle, my reputation: ah! ma chère reputation!

Madem. Matam, quand on l'a une fois perdus, on n'en est plus embarrassée.

Lady F. Fie! mademoiselle, fie! reputation is a jewel.

Madem. Qui coute bien chère, matam.

Lady F. Why, sure, you would not sacrifice your honour to your pleasure?

Madem. Je suis philosophe.

Lady F. Bless me, how you talk! Why, what if honour be a burden, mademoiselle, must it not be borne?

Madem. Chacun a sa façon. Quand quelque chose m'incommode moi, je m'en defais vite.

Lady F. Get you gone, you little naughty Frenchwoman, you! I vow and swear I must turn you out of doors, if you talk thus.

Madem. Turn me out of doors! turn yourself out of doors, and go see what de gentleman have to say to you. Tenez! Voila [*giving her her things hastily*] votre esharp, votre coife, votre masque, voilà tout. Hey! mercure, coquin! call one chair for matam, and one oder [*calling within*] for me. Va-t-en vite. [*Turning to her lady, and helping her on hastily with her things.*] Allons, matam! depêchez vous, donc. Mon dieu! quelles scruples!

Lady F. Well, for once, mademoiselle, I'll follow your advice, out of the intemperate desire I have to know who this ill-bred fellow is. But I have too much delicatesse to make a practice on't.

Madem. Belle chose, vraiment, que la delicatesse, lorsqu'il s'agit de divertir—a ça. Vous voilà équipée, partons. Hé bien! qu'avez vous, donc?

Lady F. J'ai peur.

Madem. Je n'en ai point moi.

Lady F. I dare not go.

Madem. Démeurez donc.

Lady F. Je suis poltrone.

Madem. Tant pis pour vous.

Lady F. Curiosity's a wicked devil.

Madem. C'est une charmante sainte.

Lady F. It ruined our first parents.

Madem. Elle a bien diverti leurs enfans.

Lady F. L'honneur est contre.

Madem. Le plaisir est pour.

Lady F. Must I then go?

Madem. Must you go! Must you eat, must you drink, must you sleep, must you live? De nature bid you do one, de nature bid you do toder. Vous me ferez enrager.

Lady F. But when reason corrects nature, mademoiselle——

Madem. Elle est, donc, bien insolente, c'est sa sœur ainée.

Lady F. Do you, then, prefer your nature to your reason, mademoiselle?

Madem. Oui da.

Lady F. Pourquoi?

Madem. Because my nature make me merry, my reason make me mad.

Lady F. Ah! la mèchante Françoise!

Madem. Ah! la belle Angloise! [*Exit, forcing* Lady F. *off.*

ACT II

SCENE I.—*St. James's Park*

Enter Lady FANCIFUL *and* MADEMOISELLE.

Lady F. Well, I vow, mademoiselle, I am strangely impatient to know who this confident fellow is.

Enter HEARTFREE.

Look! there's Heartfree. But, sure, it can't be him; he's a professed woman-hater. Yet who knows what my wicked eyes may have done?

Madem. Il nous approche, matam.

Lady F. Yes, 'tis he; now will he be most intolerably cavalier, though he should be in love with me.

Heart. Madam, I'm your humble servant. I perceive you have more humility and good-nature than I thought you had.

Lady F. What you attribute to humility and good-nature, sir, may, perhaps, be only due to curiosity. I had a mind to know who 'twas had ill manners enough to write that letter.

[*Throwing him the letter.*

Heart. Well, and now I hope you are satisfied?

Lady F. I am so, sir; good b'ye.

Heart. Nay, hold there! though you have done your business, I haven't done mine: by your ladyship's leave, we must have one moment's prattle together. Have you a mind to be the prettiest woman about town or not? How she stares upon me! What, this passes for an impertinent question with you now, because you think you are so already?

Lady F. Pray, sir, let me ask you a question in my turn: by what right do you pretend to examine me?

Heart. By the same right that the strong govern the weak, because I have you in my power; for you cannot get so quickly to your coach, but I shall have time enough to make you hear everything I have to say to you.

Lady F. These are strange liberties you take, Mr. Heartfree.

Heart. They are so, madam, but there's no help for it; for, know, that I have a design upon you.

Lady F. Upon me, sir?

Heart. Yes, and one that will turn to your glory and my comfort, if you will be but a little wiser than you use to be.

Lady F. Very well, sir.

Heart. Let me see: your vanity, madam, I take to be about some eight degrees higher than any woman's in the town, let t'other be who she will; and my indifference is naturally about the same pitch. Now, could you find the way to turn this indifference into fire and flame, methinks, your vanity ought to be satisfied: and this, perhaps, you might bring about upon pretty reasonable terms.

Lady F. And, pray, at what rate would this indifference be bought off, if one should have so depraved an appetite to desire it?

Heart. Why, madam, to drive a quaker's bargain, and make but one word with you, if I do part with it, you must lay down your affectation.

Lady F. My affectation, sir!

Heart. Why, I ask you nothing but what you may very well spare.

Lady F. You grow rude, sir. Come, mademoiselle, it is high time to be gone.

Madem. Allons, allons, allons!

Heart. [*stopping them*]. Nay, you may as well stand still: for hear me you shall, walk which way you please.

Lady F. What mean you, sir?

Heart. I mean to tell you that you are the most ungrateful woman upon earth.

Lady F. Ungrateful! To whom?

Heart. To nature.

Lady F. Why, what has nature done for me?

Heart. What you have undone by art. It made you handsome; it gave you beauty to a miracle, a shape without a fault, wit enough to make them relish, and so turned you loose to your own discretion, which has made such work with you, that you are become the pity of our sex, and the jest of your own. There is not a feature in your face, but you have found the way to teach it some affected convulsion; your feet, your hands, your very fingers' ends, are directed never to move without some ridiculous air or other; and your language is a suitable trumpet, to draw people's eyes upon the raree-show.

Madem. [*aside*]. Est ce qu'on fait l'amour en Angleterre comme ça?

Lady F. [*aside*]. Now I could cry for madness, but that I know he'd laugh at me for it.

Heart. Now do you hate me for telling you the truth, but that's because you don't believe 'tis so; for were you once convinced of that, you'd reform for your own sake.

Lady F. Every circumstance of nice breeding must needs appear ridiculous to one who has so natural an antipathy to good manners.

Heart. But suppose I could find the means to convince you that the whole world is of my opinion?

Lady F. Sir, though you, and all the world you talk of, should be so impertinently officious as to think to persuade me I don't know how to behave myself, I should still have charity enough for my own understanding to believe myself in the right, and all you in the wrong.

Madem. Le voilà mort.   [*Exit with* Lady F.

Heart. [*gazing at her*]. There her single clapper has published the sense of the whole sex. Well, this once I have endeavoured to wash the blackmoor white, but, henceforward, I'll sooner undertake to teach sincerity to a courtier, generosity to a usurer, honesty to a lawyer, than discretion to a woman I see has once set her heart upon playing the fool.

Enter CONSTANT.

'Morrow, Constant.

Con. Good-morrow, Jack. What are you doing here this morning?

Heart. Doing! guess, if you can. Why, I have been en-

deavouring to persuade my Lady Fanciful that she's the most
foolish woman about town.

Con. A pretty endeavour, truly!

Heart. I have told her, in as plain English as I could speak,
both what the town says of her, and what I think of her. In
short, I have used her as an absolute king would do magna charta.

Con. And how does she take it?

Heart. As children do pills; bite them, but can't swallow
them.

Con. But, pr'ythee, what has put it into your head, of all
mankind, to turn reformer?

Heart. Why, one thing was, the morning hung upon my
hands; I did not know what to do with myself; and another
was, that as little as I care for women, I could not see with
patience one that heaven had taken such wondrous pains about,
be so very industrious to make herself the Jack-pudding of the
creation.

Con. Well, now I could almost wish to see my cruel mistress
make the self-same use of what heaven has done for her; that so
I might be cured of the same disease that makes me so very
uneasy; for love, love is the devil, Heartfree.

Heart. And why do you let the devil govern you?

Con. Because I have more flesh and blood than grace and
self-denial. My dear, dear mistress—'Sdeath! that so genteel
a woman should be a saint, when religion's out of fashion!

Heart. Nay, she's much in the wrong, truly; but who knows
how far time and good example may prevail?

Con. Oh! they have played their parts in vain already; 'tis
now two years since the fellow her husband invited me to his
wedding; and there was the first time I saw that charming
woman, whom I have loved ever since; but she is cold, my
friend, still cold as the northern star.

Heart. So are all women by nature, which maketh them so
willing to be warmed.

Con. Oh! don't profane the sex: pr'ythee, think them all
angels for her sake; for she's virtuous even to a fault.

Heart. A lover's head is a good accountable thing, truly! he
adores his mistress for being virtuous, and yet, is very angry
with her, because she won't be kind.

Con. Well, the only relief I expect in my misery is to see thee
some day or other as deeply engaged as myself, which will force
me to be merry in the midst of all my misfortunes.

Heart. That day will never come, be assured, Ned. But,
pr'ythee, let me tell you how I avoid falling in love; that which
serves me for prevention may chance to serve you for a cure.

Con. Well, use the ladies moderately, then, and I'll hear you.

Heart. That using them moderately undoes us all: but I'll
use them justly, and that you ought to be satisfied with. I
always consider a woman, not as the tailor, the shoe-maker, the

tire-woman, the sempstress, and (which is more than all that), the poet makes her; but I consider her as pure nature has contrived her, and that more strictly than I should have done our old grandmother Eve, had I seen her naked in the garden; for I consider her turned inside out. Her heart well examined, I find there pride, vanity, covetousness, indiscretion; but, above all things, malice: plots eternally forging to destroy one another's reputations, and as honestly to charge the levity of men's tongues with the scandal; hourly debates how to make poor gentlemen in love with them, with no other intent but to use them like dogs when they have done; a constant desire of doing more mischief, and an everlasting war waged against truth and good-nature.

Con. Very well, sir, an admirable composition truly!

Heart. Then for her outside, I consider it merely as an outside: she has a thin, tiffany covering; just over such stuff as you and I are made of. As for her motion, her mien, her airs, and all those tricks, I know they affect you mightily. If you should see your mistress at a coronation, dragging her peacock's train, with all her state and insolence about her, 'twould strike you with all the awful thoughts that heaven itself could pretend to form you: whereas, I turn the whole matter into a jest, and suppose her strutting, in the self-same stately manner, with nothing on but her stays, and her scanty quilted under-petticoat.

Con. Hold thy profane tongue; for I'll hear no more.

Heart. What, you'll love on, then?

Con. Yes.

Heart. Yet have no hopes at all.

Con. None.

Heart. Nay, the resolution may be discreet enough: perhaps you have found out some new philosophy; that love, like virtue, is its own reward: so you and your mistress will be as well content at a distance, as others that have less learning are in coming together.

Con. No; but if she should prove kind at last, my dear Heartfree——   [*Embracing him.*

Heart. Nay, pr'ythee, don't take me for your mistress; for lovers are very troublesome.

Con. Well, who knows what time may do?

Heart. And just now he was sure that time could do nothing.

Con. Yet not one kind glance in two years is somewhat strange.

Heart. Not strange at all; she don't like you, that's all the business.

Con. Pr'ythee, don't distract me.

Heart. Nay, you are a good, handsome, young fellow, she might use you better. Come, will you go see her? perhaps she may have changed her mind; there's some hopes, as long as she's a woman.

Con. Oh! 'tis in vain to visit her: sometimes, to get a sight of

her, I visit that beast her husband; but she certainly finds some
pretence to quit the room as soon as I enter.

Heart. It's much she don't tell him you have made love to her,
too; for that's another good-natured thing usual amongst
women, in which they have several ends. Sometimes 'tis to
recommend their virtue, that they may be kind with the greater
security. Sometimes 'tis to make their husbands fight, in hopes
they may be killed, when their affairs require it should be so:
but, most commonly, 'tis to engage two men in a quarrel, that
they may have the credit of being fought for; and if the lover's
killed in the business, they cry, " Poor fellow, he had ill-luck; "
and so they go to cards.

Con. Thy injuries to women are not to be forgiven. Look
to't, if ever you fall into their hands——

Heart. They can't use me worse than they do you, that speak
well of them. Oho! here comes the knight!

Enter Sir John Brute.

Your humble servant, Sir John.

Sir J. Servant, sir.

Heart. How does all your family?

Sir J. Plague o' my family!

Con. How does your lady? I haven't seen her abroad a good
while.

Sir J. Do! I don't know how she does, not I; she was well
enough yesterday; I haven't been at home to-night.

Con. What, were you out of town?

Sir J. Out of town! No; I was drinking.

Con. You are a true Englishman; don't know your own
happiness. If I were married to such a woman, I would not be
from her a night, for all the wine in France.

Sir J. Not from her! Oons! what a time should a man have
of that!

Heart. Why, there's no division, I hope?

Sir J. No; but there's a conjunction, and that's worse: a
pox of the parson! Why the plague don't you two marry? I
fancy I look live the devil to you.

Heart. Why, you don't think you have horns, do you?

Sir J. No; I believe my wife's religion will keep her honest.

Heart. And what will make her keep her religion?

Sir J. Persecution; and, therefore, she shall have it.

Heart. Have a care, knight, women are tender things.

Sir J. And yet, methinks, 'tis a hard matter to break their
hearts.

Con. Fie, fie! you have one of the best wives in the world, and
yet you seem the most uneasy husband.

Sir J. Best wives! the woman's well enough; she has no vice
that I know of; but she's a wife: and d——n a wife! if I were

married to a hogshead of claret, matrimony would make me hate it.

Heart. Why did you marry, then? you were old enough to know your own mind.

Sir J. Why did I marry! What, you would have me intrigue, I suppose, and so have hedged myself into forty quarrels with her relations; besides buying my pardon; but more than all that, you must know I was afraid of being d——d in those days: for I kept sneaking, cowardly company, fellows that went to church, said grace to their meat, and had not the least tincture of quality about them.

Heart. But I think you have got into a better gang now.

Sir J. Zoons! sir, my Lord Rake and I are hand and glove: I believe we may get our bones broken together to-night. Have you a mind to share a frolic?

Con. Not I, truly; my talent lies in softer exercises.

Sir J. What, a down bed and a strumpet? A pox of venery, I say. Will you come and drink with me this afternoon?

Con. I can't drink to-day; but we'll come and sit an hour with you if you will.

Sir J. Pooh! pox! sit an hour! Why can't you drink?

Con. Because I'm to see my mistress.

Sir J. Who's that?

Con. Why, do you use to tell?

Sir J. Yes.

Con. So won't I.

Sir J. Why?

Con. Because it is a secret.

Sir J. Would my wife knew it! 'twould be no secret long.

Con. Why, do you think she can't keep a secret?

Sir J. No more than she could keep Lent.

Heart. Pr'ythee, tell it her, to try, Constant.

Sir J. No, pr'ythee, don't, that I mayn't be plagued with it.

Con. I'll hold you a guinea you don't make her tell it you.

Sir J I'll hold you a guinea I do.

Con. Which way?

Sir J. Why, I'll beg her not to tell it me.

Heart. Nay, if anything does it, that will.

Con. But do you think, sir——

Sir J. Oons! sir, I think a woman and a secret are the two impertinentest themes in the universe; therefore, pray, let's hear no more of my wife nor your mistress. D——n them both, with all my heart, and everything else that daggles a petticoat, except four generous whores who are drunk with my Lord Rake and I ten times in a fortnight.   [*Exit.*

Con. Here's a dainty fellow for you! and the veriest coward, too. But his usage of his wife makes me ready to stab the villain.

Heart. Lovers are short-sighted: all their senses run into that of feeling. This proceeding of his is the only thing on earth can make you fortunate. If anything can prevail with her to accept a gallant, 'tis his usage of her. Pr'ythee, take heart; I have great hopes for you: and, since I can't bring you quite off her, I'll endeavour to bring you quite on; for a whining lover is the d——dest companion upon earth.

Con. My dear friend, flatter me a little more with these hopes; for whilst they prevail, I have Elysium within me, and could melt with joy.

Heart. Pray, no melting yet. This afternoon, perhaps, we shall make some advance. In the meanwhile, let's go dine at Locket's, and let hope get you a stomach.   [*Exeunt.*

SCENE II.—Lady FANCIFUL's *House*

Enter Lady FANCIFUL and MADEMOISELLE.

Lady F. Did you ever see anything so importune, mademoiselle?

Madem. Inteed, matam, to say de trute, he want leetel good breeding.

Lady F. Good breeding! He wants to be caned, mademoiselle. An insolent fellow! And yet, let me expose my weakness, 'tis the only man on earth I could resolve to dispense my favours on, were he but a fine gentleman. Well, did men but know how deep an impression a fine gentleman makes in a lady's heart, they would reduce all their studies to that of good-breeding alone.

Enter a Servant.

Serv. Will your ladyship please to dine yet?

Lady F. Yes, let them serve. [*Exit* Servant.] Sure, this Heartfree has bewitched me, mademoiselle. I vow, 'tis a thousand pities he is not more polished; don't you think so?

Madem. Matam, I think it so great pity, that if I was in your ladyship's place, I take him home in my house, I lock him up in my closet, and I never let him go till I teach him everyting dat fine laty expect from fine gentleman.

Lady F. Why, truly, I believe I should soon subdue his brutality; for, without doubt, he has a strange penchant to grow fond of me, in spite of his aversion to the sex, else he would never have taken so much pains about me. Lord! how proud would some poor creatures be of such a conquest! but I, alas! I don't know how to receive as a favour, what I take to be so infinitely my due. But what shall I do to new mould him, mademoiselle? for till then, he's my utter aversion.

Madem. Matam, you must laugh at him in all de places dat you meet him, and turn into de redicule all he say, and all he do.

Lady F. Why, truly, satire has ever been of wondrous use to reform ill-manners. Besides, 'tis my particular talent to ridicule folks. I can be severe, strangely severe, when I will, mademoiselle. Give me the pen and ink, I find myself whimsical: I'll write to him—or, I'll let it alone, and be severe upon him that way. [*Sitting down to write and rising up again.*] Yet, active severity is better than passive. [*Sitting down.*] 'Tis as good to let it alone, too; for every lash I give him, perhaps, he'll take for a favour. [*Rising.*] Yet, 'tis a thousand pities so much satire should be lost. [*Sitting.*] But if it should have a wrong effect upon him, 'twould distract me. [*Rising.*] Well, I must write, though, after all. [*Sitting.*] Or, I'll let it alone, which is the same thing. [*Rising.*

Madem. La voilà determinée. [*Exeunt.*

ACT III

SCENE I.—Sir JOHN BRUTE'S *House*

Sir JOHN BRUTE, Lady BRUTE, *and* BELINDA *discovered, rising from the table.*

Sir J. Here, take away the things: I expect company. But, first, bring me a pipe; I'll smoke. [*To a Servant.*

Lady B. Lord! Sir John, I wonder you won't leave that nasty custom.

Sir J. Pr'ythee, don't be impertinent.

Bel. [*to* Lady B]. I wonder who those are he expects this afternoon.

Lady B. I'd give the world to know. Perhaps 'tis Constant; he comes here sometimes: if it does prove him, I'm resolved I'll share the visit.

Bel. We'll send for our work, and sit here.

Lady B. He'll choke us with his tobacco.

Bel. Nothing will choke us, when we are doing what we have a mind to. Lovewell!

Enter LOVEWELL.

Love. Madam.

Lady B. Here, bring my cousin's work and mine hither.

[*Exit* LOVEWELL, *and re-enters with their work.*

Sir J. Why, pox! can't you work somewhere else?

Lady B. We shall be careful not to disturb you, sir.

Bel. Your pipe would make you too thoughtful, uncle, if you were left alone; our prittle prattle will cure your spleen.

Sir J. Will it so, Mrs. Pert? Now I believe it will so increase it [*sitting and smoking*] I shall take my own house for a paper-mill.

Lady B. [*aside to* BEL.]. Don't let's mind him; let him say what he will.

Sir J. A woman's tongue a cure for the spleen! Oons! if a man had got the headache, they'd be for applying the same remedy.   [*Aside.*

Lady B. You have done a good deal, Belinda, since yesterday.

Bel. Yes, I have worked very hard; how do you like it?

Lady B. Oh! 'tis the prettiest fringe in the world! Well, cousin, you have the happiest fancy! pr'ythee, advise me about altering my crimson petticoat.

Sir J. D—n your petticoat! here's such a prating, a man can't digest his own thoughts for you.

Lady B. Don't answer him. [*Aside.*] Well, what do you advise me?

Bel. Why, really, I would not alter it at all. Methinks 'tis very pretty as it is.

Lady B. Ay, that's true; but you know one grows weary of the prettiest things in the world, when one has had them long.

Sir J. Yes, I have taught her that.

Bel. Shall we provoke him a little?   [*Apart to* Lady B.

Lady B. With all my heart. Belinda, don't you long to be married?

Bel. Why, there are some things in it which I could like well enough.

Lady B. What do you think you should dislike?

Bel. My husband: a hundred to one else.

Lady B. Oh! you wicked wretch! sure, you don't speak as you think?

Bel. Yes, I do: especially if he smoked tobacco.

                                        [Sir J. *looks earnestly at them.*

Lady B. Why, that, many times, takes off worse smells.

Bel. Then he must smell very ill indeed.

Lady B. So some men will, to keep their wives from coming near them.

Bel. Then those wives should cuckold them at a distance.

  [Sir J. *runs in a fury, throws his pipe at them, and drives them out.* As they run off, enter CONSTANT and HEART-FREE; Lady BRUTE *runs against* CONSTANT.

Sir J. Oons! get you gone up stairs, you confederating strumpets you, or I'll cuckold you, with a vengeance!

Lady B. Oh, lord! he'll beat us, he'll beat us! Dear Mr. Constant, save us!   [*Exit with* BELINDA.

Sir J. I'll cuckold you, with a pox!

Con. Heaven! Sir John, what's the matter?

Sir J. Sure, if women had been ready created, the devil, instead of being kicked down into hell, had been married.

Heart. Why, what new plagues have you found now?

Sir J. Why, these two gentlewomen did but hear me say I expected you here this afternoon; upon which they presently resolved to take up the room on purpose to plague me and my friends.

Con. Was that all? Why, we should have been glad of their company.

Sir J. Then I should have been weary of your's; for I can't relish both together. They found fault with my smoking tobacco, too, and said men stunk; but I had a good mind to say something.

Con. Oh! nothing against the ladies, I hope?

Sir J. The ladies! Come, will you sit down? Give us some wine, fellow. You won't smoke?

Con. No, nor drink neither, at this time; I must ask your pardon.

Sir J. What, this mistress of your's runs in your head? I'll warrant, it's some such squeamish minx as my wife, that's grown so dainty of late, she finds fault even with a dirty shirt.

Heart. That a woman may do, and not be very dainty neither.

Sir J. Come, you shall take one glass, though I send for a box of lozenges, to sweeten your mouth after it.

Con. Nay, if one glass will satisfy you, I'll drink it, without putting you to that expense.

Sir J. Why, that's honest. So, here's to you, gentlemen. A wife's the devil. To your both being married.   [*They drink.*

Heart. Oh! your most humble servant, sir.

Sir J. Well, how do you like my wine?

Con. 'Tis very good, indeed.

Heart. 'Tis admirable.

Sir J. Then take t'other glass.

Con. No, pray, excuse us now: we'll come another time, and then we won't spare it.

Sir J. This one glass, and no more. Come, it shall be your mistress's health; and that's a great compliment from me, I assure you.

Con. And 'tis a very obliging one to me; so give us the glasses.

Sir J. So, let her live——   [*Coughs in the glass.*

Heart. And be kind.

Con. What's the matter? Does it go the wrong way?

Sir J. If I had love enough to be jealous, I should take this for an ill omen; for I never drunk my wife's health in my life, but I puked in my glass.

Con. Oh! she's too virtuous to make any reasonable man jealous.

Sir J. Pox of her virtue. If I could catch her adulterating, I might be divorced from her by law.

Heart. And so pay her a yearly pension, to be a distinguished cuckold.

Enter a Servant.

Serv. Sir, there's my Lord Rake, Colonel Bully, and some other gentlemen at the Blue Posts, desire your company.

Sir J. Gadso! we are to consult about playing the devil to-night.

Heart. Well, we won't hinder business.

Sir J. Methinks, I don't know how to leave you two; but, for once, I must make bold. Or, look you! may be, the conference mayn't last long. So, if you'll wait here half-an-hour, or an hour; if I don't come then, why, then, I won't come at all.

Heart. [*apart to* CON]. A good modest proposition, truly!

Con. [*apart to* HEART.]. But let's accept on't, however. Who knows what may happen?

Heart. Well, sir, to shew you how fond we are of your company, we'll expect your return as long as we can.

Sir J. Nay, may be I mayn't stay at all; but business, you know, must be done: so, your servant. Or, hark you! if you have a mind to take a frisk with us, I have an interest with my lord; I can easily introduce you.

Con. We are much beholden to you; but, for my part, I'm engaged another way.

Sir J. What, to your mistress, I'll warrant. P'rythee, leave her to her own thoughts, and make one with us to-night.

Con. Sir, 'tis business that is to employ me.

Heart. And me; and business must be done, you know.

Sir J. Ay, women's business, though the world were consumed for't.   [*Exit.*

Con. Farewell, beast! and now, my dear friend, would my mistress be but as complaisant as some men's wives, who think it a piece of good-breeding to receive the visits of their husband's friends in his absence——

Heart. Why, for your sake, I could forgive her. But what way shall we invent to see her?

Con. Oh! never hope it: invention will prove as vain as wishes.

Enter Lady BRUTE *and* BELINDA.

Heart. What do you think now, friend?   [*Apart to* CON.
Con. I think I shall swoon.   [*Apart to* HEART.
Heart. I'll speak first, then, while you fetch breath.
                                            [*Apart to* CON.

Lady B. We think ourselves obliged, gentlemen, to come and return you thanks for your knight-errantry. We were just upon being devoured by the fiery dragon.

Bel. Did not his fumes almost knock you down, gentlemen?

Heart. Truly, ladies, we did undergo some hardships; and should have done more, if some greater heroes than ourselves hard by had not diverted him.

Con. Though I am glad of the service you are pleased to say we have done you, yet I'm sorry we could do it in no other way, than by making ourselves privy to what you would, perhaps, have kept a secret.

Lady B. For Sir John's part, I suppose he designed it no secret, since he made so much noise. And for myself, truly, I am not much concerned, since 'tis fallen only into this gentleman's hand and your's, who, I have many reasons to believe, will neither interpret nor report anything to my disadvantage.

Con. Your good opinion, madam, was what I feared I never could have merited.

Lady B. Your fears were vain, then, sir, for I'm just to everybody.

Heart. Pr'ythee, Constant, what is it you do to get the ladies' good opinions? for I'm a novice at it.

Bel. Sir, will you give me leave to instruct you?

Heart. Yes, that I will, with all my soul, madam.

Bel. Why, then, you must never be a sloven; never be out of humour; never smoke tobacco; nor drink but when you are dry.

Heart. That's hard.

Con. Nay, if you take his bottle from him, you break his heart, madam.

Bel. Why, is it possible the gentleman can love drinking?

Heart. Only by way of antidote.

Bel. Against what, pray?

Heart. Against love, madam.

Lady B. Are you afraid of being in love, sir?

Heart. I should, if there were any danger of it.

Lady B. Pray, why so?

Heart. Because I always had an aversion to being used like a dog.

Bel. Why, truly, men in love are seldom used better.

Lady B. But were you never in love, sir?

Heart. No, I thank heaven, madam.

Bel. Pray, where got you your learning, then?

Heart. From other people's experience.

Bel. That's being a spunger, sir, which is scarce honest; if you'd buy some experience with your own money, as 'twould be fairlier got, so 'twould stick longer by you.

Enter a Footman.

Foot. Madam, here's my Lady Fanciful, to wait upon your ladyship. [*Exit.*

Lady B. Shield me, kind heaven! What an inundation of impertinence is here coming upon us!

Enter Lady FANCIFUL, *who runs first to* Lady BRUTE, *then to* BELINDA, *kissing them.*

Lady F. My dear Lady Brute, and sweet Belinda, methinks 'tis an age since I saw you.

o 604

Lady B. Yet 'tis but three days; sure, you have passed your time very ill, it seems so long to you!

Lady F. Why, really, to confess the truth to you, I am so everlastingly fatigued with the addresses of unfortunate gentlemen, that were it not for the goodness of the example, I should e'en tear out these wicked eyes with my own fingers to make both myself and mankind easy. What think you on't, Mr. Heartfree, for I take you to be my faithful adviser?

Heart. Why, truly, madam, I think every project that is for the good of mankind ought to be encouraged.

Lady F. Then I have your consent, sir?

Heart. To do whatever you please, madam.

Lady F. You had a much more limited complaisance this morning, sir. Would you believe it, ladies? this gentleman has been so exceeding generous, to tell me of above fifty faults, in less time than it was well possible for me to commit two of them.

Con. Why, truly, madam, my friend there is apt to be something familiar with the ladies.

Lady F. He is, indeed, sir; but he's wondrous charitable with it; he has had the goodness to design a reformation, e'en down to my fingers' ends. 'Twas thus, I think, sir [*opening her fingers in an awkward manner*] you'd have them stand? My eyes, too, he did not like. How was it you would have directed them? thus, I think. [*Staring at him.*] Then, there was something amiss in my gait, too; I don't know well how 'twas, but, as I take it, he would have me walk like him. Pray, sir, do me the favour to take a turn or two about the room, that the company may see you. He's sullen, ladies, and won't. But, to make short, and give you as true an idea as I can of the matter, I think 'twas much about this figure in general, he would have moulded me to—but I was an obstinate woman, and could not resolve to make myself mistress of his heart, by growing as awkward as his fancy.

[*She walks awkwardly about, staring and looking ungainly; then changes on a sudden to the extremity of her usual affectation.*

Heart. Just thus women do, when they think we are in love with them, or when they are so with us.

[CONSTANT *and* Lady B. *talk together apart.*

Lady F. 'Twould, however, be less vanity for me to conclude the former, than you the latter, sir.

Heart. Madam, all I shall presume to conclude is, that if I were in love, you'd find the means to make me soon weary on't.

Lady F. Not by over fondness, upon my word, sir. But, pr'ythee, let's stop here; for you are so much governed by instinct, I know you'll grow brutish at last.

Bel. [*aside*]. Now am I sure she's fond of him. I'll try to make her jealous. Well, for my part, I should be glad to find somebody would be so free with me, that I might know my faults, and mend them.

Lady F. Then, pray, let me recommend this gentleman to you; I have known him some time, and will be surety for him, that upon a very limited encouragement on your side, you shall find an extended impudence on his.

Heart. I thank you, madam, for your recommendation; but, hating idleness, I'm unwilling to enter into a place where, I believe, there would be nothing to do. I was fond of serving your ladyship, because I knew you'd find me constant employment.

Lady F. I told you he'd be rude, Belinda.

Bel. Oh! a little bluntness is a sign of honesty, which makes me always ready to pardon it. So, sir, if you have no other objection to my service, but the fear of being idle in it, you may venture to list yourself: I shall find you work, I warrant you.

Heart. Upon those terms I engage, madam; and thus, with your leave, I take for earnest.   [*Offers to kiss her hand.*

Bel. Hold there, sir! I'm none of your earnest-givers. But, if I'm well served, I give good wages, and pay punctually.

[HEARTFREE *and* BELINDA *seem to continue talking familiarly together.*

Lady F. [*aside*]. I don't like this jesting between them. Methinks the fool begins to look as if he were in earnest; but then, he must be a fool, indeed.   Lard! what a difference there is between me and her! [*Looking at* BELINDA *scornfully.*] How I should despise such a thing, if I were a man! What a nose she has! what a chin! what a neck! Then her eyes—and the worst kissing lips in the universe! No, no, he can never like her, that's positive; yet I can't suffer them together any longer. Mr. Heartfree, do you know that you and I must have no quarrel, for all this? I can't forbear being a little severe, now and then; but women, you know, may be allowed anything.

Heart. Up to a certain age, madam.

Lady F. Which I'm not yet past, I hope.

Heart. [*aside*]. Nor ever will, I dare swear.

Lady F. [*to* Lady B]. Come, madam, will your ladyship be witness to our reconciliation?

Lady B. You are agreed, then, at last?

Heart. [*slightingly*]. We forgive.

Lady F. [*aside*]. That was a cold, ill-natured reply.

Lady B. Then there are no challenges sent between you?

Heart. Not from me, I promise. [*Aside to* CONSTANT.] But that's more than I'll do for her; for I know she can as well be hanged as forbear writing to me.

Con. That I believe. But I think we had best be going, lest she should suspect something, and be malicious.

Heart. With all my heart.

Con. Ladies, we are your humble servants. I see Sir John

is quite engaged, 'twould be in vain to expect him. Come, Heartfree. [*Exit.*

Heart. Ladies, your servant. [*To* BEL.] I hope, madam, you won't forget our bargain; I'm to say what I please to you. [*Exit.*

Bel. Liberty of speech entire, sir.

Lady F. [*aside*]. Very pretty, truly! But how the blockhead went out languishing at her; and not a look towards me! Well, people may talk, but miracles are not ceased. For, 'tis more than natural, such a rude fellow as he is, and such a little impertinent as she should be capable of making a woman of my sphere uneasy. But I can bear her sight no longer, methinks she's grown ten times uglier than Cornet. I must home and study revenge. [*To* Lady B.] Madam, your humble servant; I must take my leave.

Lady B. What, going already, madam?

Lady F. I must beg you'll excuse me this once; for, really, I have eighteen visits to return this afternoon; so, you see, I'm importuned by the women as well as the men. [*Going.*] Nay, you sha'n't go one step out of the room.

Lady B. Indeed, I'll wait upon you down.

Lady F. No, sweet Lady Brute, you know I swoon at ceremony.

Lady B. Pray, give me leave.

Lady F. You know I won't.

Lady B. Indeed I must.

Lady F. Indeed you sha'n't.

Lady B. Indeed I will.

Lady F. Indeed you sha'n't.

Lady B. Indeed I will.

Lady F. Indeed you sha'n't. Indeed, indeed, indeed you sha'n't. [*Exit running; they follow.*

Re-enter Lady BRUTE.

Lady B. This impertinent woman has put me out of humour for a fortnight. What an agreeable moment has her foolish visit interrupted! Lord! what a pleasure there is in doing what we should not do!

Enter CONSTANT.

Ah! here again!

Con. Though the renewing my visit may seem a little irregular, I hope, I shall obtain your pardon for it, madam, when you know I only left the room lest the lady who was here should have been as malicious in her remarks as she is foolish in her conduct.

Lady B. He who has discretion enough to be tender of a woman's reputation, carries a virtue about him that may atone for a great many faults.

Con. If it has a title to atone for any, its pretensions must needs be strongest, where the crime is love. But I hope it cannot be reckoned an offence to love, where it is a duty to adore.

Lady B. 'Tis an offence, a great one, where it would rob a woman of all she ought to be adored for—her virtue.

Con. Virtue! that phantom of honour, which men in every age have so condemned, they have thrown it amongst the women to scramble for.

Lady B. If it be a thing of so very little value, why do you so earnestly recommend it to your wives and daughters?

Con. We recommend it to our wives, madam, because we would keep them to ourselves; and to our daughters because we would dispose of them to others.

Lady B. 'Tis, then, of some importance, it seems, since you can't dispose of them without it.

Con. I beg you will believe I did but rally, madam. I know you judge too well of right and wrong to be deceived by arguments like those. And I hope you will have so favourable an opinion of my understanding, too, to believe the thing called virtue has worth enough with me to pass for an eternal obligation wherever 'tis sacrificed.

Lady B. It is, I think, so great a one, as nothing can repay.

Con. Yes, the making the man you love your everlasting debtor.

Lady B. When debtors once have borrowed all we have to lend, they are very apt to grow shy of their creditors' company.

Con. That, madam, is only when they are forced to borrow of usurers, and not of a generous friend. Let us choose our creditors and we are seldom so ungrateful as to shun them.

Lady B. What think you of Sir John, sir? I was his free choice.

Con. I think he's married, madam.

Lady B. Does marriage, then, exclude men from your rule of constancy?

Con. It does. Constancy's a brave, free, haughty, generous agent, that cannot buckle to the chains of wedlock. [*Following her.*] But, madam——

Lady B. But, sir, 'tis my turn to be discreet now, and not suffer too long a visit.

Con. [*catching her hand*]. By heaven, you shall not stir till you give me hopes that I shall see you again at some more convenient time and place.

Lady B. I give you just hopes enough [*breaking from him*] to get loose from you; and that's all I can afford you at this time.
[*Exit, running.*

Con. Now, by all that's great and good, she's a charming, woman! In what ecstacy of joy she has left me! for she gave me hope. Did she not say she gave me hope? Hope! Ay, what hope? Enough to make me let her go! Why, that's enough in conscience. Or, no matter how t'was spoke, hope was the word, it came from her, and it was said to me.

Enter HEARTFREE.

Ah! Heartfree, thou hast done me noble service in prattling to the young gentlewoman without there. Come to my arms, thou venerable bawd, and let me squeeze thee [*embracing him eagerly*] as a new pair of stays does a fat country girl, when she's carried to court to stand for a maid of honour.

Heart. Why, what the devil's all this rapture for?

Con. Rapture! There's ground for rapture, man! There's hopes, my Heartfree—hopes, my friend.

Heart. Hopes! of what?

Con. Why, hopes that my lady and I together (for 'tis more than one body's work), should make Sir John a cuckold.

Heart. Pr'ythee, what did she say to thee?

Con. Say! What did she not say! She said that—says she —she said—Zoons! I don't know what she said; but she looked as if she said everything I'd have her: and so, if thou'lt go to the tavern, I'll treat thee with anything that gold can buy; I'll give all my silver among the drawers, make a bonfire before the doors; swear that the Pope's turned protestant, and that all the politicians in England are of one mind.   [*Exeunt.*

SCENE II.—*A Tavern*

LORD RAKE, Sir JOHN BRUTE, *etc., discovered at a table, drinking.*

All. Huzza!

Lord R. Come, boys, charge again: so—confusion to all order. Here's liberty of conscience.

All. Huzza!

Lord R. Come, sing the song I made this morning, to this purpose.

Sir J. 'Tis wicked, I hope.

Lord R. Don't I tell you that I made it?

Sir J. My lord, I beg your pardon for doubting your taste. Come, begin.

SONG.—Colonel BULLY.

We're gayly yet, we're gayly yet,
And we're not very fow, but we're gayly yet;
Then sit ye awhile, and tipple a bit,
For we's not very fow, but we're gayly yet,
    And we're gayly yet, etc.

There were three lads, and they were clad,
There were three lasses, and them they had.

> Three trees in the orchard are newly sprung,
> And we's a git geer enough, we're but young.
>   And we're gayly yet, etc.

Then up went Ailey, Ailey, up went Ailey now;
Then up with Ailey, quo' Crumma, we's get a roaring fow.
And one was kiss'd in the barn, another was kiss'd on the green,
And t'other behind the pease-stack, till the mow flew up to
    her eyn.
>   Then up went Ailey, Ailey, etc.

> Now, fie! John Thompson, run,
>   Gin ever you run in your life,
> De'il get ye! but, hie, my dear Jack,
>   There's a mon got to bed with your wife.
>   Then up went Ailey, etc.

> Then away John Thompson run,
>   And, egad! he run with speed,
> But before he had run his length
>   The false loon had done the deed.
>   Then up went Ailey, etc.

Lord R. Well, how do you like it, gentlemen?

All. Oh! admirable!

Sir J. I would not give a fig for a song that is not full of sin and impudence.

Lord R. Then my muse is to your taste. But drink away; the night steals upon us; we shall want time to be lewd in. Hey! sally out, sirrah, and see what's doing in the camp; we'll beat up the quarters presently.

Wait. I'll bring your lordship an exact account.   [*Exit.*

Lord R. Courage, knight! victory attends you!

Sir J. And laurels shall crown me. Drink away, and be d——d!

Lord R. Again, boys! t'other glass, and no morality.

Sir J. [*drunk*]. Ay, no morality—and d——n the watch! And let the constable be married.

All. Huzza!

Enter Waiter.

Lord R. How are the streets inhabited, sirrah?

Wait. My lord, it's Sunday night, they are full of drunken citizens.   [*Exit.*

Lord R. Along, then, boys, we shall have a feast.

Col. Along, noble knight!

Sir J. Ay, along, Bully! and he that says Sir John Brute is not as drunk, and as religious as the drunkenest citizen of them all, is a liar, and the son of a whore.

Col. Why, that **was** bravely spoken, and like a free-born
Englishman.

Sir J. What's that to you, sir, whether I am an Englishman or
a Frenchman?

Col. Zoons! you are not angry, sir?

Sir J. Zoons! I am angry, sir; for, if I am a free-born Englishman, what have you to do, even to talk of my privileges?

Lord R. Why, pr'ythee, knight, don't quarrel here; leave
private animosities to be decided by daylight; let the night be
employed against the public enemy.

Sir J. My lord, I respect you, because you are a man of quality.
But I'll make that fellow know I'm within a hair's-breadth as
absolute by my privileges, as the king of France is by his prerogative. He, by his prerogative, takes money where it is not
his due; I, by my privilege, refuse paying it where I owe it.
Liberty and property, and old England! Huzza!

All. Huzza!   [*Exit Sir JOHN, reeling, the rest following.*

ACT IV

SCENE I.—*Covent Garden*

Enter Lord RAKE *and* Colonel BULLY, *with their swords drawn.*

Lord R. Is the dog dead?

Col. No, d——n him! I heard him wheeze.

Lord R. How the witch his wife howled!

Col. Ay, she'll alarm the watch presently.

Lord R. Appear, knight, then; come, you have a good cause
to fight for; there's a man murdered.

Enter Sir JOHN BRUTE.

Sir J. Is there? then let his ghost be satisfied; for I'll sacrifice
a constable to it presently, and burn his body upon his wooden
chair.

Enter a Tailor, *with a bundle under his arm.*

Col. How now! What have we got here? a thief?

Tai. No, an't please you, I'm no thief.

Lord R. That we'll see presently. Here, let the general
examine him.

Sir J. Ay, ay; let me examine him, and I'll lay a hundred
pounds I find him guilty, in spite of his teeth; for he looks
like a sneaking rascal. Come, sirrah, without equivocation, or

mental reservation, tell me of what opinion you are, and what calling; for by them I shall guess at your morals.

Tai. An't please you, I'm a dissenting journeyman woman's tailor.

Sir J. Then, sirrah, you love lying by your religion, and theft by your trade: and so, that your punishments may be suitable to your crimes, I'll have you first gagged, and then hanged.

Tai. Pray, good worthy gentlemen, don't abuse me: indeed, I am an honest man, and a good workman, though I say it that should not say it.

Sir J. No words, sirrah, but attend your fate.

Lord R. Let me see what's in that bundle.

Tai. An't please you, it's my lady's morning dress and hat.

Sir J. What lady, you reptile, you?

Tai. My Lady Brute, an't please your honour.

Sir J. My Lady Brute! my wife! the robe of my wife! With reverence let me approach it. The dear angel is always taking care of me in danger, and has sent me this suit of armour to protect me in this day of battle: on they go.

All. Oh, brave knight!

Lord R. Live, Don Quixote the second!

Sir J. Sancho, my 'squire, help me on with my armour.

Tai. Oh! dear gentleman! I shall be quite undone if you take the sack.

Sir J. Retire, sirrah! and, since you carry off your skin, go home, and be happy. [*Exit* Tailor. *They dress* Sir J.] So! how do you like my shapes now?

Lord R. To a miracle! he looks like a queen of the Amazons. But to your arms, gentlemen! the enemy's upon their march; here's the watch.

Sir J. Oons! if it were Alexander the Great, at the head of his army, I would drive him into a horsepond.

All. Huzza! Oh, brave knight!

Enter Watchmen.

Sir J. See! here he comes, with all his Greeks about him: follow me, boys.

1 Watch. Heyday! Who have we got here? stand!

Sir J. Mayhap not.

1 Watch. What are you all doing here in the streets at this time of night? And who are you, madam, that seems to be at the head of this noble crew?

Sir J. Sirrah, I am Bonduca, queen of the Welshmen; and, with a leek as long as my pedigree, I will destroy your Roman legions in an instant. Britons, strike home!

[*Snatches a* Watchman's *staff, strikes at the* Watch, *drives them off, and returns in custody.*

1 Watch. So! we have got the queen, however. We'll make

her pay well for her ransom. Come, madam, will your majesty please to walk before the constable?

Sir J. The constable's a rascal, and you are a son of a whore!

1 Watch. A most noble reply, truly! If this be her royal style, I'll warrant her maids of honour prattle prettily: but we'll teach you some of our court dialect before we part with you, princess. Away with her to the round-house.

Sir J. Hands off, you ruffians! My honour's dearer to me than my life; I hope you won't be so uncivil.

1 Watch. Away with her.   [*Exeunt.*

SCENE II.—*A chamber*

Enter HEARTFREE.

Heart. What the plague ails me? Love! No, I thank you for that; my heart's rock still. Yet, 'tis Belinda that disturbs me, that's positive. Well, what of all that? Must I love her for being troublesome? At that rate, I might love all the women I meet, egad! But hold! though I don't love her for disturbing me, yet she may disturb me, because I love her. Ay, that may be, faith. I have dreamt of her, that's certain. Well, so I have of my mother; therefore, what's that to the purpose? Ay, but Belinda runs in my mind waking—and so does many a d——d thing, that I don't care a farthing for. Methinks, though, I would fain be talking to her, and yet I have no business. Well, am I the first man that has had a mind to do an impertinent thing?

Enter CONSTANT.

Con. How now, Heartfree! What makes you up and dressed so soon? I thought none but lovers quarrelled with their beds; I expected to have found you snoring, as I used to do.

Heart. Why, faith! friend, 'tis the care I have of your affairs that makes me so thoughtful; I have been studying all night how to bring your matter about with Belinda.

Con. With Belinda?

Heart. With my lady, I mean: and, faith! I have mighty hopes on't. Sure, you must be very well satisfied with her behaviour to you yesterday?

Con. So well, that nothing but a lover's fears can make me doubt of success. But what can this sudden change proceed from?

Heart. Why, you saw her husband beat her, did you not?

Con. That's true: a husband is scarce to be borne upon any terms, much less when he fights with his wife. Methinks she should e'en have cuckolded him upon the spot, to shew, that after the battle she was master of the field.

Heart. A council of war of women would infallibly have advised her to it. But, I confess, so agreeable a woman as Belinda deserves better usage.

Con. Belinda again!

Heart. My lady, I mean. What a plague makes me blunder so to-day? [*Aside.*] A plague of this treacherous tongue.

Con. Pr'ythee, look upon me seriously, Heartfree. Now answer me directly: is it my lady, or Belinda, employs your careful thoughts thus?

Heart. My lady, or Belinda!

Con. In love, by this light! in love!

Heart. In love!

Con. Nay, never deny it; for thou'lt do it so awkwardly, 'twill but make the jest sit heavier about thee. My dear friend, I give you much joy.

Heart. Why, pr'ythee, you won't persuade me to it, will you?

Con. That she's mistress of your tongue, that's plain; and I know you are so honest a fellow, your tongue and heart always go together. But how—but how the devil—psha! Ha, ha, ha!

Heart. Heyday! Why, sure, you don't believe it in earnest?

Con. Yes, I do, because I see you deny it in jest.

Heart. Nay, but, look you! Ned—a—deny in jest—a—gadzooks! you know, I say—a—when a man denies a thing in jest—a——

Con. Ha, ha, ha!

Heart. Nay, then we shall have it: what, because a man stumbles at a word? Did you never make a blunder?

Con. Yes, for I am in love; I own it.

Heart. Then so am I:—now laugh till thy soul's glutted with mirth. But, dear Constant, don't tell the town on't.

Con. Nay, then, 'twere almost a pity to laugh at thee, after so honest a confession.

Enter a Footman.

Foot. Sir, there's a porter without with a letter; he desires to give it into your own hands.

Con. Call him in.

Enter Porter.

What, Joe, is it thee?

Port. An't please you, sir, I was ordered to deliver this into your hands, by two well-shaped ladies, at the New Exchange. I was at your honour's lodgings, and your servants sent me hither.

Con. 'Tis well: are you to carry any answer?

Port. No, my noble master. They gave me my orders, and whip, they are gone.

Con. Very well: there. [*Gives him money.*

Port. Heaven bless your honour! [*Exit.*

Con. Now let's see what honest, trusty Joe has brought us.

[Reads.] "If you and your playfellow can spare time from your business and devotions, don't fail to be at Spring Garden about eight in the evening. You'll find nothing there but women, so you need bring no other arms than what you usually carry about you." So, playfellow, here's something to stay your stomach till your mistress's dish is ready for you.

Heart. Some of our old battered acquaintance. I won't go, not I.

Con. Nay, that you can't avoid: there's honour in the case; 'tis a challenge, and I want a second.

Heart. I doubt I shall be but a very useless one to you; for I'm so disheartened by this wound Belinda has given me, I do not think I shall have courage enough to draw my sword.

Con. Oh! if that be all, come along; I'll warrant you'll find sword enough for such enemies as we have to deal withal.

[*Exeunt.*

SCENE III.—*A Hall in the* Justice's *house*

Enter Constable *and* Watchmen *with* Sir JOHN BRUTE.

Con. Come, forsooth, come along, if you please. I once, in compassion, thought to have seen you safe home this morning; but you have been so rampant and abusive all night, I shall see what the justice of peace will say to you.

Sir J. And you shall see what I'll say to the justice of peace, sirrah.   [Watchman *knocks at the door.*

Enter Servant.

Con. Is Mr. Justice at home?

Serv. Yes.

Con. Pray acquaint his worship we have got an unruly woman here, and desire to know what he'll please to have done with her.

Serv. I'll acquaint my master.   [*Exit.*

Sir J. Hark you! constable, what cuckoldy justice is this?

Con. One that knows how to deal with such romps as you are, I'll warrant you.

Enter Justice.

Just. Well, Mr. Constable, what is the matter here?

Con. An't please your worship, this here comical sort of a gentlewoman has committed great outrages to-night. She has been frolicking with my Lord Rake and his gang; they attacked the watch, and I hear there has been a man killed. I believe 'tis they have done it.

Sir J. Sir, there may have been murder, for aught I know; and 'tis a great mercy there has not been a rape, too; that fellow would have ravished me.

1 Watch. Ravish, ravish! Oh, lud! oh, lud! oh, lud! Do I look like a ravisher?

Just. Why, truly, she does seem a little masculine about the mouth.

2 Watch. Yes, and about the hands, too, an't please your worship. I did but offer, in mere civility, to help her up the steps into our apartment, and with her gripen fists——

[Sir J. *knocks him down.*

Sir J. I felled him to the ground, like an ox.

Just. Out upon this boisterous woman! out upon her!

Sir J. Mr. Justice, he would have been uncivil; it was in defence of my honour, and I demand satisfaction.

2 Watch. I hope your worship will satisfy her honour in Bridewell! that fist of her's will make an admirable hemp-beater.

Sir J. I hope you will protect me against that libidinous rascal. I am a woman of quality, and virtue, too, for all I am in an undress this morning.

Just. Why, she really has the air of a sort of a woman a little somethingish out of the common. Madam, if you expect I should be favourable to you, I desire I may know who you are.

Sir J. Sir, I am anybody, at your service.

Just. I desire to know your name.

Sir J. Sir, my name's Mary.

Just. Ay, but your surname, madam.

Sir J. Sir, my surname's the very same with my husband's.

Just. A strange woman this! Who is your husband, pray?

Sir J. Sir John——

Just. Sir John who?

Sir J. Sir John Brute.

Just. Is it possible, madam, you can be my Lady Brute?

Sir J. That happy woman, sir, am I; only a little in my merriment to-night.

Just. I am concerned for Sir John.

Sir J. Truly, so am I.

Just. I have heard he is an honest gentleman.

Sir J. As ever drank.

Just. Good lack! Indeed, lady, I'm sorry he has such a wife.

Sir J. I am sorry he has any wife at all.

Just. And so, perhaps, may he. I doubt you have not given him a very good taste of matrimony.

Sir J. Taste, sir! I have scorned to stint him to a taste; I have given him a full meal of it.

Just. Indeed, I believe so. But, pray, fair lady, may he have given you any occasion for this extraordinary conduct? does he not use you well?

Sir J. A little upon the rough sometimes.

Just. Ay, any man may be out of humour now and then.

Sir J. Sir, I love peace and quiet; and when a woman don't find that at home, she's apt, sometimes, to comfort herself with a few innocent diversions abroad.

Just. A strange woman this! Does he spend a reasonable portion of his time at home, to the comfort of his wife and children?

Sir J. He never gave his wife cause to repine at his being abroad in his life.

Just. Pray, madam, how may he be in the grand matrimonial point. Is he true to your bed?

Sir J. Sir!

Just. Is he true to your bed?

Sir J. Chaste! Oons! this fellow asks so many impertinent questions! Egad! I believe it is the justice's wife in the justice's clothes.　　　　　　　　　　　　　　　　　　　　[*Aside.*

Just. 'Tis a great pity she should have been thus disposed of. Pray, madam (and then I have done), what may be your ladyship's common method of life? if I may presume so far.

Sir J. Why, sir, much that of a woman of quality.

Just. Pray, how may you generally pass your time, madam? Your morning, for example.

Sir J. Sir, like a woman of quality, I wake about two o'clock in the afternoon; I stretch, and make a sign for my chocolate; when I have drunk three cups, I slide down again upon my back, with my arms over my head, while my two maids put on my stockings; then, hanging upon their shoulders, I am trailed to my great chair, where I sit and yawn for my breakfast; if it don't come presently, I lie down upon my couch to say my prayers, while my maid reads me the play-bills.

Just. Very well, madam!

Sir J. When the tea is brought in, I drink twelve regular dishes, with eight slices of bread and butter; and, half-an-hour after, I send to the cook, to know, if the dinner is almost ready.

Just. So, madam!

Sir J. By that time my head is half-dressed, I hear my husband swearing himself into a state of perdition that the meat's all cold upon the table; to amend which, I come down in an hour more, and have it sent back to the kitchen, to be all dressed over again.

Just. Poor man!

Sir J. When I have dined, and my idle servants are presumptuously set down at their ease to do so too, I call for my coach, to go visit fifty dear friends, of whom I hope I never shall find one at home while I shall live.

Just. So! there's the morning and afternoon pretty well disposed of. Pray, how, madam, do you pass your evenings?

Sir J. Like a woman of spirit, sir; a great spirit. Give me a box and dice—seven's the main! Oons! sir, I set you a hundred pounds! Why, do you think women are married now-a-days to sit at home and mend napkins? Oh! the lord help your head!

Just. Mercy on us! Mr. Constable, what will this age come to?

Con. What will it come to, indeed, if such women as these are not set in the stocks!

Sir J. Mr. Justice!

Just. Madam!

Sir J. Sir, I have a little urgent business calls upon me; and, therefore, I desire the favour of you to bring matters to a conclusion.

Just. Madam, if I were sure that business were not to commit more disorders, I would release you.

Sir J. None—by my virtue.

Just. Then, Mr. Constable, you may discharge her.

Sir J. Sir, your very humble servant. Will you please to accept of a bottle?

Just. I thank you kindly, madam: but I never drink in a morning. Good b'ye, madam! good b'ye!

Sir J. Mr. Justice, will you be so kind and obliging as to grant me one favour?

Just. Ay: what is it?

Sir J. That your worship would be so very obliging as to let me have the honour of a chaste salute. Won't you?

Just. Good b'ye, madam!

Sir J. Good b'ye, good sir! [*Exit* Justice]. So now, Mr. Constable, shall you and I go pick up a whore together?

Con. No, thank you, madam: my wife's enough to satisfy any reasonable man.

Sir J. [*aside*]. He, he, he! The fool is married, then. Well, you won't go?

Con. Not I, truly!

Sir J. Then I'll go by myself; and you and your wife may go to the devil.   [*Exit.*

Con. [*gazing after him*]. Why, God-a-mercy, lady.   [*Exit.*

SCENE IV.—*Spring Garden*

CONSTANT *and* HEARTFREE *cross the stage. As they go off, enter* Lady FANCIFUL *and* MADEMOISELLE, *masked, and dogging them.*

Con. So! I think we are about the time appointed: let us walk up this way.   [*Exit with* HEARTFREE.

Lady F. Good! thus far I have dogged them without being discovered. 'Tis infallibly some intrigue that brings them to Spring Garden. How my poor heart is torn and racked with fear and jealousy! Let it be anything but that flirt Belinda, and I'll try to bear it. But, if it proves her, all that's woman in me shall be employed to destroy her.

          [*Exit after* CONSTANT *and* HEARTFREE.

Re-enter CONSTANT *and* HEARTFREE. LADY FANCIFUL *and*
MADEMOISELLE *still following at a distance.*

Con. I see no females yet, that have anything to say to us.
I'm afraid we are bantered.

Heart. I wish we were, for I'm in no humour to make either
them or myself merry.

Enter Lady BRUTE *and* BELINDA, *masked, and poorly dressed.*

Con. How now! Who are these? Not our game, I hope.

Heart. If they are, we are e'en well enough served, to come a
hunting here when we had so much better game in chase elsewhere.

Lady F. [*to* MADEMOISELLE]. So, those are their ladies, without doubt.   But I'm afraid that doily stuff is not worn for want
of better clothes.   They are the very shape and size of Belinda
and her aunt.

Madem. So dey be, inteed, matam.

Lady F. We'll slip into this close arbour, where we may hear
all they say.   [*Exit with* MADEM.

Lady B. What, are you afraid of us, gentlemen?

Heart. Why, truly, I think we may, if appearances don't lie.

Bel. Do you always find women what they appear to be, sir?

Heart. No, forsooth! but I seldom find them better than they
appear to be.

Bel. Then the outside's best, you think.

Heart. 'Tis the honestest.

Con. Have a care, Heartfree! you are relapsing again.

Lady B. Why, does the gentleman use to rail at women?

Con. He has done formerly.

Bel. I suppose he had very good call for't.   They did not use
you so well as you thought you deserved, sir?

Lady B. They made themselves merry at your expense, sir?

Bel. Laughed when you sighed?

Lady B. Slept while you were waking?

Bel. Had your porter beat?

Lady B. And threw your billet-doux in the fire?

Heart. Heyday! I shall do more than rail, presently.

Bel. Why, you won't beat us, will you?

Heart. I don't know but I may.

Con. What the devil's coming here? Sir John, and drunk,
i'faith!

Enter Sir JOHN BRUTE.

Sir J. What, a pox! here's Constant, Heartfree, and two
whores, egad! Oh! you covetous rogues! What have you
never a spare punk for your friend? But I'll share with you.
                                        [*Seizes both the women.*

Heart. Why, what the plague have you been doing, knight?

Sir J. Why, I have been beating the watch, and scandalising the women of quality.

Heart. A very good account, truly!

Sir J. And what do you think I'll do next?

Con. Nay, that no man can guess.

Sir J. Why, if you'll let me sup with you, I'll treat both your strumpets.

Lady B. [*aside*]. Oh, lord! we are undone.

Heart. No, we can't sup together, because we have some affairs elsewhere. But if you'll accept of these two ladies, we'll be so complaisant to you to resign our right in them.

Bel. [*aside*]. Lord! what shall we do?

Sir J. Let me see; their clothes are such d——d clothes, they won't pawn for the reckoning.

Heart. Sir John, your servant. Raptures attend you.

Con. Adieu, ladies; make much of the gentleman.

Lady B. Why, sure, you won't leave us in the hands of a drunken fellow, to abuse us?

Sir J. Who do you call a drunken fellow, you slut you! I'm a man of quality: the king has made me a knight.

Heart. Ay, ay, you are in good hands; adieu, adieu! [*Runs off.*

Lady B. The devil's hands! let me go, or I'll—for heaven's sake protect us!

　　　[*Breaks from* Sir J. *runs to* CONSTANT, *twitching off her mask, and clapping it on again.*

Sir J. I'll devil you, you jade, you! I'll demolish your ugly face.

Re-enter HEARTFREE, BELINDA *runs to him, and shews her face.*

Heart. Hold, thou mighty man! Lookye! sir, we did but jest with you. These are ladies of our acquaintance, that we had a mind to frighten a little; but now you must leave us.

Sir J. Oons! I won't leave you, not I.

Heart. Nay, but you must, though; and, therefore, make no words on't.

Sir J. Then you are a couple of d——d uncivil fellows; and I hope your punks will give you sauce to your mutton. [*Exit.*

Lady B. Oh! I shall never come to myself again, I'm so frightened!

Con. 'Tis a narrow escape, indeed.

Bel. Women must have frolics, you see, whatever they cost them.

Heart. This might have proved a dear one, though.

Lady B. You are the more obliged to us for the risk we run upon your accounts.

Con. And I hope you'll acknowledge something due to our knight errantry, ladies. This is the second time we have delivered you.

Lady B. 'Tis true: and since we see fate has destined you for our guardians, 'twill make us the more willing to trust ourselves in your hands. But you must not have the worse opinion of us for our innocent frolic.

Heart. Ladies, you may command our opinion in everything that is to your advantage.

Bel. Then, sir, I command you to be of opinion, that women are sometimes better than they appear to be.

[Lady B. *and* CONSTANT *talk apart.*

Heart. Madam, you have made a convert of me in everything. I'm grown a fool. I could be fond of a woman.

Bel. I thank you, sir, in the name of the whole sex.

Heart. Which sex nothing but yourself could ever have atoned for.

Bel. Now has my vanity a devilish itch to know in what my merit consists.

Heart. In your humility, madam, that keeps you ignorant it consists at all.

Bel. One other compliment, with that serious face, and I hate you for ever after.

Heart. Some women love to be abused; is that it you would be at?

Bel. No, not that neither; but I'd have men talk plainly what's fit for women to hear, without putting them to a real or an affected blush.

Heart. Why, then, in as plain terms as I can find to express myself, I could love you even to matrimony itself—almost, egad!

Bel. Just as Sir John did her ladyship there——

Heart. Dear creature! do but try me.

Bel. That's the surest way, indeed, to know; but not the safest.—[*To* Lady B.]. Madam, are you not for taking a turn in the great walk? It's almost dark; nobody will know us.

Lady B. Really, I find myself something idle, Belinda: besides, I dote upon this little, odd, private corner. But don't let my lazy fancy confine you.

Con. [*aside*]. So, she would be left alone with me! that's well.

Bel. Well, we'll take one turn, and come to you again.—[*To* HEARTFREE]. Come, sir, shall we go pry into the secrets of the garden? Who knows what discoveries we may make?

Heart. Madam, I am at your service.

Con. [*aside to* HEARTFREE]. Don't make too much haste back; for, d'ye hear?—I may be busy.

Heart. Enough! [*Exit* BEL. *with* HEARTFREE.

Lady B. Sure, you think me scandalously free, Mr. Constant; I'm afraid I shall lose your good opinion of me.

Con. My good opinion, madam, is like your cruelty—never to be removed.

Lady B. Indeed I doubt you much. Why, suppose you had a wife, and she should entertain a gallant?

Con. If I gave her just cause, how should I justly condemn her?

Lady B. Ah! but you differ widely about just causes.

Con. But blows can bear no dispute.

Lady B. Nor ill manners much, truly.

Con. Then no woman on earth has so just a cause as you have. But, for heaven's sake! (for now I must be serious), if pity, or if gratitude can move you;—[*taking her hand*] if constancy and truth have power to tempt you; if love, if adoration, can affect you, give me at least some hopes, that time may do, what you, perhaps, mean never to perform: 'twill ease my sufferings, though not quench my flame.

Lady B. Your sufferings eased, your flame would soon abate; and that I would preserve, not quench it, sir.

Con. Would you preserve it, nourish it with favours; for that's the food it naturally requires.

Lady B. Yet on that natural food 'twould surfeit soon, should I resolve to grant all you would ask.

Con. And in refusing all, you starve it. Forgive me, therefore (since my hunger rages), if I at last grow wild; and, in my phrenzy, force at least this from you. [*Kissing her hand*]. Or if you'd have my flame soar higher still, then grant me this, and this, and thousands more. [*Kissing first her hand and then her neck.—Aside.*] For now's the time she melts into compassion.

Lady B. Oh, heavens! let me go.

Con. Ay, go, ay! where shall we go, my charming angel—into this private arbour? Nay, let's lose no time—moments are precious——

Lady B. And lovers wild. Pray, let us stop here; at least for this time.

Con. 'Tis impossible! he that has power over you, can have none over himself.

[*As he is forcing her into the arbour,* Lady FANCIFUL *and* MADEMOISELLE *rush out upon them, and run across the stage.*

Lady B. Ah! I'm lost!

Lady F., Madam. Fe, fe, fe!   [*Exeunt.*

Con. Death and furies! who are those?

Lady B. Oh, heavens! I'm out of my wits. If they know me, I'm ruined.

Con. Don't be frightened; ten thousand to one they are strangers to you.

Lady B. Whatever they are, I won't stay here a moment longer.

Con. Whither will you go?

Lady B. Home, as if the devil were in me! Lord! where's this Belinda now?

Enter BELINDA *and* HEARTFREE.

Oh! 'tis well you are come; I'm so frightened! Let's begone, for heaven's sake!

Bel. Lord! what's the matter?

Lady B. The devil's the matter! Here's a couple of women have done the most impertinent thing—away, away, away!

[*Exeunt.*

SCENE V.—Lady FANCIFUL'S *House*

Enter Lady FANCIFUL *and* MADEMOISELLE.

Lady F. Well, mademoiselle, did you dodge the filthy things?
Madem. O qu'oui, madame.
Lady F. And where are they?
Madem. Au logis.
Lady F. What, men and all?
Madem. Tous ensemble.
Lady F. Oh, confidence! What, carry their fellows to their own house?
Madem. C'est que le mari n'y est pas.
Lady F. No, so I believe, truly. But he shall be there, and quickly, too, if I can find him out. Well, 'tis a prodigious thing to see, when men and women get together, how they fortify one another in their impudence. But if that drunken fool, her husband, be to be found in e'er a tavern in town, I'll send him amongst them: I'll spoil their sport.
Madem. En verité, madame, ce seroit domage.
Lady F. 'Tis in vain to oppose it, mademoiselle; therefore, never go about it: for I am the steadiest creature in the world—when I am determined to do mischief. So, come along. [*Exeunt.*

SCENE VI.—Sir JOHN BRUTE'S *House*

Enter CONSTANT, HEARTFREE, Lady BRUTE, BELINDA, *and* LOVEWELL.

Lady B. But are you sure you don't mistake, Lovewell?
Lov. Madam, I saw them all go into the tavern together; and my master so drunk, he could scarce stand.
Lady B. Then, gentlemen, I believe we may venture to let you stay, and play at cards with us an hour or two; for they'll scarce part till morning.
Bel. I think it's a pity they should ever part——
Con. The company that's here, madam.
Lady B. Then, sir, the company that's here must remember to part itself in time.
Con. Madam, we don't intend to forfeit your future favours, by an indiscreet usage of this. The moment you give us the signal, we shan't fail to make our retreat.
Lady B. Upon those conditions, then, let us sit down to cards.

Enter LOVEWELL.

Lov. Oh, lord! madam, here's my master just staggering in upon you: he has been quarrelsome yonder, and they have kicked him out of the company.   [*Exit.*

Lady B. Into the closet, gentlemen, for heaven's sake!

[CONSTANT *and* HEARTFREE *run into the closet.*

Enter Sir JOHN BRUTE, *covered with dirt and blood.*

Lady B. Ah! ah! he's all over blood!

Sir J. What the plague does the woman squall for? Did you never see a man in a pickle before?

Lady B. Lord! where have you been?

Sir J. I have been at—cuffs.

Lady B. I fear that is not all. I hope you are not wounded?

Sir J. Sound as a roach, wife.

Lady B. I'm mighty glad to hear it.

Sir J. You know—I think you lie.

Lady B. 'Tis a hard fate, I should not be believed.

Sir J. 'Tis a d——d atheistical age, wife.

Lady B. I am sure I have given you a thousand tender proofs how great my care is of you. But, spite of all your cruel thoughts, I still persist; and, at this moment, if I can, persuade you to lie down and sleep a little.

Sir J. Why, do you think I am drunk, you slut you?

Lady B. Heaven forbid I should! But I'm afraid you are feverish. Pray, let me feel your pulse.

Sir J. Stand off, and be d——d.

Lady B. Why, I see your distemper in your eyes: you are all on fire. Pray, go to bed; let me entreat you.

Sir J. Come, kiss me, then.

Lady B. [*kissing him*]. There! now go.—[*Aside.*] He stinks like poison.

Sir J. I see it goes d——y against your stomach; and, there-fore,—kiss me again.

Lady B. Nay, now you fool me.

Sir J. Do it, I say.

Lady B. [*aside*]. Ah! lord have mercy upon me! Well—there! Now will you go?

Sir J. Now, wife, you shall see my gratitude: you gave me two kisses; I'll give you—two hundred. [*Kisses and tumbles her.*

Lady B. Oh, lord! pray, Sir John, be quiet! Heavens! what a pickle I am in.

Sir J. So, now, you being as dirty and as nasty as myself, we may go pig together. But, first, I must have a cup of your cold tea, wife.   [*Going to the closet.*

Lady B. [*aside*]. Oh! I am ruined! There's none there, my dear.

Sir J. I'll warrant you I'll find some, my dear.

Lady B. You can't open the door; the lock's spoiled: I have been turning and turning the key this half-hour, to no purpose. I'll send for the smith to-morrow.

Sir J. There's ne'er a smith in Europe can open a door with more expedition than I can do. As for example:—[*He bursts open the door.*] How now! What the devil have we got here? Constant, Heartfree,—and two w— again, egad! This is the worst cold tea that ever I met with in my life! " I have been turning and turning——"

Enter CONSTANT and HEARTFREE *from the closet.*

Lady B. [*aside*]. Oh, lord; what will become of us!

Sir J. Gentlemen, I am your very humble servant. I give you many thanks. I see you take care of my family: I shall do all I can to return the obligation.

Con. Sir, how oddly soever this business may appear to you, you'd have no cause to be uneasy, if you knew the truth of all things. Your lady is the most virtuous woman in the world, and nothing has passed but an innocent frolic.

Heart. Nothing else, upon my honour, sir.

Sir J. You are both very civil gentlemen; and my wife there, is a very civil gentlewoman; therefore, I don't doubt but many civil things have passed between you. Your very humble servant.

Lady B. [*aside to* CONSTANT]. Pray, begone; he's so drunk, he can't hurt us to-night, and to-morrow morning you shall hear from us.

Con. I'll obey you, madam. Sir, when you are cool, you'll understand reason better: so, then, I shall take the pains to inform you; if not, I wear a sword, sir, and so good b'ye. Come along, Heartfree.   [*Exeunt.*

Sir J. Wear a sword, sir! And what, then, sir? He comes to my house, eats my meat, lies with my wife, dishonours my family, gets a bastard to inherit my estate; and when I ask a civil account of all this.—" Sir," says he, " I wear a sword." Wear a sword, sir?—" Yes, sir," says he, " I wear a sword." It may be a good answer at cross purposes; but 'tis a d——d one to a man in my whimsical circumstances. " Sir," says he, " I wear a sword." [*To* Lady B.] And what do you wear now? Eh! tell me. [*Sitting down.*] What, you are modest, and can't! why, then, I'll tell you, you slut, you: — you wear an impudent, lewd face; a d——d designing heart; and a tail—and a tail full of——   [*Falls fast asleep.*

Lady B. So, thanks to kind heaven, he's fast for some hours!

Bel. 'Tis well he is so, that we may have time to lay our story handsomely; for we must lie like the devil to bring ourselves off.

Lady B. What shall we say, Belinda?

Bel. [*musing*]. I'll tell you; it must all light upon Heartfree and me.

Lady B. I'm beholden to you, cousin; but that would be carrying the jest a little too far. But it's late: let's, out of an excess of charity, take a small care of that nasty drunken thing there. Do but look at him, Belinda.

Bel. Ah! it's a savoury dish.

Lady B. As savoury as it is, I'm cloyed with it. Pr'ythee, call the butler to take away.

Bel. Call the butler! Call the scavenger. [*To a* Servant *within.*] Who's there? Call Razor; let him take away his master; scour him clean, with a little soap and sand, and so put him to bed.

Lady B. Come, Belinda, I'll e'en lie with you to-night, and, in the morning, we'll send for our gentlemen, to set this matter even.

Bel. With all my heart.

Lady B. Good night, my dear.

[*Making a low courtesy to* Sir JOHN.

Both. Ha, ha, ha! [*Exeunt.*

Enter RAZOR.

Razor. My lady, there, is a wag; my master, there, is a cuckold. Marriage is a slippery thing! Women have depraved appetites— My lady's a wag. I have heard all; I have seen all; I understand all; and I'll tell all: for my little Frenchwoman loves news dearly. This story will gain her heart, or nothing will.—[*To* Sir J.] Come, sir, your head's too full of fumes at present, to make room for your jealousy; but I reckon we shall have rare work with you, when your pate's empty. Come to your kennel, you cuckoldy, drunken sot, you! [*Takes him on his back.*

My master's asleep in his chair, and a snoring,
My lady's abroad, and—*Oh! rare matrimony.* [*Exit.*

ACT V

SCENE I.—Lady FANCIFUL'S *House*

Enter Lady FANCIFUL *and* MADEMOISELLE.

Lady F. But why did you not tell me before mademoiselle, that Razor and you were fond?

Madem. De modesty hinder me, matam.

Lady F. Why, truly, modesty does often hinder us from doing things we have an extravagant mind to. But does he love you well enough yet, to do anything you bid him? Do you think, to oblige you, he would speak scandal?

Madem. Matam, to oblige your ladyship, he shall speak anything.

Lady F. Why, then, mademoiselle, I'll tell you what you shall do: you shall engage him to tell his master all that passed at Spring Gardens. I have a mind he shall know what a wife and a niece he has got.

Madem. Il le fera, madame.

Enter CORNET, *who speaks apart to* MADEMOISELLE.

Corn. Mademoiselle, yonder's Mr. Razor desires to speak with you.

Madem. Tell him I come presently. [*Exit* CORNET.] Razor be dere, madame.

Lady F. That's fortunate! Well, I'll leave you together; and, if you find him stubborn, mademoiselle—harkye!—don't refuse him a few reasonable little liberties, to put him in humour.

Madem. Laissez moi faire.　　　　　　　　　[*Exit* Lady F.

RAZOR *peeps in; and, seeing* Lady FANCIFUL *gone, turns to* MADEMOISELLE, *and kisses her.*

Madem. How now, confidence!

Razor. How now, modesty!

Madem. Who makes you so familiar, sirrah?

Razor. My impudence, hussy.

Madem. Stand off, rogue-face!

Razor. Ah! mademoiselle, great news at our house.

Madem. Why, vat be de matter?

Razor. The matter! why, uptails all's the matter.

Madem. Tu te mocque de moi.

Razor. Now do you long to know the particulars—the time when—the place where—the manner how—but I won't tell you a word more.

Madem. Nay, den dou kill me Razor.

Razor. Come, kiss me, then.　　　　[*Putting his hands behind.*

Madem. Nay, pridee, tell me.

Razor. Good b'ye.　　　　　　　　　　　　　[*Going.*

Madem. Hold, hold! I will kiss dee.　　　[*Kissing him.*

Razor. So, that's civil! Why, now, my pretty Poll, my gold-finch, my little water-wagtail, you must know that—Come, kiss me again.

Madem. I won't kiss de no more.

Razor. Good b'ye.

Madem. Doucement! dere! es tu content?　　[*Kissing him.*

Razor. So, now I'll tell thee all. Why, the news is, that cuckoldom in folio is newly printed, and matrimony in quarto is just going into the press. Will you buy any books, mademoiselle.

Madem. Tu parle comme un libraire; de devil, no understand dee!

Razor. Why, then, that I may make myself intelligible to a waiting-woman, I'll speak like a valet-de-chambre: my lady has cuckolded my master.

Madem. Bon.

Razor. Which we take very ill from her hands, I can tell her that. We can't yet prove matter of fact upon her.

Madem. N'importe.

Razor. But we can prove, that matter of fact had like to have been upon her.

Madem. Ouy-da.

Razor. For we have such terrible circumstances—

Madem. Sans doute.

Razor. That any man of parts may draw tickling conclusions from them.

Madem. Fort bien.

Razor. We found a couple of tight, well-built gentlemen stuffed into her ladyship's closet.

Madem. Le diable!

Razor. And I, in my particular person, have discovered a most d——e plot, how to persuade my poor master, that all this hide and seek, this will-in-the-wisp, has no other meaning than a Christian marriage for sweet Mrs. Belinda.

Madem. Un mariage? Ah, les droles!

Razor. Don't you interrupt me, hussy!—'Tis agreed, I say; and my innocent lady, to wriggle herself out at the back door of the business, turns marriage bawd to her niece, and resolves to deliver up her fair body to be tumbled and mumbled by that young liquorish whipster, Heartfree. Now are you satisfied?

Madem. No.

Razor. Right woman! always gaping for more.

Madem. Dis be all den, dat you know?

Razor. All! ay, and a great deal too, I think.

Madem. Dou be fool, dou know noteing. Ecoute, mon pauvre Razor! Dou see des two eyes? Des two eyes have see de devil.

Razor. The woman's mad!

Madem. In Spring Garden, dat rogue Constant meet dy lady.

Razor. Bon.

Madem. I'll tell dee no more.

Razor. Nay, pr'ythee, my swan!

Madem. Come, kiss me, den.

> [*Clapping her hands behind her, as he did before.*

Razor. I won't kiss you, not I.

Madem. Adieu! [*Going.*

Razor. Hold! [*Gives her a hearty kiss.*] Now proceed.

Madem. A çà—I hide myself in one cunning place, where I hear all and see all. First, dy drunken master come mal-à-propos; but de sot no know his own dear wife, so he leave her to her sport: den de game begin. De lover say soft ting; de lady look upon de ground. [*As she speaks,* RAZOR *still acts the man, and she the woman.*] He takes her by de hand; she turn her head on oder way. Den he squeeze very hard; den she pull—very softly. Den he take her in his arms; den she give him little pat.

Den he tremble; den she sigh. Den he pull her into the arbour; den she pinch him.—

Razor. Ay, but not so hard, you baggage, you.

Madem. Den he grow bold; she grow weak. He tro her down, il tombe dessu, le diable assist, il emport tout—[RAZOR *struggles with her, as if he would throw her down.*]—Stand off, sirrah!

Razor. You have set me afire, you jade, you!

Madem. Den go to de river and quench dyself.

Razor. What an unnatural harlot this is!

Madem. Razor!   [*Looking languishingly on him.*

Razor. Mademoiselle!

Madem. Dou no love me?

Razor. Not love thee! More than a Frenchman does soup.

Madem. Den you will refuse nothing dat I bid dee?

Razor. Don't bid me hang myself, then.

Madem. No; only tell dy master all I have tell dee of dy lady.

Razor. Why, you little malicious strumpet, you! should you like to be served so?

Madem. Dou dispute, den?—Adieu!

Razor. Hold!—But why wilt thou make be such a rogue, my dear?

Madem. Voilà un vrai Anglois! il est amoureux, et cependant il veut raisonner. Va t'en au diable!

Razor. Hold, once more; in hopes thou'lt give me up thy body, I'll make a present of my honesty.

Madem. Bon ècoute donc; if dou fail me, I never see dee more. If dou obey me, je m'abandonne à toi à toi.

                          [*She kisses him, and exit.*

Razor [*licking his lips*]. Not be a rogue!—*Amor vincit omnia.*

                                          [*Exit.*

Enter Lady FANCIFUL *and* MADEMOISELLE.

Lady F. Marry, say ye? Will the two things marry?

Madem. On le va faire, madame.

Lady F. Look you, mademoiselle—in short, I can't bear it— no, I find I can't. Therefore, run and call Razor back immediately; for something must be done to stop this impertinent wedding. If I can but defer it four and twenty hours, I'll make such work about town, with that little pert slut's reputation, he shall as soon marry a witch.

Madem. [*aside*]. La voilà bien intentionée.   [*Exeunt.*

SCENE II.—CONSTANT'S *Lodgings*

Enter CONSTANT *and* HEARTFREE.

Con. But what dost think will become of this business?

Heart. 'Tis easier to think what will not become on't.

Con. What's that?

Heart. A challenge. I know the knight too well for that; his dear body will always prevail upon his noble soul to be quiet.

Con. But though he dare not challenge me, perhaps he may venture to challenge his wife.

Heart. Not if you whisper him in the ear, you won't have him do't; and there's no other way left that I see. For, as drunk as he was, he'll remember you and I were where we should not be; and I don't think him quite blockhead enough yet, to be persuaded we were got into his wife's closet only to peep into her prayer-book.

Enter a Servant, *with a letter.*

Serv. Sir, here's a letter: a porter brought it.

Con. Oh, ho! here's instructions for us. [*Reads*] "The accident that has happened has touched our invention to the quick. We would fain come off without your help, but find that's impossible. In a word, the whole business must be thrown upon a matrimonial intrigue between your friend and mine; but if the parties are not fond enough to go quite through with the matter, 'tis sufficient for our turn, they own the design. We'll find pretences enough to break the match. Adieu!"—Well, women for invention! How long would my block head have been producing this, eh! Heartfree? What, musing, man? Pr'ythee, be cheerful. What sayest thou, friend, to this matrimonial remedy?

Heart. Why, I say, it's worse than the disease.

Con. Here's a fellow for you! There's beauty and money on her side, and love up to the ears on his; and yet——

Heart. And yet, I think, I may reasonably be allowed to boggle at marrying the niece, in the very moment that you are deluding the aunt.

Con. Why, truly, there may be something in that. But have not you a good opinion enough of your own parts, to believe you could keep a wife to yourself?

Heart. I should have, if I had a good opinion enough of hers, to believe she could do as much by me. But, pr'ythee, advise me in this good and evil, this life and death, this blessing and curse, that is set before me. Shall I marry, or die a maid?

Con. Why 'faith, Heartfree, matrimony is like an army going to engage: love's the forlorn hope, which is soon cut off; the marriage knot is the main body, which may stand buff a long time; and repentance is the rear guard, which rarely gives ground as long as the main body has a being.

Heart. Conclusion, then; you advise me to rake on as you do.

Con. That's not concluded yet; for, though marriage be a lottery, in which there are wondrous many blanks, yet there is one inestimable lot in which the only heaven on earth is written. Would your kind fate but guide your hand to that, though I were wrapped in all that luxury itself could clothe me with, I should envy you.

Heart. And justly, too; for to be capable of loving one, doubtless, is better than to possess a thousand; but how far that capacity's in me, alas! I know not.

Con. But you would know?

Heart. I would so.

Con. Matrimony will inform you. Come, one flight of resolution carries you to the land of experience; where, in a very moderate time, you'll know the capacity of your soul and your body both, or I'm mistaken. [*Exeunt.*

SCENE III.—Sir John Brute's

Enter Lady Brute *and* Belinda.

Bel. Well, madam, what answer have you from them?

Lady B. That they'll be here this moment. I fancy 'twill end in a wedding: I'm sure he's a fool if it don't. Ten thousand pounds, and such a lass as you are, is no contemptible offer to a younger brother.

Enter Constant *and* Heartfree.

Good morrow, gentlemen; how have you slept after your adventure?

Heart. Some careful thoughts, ladies, on your accounts, have kept us waking.

Bel. And some careful thoughts on your own, I believe, have hindered you from sleeping. Pray how does this matrimonial project relish with you?

Heart. Why, 'faith, e'en as storming towns does with soldiers, where the hopes of delicious plunder banishes the fear of being knocked on the head.

Bel. Is it, then, possible, after all, that you dare think of downright lawful wedlock?

Heart. Madam, you have made me so foolhardy, I dare do anything.

Bel. Then, sir, I challenge you, and matrimony's the spot where I expect you.

Heart. 'Tis enough; I'll not fail. [*Aside.*] So, now I am in for Hobbes's voyage; a great leap in the dark.

Lady B. Well, gentlemen, this matter being concluded, then, have you got your lessons ready? for Sir John is grown such an atheist of late, he'll believe nothing upon easy terms.

Con. We'll find means to extend his faith, madam. But, pray, how do you find him this morning?

Lady B. Most lamentably morose; chewing the cud after last night's discovery; of which, however, he has but a confused notion, even now. But I'm afraid the valet de chambre has told him all; for they are very busy together at this moment. When I told him of Belinda's marriage, I had no other answer but a grunt; from which you may draw what conclusion you think fit.—But to your notes, gentlemen; he's here.

Enter Sir JOHN BRUTE *and* RAZOR.

Con. Good morrow, sir.

Heart. Good morrow, Sir John; I'm very sorry my indiscretion should cause so much disorder in your family.

Sir J. Disorders generally come from indiscretion, sir; 'tis no strange thing at all.

Lady B. I hope, my dear, you are satisfied there was no wrong intended you.

Sir J. None, my dove.

Bel. If not, I hope my consent to marry Mr. Heartfree will convince you; for, as little as I know of amours, sir, I can assure you, one intrigue is enough to bring four people together, without further mischief.

Sir J. And I know, too, that intrigues tend to procreation of more kinds than one. One intrigue will beget another, as soon as beget a son or a daughter.

Con. I am very sorry, sir, to see you still seem unsatisfied with a lady, whose more than common virtue, I am sure, were she my wife, should meet a better usage.

Sir J. Sir, if her conduct has put a trick upon her virtue, her virtue's the bubble, but her husband's the loser.

Con. Sir, you have received a sufficient answer already, to justify both her conduct and mine. You'll pardon me for meddling in your family affairs; but I perceive I am the man you are jealous of, and therefore it concerns me.

Sir J. Would it did not concern me, and then I should not care who it concerned.

Con. Well, sir, if truth and reason won't content you, I know but one way more, which, if you think fit, you may take.

Sir J. Lord, sir, you are very hasty: if I had been found at prayers in your wife's closet, I should have allowed you twice as much time to come to yourself in.

Con. Nay, sir, if time be all you want, we have no quarrel

Heart. I told you how the sword would work upon him.

[*Sir John muses.*

Con. Let him muse; however, I'll lay fifty pounds our foreman brings us in not guilty.

Sir J. [*aside*]. 'Tis very well—'tis very well. In spite of that young jade's matrimonial intrigue, I am a downright stinking cuckold. Here they are. Boo—[*Putting his hand to his forehead.*] Methinks, I could butt with a bull. What the plague did I marry for? I know she did not like me; but that's past. And now what shall I do with her? If I put my horns into my pocket, she'll grow insolent—if I don't, that goat there, that

stallion, is ready to whip me through the guts.   The debate then
is reduced to this; shall I die a hero, or live a rascal?   Why,
wiser men than I have long since concluded, that a living dog is
better than a dead lion. [*To* CONSTANT *and* HEARTFREE.] Gentlemen, now my wine and my passion are governable, I must own,
I have never observed anything in my wife's course of life, to
back me in my jealousy of her: but jealousy's a mark of love;
so she need not trouble her head about it, as long as I make no
more words on't.

Enter Lady FANCIFUL *disguised, and addresses* BELINDA *apart.*

Con. I'm glad to see your reason rule at last.   Give me your
hand: I hope you'll look upon me as you used to do.
Sir J. Your humble servant. [*Aside.*] A wheedling son of a
whore?
Heart. And that I may be sure you are friends with me, too,
pray give me your consent to wed your niece.
Sir J. Sir, you have it with all my heart; d——n me if you
haven't. [*Aside.*] 'Tis time to get rid of her; a young pert pimp;
she'll make an incomparable bawd in a little time.

Enter a servant who gives HEARTFREE *a letter.*

Bel. Heartfree your husband, say you?   'Tis impossible!
Lady F. Would to kind heaven it were! but 'tis too true; and
in the world there lives not such a wretch.   I'm young; and
either I have been flattered by my friends, as well as my glass,
or nature has been kind and generous to me.   I had a fortune too
was greater far than he could ever hope for; but with my heart I
am robbed of all the rest.   I am slighted and I'm beggared both
at once; I have scarcely a bare subsistence from the villain, yet
dare complain to none; for he has sworn, if ever 'tis known I am
his wife, he'll murder me.   [*Weeping.*
Bel. The traitor!
Lady F. I accidentally was told he courted you; charity soon
prevailed upon me to prevent your misery; and, as you see, I'm
still so generous even to him, as not to suffer he should do anything, for which the law might take away his life.   [*Weeping.*
Bel. Poor creature!   How I pity her!
                                        [*They continue talking aside.*
Heart. [*aside*]. Death and the devil!—Let me read it again.
[*Reads.*] "Though I have a particular reason not to let you know
who I am till I see you, yet you'll easily believe 'tis a faithful
friend that gives you this advice.   [Good !] I have a child by
Belinda—[Better and better]—which is now out at nurse—[Heaven
be praised !]—and I think the foundation laid for another—[Ha !
old true-penny !]—no rack could have tortured this story from
me; but friendship has done it.   I heard of your design to marry
her, and could not see you abused.   Make use of my advice, but
keep my secret till I ask you for it again."   [*Exit* Lady FANCIFUL.

Con. [*to* BELINDA]. Come, madam, shall we send for the parson? I doubt here's no business for the lawyers; younger brothers have nothing to settle but their hearts, and that I believe my friend here has already done very faithfully.

Bel. [*scornfully*]. Are you sure, sir, there are no old mortgages upon it?

Heart. [*coldly*]. If you think there are, madam, it mayn't be amiss to defer the mortgage till you are sure they are paid off.

Bel. We'll defer it as long as you please, sir.

Heart. The more time we take to consider on't, madam, the less apt we shall be to commit oversight: therefore, if you please, we will put it off for just nine months.

Bel. Guilty consciences make men cowards.

Heart. And they make women desperate.

Bel. I don't wonder you want time to resolve.

Heart. I don't wonder you are so quickly determined.

Bel. What does the fellow mean?

Heart. What does the lady mean?

Sir J. Zoons! what do you both mean?

[HEARTFREE *and* BELINDA *walk about.*

Razor. [*aside*]. Here is so much sport going to be spoiled, it makes me ready to weep again. A pox o' this impertinent Fanciful, and her plots, and her Frenchwoman too; I hear them tittering without still. Ecod, I'll e'en go lug them both by the ears, and discover the plot, to secure my pardon.   [*Exit.*

Con. Pr'ythee, explain, Heartfree.

Heart. A fair deliverance; thank my stars and my friend!

Bel. 'Tis well it went no farther; a base fellow!

Lady B. What can be the meaning of all this?

Bel. What's his meaning, I don't know; but mine is, that if I had married him, I had had no husband.

Heart. And what's her meaning, I don't know; but mine is, that if I had married her, I had had wife enough.

Sir J. Your people of wit have got such cramp ways of expressing themselves, they seldom comprehend one another. Pox take you both, will you speak in the language of common sense, that you may be understood?

Enter RAZOR, *pulling in* Lady FANCIFUL *and* MADEMOISELLE.

Razor. If they won't, here comes an interpreter.

Lady B. Heavens! What have we here?

Razor. A villain—but a repenting villain.

Lady B. What means this?

Razor. Nothing without my pardon.

Lady B. What pardon do you want?

Razor. Imprimis, your ladyship's, for a d——e lie made upon your spotless virtue, and set to the tune of Spring Garden. [*To* Sir JOHN.] Next at my generous master's feet I bend, for interrupting his more noble thoughts with phantoms of disgrace.

ful cuckoldom. [*To* CONSTANT.] Thirdly, I to this gentleman
apply, for making him the hero of my romance. [*To* HEARTFREE.]
Fourthly, your pardon, noble sir, I ask, for clandestinely marrying you, without either bidding of bans, bishop's license, friends'
consent, or your own knowledge. [*To* BELINDA.] And lastly, to
my good young lady's clemency I come, for pretending the corn
was sowed in the ground, before ever the plough had been in the
field.

Sir J. [*aside*]. So that, after all, 'tis a moot point whether I
am a cuckold or not.

Bel. Well, sir, upon condition you confess all, I'll pardon you
myself, and try to obtain as much from the rest of the company.
But I must know then who 'tis has put you upon all this mischief.

Razor. Satan and his equipage; woman tempted me, vice
weakened me—and so the devil overcame me: as fell Adam, so
fell I.

Bel. Then pray, Mr. Adam, will you make us acquainted with
your Eve?

Razor [*to* MADEMOISELLE]. Unmask, for the honour of France.

All. Mademoiselle!

Madem. Me ask ten thousand pardon of all de good company.

Sir J. Why, this mystery thickens instead of clearing up.
[*To* RAZOR.] You son of a whore you, put us out of our pain.

Razor. One moment brings sunshine. [*Shewing* MADEMOISELLE.]
'Tis true, this is the woman that tempted me, but this is the
serpent that tempted the woman; and if my prayers might be
heard, her punishment for so doing should be like the serpents
of old—[*Pulls off* Lady FANCIFUL'S *mask*] she should lie upon
her face all the days of her life.

All. Lady Fanciful!

Bel. Impertinent!

Lady B. Ridiculous!

All. Ha, ha, ha!

Bel. I hope your ladyship will give me leave to wish you joy,
since you have owned your marriage yourself. [*To* HEARTFREE.]
I vow 'twas strangely wicked in you to think of another wife,
when you have one already so charming as her ladyship.

All. Ha, ha, ha!

Lady F. [*aside*]. Confusion seize them, as it seizes me. Your
mirth's as nauseous as yourself. Belinda, you think you triumph
over a rival now; helas! ma pauvre fille. Where'er I'm a rival,
there's no cause for mirth. No, my poor wretch, 'tis from
another principle I have acted. I knew that thing there would
make so perverse a husband, and you so impertinent a wife, that,
lest your mutual plagues should make you run both mad, I
charitably would have broken the match. He, he, he!

[Exit, laughing affectedly.

Madem. He, he, he!   *[Exit, following her.*

All. Ha, ha, ha!

Sir J. [*aside*]. Why now, this woman will be married to somebody, too.

Bel. Poor creature! what a passion she is in! but I forgive her.

Heart. Since you have so much goodness for her, I hope you'll
pardon my offence too, madam?

Bel. There will be no great difficulty in that, since I am guilty
of an equal fault.

Heart. Then let's to church;
And if it be our chance to disagree—

Bel. Take heed! the surly husband's fate you see.

Sir J. Surly I may be, stubborn I am not.
For I have both forgiven and forgot;
If so, be these our judges, Mrs. Pert,
If they approve,
'Tis more their goodness, than our desert.   [*Exeunt.*

THE MAN OF MODE

OR, SIR FOPLING FLUTTER

A COMEDY

DRAMATIS PERSONÆ

Mr. DORIMANT,
Mr. MEDLEY,
OLD BELLAIR, } Gentlemen.
YOUNG BELLAIR,
Sir FOPLING FLUTTER.

LADY TOWNLEY,
EMILIA,
Mrs. LOVEIT, } Gentlewomen.
BELINDA,
LADY WOODVIL,
HARRIET, her daughter.

PERT and BUSY, waiting-women.
A Shoemaker.
An Orange-Woman.
Three Slovenly Bullies.
Two Chairmen.
Mr. SMIRK, a parson.
HANDY, a valet-de-chambre.
Pages, Footmen, etc.

SCENE—LONDON.

THE DUCHESS

MADAM, Poets, however they may be modest otherwise, have always too good an opinion of what they write. The world, when it sees this play dedicated to your Royal Highness, will conclude I have more than my share of that vanity. But I hope the honour I have of belonging to you will excuse my presumption. 'Tis the first thing I have produced in your service, and my duty obliges me to what my choice durst not else have aspired.

I am very sensible, madam, how much it is beholding to your indulgence for the success it had in the acting, and your protection will be no less fortunate to it in the printing; for all are so ambitious of making their court to you, that none can be severe to what you are pleased to favour.

This universal submission and respect is due to the greatness of your rank and birth; but you have other illustrious qualities which are much more engaging. Those would but dazzle, did not these really charm the eyes and understandings of all who have the happiness to approach you.

Authors, on these occasions, are never wanting to publish a particular of their patron's virtues and perfections; but your Royal Highness's are so eminently known, that, did I follow their examples, I should but paint those wonders here of which every one already has the idea in his mind. Besides, I do not think it proper to aim at that in prose which is so glorious a subject for verse; in which hereafter if I show more zeal than skill, it will not grieve me much, since I less passionately desire to be esteemed a poet than to be thought,

Madam,
Your Royal Highness's
most humble, most obedient,
and most faithful servant,

GEORGE ETHEREGE.

PROLOGUE

BY SIR CAR SCROOPE, BARONET

LIKE dancers on the ropes poor poets fare,
Most perish young, the rest in danger are;
This, one would think, should make our authors wary,
But, gamester like, the giddy fools miscarry.
A lucky hand or two so tempts 'em on,
They cannot leave off play till they 're undone.
With modest fears a muse does first begin,
Like a young wench newly enticed to sin;
But tickled once with praise, by her good will,
The wanton fool would never more lie still.
'Tis an old mistress you 'll meet here to-night,
Whose charms you once have look'd on with delight;
But now of late such dirty drabs have known ye,
A muse o'th' better sort's ashamed to own ye.
Nature well drawn, and wit, must now give place
To gaudy nonsense and to dull grimace:
Nor is it strange that you should like so much
That kind of wit, for most of yours is such.
But I 'm afraid that while to France we go,
To bring you home fine dresses, dance, and show,
The stage, like you, will but more foppish grow.
Of foreign wares why should we fetch the scum
When we can be so richly served at home?
For, heaven be thank'd, 'tis not so wise an age
But your own follies may supply the stage.
Though often plough'd, there 's no great fear the soil
Should barren grow by the too frequent toil,
While at your doors are to be daily found
Such loads of dunghill to manure the ground.
'Tis by your follies that we players thrive,
As the physicians by diseases live;
And as each year some new distemper reigns,
Whose friendly poison helps t'increase their gains,
So among you there starts up every day
Some new unheard-of fool for us to play.
Then for your own sakes be not too severe,
Nor what you all admire at home, damn here:
Since each is fond of his own ugly face,
Why should you, when we hold it, break the glass?

THE MAN OF MODE

OR, SIR FOPLING FLUTTER

ACT I

SCENE I.—*A Dressing-room. A table covered with a toilet; clothes laid ready*

Enter DORIMANT *in his gown and slippers, with a note in his hand made up, repeating verses.*

Dor. Now for some ages had the pride of Spain
　　Made the sun shine on half the world in vain.

　　　　　　　　　　　　[*Then looking on the note.*

[*For* Mrs. LOVEIT.] What a dull insipid thing is a *billet-doux* written in cold blood, after the heat of the business is over ! It is a tax upon good-nature which I have here been labouring to pay, and have done it, but with as much regret as ever fanatic paid the Royal Aid or Church Duties. 'Twill have the same fate, I know, that all my notes to her have had of late, 'twill not be thought kind enough. Faith, women are i' the right when they jealously examine our letters, for in them we always first discover our decay of passion.——Hey! Who waits?

Enter HANDY

Handy. Sir——

Dor. Call a footman.

Handy. None of 'em are come yet.

Dor. Dogs! Will they ever lie snoring a-bed till noon?

Handy. 'Tis all one, sir: if they're up, you indulge 'em so they're ever poaching after whores all the morning.

Dor. Take notice henceforward, who's wanting in his duty, the next clap he gets, he shall rot for an example. What vermin are those chattering without?

Handy. Foggy Nan the orange-woman and swearing Tom the shoemaker.

Dor. Go; call in that overgrown jade with the flasket of guts before her; fruit is refreshing in a morning. [*Exit* HANDY.

　　　　It is not that I love you less
　　　　Than when before your feet I lay.

437

Enter ORANGE-WOMAN *with* HANDY.

How now, Double Tripe! what news do you bring?

Or.-Wom. News! Here's the best fruit has come to town t'year; gad, I was up before four o'clock this morning, and bought all the choice i' the market.

Dor. The nasty refuse of your shop.

Or-Wom. You need not make mouths at it; I assure you 'tis all culled ware.

Dor. The citizens buy better on a holiday in their walk to Totnam.[1]

Or.-Wom. Good or bad, tis all one; I never knew you commend anything. Lord! would the ladies had heard you talk of 'em as I have done. Here, bid your man give me an angel.

                                        [*Sets down the fruit.*

Dor. Give the bawd her fruit again.

Or.-Wom. Well, on my conscience, there never was the like of you. God's my life, I had almost forgot to tell you there is a young gentlewoman lately come to town with her mother, that is so taken with you.

Dor. Is she handsome?

Or.-Wom. Nay, gad, there are few finer women, I tell you but so, and a hugeous fortune, they say. Here, eat this peach, it comes from the stone; 'tis better than any Newington y' have tasted.

Dor. This fine woman, I'll lay my life,

                                        [*Taking the peach.*

is some awkward, ill-fashioned, country toad, who, not having above four dozen of black hairs on her head, has adorned her baldness with a large white fruz, that she may look sparkishly in the forefront of the King's box at an old play.

Or.-Wom. Gad, you'd change your note quickly if you did but see her.

Dor. How came she to know me?

Or.-Wom. She saw you yesterday at the Change; she told me you came and fooled with the woman at the next shop.

Dor. I remember there was a mask observed me indeed. Fooled, did she say?

Or.-Wom. Ay, I vow she told me twenty things you said too; and acted with her head and with her body so you——

---

[1] Cf. *The Virtuoso* (v.): "The suburb fools trudge to Lamb's Conduit or Totnam." Later on the walk became more modish:

> When the sweet breathing spring unfolds the buds
>
> .   .   .   .   .   .
>
> Then Totenham fields with roving beauty swarms.
>
>   GAY, *Epistle to Pulteney.*

Enter MEDLEY.

Med. Dorimant, my life, my joy, my darling sin, how dost thou?

Or.-Wom. Lord! what a filthy trick these men have got of kissing one another!   [*She spits.*

Med. Why do you suffer this cartload of scandal to come near you and make your neighbours think you so improvident to need a bawd?

Or.-Wom. Good, now we shall have it! you did but want him to help you; come, pay me for my fruit.

Med. Make us thankful for it, huswife; bawds are as much out of fashion as gentlemen-ushers: none but old formal ladies use the one, and none but foppish old strangers employ the other —go, you are an insignificant brandy bottle.

Dor. Nay, there you wrong her, three quarts of canary is her business.

Or.-Wom. What you please, gentlemen.

Dor. To him! give him as good as he brings.

Or.-Wom. Hang him, there is not such another heathen in the town again, except it be the shoemaker without.

Med. I shall see you hold up your hand at the bar next sessions for murder, huswife; that shoemaker can take his oath you are in fee with the doctors to sell green fruit to the gentry, that the crudities may breed diseases.

Or.-Wom. Pray give me my money.

Dor. Not a penny; when you bring the gentlewoman hither you spoke of, you shall be paid.

Or.-Wom. The gentlewoman! the gentlewoman may be as honest as your sister, for aught as I know. Pray pay me, Mr. Dorimant, and do not abuse me so; I have an honester way of living, you know it.

Med. Was there ever such a restiff bawd?

Dor. Some jade's tricks she has, but she makes amends when she's in good-humour. Come, tell me the lady's name, and Handy shall pay you.

Or.-Wom. I must not, she forbid me.

Dor. That's a sure sign she would have you.

Med. Where does she live?

Or.-Wom. They lodge at my house.

Med. Nay, then she's in a hopeful way.

Or.-Wom. Good Mr. Medley, say your pleasure of me, but take heed how you affront my house. God's my life, in a hopeful way!

Dor. Prithee, peace! what kind of woman's the mother?

Or.-Wom. A goodly grave gentlewoman. Lord! how she talks against the wild young men o' the town! As for your part, she thinks you an arrant devil; should she see you, on my conscience she would look if you had not a cloven foot.

Dor. Does she know me?

Or.-Wom. Only by hearsay; a thousand horrid stories have been told her of you, and she believes 'em all.

Med. By the character, this should be the famous Lady Woodvil and her daughter Harriet.

Or.-Wom. The devil's in him for guessing, I think.

Dor. Do you know 'em?

Med. Both very well; the mother's a great admirer of the forms and civility of the last age.

Dor. An antiquated beauty may be allowed to be out of humour at the freedoms of the present. This is a good account of the mother; pray, what is the daughter?

Med. Why, first she's an heiress, vastly rich.

Dor. And handsome?

Med. What alteration a twelvemonth may have bred in her I know not, but a year ago she was the beautifullest creature I ever saw; a fine, easy, clean shape; light brown hair in abundance; her features regular; her complexion clear and lively; large wanton eyes; but above all, a mouth that has made me kiss it a thousand times in imagination, teeth white and even, and pretty pouting lips, with a little moisture ever hanging on them, that look like the Provence rose fresh on the bush, ere the morning sun has quite drawn up the dew.

Dor. Rapture, mere rapture!

Or.-Wom. Nay, gad, he tells you true; she's a delicate creature.

Dor. Has she wit?

Med. More than is usual in her sex, and as much malice. Then she's as wild as you would wish her, and has a demureness in her looks that makes it so surprising.

Dor. Flesh and blood cannot hear this, and not long to know her.

Med. I wonder what makes her mother bring her up to town; an old doting keeper cannot be more jealous of his mistress.

Or.-Wom. She made me laugh yesterday; there was a judge came to visit 'em, and the old man, she told me, did so stare upon her, and when he saluted her smacked so heartily; who would think it of 'em?

Med. God a mercy, a judge! [1]

Dor. Do 'em right, the gentlemen of the long robe have not been wanting by their good examples to countenance the crying sin o' the nation.

Med. Come, on with your trappings; 'tis later than you imagine.

Dor. Call in the shoemaker, Handy.

Or.-Wom. Good Mr. Dorimant, pay me; gad, I had rather give you my fruit than stay to be abused by that foul-mouthed rogue; what you gentlemen say, it matters not much, but such a dirty fellow does one more disgrace.

[1] The first edition (1676) has "God-a-mercy, Judge": the correction seems to be necessary.

Dor. Give her ten shillings, and be sure you tell the young gentlewoman I must be acquainted with her.

Or.-Wom. Now do you long to be tempting this pretty creature. Well, heavens mend you!

Med. Farewell.   [*Exeunt* ORANGE-WOMAN *and* HANDY.
Dorimant, when did you see your *pis-aller*, as you call her Mrs. Loveit?

Dor. Not these two days.

Med. And how stand affairs between you?

Dor. There has been great patching of late, much ado; we make a shift to hang together.

Med. I wonder how her mighty spirit bears it.

Dor. Ill enough, on all conscience; I never knew so violent a creature.

Med. She's the most passionate in her love, and the most extravagant in her jealousy, of any woman I ever heard of. What note is that?

Dor. An excuse I am going to send her for the neglect I am guilty of.

Med. Prithee read it.

Dor. No; but if you will take the pains you may.

Med. [*reads*]. "I never was a lover of business, but now I have a just reason to hate it, since it has kept me these two days from seeing you. I intend to wait upon you in the afternoon, and in the pleasure of your conversation forget all I have suffered during this tedious absence." This business of yours, Dorimant, has been with a vizard at the playhouse; I have had an eye on you. If some malicious body should betray you, this kind note would hardly make your peace with her.

Dor. I desire no better.

Med. Why, would her knowledge of it oblige you?

Dor. Most infinitely; next to the coming to a good understanding with a new mistress, I love a quarrel with an old one; but the devil's in't, there has been such a calm in my affairs of late, I have not had the pleasure of making a woman so much as break her fan, to be sullen, or forswear herself these three days.

Med. A very great misfortune. Let me see, I love mischief well enough to forward this business myself; I'll about it presently and though I know the truth of what you've done will set her a-raving, I'll heighten it a little with invention, leave her in a fit o' the mother, and be here again before you're ready.

Dor. Pray stay; you may spare yourself the labour; the business is undertaken already by one who will manage it with as much address, and I think with a little more malice than you can.

Med. Who i' the devil's name can this be?

Dor. Why the vizard—that very vizard you saw me with.

Med. Does she love mischief so well as to betray herself to spite another?

Dor. Not so neither, Medley. I will make you comprehend the mystery: this mask, for a farther confirmation of what I have been these two days swearing to her, made me yesterday at the playhouse make her a promise before her face utterly to break off with Loveit; and because she tenders my reputation, and would not have me do a barbarous thing, has contrived a way to give me a handsome occasion.

Med. Very good.

Dor. She intends, about an hour before me, this afternoon to make Loveit a visit, and (having the privilege, by reason of a professed friendship between 'em) to talk of her concerns.

Med. Is she a friend?

Dor. Oh, an intimate friend!

Med. Better and better; pray proceed.

Dor. She means insensibly to insinuate a discourse of me, and artificially raise her jealousy to such a height, that transported with the first motions of her passion, she shall fly upon me with all the fury imaginable as soon as ever I enter; the quarrel being thus happily begun, I am to play my part, confess and justify all my roguery, swear her impertinence and ill-humour makes her intolerable, tax her with the next fop that comes into my head, and in a huff march away; slight her, and leave her to be taken by whosoever thinks it worth his time to lie down before her.

Med. This vizard is a spark, and has a genius that makes her worthy of yourself, Dorimant.

Enter HANDY, *Shoemaker, and Footman.*

Dor. You rogue there, who sneak like a dog that has flung down a dish, if you do not mend your waiting I'll uncase you, and turn you loose to the wheel of fortune. Handy, seal this, and let him run with it presently. [*Exeunt* HANDY [1] *and Footman.*

Med. Since you're resolved on a quarrel, why do you send her this kind note?

Dor. To keep her at home in order to the business. [*To the Shoemaker.*] How now, you drunken sot?

Shoem. 'Zbud, you have no reason to talk; I have not had a bottle of sack of yours in my belly this fortnight.

Med. The orange-woman says your neighbours take notice what a heathen you are, and design to inform the bishop and have you burned for an atheist.

Shoem. Damn her, dunghill! if her husband does not remove her, she stinks so the parish intend to indict him for a nuisance.

Med. I advise you like a friend, reform your life; you have brought the envy of the world upon you by living above yourself. Whoring and swearing are vices too genteel for a shoemaker.

Shoem. 'Zbud, I think you men of quality will grow as un-

---

[1] Who presently returns, though the entry is not marked.

reasonable as the women; you would engross the sins o' the nation; poor folks can no sooner be wicked, but they're railed at by their betters.

Dor. Sirrah, I'll have you stand i' the pillory for this libel.

Shoem. Some of you deserve it, I'm sure; there are so many of 'em, that our journeymen nowadays, instead of harmless ballads, sing nothing but your damned lampoons.

Dor. Our lampoons, you rogue?

Shoem. Nay, good master, why should not you write your own commentaries as well as Cæsar?

Med. The rascal's read, I perceive.

Shoem. You know the old proverb—ale and history.

Dor. Draw on my shoes, sirrah.

Shoem. Here's a shoe—

Dor. Sits with more wrinkles than there are in an angry bully's forehead.

Shoem. 'Zbud, as smooth as your mistress's skin does upon her; so strike your foot in home. 'Zbud, if e'er a *monsieur* of 'em all make more fashionable wear, I'll be content to have my ears whipped off with my own paring-knife.

Med. And served up in a *ragoût* instead of coxcombs to a company of French shoemakers for a collation.

Shoem. Hold, hold! damn 'em, caterpillars! let 'em feed upon cabbage. Come, master, your health this morning next my heart now.

Dor. Go, get you home, and govern your family better; do not let your wife follow you to the alehouse, beat your whore, and lead you home in triumph.

Shoem. 'Zbud, there's never a man i' the town lives more like a gentleman with his wife than I do. I never mind her motions, she never inquires into mine; we speak to one another civilly, hate one another heartily, and because 'tis vulgar to lie and soak together, we have each of us our several settle-bed.

Dor. Give him half-a-crown.

Med. Not without he will promise to be bloody drunk.

Shoem. Tope's the word i' the eye of the world, for my master's honour, Robin.

Dor. Do not debauch my servants, sirrah.

Shoem. I only tip him the wink; he knows an alehouse from a hovel.   [*Exit Shoemaker.*

Dor. My clothes, quickly.

Med. Where shall we dine to-day?

Enter BELLAIR.

Dor. Where you will; here comes a good third man.

Bell. Your servant, gentlemen.

Med. Gentle sir, how will you answer this visit to your honourable mistress? 'Tis not her interest you should keep company with men of sense, who will be talking reason.

Bell. I do not fear her pardon, do you but grant me yours for my neglect of late.

Med. Though you've made us miserable by the want of your good company, to show you I am free from all resentment, may the beautiful cause of our misfortune give you all the joys happy lovers have shared ever since the world began.

Bell. You wish me in heaven, but you believe me on my journey to hell.

Med. You have a good strong faith, and that may contribute much towards your salvation. I confess I am but of an untoward constitution, apt to have doubts and scruples, and in love they are no less distracting than in religion; were I so near marriage, I should cry out by fits as I ride in my coach, *Cuckold, Cuckold,* with no less fury than the mad fanatic does *Glory* in Bedlam.

Bell. Because religion makes some run mad, must I live an atheist?

Med. Is it not great indiscretion for a man of credit, who may have money enough on his word, to go and deal with Jews who for little sums make men enter into bonds and give judgments?

Bell. Preach no more on this text, I am determined, and there is no hope of my conversion.

Dor. [*to* HANDY, *who is fiddling about him*]. Leave your unnecessary fiddling; a wasp that's buzzing about a man's nose at dinner is not more troublesome than thou art.

Handy. You love to have your clothes hang just, sir.

Dor. I love to be well dressed, sir; and think it no scandal to my understanding.

Handy. Will you use the essence, or orange-flower water?

Dor. I will smell as I do to-day, no offence to the ladies' noses.

Handy. Your pleasure, sir.

Dor. That a man's excellency should lie in neatly tying of a ribbon or a cravat! How careful's nature in furnishing the world with necessary coxcombs?

Bell. That's a mighty pretty suit of yours, Dorimant.

Dor. I am glad't has your approbation.

Bell. No man in town has a better fancy in his clothes than you have.

Dor. You will make me have an opinion of my genius.

Med. There is a great critic, I hear, in these matters lately arrived piping hot from Paris.

Bell. Sir Fopling Flutter. you mean.

Med. The same.

Bell. He thinks himself the pattern of modern gallantry.

Dor. He is indeed the pattern of modern foppery.

Med. He was yesterday at the play, with a pair of gloves up to his elbows and a periwig more exactly curled than a lady's head newly dressed for a ball.

Bell. What a pretty lisp he has!

Dor. Ho! that he affects in imitation of the people of quality in France.

Med. His head stands for the most part on one side, and his looks are more languishing than a lady's when she lolls at stretch in her coach or leans her head carelessly against the side of a box i' the playhouse.

Dor. He is a person indeed of great acquired follies.

Med. He is like many others, beholding to his education for making him so eminent a coxcomb; many a fool had been lost to the world had their indulgent parents wisely bestowed neither learning nor good breeding on 'em.

Bell. He has been, as the sparkish word is, brisk upon the ladies already; he was yesterday at my Aunt Townley's, and gave Mrs. Loveit a catalogue of his good qualities under the character of a complete gentleman, who, according to Sir Fopling, ought to dress well, dance well, fence well, have a genius for love-letters, an agreeable voice for a chamber, be very amorous, something discreet, but not over-constant.

Med. Pretty ingredients to make an accomplished person.

Dor. I am glad he pitched upon Loveit.

Bell. How so?

Dor. I wanted a fop to lay to her charge, and this is as pat as may be.

Bell. I am confident she loves no man but you.

Dor. The good fortune were enough to make me vain, but that I am in my nature modest.

Bell. Hark you, Dorimant; with your leave, Mr. Medley, 'tis only a secret concerning a fair lady.

Med. Your good breeding, sir, gives you too much trouble; you might have whispered without all this ceremony.

Bell. [*to* DORIMANT]. How stand your affairs with Belinda of late?

Dor. She's a little jilting baggage.

Bell. Nay, I believe her false enough, but she's ne'er the worse for your purpose; she was with you yesterday in a disguise at the play.

Dor. There we fell out, and resolved never to speak to one another more.

Bell. The occasion?

Dor. Want of courage to meet me at the place appointed. These young women apprehend loving as much as the young men do fighting at first; but once entered, like them too, they all turn bullies straight.

Enter HANDY [1]

Handy [*to* BELLAIR]. Sir, your man without desires to speak with you.

Bell. Gentlemen, I'll return immediately. [*Exit* BELLAIR.

[1] Whose previous exit had not been noticed.

Med. A very pretty fellow this.

Dor. He's handsome, well-bred, and by much the most tolerable of all the young men that do not abound in wit.

Med. Ever well-dressed, always complaisant, and seldom impertinent; you and he are grown very intimate, I see.

Dor. It is our mutual interest to be so: it makes the women think the better of his understanding and judge more favourably of my reputation; it makes him pass upon some for a man of very good sense and I upon others for a very civil person.

Med. What was that whisper?

Dor. A thing which he would fain have known, but I did not think it fit to tell him; it might have frighted him from his honourable intentions of marrying.

Med. Emilia, give her her due, has the best reputation of any young woman about the town who has beauty enough to provoke detraction; her carriage is unaffected, her discourse modest, not at all censorious nor pretending, like the counterfeits of the age.

Dor. She's a discreet maid, and I believe nothing can corrupt her but a husband.

Med. A husband?

Dor. Yes, a husband; I have known many women make a difficulty of losing a maidenhead who have afterwards made none of a cuckold.

Med. This prudent consideration, I am apt to think, has made you confirm poor Bellair in the desperate resolution he has taken.

Dor. Indeed, the little hope I found there was of her, in the state she was in, has made him by my advice contribute something towards the changing of her condition.

Enter BELLAIR.

Dear Bellair, by heavens I thought we had lost thee; men in love are never to be reckoned on when we would form a company.

Bell. Dorimant I am undone; my man has brought the most surprising news i' the world.

Dor. Some strange misfortune is befallen your love.

Bell. My father came to town last night, and lodges i' the very house where Emilia lies.

Med. Does he know it is with her you are in love?

Bell. He knows I love, but knows not whom, without some officious sot has betrayed me.

Dor. Your Aunt Townley is your confidante and favours the business.

Bell. I do not apprehend any ill office from her; I have received a letter, in which I am commanded by my father to meet him at my aunt's this afternoon; he tells me farther he has made a match for me, and bids me resolve to be obedient to his will or expect to be disinherited.

Med. Now's your time, Bellair; never had lover such an opportunity of giving a generous proof of his passion.

Bell. As how, I pray?

Med. Why, hang an estate, marry Emilia out of hand, and provoke your father to do what he threatens; 'tis but despising a coach, humbling yourself to a pair of goloshes, being out of countenance when you meet your friends, pointed at and pitied wherever you go by all the amorous fops that know you, and your fame will be immortal.

Bell. I could find in my heart to resolve not to marry at all.

Dor. Fie, fie! that would spoil a good jest and disappoint the well-natured town of an occasion of laughing at you.

Bell. The storm I have so long expected hangs o'er my head and begins to pour down upon me; I am on the rack, and can have no rest till I'm satisfied in what I fear; where do you dine?

Dor. At Long's or Locket's.[1]

Med. At Long's let it be.

Bell. I'll run and see Emilia, and inform myself how matters stand; if my misfortunes are not so great as to make me unfit for company, I'll be with you. [*Exit* BELLAIR

Enter a Footman with a letter.

Foot. [*to* DORIMANT]. Here's a letter, sir.

Dor. The superscription's right: *For Mr. Dorimant.*

Med. Let's see: the very scrawl and spelling of a true-bred whore.

Dor. I know the hand; the style is admirable, I assure you.

Med. Prithee read it.

Dor. [*reads*]. "I told a you you dud not love me, if you dud, you would have seen me again e'er now; I have no mony, and am very mallicolly; pray send me a guynie to see the operies. Your servant to command, Molly."

Med. Pray let the whore have a favourable answer, that she may spark it in a box and do honour to her profession.

Dor. She shall, and perk up i' the face of quality. Is the coach at door?

Handy. You did not bid me send for it.

Dor. Eternal blockhead! [HANDY *offers to go out.*] Hey, sot.

Handy. Did you call me, sir?

Dor. I hope you have no just exception to the name, sir?

Handy. I have sense, sir.

Dor. Not so much as a fly in winter.——How did you come, Medley?

Med. In a chair.

---

[1] Famous ordinaries; the former in the Haymarket, the latter near Charing Cross. "I'll marry a drawer," says Lady Wishfort in *The Way of the World*, iii, 1, "to have him poisoned in his wine. I'll send for Robin from Locket's immediately." Compare, too, *Love for Love*, iii, 3.

Footman. You may have a hackney coach if you please, sir.

Dor. I may ride the elephant if I please, sir; call another chair, and let my coach follow to Long's.

[*Exeunt singing, Be calm, ye great parents, etc.*

ACT II

SCENE I

Enter my Lady TOWNLEY *and* EMILIA.

Lady Town. I was afraid, Emilia, all had been discovered.

Emil. I tremble with the apprehension still.

Lady Town. That my brother should take lodgings i' the very house where you lie!

Emil. 'Twas lucky we had timely notice to warn the people to be secret; he seems to be a mighty good-humoured old man.

Lady Town. He ever had a notable smirking way with him.

Emil. He calls me rogue, tells me he can't abide me, and does so bepat me.

Lady Town. On my word you are much in his favour then.

Emil. He has been very inquisitive, I am told, about my family, my reputation, and my fortune.

Lady Town. I am confident he does not i' the least suspect you are the woman his son's in love with.

Emil. What should make him then inform himself so particularly of me?

Lady Town. He was always of a very loving temper himself; it may be he has a doting fit upon him; who knows?

Emil. It cannot be.

Enter YOUNG BELLAIR.

Lady Town. Here comes my nephew. Where did you leave your father?

Y. Bell. Writing a note within. Emilia, this early visit looks as if some kind jealousy would not let you rest at home.

Emil. The knowledge I have of my rival gives me a little cause to fear your constancy.

Y. Bell. My constancy! I vow——

Emil. Do not vow——Our love is frail as is our life, and full as little in our power; and are you sure you shall outlive this day?

Y. Bell. I am not; but when we are in perfect health 'twere an idle thing to fright ourselves with the thoughts of sudden death

Lady Town. Pray what has passed between you and your father i' the garden?

Y. Bell. He's firm in his resolution, tells me I must marry Mrs. Harriet, or swears he'll marry himself and disinherit me; when I saw I could not prevail with him to be more indulgent, I dissembled an obedience to his will which has composed his passion, and will give us time, and I hope opportunity, to deceive him.

Enter OLD BELLAIR *with a note in his hand.*

Lady Town. Peace, here he comes.

O. Bell. Harry, take this, and let your man carry it for me to Mr. Fourbes's chamber, my lawyer, i' the Temple.

　　　　　　　　　　　　　Exit YOUNG BELLAIR.

[*To* EMILIA.] Neighbour, adod, I am glad to see thee here; make much of her, sister, she's one of the best of your acquaintance; I like her countenance and her behaviour well, she has a modesty that is not common i' this age, adod, she has.

Lady Town. I know her value, brother, and esteem her accordingly.

O. Bell. Advise her to wear a little more mirth in her face, adod, she's too serious.

Lady Town. The fault is very excusable in a young woman.

O. Bell. Nay, adod, I like her ne'er the worse, a melancholy beauty has her charms; I love a pretty sadness in a face which varies now and then, like changeable colours, into a smile.

Lady Town. Methinks you speak very feelingly, brother.

O. Bell. I am but five-and-fifty, sister, you know, an age not altogether insensible! [*To* EMILIA.] Cheer up, sweetheart, I have a secret to tell thee may chance to make thee merry; we three will make collation together anon; i' the meantime mum, I can't abide you; go, I can't abide you.

Enter YOUNG BELLAIR.

Harry, come, you must along with me to my Lady Woodvil's. I am going to slip the boy at a mistress.

Y. Bell. At a wife, sir, you would say.

O. Bell. You need not look so grum, sir; a wife is no curse when she brings the blessing of a good estate with her; but an idle town flirt, with a painted face, a rotten reputation, and a crazy fortune, adod, is the devil and all; and such a one I hear you are in league with.

Y. Bell. I cannot help detraction, sir.

O. Bell. Out, a pise o' their breeches, there are keeping fools enough for such flaunting baggages, and they are e'en too good for 'em. [*To* EMILIA.] Remember night, go, you're a rogue, you're a rogue; **fare you** well, fare you well; come, come, come along, sir.　　　　　　　　[*Exeunt* OLD *and* YOUNG BELLAIR.

Lady Town. On my word the old man comes on apace; I'll lay my life he's smitten.

Emil. This is nothing but the pleasantness of his humour.

Lady Town. I know him better than you; let it work, it may prove lucky.

Enter a Page.

Page. Madam, Mr. Medley has sent to know whether a visit will not be troublesome this afternoon?

Lady Town. Send him word his visits never are so.

[*Exit Page.*

Emil. He's a very pleasant man.

Lady Town. He's a very necessary man among us women; he's not scandalous i' the least, perpetually contriving to bring good company together, and always ready to stop up a gap at ombre; then he knows all the little news o' the town.

Emil. I love to hear him talk o' the intrigues; let 'em be never so dull in themselves, he'll make 'em pleasant i' the relation.

Lady Town. But he improves things so much one can take no measure of the truth from him. Mr. Dorimant swears a flea or a maggot is not made more monstrous by a magnifying glass than a story is by his telling it.

Emil. Hold, here he comes.

Enter MEDLEY.

Lady Town. Mr. Medley.

Med. Your servant, madam.

Lady Town. You have made yourself a stranger of late.

Emil. I believe you took a surfeit of ombre last time you were here.

Med. Indeed I had my bellyful of that termagant lady-dealer; there never was so insatiable a carder, an old gleeker never loved to sit to't like her; I have played with her now at least a dozen times till she's worn out all her fine complexion, and her tour [1] would keep in curl no longer.

Lady Town. Blame her not, poor woman; she loves nothing so well as a black ace.

Med. The pleasure I have seen her in when she has had hope in drawing for a matadore! [2]

Emil. 'Tis as pretty sport to her as persuading masks off is to you to make discoveries.

Lady Town. Pray, where's your friend Mr. Dorimant?

Med. Soliciting his affairs; he's a man of great employment, has more mistresses now depending than the most eminent lawyer in England has causes.

Emil. Here has been Mrs. Loveit, so uneasy and out of humour these two days.

---

[1] Headdress.   [2] A game at cards.

Lady Town. How strangely love and jealousy rage in that poor woman!

Med. She could not have picked out a devil upon earth so proper to torment her; he has made her break a dozen or two of fans already, tear half a score points in pieces, and destroy hoods and knots without number.

Lady Town. We heard of a pleasant serenade he gave her t'other night.

Med. A Danish serenade, with kettledrums and trumpets.

Emil. Oh, barbarous!

Med. What, you are of the number of the ladies whose ears are grown so delicate since our operas,[1] you can be charmed with nothing but *flutes douces* [2] and French hautboys.

Emil. Leave your raillery, and tell us is there any new wit come forth, songs or novels?

Med. A very pretty piece of gallantry by an eminent author called *The Diversions of Brussels* [3]; very necessary to be read by all old ladies who are desirous to improve themselves at questions and commands, blindman's buff, and the like fashionable recreations.

Emil. Oh, ridiculous!

Med. Then there is *The Art of Affectation,* written by a late beauty of quality, teaching you how to draw up your breasts, stretch up your neck, to thrust out your breech, to play with your head, to toss up your nose, to bite your lips, to turn up your eyes, to speak in a silly soft tone of a voice, and use all the foolish French words that will infallibly make your person and conversation charming, with a short apology at the latter end, in the behalf of young ladies who notoriously wash and paint, though they have naturally good complexions.

Emil. What a deal of stuff you tell us?

Med. Such as the town affords, madam.   The Russians hearing the great respect we have for foreign dancing have lately sent over some of the best balladines, who are now practising a famous ballet, which will be sudddenly danced at the Bear Garden.

Lady Town. Pray forbear your idle stories, and give us an account of the state of love as it now stands.

---

[1] "I saw an Italian opera in music, the first that had been in England of the kind."—Evelyn, 5 Jan., 1674.

[2] Here, and later on (iv, 1), variously spelt *flute doux* and *flutes deux.* It has been suggested (*Notes and Queries,* 7th S., v, 135) that *flutes douces* is the right reading, and this has been adopted. The *flute douce* may have been something like the *flute d'amour,* or *Liebesflöte,* "an old form of flute with a narrow bore, supposed to have a smooth and fascinating quality."

[3] Possibly one of the romances which Pepys read surreptitiously. Was it by any chance the basis of D'Urfey's play, *The Campaigners, or Pleasant Adventures at Brussels,* 1698, in which, by the way, we have a footman called Mascarillo?

Med. Truly there has been some revolutions in those affairs, great chopping and changing among the old, and some new lovers, whom malice, indiscretion, and misfortune have luckily brought into play.

Lady Town. What think you of walking into the next room, and sitting down before you engage in this business?

Med. I wait upon you, and I hope (though women are commonly unreasonable) by the plenty of scandal I shall discover to give you very good content, ladies. [*Exeunt.*

SCENE II

Enter Mrs. Loveit *and* Pert. *Mrs.* Loveit *putting up a letter, then pulling out her pocket-glass, and looking in it.*

Lov. Pert.

Pert. Madam.

Lov. I hate myself, I look so ill to-day.

Pert. Hate the wicked cause on't, that base man Mr. Dorimant, who makes you torment and vex yourself continually.

Lov. He is to blame, indeed.

Pert. To blame to be two days without sending, writing, or coming near you, contrary to his oath and covenant! 'twas to much purpose to make him swear: I'll lay my life there's not an article but he has broken——talked to the vizards i' the pit; waited upon the ladies from the boxes to their coaches; gone behind the scenes and fawned upon those little insignificant creatures the players; 'tis impossible for a man of his inconstant temper to forbear, I'm sure.

Lov. I know he is a devil, but he has something of the angel yet undefaced in him, which makes him so charming and agreeable that I must love him be he never so wicked.

Pert. I little thought, madam, to see your spirit tamed to this degree, who banished poor Mr. Lackwit but for taking up another lady's fan in your presence.

Lov. My knowing of such odious fools contributes to the making of me love Dorimant the better.

Pert. Your knowing of Mr. Dorimant, in my mind, should rather make you hate all mankind.

Lov. So it does, besides himself.

Pert. Pray, what excuse does he make in his letter?

Lov. He has had business.

Pert. Business in general terms would not have been a current excuse for another; a modish man is always very busy when he is in pursuit of a new mistress.

Lov. Some fop has bribed you to rail at him; he had business, I will believe it, and will forgive him.

Pert. You may forgive him anything, but I shall never forgive him his turning me into ridicule, as I hear he does.

Lov. I perceive you are of the number of those fools his wit has made his enemies.

Pert. I am of the number of those he's pleased to rally, madam; and if we may believe Mr. Wagfan and Mr. Caperwell, he sometimes makes merry with yourself too among his laughing companions.

Lov. Blockheads are as malicious to witty men as ugly women are to the handsome; 'tis their interest, and they make it their business to defame 'em.

Pert. I wish Mr. Dorimant would not make it his business to defame you.

Lov. Should he, I had rather be made infamous by him than owe my reputation to the dull discretion of those fops you talk of.

Enter BELINDA.

Belinda!   [*Running to her.*

Bel. My dear.

Lov. You have been unkind of late.

Bel. Do not say unkind, say unhappy!

Lov. I could chide you; where have you been these two days?

Bel. Pity me rather, my dear, where I have been so tired with two or three country gentlewomen, whose conversation has been more insufferable than a country fiddle.

Lov. Are they relations?

Bel. No, Welsh acquaintance I made when I was last year at St. Winifred's; they have asked me a thousand questions of the modes and intrigues of the town, and I have told 'em almost as many things for news that hardly were so when their gowns were in fashion.

Lov. Provoking creatures, how could you endure 'em?

Bel. [*aside*]. Now to carry on my plot; nothing but love could make me capable of so much falsehood; 'tis time to begin, lest Dorimant should come before her jealousy has stung her.

[*Laughs, and then speaks on.*

I was yesterday at a play with 'em, where I was fain to show 'em the living, as the man at Westminster does the dead; that is Mrs. Such-a-one, admired for her beauty; this is Mr. Such-a-one, cried up for a wit; that is sparkish Mr. Such-a-one, who keeps reverend Mrs. Such-a-one, and there sits fine Mrs. Such-a-one, who was lately cast off by my Lord Such-a-one.

Lov. Did you see Dorimant there?

Bel. I did, and imagine you were there with him and have no mind to own it.

Lov. What should make you think so?

Bel. A lady masked in a pretty *déshabillé*, whom Dorimant entertained with more respect than the gallants do a common vizard.

Lov. [*aside*]. Dorimant at the play entertaining a mask, oh heavens!

Bel. [*aside*]. Good.

Lov. Did he stay all the while?

Bel. Till the play was done, and then led her out, which confirms me it was you.

Lov. Traitor!

Pert. Now you may believe he had business, and you may forgive him too.

Lov. Ungrateful, perjured man!

Bel. You seem so much concerned, my dear, I fear I have told you unawares what I had better have concealed for your quiet.

Lov. What manner of shape had she?

Bel. Tall and slender, her motions very genteel; certainly she must be some person of condition.

Lov. Shame and confusion be ever in her face when she shows it!

Bel. I should blame your discretion for loving that wild man, my dear; but they say he has a way so bewitching that few can defend their hearts who know him.

Lov. I will tear him from mine, or die i' the attempt.

Bel. Be more moderate.

Lov. Would I had daggers, darts, or poisoned arrows in my breast, so I could but remove the thoughts of him from thence!

Bel. Fie, fie! your transports are too violent, my dear. This may be but an accidental gallantry, and 'tis likely ended at her coach.

Pert. Should it proceed farther, let your comfort be, the conduct Mr. Dorimant affects will quickly make you know your rival, ten to one let you see her ruined, her reputation exposed to the town; a happiness none will envy her but yourself, madam.

Lov. Whoe'er she be, all the harm I wish her is, may she love him as well as I do, and may he give her as much cause to hate him!

Pert. Never doubt the latter end of your curse, madam.

Lov. May all the passions that are raised by neglected love, jealousy, indignation, spite, and thirst of revenge, eternally rage in her soul as they do now in mine!

[*Walks up and down with a distracted air.*

Enter a Page.

Page. Madam, Mr. Dorimant.

Lov. I will not see him.

Page. I told him you were within, madam.

Lov. Say you lied, say I'm busy, shut the door; say anything.

Page. He's here, madam.

Enter DORIMANT.

Dor.   They taste of death who do at Heaven arrive,
          But we this paradise approach alive.

[*To* LOVEIT.] What, dancing the galloping nag without a fiddle?

> [*Offers to catch her by the hand; she flings away and walks on.*

I fear this restlessness of the body, madam [*Pursuing her.*] proceeds from an unquietness of the mind. What unlucky accident puts you out of humour; a point ill washed, knots spoiled i' the making up, hair shaded awry, or some other little mistake in setting you in order?

Pert. A trifle, in my opinion, sir, more inconsiderable than any you mention.

Dor. Oh, Mrs Pert, I never knew you sullen enough to be silent; come, let me know the business.

Pert. The business, sir, is the business that has taken you up these two days; how have I seen you laugh at men of business, and now to become a man of business yourself!

Dor. We are not masters of our own affections, our inclinations daily alter; now we love pleasure, and anon we shall dote on business: human frailty will have it so, and who can help it?

Lov. Faithless, inhuman, barbarous man!——

Dor. Good, now the alarm strikes.——

Lov. Without sense of love, of honour, or of gratitude, tell me —for I will know—what devil, masked she were you with at the play yesterday?

Dor. Faith, I resolved as much as you, but the devil was obstinate and would not tell me.

Lov. False in this as in your vows to me! you do know.

Dor. The truth is, I did all I could to know.

Lov. And dare you own it to my face? Hell and furies!

> [*Tears her fan in pieces.*

Dor. Spare your fan, madam; you are growing hot, and will want it to cool you.

Lov. Horror and distraction seize you, sorrow and remorse gnaw your soul, and punish all your perjuries to me!—— [*Weeps.*

Dor.   So thunder breaks the cloud in twain,
          And makes a passage for the rain.

> [*Turning to* BELINDA.

Belinda, you are the devil that have raised this storm; you were at the play yesterday, and have been making discoveries to your dear.

Bel. You're the most mistaken man i' the world.

Dor. It must be so, and here I vow revenge; resolve to pursue and persecute you more impertinently than ever any loving fop did his mistress, hunt you i' the Park, trace you i' the Mall, dog you in every visit you make, haunt you at the plays and i' the

Drawing-room, hang my nose in your neck, and talk to you whether you will or no, and ever look upon you with such dying eyes, till your friends grow jealous of me, send you out of town, and make the world suspect your reputation. [*In a lower voice.* At my Lady Townley's when we go from hence.

[*He looks kindly on* BELINDA.

Bel. I'll meet you there.

Dor. Enough.

Lov. Stand off, you shall not stare upon her so.

[*Pushing* DORIMANT *away.*

Dor. Good! There's one made jealous already.

Lov. Is this the constancy you vowed?

Dor. Constancy at my years! 'tis not a virtue in season; you might as well expect the fruit the autumn ripens i' the spring.

Lov. Monstrous principle!

Dor. Youth has a long journey to go, madam: should I have set up my rest at the first inn I lodged at, I should never have arrived at the happiness I now enjoy.

Lov. Dissembler, damned dissembler!

Dor. I am so, I confess; good nature and good manners corrupt me. I am honest in my inclinations, and would not, were't not to avoid offence, make a lady a little in years believe I think her young, wilfully mistake art for nature, and seem as fond of a thing I am weary of as when I doted on't in earnest.

Lov. False man!

Dor. True woman!

Lov. Now you begin to show yourself!

Dor. Love gilds us over and makes us show fine things to one another for a time, but soon the gold wears off, and then again the native brass appears.

Lov. Think on your oaths, your vows and protestations, perjured man.

Dor. I made 'em when I was in love.

Lov. And therefore ought they not to bind? Oh, impious!

Dor. What we swear at such a time may be a certain proof of a present passion; but to say truth, in love there is no security to be given for the future.

Lov. Horrid and ungrateful, begone, and never see me more.

Dor. I am not one of those troublesome coxcombs, who because they were once well received take the privilege to plague a woman with their love ever after; I shall obey you, madam, though I do myself some violence.

[*He offers to go, and* LOVEIT *pulls him back.*

Lov. Come back, you shall not go. Could you have the ill-nature to offer it?

Dor. When love grows diseased, the best thing we can do is to put it to a violent death; I cannot endure the torture of a lingering and consumptive passion.

Lov. Can you think mine sickly?

Dor. Oh, 'tis desperately ill! What worse symptoms are there than your being always uneasy when I visit you, your picking quarrels with me on slight occasions, and in my absence kindly listening to the impertinencies of every fashionable fool that talks to you?

Lov. What fashionable fool can you lay to my charge?

Dor. Why, the very cock-fool of all those fools, Sir Fopling Flutter.

Lov. I never saw him in my life but once.

Dor. The worse woman you, at first sight to put on all your charms, to entertain him with that softness in your voice and all that wanton kindness in your eyes you so notoriously affect when you design a conquest.

Lov. So damned a lie did never malice yet invent. Who told you this?

Dor. No matter; that ever I should love a woman that can dote on a senseless caper, a tawdry French ribbon, and a formal cravat.

Lov. You make me mad.

Dor. A guilty conscience may do much; go on, be the game-mistress o' the town, and enter all our young fops as fast as they come from travel.

Lov. Base and scurrilous!

Dor. A fine mortifying reputation 'twill be for a woman of your pride, wit, and quality!

Lov. This jealousy's a mere pretence, a cursed trick of your own devising; I know you.

Dor. Believe it, and all the ill of me you can: I would not have a woman have the least good thought of me that can think well of Fopling; farewell; fall to, and much good may [it] do you with your coxcomb.

Lov. Stay, oh! stay, and I will tell you all.

Dor. I have been told too much already.

[*Exit* DORIMANT.

Lov. Call him again.

Pert. E'en let him go, a fair riddance.

Lov. Run, I say; call him again. I will have him called.

Pert. The devil should carry him away first, were it my concern.

[*Exit* PERT.

Bel. He's frightened me from the very thoughts of loving men; for heaven's sake, my dear, do not discover what I told you; I dread his tongue as much as you ought to have done his friendship.

Enter PERT.

Pert. He's gone, madam.

Lov. Lightning blast him!

Pert. When I told him you desired him to come back, he smiled, made a mouth at me, flung into his coach, and said——

Lov. What did he say?

Pert. "*Drive away*"; and then repeated verses.

Lov. Would I had made a contract to be a witch, when first I entertained this great devil, monster, barbarian; I could tear myself in pieces. Revenge, nothing but revenge can ease me: plague, war, famine, fire, all that can bring universal ruin and misery on mankind; with joy I'd perish to have you in my power but this moment.   [*Exit* LOVEIT.

Pert. Follow, madam; leave her not in this outrageous passion.
                                   [PERT *gathers up the things.*

Bel. He's given me the proof which I desired of his love:
But 'tis a proof of his ill-nature too;
I wish I had not seen him use her so.
I sigh to think that Dorimant may be
One day as faithless and unkind to me.   [*Exeunt.*

ACT III

SCENE I.—Lady WOODVIL's *Lodgings.*

Enter HARRIET *and* BUSY *her woman.*

Busy. Dear madam! Let me set that curl in order.

Har. Let me alone, I will shake 'em all out of order.

Busy. Will you never leave this wildness?

Har. Torment me not.

Busy. Look! there's a knot falling off.

Har. Let it drop.

Busy. But one pin, dear madam.

Har. How do I daily suffer under thy officious fingers!

Busy. Ah, the difference that is between you and my Lady Dapper! How uneasy she is if the least thing be amiss about her!

Har. She is indeed most exact; nothing is ever wanting to make her ugliness remarkable.

Busy. Jeering people say so.

Har. Her powdering, painting, and her patching never fail in public to draw the tongues and eyes of all the men upon her.

Busy. She is indeed a little too pretending.

Har. That women should set up for beauty as much in spite of nature as some men have done for wit!

Busy. I hope, without offence, one may endeavour to make oneself agreeable.

Har. Not when 'tis impossible. Women then ought to be no more fond of dressing than fools should be talking. Hoods and modesty, masks and silence, things that shadow and conceal: they should think of nothing else.

Busy. Jesu! madam, what will your mother think is become of you? For heaven's sake, go in again.

Har. I won't.

Busy. This is the extravagant'st thing that ever you did in your life, to leave her and a gentleman who is to be your husband.

Har. My husband! Hast thou so little wit to think I spoke what I meant when I overjoyed her in the country with a low curtsey and *What you please, madam, I shall ever be obedient?*

Busy. Nay, I know not, you have so many fetches.

Har. And this was one to get her up to London; nothing else, I assure thee.

Busy. Well, the man, in my mind, is a fine man.

Har. The man indeed wears his clothes fashionably, and has a pretty negligent way with him, very courtly and much affected; he bows, and talks, and smiles so agreeably as he thinks.

Busy. I never saw anything so genteel.

Har. Varnished over with good breeding many a blockhead makes a tolerable show.

Busy. I wonder you do not like him.

Har. I think I might be brought to endure him, and that is all a reasonable woman should expect in a husband; but there is duty i' the case——and like the haughty Merab,

> I find much aversion in my stubborn mind,
> Which is bred by being promised and design'd.

Busy. I wish you do not design your own ruin! I partly guess your inclinations, madam,——that Mr. Dorimant——

Har. Leave your prating, and sing some foolish song or other.

Busy. I will: the song you love so well ever since you saw Mr. Dorimant.

Song

> When first Amintas charm'd my heart,
>   My heedless sheep began to stray;
> The wolves soon stole the greatest part,
>   And all will now be made a prey.
>
> Ah! let not love your thoughts possess,
> 'Tis fatal to a shepherdess;
> The dangerous passion you must shun,
> Or else, like me, be quite undone.

Har. Shall I be paid down by a covetous parent for a purchase? I need no land; no, I'll lay myself out all in love. It is decreed——

Enter YOUNG BELLAIR.

Y. Bell. What generous resolution are you making, madam?

Har. Only to be disobedient, sir.

Y. Bell. Let me join hands with you in that.

Har. With all my heart; I never thought I should have given you mine so willingly. Here I, Harriet——

Y. Bell. And I, Harry——

Har. Do solemnly protest——

Y. Bell. And vow——

Har. That I with you——

Y. Bell. And I with you——

Both. Will never marry.

Har. A match!

Y. Bell. And no match! How do you like this indifference now?

Har. You expect I should take it ill, I see.

Y. Bell. 'Tis not unnatural for you women to be a little angry [if] you miss a conquest, though you would slight the poor man were he in your power.

Har. There are some, it may be, have an eye like Bartholomew, big enough for the whole fair, but I am not of the number, and you may keep your gingerbread: 'twill be more acceptable to the lady whose dear image it wears, sir.

Y. Bell. I must confess, madam, you came a day after the fair

Har. You own then you are in love.

Y. Bell. I do.

Har. The confidence is generous, and in return I could almost find in my heart to let you know my inclinations.

Y. Bell. Are you in love?

Har. Yes, with this dear town, to that degree I can scarce endure the country in landscapes and in hangings.

Y. Bell. What a dreadful thing 'twould be to be hurried back to Hampshire?

Har. Ah! name it not!

Y. Bell. As for us, I find we shall agree well enough! Would we could do something to deceive the grave people!

Har. Could we delay their proceeding, 'twere well; a reprieve is a good step towards the getting of a pardon.

Y. Bell. If we give over the game we are undone; what think you of playing it on booty?

Har. What do you mean?

Y. Bell. Pretend to be in love with one another; 'twill make some dilatory excuses we may feign pass the better.

Har. Let us do 't, if it be but for the dear pleasure of dissembling.

Y. Bell. Can you play your part?

Har. I know not what 'tis to love, but I have made pretty remarks by being now and then where lovers meet. Where did you leave their gravities?

Y. Bell. I' th' next room; your mother was censuring our modern gallant.

Enter OLD BELLAIR *and* Lady WOODVIL.

Har. Peace! Here they come, I will lean against this wall and look bashfully down upon my fan, while you like an amorous spark modishly entertain me.

Lady Wood. Never go about to excuse 'em; come, come. it was not so when I was a young woman.

O. Bell. Adod, they're something disrespectful.

Lady Wood. Quality was then considered, and not rallied by every leering fellow.

O. Bell. Youth will have its jest, adod it will.

Lady Wood. 'Tis good breeding now to be civil to none but players and Exchange women; they are treated by 'em as much above their condition as others are below theirs.

O. Bell. Out, a pise on 'em! talk no more; the rogues ha' got an ill habit of preferring beauty, no matter where they find it.

Lady Wood. See your son and my daughter, they have improved their acquaintance since they were within.

O. Bell. Adod, methinks they have; let's keep back and observe.

Y. Bell. Now for a look and gestures that may persuade 'em I am saying all the passionate things imaginable.

Har. Your head a little more on one side, ease yourself on your left leg, and play with your right hand.

Y. Bell. Thus, is it not?

Har. Now set your right leg firm on the ground, adjust your belt, then look about you.

Y. Bell. A little exercising will make me perfect.

Har. Smile, and turn to me again very sparkish.

Y. Bell. Will you take your turn and be instructed?

Har. With all my heart.

Y. Bell. At one motion play your fan, roll your eyes, and then settle a kind look upon me.

Har. So.

Y. Bell. Now spread your fan, look down upon it, and tell the sticks with a finger.

Har. Very modish!

Y. Bell. Clap your hand up to your bosom, hold down your gown; shrug a little, draw up your breasts, and let 'em fall again gently, with a sigh or two, etc.

Har. By the good instructions you give, I suspect you for one of those malicious observers who watch people's eyes and from innocent looks make scandalous conclusions.

Y. Bell. I know some, indeed, who, out of mere love to mischief, are as vigilant as jealousy itself, and will give you an account of every glance that passes at a play and i' th' circle.[1]

[1] In Hyde Park.

Har. 'Twill not be amiss now to seem a little pleasant.

Y. Bell. Clap your fan then in both your hands, snatch it to your mouth, smile, and with a lively motion fling your body a little forwards. So,——now spread it; fall back on the sudden, cover your face with it, and break out in to a loud laughter—— take up! look grave, and fall a-fanning of yourself——admirably well acted.

Har. I think I am pretty apt at these matters.

O. Bell. Adod, I like this well.

Lady Wood. This promises something.

O. Bell. Come! there is love i' th' case, adod there is, or will be; what say you, young lady?

Har. All in good time, sir; you expect we should fall to and love, as gamecocks fight, as soon as we are set together; adod, you're unreasonable!

O. Bell. Adod, sirrah, I like thy wit well.

Enter a Servant.

Serv. The coach is at the door, madam.

O. Bell. Go, get you and take the air together.

Lady Wood. Will not you go with us?

O. Bell. Out a pise. Adod, I ha' business and cannot. We shall meet at night at my sister Townley's.

Y. Bell. [*aside*]. He's going to Emilia. I overheard him talk of a collation.   [*Exeunt.*

SCENE II

Enter Lady Townley, Emilia, *and* Mr. Medley.

Lady Town. I pity the young lovers we last talked of; though, to say truth, their conduct has been so indiscreet they deserve to be unfortunate.

Med. You've had an exact account, from the great lady i' th' box down to the little orange-wench.

Emil. You're a living libel, a breathing lampoon; I wonder you are not torn in pieces.

Med. What think you of setting up an office of intelligence for these matters? The project may get money.

Lady Town. You would have great dealings with country ladies.

Med. More than Muddiman [1] has with their husbands.

---

[1] Was this the gentleman whom Pepys found "a good scholar, an arch rogue"?—*Diary,* 10th January, 1660. Mentioned also in the *Letterbook,* 23rd January, 1688.

Enter BELINDA.

Lady Town. Belinda, what has been become of you? we have not seen you here of late with your friend Mrs. Loveit.

Bel. Dear creature, I left [her] but now so sadly afflicted.

Lady Town. With her old distemper, jealousy?

Med. Dorimant has played her some new prank.

Bel. Well, that Dorimant is certainly the worst man breathing.

Emil. I once thought so.

Bel. And do you not think so still?

Emil. No, indeed!

Bel. Oh, Jesu!

Emil. The town does him a great deal of injury, and I will never believe what it says of a man I do not know again, for his sake.

Bel. You make me wonder!

Lady Town. He's a very well-bred man.

Bel. But strangely ill-natured.

Emil. Then he's a very witty man.

Bel. But a man of no principles.

Med. Your man of principles is a very fine thing indeed!

Bel. To be preferred to men of parts by women who have regard to their reputation and quiet. Well, were I minded to play the fool, he should be the last man I'd think of.

Med. He has been the first in many lady's favours, though you are so severe, madam.

Lady Town. What he may be for a lover I know not, but he's a very pleasant acquaintance, I am sure.

Bel. Had you seen him use Mrs. Loveit as I have done, you would never endure him more.

Emil. What, he has quarrelled with her again?

Bel. Upon the slightest occasion; he's jealous of Sir Fopling.

Lady Town. She never saw him in her life but yesterday, and that was here.

Emil. On my conscience, he's the only man in town that's her aversion; how horribly out of humour she was all the while he talked to her!

Bel. And somebody has wickedly told him——

Emil. Here he comes.

Enter DORIMANT.

Med. Dorimant! you are luckily come to justify yourself—— here's a lady——

Bel. Has a word or two to say to you from a disconsolate person.

Dor. You tender your reputation too much, I know, madam, to whisper with me before this good company.

Bel. To serve Mrs. Loveit, I'll make a bold venture.

Dor. Here's Medley, the very spirit of scandal.

Bel. No matter!

Emil. 'Tis something you are unwilling to hear, Mr. Dorimant.

Lady Town. Tell him, Belinda, whether he will or no.

Bel. [*aloud*]. Mrs. Loveit——

Dor. Softly, these are laughers, you do not know'em.

Bel. [*to* DORIMANT, *apart*]. In a word, you've made me hate you, which I thought you never could have done.

Dor. In obeying your commands.

Bel. 'Twas a cruel part you played! how could you act it?

Dor. Nothing is cruel to a man who could kill himself to please you; remember, five o'clock to-morrow morning.

Bel. I tremble when you name it.

Dor. Be sure you come.

Bel. I shall not.

Dor. Swear you will.

Bel. I dare not.

Dor. Swear, I say.

Bel. By my life! by all the happiness I hope for——

Dor. You will.

Bel. I will.

Dor. Kind.

Bel. I am glad I've sworn, I vow I think I should ha' failed you else!

Dor. Surprisingly kind! In what temper did you leave Loveit?

Bel. Her raving was prettily over, and she began to be in a brave way of defying you and all your works. Where have you been since you went from thence?

Dor. I looked in at the play.

Bel. I have promised, and must return to her again.

Dor. Persuade her to walk in the Mall [1] this evening.

Bel. She hates the place, and will not come.

Dor. Do all you can to prevail with her.

Bel. For what purpose?

Dor. Sir Fopling will be here anon; I'll prepare him to set upon her there before me.

Bel. You persecute her too much; but I'll do all you'll ha' me.

Dor. [*aloud*]. Tell her plainly, 'tis grown so dull a business I can drudge on no longer.

Emil. There are afflictions in love, Mr. Dorimant.

Dor. You women make 'em, who are commonly as unreasonable in that as you are at play; without the advantage be on your side a man can never quietly give over when he's weary.

Med. If you would play without being obliged to complaisance, Dorimant, you should play in public places.

[1] i.e. Pall Mall, which roused the enthusiasm of even the fastidious Gay:

> "O bear me to the paths of fair Pell Mell."
>
> *Trivia*, ii, 257.

Dor. Ordinaries were a very good thing for that, but gentlemen do not of late frequent 'em; the deep play is now in private houses. [BELINDA *offering to steal away.*

Lady Town. Belinda, are you leaving us so soon?

Bel. I am to go to the Park with Mrs. Loveit, madam.
[*Exit* BELINDA.

Lady Town. This *confidence* will go nigh to spoil this young creature.

Med. 'Twill do her good, madam. Young men who are brought up under practising lawyers prove the abler counsel when they come to be called to the Bar themselves.

Dor. The town has been very favourable to you this afternoon, my Lady Townley; you use to have an *embarras* of chairs and coaches at your door, an uproar of footmen in your hall, and a noise of fools above here.

Lady Town. Indeed my house is the general *rendezvous*, and, next to the playhouse, is the common refuge of all the young idle people.

Emil. Company is a very good thing, madam, but I wonder you do not love it a little more chosen.

Lady Town. 'Tis good to have an universal taste; we should love wit, but for variety be able to divert ourselves with the extravagancies of those who want it.

Med. Fools will make you laugh.

Emil. For once or twice; but the repetition of their folly after a visit or two grows tedious and unsufferable.

Lady Town. You are a little too delicate, Emilia.

Enter a Page.

Page. Sir Fopling Flutter, madam, desires to know if you are to be seen.

Lady Town. Here's the freshest fool in town, and one who has not cloyed you yet. Page!

Page. Madam!

Lady Town. Desire him to walk up. [*Exit Page.*

Dor. Do not you fall on him, Medley, and snub him. Soothe him up in his extravagance; he will show the better.

Med. You know I have a natural indulgence for fools, and need not this caution, sir.

Enter Sir FOPLING FLUTTER, *with his Page after him.*

Sir Fop. Page, wait without. Madam [*To* Lady TOWNLEY.], I kiss your hands. I see yesterday was nothing of chance; the *belles assemblées* form themselves here every day. Lady [*To* EMILIA.], your servant. Dorimant, let me embrace thee; without lying, I have not met with any of my acquaintance who retain so much of Paris as thou dost—the very air thou hadst when the

marquis mistook thee i' th' Tuileries, and cried, *He! Chevalier!*
and then begged thy pardon.

Dor. I would fain wear in fashion as long as I can, sir; 'tis a
thing to be valued in men as well as baubles.

Sir Fop. Thou art a man of wit, and understandest the town;
prithee let thee and I be intimate, there is no living without
making some good man the confidant of our pleasures.

Dor. 'Tis true! but there is no man so improper for such a
business as I am.

Sir Fop. Prithee, why hast thou so modest an opinion of
thyself?

Dor. Why, first, I could never keep a secret in my life, and then
there is no charm so infallibly makes me fall in love with a woman
as my knowing a friend loves her. I deal honestly with you.

Sir Fop. Thy humour's very gallant, or let me perish; I knew
a French count so like thee.

Lady Town. Wit, I perceive, has more power over you than
beauty, Sir Fopling, else you would not have let this lady stand
so long neglected.

Sir Fop. [*to* EMILIA]. A thousand pardons, madam; some
civilities due, of course, upon the meeting a long absent friend.
The *éclat* of so much beauty, I confess, ought to have charmed
me sooner.

Emil. The *brilliant* of so much good language, sir, has much
more power than the little beauty I can boast.

Sir Fop. I never saw anything prettier than this high work
on your *point d'Espagne.*——

Emil. 'Tis not so rich as *point de Venise.*——

Sir Fop. Not altogether, but looks cooler, and is more proper
for the season. Dorimant, is not that Medley?

Dor. The same, sir.

Sir Fop. Forgive me, sir; in this *embarras* of civilities I could
not come to have you in my arms sooner. You understand an
equipage the best of any man in town, I hear.

Med. By my own you would not guess it.

Sir Fop. There are critics who do not write, sir.

Med. Our peevish poets will scarce allow it.

Sir Fop. Damn 'em, they'll allow no man wit who does not
play the fool like themselves, and show it! Have you taken
notice of the *calèche* I brought over?

Med. Oh, yes! It has quite another air than the English
makes.

Sir Fop. 'Tis as easily known from an English tumbril as an
Inns of Court man is from one of us.

Dor. Truly, there is a *bel-air* in *calèches* as well as men.

Med. But there are few so delicate to observe it.

Sir Fop. The world is generally very *grossier* here, indeed.

Lady Town. He's very fine.

Emil. Extreme proper.

Sir Fop. A slight suit I made to appear in at my first arrival, not worthy your consideration, ladies.

Dor. The pantaloon is very well mounted.

Sir Fop. The tassels are new and pretty.

Med. I never saw a coat better cut.

Sir Fop. It makes me show long-waisted, and, I think, slender.

Dor. That's the shape our ladies dote on.

Med. Your breech, though, is a handful too high in my eye, Sir Fopling.

Sir Fop. Peace, Medley; I have wished it lower a thousand times, but a pox on't, 'twill not be.

Lady Town. His gloves are well fringed, large and graceful.

Sir Fop. I was always eminent for being *bien-gante*.

Emil. He wears nothing but what are originals of the most famous hands in Paris.

Sir Fop. You are in the right, madam.

Lady Town. The suit?

Sir Fop. Barroy.[1]

Emil. The garniture?

Sir Fop. Le Gras.

Med. The shoes?

Sir Fop. Piccat.

Dor. The periwig?

Sir Fop. Chedreux.[2]

Lady Town. and Emil. The gloves?

Sir Fop. Orangerie: you know the smell, ladies. Dorimant, I could find in my heart for an amusement to have a gallantry with some of our English ladies.

Dor. 'Tis a thing no less necessary to confirm the reputation of your wit than a duel will be to satisfy the town of your courage.

Sir Fop. Here was a woman yesterday——

Dor. Mistress Loveit.

Sir Fop. You have named her.

Dor. You cannot pitch on a better for your purpose.

Sir Fop. Prithee, what is she?

Dor. A person of quality, and one who has a rest of reputation enough to make the conquest considerable. Besides, I hear she likes you too.

Sir Fop. Methought she seemed, though, very reserved and uneasy all the time I entertained her.

---

[1] Perhaps this should be *Barri*. The "drap du Barri" was later on extremely fashionable.

[2] A species of perruque, so called from the name of its inventor. Dryden wore a chedreux and a sword when he ate tarts with Mrs. Reeve at the Mulberry Garden, and Oldham, in his imitation of the Third Satire of Juvenal, has:

> "Their tawdry clothes, pulvilios, essences;
> Their chedreux perruques and their vanities."

Dor. Grimace and affection. You will see her i' th' Mall to-night.

Sir Fop. Prithee let thee and I take the air together.

Dor. I am engaged to Medley, but I'll meet you at St. James's and give you some information upon the which you may regulate your proceedings.

Sir Fop. All the world will be in the Park to-night: ladies, 'twere pity to keep so much beauty longer within doors and rob the Ring of all those charms that should adorn it.——Hey, page!

Enter Page, and goes out again.

See that all my people be ready. Dorimant, *au revoir !*

[*Exit* Sir Fopling.

Med. A fine mettled coxcomb.

Dor. Brisk and insipid.

Med. Pert and dull.

Emil. However you despise him, gentlemen, I'll lay my life he passes for a wit with many.

Dor. That may very well be; nature has her cheats, stums a brain, and puts sophisticate dulness often on the tasteless multitude for true wit and good-humour. Medley, come.

Med. I must go a little way, I will meet you i' the Mall.

Dor. I'll walk through the garden thither. [*To the Women.*] We shall meet anon and bow.

Lady Town. Not to-night; we are engaged about a business the knowledge of which may make you laugh hereafter.

Med. Your servant, ladies.

Dor. Au revoir ! as Sir Fopling says.

[*Exeunt* Medley *and* Dorimant.

Lady Town. The old man will be here immediately.

Emil. Let's expect him i' th' garden.

Lady Town. Go, you are a rogue.

Emil. I can't abide you.   [*Exeunt.*

SCENE III.—*The Mall*

Enter Harriet *and* Young Bellair, *she pulling him.*

Har. Come along.

Y. Bell. And leave your mother?

Har. Busy will be sent with a hue and cry after us; but that's no matter.

Y. Bell. 'Twill look strangely in me.

Har. She'll believe it a freak of mine and never blame your manners.

Y. Bell. What reverend acquaintance is that she has met?

Har. A fellow-beauty of the last King's time, though by the ruins you would hardly guess it. [*Exeunt.*

Enter DORIMANT, *who crosses the stage.*

Enter YOUNG BELLAIR *and* HARRIET.

Y. Bell. By this time your mother is in a fine taking.

Har. If your friend Mr. Dorimant were but here now, that she might find me talking with him.

Y. Bell. She does not know him, but dreads him, I hear, of all mankind.

Har. She concludes if he does but speak to a woman she's undone; is on her knees every day to pray heaven defend me from him.

Y. Bell. You do not apprehend him so much as she does.

Har. I never saw anything in him that was frightful.

Y. Bell. On the contrary, have you not observed something extreme delightful in his wit and person?

Har. He's agreeable and pleasant I must own, but he does so much affect being so, he displeases me.

Y. Bell. Lord, madam, all he does and says is so easy and so natural.

Har. Some men's verses seem so to the unskilful, but labour i' the one and affectation in the other to the judicious plainly appear.

Y. Bell. I never heard him accused of affectation before.

Enter DORIMANT, *who stares upon her.*

Har. It passes on the easy town, who are favourably pleased in him to call it humour.

[*Exeunt* YOUNG BELLAIR *and* HARRIET.

Dor. 'Tis she! it must be she, that lovely hair, that easy shape, those wanton eyes, and all those melting charms about her mouth which Medley spoke of; I'll follow the lottery, and put in for a prize with my friend Bellair. [*Exit* DORIMANT *repeating :*

In love the victors from the vanquish'd fly;
They fly that wound, and they pursue that die.

Enter YOUNG BELLAIR *and* HARRIET, *and after them* DORIMANT, *standing at a distance.*

Y. Bell. Most people prefer High Park [1] to this place.

Har. It has the better reputation, I confess; but I abominate the dull diversions there, the formal bows, the affected smiles, the silly by-words, and amorous tweers in passing; here one meets with a little conversation now and then.

---

[1] i.e. Hyde Park, *the* park *par excellence*; references to it are endless. The great resort there was the so-called Ring. The name *High* Park seems unusual.

Y. Bell. These conversations have been fatal to some of your sex, madam.

Har. It may be so; because some who want temper have been undone by gaming, must others who have it wholly deny themselves the pleasure of play?

Dor. Trust me, it were unreasonable, madam.

                              [*Coming up gently, and bowing to her.*
Har. Lord! who's this?   [*She starts, and looks grave.*

Y. Bell. Dorimant.

Dor. Is this the woman your father would have you marry?

Y. Bell. It is.

Dor. Her name?

Y. Bell. Harriet.

Dor. I am not mistaken, she's handsome.

Y. Bell. Talk to her, her wit is better than her face; we were wishing for you but now.

Dor. [*to* HARRIET]. Overcast with seriousness o' the sudden! A thousand smiles were shining in that face but now; I never saw so quick a change of weather.

Har. [*aside*]. I feel as great a change within; but he shall never know it.

Dor. You were talking of play, madam; pray what may be your stint?

Har. A little harmless discourse in public walks, or at most an appointment in a box barefaced at the playhouse; you are for masks and private meetings where women engage for all they are worth, I hear.

Dor. I have been used to deep play, but I can make one at small game when I like my gamester well.

Har. And be so unconcerned you'll ha' no pleasure in it.

Dor. Where there is a considerable sum to be won the hope of drawing people in makes every trifle considerable.

Har. The sordidness of men's natures, I know, makes 'em willing to flatter and comply with the rich, though they are sure never to be the better for 'em.

Dor. 'Tis in their power to do us good, and we despair not but at some time or other they may be willing.

Har. To men who have fared on this town like you, 'twould be a great mortification to live on hope; could you keep a Lent for a mistress?

Dor. In expectation of a happy Easter, and though time be very precious, think forty days well lost to gain your favour.

Har. Mr. Bellair! let us walk, 'tis time to leave him; men grow dull when they begin to be particular.

Dor. You're mistaken, flattery will not ensue, though I know you're greedy of the praises of the whole Mall.

Har. You do me wrong.

Dor. I do not; as I followed you I observed how you were pleased when the fops cried: "She's handsome, very handsome,

By God she is," and whispered aloud your name, the thousand several forms you put your face into; then, to make yourself more agreeable, how wantonly you played with your head, flung back your locks, and looked smilingly over your shoulder at 'em.

Har. I do not go begging the men's, as you do the ladies' good liking, with a sly softness in your looks and a gentle slowness in your bows as you pass by 'em——as thus, sir; ——   [*Acts him.* Is not this like you?

Enter Lady WOODVIL *and* BUSY.

Y. Bell. Your mother, madam.
                    [*Pulls* HARRIET; *she composes herself.*
Lady Wood. Ah, my dear child Harriet!
Busy. Now is she so pleased with finding her again she cannot chide her.
Lady Wood. Come away!
Dor. 'Tis now but high Mall, madam, the most entertaining time of all the evening.
Har. I would fain see that Dorimant, mother, you so cry out for a monster; he's in the Mall, I hear.
Lady Wood. Come away then! the plague is here, and you should dread the infection.
Y. Bell. You may be misinformed of the gentleman.
Lady Wood. Oh, no! I hope you do not know him! He is the prince of all the devils in the town, delights in nothing but in rapes and riots.
Dor. If you did but hear him speak, madam!
Lady Wood. Oh! he has a tongue, they say, would tempt the angels to a second fall.

Enter Sir FOPLING *with his Equipage, six Footmen and a Page.*

Sir Fop. Hey, Champagne, Norman, La Rose, La Fleur, La Tour, La Verdue.   Dorimant!——
Lady Wood. Here, here he is among this rout, he names him; come away, Harriet, come away.
                [*Exeunt* Lady WOODVIL, HARRIET, BUSY, *and* YOUNG BELLAIR.
Dor. This fool's coming has spoiled all; she's gone, but she has left a pleasing image of herself behind that wanders in my soul ——It must not settle there.
Sir Fop. What reverie is this?   Speak, man.
Dor.   Snatch'd from myself, how far behind
                Already I behold the shore!

Enter MEDLEY.

Med. Dorimant, a discovery!   I met with Bellair.
Dor. You can tell me no news, sir; I know all.
Med. How do you like the daughter?

Dor. You never came so near truth in your life as you did in her description.

Med. What think you of the mother?

Dor. Whatever I think of her, she thinks very well of me, I find.

Med. Did she know you?

Dor. She did not; whether she does now or no, I know not. Here was a pleasant scene towards, when in came Sir Fopling, mustering up his equipage, and at the latter end named me and frighted her away.

Med. Loveit and Belinda are not far off, I saw 'em alight at St. James's.

Dor. [*whispers*]. Sir Fopling, hark you, a word or two. Look you do not want assurance.

Sir Fop. I never do on these occasions.

Dor. Walk on, we must not be seen together; make your advantage of what I have told you; the next turn you will meet the lady.

Sir Fop. Hey——Follow me all.

[*Exeunt* Sir FOPLING *and his Equipage.*

Dor. Medley, you shall see good sport anon between Loveit and this Fopling.

Med. I thought there was something toward by that whisper

Dor. You know a worthy principle of hers?

Med. Not to be so much as civil to a man who speaks to her in the presence of him she professes to love.

Dor. I have encouraged Fopling to talk to her to-night.

Med. Now you are here she will go nigh to beat him.

Dor. In the humour she's in, her love will make her do some very extravagant thing, doubtless.

Med. What was Belinda's business with you at my Lady Townley's?

Dor. To get me to meet Loveit here in order to an *éclaircisse-ment.* I made some difficulty of it, and have prepared this *rencontre* to make good my jealousy.

Med. Here they come!

Enter LOVEIT, BELINDA, *and* PERT.

Dor. I'll meet her and provoke her with a deal of dumb civility in passing by, then turn short and be behind her when Sir Fopling sets upon her

         See how unregarded now
         That piece of beauty passes.

[*Exeunt* DORIMANT *and* MEDLEY.

Bel. How wonderful respectfully he bowed!

Pert. He's always over-mannerly when he has done a mischief.

Bel. Methought indeed at the same time he had a strange despising countenance.

Pert. The unlucky look, he thinks, becomes him.

Bel. I was afraid you would have spoke to him, my dear.

Lov. I would have died first; he shall no more find me the loving fool he has done.

Bel. You love him still!

Lov. No.

Pert. I wish you did not.

Lov. I do not, and I will have you think so. What made you hale me to this odious place, Belinda?

Bel. I hate to be hulched up in a coach; walking is much better.

Lov. Would we could meet Sir Fopling now!

Bel. Lord! would you not avoid him?

Lov. I would make him all the advances that may be.

Bel. That would confirm Dorimant's suspicion, my dear.

Lov. He is not jealous, but I will make him so, and be revenged a way he little thinks on.

Bel. [*aside*]. If she should make him jealous, that may make him fond of her again: I must dissuade her from it. Lord! my dear, this will certainly make him hate you.

Lov. 'Twill make him uneasy, though he does not care for me; I know the effects of jealousy on men of his proud temper.

Bel. 'Tis a fantastic remedy, its operations are dangerous and uncertain.

Lov. 'Tis the strongest cordial we can give to dying love, it often brings it back when there's no sign of life remaining. But I design not so much the reviving his, as my revenge.

Enter Sir FOPLING *and his Equipage.*

Sir Fop. Hey! bid the coachman send home four of his horses, and bring the coach to Whitehall; I'll walk over the Park——Madam, the honour of kissing your fair hands is a happiness I missed this afternoon at my Lady Townley's.

Lov. You were very obliging, Sir Fopling, the last time I saw you there.

Sir Fop. The preference was due to your wit and beauty. Madam, your servant; there never was so sweet an evening.

Bel. 'T has drawn all the rabble of the town hither.

Sir Fop. 'Tis pity there's not an order made that none but the *beau monde* should walk here.

Lov. 'Twould add much to the beauty of the place. See what a sort of nasty fellows are coming.

Enter three ill-fashioned Fellows, singing,

'Tis not for kisses alone, etc.

Lov. Fo! Their periwigs are scented with tobacco so strong——

Sir Fop. It overcomes our pulvillio [1]——Methinks I smell the coffee-house they came from.

1 Man. Dorimant's convenient, Madam Loveit.

2 Man. I like the oily buttock with her.

3 Man. What spruce prig is that?

1 Man. A caravan lately come from Paris.

2 Man. Peace, they smoke. [2]

There's something else to be done, etc.

[*All of them coughing; exeunt, singing.*

Enter DORIMANT *and* MEDLEY.

Dor. They're engaged.

Med. She entertains him as if she liked him.

Dor. Let us go forward; seem earnest in discourse, and show ourselves. Then you shall see how she'll use him.

Bel. Yonder's Dorimant, my dear.

Lov. [*aside*]. I see him, he comes insulting; but I will disappoint him in his expectation. [*To* Sir FOPLING.] I like this pretty nice humour of yours, Sir Fopling. With what a loathing eye he looked upon those fellows!

Sir Fop. I sat near one of 'em at a play to-day, and was almost poisoned with a pair of cordovan gloves he wears.

Lov. Oh! filthy cordovan, how I hate the smell!

[*Laughs in a loud affected way.*

Sir Fop. Did you observe, madam, how their cravats hung loose an inch from their neck, and what a frightful air it gave 'em?

Lov. Oh! I took particular notice of one that is always spruced up with a deal of dirty sky-coloured ribbon.

Bel. That's one of the walking flageolets who haunt the Mall o' nights.

Lov. Oh! I remember him; he's a hollow tooth enough to spoil the sweetness of an evening.

Sir Fop. I have seen the tallest walk the streets with a dainty pair of boxes neatly buckled on.

Lov. And a little footboy at his heels pocket-high, with a flat cap——a dirty face.

Sir Fop. And a snotty nose.

Lov. Oh——odious! there's many of my own sex with that Holborn equipage trip to Gray's Inn Walks, and now and then travel hither on a Sunday.

Med. She takes no notice of you.

Dor. Damn her! I am jealous of a counterplot!

[1] A favourite essence.

"The patch, the powder-box, pulville-perfumes."
GAY, *The Fan*, i, 129.

"Have you pulvilled the coachman?"—*The Way of the World*, iv, 1.

[2] i.e. suspect that we are talking about them.

Lov. Your liveries are the finest, Sir Fopling.——Oh, that page! that page is the prettily'st dressed——They are all Frenchmen?

Sir Fop. There's one damned English blockhead among 'em, you may know him by his mien.

Lov. Oh! that's he, that's he! what do you call him?

Sir Fop. Hey!——I know not what to call him.——

Lov. What's your name?

Footman. John Trott, madam!

Sir Fop. Oh, unsufferable! Trott, Trott, Trott! there's nothing so barbarous as the names of our English servants. What countryman are you, sirrah?

Footman. Hampshire, sir.

Sir Fop. Then Hampshire be your name. Hey, Hampshire!

Lov. Oh, that sound! that sound becomes the mouth of a man of quality!

Med. Dorimant, you look a little bashful on the matter.

Dor. She dissembles better than I thought she could have done.

Med. You have tempted her with too luscious a bait: she bites at the coxcomb.

Dor. She cannot fall from loving me to that?

Med. You begin to be jealous in earnest.

Dor. Of one I do not love?

Med. You did love her.

Dor. The fit has long been over.

Med. But I have known men fall into dangerous relapses when they have found a woman inclining to another.

Dor. [*to himself*]. He guesses the secret of my heart! I am concerned, but dare not show it lest Belinda should mistrust all I have done to gain her.

Bel. [*aside*]. I have watched his look, and find no alteration there: did he love her, some signs of jealousy would have appeared.

Dor. I hope this happy evening, madam, has reconciled you to the scandalous Mall; we shall have you now hankering here again.

Lov. Sir Fopling, will you walk?

Sir Fop. I am all obedience, madam.

Lov. Come along then, and let's agree to be malicious on all the ill-fashioned things we meet.

Sir Fop. We'll make a *critique* on the whole Mall, madam.

Lov. Belinda, you shall engage——

Bel. To the reserve of our friends, my dear.

Lov. No, no exceptions——

Sir Fop. We'll sacrifice all to our diversion.

Lov. All—all——

Sir Fop. All.

Bel. All? Then let it be.

     [*Exeunt* Sir FOPLING, LOVEIT, BELINDA, *and* PERT, *laughing*.

Med. Would you had brought some more of your friends, Dorimant, to have been witnesses of Sir Fopling's disgrace and your triumph.

Dor. 'Twere unreasonable to desire you not to laugh at me; but pray do not expose me to the town this day or two.

Med. By that time you hope to have regained your credit?

Dor. I know she hates Fopling, and only makes use of him in hope to work me on again; had it not been for some powerful considerations which will be removed to-morrow morning, I had made her pluck off this mask and show the passion that lies panting under.

Enter a Footman.

Med. Here comes a man from Bellair, with news of your last adventure.

Dor. I am glad he sent him. I long to know the consequence of our parting.

Footman. Sir, my master desires you to come to my Lady Townley's presently, and bring Mr. Medley with you. My Lady Woodvil and her daughter are there.

Med. Then all's well, Dorimant.

Footman. They have sent for the fiddles and mean to dance! He bid me tell you, sir, the old lady does not know you, and would have you own yourself to be Mr. Courtage. They are all prepared to receive you by that name.

Dor. That foppish admirer of quality who flatters the very meat at honourable tables, and never offers love to a woman below a lady-grandmother.

Med. You know the character you are to act, I see.

Dor. This is Harriet's contrivance——wild, witty, lovesome, beautiful and young——come along, Medley.

Med. This new woman would well supply the loss of Loveit.

Dor. That business must not end so; before to-morrow's sun is set I will revenge and clear it:

And you and Loveit to her cost shall find,
I fathom all the depths of womankind. 　　　　[*Exeunt.*

ACT IV

SCENE I.—*The scene opens with the fiddles playing a country dance*

Enter DORIMANT, Lady WOODVIL, YOUNG BELLAIR, *and* Mrs. HARRIET, OLD BELLAIR, *and* EMILIA, Mr. MEDLEY *and* Lady TOWNLEY, *as having just ended the dance.*

O. Bell. So, so, so, a smart bout, a very smart bout, adod!

Lady Town. How do you like Emilia's dancing, brother?

O. Bell. Not at all, not at all.

Lady Town. You speak not what you think, I am sure.

O. Bell. No matter for that; go, bid her dance no more, it don't become her, it don't become her, tell her I say so. [*Aside.*] Adod, I love her.

Dor. [*to* Lady WOODVIL]. All people mingle nowadays, madam, and in public places women of quality have the least respect showed 'em.

Lady Wood. I protest you say the truth, Mr. Courtage.

Dor. Forms and ceremonies, the only things that uphold quality and greatness, are now shamefully laid aside and neglected.

Lady Wood. Well! this is not the women's age, let 'em think what they will; lewdness is the business now, love was the business in my time.

Dor. The women indeed are little beholding to the young men of this age; they're generally only dull admirers of themselves, and make their court to nothing but their periwigs and their cravats, and would be more concerned for the disordering of 'em, though on a good occasion, than a young maid would be for the tumbling of her head or handkerchief.

Lady Wood. I protest you hit 'em.

Dor. They are very assiduous to show themselves at Court well dressed to the women of quality, but their business is with the stale mistresses of the town, who are prepared to receive their lazy addresses by industrious old lovers who have cast 'em off and made 'em easy.

Har. He fits my mother's humour so well, a little more and she'll dance a kissing dance with him anon.

Med. Dutifully observed, madam.

Dor. They pretend to be great critics in beauty; by their talk you would think they liked no face, and yet can dote on an ill one if it belong to a laundress or a tailor's daughter; they cry a woman's past her prime at twenty, decayed at four-and-twenty, old and unsufferable at thirty.

Lady Wood. Unsufferable at thirty! That they are in the wrong, Mr. Courtage, at five-and-thirty there are living proofs enough to convince 'em.

Dor. Ay, madam, there's Mrs. Setlooks, Mrs. Droplip, and my Lady Lowd; show me among all our opening buds a face that promises so much beauty as the remains of theirs.

Lady Wood. The depraved appetite of this vicious age tastes nothing but green fruit, and loathes it when 'tis kindly ripened.

Dor. Else so many deserving women, madam, would not be so untimely neglected.

Lady Wood. I protest, Mr. Courtage, a dozen such good men as you would be enough to atone for that wicked Dorimant and all the under-debauchees of the town.

[HARRIET, EMILIA, YOUNG BELLAIR, MEDLEY, *and* Lady TOWNLEY *break out into laughter.*

What's the matter there?

Med. A pleasant mistake, madam, that a lady has made, occasions a little laughter.

O. Bell. Come, come, you keep 'em idle, they are impatient till the fiddles play again.

Dor. You are not weary, madam?

Lady Wood. One dance more; I cannot refuse you, Mr. Courtage. [*They dance.*

Emil. You are very active, sir.

[*After the dance* OLD BELLAIR *singing and dancing up to* EMILIA.

O. Bell. Adod, sirrah, when I was a young fellow I could ha' capered up to my woman's gorget.

Dor. You are willing to rest yourself, madam?

Lady Town. We'll walk into my chamber and sit down.

Med. Leave us Mr. Courtage, he's a dancer, and the young ladies are not weary yet.

Lady Wood. We'll send him out again.

Har. If you do not quickly, I know where to send for Mr. Dorimant.

Lady Wood. This girl's head, Mr. Courtage, is ever running on that wild fellow.

Dor. 'Tis well you have got her a good husband, madam; that will settle it.

[*Exeunt* Lady TOWNLEY, Lady WOODVIL, *and* DORIMANT.

O. Bell. [*to* EMILIA]. Adod, sweetheart, be advised, and do not throw thyself away on a young idle fellow.

Emil. I have no such intention, sir.

O. Bell. Have a little patience, thou shalt have the man I spake of. Adod, he loves thee, and will make a good husband; but no words.

Emil. But, sir.——

O. Bell. No answer——out a pise! peace! and think on't.

Enter DORIMANT.

Dor. Your company is desired within, sir.

O. Bell. I go, I go, good Mr. Courtage—— [*To* EMILIA.] Fare you well; go, I'll see you no more.

Emil. What have I done, sir?

O. Bell. You are ugly, you are ugly; is she not, Mr. Courtage?

Emil. Better words, or I shan't abide you.

O. Bell. Out a pise——adod, what does she say? Hit her a pat for me there. [*Exit* OLD BELLAIR.

Med. You have charms for the whole family.

Dor. You'll spoil all with some unseasonable jest, Medley.

Med. You see I confine my tongue and am content to be a bare spectator, much contrary to my nature.

Emil. Methinks, Mr. Dorimant, my Lady Woodvil is a little fond of you.

Dor. Would her daughter were!

Med. It may be you may find her so; try her, you have an opportunity.

Dor. And I will not lose it. Bellair, here's a lady has something to say to you.

Y. Bell. I wait upon her. Mr. Medley, we have both business with you.

Dor. Get you all together then. [*To* HARRIET.] That demure curtsey is not amiss in jest, but do not think in earnest it becomes you.

Har. Affectation is catching, I find; from your grave bow I got it.

Dor. Where had you all that scorn and coldness in your look?

Har. From nature, sir; pardon my want of art: I have not learnt those softnesses and languishings which now in faces are so much in fashion.

Dor. You need 'em not; you have a sweetness of your own, if you would but calm your frowns and let it settle.

Har. My eyes are wild and wandering like my passions, and cannot yet be tied to rules of charming.

Dor. Women, indeed, have commonly a method of managing those messengers of love; now they will look as if they would kill, and anon they will look as if they were dying. They point and rebate [1] their glances the better to invite us.

Har. I like this variety well enough, but hate the set face that always looks as it would say, Come, love me—a woman who at plays makes the *doux yeux* to a whole audience and at home cannot forbear 'em to her monkey.

Dor. Put on a gentle smile, and let me see how well it will become you.

Har. I am sorry my face does not please you as it is, but I shall not be complaisant and change it.

[1] A fencing term.

Dor. Though you are obstinate, I know 'tis capable of improvement, and shall do you justice, madam, if I chance to be at Court when the critics of the circle pass their judgment; for thither you must come.

Har. And expect to be taken in pieces, have all my features examined, every motion censured, and on the whole be condemned to be but pretty, or a beauty of the lowest rate. What think you?

Dor. The women, nay, the very lovers who belong to the drawing-room, will maliciously allow you more than that; they always grant what is apparent that they may the better be believed when they name concealed faults they cannot easily be disproved in.

Har. Beauty runs as great a risk exposed at Court as wit does on the stage, where the ugly and the foolish all are free to censure.

Dor. [*aside*]. I love her, and dare not let her know it; I fear she has an ascendant o'er me, and may revenge the wrongs I have done her sex. [*To her.*] Think of making a party, madam, love will engage.

Har. You make me start! I did not think to have heard of love from you.

Dor. I never knew what 'twas to have a settled ague yet, but now and then have had irregular fits.

Har. Take heed! sickness after long health is commonly more violent and dangerous.

Dor. [*aside*]. I have took the infection from her, and feel the disease now spreading in me—— [*To her.*] Is the name of love so frightful that you dare not stand it?

Har. 'Twill do little execution out of your mouth on me, I am sure.

Dor. It has been fatal——

Har. To some easy women, but we are not all born to one destiny; I was informed you use to laugh at love, and not make it.

Dor. The time has been, but now I must speak——

Har. If it be on that idle subject, I will put on my serious look, turn my head carelessly from you, drop my lip, let my eyelids fall and hang half o'er my eyes—thus—while you buzz a speech of an hour long in my ear, and I answer never a word; why do you not begin?

Dor. That the company may take notice how passionately I make advances of love, and how disdainfully you receive 'em.

Har. When your love's grown strong enough to make you bear being laughed at, I'll give you leave to trouble me with it: till when, pray forbear, sir.

Enter Sir FOPLING *and others in masks.*

Dor. What's here, masquerades?

Har. I thought that foppery had been left off and people might have been in private with a fiddle.

Dor. 'Tis endeavoured to be kept on foot still by some who find themselves the more acceptable the less they are known.

Y. Bell. This must be Sir Fopling.

Med. That extraordinary habit shows it.

Y. Bell. What are the rest?

Med. A company of French rascals whom he picked up in Paris and has brought over to be his dancing equipage on these occasions. Make him own himself; a fool is very troublesome when he presumes he is incognito.

Sir Fop. [*to* HARRIET]. Do you know me?

Har. Ten to one but I guess at you.

Sir Fop. Are you women as fond of a vizard as we men are?

Har. I am very fond of a vizard that covers a face I do not like, sir.

Y. Bell. Here are no masks, you see, sir, but those which came with you; this was intended a private meeting, but because you look like a gentleman, if you discover yourself, and we know you to be such, you shall be welcome.

Sir Fop. [*pulling off his mask*]. Dear Bellair.

Med. Sir Fopling! how came you hither?

Sir Fop. Faith, I was coming late from Whitehall, after the King's *couchée*, one of my people told me he had heard fiddles at my Lady Townley's, and——

Dor. You need not say any more, sir.

Sir Fop. Dorimant, let me kiss thee.

Dor. [*whispers*]. Hark you, Sir Fopling.

Sir Fop. Enough, enough—Courtage. A pretty kind of young woman that, Medley; I observed her in the Mall; more *éveillée* [1] than our English women commonly are; prithee, what is she?

Med. The most noted *coquette* in town; beware of her.

Sir Fop. Let her be what she will, I know how to take my measures; in Paris the *mode* is to flatter the *prude*, laugh at the *faux-prude*, make serious love to the *demi-prude*, and only rally with the *coquette*. Medley, what think you?

Med. That for all this smattering of the mathematics, you may be out in your judgment at tennis.

Sir Fop. What a *coq-à-l'âne* is this! I talk of women, and thou answer'st tennis.

Med. Mistakes will be for want of apprehension.

Sir Fop. I am very glad of the acquaintance I have with this family.

Med. My lady truly is a good woman.

Sir Fop. Ah! Dorimant—Courtage I would say—would thou hadst spent the last winter in Paris with me. When thou wert

---

[1] Cf. the *Spectator*, No. 45, on the "Invasion of French Manners": "The whole behaviour of the French is to make the sex (women) more fantastical, or (as they are pleased to call it) more *awakened*."

there La Corneus and Sallyes[1] were the only habitudes we had; a comedian would have been a *bonne fortune*. No stranger ever passed his time so well as I did some months before I came over. I was well received in a dozen families where all the women of quality used to visit; I have intrigues to tell thee more pleasant than ever thou read'st in a novel.

Har. Write'em, sir, and oblige us women; our language wants such little stories.

Sir Fop. Writing, madam, is a mechanic part of wit; a gentleman should never go beyond a song or a billet.

Har. Bussy was a gentleman.

Sir Fop. Who, d'Ambois?[2]

Med. Was there ever such a brisk blockhead?

Har. Not d'Ambois, sir, but Rabutin[3]—he who writ *The Loves of France*.

Sir Fop. That may be madam: many gentlemen do things that are below'em. Damn your authors, Courtage; women are the prettiest things we can fool away our time with.

Har. I hope ye have wearied yourself to-night at Court sir, and will not think of fooling with anybody here.

Sir Fop. I cannot complain of my fortune there, madam—— Dorimant——

Dor. Again!

Sir Fop. Courtage, a pox on't! I have something to tell thee.

---

[1] So the old editions. Possibly Etherege wrote *Cornuel* and *Selles*. Readers of Madame de Sévigné will remember allusions to a Madame Cornuel whose epigrams were deservedly admired. She is mentioned in Bussy's letters, plays some part in the *Histoire Amoureuse* (*Memoires*, vol. ii, pp. 350–8), and altogether seems to have been a distinguished figure in French society. Very probably Etherege knew her, at least by fame, and may be referring to her here. Madame Selles is less tangible. Bussy, however, mentions a lady of that name who had attracted some attention by "une petite histoire de ses amours." This *histoire* is spoken of several times in the *Correspondance* (vol. ii, pp. 134–7), and its author may have presided over one of the fashionable *salons* of the time. At any rate, it should be noticed that all the names which occur in the play—Candale, Merille, Lambert, etc.—are those of contemporaries, and all through Etherege is bent on showing his close familiarity with the great world of Paris.

[2] To whom is Etherege referring?—the great French cardinal and minister, or the nobleman whose adventures are chronicled in Dumas' *La Dame de Monsoreau*?

[3] Bussy-Rabutin, Roger, Comte de; born 1618, died 1693; a cousin of Madame de Sévigné, with whom he corresponded. A complete edition of his *Memoires* and *Correspondance* was published at Paris, 1857–9. Etherege speaks so familiarly of him that one is tempted to think he knew the author of the *Histoire Amoureuse*, and I hoped—vainly, however—to find some reference in the letters to the English dramatist. Of Bussy's numerous works the fame of the *Histoire Amoureuse des Gaules* alone has survived. It appears to have been extremely popular, possessing "a thousand irresistible graces," according to the dictum of that politest of eighteenth-century critics, the ingenious and courtly Major Pack (*Works*, ed. 1729).

When I had made my court within, I came out and flung myself upon the mat under the State i' th' outward room i' th' midst of half a dozen beauties who were withdrawn to jeer among themselves, as they called it.

Dor. Did you know 'em?

Sir Fop. Not one of 'em by heavens! not I. But they were all your friends.

Dor. How are you sure of that?

Sir Fop. Why we laughed at all the town; spared nobody but yourself; they found me a man for their purpose.

Dor. I know you are malicious to your power.

Sir Fop. And faith I had occasion to show it for I never saw more gaping fools at a ball or on a Birthday.

Dor. You learned who the women were?

Sir Fop. No matter; they frequent the drawing-room.

Dor. And entertain themselves pleasantly at the expense of all the fops who come there.

Sir Fop. That's their business; faith, I sifted 'em, and find they have a sort of wit among them——Ah! filthy.

[*Pinches a tallow candle.*

Dor. Look, he has been pinching the tallow candle.

Sir Fop. How can you breathe in a room where there's grease frying? Dorimant, thou art intimate with my lady, advise her for her own sake, and the good company that comes hither, to burn wax lights.

Har. What are these masquerades who stand so obsequiously at a distance?

Sir Fop. A set of *balladins* whom I picked out of the best in France, and brought over with a *flutes douces* or two, my servants; they shall entertain you.

Har. I had rather see you dance yourself, Sir Fopling.

Sir Fop. And I had rather do it—all the company knows it —but, madam——

Med. Come, come, no excuses, Sir Fopling.

Sir Fop. By heavens, Medley!

Med. Like a woman, I find you must be struggled with before one brings you to what you desire.

Har. [*aside*]. Can he dance?

Emil. And fence and sing too, if you'll believe him.

Dor. He has no more excellence in his heels than in his head. He went to Paris a plain bashful English blockhead, and is returned a fine undertaking French fop.

Med. I cannot prevail.

Sir Fop. Do not think it want of complaisance, madam.

Har. You are too well bred to want that, Sir Fopling. I believe it want of power.

Sir Fop. By heavens! and so it is. I have sat up so damned late and drunk so cursed hard since I came to this lewd town, that

I am fit for nothing but low dancing now, a *corant, bourée,*[1] or a *menuet;* but St. André tells me, if I will but be regular, in one month I shall rise again.   Pox on this debauchery!

[Endeavours at a caper.

Emil. I have heard your dancing much commended.

Sir Fop. It had the good fortune to please in Paris. I was judged to rise within an inch as high as the *basque,* in an entry I danced there.

Har. I am mightily taken with this fool; let us sit.   Here's a seat, Sir Fopling.

Sir Fop. At your feet, madam; I can be nowhere so much at ease: by your leave, gown.

Har. and Emil. Ah! you'll spoil it.

Sir Fop. No matter, my clothes are my creatures; I make 'em to make my court to you ladies, hey——   *[Dance.*
Qu'on commence—to an English dancer English motions.   I was forced to entertain this fellow, one of my set miscarrying—— Oh, horrid! leave your damned manner of dancing, and put on the French air; have you not a pattern before you——pretty well!   Imitation in time may bring him to something.

After the dance enter OLD BELLAIR, Lady WOODVIL, *and Lady* TOWNLEY.

O. Bell. Hey, adod! what have we here, a mumming?

Lady Wood. Where's my daughter——Harriet?

Dor. Here, here, madam.   I know not but under these disguises there may be dangerous sparks; I gave the young lady warning.

Lady Wood. Lord!   I am so obliged to you, Mr. Courtage.

Har. Lord! how you admire this man.

Lady Wood. What have you to except against him?

Har. He's a fop.

Lady Wood. He's not a Dorimant, a wild extravagant fellow of the times.

Har. He's a man made up of forms and commonplaces sucked out of the remaining lees of the last age.

Lady Wood. He's so good a man, that were you not engaged——

Lady Town. You'll have but little night to sleep in.

Lady Wood. Lord! 'tis perfect day——

Dor. [*aside*]. The hour is almost come I appointed Belinda, and I am not so foppishly in love here to forget: I am flesh and blood yet.

Lady Town. I am very sensible, madam.

---

[1] For the former, cf. *Henry V,* iii, 5, 33:
            "And teach lavoltas high and swift corantos."
For a note on the *bourée* Ashton's *Social Life in the Reign of Queen Anne* (i, 100) may be consulted.

Lady Wood. Lord, madam!

Har. Look, in what struggle is my poor mother yonder?

Y. Bell. She has much ado to bring out the compliment.

Dor. She strains hard for it.

Har. See, see! her head tottering, her eyes staring, and her under lip trembling

Dor. [*aside*]. Now, now she's in the very convulsions of her civility. 'Sdeath, I shall lose Belinda. I must fright her hence; she'll be an hour in this fit of good manners else. [*To* Lady Woodvil.] Do you not know Sir Fopling, madam?

Lady Wood. I have seen that face   Oh, heaven! 'tis the same we met in the Mall; how came he here?

Dor. A fiddle in this town is a kind of fop-call; no sooner it strikes up but the house is besieged with an army of masquerades straight.

Lady Wood. Lord! I tremble, Mr. Courtage; for certain Dorimant is in the company.

Dor. I cannot confidently say he is not; you had best begone. I will wait upon you; your daughter is in the hands of Mr. Bellair.

Lady Wood. I'll see her before me. Harriet, come away.

Y. Bell. Lights! lights!

Lady Town. Light down there.

O. Bell. Adod, it needs not

Dor. Call my Lady Woodvil's coach to the door quickly.

[*Exeunt* Dorimant *and* Young Bellair, *with the Ladies.*

O. Bell. Stay, Mr. Medley, let the young fellows do that duty; we will drink a glass of wine together. 'Tis good after dancing; what mumming spark is that?

Med. He is not to be comprehended in few words.

Sir Fop. Hey! La Tour.

Med. Whither away, Sir Fopling?

Sir Fop. I have business with Courtage——

Med. He'll but put the ladies into their coach, and come up again.

O. Bell. In the meantime I'll call for a bottle.

[*Exit* Old Bellair.

Enter Young Bellair.

Med. Where's Dorimant?

Y. Bell. Stolen home; he has had business waiting for him there all this night, I believe, by an impatience I observed in him.

Med. Very likely; 'tis but dissembling drunkenness, railing at his friends, and the kind soul will embrace the blessing and forget the tedious expectation.

Sir Fop. I must speak with him before I sleep.

Y. Bell. Emilia and I are resolved on that business.

Med. Peace, here's your father.

Enter OLD BELLAIR *and Butler, with a bottle of wine.*

O. Bell. The women are all gone to bed. Fill, boy; Mr. Medley, begin a health.

Med. [*whispers*]. To Emilia.

O. Bell. Out, a pise! she's a rogue, and I'll not pledge you.

Med. I know you will.

O. Bell. Adod, drink it then.

Sir Fop. Let us have the new *bachique.*

O. Bell. Adod, that is a hard word; what does it mean, sir?

Med. A catch or drinking song.

O. Bell. Let us have it then.

Sir Fop. Fill the glasses round, and draw up in a body.   Hey! music!

THEY SING

The pleasures of love and the joys of good wine
To perfect our happiness wisely we join.
We to beauty all day
Give the sovereign sway,
And her favourite nymphs devoutly obey.
At the plays we are constantly making our court,
And when they are ended we follow the sport,
To the Mall and the Park,
Where we love till 'tis dark;
Then sparkling champagne
Puts an end to their reign;
It quickly recovers
Poor languishing lovers,
Makes us frolic and gay, and drowns all our sorrow;
But, alas! we relapse again on the morrow.
Let ev'ry man stand
With his glass in his hand,
And briskly discharge at the word of command.
Here's a health to all those
Whom to-night we depose:
Wine and beauty by turns great souls should inspire.
Present altogether, and now, boys, give fire!

O. Bell. Adod, a pretty business, and very merry.

Sir Fop. Hark you, Medley, let you and I take the fiddles, and go waken Dorimant.

Med. We shall do him a courtesy, if it be as I guess.   For after the fatigue of this night, he'll quickly have his bellyful, and be glad of an occasion to cry: Take away, Handy.

Y. Bell. I'll go with you, and there we'll consult about affairs, Medley.

O. Bell. [*looks at his watch*]. Adod, 'tis six o'clock.

Sir Fop. Let's away then.

O. Bell. Mr. Medley, my sister tells me you are an honest man, and, adod, I love you. Few words and hearty—that's the way with old Harry, old Harry.

Sir Fop. Light your *flambeaux.* Hey!

O. Bell. What does the man mean?

Med. 'Tis day, Sir Fopling.

Sir Fop. No matter. Our serenade will look the greater.

[*Exeunt omnes.*

SCENE II.—DORIMANT's *Lodging. A table, a candle, a toilet, etc.*
HANDY *tying up linen*

Enter DORIMANT *in his gown, and* BELINDA.

Dor. Why will you be gone so soon?

Bel. Why did you stay out so late?

Dor. Call a chair, Handy. [*Exit* HANDY.
What makes you tremble so?

Bel. I have a thousand fears about me. Have I not been seen, think you?

Dor. By nobody but myself and trusty Handy.

Bel. Where are all your people?

Dor. I have dispersed 'em on sleeveless [1] errands. What does that sigh mean?

Bel. Can you be so unkind to ask me?—Well—[*Sighs.*] were it to do again——

Dor. We should do it, should we not?

Bel. I think we should; the wickeder man you to make me love so well. Will you be discreet now?

Dor. I will.

Bel. You cannot.

Dor. Never doubt it.

Bel. I will not expect it.

Dor. You do me wrong.

Bel. You have no more power to keep the secret than I had not to trust you with it.

Dor. By all the joys I have had, and those you keep in store——

Bel. You'll do for my sake what you never did before——

Dor. By that truth thou hast spoken, a wife shall sooner betray herself to her husband——

Bel. Yet I had rather you should be false in this, than in any other thing you promised me.

Dor. What's that?

Bel. That you would never see Loveit more but in public places, in the Park, at Court, and plays.

Dor. 'Tis not likely a man should be fond of seeing a damned old play when there is a new one acted.

Bel. I dare not trust your promise.

[1] i.e. fruitless: "on a sleeveless errand."—*Troilus and Cressida*, v, 4.

Dor. You may.

Bel. This does not satisfy me. You shall swear you never will see her more.

Dor. I will! A thousand oaths——By all——

Bel. Hold——You shall not, now I think on't better.

Dor. I will swear.

Bel. I shall grow jealous of the oath, and think I owe your truth to that, not to your love.

Dor. Then, by my love, no other oath I'll swear.

Enter HANDY.

Handy. Here's a chair.

Bel. Let me go.

Dor. I cannot

Bel. Too willingly, I fear.

Dor. Too unkindly feared   When will you promise me again?

Bel. Not this fortnight

Dor. You will be better than your word.

Bel. I think I shall. Will it not make you love me less? [*Starting.*] Hark! what fiddles are these? [*Fiddles without.*

Dor. Look out Handy.   [*Exit* HANDY *and returns.*

Handy. Mr. Medley, Mr. Bellair, and Sir Fopling; they are coming up.

Dor. How got they in?

Handy. The door was open for the chair.

Bel. Lord! let me fly——

Dor. Here, here, down the back stairs. I'll see you into your chair.

Bel. No, no, stay and receive 'em, and be sure you keep your word and never see Loveit more: let it be a proof of your kindness.

Dor. It shall——Handy, direct her. Everlasting love go along with thee.   [*Kissing her hand.*
    [*Exeunt* BELINDA *and* HANDY.

Enter YOUNG BELLAIR, MEDLEY, *and* Sir FOPLING.

Y. Bell. Not a-bed yet!

Med. You have had an irregular fit, Dorimant?

Dor. I have.

Y. Bell. And is it off already?

Dor. Nature has done her part, gentlemen; when she falls kindly to work, great cures are effected in little time, you know.

Sir Fop. We thought there was a wench in the case by the chair that waited. Prithee make us a *confidence*.

Dor. Excuse me.

Sir Fop. Le sage Dorimant! was she pretty?

Dor. So pretty she may come to keep her coach and pay parish duties if the good humour of the age continue.

Med. And be of the number of the ladies kept by public-spirited men for the good of the whole town.

Sir Fop. Well said, Medley.

[Sir FOPLING *dancing by himself.*

Y. Bell. See, Sir Fopling dancing.

Dor. You are practising and have a mind to recover, I see.

Sir Fop. Prithee, Dorimant, why hast not thou a glass hung up here? A room is the dullest thing without one.

Y. Bell. Here is company to entertain you.

Sir Fop. But I mean in case of being alone. In a glass a man may entertain himself

Dor. The shadow of himself indeed.

Sir Fop. Correct the errors of his motions and his dress.

Med. I find, Sir Fopling, in your solitude you remember the saying of the wise man, and study yourself.

Sir Fop. 'Tis the best diversion in our retirements. Dorimant, thou art a pretty fellow, and wear'st thy clothes well, but I never saw thee have a handsome cravat. Were they made up like mine, they'd give another air to thy face. Prithee let me send my man to dress thee but one day. By heavens! an Englishman cannot tie a ribbon.

Dor. They are something clumsy-fisted

Sir Fop. I have brought over the prettiest fellow that ever spread a toilet; he served some time under Merille,[1] the greatest *genie* in the world for a *valet-de-chambre.*

Dor. What, he who formerly belonged to the Duke of Candale?[2]

Sir Fop. The same, and got him his immortal reputation.

Dor. You've a very fine *brandenburgh* on, Sir Fopling.

Sir Fop. It serves to wrap me up after the fatigue of a ball.

Med. I see you often in it, with your periwig tied up.

Sir Fop. We should not always be in a set dress; 'tis more *en cavalier* to appear now and then in a *déshabillé.*

Med. Pray how goes your business with Loveit?

Sir Fop. You might have answered yourself in the Mall last night. Dorimant! did you not see the advances she made me? I have been endeavouring at a song.

---

[1] Mentioned in the *Histoire Amoureuse* as "le prinicpal confident du duc" (i.e. Candale).—Bussy's *Memoires*, vol. ii, p. 322. Subsequently he passed into the service of the Duke of Orleans; cf. the *Correspondance* vol. ii, p. 313 ("valet de chambre de M. le duc d'Orléans"), and vol. iii, p. 240, where he has risen to the dignity of "premier valet de chambre de Monsieur."

[2] Often referred to in Bussy's *Memoires*. The allusion to his "immortal reputation" is explained by a passage in the *Histoire Amoureuse*: "Le duc de Candale avait les yeux bleus, le nez bien fait, les traits irreguliers, la bouche grande et désagréable mais de fort belles dents, les cheveux blonds-dorés, en la plus grande quantité du monde. Sa taille était admirable et s'habillait bien, et les plus propres tâchaient de l'imiter. Il avait l'air d'un homme de grande qualité, il tenait un des premiers rangs en France." Doubtless the duke's love-affair with Madame Olonne served as a title to distinction.

Dor. Already!

Sir Fop. 'Tis my *coup d'essai* in English; I would fain have thy opinion of it.

Dor. Let's see it.

Sir Fop. Hey, Page! give me my song——Bellair, here, thou hast a pretty voice, sing it.

Y. Bell. Sing it yourself, Sir Fopling.

Sir Fop. Excuse me.

Y. Bell. You learnt to sing in Paris.

Sir Fop. I did, of Lambert,[1] the greatest master in the world; but I have his own fault, a weak voice, and care not to sing out of a *ruelle.*[2]

Dor. A *ruelle* is a pretty cage for a singing fop, indeed.

YOUNG BELLAIR *reads the song.*

> How charming Phyllis is! how fair!
>   Ah, that she were as willing
> To ease my wounded heart of care,
>   And make her eyes less killing!
> I sigh! I sigh! I languish now,
>   And love will not let me rest;
> I drive about the Park, and bow
>   Still as I meet my dearest.

Sir Fop. Sing it, sing it, man; it goes to a pretty new tune, which I am confident was made by Baptiste.[3]

Med. Sing it yourself, Sir Fopling; he does not know the tune.

Sir Fop. I'll venture.   [Sir FOPLING *sings.*

Dor. Ay, marry, now 'tis something. I shall not flatter you, Sir Fopling; there is not much thought in 't, but 'tis passionate, and well turned.

Med. After the French way.

Sir Fop. That I aimed at. Does it not give you a lively image of the thing? Slap down goes the glass, and thus we are at it.

Dor. It does indeed. I perceive, Sir Fopling, you'll be the

---

[1] Michel Lambert, "maître de la musique de la chambre du roi"; born 1610, died July 1696.

[2] Properly the *ruelle* was the space in a bedroom between the bed and the wall: "Se disait particulièrement des chambres à coucher sous Louis XIV, des alcôves de certaines dames de qualité, servant de salon de conversation et où régnait souvent le ton précieux."—Littré. Turning to *Les Précieuses* (scene ix), we find Mascarille saying: "Et vous verrez courir de ma façon, dans les belles ruelles de Paris, deux cents chansons, autant de sonnets." The use of the word here is one of those intimate touches in which Etherege delights.

[3] "The present great composer," says Pepys, 18th June, 1666. Baptiste—his real name was Baptiste Anet—was a pupil of Corelli; as a violinist he had a great reputation. He settled in Paris, but being badly received by Louis XIV eventually retired into Poland, where he died.

very head of the sparks who are lucky in compositions of this nature.

Enter Sir FOPLING'S *Footman.*

Sir Fop. La Tour, is the bath ready?

Footman. Yes, sir.

Sir Fop. Adieu donc, mes chers.   [*Exit* Sir FOPLING.

Med. When have you your revenge on Loveit, Dorimant?

Dor. I will but change my linen, and about it.

Med. The powerful considerations which hindered have been removed then?

Dor. Most luckily this morning; you must along with me, my reputation lies at stake there.

Med. I am engaged to Bellair.

Dor. What's your business?

Med. Ma-tri-mony, an't like you.

Dor. It does not, sir.

Y. Bell. It may in time, Dorimant; what think you of Mrs. Harriet?

Dor. What does she think of me?

Y. Bell. I am confident she loves you.

Dor. How does it appear?

Y. Bell. Why, she's never well but when she's talking of you; but then she finds all the faults in you she can. She laughs at all who commend you; but then she speaks ill of all who do not.

Dor. Women of her temper betray themselves by their over-cunning. I had once a growing love with a lady who would always quarrel with me when I came to see her, and yet was never quiet if I stayed a day from her.

Y. Bell. My father is in love with Emilia.

Dor. That is a good warrant for your proceedings: go on and prosper; I must to Loveit. Medley, I am sorry you cannot be a witness.

Med. Make her meet Sir Fopling again in the same place, and use him ill before me.

Dor. That may be brought about, I think. I'll be at your aunt's anon, and give you joy, Mr. Bellair.

Y. Bell. You had not best think of Mrs. Harriet too much; without church security there's no taking up there.

Dor. I may fall into the snare too.   But

> The wise will find a difference in our fate;
> You wed a woman, I a good estate.   [*Exeunt.*

SCENE III

Enter the Chair with BELINDA; *the Men set it down and open it.*
BELINDA *starting.*

Bel. [*surprised*]. Lord! where am I? in the Mall? Whither
have you brought me?

1 Chairman. You gave us no directions, madam.

Bel. [*aside*]. The fright I was in made me forget it.

1 Chairman. We use to carry a lady from the squire's hither.

Bel. [*aside*]. This is Loveit; I am undone if she sees me.
Quickly carry me away.

1 Chairman. Whither, an't like your honour?

Bel. Ask no questions.

Enter LOVEIT'S *Footman.*

Footman. Have you seen my lady, madam?

Bel. I am just come to wait upon her.

Footman. She will be glad to see you, madam. She sent me
to you this morning to desire your company, and I was told you
went out by five o'clock.

Bel. [*aside*]. More and more unlucky!

Footman. Will you walk in, madam?

Bel. I'll discharge my chair and follow. Tell your mistress
I am here.   [*Exit Footman.*
                                       [*Gives the Chairmen money.*
Take this, and if ever you should be examined, be sure you say
you took me up in the Strand, over against the Exchange, as
you will answer it to Mr. Dorimant.

Chairmen. We will, an't like your honour.
                                           [*Exeunt Chairmen.*

Bel. Now to come off, I must on——

      In confidence and lies some hope is left;
      'Twere hard to be found out in the first theft. [*Exit*

ACT V

SCENE I

Enter Mistress Loveit *and* Pert, *her woman.*

Pert. Well, in my eyes Sir Fopling is no such despicable person.
Lov. You are an excellent judge!
Pert. He's as handsome a man as Mr. Dorimant, and as great a gallant.
Lov. Intolerable! is't not enough I submit to his impertinences, but I must be plagued with yours too?
Pert. Indeed, madam——
Lov. 'Tis false, mercenary malice——

Enter her Footman.

Footman. Mrs. Belinda, madam
Lov. What of her?
Footman. She's below.
Lov. How came she?
Footman. In a chair; ambling Harry brought her.
Lov. He bring her! His chair stands near Dorimant's door, and always brings me from thence——Run and ask him where he took her up; go, there is no truth in friendship neither. Women as well as men—all are false, or all are so to me at least.
Pert. You are jealous of her too.
Lov. You had best tell her I am. 'Twill become the liberty you take of late. This fellow's bringing of her, her going out by five o'clock——I know not what to think.

Enter Belinda.

Belinda, you are grown an early riser, I hear.
Bel. Do you not wonder, my dear, what made me abroad so soon?
Lov. You do not use to be so.
Bel. The country gentlewomen I told you of (Lord! they have the oddest diversions!) would never let me rest till I promised to go with them to the markets this morning to eat fruit and buy nosegays.
Lov. Are they so fond of a filthy nosegay?
Bel. They complain of the stinks of the town, and are never well but when they have their noses in one.
Lov. There are essences and sweet waters.
Bel. Oh! they cry out upon perfumes they are unwholesome; one of 'em was falling into a fit with the smell of these *narolii.*

Lov. Methinks, in complaisance you should have had a nosegay too.

Bel. Do you think, my dear, I could be so loathsome to trick myself up with carnations and stock gillyflowers? I begged their pardon, and told them I never wore anything but orange flowers and tuberose. That which made me willing to go was a strange desire I had to eat some fresh nectarines.

Lov. And had you any?

Bel. The best I ever tasted.

Lov. Whence came you now?

Bel. From their lodgings, where I crowded out of a coach, and took a chair to come and see you, my dear.

Lov. Whither did you send for that chair?

Bel. 'Twas going by empty.

Lov. Where do these country gentlewomen lodge, I pray?

Bel. In the Strand, over against the Exchange.

Pert. That place is never without a nest of 'em; they are always as one goes by fleering in balconies or staring out of windows.

Enter Footman.

Lov. [*whispers to the Footman*]. Come hither.

Bel. [*aside*]. This fellow by her order has been questioning the chairmen—I threatened 'em with the name of Dorimant; if they should have told truth I am lost for ever.

Lov. In the Strand, said you?

Footman. Yes, madam, over against the Exchange.

[*Exit Footman.*

Lov. She's innocent, and I am much to blame.

Bel. [*aside*]. I am so frighted my countenance will betray me.

Lov. Belinda! what makes you look so pale?

Bel. Want of my usual rest, and jolting up and down so long in an odious hackney.

Enter Footman.

Footman. Madam, Mr. Dorimant!

Lov. What makes him here?

Bel. [*aside*]. Then I am betrayed indeed; he's broke his word, and I love a man that does not care for me.

Lov. Lord! you faint, Belinda.

Bel. I think I shall; such an oppression here on the sudden.

Pert. She has eaten too much fruit, I warrant you.

Lov. Not unlikely!

Pert. 'Tis that lies heavy on her stomach.

Lov. Have her into my chamber, give her some surfeit water, and let her lie down a little.

Pert. Come, madam, I was a strange devourer of fruit when I was young, so ravenous——

[*Exit* BELINDA, PERT *leading her off.*

Lov. Oh, that my love would be but calm awhile! that I might receive this man with all the scorn and indignation he deserves.

Enter DORIMANT.

Dor. Now for a touch of Sir Fopling to begin with. Hey——page——give positive order that none of my people stir——let the *canaille* wait as they should do: since noise and nonsense have such powerful charms,

> I, that I may successful prove,
> Transform myself to what you love.

Lov. If that would do, you need not change from what you are; you can be vain and loud enough.

Dor. But not with so good a grace as Sir Fopling. Hey, Hampshire!——Oh! that sound! that sound becomes the mouth of a man of quality.

Lov. Is there a thing so hateful as a senseless mimic?

Dor. He's a great grievance indeed to all who like yourself, madam, love to play the fool in quiet.

Lov. A ridiculous animal who has more of the ape than the ape has of the man in him.

Dor. I have as mean an opinion of a sheer mimic as yourself; yet were he all ape I should prefer him to the gay, the giddy, brisk, insipid, noisy fool you dote on.

Lov. Those noisy fools, however you despise 'em, have good qualities, which weigh more (or ought at least) with us women than all the pernicious wit you have to boast of.

Dor. That I may hereafter have a just value for their merit, pray do me the favour to name 'em.

Lov. You'll despise 'em as the dull effects of ignorance and vanity, yet I care not if I mention some. First, they really admire us, while you at best but flatter us well.

Dor. Take heed! fools can dissemble too——

Lov. They may, but not so artificially as you: there is no fear they should deceive us. Then they are assiduous, sir; they are ever offering us their service, and always waiting on our will.

Dor. You owe that to their excessive idleness; they know not how to entertain themselves at home, and find so little welcome abroad, they are fain to fly to you who countenance 'em as a refuge against the solitude they would be otherwise condemned to.

Lov. Their conversation too diverts us better.

Dor. Playing with your fan, smelling to your gloves, commending your hair, and taking notice how 'tis cut and shaded after the new way.

Lov. Were it sillier than you can make it, you must allow 'tis pleasanter to laugh at others than to be laughed at ourselves, though never so wittily. Then though they want skill to flatter us, they flatter themselves so well they save us the labour; we need not take that care and pains to satisfy 'em of our love, which we so often lose on you.

Dor. They commonly indeed believe too well of themselves, and always better of you than you deserve.

Lov. You are in the right; they have an implicit faith in us which keeps 'em from prying narrowly into our secrets, and saves us the vexatious trouble of clearing doubts which your subtle and causeless jealousies every moment raise.

Dor. There is an inbred falsehood in women which inclines 'em still to them whom they may most easily deceive.

Lov. The man who loves above his quality does not suffer more from the insolent impertinence of his mistress than the woman who loves above her understanding does from the arrogant presumptions of her friend.

Dor. You mistake the use of fools: they are designed for properties, and not for friends. You have an indifferent stock of reputation left yet. Lose it all like a frank gamester on the square; 'twill then be time enough to turn rook and cheat it up again on a good substantial bubble.

Lov. The old and the ill-favoured are only fit for properties indeed, but young and handsome fools have met with kinder fortunes.

Dor. They have, to the shame of your sex be it spoken; 'twas this, the thought of this, that made me, by a timely jealousy, endeavour to prevent the good fortune you are providing for Sir Fopling——but against a woman's frailty all our care is vain.

Lov. Had I not with a dear experience bought the knowledge of your falsehood, you might have fooled me yet. This is not the first jealousy you have feigned to make a quarrel with me and get a week to throw away on some such unknown inconsiderable slut as you have been lately lurking with at plays.

Dor. Women, when they would break off with a man, never want th' address to turn the fault on him.

Lov. You take a pride of late in using of me ill, that the town may know the power you have over me, which now (as unreasonably as yourself) expects that I (do me all the injuries you can) must love you still.

Dor. I am so far from expecting that you should, I begin to think you never did love me.

Lov. Would the memory of it were so wholly worn out in me that I did doubt it too! What made you come to disturb my growing quiet?

Dor. To give you joy of your growing infamy.

Lov. Insupportable! insulting devil! this from you, the only author of my shame! This from another had been but justice, but from you 'tis a hellish and inhuman outrage. What have I done?

Dor. A thing that puts you below my scorn and makes my anger as ridiculous as you have made my love.

Lov. I walked last night with Sir Fopling.

Dor. You did, madam, and you talked and laughed aloud, ha, ha, ha!——Oh! that laugh! that laugh becomes the confidence of a woman of quality.

Lov. You, who have more pleasure in the ruin of a woman's reputation than in the endearments of her love, reproach me not with yourself, and I defy you to name the man can lay a blemish on my fame.

Dor. To be seen publicly so transported with the vain follies of that notorious fop, to me is an infamy below the sin of prostitution with another man.

Lov. Rail on, I am satisfied in the justice of what I did; you had provoked me to't.

Dor. What I did was the effect of a passion whose extravagances you have been willing to forgive.

Lov. And what I did was the effect of a passion you may forgive if you think fit.

Dor. Are you so indifferent grown?

Lov. I am.

Dor. Nay! then 'tis time to part. I'll send you back your letters you have so often asked for. I have two or three of 'em about me.

Lov. Give 'em me.

Dor. You snatch as if you thought I would not——there—— and may the perjuries in 'em be mine if e'er I see you more.

　　　　　　　　　　　　　[Offers to go, she catches him.

Lov. Stay!

Dor. I will not.

Lov. You shall.

Dor. What have you to say?

Lov. I cannot speak it yet.

Dor. Something more in commendation of the fool. Death! I want patience, let me go.

Lov. [*aside*]. I cannot. I can sooner part with the limbs that hold him. I hate that nauseous fool, you know I do.

Dor. Was it the scandal you were fond of then?

Lov. You'd raised my anger equal to my love, a thing you ne'er could do before, and in revenge I did——I know not what I did.——Would you would not think on't any more!

Dor. Should I be willing to forget it, I shall be daily minded of it, 'twill be a commonplace for all the town to laugh at me; and Medley, when he is rhetorically drunk, will ever be declaiming on it in my ears.

Lov. 'Twill be believed a jealous spite! Come, forget it.

Dor. Let me consult my reputation; you are too careless of it [*pauses*]. You shall meet Sir Fopling in the Mall again to-night.

Lov. What mean you?

Dor. I have thought on't, and you must: 'tis necessary to

justify my love to the world; you can handle a coxcomb as he deserves when you are not out of humour, madam.

Lov. Public satisfaction for the wrong I have done you! This is some new device to make me more ridiculous.

Dor. Hear me.

Lov. I will not.

Dor. You will be persuaded.

Lov. Never.

Dor. Are you so obstinate?

Lov. Are you so base?

Dor. You will not satisfy my love?

Lov. I would die to satisfy that, but I will not to save you from a thousand racks do a shameless thing to please your vanity.

Dor. Farewell, false woman!

Lov. Do! go!

Dor. You will call me back again.

Lov. Exquisite fiend! I knew you came but to torment me.

Enter BELINDA *and* PERT.

Dor. [*surprised*]. Belinda here!

Bel. [*aside*]. He starts and looks pale; the sight of me has touched his guilty soul.

Pert. 'Twas but a qualm, as I said, a little indigestion; the surfeit water did it, madam, mixed with a little *mirabilis*.

Dor. I am confounded, and cannot guess how she came hither!

Lov. 'Tis your fortune, Belinda, ever to be here when I am abused by this prodigy of ill-nature.

Bel. I am amazed to find him here! How has he the face to come near you?

Dor. [*aside*]. Here is fine work towards! I never was at such a loss before.

Bel. One who makes a public profession of breach of faith and ingratitude; I loathe the sight of him.

Dor. [*aside*]. There is no remedy; I must submit to their tongues now, and some other time bring myself off as well as I can.

Bel. Other men are wicked, but then they have some sense of shame: he is never well but when he triumphs, nay, glories to a woman's face in his villainies.

Lov. You are in the right, Belinda; but methinks your kindness for me makes you concern yourself too much with him.

Bel. It does indeed, my dear; his barbarous carriage to you yesterday made me hope you ne'er would see him more, and the very next day to find him here again provokes me strangely; but, because I know you love him, I have done.

Dor. You have reproached me handsomely, and I deserve it for coming hither; but——

Pert. You must expect it, sir; all women will hate you for my lady's sake.

Dor. [*aside to* BELINDA]. Nay, if she begins too, 'tis time to fly; I shall be scolded to death else. I am to blame in some circumstances, I confess; but as to the main, I am not so guilty as you imagine. I shall seek a more convenient time to clear myself.

Lov. Do it now! what impediments are here?

Dor. I want time, and you want temper.

Lov. These are weak pretences!

Dor. You were never more mistaken in your life, and so farewell.   [DORIMANT *flings off*.

Lov. Call a footman, Pert, quickly; I will have him dogged.

Pert. I wish you would not for my quiet and your own.

Lov. I'll find out the infamous cause of all our quarrels, pluck her mask off, and expose her barefaced to the world.

Bel. [*aside*]. Let me but escape this time I'll never venture more.

Lov. Belinda! you shall go with me.

Bel. I have such a heaviness hangs on me with what I did this morning, I would fain go home and sleep, my dear.

Lov. Death and eternal darkness! I shall never sleep again. Raging fevers seize the world, and make mankind as restless all as I am!   [*Exit* LOVEIT.

Bel. I knew him false, and helped to make him so. Was not her ruin enough to fright me from the danger? It should have been, but love can take no warning.   [*Exit* BELINDA.

SCENE II.——Lady TOWNLEY's *house*

Enter MEDLEY, YOUNG BELLAIR, Lady TOWNLEY. EMILIA, *and Chaplain.*

Med. Bear up, Bellair, and do not let us see that repentance in thine we daily do in married faces.

Lady Town. This wedding will strangely surprise my brother when he knows it.

Med. Your nephew ought to conceal it for a time, madam, since marriage has lost its good name; prudent men seldom expose their own reputations till 'tis convenient to justify their wives.

O. Bell. [*without*]. Where are you all there? Out, adod, will nobody hear?

Lady Town. My brother! quickly, Mr. Smirk, into this closet; you must not be seen yet.   [*He goes into the closet.*

Enter OLD BELLAIR *and* Lady TOWNLEY's *Page.*

O. Bell. Desire Mr. Fourbes to walk into the lower parlour, I will be with him presently. [*To* YOUNG BELLAIR.] Where have you been, sir, you could not wait on me to-day?

Y. Bell. About a business.

O. Bell. Are you so good at business? Adod, I have a business too you shall despatch out of hand, sir. Send for a parson, sister; my Lady Woodvil and her daughter are coming.

Lady Town. What need you huddle up things thus!

O. Bell. Out a pise! youth is apt to play the fool, and 'tis not good it should be in their power.

Lady Town. You need not fear your son.

O. Bell. He's been idling this morning, and, adod, I do not like him. [*To* EMILIA.] How dost thou do, sweetheart?

Emil. You are very severe, sir; married in such haste.

O. Bell. Go to, thou'rt a rogue, and I will talk with thee anon. Here's my Lady Woodvil come.

Enter Lady WOODVIL, HARRIET, *and* BUSY.

Welcome, madam; Mr. Fourbes is below with the writings.

Lady Wood. Let us down, and make an end then.

O. Bell. Sister, show the way. [*To* YOUNG BELLAIR, *who is talking to* HARRIET.] Harry, your business lies not there yet; excuse him till we have done, lady, and then, adod, he shall be for thee. Mr. Medley, we must trouble you to be a witness.

Med. I luckily came for that purpose, sir.

[*Exeunt* OLD BELLAIR, MEDLEY, YOUNG BELLAIR, Lady
TOWNLEY, *and* Lady WOODVIL.

Busy. What will you do, madam?

Har. Be carried back and mewed up in the country again, run away here, anything rather than be married to a man I do not care for——Dear Emilia, do thou advise me.

Emil. Mr. Bellair is engaged you know.

Har. I do; but know not what the fear of losing an estate may fright him to.

Emil. In the desperate condition you are in you should consult with some judicious man; what think you of Mr. Dorimant?

Har. I do not think of him at all.

Busy. She thinks of nothing else, I am sure.

Emil. How fond your mother was of Mr. Courtage!

Har. Because I contrived the mistake to make a little mirth you believe I like the man.

Emil. Mr. Bellair believes you love him.

Har. Men are seldom in the right when they guess at a woman's mind; would she whom he loves loved him no better!

Busy [*aside*]. That's e'en well enough, on all conscience.

Emil. Mr. Dorimant has a great deal of wit.

Har. And takes a great deal of pains to show it.

Emil. He's extremely well-fashioned.

Har. Affectedly grave or ridiculously wild and apish.

Busy. You defend him still against your mother.

Har. I would not were he justly rallied, but I cannot hear any one undeservedly railed at.

Emil Has your woman learnt the song you were so taken with?

Har. I was fond of a new thing; 'tis dull at second hearing.

Emil. Mr. Dorimant made it.

Busy. She knows it, madam, and has made me sing it at least a dozen times this morning.

Har. Thy tongue is as impertinent as thy fingers.

Emil. You have provoked her.

Busy. 'Tis but singing the song,[1] and I shall appease her.

Emil. Prithee do.

Har. She has a voice will grate your ears worse than a cat-call, and dresses so ill she's scarce fit to trick up a yeoman's daughter on a holiday.

Busy [*sings*].

> As Amoret with Phyllis sat
>   One evening on the plain,
> And saw the charming Strephon wait
>   To tell the nymph his pain,
>
> The threatening danger to remove
>   She whisper'd in her ear,
> Ah, Phyllis! if you would not love,
>   This shepherd do not hear.
>
> None ever had so strange an art
>   His passion to convey
> Into a listening virgin's heart,
>   And steal her soul away.
>
> Fly, fly betimes, for fear you give
>   Occasion for your fate.
> In vain, said she, in vain I strive,
>   Alas! 'tis now too late.

Enter DORIMANT.

Dor. Music so softens and disarms the mind——

Har. That not one arrow does resistance find.

Dor. Let us make use of the lucky minute then.

Har. [*aside, turning from* DORIMANT]. My love springs with my blood into my face, I dare not look upon him yet.

Dor. What have we here, the picture of celebrated beauty giving audience in public to a declared lover?

Har. Play the dying fop and make the piece complete, sir.

---

[1] "A translation," says Coxeter (MS. note in his copy of Gildon's *Lives*), "from the French of Madame la Comtesse de la Suze in Le Recüeil des Pièces Gallantes." The version was by Sir Car Scroope; indeed all the old editions prefix to the verses a note—"Song by Sir C. S."

Dor. What think you if the hint were well improved—the whole mystery of making love pleasantly designed and wrought in a suit of hangings?

Har. 'Twere needless to execute fools in effigy who suffer daily in their own persons.

Dor. [*aside to* EMILIA]. Mrs. Bride, for such I know this happy day has made you.

Emil. Defer the formal joy you are to give me and mind your business with her. [*Aloud.*] Here are dreadful preparations, Mr. Dorimant, writings sealing, and a parson sent for.

Dor. To marry this lady?

Busy. Condemned she is, and what will become of her I know not, without you generously engage in a rescue.

Dor. In this sad condition, madam, I can do no less than offer you my service.

Har. The obligation is not great; you are the common sanctuary for all young women who run from their relations.

Dor. I have always my arms open to receive the distressed. But I will open my heart, and receive you where none yet did ever enter: you have filled it with a secret, might I but let you know it——

Har. Do not speak it if you would have me believe it; your tongue is so famed for falsehood 'twill do the truth an injury.

[*Turns away her head.*

Dor. Turn not away then; but look on me and guess it.

Har. Did you not tell me there was no credit to be given to faces? that women nowadays have their passions as much at will as they have their complexions, and put on joy and sadness, scorn and kindness, with the same ease they do their paint and patches [1]——Are they the only counterfeits?

Dor. You wrong your own while you suspect my eyes; by all the hope I have in you, the inimitable colour in your cheeks is not more free from art than are the sighs I offer.

Har. In men who have been long hardened in sin we have reason to mistrust the first signs of repentance.

Dor. The prospect of such a heaven will make me persevere and give you marks that are infallible.

Har. What are those?

Dor. I will renounce all the joys I have in friendship and in wine, sacrifice to you all the interest I have in other women——

Har. Hold!—though I wish you devout I would not have you turn fanatic—Could you neglect these awhile and make a journey into the country?

Dor. To be with you I could live there and never send one thought to London.

[1] When the custom of patching (to which the *Spectator* objected so strongly, No. 81) first became fashionable is not quite clear. Shadwell, however, in *The Virtuoso*, writes: "They have so many tricks to disguise themselves, washing, painting, patching."

Har. Whate'er you say, I know all beyond High Park's a desert to you, and that no gallantry can draw you farther.

Dor. That has been the utmost limit of my love, but now my passion knows no bounds, and there's no measure to be taken of what I'll do for you from anything I ever did before.

Har. When I hear you talk thus in Hampshire I shall begin to think there may be some truth enlarged upon.

Dor. Is this all?——will you not promise me?——

Har. I hate to promise! What we do then is expected from us, and wants much of the welcome it finds when it surprises.

Dor. May I not hope?

Har. That depends on you and not on me; and 'tis to no purpose to forbid it. [*Turns to* BUSY.

Busy. Faith, madam, now I perceive the gentleman loves you too; e'en let him know your mind, and torment yourselves no longer.

Har. Dost think I have no sense of modesty?

Busy. Think, if you lose this you may never have another opportunity.

Har. May he hate me—a curse that frights me when I speak it—if ever I do a thing against the rules of decency and honour!

Dor. [*to* EMILIA]. I am beholding to you for your good intentions, madam.

Emil. I thought the concealing of our marriage from her might have done you better service.

Dor. Try her again.

Emil. What have you resolved, madam? The time draws near.

Har. To be obstinate, and protest against this marriage.

Enter Lady TOWNLEY *in haste.*

Lady Town. [*To* EMILIA]. Quickly, quickly, let Mr. Smirk out of the closet. [SMIRK *comes out of the closet.*

Har. A parson! had you laid him in here?

Dor. I knew nothing of him.

Har. Should it appear you did, your opinion of my easiness may cost you dear.

Enter OLD BELLAIR, YOUNG BELLAIR, MEDLEY, *and* Lady WOODVIL.

O. Bell. Out a pise! the canonical hour is almost past. Sister, is the man of God come?

Lady Town. He waits your leisure.

O. Bell. By your favour, sir. Adod, a pretty spruce fellow! what may we call him?

Lady Town. Mr. Smirk, my Lady Biggot's chaplain.

O. Bell. A wise woman! adod, she is. The man will serve for the flesh as well as the spirit. Please you, sir, to commission a young couple to go to bed together i' God's name? Harry.

Y. Bell. Here, sir.

O. Bell. Out a pise! without your mistress in your hand!

Smirk. Is this the gentleman?

O. Bell. Yes, sir.

Smirk. Are you not mistaken, sir?

O. Bell. Adod, I think not, sir.

Smirk. Sure you are, sir.

O. Bell. You look as if you would forbid the banns; Mr. Smirk, I hope you have no pretension to the lady?

Smirk. Wish him joy, sir! I have done him the good office to-day already.

O. Bell. Out a pise! what do I hear?

Lady Town. Never storm, brother, the truth is out.

O. Bell. How say you, sir? is this your wedding-day?

Y. Bell. It is, sir.

O. Bell. And, adod, it shall be mine too; give me thy hand, sweetheart. [*To* EMILIA.] What dost thou mean? give me thy hand, I say.　　　　　　　[EMILIA *kneels, and* YOUNG BELLAIR.

Lady Town. Come, come, give her your blessing; this is the woman your son loved and is married to.

O. Bell. Ha! cheated! cozened! and by your contrivance, sister!

Lady Town. What would you do with her? She's a rogue, and you can't abide her.

Med. Shall I hit her a pat for you, sir?

O. Bell. Adod, you are all rogues, and I never will forgive you.

Lady Town. Whither! whither away?

Med. Let him go and cool awhile.

Lady Wood. [*to* DORIMANT]. Here's a business broke out now; Mr. Courtage, I am made a fine fool of.

Dor. You see the old gentleman knows nothing of it.

Lady Wood. I find he did not. I shall have some trick put upon me if I stay in this wicked town any longer. Harriet! dear child! where art thou? I'll into the country straight.

O. Bell. Adod, madam, you shall hear me first.

Enter LOVEIT *and* BELINDA.

Lov. Hither my man dogged him.

Bel. Yonder he stands, my dear.

Lov. I see him. [*Aside.*] And with the face that has undone me! Oh, that I were but where I might throw out the anguish of my heart! here it must rage within and break it.

Lady Town. Mrs. Loveit, are you afraid to come forward?

Lov. I was amazed to see so much company here in a morning, the occasion sure is extraordinary.

Dor. [*aside*]. Loveit and Belinda! the devil owes me a shame to-day, and I think never will have done paying it.

Lov. Married! dear Emilia! how am I transported with the news?

Har. [*to* DORIMANT] I little thought Emilia was the woman Mr. Bellair was in love with; I'll chide her for not trusting me with the secret.

Dor. How do you like Mrs. Loveit?

Har. She's a famed mistress of yours, I hear.

Dor. She has been on occasion.

O. Bell. [*to* Lady WOODVIL]. Adod, madam, I cannot help it.

Lady Wood. You need make no more apologies, sir.

Emil. [*to* LOVEIT]. The old gentleman's excusing himself to my Lady Woodvil.

Lov. Ha, ha, ha! I never heard of anything so pleasant.

Har. [*to* DORIMANT]. She's extremely overjoyed at something.

Dor. At nothing; she is one of those hoiting ladies who gaily fling themselves about and force a laugh when their aching hearts are full of discontent and malice.

Lov. Oh, heaven! I was never so near killing myself with laughing. Mr. Dorimant, are you a brideman?

Lady Wood. Mr. Dorimant! Is this Mr. Dorimant, madam?

Lov. If you doubt it, your daughter can resolve you, I suppose.

Lady Wood. I am cheated too, basely cheated.

O. Bell. Out a pise! what's here? more knavery yet?

Lady Wood. Harriet! on my blessing, come away, I charge you.

Har. Dear mother, do but stay and hear me.

Lady Wood. I am betrayed, and thou art undone, I fear.

Har. Do not fear it. I have not, nor never will do anything against my duty; believe me, dear mother, do.

Dor. [*to* LOVEIT]. I had trusted you with this secret, but that I knew the violence of your nature would ruin my fortune, as now unluckily it has. I thank you, madam.

Lov. She's an heiress, I know, and very rich.

Dor. To satisfy you I must give up my interest wholly to my love; had you been a reasonable woman, I might have secured 'em both and been happy.

Lov. You might have trusted me with anything of this kind, you know you might. Why did you go under a wrong name?

Dor. The story is too long to tell you now—be satisfied, this is the business, this is the mask has kept me from you.

Bel. [*aside*]. He's tender of my honour, though he's cruel to my love.

Lov. Was it no idle mistress then?

Dor. Believe me, a wife, to repair the ruins of my estate that needs it.

Lov. The knowledge of this makes my grief hang lighter on my soul; but I shall never more be happy.

Dor. Belinda!

Bel. Do not think of clearing yourself with me, it is impossible. Do all men break their words thus?

Dor. Th' extravagant words they speak in love; 'tis as unreasonable to expect we should perform all we promise then, as do all we threaten when we are angry.   When I see you next——

Bel. Take no notice of me, and I shall not hate you.

Dor. How came you to Mrs. Loveit?

Bel. By a mistake the chairmen made for want of my giving them directions.

Dor. 'Twas a pleasant one.   We must meet again.

Bel. Never.

Dor. Never?

Bel. When we do, may I be as infamous as you are false.

Lady Town. Men of Mr. Dorimant's character always suffer in the general opinion of the world.

Med. You can make no judgment of a witty man from common fame, considering the prevailing faction, madam.

O. Bell. Adod, he's in the right.

Med. Besides, 'tis a common error among women to believe too well of them they know and too ill of them they don't.

O. Bell. Adod, he observes well.

Lady Town. Believe me, madam, you will find Mr. Dorimant as civil a gentleman as you thought Mr. Courtage.

Har. If you would but know him better——

Lady Wood. You have a mind to know him better; come away! You shall never see him more.

Har. Dear mother, stay!

Lady Wood. I won't be consenting to your ruin.

Har. Were my fortune in your power

Lady Wood. Your person is.

Har. Could I be disobedient I might take it out of yours, and put it into his.

Lady Wood. 'Tis that you would be at; you would marry this Dorimant?

Har. I cannot deny it; I would, and never will marry any other man.

Lady Wood. Is this the duty that you promised?

Har. But I will never marry him against your will——

Lady Wood [*aside*]. She knows the way to melt my heart. [*To* HARRIET.]   Upon yourself light your undoing.

Med. [*to* OLD BELLAIR]. Come, sir, you have not the heart any longer to refuse your blessing

O. Bell. Adod, I ha' not——Rise, and God bless you both! Make much of her, Harry, she deserves thy kindness. [*To* EMILIA.]   Adod, sirrah, I did not think it had been in thee.

Enter Sir FOPLING *and his Page.*

Sir Fop. 'Tis a damned windy day; hey, page?   Is my periwig right?

Page. A little out of order, sir.

Sir Fop. Pox o' this apartment! it wants an antechamber to adjust oneself in. [*To* LOVEIT.] Madam, I came from your house, and your servants directed me hither.

Lov. I will give order hereafter they shall direct you better.

Sir Fop. The great satisfaction I had in the Mall last night has given me much disquiet since.

Lov. 'Tis likely to give me more than I desire.

Sir Fop. What the devil makes her so reserved? Am I guilty of an indiscretion, madam?

Lov. You will be of a great one if you continue your mistake, sir.

Sir Fop. Something puts you out of humour.

Lov. The most foolish inconsiderable thing that ever did.

Sir Fop. Is it in my power?

Lov. To hang or drown it; do one of 'em, and trouble me no more.

Sir Fop. So *fière*? *Serviteur, madame.* Medley, where's Dorimant?

Med. Methinks the lady has not made you those advances to-day she did last night, Sir Fopling.

Sir Fop. Prithee do not talk of her.

Med. She would be a *bonne fortune*

Sir Fop. Not to me, at present.

Med. How so?

Sir Fop. An intrigue now would be but a temptation to me to throw away that vigour on one which I mean shall shortly make my court to the whole sex in a *ballet*.

Med. Wisely considered, Sir Fopling.

Sir Fop. No one woman is worth the loss of a cut in a caper.

Med. Not when 'tis so universally designed.

Lady Wood. Mr. Dorimant, every one has spoke so much in your behalf that I can no longer doubt but I was in the wrong.

Lov. There's nothing but falsehood and impertinence in this world; all men are villains or fools. Take example from my misfortunes, Belinda; if thou wouldst be happy, give thyself wholly up to goodness.

Har. [*To* LOVEIT]. Mr. Dorimant has been your God Almighty long enough; 'tis time to think of another.

Lov. Jeered by her! I will lock myself up in my house, and never see the world again.

Har. A nunnery is the more fashionable place for such a retreat, and has been the fatal consequence of many a *belle passion*.

Lov. Hold, heart! till I get home; should I answer 'twould make her triumph greater.   [*Is going out.*

Dor. Your hand, Sir Fopling

Sir Fop. Shall I wait upon you, madam?

Lov. Legion of fools, as many devils take thee!

[*Exit* LOVEIT.

Med. Dorimant! I pronounce thy reputation clear   and

henceforward when I would know anything of woman, I will consult no other oracle.

Sir Fop. Stark mad, by all that's handsome! Dorimant, thou hast engaged me in a pretty business.

Dor. I have not leisure now to talk about it.

O. Bell. Out a pise! what does this Man of Mode do here again?

Lady Town. He'll be an excellent entertainment within, brother, and is luckily come to raise the mirth of the company.

Lady Wood. Madam, I take my leave of you.

Lady Town. What do you mean, madam?

Lady Wood. To go this afternoon part of my way to Hartley.

O. Bell. Adod, you shall stay and dine first; come, we will all be good friends, and you shall give Mr. Dorimant leave to wait upon you and your daughter in the country.

Lady Wood. If his occasions bring him that way, I have now so good an opinion of him he shall be welcome.

Har. To a great rambling lone house that looks as it were not inhabited, the family's so small; there you'll find my mother, an old lame aunt, and myself, sir, perched up on chairs at a distance in a large parlour, sitting moping like three or four melancholy birds in a spacious volery. Does not this stagger your resolution?

Dor. Not at all, madam. The first time I saw you you left me with the pangs of love upon me, and this day my soul has quite given up her liberty.

Har. This is more dismal than the country, Emilia; pity me who am going to that sad place. Methinks I hear the hateful noise of rooks already—knaw, knaw, knaw. There's music in the worst cry in London, *My dill and cucumbers to pickle.*[1]

O. Bell. Sister, knowing of this matter, I hope you have provided us some good cheer.

Lady Town. I have, brother, and the fiddles too.

O. Bell. Let 'em strike up then; the young lady shall have a dance before she departs.   [*Dance.*

[*After the dance.*] So, now we'll in and make this an arrant wedding-day

[*To the pit.*] And if these honest gentlemen rejoice,

          Adod, the boy has made a happy choice.

                                        [*Exeunt omnes*

---

[1] Addison thought differently: "I am always pleased with that particular time of the year which is proper for the pickling of dill and cucumbers; but, alas! this cry, like the song of the nightingale, is not heard above two months. It would therefore be worth while to consider whether the same air might not in some cases be adapted to other words."—In the classic dissertation on London "Cries," *Spectator*, No. 251.

THE EPILOGUE

BY MR. DRYDEN

Most modern wits such monstrous fools have shown,
They seem'd not of heaven's making, but their own.
Those nauseous harlequins in farce may pass,
But there goes more to a substantial ass;
Something of man must be exposed to view,
That, gallants, they may more resemble you:
Sir Fopling is a fool so nicely writ,
The ladies would mistake him for a wit,
And when he sings, talks loud, and cocks, would cry,
I vow, methinks he's pretty company ! [1]
So brisk, so gay, so travell'd, so refined,
As he took pains to graft upon his kind.
True fops help nature's work, and go to school
To file and finish God Almighty's fool.
Yet none Sir Fopling him, or him, can call [1];
He's knight o' th' shire, and represents ye all.
From each he meets he culls whate'er he can,
Legion's his name, a people in a man:
His bulky folly gathers as it goes,
And, rolling o'er you, like a snowball grows.
His various modes from various fathers follow;
One taught the toss, and one the new French wallow
His sword-knot this, his cravat this design'd,
And this the yard-long snake he twirls behind.
From one the sacred periwig he gain'd,
Which wind ne'er blew, nor touch of hat profaned
Another's diving bow he did adore,
Which with a shog casts all the hair before;
Till he, with full decorum, brings it back,
And rises with a water-spaniel shake.
As for his songs (the ladies' dear delight)
Those sure he took from most of you who write.
Yet every man is safe from what he fear'd,
For no one fool is hunted from the herd.

[1] This, with what follows, is not unsuggestive of Shadwell's prologue
to *The Virtuoso*:

> Yet no one coxcomb in this play is shown,
> No one man's humour makes a part alone,
> But scatter'd follies gather'd into one.

Already Published

Mary Shelley's FRANKENSTEIN
First of the science-fiction novels.

256 pages
No. 1616.

GOLDEN TREASURY OF LONGER POEMS
Great narrative poems.

448 pages
No. 1746.

Boccaccio's DECAMERON
The first forty tales in the unabridged Rigg translation.

320 pages
No. 1845.

Wilde's PLAYS, PROSE WRITINGS AND POEMS
includes the novel 'The Picture of Dorian Gray', the dialogue 'The Critic as Artist', and the plays 'The Importance of Being Earnest', 'Lady Windermere's Fan', and the prose piece 'Soul of Man Under Socialism'.

448 pages
No. 1858.

GHOST STORIES
A fine, shivering collection.

384 pages
No. 1952.

Conrad's THE NIGGER OF THE 'NARCISSUS', TYPHOON and THE SHADOW LINE
Three great sea yarns by the writer on ships and the sea.

320 pages
No. 1980.

Boswell's LIFE OF JOHNSON
The greatest life in English, unabridged. Two volumes.

672 pages
No. 1001.
656 pages
No. 1002.

Jane Austen's PRIDE AND PREJUDICE
The great comedy of English society in the eighteenth century.

352 pages
No. 1002.

Balzac's WILD ASS'S SKIN
A bargain with destiny.

256 pages
No. 1026.

Ibsen's PLAYS
'A Doll's House', 'The Wild Duck' and 'Lady from the Sea', R. Farquharson Sharp, Eleanor Marx-Aveling and Linda Hannås translations.

272 pages
No. 1494.

A BOOK OF NONSENSE
Edward Lear, Lewis Carroll and others. Illustrated.

256 pages
No. 1806.

De Quincey's CONFESSIONS OF AN ENGLISH OPIUM-EATER
The subtle masterpiece of English prose: a dream-fantasy-cum-autobiography. Introduction by Professor John E. Jordan, a De Quincey specialist.

288 pages
No. 1223.

☆ **Everyman Paperbacks** ☆ **Uniform with this volume** ☆

Charles Dickens's HARD TIMES

Dickens's abiding picture of the harsh conditions of a not-so-distant industrial England: the 'Paradise' of the Gradgrinds and Bounderbys. G. K. Chesterton writes a long Introduction.

288 pages
No. 1292.

Melville's MOBY DICK

The greatest sea-story ever written.

544 pages
No. 1179.

THE GOLDEN TREASURY

The world's most famous volume of poetry.

352 pages
No. 1096.

Swift's GULLIVER'S TRAVELS

'Word-for-word' text—the complete Gulliver.

336 pages
No. 1060.

RUSSIAN SHORT STORIES

Translation and Introduction by Rochelle S. Townsend. Pushkin, Tolstoy, Kuprin, Gorky and Chehov in the best translation.

304 pages
No. 1758.

Summer 1961

Jane Austen's EMMA

A handsome, clever, rich, match-making heroine—whose summer-like schemes end in temperamental storms.

448 pages
No. 1024.

Lewis Carroll's ALICE IN WONDERLAND

Carroll's own illustrations are included.

112 pages
No. 1836.

Joseph Conrad's THE SECRET AGENT

Conrad's vivid story of anarchists—at work in London.

328 pages
No. 1282.

TALES OF DETECTION

A hundred years of detective fiction are represented in this anthology. Dorothy L. Sayers writes a long Introduction.

416 pages
No. 1928.

INTERNATIONAL MODERN PLAYS

Five great plays. Strindberg's 'Lady Julie', Hauptmann's 'Hannele', Čapek's 'The Life of the Insects', Cocteau's 'The Infernal Machine' and Chiarelli's 'The Mask and the Face'.

320 pages
No. 1989.

Summer publications—continued

George Eliot's THE MILL ON THE FLOSS

The novelist readers are rediscovering in the 60's is here seen at her ripest in observing the pastoral life.

512 pages
No. 1325.

Autumn 1961

Darwin's VOYAGE OF THE 'BEAGLE'

An engrossing account of South America—wild life, plants, rocks, natural phenomena of all kinds—as only Darwin could see and describe them.

512 pages
No. 1104.

Samuel Butler's THE WAY OF ALL FLESH

Introduction by A. J. Hoppé. Witty, observant novel of parents and children and the ways that divide them.

384 pages
No. 1895.

Dickens's GREAT EXPECTATIONS

A marvel of construction—this autumnal novel of the great 'Boz'.

480 pages
No. 1234.

Flaubert's SENTIMENTAL EDUCATION

The French perfectionist of style here writes an unforgettable love story drawn from personal experience.

416 pages
No. 1969.

John Keats's POEMS

Edited with an Introduction by Gerald Bullett. Contains every poem published with a selection of poems discovered since Keats' death. The cheapest Keats on the market.

384 pages
No. 1101.

FRENCH SHORT STORIES OF THE 19TH AND 20TH CENTURIES

Selected by F. C. Green, M.A., Ph.D., Professor of French at the University of Edinburgh, from nineteenth and twentieth centuries.

384 pages
No. 1896.